New & Expanded Edition

Definitive
Opera
Encyclopedia

This is a **FLAME TREE** book
First published in 2017

Publisher and Creative Director: Nick Wells
Senior Project Editor: Sonya Newland
Editors: Polly Prior & Laura Bulbeck
Digital Manager: Chris Herbert
Indexer: Helen Snaith

Special thanks to:
Gillian Whitaker, Julia Rolf

FLAME TREE PUBLISHING
6 Melbray Mews
London SW6 3NS
United Kingdom

www.flametreepublishing.com

17 19 21 20 18
1 3 5 7 9 10 8 6 4 2

ISBN: 978-1-78361-990-0

A copy of the CIP data for this book is available at the British Library
upon request.

Publisher's note:
This publication is an expanded revised and updated edition of text that
previously appeared in the Illustrated Encyclopedia of Opera (2004).

Decorations and ornaments throughout are based on 19th Century engravings
and have been recreated at the Flame Tree Studio.

Printed in Italy

New & Expanded Edition

Definitive Opera Encyclopedia

Founding Editor: Stanley Sadie

Consultant Editor: Sarah Gabriel

Foreword by

Philip Langridge

FLAME TREE PUBLISHING

CONTENTS

HOW TO USE THIS BOOK

This book comprises an introductory section on the development of opera, from its roots in the musical theatre of ancient Greece, followed by seven chronologically organized chapters from The Early and Middle Baroque to The Modern Era. Each chapter is divided into a number of sections. Common to each chapter are the following:

Introduction: Gives vital information about the relevant period, clarifying the backdrop against which the music developed and setting it and its protagonists in their social, historical and cultural context.

Genres and Styles: Details the creation of new musical styles, performance styles and compositional techniques, as well as the development of those that already existed. (NB there is no Genres and Styles section in Chapter 5.)

Personalities: Biographies of the key figures in opera of the time – from the major composers to those that were less prolific – along with details and synopses of the major operas. This section also includes biographies of librettists and singers of the period.

THEMES

At the end of each section are short entries covering a range of themes. The theme is indicated by an icon and a cross-reference is given to the next entry of the same theme.

⚜ **Techniques** – Introduces developments in the composition and structure of opera, with discussion of the innovations and various genres particular to each era.

⚫ **Houses and Companie**s – Provides information about the world's most celebrated opera houses and performance companies, as well as famous patrons and related societies and factions.

☻ **The Voice** – Explores developments in vocal techniques, the different types of voice that dominated each era and style, and how the composers tailored their operas to showcase the singers' vocal abilities.

✄ **Performance** – Highlights different types of opera-related performance and developments in how the operas themselves were performed and staged, including contemporary eyewitness accounts of opera stagings.

𝒞 **Stage and Scene** – Examines the more practical side of opera's history, including set designs and stage machinery, as well as issues such as censorship.

CROSS-REFERENCING

A system of cross-referencing has been used in which terms or names that have an entry elsewhere in the encyclopedia are indicated in bold. Any term that may require further explanation can be found in the glossary at the end of the book. Names are emboldened when the individual has his or her own entry in one of the Personalities sections.

NAMES, DATES AND TRANSLATIONS

Full names and dates are given for musicological figures the first time they are mentioned. Opera titles are translated the first time they are mentioned if not in English, and the year in which they were first performed is given. Titles of arias and excerpts are also translated where necessary.

FOREWORD

ONE **WHO STRIVES** to create beauty, to liberate from the marble mass of language the slender forms of an art ...' sings Gustav von Aschenbach in Benjamin Britten's *Death in Venice*. This could be written on my tombstone. It is the very essence of an artist's work. It is what we strive to do and what we hope to see and hear in performance. When I am performing as a singer, I often ask myself if I am communicating successfully with the listener. This in part also depends upon whether the listener is able to enter fully into the discussion, because that is how we should describe a performance: a discussion between performer and audience. The audience needs to take part in order for it to be a real discussion. This is one reason for using a book like this, to have a better understanding of the language, history, style, story etc. of any opera in order to take part in the discussion.

I know that *The Encyclopedia of Opera* looks a pretty forbidding title, but flicking through the pages it seems much more like a novel by the same name. For instance, you can easily imagine what it must have been like around the year 1600 when the good old Camerata were creating this magic formula, when real horses were used in performances of Monteverdi's *Il Combattimento di Tancredi e Clorinda*, and when the words, the music and the drama were of equal importance. Just imagine creating such a wonderful art form which has survived for 400 years, almost unchanged.

We have, of course, strayed quite a lot from those early ideals, having seen some terribly grand singers, before whom everyone bowed, the great and mighty conductor under whose baton everyone cowered, and finally the rise of the director, who has reigned supreme with all those seemingly crazy ideas on stage. In addition, there have been the opera companies begging for money to support themselves, with the politicians not far behind, and all of us musicians, singers, designers and directors trying to stage the operas as works of art.

I have been fortunate in singing in so many of the styles which you will find discussed in this book. Monteverdi has always been a particular favourite of mine, and his *L'incoronazione di Poppea* comes top of my list. I love the way in which Monteverdi contrasted between a tragic scene (Senaca's death, for example) and a comic one (the scene with Lucano and Nero), placed right next to one another. Mozart did the same in his operas (*Die Zauberflöte*, for instance), and one can trace this expressive device down through the years. Singing Rameau's *Les Boreades* was a huge thrill, and at that time we were probably performing it for the first time ever. I found it to be an opera which points forward to Wagner and back to Monteverdi at the same time. His use of the recitative as aria and vice versa is extraordinary. How on earth did these composers get their inspiration? Inspiration? That is what Pfitzner's *Palestrina* deals with. It tells of the awful dilemma a composer finds himself in when his inspiration dries up. Interesting thought: a composer composing an opera about a composer with writer's block! I can only marvel at the brilliance of these composers, who just seem to come up with such amazing ideas.

Janáček said that speech melodies are windows into people's souls. Debussy said that music is a dream from which the veil has been lifted, and that it is not even the expression of a feeling, it is the feeling itself. With words like that ringing in your ears you would be foolish not to join the discussion. You can visit any opera house to hear a live performance, listen to CDs of any of these operas and even see them on DVD. Opera is more popular now than ever, and much more accessible. I cannot imagine life without music, and when this is allied to words and theatre, the sky is the limit.

Philip Langridge

INTRODUCTION

O PERA IS PERHAPS the most elaborate of all art forms. It may call on the skills of poet, composer, scenographer, director and choreographer to create a 'complete artwork' (or, to call on Wagner's term, *Gesamtkunstwerk*). It can offer its creators a breadth of resource unknown to most other art forms, partly because of the simultaneous appeal it makes to several different susceptibilities, but also because music can open up possibilities of strengthening, subtilizing or inflecting, or even contradicting, any words that are uttered on the stage, and may even carry information about words or feelings or the characters that are left unspoken or are indeed unknown to the characters themselves.

In Gluck's *Iphigénie en Tauride*, for example, when Orestes tells himself and us that 'Le calme rentre dans mon coeur' ('Calm returns to my heart'), we in the audience know – from the uneasy throb of the violas in the orchestra – that his newfound calm is illusory. When, in Wagner's *Die Walküre*, Sieglinde tells the tale of the mysterious stranger who intruded upon her wedding feast, the orchestra tells us precisely who this was. The music may elucidate the emotional relationship between characters in an ensemble, as in the famous quartet in Verdi's *Rigoletto*. It can symbolize and powerfully reinforce what is expressed: for example, when two lovers begin a duet singing singly and end it singing in mellifluous thirds or sixths – as they usually do – it will stress their growing mutuality of feeling and identity of purpose.

In everyday life, people do not very often sing to convey their thoughts; in opera they do. Opera is not a naturalistic art; it depends on the acceptance by its audience of a series of conventions, of which the coupling of music and words is the central one. But in the course of its history there have been numerous attempts to make it less dependent on what, in a changing society, has come to be regarded as artificiality and, often, as representative of an outmoded world. The 'reforms' of the early eighteenth-century Italian librettists, of Gluck and his colleagues, of Wagner, and of various groups in the twentieth century have all been of this kind. The disputes to which they gave rise have sometimes focused on the claims of primacy between words and music (a topic which several composers have even treated as the subject matter of an opera, for example Salieri and Richard Strauss).

Often such disputes devolve on the issue of 'set-piece' arias or duets and whether they should be separated, by clear breaks in musical texture, or should be welded into a more nearly continuous whole. Traditions differ, geographically and temporally, and are closely related to social and linguistic factors. Verdi once remarked: 'If only there could be no cavatinas, no duets, no trios, no choruses, no finales etc., and if only the whole opera could be, as it were, all one number, I should find that sensible and right.' But he knew better than to compose operas like that for an Italian audience.

What music can tell us about human behaviour, and the different ways in which composers have chosen to use music to enrich our understanding: that is the central stuff of the history of opera, and it is what this book tries to clarify and illuminate.

Stanley Sadie

THE ROOTS
OF OPERA

O pera, with its unique blend of poetry, drama and music, has come a long way from its humble beginnings in ancient Greek theatre. The grandiose, all-encompassing music dramas of Verdi and Wagner may seem a world away from the era of Aristotle and Plato, but this noble civilization, which held music and theatre in high regard as both art forms and means of entertainment, was to play a crucial role in the development of opera.

Sadly, no music from ancient Greece survives today, but we can gain a fairly accurate picture by piecing together information from contemporary writings, surviving plays and depictions on pottery and other artefacts. The great dramas and tragedies of the period were punctuated by musical and lyrical interludes, and it was here that the concept began to emerge of using music and song to convey narratives and reflect characters' emotions.

In the strictly religious Europe of the Middle Ages, the use of music in drama was mainly restricted to sacred settings. This took one of two forms: the liturgical drama, performed in Latin as part of a church service, or the mystery play, aimed at the general public but retaining a basis in Biblical stories. Meanwhile, in Japan, the Nō theatre combined structured drama with music and song, in performances reminiscent of those of ancient Greece.

However, it was in the Renaissance period that the direct influence of ancient Greek theatre began to take hold. The humanist movement, which flourished in fifteenth-century Florence, revered above all else the works of the classical civilizations. Architects and artists such as Filippo Brunelleschi (1377–1446 and Michelangelo Buonarotti (1475–1564) took as their inspiration the buildings and sculptures of ancient Greece and Rome, and so it followed that musicians and composers were similarly inspired.

The *intermedi* of Renaissance Florence took place between the acts of plays and involved music, singing and elaborate costumes and sets. These became a popular form of court entertainment for the powerful de' Medici family, and were a precursor to the grandeur of Baroque opera productions. Composers such as **Jacopo Peri** (1561–1633), **Giulio Caccini** (*c.* 1545–1618) and **Claudio Monteverdi** (1567–1643) used Greek and Roman mythology as a basis for their musical dramas, and it was from these early works such as *Orfeo* that opera as we know it began to emerge.

The Roots of Opera
MUSIC IN CLASSICAL ANTIQUITY

The musical culture of ancient Greece has had a profound influence on the history of Western music. However, its legacy is particularly evident in the emergence of opera in the early seventeenth century. Even though we have little idea about what ancient Greek music actually sounded like – composers and musicians did not write their music down – there are plenty of sources of information about it. Philosophers such as Plato and Aristotle discussed it in their treatises, theorists analysed its melodies and rhythms, craftsmen painted musical scenes on their pottery bowls, and, of course, we have the works of the great tragedians themselves – the plays of Aeschylus, Sophocles and Euripides.

GREEK DRAMA

In the fifth century BC, the city-state of Athens witnessed a great flourishing of artistic and intellectual achievement, among the greatest of which was the development of tragedy. The dramas of ancient Greece had their origins in choral dances performed by ordinary citizens in ritual ceremonies, and these two aspects of the tragedy – the ritual and the choral – remained among the most important of its defining features, even when the element of story-telling (drama as we understand it today) assumed a more prominent role.

Greek tragedies were performed as part of the formal celebrations at the Great Dionysia, a festival of Dionysos, the god of wine, music and poetry. The three most famous tragedians were Aeschylus (525–456 BC), Sophocles (*c.* 496–406 BC) and Euripides (*c.* 485–*c.* 406 BC), and their works were revered in antiquity just as much as they are today. Aeschylus was the oldest of the trio. He wrote over 90 plays, of which only seven survive. Of these, the *Oresteia*, a trilogy of three tragedies, is perhaps the most famous: it was performed in 458 BC and won the festival competition.

Sophocles wrote over 120 dramas, but again only seven survive, among them the famous *Oedipus Tyrannos* ('Oedipus the King'). Euripides, the youngest of the great tragedians, wrote about 90 plays, of which 19 are still known today.

THE GREEK THEATRE

The Theatre of Dionysos in Athens, where the tragedies were performed, stood at the foot of the south-eastern end of the Acropolis in the sanctuary of Dionysos. Like other Greek theatres, it was a vast space, wholly open to the sky, and by the fourth century it could seat around 20,000 spectators. The audience sat in tiers of seats that were arranged in a horseshoe shape carved out of the rock of the Acropolis, and looked down upon the action below them. This was known as the *theatron*, 'the place for seeing'. At the centre of the horseshoe was a flat, circular piece of ground, called the *orchéstra*, 'the place for dancing', which housed the altar of Dionysos and was where the *choros* of citizens performed their songs and dances. Behind this, facing the audience, was the *skéne*, or stage. In the fifth century BC this was a temporary, single-storey wooden building, sometimes painted with rudimentary scenery to represent the setting of the drama. It had a platform slightly raised above the level of the *orchéstra*, on which the solo actors performed. Characters representing gods often appeared on the roof of the *skéne* to address the mortals below. Later, in the fourth century, when the Theatre of Dionysos was enlarged, the *skéne* was rebuilt of stone in two storeys and decorated with statues of the great dramatists. Inside the *skéne* and invisible to the audience was the 'backstage' area, which also housed the *méchane*, 'mechanical device' – a kind of crane or hoist that, from the time of Euripides onwards, was used to lift characters into the air, usually to represent flying.

MUSIC IN ANCIENT GREEK CULTURE

In performances of tragedy, as in other forms of Greek poetry, the words and the musical sounds were closely bound together. In particular, the melodic line exactly followed the intonations of the poetic language, reflecting the rise and fall of the singer's recitation of the text, and the rhythms were precisely those of the poetic metre used in the verse. Greek music was monodic – that is, it was a single melodic line, without harmony of any kind. In fact, so intimately connected were poetry, music and dance, that the Greek idea of music – or *mousiké* – encompassed all these aspects of performance – not just what we today understand as 'music'.

Music held a particularly important place in the culture of ancient Greece and it exerted serious moral and emotional effects on the character of both performer and listener. Music was therefore of great concern in the education of children and in the everyday lives of adults. As music theory progressed and different styles of music were analysed and given names, so philosophers began to assign moral characters to each style. This theory, known as the doctrine of *éthos* ('character'), found its most influential proponent in the works of Plato (*c*. 485–*c*. 406 BC). According to Plato, the Dorian style of music was associated with virility and courage and was especially appropriate for choral music, the Phrygian was sober and thoughtful, and the Ionian and Lydian styles induced excitability, moral weakness and effeminacy.

These views were shared by Plato's pupil, Aristotle (384–322 BC), but whereas Plato argued that the power of musicians and poets over people's emotions and characters was so great that they should be banished from the city, Aristotle took a more moderate view. For him, music could be used educationally – by using the Dorian mode – to instil the ideal, manly virtues, but was also valuable as a means of entertainment and relaxation. In his view, the strong and varied emotions had a beneficial effect on an audience: by providing an outlet for extreme feelings, tragedy had a purifying effect (*catharsis*) on the soul.

❈ GREEK TRAGEDY ∾ p. 19

The performers in the Greek tragedy were of two distinct types: the *choros* and the solo actors. The *choros* was a group of 12 or 15 adult men drawn from the general citizenry of Athens. Its role was largely passive in the drama, usually commenting upon the action or sympathizing with the solo characters.

Although the *choros* (and particularly its leader, the *choregos*) engaged in dialogue with the solo actors, its most important role was the performance of lyric songs. These were formal episodes in the tragedy, reflecting upon the action, and involved dancing, poetry and singing, often to the accompaniment of the *aulos* – a type of wind instrument rather like an oboe.

Sometimes the *choros* was divided into two groups, with one answering or debating with the other. The solo actors in the tragedy (no more than three) were also all adult males, even when representing female characters. They were professional performers, skilled in acting and singing. They wore masks over their faces that showed the essential character of their role. Although they did perform formal songs, such as laments, their singing was probably more a kind of chant – more musical than everyday speech, but not quite the same as song.

The Roots of Opera

MUSIC IN MEDIEVAL DRAMA

In the Middle Ages, two distinct forms of music drama existed: the liturgical dramas that took place in churches as a part of the service – and were therefore in Latin; and the 'mystery' or 'miracle' plays that were performed outside churches in the everyday language of the people.

LITURGICAL DRAMAS

Liturgical dramas were performed only by members of the clergy, and formed part of the church service on particular occasions. The earliest known drama dates from the ninth century and recreates the scene from the Gospels when the Marys visited the tomb of Christ and spoke with an angel. It was often performed as part of the **Mass** on Easter Day. Later plays also took place on other major Christian festivals, particularly Christmas. There is some evidence that basic scenery and costumes were occasionally used, especially for the more elaborate plays.

In the Middle Ages, all the words of the Mass and other church services were chanted or sung, with each set of words having its own melody. The music for the liturgical dramas was no different, with the texts and verses of the plays set in the same traditional **plainchant** style. Sometimes chants were drawn directly from the liturgical services, but melodies were also often written especially for the plays.

'MYSTERY' PLAYS

'Mystery' plays were performed throughout Europe from the fourteenth century to the Reformation in the sixteenth century. Their subject matter was religious and they were generally enacted out in the open air as part of the celebrations of a holy day (or 'holiday'). Many of the plays tell of the whole history of the world, from the Creation to the Last Judgement, taking in all the major stories from the Bible. These plays were performed by craftsmen, with each guild being responsible for a particular scene. The choice of guild was often closely connected to the subject matter of the scene – for example, the carpenters might be in charge of the story of Noah's Ark, and the butchers of the telling of the Crucifixion. While some plays were designed for performance on a fixed wooden stage, others took place on a succession of wagons as part of a procession through the town's streets.

Although these plays were largely spoken, they also included many musical items – songs, instrumental music and dances. Unfortunately, very few of these pieces were written down in notation, because they were usually already well known to both the performers and audience. The melodies were generally taken from popular songs of the time, liturgical plainchant and dance tunes. Almost no music was specially written for the mystery plays.

JAPANESE NO THEATRE ~ p. 13

Several other non-Western cultures have developed genres of musical performance similar to that of opera – they combine music, song, story-telling and theatrical presentation. The most famous of these is the Nō theatre of Japan.

Nō theatre was essentially established in the fourteenth and fifteenth centuries by the two great playwrights Kan'ami (1333–84) and his son Zeami (1363–1443). These two men drew upon earlier traditions of music and drama to form the highly stylized art that is still performed today. There are five types of Nō play: plays about gods; plays about men; plays about women (usually those that are young and beautiful); plays featuring mad women; and plays concerning supernatural beings. Originally, a performance consisted of a play from each category, with a comic play – known as a *kyōgen* – inserted between each Nō. Such performances could last an entire day.

Nō actors – all of whom are men – are of three types: the principal, who wears a mask and represents the main character of the story; the secondary, who enters into dialogue with the principal; and the comic actor who performs the *kyōgen*. There is also a chorus of eight people that sets the scene and comments on the action, often voicing the other characters' thoughts and feelings. Accompanying the actors and chorus, as well as performing purely instrumental music and dances, are a flute-player (who plays the bamboo *nōkan*) and three drummers.

Nō theatre is performed on a square stage, with a pillar in each corner supporting a roof. The instrumentalists sit at the back, and the chorus kneels on either side of the stage. Traditionally, Nō plays took place outside, but for the last 100 years or so they have often been performed inside buildings specially constructed for the purpose. Today, Tokyo has several such theatres, including the National Nō Theatre, and other major cities in Japan also have dedicated theatres. Nō theatre is still a popular form of entertainment in Japan.

The Roots of Opera
MUSIC IN THE RENAISSANCE

The Renaissance, with its renewed interest in the music of the ancient world, is where the true roots of opera lie. The word 'Renaissance' means 'rebirth' and refers to the revival of the artistic and intellectual ideals of classical civilization following the intervening Middle Ages. The Renaissance began in Italy in the late fourteenth century and later spread to other countries throughout Europe, but it was in Italy that the immediate predecessors of modern opera began to take shape in the fifteenth century.

INTERMEDI

One of the most important precursors of opera was the *intermedio*. *Intermedi* were a series of interludes that were inserted between the acts of a play, initially as a means of dividing up the action or marking the passage of time between events in the main drama. They were an aristocratic entertainment, often performed to celebrate occasions such as court weddings, and usually involved singing, dancing, instrumental music and elaborate stage effects. Their subject matter often reflected the fashionable Renaissance themes of stories from classical myths, allegories and pastoral scenes.

The earliest *intermedi* took place in Ferrara in the late fifteenth century, but the genre reached its height at the court of the Medici family of Florence in the sixteenth. By this time, the *intermedi* were often more important parts of the entertainment than the original drama. The scenery and costumes could be spectacular and the finest musicians, singers and dancers were employed to perform the musical numbers. The importance of the *intermedi* for the development of opera at the very end of the sixteenth century lies in the close association between drama and music, and in the intellectual environment in which the most influential *intermedi* were performed. The 1589 *intermedi* of Florence, for example, involved many of the musicians and thinkers who were later responsible for the first genuine operas. They used these courtly entertainments as a means of presenting their ideas and putting their theories about the music of the ancient world into practice.

THE FLORENTINE CAMERATA

The Camerata ('club' or 'society') was a group of intellectuals with aristocratic connections that met in Florence during the 1570s and 1580s. Led by Count Giovanni de' Bardi, its members came together principally to discuss the music of the ancient Greeks with the aim of influencing the composition of contemporary music. Among its chief members were Vincenzo Galilei, an expert in the music of the ancient world (and the father of Galileo), and the composers Guilio Caccini and Jacopo Peri, both of whom went on to write the earliest genuine operas.

THE RECREATION OF THE GREEK IDEAL

The principal concern of the Camerata was to recreate as far as possible the character of ancient music. Although they had no actual examples of Greek melodies to go on, they closely studied the writings of the classical music theorists and philosophers (particularly Plato and Aristotle). Several ideas particularly interested the Camerata: the complete union of melody and poetry that its members saw in the performance of song and dramas (especially tragedies) in the ancient world, and the legendary powers of music over the human soul and emotions. As a result of their discussions, the Camerata proposed an ideal style of music in which poetry and melody became equals. The music should not obscure the words – for example by having more than one melody performed at the same time, or by distorting the natural rhythms of speech. It should also reflect the subject matter of the poetry and reinforce the meaning of the words in order to achieve the maximum emotional impact on the listener. Music was reunited with drama and poetry once more.

※ THE FLORENTINE INTERMEDI OF 1589 ∾ p. 52

The six *intermedi* composed to celebrate the marriage of Ferdinando de' Medici of Florence and Christine of Lorraine in 1589 were the most spectacular and expensive ever seen. So lavish was the presentation that it completely dominated the play it accompanied – *La pellegrina* ('The Pilgrim') by Girolamo Bargagli. All the texts and music survive, together with the designs for the costumes and sets. The *intermedi* were devised by Giovanni de' Bardi (1534–1612) on the theme of the power of music in the ancient world, with texts written by Bardi, Ottavio Rinuccini (1562–1621) and Laura Guidiccioni (fl. 1550). The music was composed largely by Cristofano Malvezzi (1547–99) and Luca Marenzio (1550–99), with contributions by others, including Peri, Caccini and Bardi.

The individual scenes included: the Harmony of the Spheres (*Intermedio* 1); the contest in song between the Muses and the Pierides (*Intermedio* 2); the story of the singer Arion and his rescue by a dolphin (*Intermedio* 5); and the descent of Rhythm and Harmony from heaven to earth (*Intermedio* 6). The music for each of these scenes began with an instrumental *sinfonia*, and continued with a mixture of solo songs performed by virtuoso singers and elaborate choral madrigals requiring 60 singers and over 20 instruments.

THE ROOTS OF OPERA: MUSIC IN THE RENAISSANCE

EARLY AND MIDDLE BAROQUE

As part of the Renaissance (literally 'rebirth'), which began in Italy in around 1450, the Baroque era was a revolution within a revolution. It saw a break from the Medieval view of humanity as innately sinful. Instead, Renaissance thinking cast individuals as a dynamic force in their own right and gave free rein to human imagination, ingenuity and self-expression. The Protestant movement, which rejected the ethos of the established Catholic Church after 1517, was typical of the often-aggressive individuality of the Renaissance age.

The meaning of the word 'baroque', coined by opponents of the new and shocking departure from ascetic Christian tradition, reflected the fundamental change in mindset the Renaissance involved. It derived from the Italian *barroco*, meaning 'an obstacle to logic', or from the Portuguese *barroco* and Spanish *barrueco*, meaning 'an irregularly shaped pearl'. 'Baroque' later came to mean anything imperfect, bizarre, contorted or generally contrary to established rules.

The impact was intense and all-pervasive. The flamboyant Baroque style affected all artistic forms, giving a new grandeur to architecture, rich, brilliant colour to painting and a more sensuous and fluid realism to sculpture. In particular, painting and sculpture depicted real, flesh-and-blood humans rather than stiff, insipid figures.

In the theatre, plays plumbed new depths of emotion and explored the dark complexities of love, hate, revenge and despair. The recasting of music was just as startling. Until the Baroque style evolved, music had been dominated by the simpler, restrained sound of sacred works designed to invoke religious devotion and typify the other-worldliness of faith. Baroque composers broadened these horizons by turning musical performances into entertainments that explored emotional depths and rich harmonic textures. Baroque opera introduced interplay between orchestra and performers and an entirely novel feature – the visual attractions of costumed performers and stage scenery.

KEY EVENTS

1477	Chaucer's *Canterbury Tales* first printed
1485	Henry Tudor becomes Henry VII
1405	Leonardo da Vinci paints *Last Supper*
1517	Martin Luther launches the Protestant Reformation in Europe
1527	Sack of Rome by imperial forces
1531	Michelangelo begin the *Last Judgement* in the Sistine Chapel
1572	St Bartholomew's Day Massacre in Paris
1598	Huguenots granted freedom of worship
1599	Globe Theatre built in London
1603	Death of Elizabeth I; James VI of Scotland becomes James I of England
1610	Galileo observes Jupiter's moons
1611	Authorized King James Bible is issued
1618	Beginning of the Thirty Years' War
1630	Tirso de Molina writes *El burlador de Sevilla* – the first dramatization of the Don Juan legend
1642	English Civil War breaks out
1661	Louis XIV begins absolute rule in France
1666	Great Fire of London destroys many buildings in the city
1675	Christopher Wren rebuilds St Paul's Cathedral

Early and Middle Baroque
INTRODUCTION

Opera began as an elite art. The first operas were created and performed for small, select audiences at wealthy courts in such cultural centres as Florence, Mantua, Parma and Rome. However, in 1637 the first public theatre in Venice, the Teatro San Cassiano opened, and the 'invitation only' nature of opera changed. The Venetian opera houses were funded by the city's patrician families, and paid for mostly by the sale of subscription boxes to the wealthy. Opera was expensive to produce, and although the opera houses were 'public', access to productions was usually limited to those with money to spare.

ITALIAN ORIGINS AND MONTEVERDI

Opera – a tradition that brings together art, architecture, music and literature – was the most enduring result of the Baroque's dramatic impulse. The operas of the seventeenth century are an index of the latest developments in all these arts. The plots of the operas were drawn mostly from mythology or history, but the telling of these tales reflected the current literary ideals.

L'Orfeo, favola in musica ('Orpheus, a Legend in Music', 1607), written by **Claudio Monteverdi** (1567–1643) and first staged in Mantua, recounted the tragic tale of the legendary musician Orpheus, who never recovered from the death of his wife, Euridice: he spent the rest of his life mourning for her and singing of his loss. The popularity of this poignant theme was evident from the start. Within a year, another opera had been written on the same subject, and before the seventeenth century was out, a further 21 had been performed.

Monteverdi was an undisputed trendsetter, and in more than his choice of subject. *L'Orfeo* displayed a novel approach – more dramatic, more lyrical and much more expressive than its predecessors. The popular appeal of this first undisputed masterpiece of Baroque opera and the works that followed it was soon evident. Within a short time, Venice, where Monteverdi settled in 1613 as *maestro di cappella* at the Cathedral of St Mark's, became the first centre of Italian opera. There, opera began to evolve, as audiences demanded more drama and more action on stage. An **overture**, at first consisting of a short fanfare of instruments, was introduced to start the performance. Opera plots became more violent and exciting, and stage effects more spectacular. The **aria** introduced by Monteverdi became more prominent. The seamless musical style known as **bel canto** – 'beautiful singing' – also developed in Venice. By that time, Rome had replaced Venice as the centre of Italian opera. Rome was succeeded later in the seventeenth century by Naples.

THE ARRIVAL OF OPERA IN GERMANY AND FRANCE

The popularity of opera quickly spread outside Italy. Italian opera was adopted wholesale in Germany and Austria, and dominated the scene for several years. German-language operas did not appear until after 1678, when the Oper am Gänsemarkt was established in Hamburg. Italian opera arrived in France in 1645 but had only limited success. In the event, the individualistic French preferred to develop their own genre. In 1664, **Jean-Baptiste Lully** (1632–87), court composer to King Louis XIV, started to compose **comédie-ballets**, which bore some resemblance to opera in their use of **recitative** and melodious airs, with dances added to the performances.

VERNACULAR OPERA
IN FRANCE AND SPAIN

The first French opera was *Pomone* (1671), composed by Robert Cambert (*c.* 1628–77), with a **libretto** written by the poet Pierre Perrin (1620–75). Spain developed its own native form of opera, the *zarzuela*, also in the seventeenth century. This musical drama with spoken dialogue took its name from the hunting lodge owned by King Philip IV near Madrid, where *zarzuela* and other dramatic performances took place. Although characteristically Spanish, *zarzuela* was Italianate in form and included arias, recitatives, duets, choruses and dances, as well as popular songs performed between the acts.

AN ENGLISH OPERA AT LAST

The typically English opera was slow to develop, and did not appear in full form until the twentieth century. Instead, English audiences were offered French-style **semi-operas** that featured spoken dialogue. One brilliant exception was *Dido and Aeneas* (1689) by **Henry Purcell** (1659–95) – an outstanding all-English, all-sung opera that was written for a girls' school in Chelsea, London.

◉ THE TEATRO SAN CASSIANO,
VENICE ∾ p. 43

∾ p. 43

When the Teatro San Cassiano, the first public opera house, opened in 1637, the Venetian nobility rapidly decamped from the private homes in which performances had previously been given and rented the best box seats for each opera season. The public had to make do with the lower *parterre*, or 'pit'.

The San Cassiano was built and owned by an aristocratic family, the Trons. The first opera staged there was *L'Andromeda* (1637), with music by Francesco Manelli and libretto by Benedetto Ferrari. Ferrari and Manelli were in charge of production for two years before handing

over control to a company led by the composer **Francesco Cavalli** (1602–76). For the next six years, Cavalli wrote all the operas performed at San Cassiano, except Monteverdi's *Il ritourno d'Ulisse* in patria ('Ulysses' Return Home', 1640).

As more and more opera houses opened in Venice – 11 by the end of the seventeenth century – fewer and fewer operas were produced at San Cassiano. Ultimately, the Teatro was upstaged by larger opera houses that were able to accommodate more elaborate performances. Although in decline, San Cassiano remained open for another century until it finally closed in 1807, after 170 years.

Early and Middle Baroque
GENRES AND STYLES

Opera developed from a mixture of genres, styles and techniques that combined to create a distinctly new form of music. Among opera's many novel aspects, one of the most significant was its secular nature. Opera essentially upended the basic principle of church music. For religious purposes, words had to predominate over the music. With opera, it was the other way around – plots, characters and lyrics were important, but they served the musical agenda.

A BREAK WITH SACRED TRADITION
– DRAMMA PER MUSICA

In Renaissance times, secularism was tantamount to heresy, and heresy incurred severe punishment, including torture and burning. It was no small matter, therefore, when the effect of secularism on opera made it an obvious culprit. The evidence was there in opera's reliance on the pagan myths of ancient Greece, its strong emotional content, its emphasis on human, rather than religious motivations and the flamboyant materialism of its spectacular staging. Opera broke another basic tradition of religious music – that the libretto should consist of sacred texts. Instead, opera had its own libretto, the *dramma per musica* ('drama for music'), which dealt with heroic or serious but not necessarily religious themes. In these circumstances, it was inevitable that opera should become subject to papal prohibition orders.

NEW MUSICAL FORMS
EVOLVED – MONODY

The pope, however, could not exercise a blanket ban in Italy, which in Renaissance times was a mass of city-states with their own rulers, their own laws – and their own opera houses. Religious authorities were able to exert less pressure of the sort that had controlled the arts in Medieval times, so that new musical forms were able to evolve. One of them was monody, the solo song that became popular in Florence and Venice in the first half of the seventeenth century. Monody, which was accompanied by a continuo (bass line), often played on a harpsichord or lute, came in two forms. The first was the **madrigal** type, which had an elaborately decorated vocal line. The second, established by Caccini around 1601–02, was the aria type, in which the principal melody was repeated with variations. Monody was emotional and highly ornamented, with varied rhythms and leaps between notes that greatly heightened its dramatic effect.

RECITATIVE

Recitative, a part-spoken, part-sung musical line based on natural speech rhythms and pitch, was regarded as largely synonymous with monody. During the seventeenth century, recitatives acted as a link between one aria and the next, but this was not their only function. Their words could also further the plot or give insights into the characters, without letting go of the musical line. Another French innovation, the ***ballet de cour***, or 'royal court ballet', featured a recitative at the start of each act, where it served as a narrative to explain the action or 'plot' demonstrated by the dance.

ENSEMBLE

Like the ballet, opera was a genre requiring the precise, skilful teamwork known as **ensemble** playing. The expression came from the French word *ensemble*, meaning 'together'. As opera scores began to include duets – usually 'love' duets – trios, quartets and quintets, great precision, timing and tone control were required of the singers. This is not to suggest that the solo performer, singing an aria and therefore responsible for delivering the major share of the music, was under less demanding discipline. In early Baroque opera, the aria – which in Italian meant 'air' and was a lyrical piece for solo voice – was usually accompanied by a continuo with **ritornellos**, or short orchestral interludes between the verses. In early Baroque arias, there were four or more verses. The number of verses was reduced to two after 1650, and subsequently, the two-verse aria became standard. In Venice, arias were written in double or triple time or a mixture of both until around 1660.

SACRA RAPPRESENTAZIONE IN ITALY

Opera, however, did not have a monopoly of the aria. Arias were also centrepieces in **cantatas**, the vocal chamber music of the Baroque era, and in **oratorios**. Although the oratorio shared with opera the basic ingredients of soloists, chorus and orchestra, oratorios placed much more emphasis on choral singing, and the two genres had different purposes. Opera rapidly developed as a secular art form, whereas oratorio was firmly sacred music. In the mid-sixteenth century, some time before it helped to 'father' opera, the groundwork of oratorio was laid in 'spiritual exercises' at the Congregation of the Oratorio of St Filippo Neri in Rome. In its turn, oratorio had its own 'sire', which also contributed to the development of opera – the *sacra rappresentazione*, or 'sacred opera', a religious play with musical accompaniment.

DIVERTISSEMENT IN FRANCE

While Italy was the chief and most prolific influence in developing 'true' opera, other European countries took to the new genre with enthusiasm and developed their own operatic traditions. The French, for example, introduced the **divertissement** ('entertainment') – a section of vocal solos, ensembles and dances that are usually ancillary to the work's main action. The *grands divertissements* devised for King Louis XIV in 1664 and 1674, complete entertainments in their own right, featured two or more singers who represented allegorical or mythological figures.

Like these 'big diversions', the *tragédie en musique* or **tragédie lyrique** – the musical or lyrical tragedy – had links with the French royal court. The *tragédie en musique* was first established by Cambert and afterwards developed by Lully and **Jean-Philippe Rameau** (1683–1764). The libretto concentrated on the themes of courtly love and knightly behaviour, and the performance included ballet scenes, recitatives, choruses and airs, which used minuet and other dance rhythms.

AIR

The French shared another innovation, the air, with the English. The air – a term for a light tune or song – appeared in France after 1571 as the *air de cour*, or court song. The first *airs de cour* were solo or ensemble songs with lute accompaniment. The genre reached England in 1597 with the publication of the first of four books of *Ayres for Voice and Lute* by John Dowland (1563–1626). The other three appeared in 1600, 1603 and 1612.

Overall, however, the English failed to make a characteristic mark on opera. The only noteworthy example to come out of England in the Baroque era was Purcell's *Dido and Aeneas*. Purcell was nevertheless a considerable composer for the theatre. He wrote songs and instrumental music for plays and co-wrote five semi-operas. These were more spoken dialogue than opera but included *divertissements* and various musical scenes and shared some characteristics with the English court entertainment known as the **masque**.

MASQUES

The masque developed out of fifteenth-century English and Italian entertainments in which masks were used as a disguise. Introduced at court by King Henry VIII (1491–1547), the masque was a mixture of songs with recitatives, dialogue, dances, energetic 'revels' and provocative interplay between performers and audience. The staging of masques could be extremely elaborate. After 1660, they moved from the royal court to the theatre, to become a public entertainment.

❈ *BEL CANTO* ∽ p. 19

Bel canto – beautiful singing – is a vocal technique that is deliberately designed to sound effortless but is, in reality, extremely difficult to achieve. Although the technique reached full flower in the nineteenth century, especially in the operas of **Vincenzo Bellini** (1801–35), elements of *bel canto* style first appeared in the Baroque era, in Venetian opera of the mid-seventeenth century. The technique goes back even further, though, to Medieval teachers who encouraged singers to achieve an even continuity of tone and pass from one musical phrase to the next without a pause. The smooth, sustained legato characteristic of *bel canto*, in which the singer scarcely seems to take a breath, requires superlative tone, elegant phrasing and expressive delivery, all combined in seamless fashion to provide an uninterrupted musical line. Although *bel canto* can appear to lack vocal fire when compared to the extra-musical dramatics of **verismo**, it is by no means without drama or emotion and was used to great effect by its most illustrious twentieth-century practitioners, **Maria Callas** (1923–77) and Tito Schipa (1888–1965). Long identified as the traditional Italian art of singing, the term *bel canto* was first used some time before 1840 by Italian composer and singer Nicola Vaccai.

SOUNDS FAMILIAR

MELODIES FROM THE OPERA – THE OVERTURE

The Florentine composer **Antonio Cesti** (1623–69) introduced the idea of putting melodies in an opera into its overture, as a kind of 'trailer' to the music that was to come and to set the mood. He first did this in his famous *Il pomo d'oro* ('The Golden Apple', 1668).

❈ MONTEVERDI'S INNOVATIONS ∽ p. 51

Claudio Monteverdi was a great innovator who achieved the quantum leap of musical style that largely freed opera from its Medieval and religious origins. To achieve this, he broke some rules, put his own interpretations on others and made changes that, in seventeenth-century terms, were revolutionary. The recitative, for example, was already an established pattern in singing, but Monteverdi used it in a new way, as a lead-in to an aria.

Orchestras in the seventeenth century were relatively small, which limited their dramatic impact. Monteverdi expanded the size of his orchestra to some 40 instruments, thus broadening and deepening the sound. It was common practice, too, for music to be played by any available combination of instruments. Monteverdi sought more precise effects by allocating certain passages of music in his operas to instruments of his choice. A further innovation, again uncommon in seventeenth-century orchestration, was Monteverdi's frequent changes of harmony and key. This variability increased an opera's dramatic feel, alerted the audience to new musical developments in the score and generally kept their attention at a peak of interest.

Early and Middle Baroque
PERSONALITIES

Blow, John
1649–1708, **ENGLISH**

John Blow, an influential figure in English music, was a gentleman of the Chapel Royal, organist there and later, in 1700, its official composer. Among his students was the brilliant Henry Purcell. Blow's own compositions were considerable. Besides his church music, which included over 100 anthems, he provided music for entertainments at the royal court. These were typically Baroque in their emphasis on emotion and included some 90 songs, together with duets, 70 pieces for harpsichord and his only work for the stage, *Venus and Adonis* (*c.* 1682). This short opera, which Blow described as a 'masque for the entertainment of the king', was written for King Charles II, who had appointed him court composer. *Venus and Adonis*, in which Charles's mistress and her daughter took part, showed distinct French influences in the dances. Blow's opera foreshadowed Purcell's *Dido and Aeneas*, composed two years later. Blow's 'Ode on the Death of Mr Henry Purcell (1696)', a duet with instrumental accompaniment, eloquently expressed his sadness at the untimely demise of his young friend and sometime student.

Busenello, Gian Francesco
1598–1659, **ITALIAN**

Venetian-born librettist Gian Francesco Busenello had a particular talent for the commercial operas that became fashionable in Italy in the first half of the seventeenth century. Busenello possessed a certain cynical realism about life that served him and his composers well when it came to insights into human behaviour. Busenello was never judgemental in his treatment of his operatic characters, even the most villainous. Instead, he viewed them with sardonic tolerance and an acute sense of humour, which made them more believable. Busenello began writing libretti somewhat late in life, and his output was not extensive. He wrote only five or six in all, starting with Cavalli's *Gli amore di Apollo e di Dafne* ('The Love of Apollo and Daphne', 1640). Busenello provided libretti for three other Cavalli operas, but his greatest achievement was his work for Monteverdi in *L'incoronazione di Poppea* (1642).

Caccini, Francesca
1587–c. 1637, **ITALIAN**

Francesca Caccini was the daughter of composer and singer **Giulio Caccini** (1551–1618). She sang at lavish musical entertainments staged in Florence and also performed in Paris with her mother and sister in 1604–05. Francesca, known as *La Cecchina* ('The Little Fairy'), was extremely versatile: she was not only a singer, but a talented performer on the harpsichord, guitar and lute, and a composer in her own right. Her first compositions were festive ballets, such as *Il ballo delle zigane* ('The Ballet of the Gypsies', 1615). She then graduated to monody in her *Primo libro della musiche* ('First Book of Music', 1618). From there, Caccini collaborated with Marco di Gagliano on the sacred work *Il martirio di Sant'Agata* ('The Martyrdom of Saint Agatha', 1622) and wrote the opera *La liberazione di Ruggiero dall'isola d'Alcina* ('Ruggiero's Liberation from Alcina's Island', 1625). This was the first opera known to be composed by a woman.

Caccini, Giulio
1551–1618, **ITALIAN**

At age 13, Giulio Caccini arrived at the court of the de' Medici family in Florence and very quickly proved himself immensely gifted in several musical skills – as singer, composer, teacher, lutenist and harpist. In 1598,

Caccini helped Peri compose *Dafne*. In 1600, he became superintendent of musicians and actors at the ducal court of Tuscany. In the same year, Caccini wrote his first opera, *Il rapimento di Cefalo* ('The Kidnapping of Cefalo') and his second, *Euridice*, with libretto by Ottavio Rinuccini. This *Euridice* was first performed in 1602. There was some dispute with Peri, who also used Rinuccini's text and acknowledged that his score included some of Caccini's music: this was not good enough for Caccini, who claimed that he, and not Peri, had 'invented' the operatic style. However, Caccini's greatest contribution to music and opera did not lie with his compositions but with his book *Le nuove musiche* ('The New Music'), published in 1602. Here, Caccini made a powerful case for the radical changes of style and mood that revolutionized music in the Baroque period and prompted the birth of opera.

Euridice

by Giulio Caccini
Premiered: 1602, Florence
Libretto by Ottavio Rinuccini, after Ovid

PROLOGUE

The figure of Tragedy introduces the opera, explaining that to make the story suitable for marriage celebrations, the original ending has been altered.

ACT I

The act opens in an Arcadian village, with Euridice preparing for her marriage to Orfeo, along with nymphs and shepherds who sing of the couple's beauty. Orfeo is similarly celebrating with his friend Arceto and other shepherds, when a messenger, Dafne, enters bearing bad news: Euridice has been bitten by a snake and has died, whispering Orfeo's name with her dying breath. The nymphs and shepherds join Orfeo in a melancholy lament.

ACT II

Orfeo, escorted by Venere, arrives in the underworld. He pleads with Plutone, the ruler there, to return Euridice to him, but Plutone explains that this is not how things happen in the underworld. However, the beauty of Orfeo's song touches the hearts of Proserpina (Plutone's wife), Venere and Charon, the boatman of the dead. These divinities add their pleas to Orfeo's, and Plutone eventually agrees to free Euridice.

ACT III

Meanwhile, the nymphs and shepherds are concerned about what has happened to Orfeo and Euridice. A shepherd, Arminta, arrives with the happy news that the couple are well and are on their way home. When Orfeo and Euridice return to the village, Orfeo sings a song of joy, which is followed by much rejoicing and dancing throughout the village. The opera closes with a celebration of the victory of love over death.

Calderón de la Barca, Pedro
1600–81, SPANISH

Pedro Calderón de la Barca, one of Spain's greatest playwrights, made an important venture into the world of opera with his libretto for **Juan Hidalgo**'s (*c.* 1612–85) *La púrpura de la rosa* ('The Colour of the Rose', *c.* 1660) – the first Spanish opera performed in Madrid. The same year, Calderón provided Hidalgo with another libretto, this time for the composer's *Celos aun del aire matan* ('Even Jealousy of the Air Can Kill', *c.* 1660). Although Calderón's output for opera was not great, the plots of his plays – notably his so-called 'revenge' dramas – explored similar territory. Calderón's work also retains a modern appeal. His most famous play, *La vida es sueño* ('Life is a Dream', 1635), which dealt with free will and predestination, was turned into an opera by the American composer Lewis Spratlan (b. 1940) and won the Pulitzer Prize in Music in 2000.

Campra, André
1660–1744, **FRENCH**

Born in Aix-en-Provence, Campra became a church musician in Arles and Toulouse, and composed sacred music that was much admired. In 1694, Campra moved to Paris to become master of music at the cathedral of Nôtre Dame. Three years later, he produced his **opéra-ballet**, *L'Europe galante* (1697). With this work, Campra was straying into secular territory and became worried that his church position might be jeopardized. This was why *L'Europe galante* was published anonymously and why Campra borrowed his brother's name for his other early compositions of the same type. Fortunately he did not have to maintain this subterfuge for too long. He left Nôtre Dame in 1700 and embarked on a prolific career as a composer of opera. Campra's sizable output included some 40 dramatic works, from short *divertissements* to full-length operas. Jean-Baptiste Lully, the 'father' of French opera, exerted a strong influence over Campra's output, which won him great popularity and acclaim. Among his many honours and awards was an appointment, in 1722, as *Sons Maître de Musique de la Chappelle Royale* (Deputy Music Master of the Chapel Royal).

Cavalieri, Emilio de'
c. 1550–1602, **ITALIAN**

Emilio de' Cavalieri – composer, teacher, dancer and organist – was born in Rome. At the de' Medici court in Florence, he organized the family's spectacular celebrations and was also involved with the innovative Camerata group and their experiments into the stile *rappresentativo* (representative style). In 1589, Cavalieri contributed madrigals and concluding music for the *intermedi* (interludes) staged in Florence; the chorus that began the finale became one of the most popular melodies of its time. However, like Peri, Cavalieri fell foul of Giulio Caccini. Cavalieri wrote *La contesa fra Guinon e Minerva* ('The Dispute between Guinon and Minerva', 1600) for the wedding of King Henry VI of Spain. Caccini's *Il rapimento di Cefalo* was also to be performed on this occasion, but Caccini sabotaged Cavalieri's attempts to take control of the production. In disgust, Cavalieri returned to Rome. There he introduced the new style of music to a new audience with a sacred opera, sometimes called the first oratorio, *La rappresentazione di anima e di corpo* ('The Story of the Soul and the Body'). This presaged the role of Rome as a major centre of Baroque opera some 30 years later.

La Rappresentatione di Animo e di Corpo ('The Story of the Soul and the Body')
by Emilio de' Cavalieri
Premiered: 1600, Rome
Libretto by Agostino Manni and Dorisio Isorelli

PROLOGUE
The figures of Avveduto and Prudenzio (both mean 'Prudence') discuss at length the various facets of human nature and appeal to the audience to learn from what they will see in this allegorical opera.

ACT I
The character Tempo (Time) presents a monologue on the transience of human life and Intelletto (Intellect) discusses spiritual hopes and desires. There follows a dialogue between Corpo (Body) and Anima (Soul) about their contrasting needs. The act concludes with a chorus that discusses the role of the heavens in helping men overcome everyday obstacles and dangers.

ACT II
Consiglio (Counsel) arranges a test for Anima and Corpo, in which they must resist the sins of the flesh offered by Mondo (the World) and Vita Mondana (Worldy Life). Piacere (Pleasure)

appears with some cohorts and attempts to seduce Anima and Corpo. Corpo is about to give in, but Anima, disgusted, sends Piacere away. Anima appeals to the heavens for help and is answered by an echo. A guardian angel descends and assists them in resisting the temptations. The seduction ends when the silhouette of Morte (Death) is seen. Corpo laments the difficult choices he must make, and the chorus praises heavenly rewards.

ACT III

Intelletto and Consiglio present the two afterlife existences. They are aided alternately in their descriptions by damned spirits (who sing in a low register) and blessed spirits (who sing at a brighter pitch). Anima, Corpo, Consiglio and Intelletto discuss each issue as it is raised. Anima and Corpo resolve to reach heaven and invite everyone to rejoice in praise of the Lord.

Cavalli, Francesco

1602–76, **ITALIAN**

Francesco Cavalli was in the right place at the right time when the first opera house, the Teatro San Cassiano, opened in Venice in 1637. The following year, Cavalli, with Orazio Persiani (fl. 1640) as librettist, produced *La nozze di Teti e di Peleo* ('The Wedding of Teti and Peleo', 1638) for the San Cassiano. In the next 10 years, Cavalli composed 10 more operas, including *Egisto* (1643). He also became manager of the San Cassiano, together with the librettist **Giovanni Faustini** (1615–51). Together, they firmly established the stile *rappresentazione*. In 1650, the San Cassiano closed due to financial difficulties, but it reopened in 1658. Cavalli returned as musical director, contracted to write one opera a year. He was banned from working for any other Venetian opera house but was permitted to accept work from outside Venice. In 1662, he wrote *Ercole amante* ('Hercules in Love') for the marriage of King Louis XIV of France, but it was so badly received

that Cavalli was reluctant to write any more operas. Eventually, however, he relented and wrote six more; two of the works were never staged but three are still performed today.

Egisto

by Francesco Cavalli
Premiered: 1643, Venice
Libretto by Giovanni Faustini

BACKGROUND

Egisto and Clori, two lovers from Delos, have been captured by pirates and sold to different masters. On the day of her marriage to Lidio, Climene has also been captured and sold to the same master as Egisto.

ACT I

One year later, Egisto and Climene have escaped and returned to her home island of Zakynthos, both anxious to be reunited with their former lovers. Unfortunately, however, they discover that Clori and Lidio have fallen in love. Climene's brother, Ipparco, also happens to have fallen for Clori and is encouraged by his servant Dema to take his vengeance against Lidio. After overhearing the declarations of love between Clori and Lidio, Egisto and Climene appeal to Amor to help them exact their revenge; instead of helping them however, he is encouraged by Venus to drive Egisto mad.

ACT II

Clori pretends not to recognize Egisto, claiming that he must be mad to think they were ever lovers. When confronted by Climene, Lidio tells her that she has been replaced in his affections by Clori. Egisto advises Lidio that his love for Clori will bring nothing but sorrow. Amor is captured by Semele, Fedra, Didone and Hero, all of whom had been wronged by love, and Amor appeals to Apollo (an ancestor of Egisto) to release him.

ACT III

To uphold his sister's honour and rid himself of a rival, Ipparco resolves to kill Lidio. He captures him and then urges Climene to stab her former lover, but she hesitates, asking the gods to forgive him and requesting her own death instead. This reawakens Lidio's love for Climene and they are reunited. Egisto has now been driven mad, but Clori's heart is softened by his suffering. All four lovers return to their original pairs through the power of Amor.

Cesti, Antonio
1623–69, ITALIAN

Musically speaking, Florentine composer Antonio Cesti led a double life. He wrote operas for the Venetian opera houses but also provided music for the courts at Innsbruck and Vienna. Either way, he was involved in basically secular entertainment, despite the fact that he was in holy orders. At age 14, Cesti had joined the Minorite friars, but his roving eye, which ill-suited him for the religious life, was encouraged by his contacts with Venice and the glamorous ducal courts of Austria. A series of scandals and indiscretions led him to resign from the Church in 1659, but earlier he had written *Orontea* (1649) and *Cesare amante* ('Caesar in Love', 1651) for Venetian audiences. In 1652, Cesti was appointed *Kappellmeister* to the Austrian Archduke Ferdinand Karl and produced several operas, including the most successful, *La Dori* ('The Faithful Slave', 1657). From there, Cesti moved to imperial Vienna, where his most famous opera, *Il pomo d'oro* ('The Golden Apple'), was staged in 1668. Another opera, *Genserico* (1669), is also sometimes attributed to Cesti.

Il pomo d'oro ('The Golden Apple')
by Antonio Cesti
Premiered: 1668, Vienna
Libretto by Francesco Sbarra

PROLOGUE

Personifications of the Habsburg territories gather in praise of Austria and its emperor, Leopold I.

ACT I

During a banquet in Giove's palace, Discordia, goddess of strife, throws a golden apple inscribed 'to the most beautiful' among the assembled goddesses. Venere, Pallade and Giunone all claim it, and Giove decrees that the prince Paride will decide. Paride and the nymph Ennone are together on Mount Ida when Mercurio brings news of Giove's decree. The shepherd Aurindo reveals his love for Ennone. At Paride's palace Giunone, Pallade and Venere try to win the apple, which goes to Venere when she offers Elena in exchange.

ACT II

Paride prepares to leave to claim Elena, but still affirms his love for Ennone. At the mouth of hell Caronte is cheered at the prospect of many new arrivals resulting from the coming war. Pallade calls on Cecrope, King of Athens, to defend her honour.

ACT III

Giunone orders Eolo, god of the winds, to destroy Paride's ship. Ennone laments her loss, while Aurindo's hopes are raised.

Venere persuades Marte to support Paride and the Trojans. When Eolo unleashes the winds, Venere also persuades Nettuno to calm the seas so that Paride can continue to look for Elena. Marte defeats the Athenians and captures Cecrope.

ACT IV

The temple of Pallade is destroyed by an earthquake, and the remaining Athenian forces depart for battle. Venere and Marte taunt Cecrope, but news comes of the approaching Athenians, whom Pallade helps in the battle.

ACT V

Ennone accepts that she has lost Paride and submits to Aurindo. Giove destroys the tower on which the golden apple is standing, and it is finally awarded to Empress Margherita.

Charpentier, Marc-Antoine

c. 1645–1704, FRENCH

Marc-Antoine Charpentier, a Parisian, was on hand to step into the breach after Lully quarrelled with the French playwright **Jean-Baptiste Poquelin Molière** (1622–73), whose works Lully had been setting to music. As a result, Charpentier wrote the music for Molière's *Le mariage forcé* ('The Forced Marriage', 1672) and *Le malade imaginaire* ('The Hypochondriac', 1673). Lully, however, was an expert at court intrigue, and he managed to sideline Charpentier. Molière had great regard for Charpentier and his abilities, but the renowned playwright died in 1673. All the same, Charpentier maintained his connection with Molière's theatre, the Comédie-Française, and many of his *divertissements* were staged there, including *Les amours de Vénus et d'Adonis* ('The Loves of Venus and Adonis', 1678). *Vénus et d'Adonis* proved so popular that it was still being performed there more than 70 years later. Charpentier's

pastorales, such as *La noce du village* ('The Village Wedding', 1692), were equally well received. His masterpiece, however, was a *tragédie lyrique*, *Médée* (1693), based on a play of the same name by **Pierre Corneille** (1606–84).

Cicognini, Giacinto

1606–51, ITALIAN

Florentine librettist Giacinto Cicognini followed in a famous father's footsteps. Jacopo Cicognini (1577–1633), had been among the pioneers who introduced Spanish theatre to Italian audiences. Jacopo was also a librettist; he wrote *Andromeda* (1618) for another Florentine, the composer Domenico Belli. Giacinto Cicognini initially intended to become a lawyer, but the stage proved much more seductive, and he renounced the courts for the theatre. Naturally enough, considering his father's work and interest in Spain, Giacinto's libretti show strong Spanish influences. This is especially evident in the elegance of Giacinto's verse. His best-known libretto was written for Cavalli's *Giasone* (1649) and, in the same year, he wrote *Orontea* for Cesti. Another libretto for *Gli amore di Alessandro Magno e di Rossana* ('The Love of Alexander the Great and Roxane') by Francesco Luzzo (1628–58) appeared in 1651, the year Giacinto died.

Corneille, Pierre

1606–84, FRENCH

Pierre Corneille, the renowned playwright, wrote verse dramas on heroic and classical themes that were tailor-made for operatic treatment. Corneille's list of plays that were turned into libretti is not nearly as long as William Shakespeare's or Sir Walter Scott's, but it is impressive enough. Corneille's verse dramas were still attracting composers in the early twentieth century. In all, 13 of his plays were turned into 41 operas between 1664 and 1916. By far the most popular was *El Cid* ('The Lord', 1637). *El Cid*, more properly called Rodrigo Diaz de Vivar, was the Spanish folk hero of numerous legends that told of his fight on behalf of Christian kings against the Moorish rulers of Spain. Between 1706 and 1916, no fewer than 20 operas were based on this play with music by such composers as **George Frideric Handel** (1685–1759) and **Jules Massenet** (1842–1912).

Dryden, John
1631–1700, ENGLISH

John Dryden, the poet, playwright and critic, made his name writing 'heroic' verse and other dramas in the Restoration period, which followed the return of King Charles II (1630–85) from exile in 1660. The restoration of the king to his throne was fortuitous for Dryden and other playwrights. During the dreary years of Puritan rule that followed the English Civil War and the execution in 1649 of the new king's father, Charles I, all theatres had been closed, and performances elsewhere – even in taverns or private houses – were forbidden by law. Dryden took full advantage of the reopening of the theatres in 1660. He wrote two plays for operatic performance – *Albion and Albianus* (1685) and *King Arthur* (1691). Dryden, together with another dramatist, Sir Robert Howard, also provided the text for Purcell's semi-opera *The Indian Queen* (1695).

Faustini, Giovanni
1615–51, ITALIAN

Librettist and theatre manager Giovanni Faustini, who was born in Venice, wrote 11 libretti for Venetian opera houses in nine years – between 1642 and 1651 – and 10 of them were set to music by Francesco Cavalli. Cavalli owed a great deal to Faustini's skill and to his unerring 'feel' for the pseudo-historical subjects of most of his libretti. Faustini also possessed an instinct for devising plots that had maximum popular appeal and would ensure financial success. His libretti were beautifully constructed and designed to wring the utmost drama out of the situations depicted on stage. He had a good understanding of the music and how it could heighten drama and made sure that his libretti offered composers plenty of scope for musical characterization. Faustini's best-known libretti, both written for Cavalli, were *Ormindo* (1644) and *Calisto*, which was first performed in 1651, the same year as Faustini's premature death.

Feind, Barthold
1678–1721, GERMAN

In 1705, Barthold Feind – whose real name was Aristobulos Eutropius or Aristobulos Wahrmund – was practising law in his home city, Hamburg, when he wrote his first libretto for **Reinhard Keiser** (1674–1739), *Octavia*. Keiser needed a replacement at this time, after the death of Christian Heinrich Postel, who had been his librettist for nine years. Feind, however, was more than a substitute. He had his own strengths as a librettist. His forté was his handling of the comic elements in his libretti and his deft way with satire and parody. In 1706, Feind produced two more libretti for Keiser and another text in 1708 for Christophe Graupner. The mixture of German and Italian elements found in Feind's libretti had been typical of Postel's work and, together with French influences, also marked the music of Keiser.

Hidalgo, Juan
c. 1612–85, SPANISH

Most works by Juan Hidalgo, who was born in Madrid, were intended for church performance. However, Hidalgo was greatly attracted to Italian opera. While it would not have been acceptable for him to use the opera style in church music, he did introduce it into several of his secular songs and other vocal settings. This led to collaboration with the famous Spanish dramatist Pedro Calderón de la Barca (1600–81), who was master of the revels of the Spanish king, Philip IV. The partnership was to be epoch-making in the context of Spanish music. Together, Hidalgo and Calderón produced the first Spanish opera, *La púrpura de la rosa* ('The Colour of the Rose', *c.* 1660). Unfortunately, neither the text nor the music of *La púrpura* have survived, but it was followed in the same year by another opera that is extant, *Celos aun del aire matan* ('Even Jealousy of the Air Can Kill', *c.* 1660). Another important composition by Hidalgo was the first *zarzuela*, his *Los cielos hacen estrellas* ('The Skies have Stars', 1672) which established the traditional form of Spanish opera.

Keiser, Reinhard
1674–1739, **GERMAN**
Reinhard Keiser was born in Teuchern, Germany. When his mentor, Johann Sigismud Kusser (1660–1727) relocated to Hamburg in around 1693, Keiser succeeded him as *Kappellmeister* in Brunswick. There, Keiser produced Kusser's first opera, *Basilius* (1694), and wrote several operas of his own, but after only three years he followed his mentor to Hamburg. Keiser formed a partnership with the librettist Christian Heinrich Postel. A series of successful operas staged at the Theater am Gänsemarkt followed, beginning with *Adonis* (1697) and continuing at the rate of five every season. As co-proprietor of the theatre after 1702, Keiser oversaw performances of the early works of Handel, among others. Afterwards, as sole director, Keiser made Hamburg the premier operatic centre in Germany. His own music contributed much to

this reputation. Keiser's *Claudius* (1703), *Octavia* (1705) and *Croesus* (1710) demonstrated a lyricism and emotional power that was said to match the best of the Italian and French operas. The exact number of operas written by Keiser is unknown, although estimates have been made of around 75 or 100; however, of this prolific output only 19 complete operas have survived.

Octavia
by Reinhard Keiser
Premiered: 1705, Hamburg
Libretto by Barthold Feind

ACT I
King Tiridates of Armenia and his queen, Ormoena, have been captured and brought to Rome, where Nero falls in love with the beautiful Ormoena. Before he can marry her, however, Nero must first rid himself of his own virtuous wife, Octavia.

ACT II
Nero orders Octavia to commit suicide, either by poison or with a dagger. Ever obedient, Octavia prepares to stab herself but is stopped at the last minute by the patrician Piso, who is devoted to her. He swears to avenge Nero's treatment of Octavia and raises a rebellion that forces Nero to flee the city.

ACT III
Octavia, however, has other plans. Acting on a suggestion by the philosopher Seneca, she dresses as her own ghost and appears before Nero. He is horrified at the thought of what he has done and is stricken with remorse at Octavia's 'death'. Meanwhile, the rebels have been defeated. His loyal supporters tell Nero that Octavia is still alive. He is overjoyed at the news and even pardons Piso, since it was his action that saved Octavia's life. Tiridates is restored to his kingdom, and Ormoena happily returns to her husband.

Landi, Stefano
c. 1586–1639, **ITALIAN**

Stefano Landi, who was born and gained his musical training in Rome, became *maestro di cappella* to the bishop of Padua in around 1618. The next year, Landi's *La morte d'Orfeo* ('The Death of Orpheus', 1619) was performed in Rome, where the composer returned in 1620. Four years later, Landi was appointed *maestro di cappella* at Santa Maria dei Monti, and he joined the papal choir in 1629. Landi's opera *Il Sant'Alessio* ('Saint Alexius', 1632) was performed at the opening of the opera house in the Barberini palace. Both *La morte d'Orfeo* and *Il Sant'Alessio* were innovative and seminal works. The *forme*, the first secular opera to be performed in Rome, began a tradition for impressive choral scenes and spectacular endings that became characteristic of Roman opera.

Il Sant'Alessio was on an even grander scale than its predecessor, with greater realism and drama and a hero who broke with established practice by typifying, not the mythological figures of earlier Baroque opera, but a real-life human being. In *Il Sant'Alessio*, Landi anticipated the opera overture with orchestral sinfonias that were performed before the start of each act.

Il Sant'Alessio ('Saint Alexius')
by Stefano Landi
Premiered: 1632, Rome
Libretto by Giulio Rospigliosi

PROLOGUE
The figure of Roma (Rome), surrounded by a chorus of slaves, dedicates the performance to the Prince of Polonia (Poland).

ACT I
Eufemiano, a Roman senator and Alessio's father, encounters Adrasto, a knight returning from war. While pleased to see Adrasto, Eufemiano mourns the disappearance of his son Alessio. Meanwhile, Alessio, an ascetic, is offered lodgings at his father's house by the pages Marzio and Curzio. Taking him for a beggar, they mock him. In hell, the devil resolves to tempt Alessio away from his holy life. Alessio's grieving wife and mother are comforted by their nurse. Curzio arranges a rustic dance to entertain everyone.

ACT II
Eufemiano laments the loss of his son. The devil reveals his plan to trick Alessio into returning to the joys of worldly pleasures: Alessio's wife will go off in search of him, and Alessio will feel guilty and reveal himself. Dressed as a pilgrim, Alessio's wife prepares to leave, accompanied by Alessio's mother. Alessio, as the beggar, tries to dissuade them. Seeing the grief he is causing his family, he considers revealing his identity and is encouraged to do so by the devil, disguised as a hermit. An angel appears, warning Alessio against the devil and comforting him with news of his approaching death and the joys that he can expect in heaven. Alessio sings of the pleasure he will find when his earthly existence is over. A light-hearted scene follows in which the devil and Marzio taunt each other. The figure of Religione (Religion) then praises Alessio's constancy, urging others to follow his example. Eufemiano, still grieving, is comforted by news of a celestial voice that has been heard in the cathedral.

ACT III
His mission unaccomplished, the devil returns to hell. A papal ambassador brings news of Alessio's death, and his family mourns as they hear a letter he has written to them. Angels encourage everyone to celebrate along with Religione, who praises Alessio's admirable conduct and dedicates a church to him.

Legrenzi, Giovanni
1626–90, **ITALIAN**

Giovanni Legrenzi composed his first operas at Ferrara, where he became *maestro di cappella* at the Accademia dello Spirito Santo in 1656. He began with *Nino il giusto* ('Nino the Just', 1662) and in the next three years produced *Achille in Sciro* (1663) and *Zenobia e Radamisto* (1665). Subsequently, Legrenzi led a nomadic life, travelling around Europe until 1677, when he was appointed director of the Ospedali dei Mendicanti (the Beggars' Hospital) in Venice. Legrenzi wrote some 14 operas for the opera houses in Venice; many of these works have been lost. After becoming the first *maestro di cappella* at St Mark's in 1685, he abandoned the theatre and instead confined himself to instrumental and church music.

The Venetian operatic tradition culminated with Legrenzi's works, which were partly modelled on those of Monteverdi and Cavalli and included an ingenious genre, the heroic-comic opera, including *Totila* (1677), *Giustino* (1683) and *I due Cesari* ('The Two Caesars', 1683). In all these operas, Legrenzi provided elaborate musical treatment for historical themes, as well as dramatic and also comic scenes. One important innovation by Legrenzi was his emphasis on orchestral accompaniment and instrumental melodies, which anticipated practices later developed by the so-called Neapolitan school.

Lully, Jean-Baptiste
1632–87, FRENCH

Jean-Baptiste Lully was a French composer with an Italian background. He was born in Florence on 28 November 1632. His original name, later gallicized, was Giovanni Battista Lulli. In 1646, aged 14, he was placed with a noble household in Paris as a singer, dancer and violinist, and he became familiar with both French and Italian music. In 1653, he caught the attention of King Louis XIV.

COMPOSITIONS FOR THE COURT OF LOUIS XIV

Although discomfited by the composer's homosexual tendencies, King Louis thought a great deal of Lully and appointed him royal composer of instrumental music. By 1662, Lully was a naturalized Frenchman

---

and he became music master to the French royal family. He produced numerous scores for the *comédies-ballets* performed at Louis' lavish court. After 1671, when Robert Cambert's *Pomone* received its first performance, Lully progressed to opera. Devious and opportunistic, Lully bought the 'franchise' to present operas that had been reserved to Cambert's librettist, Pierre Perrin, after Perrin was imprisoned in 1672. Subsequently, Lully became a prolific composer of opera in the peculiarly French genre known as *tragédie lyrique*, which he promoted together with his librettist, **Philippe Quinault** (1635–88). Lully wrote 13 operas of this type, beginning with *Cadmus et Hermione* (1673) and ending with *Armide* (1686). Quinault was librettist for all but two.

MORE SOBER COMPOSITIONS

After 1683, when King Louis married the highly respectable Mme de Maintenon, the tone of the court became much more sober. Lully turned to writing sacred music and produced 13 'great' and 14 'small' **motets**, as well as his *Te Deum* (1677) and *De Profundis* (1683). Sadly, during a performance of the *Te Deum* early in 1687, Lully injured his foot with the point of the cane he was using to beat time. The injury became gangrenous and he died on 22 March 1687.

Alceste, ou le triomphe d'Alcide

Composed in 1674, Lully's *Alceste, ou le triomphe d'Alcide*, a *tragédie lyrique* with a prologue and five acts, had a double link with ancient Greek culture. The libretto, by Philippe Quinault, was based on *Alcestis*, a tragedy by the ancient Greek dramatist Euripides that in turn derived from the legend of Alcestis, wife of Admetus, King of Thessaly: Admetus had been promised immortality as long as he could find someone to die in his place. Alcestis volunteers to die for him but is prevented by the hero Hercules, who fights off Death in order to save her.

Lully wrote *Alceste*, which debuted at the Paris Opéra in 1674, to celebrate the French King Louis XIV's triumph in battle in Franche-Comté. Much of Lully's output while in Louis' employ was produced to satisfy the King's own taste in music, and *Alceste* was no exception. The staging of the opera was suitably spectacular, and knowing the French fondness for dancing, Lully provided ballet interludes. He also catered for audience preferences by providing a comic sub-plot and catchy tunes. This made *Alceste* a popular success, although the sensibilities of some critics were affronted, perhaps because they resented Lully's power.

Alceste, ou le triomphe d'Alcide ('Alceste, or the Triumph of Alcide')

by Jean-Baptise Lully
Composed: 1674
Premiered: 1674, Paris
Libretto by Philippe Quinault, after Euripides

PROLOGUE

Nymphs on the banks of the River Seine sing and dance with La Gloire (Glory), eagerly awaiting the victorious return of the King from battle.

ACT I

The beautiful and widely courted Alceste selects as her husband Admète, King of Thessaly. Present at her wedding, and also in love with Alceste, are Alcide (Hercules) and Licomède, King of the island of Scyros. A sub-plot is introduced that reflects the main story, involving the confidants of Alcide and Licomède courting Alceste's confidante. Licomède organizes a feast, that various nymphs and spirits of the sea attend. In the confusion, he abducts Alceste, assisted safely to his homeland by his sister, the sea-nymph Thetis, and other supernatural beings.

ACT II

On Scyros, Licomède is unsuccessful in wooing Alceste. Alcide and Admète arrive to rescue her, and a fierce battle ensues. Due largely to Alcide's strength and valour, Licomède is vanquished, but Admète is mortally wounded in the battle and exchanges poignant dying words with Alceste. However, the divine Apollon intervenes, declaring that he will return Admète's life to him if someone will agree to die in his place.

ACT III

Alceste grieves for Admète and ponders over the problem of who is to die in order to restore her husband's life. Her confidante and Admète's father each outline their unsuitability for the task. Shortly Admète enters, desiring to know to whom he owes his return to health. It transpires it is Alceste who has sacrificed her life for his; Admète is heartbroken. Alcide declares his love for Alceste and offers to go down to the underworld to retrieve her, on the condition that Admète give Alceste up to him on their return. Admète agrees.

ACT IV

Alcide descends to the underworld and crosses the River Styx. There is a feast in progress, given by Pluton and Proserpine in honour of Alceste, which is interrupted by the news that Alcide has arrived to claim her and return her to the world of the living. Pluton, ruler of the underworld, is impressed by Alcide and agrees that the pair can leave.

ACT V

An arc de triomphe is erected and a huge feast given by Admète, to celebrate Alceste's and Alcide's return. Alceste reveals to Alcide that all of her love for Admète has returned, and Alcide heroically restores Alceste to her husband; the couple are reunited amid much rejoicing. Apollon and the Muses join in the celebrations, praising the happy couple and Alcide's noble sense of honour.

Recommended Recording:

Alceste, La Grande Ecurie et la Chambre du Roy; Jean-Claude Malgoire, conductor; Astrée E 8527; Soloists: Colette Alliot-Lugaz (Alceste), Sophie Marin-Degor (Céphise), Howard Crook (Admète), Gilles Ragon (Lychas), Jean-Philippe Lafont (Alcide), François Loup (Lycomède)

TIMELINE

1632	Born as Giovanni Battista Lulli in Florence, Italy
1646	Moves to France and changes name to Jean-Baptiste Lully
1653	Enters service of Louis XIV as ballet dancer and instrumental composer
c. 1656	Becomes leader of band of les petits violins du Roi
1662	Appointed music master to the royal family
1664	Collaborates with Molière on *Le marriage force*, first in series of *comédies-ballets*
1664	Writes *Miserere*
1670	Lully performs in his *comédie-ballet*, *Le bourgeois gentilhomme*
1672	Obtains exclusive rights from King Louis to arrange operatic performances in Paris
1673	Produces his first *tragedie lyrique*, Cadmus et Hermione
1674	*Alceste* premieres spectacularly in Paris
1677	Lully composes *Te Deum*
1683	Louis XIV marries, and Lully composes *De Profundis*
1686	Premiere of *Acis et Galathée*
1687	Lully dies of gangrene of the foot in Paris
1687	Posthumous production of *Achille et Polixène*

ALCESTE: PROLOGUE

In the prologue to *Alceste*, the purpose of the opera is made clear by the mythological Nymph of the River Seine, as she laments the absence of King Louis XIV who is away fighting against the forces of the Burgundian state of Franche-Comté.

OPERAS

1672	Les fêtes de l'amour et de Bacchus
1673	Cadmus et Hermione
1674	Alceste, ou le triomphe d'Alcide
1675	Thésée
1676	Atys
1677	Isis
1678	Psyché
1679	Bellérophon
1680	Proserpine
1682	Persée
1683	Phaéton
1684	Amadis de Gaule
1685	Roland
1686	Armide
1686	Acis et Galathée
1687	Achille et Polixène

Marais, Marin
1656–1728, FRENCH

Marin Marais, who was born in Paris, was both a composer and a player of the viola da gamba. He spent his life in Paris or Versailles, where he was one of many musicians employed by King Louis XIV. Marais became a member of the Académie Royale de Musique and co-directed its orchestra with Pascal Colasse. For 15 years, between 1695 and 1710, Marais became renowned for his virtuoso instrumental performances, and in 1676 he was summoned to the Palace of Versailles to play for the king. In 1679, he was appointed to an official post as a viola da gamba performer. Marais remained at Versailles until he retired in 1725. His instrumental music was much admired, and so were his four operas, which he modelled on those of his teacher, Lully. All Marais' operas were produced in

Paris. The first, *Alcide*, premiered in 1693, followed by *Ariane et Bacchus* (1695) and *Alcyone* (1706). *Alcyone* was noteworthy for its musical representation of a storm, one of the earliest to be produced in opera. Marais' fourth opera, *Sémélé*, was produced in 1709.

Minato, Count Nicolo
c. 1627–98, **ITALIAN**

Poet and librettist Count Nicolo Minato wrote 11 texts for the Venetian opera houses, including Cavalli's *Pompeo Magna* ('Pompey the Great', 1666). In 1669, the Emperor of Austria, Leopold I, appointed Minato his court poet, and some very exciting opportunities opened up for the count. At that time, the court composer was Antonio Draghi (*c.* 1634–1700). Minato joined forces with Draghi to produce no fewer than 170 libretti. Another member of the team was the designer Ludovico Burnacini, who staged the Draghi-Minato operas. As he had already demonstrated in Venice, Minato had a particular fondness for historical subjects, and he produced *Gundeberga* (1672), one of the earliest libretti, based on a story from German history. Other libretti were set in the ancient world – *Temistocle in Persia* ('Themistocles in Persia', 1681) in ancient Greece, and *Sciopione preservatore di Roma* ('Scipio, Saviour of Rome', 1690) in ancient Rome.

Molière, Jean-Baptiste Poquelin
1622–73, **FRENCH**

The playwright, actor and *impresario* Molière was the brightest star in seventeenth-century French theatre, writing plays that lived on long after his time, some of them in the form of operas. In all, 17 of Molière's plays have been turned into 75 operas since 1706, over half of them in the twentieth century. Lully provided music for plays by Molière. So did Charpentier towards the end of Molière's life, when he wrote music for *Le mariage forcé* and *Le malade imaginaire*. Molière came from a wealthy background. He was attracted to the theatre as a very young man, embarking on his first theatrical venture in 1643, when he was only 21. Ultimately, Molière's plays and his actors came to the attention of King Louis XIV, who absorbed the entire company into his household in 1665.

Monteverdi, Claudio
1567–1643, **ITALIAN**

Claudio Giovanni Antonio Monteverdi was born in Cremona and began his illustrious career as a choirboy in the town's cathedral. By the time he was 20, he had already published the first of his eventual nine books of secular madrigals. He was also a skilled composer of motets. Monteverdi's horizons expanded in 1591 when he joined the court orchestra of Vincenzo Gonzaga, Duke of Mantua, as a string instrumentalist.

AN AMBITIOUS YOUNG MAN

The young Monteverdi was full of ambition, and aspired to succeed the Flemish composer Giaches de Wert as *maestro di cappella* in Mantua. In the event, he was upstaged by an older musician, Benedetto Pallavicino, and was forced to wait until Pallavicino's death five years later before he achieved his goal. However, his new position did not bring Monteverdi a comfortable berth. The influence of the Camerata group in Florence and the push for heightened emotion and expression in opera were already spreading. Monteverdi was attracted by these radical changes and was soon regarded as the leading exponent of the new forms of harmony and orchestration. This led him into conflict with the conservative theorist Giovanni Maria Artusi. The argument brought Monteverdi to the fore as a leader of the progressives, who embraced the new, if revolutionary, style in opera.

AN INNOVATIVE OPERA: *ORFEO*

Monteverdi's *Orfeo*, produced in Mantua in 1607, made the case for the progressive approach, and the message was reinforced by his next work, *Arianna* (1608). This was a particularly fraught time for Monteverdi, for both these operas were accompanied by tragedy in his personal life.

In 1607, the year of *Orfeo*, Monteverdi's wife, Claudia de Cattaneis, died and left him with three young children. In 1608, Caterina Martinelli, a young singer who lived with Monteverdi and who was due to take the title role in *Arianna*, died of smallpox. A replacement took over, and the first performance of the opera went ahead as scheduled. Like *Orfeo*, it was a great success, but the achievement had its down side: the acclaim appeared to intensify the dispute with Artusi and other conservatives, and a disenchanted Monteverdi left Mantua for his home town of Cremona. He pleaded poor health and insufficient pay but could not entirely free himself from Mantua. However, the Gonzaga family still had a lien on his services and did not release him until Duke Vincenzo died in 1612.

MAESTRO DI CAPPELLA
AT ST MARK'S

The following year, Monteverdi was appointed *maestro di cappella* at the Cathedral of St Mark's in Venice – a prestigious post he held until his death 30 years later. His duties were not onerous, however, and left Monteverdi with plenty of time for other work. He was now a well-respected figure in the music and opera world, and commissions regularly came his way. Two, ironically from Mantua, included a ballet, *Tirsi e Clori* (1616), and another opera, *La finta pazza Licori* ('Licori's Fake Madness', 1627). Meanwhile, Monteverdi's books of madrigals continued to appear. The eighth was published in 1638, the ninth, printed posthumously, in 1651.

MONTEVERDI'S MASTERPIECE

In 1637, when the world's first public opera house, San Cassiano, opened in Venice, Monteverdi was already on hand to compose operas for performance there. *Arianna* was revived for San Cassiano in 1640, and three new Monteverdi operas were premiered in the next three years. The third was Monteverdi's masterpiece, *L'incoronazione di Poppea* ('The Coronation of Poppea', 1642), which was first performed in the autumn. Soon afterwards, Monteverdi went home to Cremona for the last time. He died on 29 November 1643, soon after his return to Venice.

L'Orfeo, favola in musica

L'Orfeo, favola in musica consists of a prologue and five acts – a prolonged performance for its time. Monteverdi used several devices to extend the action of the opera. He wrote recitatives to be performed between the duets, as well as polyphonic madrigals, of which he was a master. Further additions included dances.

The opera, commissioned by the Gonzaga family for the carnival of 1606–07, was first produced privately in Mantua at the Accademia degli Invaghiti in February 1607. The performance was something of a relief to Monteverdi, who had been forced to overcome a crisis – a shortage of **castrati** (male sopranos) in Mantua. Monteverdi had to recruit a castrato from Pisa, but he intensified the crisis by arriving late. The composer had to give him a crash course to enable him to memorize words and music in record time. Copies of Striggio's libretto were specially printed and distributed among the audience so that they could follow the performance while it was in progress. It was so successful that Duke Vincenzo Gonzaga ordered a second performance. A third was planned but never took place. *Orfeo* was published in 1609, with a dedication to the Duke.

L'Orfeo, favola in musica ('Orpheus, a Legend in Music')
by *Claudio Monteverdi*
Composed: 1606
Premiered: 1607, Mantua
Libretto by Alessandro Striggio, after Ottavio Rinuccini and Ovid

PROLOGUE
The figure of Music welcomes the audience and flatters the patrons (the Gonzaga family), telling of the magic and power of music and asking for silence during the performance.

ACT I
In the fields of Thrace, nymphs and shepherds gather to celebrate the long-awaited marriage of demi-god Orfeo to beautiful Euridice. Amid joyous dancing and singing and teasing lovers' games, Orfeo delivers a romantic aria to Euridice. The pair then leave for the wedding.

ACT II
Returning from the wedding, Orfeo sings with the shepherds about how wonderful life is now that he has married Euridice and how miserable his life was before the wedding. A messenger, Silvia, arrives with bad news; she tells Orfeo that Euridice has suffered a snake bite and has died, whispering Orfeo's name in her final breath. The grieving Orfeo resolves to fetch his bride back from the underworld, while Silvia, mortified by the terrible news she has had to bear, shuts herself away.

ACT III
Hope escorts Orfeo to the entrance of the underworld, where she leaves him. There he encounters Charon, the boatman of the dead, who ferries souls across the River Styx. Charon is unwilling to let him pass, but Orfeo sings to him and plays his lyre until the boatman is lulled to sleep. Orfeo then crosses the river and enters the underworld.

ACT IV
Proserpina, the wife of Plutone, ruler of the underworld, is profoundly affected by Orfeo's music and pleads with her husband to release Euridice. Plutone agrees that Euridice may follow Orfeo out of the underworld, on the condition that Orfeo does not turn around. As they make their way along, Orfeo is seized with doubt and looks behind him to check that Euridice is there. Euridice must now leave Orfeo and remain in the underworld for eternity.

ACT V
Back in the fields of Thrace, the inconsolable Orfeo is comforted by Eco. His divine father, Apollo the sun god, descends from the heavens on a cloud. He then returns into the sky, taking Orfeo with him. From this heavenly viewpoint, Orfeo can gaze forever upon Euridice's starry image, as she has been transformed into a constellation.

Recommended Recording:
Orfeo, Le Concert d'Astrée; Emmanuelle Haïm, conductor; Virgin Classics 7243 5 45642 2; Soloists: Natalie Dessay (Musica), Patrizia Ciofi (Euridice), Alice Coote (Silvia), Ian Bostridge (Orfeo), Christopher Maltman (Apollo)

L'incoronazione di Poppea

L'incoronazione de Poppea, composed in 1642, has been called Monteverdi's greatest opera. It was one of the first operas to be based on history rather than mythology. The action takes place in Rome in ad 65. The eponymous heroine is the mistress and, later, wife of the Emperor Nero. The libretto was by Busenello, who took his text from the annals of the ancient Roman historian Tacitus (AD 55–120). The opera received its first performance in Venice in 1643. Poppea was written when Monteverdi was 76 and, by the standards of the seventeenth century, a very old man. Comparisons have been made with **Giuseppe Verdi** (1813–1901), who wrote his last opera, Falstaff (1893), in old age. Modern research has revealed that Poppea may not have been all Monteverdi's own work. It was ascribed to him by Cristoforo Ivanovich (1628–89), an Italian librettist and theatre historian, but neither of the two extant scores of the opera mentions the composer. It appears that Monteverdi was assisted by other composers, notably Francesco Sacrati (1605–50). Sacrati is believed to have written the finale scene and most of the music sung by Ottone, who attempts to kill Poppea after she has jilted him.

L'incoronazione di Poppea ('The Coronation of Poppea')

by Claudio Monteverdi
Composed: 1642
Premiered: 1643, Venice
Libretto by Gian Francesco Busenello, after Tacitus and Suetonius

PROLOGUE

The figures of Fortuna (Fortune) and Virtù (Virtue) argue over who has the most power over mortals. Amore (Love, or Cupid) joins them, insisting that his superior power will shortly be proven.

ACT I

Poppea's husband, Ottone, returns to her palace to find Nero's guard outside, confirming that she has taken Nero as her lover. Poppea and Nero take leave of each other, and Poppea confides in her nurse, Arnalta, her desire to be crowned empress. Meanwhile, Nero's wife, Empress Octavia, laments her husband's infidelity and is comforted by Seneca, a statesman and philospher. Returning home to his palace, Nero declares his intention to divorce Octavia and marry Poppea, making her empress. Seneca argues against this on both moral and political grounds, causing Nero's temper to rise against him. Later, Poppea, overheard by Ottone, convinces Nero that Seneca is an obstacle to their love and must die. Ottone is then rebuked by Drusilla, a noblewoman who is in love with him, over his continuing love for Poppea. Ottone pledges himself to Drusilla.

ACT II

The captain of Nero's guards, Liberto, delivers Seneca's death sentence from the emperor. Seneca gathers the members of his household around him and kills himself. While Poppea, overjoyed at the news of Seneca's death, prays to Amore, Octavia orders Ottone to kill Poppea. He hesitates, torn between his love for her and her cruel betrayal, but eventually he agrees and asks Drusilla to help him by lending him some of her clothes. Dressed as Drusilla, Ottone creeps into Poppea's chamber as she sleeps and tries to kill her. Cupid, however, protects her, and Ottone is unsuccessful. Poppea sees Ottone fleeing, pursued by Arnalta, and assumes that the figure is Drusilla.

ACT III

Drusilla is arrested for the attempted murder of Poppea and, to shield Ottone, pleads guilty and is sentenced to death. Ottone then comes forward, explaining that he was acting under Octavia's orders. This makes the situation fairly straightforward for Nero, who can now banish Octavia, as well as Ottone and

Drusilla, and crown Poppea empress as planned. Poppea is invited to ascend the imperial throne and is crowned by consuls in the name of the Roman Senate. Amore then descends from heaven with Venus and crowns Poppea goddess of beauty on Earth.

Recommended Recording:

L'incoronazione di Poppea, Concerto Vocale; René Jacobs, conductor; Harmonia Mundi HMC 901330.32; Soloists: Danielle Borst (Poppea), Guillemette Laurens (Nerone), Jennifer Larmore (Ottavia), Axel Köhler (Ottone), Michael Schopper (Seneca)

OPERAS	
1607	*L'Orfeo, favola in musica*
1608	(lost) *Arianna*
1608	(lost) *L'idropica*
1616	(lost) *Le nozze di Tetide*
1620	(lost) *Andromeda*
1624	(lost) *Apollo* (including *Il combattimento di Tancredi e Clorinda*)
1627	(lost) *La finta pazza Licori*
1628	(lost) *Gli amori di Diana e di Endimione*
1628	(lost) *Mercurio e Marte*
1630	(lost) *Proserpina rapita*
1640	*Il ritorno d'Ulisse in patria*
1641	(lost) *Le nozze d'Enea con Lavinia*
1642	*L'incoronazione di Poppea*

TIMELINE	
1567	Claudio Monteverdi born in Cremona, Italy
1587	Publishes first of nine books of secular madrigals
1591	Joins court of Duke Vincenzo I Gonzaga, Mantua, as string player
1601	Becomes *maestro di cappella* at Vincenzo I's Mantuan court
1605	Fifth book of madrigals published
1607	Premiere of *Orfeo* in Mantua; Monteverdi's wife dies
1608	*Arianna* (music of which is now mostly lost) premieres in Mantua
1610	*Vespers* first performed, Mantua
1612	Released from court of Gonzaga after death of Vincenzo I
1613	Moves to Venice; becomes *maestro di cappella* at St Mark's Cathedral
1624	Composes *Il combattimento di Tancredi*
1630	Austrian troops sack St Mark's and destroy 12 of Monteverdi's operas; plague ravages Venice
1632	Monteverdi admitted to holy orders

1637	World's first public opera house, San Cassiano, opens in Venice
1638	Eighth book of madrigals published
1640	Monteverdi writes *Il ritorno d'Ulisse in patria* for Venetian public opera
1642	Composes *L'incoronazione di Poppea*
1643	*Poppea* premieres in Venice
1643	Monteverdi dies in Venice
1651	Ninth and final book of madrigals published posthumously

Peri, Jacopo
1561–1633, ITALIAN

Like his rival and fellow Roman Giulio Caccini, Jacopo Peri possessed several musical talents. He was a composer, singer and harpist. In 1588, also like Caccini, Peri joined the Medici court in Florence. At age 27, he was, it seems, an attractive addition to one of the most glittering courts in Europe, where his singing was greatly admired and his long blond tresses earned him the nickname *Il Zazzerino* ('little shock of hair'). Peri sang in the spectacular entertainments at the Medici court, composing some music for the performances, and he also became drawn to the Camerata and their promotion of the *stile rappresentativo*, the radical 'representative style' in music. In 1598, Peri became the first to write a complete work, *Dafne*, in the new style. Peri also took a major part in his own composition, as the ancient Greek god Apollo. *Euridice* followed in 1600, with Peri this time taking the important role of Orpheus, Euridice's bereaved husband. The opera was written to celebrate the marriage of King Henri IV of France to Maria de' Medici. Published in 1601, *Euridice* is the earliest opera for which the complete score survives.

Purcell, Henry
1659–95, ENGLISH

Henry Purcell was one of the greatest Baroque composers and, as the diarist John Evelyn put it after his death, was 'esteemed the best composer of any Englishman hitherto'. Often compared to **Wolfgang Amadeus Mozart** (1756–91), Purcell exercised a similar mastery over many different types of composition – dramatic, sacred, vocal and instrumental. Tragically, like Mozart, Purcell died young, in his mid-thirties, leaving behind a prolific body of work.

FROM A MUSICAL FAMILY

Purcell came from a musical family. Apart from Henry himself, the most notable member of the family was his younger brother Daniel (c. 1660–1717), who served as organist at Magdalen College, Oxford and at St Andrew's Church in London. In 1695, the year Purcell died, Daniel sought to follow in his illustrious brother's footsteps and became a composer of music for the London theatre.

A BRIEF BUT METEORIC CAREER

Purcell began his short but brilliant career as a chorister in the Chapel Royal. He went on to become organ maker and afterwards keeper of instruments to King Charles II in 1683, at a salary of £60 a year. Already Purcell had begun to compose, producing his first instrumental music in 1680 and his first songs three years later. Purcell's first foray into music for the theatre, *Dido and Aeneas*, was also his first and only true opera, in that it featured music throughout. Although he never wrote another opera as such, Purcell did not abandon the genre entirely. He wrote songs and **incidental music** for more than 40 stage plays. In 1690, he contributed a considerable portion of the music to *Dioclesian*, the first of five semi-operas, providing *divertissements*, songs, choruses and dances. Dioclesian was followed by *King Arthur* (1691), *The Fairy Queen* (1692), *The Tempest* (c. 1695) and *The Indian Queen* (1695). Purcell died of consumption at Westminster on 21 November 1695.

Dido and Aeneas

Although ostensibly 'English', *Dido and Aeneas* owes its ancestry to Italian and French operatic influences. Although the recitatives follow the rhythms and inflexions of the English language, they were clearly modelled on Italian monody. Purcell followed the already established tradition of taking the plots of operas from ancient myth and legend. This one came from ancient Rome, as the hero, the Trojan prince Aeneas, was by tradition an ancestor of the Romans. The story for Dido and Aeneas was taken from Book Four of the *Aeneid*, a drama in verse by the Roman poet Virgil, who took 11 years to complete it.

Purcell's opera comprises a prologue and three acts, with a libretto by Irish dramatist Nahum Tate. The first performance took place at Josias Priest's School for Young Gentlewomen in Chelsea, in the spring of 1689. This work is not *grand opéra*, despite its elemental theme, but makes fairly modest vocal demands on its small cast. It is therefore likely that the first performers of *Dido and Aeneas* were the Chelsea schoolgirls. The initial public performance was given in London in 1700. The opera was revived in the late-nineteenth century.

Dido and Aeneas

by Henry Purcell
Composed: 1683–84
Premiered: c. 1689, London
Libretto by Nahum Tate, after Virgil

PROLOGUE

The Trojan Prince Aeneas has arrived at Carthage, having been shipwrecked on his way to Italy, where he was bound by Fate to found a new Troy. Belinda, lady-in-waiting and confidante of Dido, Queen of Carthage, sees Aeneas approaching the castle and requests that the court present him with an entertainment. There follows an allegorical dance featuring Phoebus and Venus.

ACT I

Dido is tormented by her love for Aeneas, but Belinda reassures her that the Prince returns her feelings. The courtiers, eager for a union between Carthage and Troy, offer further encouragement. Aeneas arrives with his attendants and declares his love for Dido, causing her to accept her own love for him. The act concludes with a triumphal dance.

ACT II

A sorceress summons witches to her cave, and together they gleefully plot Aeneas's departure, Dido's ruin and the destruction of Carthage. Their idea is to send one of their kind, disguised as Mercury, to persuade Aeneas that the gods want him to leave Carthage immediately. They then conjure up a storm so that a royal hunting party will be obliged to return to the palace. Meanwhile, Dido and Aeneas are in the forest with a group of courtiers when the witches' storm breaks, and they flee for cover. Aeneas is approached by 'Mercury', sent by the sorceress; he tells Aeneas that on Jove's command he must leave Carthage. Aeneas accepts his destiny, but not without sorrow for having to leave Dido. The act ends with a witches' chorus.

ACT III

On the quayside, Aeneas's men prepare for their departure with a sailors' song. The sorceress and witches look on with much joy and laughter; they comment on the proceedings and further plan Aeneas' death at sea, Dido's suicide and Carthage's ruin by fire. A witches' dance ends the scene. Back at the palace, Dido laments her cruel fate. Aeneas goes to her and declares that he will defy Fate and stay in Carthage, but Dido in her anger and self-pity rejects him. After Aeneas has left, Belinda attempts unsuccessfully to console Dido. The queen sings her final lament, considered to be one of opera's most beautiful and moving arias, and then kills herself. The opera concludes with the dance of the Cupids, who gather around Dido's tomb and scatter roses.

OPERAS	
1689	*Dido and Aeneas*
1690	*Dioclesian*
1691	*King Arthur*
1692	*The Fairy Queen*
1695	*The Indian Queen*
1695	*The Tempest*, or *The Enchanted Isle*

TIMELINE	
1659	Henry Purcell born in London
c. 1668	Becomes chorister in the Chapel Royal
1670	First musical composition in honour of Charles II's birthday
1674	Appointed as tuner of organ, Westminster Abbey, London
1677	Purcell becomes court composer
1679	Succeeds John Blow as organist of Westminster Abbey
1680	Writes first welcome **ode**, 'Welcome, Viceregent', for Charles II
1680	Completes his fantasies for viols; marries and eventually has six children
1682	Appointed one of three organists at the Chapel Royal
1685	Writes 'My Heart is Inditing' for coronation of James II
1689	Writes ode for Queen Mary, 'Now does the glorious day appear'
1689	*Dido and Aeneas* premieres in Chelsea
1691	*King Arthur* is produced
1692	Premiere of The Fairy Queen
1694	'Te Deum' and 'Jubilate' are performed for St Cecilia's Day
1695	Purcell's music accompanies Queen Mary's funeral
1695	The Indian Queen appears
1695	Purcell dies from tuberculosis in London, and is buried at Westminster Abbey

Quinault, Philippe
1635–88, FRENCH

Philippe Quinault was a well-known playwright when he decided to switch to the writing of opera libretti. The techniques of plays and operas – spoken and sung drama – diverged considerably, but Quinault succeeded in transferring his skills from one genre to the other. It was risky, but the star prize was collaboration with Lully, the progenitor of French opera and protégé of the mighty Louis XIV. Although Quinault developed the *tragédie lyrique* for Lully and so later influenced French *grand opéra*, there were certain restraints. Libretti had to contain formal scenes, stereotyped sentiments and the required references to royal glory and eminence. Emotion was always under control, heroes attained their objectives without undue strain and love was idyllic rather than passionate. Pantomime, dance and spectacle were regular ingredients. King Louis had to approve of everything, so that both Quinault and Lully planned their operas with royal tastes in mind.

Rasi, Francesco
1574–1620, ITALIAN

Composer and **tenor** Francesco Rasi took part in the first performances of Peri's *Euridice* and Caccini's *Rapimento di Cefalo* in Florence in 1600. By then he was already an experienced and much-admired performer, after 10 years in the service of aristocratic patrons, including Duke Fernando I of Tuscany before 1594, and, after 1598 the Gonzaga family, who ruled Mantua between 1328 and 1708 and were important patrons of music. Rasi was still in Mantua in 1607, when he is believed to have created the title role in Monteverdi's *Orfeo*. He also took part in the first version of *Dafne* composed by Marco di Gagliano (1582–1643), performed in Mantua in 1608. In 1617, Rasi doubled as composer and librettist for *Cibele ed Ati*, an opera written to celebrate the marriage of Ferdinando Gonzaga. The music has been lost, but Rasi's text has survived.

Renzi, Anna
c. 1620–c. 1660, ITALIAN

Singer Anna Renzi created the part of Ottavia, the neglected wife of Emperor Nero in Monteverdi's *L'incoronazione de Poppea*, in 1642, and she sang many other operatic roles in Venice. Renzi was one of the first female opera singers and also one of the first, if not *the* first, singers to achieve the status of a prima donna. She was an impressive actress, possessed a

fine **treble** voice and, it appears, had a fan following. In 1642, the librettist and poet Giulio Strozzi (1583–1652) wrote a book about her – *Le glorie della Signora Anna Renzi romana* ('The Glory of the Roman [singer] Signora Anna Renzi'), in which he described her in glowing terms: 'Our Signora Anna ... was endowed with such lifelike expression that her responses and speeches seem not memorized but born at the very moment. In sum ... she transforms herself completely into the person she represents.'

Rinuccini, Ottavio
1562–1621, ITALIAN

Ottavio Rinuccini, a member of the Bardi Camerata, wrote his first libretti for sophisticated Florentine entertainments. In 1598, Rinuccini produced the first opera libretto, Peri's *Dafne* (1598). A musical setting of *Dafne* composed by Heinrich Schütz in 1627 may have been the first German opera. Rinuccini's libretto *Euridice* was set to music by both Peri (1600) and Caccini (1602) and in 1608, Rinuccini wrote his most famous text, for Monteverdi's *Arianna*. However, although Monteverdi considered him to be the best librettist of his time, he turned down Rinuccini's next text, *Narciso ed Ecco* ('Narcissus and Echo'), because of its unhappy ending. The sources for Rinuccini's libretti were the Roman poet Ovid and the lyrical pastoral legend. His verse, which was well suited to the natural delivery of words, set the style for many librettists after him.

Le Rochois, Marthe
c. 1658–1728, FRENCH

Soprano Marthe Le Rochois, who was born in Caen in northern France, may have been a pupil of the French composer and singer Michel Lambert and afterwards of Lambert's son-in-law, Jean-Baptiste Lully. Lully greatly admired Le Rochois, who made her debut at the Paris Opéra in 1678 and remained a performer there for the next 20 years. Le Rochois created several roles in Lully's operas, including parts in *Proserpine* (1680), *Persée* (1682), *Amadis de Gaule* (1684) and *Roland* (1685). In 1686, she was also the first soprano to sing the title role in *Armide et Rénaud*, Lully's opera set at the time of the Crusades. Rochois appears to have been one of those stage performers who lack obvious physical attractions yet have a certain fascination for their audiences. In Le Rochois' case, her advantages were vivacity and a sensual aura, which enabled her to outclass the many more obviously beautiful singers of her day.

Rospigliosi, Giulio (Pope Clement IX)
1600–69, ITALIAN

Priest and librettist Giulio Rospigliosi served the opera-loving Barberini pope Urban VIII. Urban's family gave Rospigliosi a magnificent setting for his libretto for *Il Sant'Alessio* (1632) by Stefano Landi, which was performed at the opening of the opera house in the Barberini palace in 1632. Three more libretti in the next decade included Rossi's *Il palazzo incantato.* Rospigliosi borrowed from **commedia dell'arte** to make his comic characters more lifelike and produced the first thoroughly comic opera libretto for *Chi suffre, speri* ('Who Suffers May Hope', 1639) with music by Domenico Mazzocchi and Marco Marazzoli. Rospigliosi continued with libretti for two comic operas by Antonio Maria Abbatini: *Dal male il bene* ('Good from Bad', 1653) and *La Baltesara* ('The Girl from Balthesar', 1668). The latter was performed two years after Rospigliosi was elected pope, as Clement IX.

Rossi, Luigi
c. *1597–1653,* ITALIAN

Luigi Rossi served for a time at the Neapolitan court before joining the Borghese family in his native city of Rome

in 1621. Twenty years later, he entered the service of the Barberini family, who were influential patrons of opera. Rossi's first opera, *Il palazzo incantato* ('The Enchanted Palace', 1642), received its first performance in the Barberini palace. The production was lavish, and Rossi's opera became one of the most admired in the Italian Baroque repertoire.

The Barberini family were exiled from Italy in 1644, and in 1646 Luigi Rossi followed them to Paris, where King Louis XIV's influential chief minister, Jules Mazarin, invited the composer to attend the court. Rossi's arrival was fortuitous, since Mazarin had been attempting for some time to introduce Italian opera in France. Rossi's *Orfeo* (1647) was all Mazarin could have hoped for. The opera represented the height of the luxurious and spectacular Roman opera of the seventeenth century, and it created enormous interest in France. This *Orfeo* was strong on visual effects, and Rossi's music was both lyrical and expressive.

Orfeo
by Luigi Rossi
Premiered: 1647, Paris
Libretto by Francesco Buti

PROLOGUE
The figure of Vittoria (Victory) and French soldiers sing of their victories and the power of their kingdom.

ACT I
Euridice and her father, Endimione, consult a soothsayer regarding her forthcoming wedding to Orfeo. The omens are bad. Orfeo and Euridice celebrate their love for each other, while Aristeo, son of Bacco (Bacchus), laments his fate: he too is in love with Euridice. Having confided in his satyr, he calls for Venere (Venus) to prevent the marriage. Venere descends with Amore (Love) and the three Grazie

(Graces), promising to help. Venere plans to trick Euridice into returning Aristeo's love. During the wedding ceremony, the torches are extinguished – a bad omen. Orfeo and Euridice proclaim their love.

ACT II

Disguised as an old woman, Venere approaches Euridice. She speaks of the bad omens surrounding Euridice's marriage to Orfeo and offers Aristeo as an alternative husband, but Euridice refuses. The gods scold Amore for his part in the deception; he promises to help Orfeo and Euridice, and reveals the truth to Orfeo. The Grazie tell Venere of Amore's betrayal; she swears vengeance. Endimione and the soothsayer pray to Venere, but Guinone (Juno) tells them to pray to her instead; she will protect the lovers. At the temple, Euridice sings of love, but she is bitten by a snake and dies.

ACT III

As all mourn Euridice's death, Orfeo is escorted to the underworld. Aristeo is driven mad by Euridice's spirit and, mocked by Momo and the satyr, kills himself. Giunone sends Gelosia (Jealousy) to Proserpina and argues with the jubilant Venere. Gelosia tells Proserpina that her husband, Plutone (Pluto), may betray her for Euridice; Proserpina and Caronte (Charon) persuade Plutone to listen to Orfeo. Orfeo asks to be reunited with Euridice. Plutone agrees, on the condition that Orfeo not look back as they leave. Caronte reveals that Orfeo has not obeyed, and Euridice disappears. Venere entices Bacco to avenge Aristeo's death; he orders the deaths of Orfeo and Euridice. Giove (Jupiter) transforms the two lovers and Orfeo's lyre into constellations.

Sartorio, Antonio
1630–80, ITALIAN

Nothing is known of the first 30 years of Antonio Sartorio's life, except that he was Venetian. He made his first appearance in the historical records in 1661, when the first of his 15 operas, Gl'amori infruttuosi di Pirro ('Pirro's Hopeless Love', 1661) was performed in Venice. In 1664, Sartorio was appointed Kappellmeister at the ducal court of Brunswick-Lüneberg, and he remained in the post until 1675. However, he journeyed every year to Venice, where he hired musicians and oversaw the production of his operas at carnival time. In 1676, Sartori returned to Venice as maestro di cappella at St Mark's. His operas mark the height of the Venetian opera tradition and introduced several ingredients that later became standard fare: most notable among them was the lament. Sartorio was yet another composer to produce an opera on the tragic theme of Orpheus, in his case in 1672. His Orfeo created such a sensation that it eclipsed Cavalli's opera Massenzio (1673), which seemed so dull by comparison that the management of the Teatro San Luca feared an anti-climax and its performance was cancelled.

Scarlatti, Alessandro
1660–1725, ITALIAN

Sicilian-born Alessandro Scarlatti came to the attention of the Italian opera world with his first opera, Gli equivoci nel sembiante ('Mistaken Identities', 1679), which he wrote when he was only 19. The work was soon being staged by opera houses outside Rome, but this was not the limit of Scarlatti's new renown. At around the same time, he was appointed maestro di cappella to the generous patron of the arts Queen Christina of Sweden. By the time he was 24 and the composer of six operas, Scarlatti was maestro di cappella to the Viceroy of Naples and also director of the city's Teatro San Bartolomeo.

By 1702, Scarlatti had written at least 40 operas, but life and work in Naples seemed to pall and Scarlatti resigned his position. He hoped to join the de' Medici court in Florence and sent four operas to Prince Ferdinand de' Medici as proof of his abilities, but nothing came of this. In 1708, Scarlatti returned to Naples where he scored two of his most brilliant successes, with *Tigrane* (1715) and *Cambise* (1719). Ultimately Scarlatti's connection with Naples helped to establish the city as a centre of opera during the eighteenth century.

Mitridate Eupatore

by Alessandro Scarlatti
Premiered: 1707, Venice
Libretto by Girolamo Frigimelica Roberti

ACT I

King Farnace and Stratonica, Mitridate's mother, have usurped the Pontus throne by killing Mitridate's father. Mitridate, the true heir, has sought refuge in Egypt; his sister, Laodice, awaits his return and dreams of avenging her father's death. Egypt and Pontus are set to form an alliance and Laodice is called to court, where she is mocked by Farnace and argues with her mother.

ACT II

Mitridate and his wife, Issicratea (calling herself Antigono), arrive at court, disguised as Egyptian ambassadors. They tell Stratonica that Mitridate is nearby and Farnace calls for his death; the 'ambassadors' agree to bring him Mitridate's head in exchange for peace between their kingdoms. Laodice promises to help the 'ambassadors', if they will spare her brother's life.

ACT III

In front of the temple, Farnace addresses his people. Stratonica tells the crowd that she is willing to sacrifice her son for their benefit. Mitridate also appears, as the ambassador, promising to honour their agreement. Laodice's husband, Nicodemo, tells her what the 'ambassador' has announced. Laodice resolves to intervene and save Mitridate.

ACT IV

On the shore with Pelopida, Farnace's confidant, Laodice sees armed men arrive with the urn. Believing it to contain Mitridate's head, she mourns the loss of her brother. Mitridate recognizes her and, when they are alone, reveals his identity. The siblings are joyfully reunited. With renewed hope, Laodice shows her contempt for Stratonica and Farnace.

ACT V

Farnace arrives to claim the urn containing Mitridate's head and attempts to kill the 'ambassador'; Mitridate's sword is quicker, and Farnace is killed. Stratonica launches herself at her son but is killed by Issicratea. Nicodemo announces to the people that Farnace's tyranny is over and Mitridate has returned. Laodice crowns Mitridate, who then crowns Issicratea. Everyone rejoices at the siblings' revenge and the restoration of peace to the land.

Siface, Giovanni Francesco Grossi

1653–97, **ITALIAN**

Castrato Siface made his singing debut in Rome in 1672. He enjoyed considerable early success in Italy and created a sensation in Venice as Syphax in Cavalli's *Sciopine affricano* ('Scipio Africanus', 1685). Siface became so identified with the part that 'Syphax' became his nickname. Siface was taken up by many important personalities, including ex-Queen Christina of Sweden and by Henry Purcell in England; Purcell wrote a piece for harpsichord entitled 'Sefauci's Farewell' when the singer left England in 1687. Siface, praised as the finest living musician, received an almost hysterical reception in 1688 when he sang in Modena, Naples, Parma and Bologna. Unfortunately, Siface developed an ego to match his talents and his arrogance led to his murder near Ferrara by thugs hired by the family of a girl with whom he had been having a love affair.

Stradella, Alessandro
1639–82, ITALIAN

Alessandro Stradella was in his native Rome, writing *intermezzi* and other music for revivals of operas by Cavalli and Cesti, when he became embroiled in a quarrel with the Catholic authorities. He then had to leave Rome and decamped to Genoa, where he arrived in 1678. By that time, Stradella had composed several operas, and three were performed at Genoa's Teatro Falcone: *Trespolo tutore* ('The Guardian Trestle', 1677), *La forza dell'amor patterno* ('The Power of Paternal Love', 1678) and *Le gare dell'amor eroico* ('The Contests of Heroic Love', 1679). The first was a comic opera and one of the first in which a bass was cast in the leading male role.

Stradella's operas have been considered by some to prefigure the Neapolitan opera later developed by Alessandro Scarlatti. In addition to composition, Stradella was a music teacher and one of his students was a nobleman's mistress. Stradella abducted her. The nobleman gave chase and almost killed the composer. Far from being cured by this experience, Stradella became involved with another woman associated with vengeful men: her brothers, who disapproved of the liaison, ambushed Alessandro Stradella and murdered him.

Strozzi, Barbara
1619–67, ITALIAN

Venetian-born Barbara Caterina Strozzi, singer and composer, was the daughter of the poet and librettist Giulio Strozzi by one of his servants. Although she was the principal singer at the Accademia degli Unisoni in Perugia, which had been founded by her father in 1634, her most important contribution to music was as one of the principal women composers of the Baroque era. In 1644, Barbara Strozzi composed her *Il primo libro de madrigali* ('First Book of Madrigals'), and by 1664 no fewer than 125 songs and other pieces of vocal music by Strozzi had been published. This included eight books of music, containing 100 songs for solo voice. The last of her published works, *Arie* ('Melodies'), consisted of six arias, five cantatas and one serenade for soprano. Music for the solo voice dominated the work of Strozzi, although some of her books contain songs with orchestral accompaniment.

◉ BAROQUE OPERA IN NAPLES
～ p. 44

Opera first reached Naples when Venetian companies brought their productions to the city after 1648. At that time, the city was recovering from the spate of murders and massacres that had taken place during the revolt against Spanish rule led by the fisherman Tommaso Aniello Masaniello. Masaniello was killed in 1647 by agents working for the Spanish Viceroy Count d'Onate. The introduction of opera in Naples was part of the count's subsequent attempts to calm the populace. What d'Onate actually accomplished was the establishment of a tradition of opera in Naples that has lasted to the present day. Among the first operas to be seen there were *Ciro* (1653–54) by Francesco Provenzale and *Orontea* (1654) by Francesco Cirillo. Subsequently, the Venetian repertory gave operatic performances at the Teatro San Bartolomeo. After 1676, operas were produced at the Teatro for royal occasions, a task taken over in 1684 by Alessandro Scarlatti. The energetic, inventive Scarlatti was a great boon to the cause of Neapolitan opera. The San Bartolomeo was enlarged to hold bigger audiences, and while he remained in Naples, Scarlatti claimed to have written 80 operas for the Teatro, though half that number was more likely.

EARLY AND MIDDLE BAROQUE: PERSONALITIES

● THE BARBERINI FAMILY ∿ p. 77

The writing and performance of Baroque music and opera relied heavily on wealthy patrons, who often employed musicians in their private orchestras and opera houses. Among these patrons were the aristocratic Barberini family, who made their fortune in the Florentine cloth business. Moving to Rome, the Barberini became one of the city's most powerful family dynasties.

Maffeo Barberini (1568–1644), elected Pope Urban VIII in 1623, was an influential opera enthusiast, and Roman opera basked in the favours that flowed from his direction. Composers such as Landi and Rossi received financial support and a magnificent new opera house for their works: the family had the auditorium – audience capacity 3,000 – built in the Barberini palace. Landi's *Il Sant'Alessio*, performed in 1632, was among many operas staged there. However, the golden age of Barberini opera was brief. After Pope Urban died, his family was sued by his successor, Innocent X, for lavishing papal funds on expensive opera productions. The Barberini fled to Paris, where their cause was championed by chief minister Cardinal Jules Mazarin. The family was reconciled with Innocent and reinstated in Rome after Mazarin threatened to invade the Papal States. Their opera house reopened in 1653 and, with occasional closures, was used until the end of the seventeenth century.

⑨ THE CASTRATI ∿ p. 44

A castrato was a male singer whose boyish singing voice was preserved by castrating him before his voice changed during puberty. The castrato had an important part to play in the performance of opera, since women were barred from performing on stage and the male soprano or **contralto** was employed instead. If anything, a castrato's voice was the more effective, since castration did not entirely eliminate maleness. This was especially significant in terms of the strength of the lungs, which made the castrato voice more flexible, more penetrating and more sensuous than female voices could normally manage.

Castrati were first mentioned as early as 1562, when they were employed in religious services; the church went on using castrati for another three centuries. The advent of opera in the seventeenth century gave these singers an additional outlet – and a chance for riches and fame that the church could not offer. The opera house also provided an opportunity for lavish praise that flattered the proverbial vanity of the castrati. For example, the tone of one castrato was said to put a nightingale to shame with a sound that seemed barely human. The creation of castrati became illegal in 1870.

⑨ SINGING VIBRATO IN BAROQUE OPERA ∿ p. 52

The revolution in opera that came about in the Baroque period required singers to acquire new techniques and disciplines. The idea was to elicit a greater emotional response from opera audiences, hold their attention and engage them more fully in the plot and its characters. One way these aims could be achieved was through judicious use of vocal ornamentation, such as vibrato. Singing vibrato required a singer to make the voice fluctuate in pitch, intensity and in its own distinctive sound, the timbre. Getting it right required great skill and control, since vibrato could easily degenerate into an unattractive 'wobble'. However, when it was performed by well-trained singers, either as a group or solo, vibrato gave added depth and expressiveness to the music. Lavish use of vibrato was not a general rule in Baroque opera. Controlled vibrato, known as 'intensity vibrato', was preferred, and this was normally confined to the cadence point, the 'full stop' at the end of a musical phrase. This ornamentation was always sung on the beat. Sometimes the ornament was notated on the opera score; at other times it was left to the singer to interpolate into the performance.

🎵 STAGING BAROQUE OPERA
∿ p. 45

Baroque opera featured lavish staging, spectacle and excitement. Stages were given added depth to allow for greater perspective and more vivid scenic effects. Steps were built leading from the stage into the auditorium, bringing the audience closer to the action. The 'chariot and pole' device enabled scene changes to be made in seconds. 15 or 20 scene changes could be involved. Candles, torches and smoke depicted blazing hellfire or provided effects for the 'magical' descent of golden chariots from heaven that brought the gods to Earth. Flashes of lightning were produced by the covering and uncovering of flaming torches. 'Thunder' sounded as cannon balls were rolled down a stepped incline. Careful siting of the lights in the wings and the practice of dropping or raising cylinders or boxes of tin or black metal over the lamps made it possible to dim the stage for some scenes yet switch quickly to scenes requiring more illumination. To avoid the greatest danger of the candlelit era – setting fire to the theatre – lights were placed where they could not be dislodged, however vigorous the action on stage and however much the scenery might shake.

🎵 WORDS FOR THE MUSIC –
THE LIBRETTO ∿ p. 45

A libretto – Italian for 'small book' – enabled audiences to read the words of an opera or, in the case of a foreign language, a translation. Some of the earliest libretti were quite substantial in size, around 21.6 cm. However, they were not too unwieldy and were read by members of the audience, in confined seating space, while the performance was going on. The auditoriums of opera houses and theatres were lit by candles, which were dimmed while the performance was taking place. Instead, individual candles were available as an aid to reading. Some early libretti that have survived show grease spots where candle wax dripped onto the pages.

A libretto normally began with a preface dedicated to the librettist's patron and then went on to a prologue explaining the context of the opera's action. A list of characters came next, then details of the scene-changes, the dances to be featured and sometimes notes about the scenic effects on stage. In Italy, where the Church was always on the lookout for pagan references in the texts of Baroque operas, the librettist also had to affirm his own devout Roman Catholic faith.

🎵 COMMEDIA DELL'ARTE ∿ p. 48

The *commedia dell'arte*, which originated in Italy in the sixteenth century, was a forerunner of opera. The influence of *commedia dell'arte* was evident in both the cast lists and the plots of operas. There were, for example, slapstick sequences called *zanni* and comic servants, an elderly parent or guardian, usually named Pantalone, and his faithful sidekick Il dottore Gratiano. The beautiful but despairing heroine was usually involved in an unsuitable love match with an impoverished, but romantic, young man. On hand to help solve the dilemma was her maid, who acted as her confidante. Likewise, *commedia dell'arte* plots had ready-made features, such as disguise, mistaken identity, confusion over twins, lovers pretending to be servants and girls trapped in betrothals to rich old men. These ingredients are found in several operas written by composers from Mozart to Verdi, among many others.

Commedia dell'arte was popular all over Europe and influenced such playwrights as Shakespeare, Molière and Beaumarchais, all of whom wrote plays with plots that lent themselves easily to operatic treatment and were later turned into operas. The *commedia* characters and type of plot were directly translated to opera in *I pagliacci* ('The Clowns', 1892) by **Ruggero Leoncavallo** (1857–1919).

LATE BAROQUE

By the beginning of the eighteenth century, opera was established in some form in most major European centres. The basic types of serious and comic opera in both Italian and French traditions shared similarities, although the content and style of an operatic entertainment could vary according to whether it was intended to flatter a private patron, resound with a public audience, or to celebrate a state event such as a wedding or coronation.

The most important operatic centres in Italy during the early eighteenth century were Naples in the south and Venice in the north. Opera became popular in Naples, not least because it was a form of entertainment that the Spanish viceroy enjoyed, and most significant festive events and state celebrations were commemorated with opera performances. Several theatres had been established during the previous century, although their early eighteenth-century incarnations were rarely the same building. For instance, the Teatro San Bartolomeo was burnt down after shivering patrons had failed to extinguish a fire they had lit inside their box. The grandest theatres such as the Teatro San Carlo (named after the Spanish king) specialized in serious opera. Neapolitan serious operas often included comic subplots, frequently concerning the servants' observations about the behaviour of their noble employers, and smaller opera houses presented entirely comic operas performed in a vernacular Neapolitan dialect.

Despite the decline of its once immense political significance, Venice

boasted a vibrant operatic scene that was predominantly active from the winter carnival until the public theatres closed at the start of Lent each year. Native composers such as Gasparini, Vivaldi and Pollarolo dominated Venetian opera until the Neapolitan school, including Leo, Vinci and Porpora, became popular from the late 1720s. Theatres such as San Giovanni Grisostomo seated only a few hundred people, and those who sat in the stalls could not always see much, despite the theatres being small compared to modern opera houses.

KEY EVENTS

1702	War of the Spanish Succession begins
1706	Thomas Newcomen invents the first practical working steam engine
1709	Battle of Poltava: Peter the Great consolidates Russia's power by defeating Sweden
1710	Bishop George Berkeley publishes *A Treatise Concerning the Principles of Human Knowledge*
1713	Treaty of Utrecht ends the War of the Spanish Succession
1718	Gabriel Fahrenheit invents the mercury thermometer
1719	Daniel Defoe publishes *Robinson Crusoe*
1720	The South Sea Bubble, the first international stock-market crisis, causes financial panic in Paris and London
1720	Jonathan Swift publishes *Gulliver's Travels*
1728	John Gay's *Beggar's Opera* opens in London
1733	John Kay invents the flying shuttle loom
1730	John Wesley founds the Methodist movement
1740	War of the Austrian Succession begins
1742	Handel's *Messiah* is first performed in Dublin
1745	Second Jacobite Rebellion led by Prince Charles Edward Stuart
1748	Peace of Aix-la-Chapelle ends the War of the Spanish Succession
1740	Henry Fielding publishes *Tom Jones*

Late Baroque

INTRODUCTION

The traditions and styles of opera from Venice and Naples dominated operatic life in Rome, although for a short time public opera performances were forbidden in the papal city. The influence of Italian opera stretched much further, and companies were established outside Italy – most notably the Dresden opera house at the court of the Elector of Saxony, and in London by the Royal Academy of Music. It was only in France that a distinct national school of opera flourished without being substantially indebted towards Italian singers, librettists and musical style.

THE IDOLIZATION OF SINGERS

Opera audiences in London were primarily aristocratic or the well-educated upper-middle class, but in Italy and France opera was relatively more accessible to the wider public, especially the less serious forms of opera in Naples and Paris. Opera performances were undeniably a social event where prominent members of society could meet publicly or, indeed, illicitly, and it is easy to underestimate the fascination audiences had with discussing the merits and foibles of the most famous singers.

CASTRATO STATUS

In addition to the usual gossip and adulation that surrounded the *prima donna*, audiences were equally passionate about the leading man, the *primo uomo*. He was almost always a **castrato** – a singer who had shown musical potential while a boy that was enough to justify his parents authorizing his castration in order to preserve his voice and enable him to train as a professional singer. Castration for this purpose was technically forbidden, but the financial rewards and popularity for a successful castrato were large enough to tempt many parents to find ways to ensure that their son needed the operation for alleged medical reasons. We do not know exactly what the castrati sounded like in their early eighteenth-century prime, but they were reputed to be tall and possessed a powerful stage presence that complemented their casting in godlike or majestic roles, which promoted ideas of heroism and dignity.

However, the concept of the castrated hero was not universally admired: it was never widely accepted in London despite **George Frideric Handel**'s (1685–1759) successful operas starring **Senesino** (*c.* 1680–*c.* 1759) and **Giovanni Carestini** (*c.* 1704–*c.* 1760), and it was ridiculed and scorned in France, where they instead preferred youthful lovers and heroes to be sung by high-tenors (haute-contre). By the end of Handel's career, he rarely used castrati in his English **oratorios**, and had instead trained native English singers such as the tenor John Beard. The voice fell out of fashion, although the castrato Crescentini was reputed to have been Napoleon's favourite singer, and both **Wolfgang Amadeus Mozart** (1756–91) and **Gioachino Rossini** (1792–1868) composed castrato roles.

THE OPERA HOUSE ORCHESTRA

Most early eighteenth-century opera houses were small, and could not accommodate anything larger than a chamber orchestra. Thus, opera-house orchestras during the period were smaller than their nineteenth-century successors. The modern orchestra pit did not then exist, and the orchestra were usually seated on the floor at the front of the stalls, level with the first row of the audience. Most operas were scored for a band of strings, oboes and continuo, but the exact constitution of an opera orchestra could vary according to local traditions, the preferences of the composer and the availability of less common instruments such as recorders, flutes, trumpets and horns. Several eyewitness accounts reveal that Handel's opera orchestra tended to have over 20 violins (including violas), three or four cellos, two double basses, between two and four oboes, up to four bassoons and the continuo section. The continuo section played in **recitatives** and formed the foundations upon which the orchestrations were based, and Handel's continuo section almost certainly comprised two harpsichords, one cello and a theorbo. The continuo section could occasionally be enhanced by exotic instruments such as the addition of viols and harp in Cleopatra's 'V'adoro pupille' in Handel's *Giulio Cesare in Egitto* ('Julius Caesar in Egypt', 1724). **Nicola Antonio Porpora**'s *Flavio Anicio Olibrio* (1711) requires lute, theorbo, viola da gamba, cello, double bass and harpsichord to contribute towards the continuo line, although it is unlikely that they all played together in every **aria**.

STANDARDIZATION OF FORMS

Each operatic tradition had within it different types of opera. Serious operas were the highest regarded form of music dramas, Italian **opera seria** and French **tragédie lyrique**. Comic opera also developed within both cultures, and **opéra-ballet** also became popular in France. In Italy, the comic **intermezzo** performed between the acts of an *opera seria* rapidly gave birth to fully developed **opera buffa**. Serious opera was certainly a forum for composers and librettists to create allegories that their audience could identify with. However, it was unwise to produce operas that contained unflattering parallels with contemporary events or satirical attacks in an age when court and public opera houses alike depended on the patronage and support of the nobility and royal family.

PEDAGOGICAL AND POLITICAL ASPECTS OF OPERA

Most commentaries concealed within late Baroque operas were intended to elevate and instruct audiences. For example, the righteous indignation or bravery of a hero could represent how a decent citizen ought to react to injustice or carnal temptation. Recurring themes, such as the tribulation of lovers overcome by notable fidelity, or a tyrant demonstrating clemency or restoring the throne to its rightful occupant, were intended to resonate with audiences and show an example of how true nobility should be achieved through behaviour rather than be a simple property of birthright. While the political content of opera tended to be generalized and concentrated on promoting enlightened principles, the most important political function of opera was certainly its role as an ostentatious public celebration of state events.

𝄞 THE VISUAL ASPECT ∾ p. 121

Although early eighteenth-century operas were unashamedly designed to exploit the virtuosity of expensive singers, they were also regarded as an opportunity to fuse all the arts, in which the librettist's poetry and the composer's music were complemented by sumptuous costumes and scenery painted by master craftsmen. The mechanical wings in Baroque theatre allowed swift scene changes that could surprise and entertain an audience visually, and inventive designers produced astonishing mechanical stage effects such as moving clouds, shipwrecks and even chariots that allowed a godlike character to descend and instigate the reconciliation of opposing parties at the end of an opera. New costumes and scenery were major attractions of a new opera, although materials were frequently recycled so the environments of a medieval crusader could look suspiciously identical to Alexander the Great in Persia.

Late Baroque
GENRES AND STYLES

In the late Baroque era, opera was the most widely cultivated musical form. It had its own social and economic subculture and engaged many of the finest composers. By the early eighteenth century, most of the principal cities in Europe had imported opera from Italy and modified it to suit the local audiences' taste. In France, opera remained closely linked with the traditions of courtly entertainment established by Jean-Baptise Lully (1632–87), whose *tragédie lyriques* had developed into *opéra-ballet*.

ITALY

Early eighteenth-century Italian opera was governed by conventions, but, within those rules, imaginative composers invented an enormous variety of musical moods and first-rate dramas. The most notable dominant convention was the **da capo aria**, which constructed opportunities for expensive singers to show off their skill, but could also effectively communicate the intensity of a dramatic moment. *Da capo* arias revealed the emotions of characters, but they rarely carried the plot forward. This was instead achieved through simple recitative, composed in a conversational manner and usually accompanied only by the harpsichord and cello. Recitative was closer to speech in its rhythms, and text tended to be more direct and less contemplative than arias. However, particularly important dramatic moments, such as a pivotal event for an individual character that has immense impact on their destiny, could be set to orchestral recitative for special effect. These were usually powerful recitatives accompanied by the entire string section of the orchestra. Several of the most celebrated examples were created for the castrato Senesino in Handel's London operas.

OPERA SERIA, OPERA BUFFA AND INTERMEZZO

There were three basic types of operatic entertainments: *opera seria*, *opera buffa* and the *intermezzo*. The most highly esteemed of these forms was *opera seria*, which tended to focus on admirable behaviour such as clemency, heroism and fidelity. Naturally, in order to establish those principles, *opera seria* also explored the opposing emotions of rage, treachery and illicit lust. Only a minority were uncompromisingly serious and tragic, and most concluded with a *lieto fine* ('happy ending'). It is a fallacy that *opera seria* was without humanism or humour, but resolutions usually portrayed morally uplifting reconciliation or the restoration of the correct and natural order of things.

The comic style of *opera buffa* developed in Naples, and could ridicule its more aristocratic sibling with its focus on the foolish or ridiculous behaviour of common folk, often set in a vernacular Neapolitan dialect instead of the highbrow literary style of *opera seria* **libretti**. Similarly, the plots of *intermezzi* were more concerned about everyday life than promoting paragons of virtue, and featured a comic plot contained within a few short scenes that featured only two or three characters. However, these were usually designed as an intermediary entertainment between the acts of an *opera seria*.

FRANCE

France maintained an operatic tradition distinct from the rest of Europe. Italian operas tended to be structured into three long acts and rarely featured a chorus or dancers. In contrast, French operas frequently featured a prominent chorus, plenty of ballets and followed Lully's model, with five shorter acts. A unique genre was *opéra-ballet*, which grew out of Lully's **ballet de cour** and could contain a different exotically located story within each act, with the overall whole connected only by a tenuous theme. Unlike the imported Italian fashion that seemed exotic in London, Dresden, Vienna and Hamburg, Parisian audiences reacted with hostility to anything that attempted to increase Italian influence in their operas, and the spectre of Lully remained potent even towards the end of the eighteenth century. However, as in Italy, the popular **opéra comique** was artistically overshadowed by the grandest genre *tragédie en musique*, which often depicted powerful stories taken from classical mythology.

RECIT

French *recit* could shift metre unpredictably, and there was the additional form of 'measured' recitative that inclined towards greater expressive flexibility by emphasizing important moments with repeated figures or by elaborating the singer's declamation. Accompanied recitatives were an integral part of the action in French operas, and no Italian composer created more astonishingly vivid examples than **Jean-Philippe Rameau** (1683–1764). An air was usually in binary form, but not always discernible from *recit*. An **ariette**, despite its misleading title, was the equivalent of the Italian *aria di bravura*, and Rameau's preference for ariette form was one of the most controversial aspects of his *Hippolyte et Aricie* (1733) that enraged the guardians of Lully's musical temple.

GERMANY

An independent German style of opera did not flourish during the late Baroque period, and the many attempts made to produce vernacular German operas remain obscurities. The most widely respected German-born opera composers were Handel and **Johann Hasse** (1699–1783), who both acquired their mastery and reputation after they travelled south of the Alps to Italy. Hasse later enjoyed a long relationship with the Elector of Saxony's court at Dresden, but the operas produced there were essentially Italian in all respects.

Handel only composed his first few operas in Germany, of which only *Almira* (1705) survives: its odd mixture of German recitative, Italian arias and French ballets were tailored for the peculiar tradition that had been established by **Reinhard Keiser** (1674–1739) – the prolific, yet inconsistent, music director of the Hamburg opera house. **Georg Philipp Telemann** (1681–1767) also subsequently mixed Italian and German styles for Hamburg, although the consequent products of this mixture seem uneven and unsatisfying today despite frequent moments of musical brilliance. It was only in the later eighteenth century that a German school of operatic style began to be firmly established.

ENGLAND

Attempts to establish a native school of English opera were perpetually frustrated, not least because **Henry Purcell**'s (1659–95) premature death had robbed him of the opportunity to develop beyond the theatrical limitations of **semi-opera**. The musician Thomas Clayton and author Joseph Addison's *Rosamund* (1707) was a pioneering attempt at English opera but it failed, and John Eccles' opera *Semele* (1707), composed to a libretto by William Congreve and later set as an oratorio by Handel, was cancelled by an anxious management before it could be publicly performed. Attempts to mix the Italian and English language together could not sustain popularity in London, despite a similar compromise becoming popular in Germany. During the early years of the eighteenth century, Italian opera became fashionable, perhaps because English gentlemen had enjoyed experiences of it while on the grand tour (an extended trip to experience the civilization of Italy that was believed to crown the education of every young aristocratic Englishman). The production of *Pyrrhus and Demetrius* (1709) at the Queen's Theatre on the Haymarket successfully presented music by **Alessandro Scarlatti** (1660–1725), and such events paved the way for Handel's *Rinaldo* (1711), which was the first opera composed entirely in Italian specifically for a London audience.

ITALIAN IMPORT OPERA

Imported Italian opera dominated the London stage thereafter, although in the 1710s composers Johann Christoph Pepusch, Johann Ernest Galliard and Eccles turned their attention to **masques**, which were like short one-act English operas. These could be performed as interludes in spoken plays, but Handel's masque *Acis and Galatea* (1718) was composed for a private performance. The most talented native composers did not successfully compete directly with Handel's Italian operas, and instead devoted most of their efforts to providing masques and incidental theatre music, although **Thomas Arne** (1710–78) produced English opera during the 1730s. Meanwhile, the poet **John Gay** (1685–1732) invented the genre of 'ballad opera' with his popular *The Beggar's Opera* (1728), which made prominent use of adopted popular tunes, but it was essentially a political vehicle rather than a credible music drama. When Handel eventually gave up composing Italian operas for dwindling English audiences, he continued to dominate serious music theatre in London with his oratorios. Despite the varying degrees of success

generated by Arne's renewed attempts to establish English opera following Handel's death, there were few talented opera composers active between Purcell's death and the emergence of **Benjamin Britten** (1913–76) in the twentieth century.

❋ THE BEGGAR'S OPERA ∿ p. 82

Although endeavours to formulate a native style of English opera were all doomed to long-term failure, John Gay's spoof *The Beggar's Opera* was tremendously successful. Gay chose existing popular tunes, but Johann Christoph Pepusch provided the musical substance of the arrangements. Like Handel, Pepusch was an immigrant composer from Germany who had worked for James Brydges, the Earl of Carnarvon, during the 1710s. In fact, the so-called 'ballad opera' is hardly an opera at all, and contains over 60 short songs, based on country dances, folk tunes from Scotland and France, and an occasional sliver of Purcell and Handel. Unlike the Royal Academy of Music's expensive Italian singers, Gay and Pepusch's entertainment featured actors who were not trained singers.

The alleged influence of *The Beggar's Opera* on Handel's increasingly difficult career, composing Italian operas for London, has often been overstated. It was

51

primarily a satire directed at the Whig government, although it incidentally pokes a little fun at the loftier world of Italian opera during the process. We can imagine that the prime minister, Sir Robert Walpole, who attended the first performance, was not amused by the Tory Gay's frequent references to the low moral standards and corruption of politicians.

⟲ THE DA CAPO ARIA ∿ p. 78

A *da capo* aria is a simple formula dictated by the two-part organization of an aria's libretto text. Its mood could vary between rage, jealousy, despair or joy, according to the demands of the location of the plot. The singer's text can either directly describe their predicament, or take the form of a simile that has allegorical relevance to the course they must pursue.

The first section in which a character expresses a particular emotion has an orchestral introduction (a **ritornello**), a dynamic opening vocal statement, and then subsequent development of that theme before a closing *ritornello*. Then, in a shorter middle section, usually in a different but related key, the character clarifies, contradicts or explores a wider context for the emotion, before consolidating his or her emotional response to events with an entire repeat of the first section. In this repeat of the entire first section, known as the *da capo*, the singer was expected to embellish the vocal line with difficult ornaments and to conclude the aria with an extempore cadenza.

⬕ AN EYEWITNESS ACCOUNT ∿ p. 79

Pierre-Jacques Fougeroux visited London and attended Handel's operas *Tolomeo*, *Siroe* and *Admeto* during the Royal Academy of Music's final season in 1727–28. His account of what he saw and heard is invaluable:

The Opera, which was once negligible, has become a spectacle of some importance in the last three years. They have sent for the best voices [and] the most skilled instrumentalists from Italy ... the orchestra consisted of 24 violins led by the Castrucci brothers, two harpsichords (one of which was played by the German Indel [Handel], a great player and great composer), one archlute, three cellos, two double basses, three bassoons and sometimes flutes and trumpets. This orchestra makes a very loud noise. As there is no middle part in the harmony, the 24 violins usually divide only into firsts and seconds, which sounds extremely brilliant and is beautifully played. The two harpsichords [and] the archlute fill in the middle of the harmony. They use only a cello, the two harpsichords and the archlute to accompany the recitatives. The music is good and thoroughly in the Italian style, although there are some tender pieces in the French style ... The auditorium is small and in very poor taste; the stage is quite large, with poor scenery. There is no amphitheatre, only a pit, with large curved benches uncomfortably together ... The sides of the stage are decorated with columns, which have mirrors fixed along them with brackets and several candles; ... Instead of chandeliers there are ugly wooden candlesticks suspended by strings like those used by tightrope walkers. Nothing could look more wretched, yet there are candles everywhere.

[English translation of Fougeroux's letter 'Voiage d'Angleterre' is taken from Donald Burrows: Handel, Oxford, 1994, pp. 460–62]

Late Baroque
PERSONALITIES

Arne, Thomas Augustine
1710–78, ENGLISH

Arne was born in Covent Garden, so it is not surprising that he spent most of his life providing music for the theatre. In 1732 he formed an English opera company with Lampe and Carey, and their first production *Amelia* (1732) featured his sister Susanna (later Mrs Cibber, for whom Handel composed 'He was despised'). Arne performed Handel's *Acis and Galatea* for the public in a London theatre in 1732 before Handel had considered the possibility of doing so himself, having composed it for a private performance 14 years previously. He subsequently created English comic operas at Lincoln's Inn Fields Theatre, including *Rosamond* (1733).

In 1737, Arne married Cecilia Young – a renowned **soprano** who had performed in Handel's operas *Ariodante* and *Alcina*. Arne was invited to compose a musical setting of Milton's *Comus* (1738), which established his reputation as a serious composer, and he then composed the masque *Alfred* (1740), which became popular in London due to the final number 'Rule, Britannia'. He triumphed with his serious English opera *Artaxerxes* (1762). His only attempt at Italian opera, *L'Olimpiade* ('The Olympiad', 1765), was lost, probably with most of his music, in a fire at Covent Garden in 1808. Arne, more than any native English composer, had a knack of blending Italianate *coloratura* with English idioms, but even today he remains in the shadow of Handel.

Bononcini, Giovanni
1670–1747, ITALIAN

Bononcini was orphaned at the age of eight, and moved to Bologna, where he studied music and was accepted into the Accademia Filarmonica in 1686. By 1692, Bononcini had moved to Rome, where he met Silvio Stampiglia. They collaborated on several operas, including *Il trionfo di Camilla* ('The Triumph of Camilla', 1696), which was an enormous success in Naples. It was revived in 19 other Italian cities, and was produced in an adapted version in London by Nicolini and Swiney in 1706.

Bononcini was the favourite composer of Emperor Joseph I, and was based in Vienna between 1697 and 1712. In 1719, the Earl of Burlington secured Bononcini's services for the Royal Academy of Music in London, where the composer enjoyed tremendous popularity for several seasons. His last opera, *Astianatte* (1727), was blighted by the repercussions of the rivalry between Faustina and Cuzzoni, and he did compose for the stage again. Bononcini directed private performances of his own music for the Duchess of Marlborough until 1731, and he was a prominent member of the Academy of Ancient Musick in London until he was discredited in the early 1730s for plagiarizing a **madrigal** composed by Antonio Lotti (*c.* 1667–1740). Bononcini's melodic style was considered agreeable and pleasant, and he was admired for his expressive setting of Italian texts.

Bordoni, Faustina
1697–1781, ITALIAN

Venetian mezzo-soprano Faustina was brought up by the composers Alessandro (1669–1750) and Benedetto Marcello (1686–1739). She made her debut in Pollarolo's *Ariodante* in 1716, and was based in her home city until 1725, singing in operas by her teacher Gasparini, as well as Albinoni and Lotti. Between 1726 and 1728, she performed in London alongside Senesino and Cuzzoni in Handel's 'Rival Queens' operas. The legendary enmity between Faustina and

Cuzzoni culminated in 1727 when they came to blows on stage in a performance of Bononcini's *Astianatte*. Faustina married the composer Hasse in 1730 – the librettist **Pietro Metastasio** (1698–1782) described them as 'truly an exquisite couple'. Faustina appeared in many of her husband's *opera seria* composed for Dresden, and eventually retired in 1751. In 1773, she and her husband settled in Venice, where both of their daughters trained as singers.

Boyce, William
1711–79, ENGLISH

Boyce trained as a choirboy at St Paul's Cathedral, and between 1734 and 1768 he held organist posts. He is most regarded for his symphonies, trio sonatas and church anthems. Although the composition of music for the theatre was not a dominant part of his career, Boyce was a skilful composer who was more consistent than Arne and closer to the legacy of Purcell than Handel. His earliest dramatic works were initially conceived as concert works, although *The Secular Masque* (1746) was performed at Drury Lane in 1750 with contributions by the famous theatre singers Kitty Clive and John Beard, who both sang for Handel. Boyce regularly provided music for the actor David Garrick's Drury Lane theatre company between 1749 and 1751, including a pastoral masque for Moses Mendez's *The Chaplet* (1749) that was his biggest theatrical success. *The Rehearsal* (1750) was a satire on contemporary *opera buffa* that featured several fine songs, and Boyce contributed music for Garrick's production of *Romeo and Juliet* (1750) that was blatant competition against Arne's similar production at Covent Garden. Boyce seems to have lost enthusiasm for the theatre during the 1750s, although the song 'Heart of Oak' from Garrick's *Harlequin's Invasion* (1759) was a popular hit.

Caldara, Antonio
c. 1670–1736, ITALIAN

Caldara was probably taught by **Giovanni Legrenzi** (1626–90) and was a choirboy at St Mark's in Venice. His earliest operas were composed for Venice, while he was working as a cellist at St Mark's. He was appointed *maestro di cappella* at Mantua to the last Gonzaga duke until about 1707, and then worked at Rome for Prince Ruspoli until about 1716. His most fertile years were spent in Vienna, where he was vice-*Kapellmeister* to Emperor Charles VI, and produced more than 35 dramatic works at the Habsburg court across 20 years. Meanwhile, the prolific Caldara also composed several operas for Salzburg. He was the first composer regularly to set libretti by reformers **Apostolo Zeno** (1669–1750) and Metastasio.

Caldara was one of the few composers of the era who regularly used choral forces in his operas, although his musical style for Vienna was required to be more conservative than it had been in Venice and Rome. Other composers must have admired Caldara's work: his lost setting of Stampiglia's *La partenope* (1708) for Venice probably impressed Handel, who was in Venice at the time, and composed his own setting for London many years later. Many of Caldara's operas have survived, but have not yet been adequately explored.

Carestini, Giovanni
c. 1704–c. 1760, ITALIAN

Carestini studied in Milan from the age of 12, and gave his debut there in 1719. He studied with Antonio Maria Bernacchi, and sang alongside his teacher in his Roman debut of Alessandro Scarlatti's *La Griselda* (1721). He spent most of the 1720s singing in operas by **Leonardo Vinci** (*c.* 1696–1730), Porpora and Hasse at Rome, Naples and Venice. Initially a soprano, when he arrived in London in 1733 his voice had settled as a **mezzo-soprano**. During two seasons Handel created impressive new roles for Carestini in *Arianna*, *Ariodante* and *Alcina*. Carestini returned to Italy, and during the remainder of his career he also sang at Dresden, Berlin and St Petersburg. Hasse commented that 'he who has not heard Carestini is not acquainted with the most perfect style of singing'.

Cuzzoni, Francesca
1696–1778, ITALIAN

Singer Cuzzoni was born and trained in Parma, where she gave her first performance in 1714. She first appeared with Faustina Bordoni in Venice in 1718, and they sang together several times during the early 1720s. Her London debut in Handel's *Ottone* (1722) was a sensation. Handel composed notable roles for her including Cleopatra (*Giulio Cesare*), Asteria (*Tamerlano*), and the title role in *Rodelinda*. Cuzzoni sang in every Royal Academy opera until its closure in 1728, although this almost ended prematurely when only the intervention of the king could prevent the academy from dismissing her after the notorious on-stage brawl with Faustina. She returned to Italy and performed in several operas by Hasse, before joining the 'Opera of the Nobility' in 1734. In the late 1730s she sang for Leo and Caldara, but afterwards her career faded and she died in poverty.

Danchet, Antoine
1671–1748, FRENCH

Librettist Danchet was born on 7 September 1671 at Riom in Auvergne. His first theatrical text, *Vénus* (1698), was privately performed at Paris. This was also his first collaboration with composer **André Campra** (1660–1744). Between 1698 and 1735 Danchet and Campra produced several pastorals, ballets and *opéra ballets*, and 11 *tragedies lyriques*

including *Hésione* (1700), Cariselli (1702, using fragments of music by Lully), *Tancrède* (1702), *Télémaque* (1704) and *Idomonée* (1712). From 1727, Danchet was director of the Académie Française. Voltaire commented that Danchet's operas were less bad than his spoken plays. He is best known for having written the French libretto upon which Mozart's *Idomeneo* is based, although his original contained a much stronger supernatural element.

Durastanti, Margherita
fl. 1700–34, ITALIAN

The soprano Durastanti's first known appearance was at Venice in 1700. By 1707 she was employed by the Marquis Ruspoli in Rome, where she first met Handel, who composed several superb **cantatas** for her. Durastanti worked in Venice from 1709 until 1712, where she sang in nine operas by Lotti and the title role in Handel's *Agrippina*. She sang in Lotti's *Teofane* (1729) in Dresden, where Handel heard her and engaged her to join the Royal Academy of Music in London. Handel composed prominent roles for her in *Radamisto*, *Ottone* and *Giulio Cesare*. A second brief spell working for Handel in 1733–34 meant that she had a longer working relationship with the composer than any other musician, but the alterations Handel made to *Arianna* suggest that her stamina and range had diminished.

Farinelli
1705–82, ITALIAN

Carlo Broschi, known as 'Farinelli', studied with Porpora, and made his stage debut as a castrato in Naples when he was only 15 years old. By 1723, he was taking lead roles in his teacher's operas. Farinelli was remarkably successful across Europe, and in 1734 he reunited with Porpora to work in London for the 'Opera of the Nobility'. While at the peak of his fame, Farinelli suddenly quit in 1737 and spent over two decades in the service of Philip V of Spain, where his duties were not all directly associated with music and opera. He retired to Bologna in 1759 and became a respected figure visited by Mozart, Casanova and Emperor Joseph II. Today, Farinelli is known as the most famous castrato, largely due to Gérard Corbiau's controversial and mostly fictional film *Farinelli, il castrato* (1994).

Fel, Marie
1713–94, FRENCH

The daughter of a Bordeaux organist, Marie Fel studied singing with Mme Van Loo, and gave her operatic debut in October 1734. Mentioned in Rousseau's *Confessions*, Fel was one of the most famous singers of the Académie Royale de Musique, and was a regular soloist at the Concert Spirituel and the Concerts chez la Reine. From 1739, she performed in many productions, including most of Rameau's operas: she created leading roles in *Castor et Pollux*, Dardanus, *Les indes galantes*, *Platée* and *Zoroastre*. The technique and quality of Fel's singing, along with that of other singers such as her pupil Sophie Arnould, allowed Rameau to compose a more prominent number of demanding *ariettes* in his later operas. Fel also sang in works by Lully, Campra and Jean-Joseph de Mondonville (1711–72). She retired in 1758.

Fux, Johann Joseph
1660–1741, GERMAN

Fux studied music at Graz, and became a talented organist and church musician. He probably travelled to Italy during the 1680s, and his *a capella* **Masses** influenced by **Giovanni Pierluigi de Palestrina** (*c.* 1525–94) attracted the admiring attention of Emperor Leopold I in 1698. Based in Vienna for the remainder of his life, Fux was a respected composer of church music, but his visit to Rome in 1700 attracted him to composing operas

and oratorios. Most of Fux's 18 operas are settings of libretti by Pietro Pariati (1665–1733), although he also set some texts by Stampiglia, Zeno and Metastasio. His greatest triumph was *Costanza e Fortezza* (1723), performed in Prague to celebrate his patron Charles VI's coronation as King of Bohemia, although, owing to ill health, Fux's able assistant Caldara conducted the performances. However, Fux is most remembered for his scholarly book *Gradus ad Parnassum* (1725), which was a treatise on counterpoint that influenced the greatest Viennese choral composers of the late eighteenth century, including Mozart and **Joseph Haydn** (1732–1809). Fux was a respected teacher who trained Gottlieb Muffat and **Jan Dismas Zelenka** (1679–1745), and in his frail later years was assisted by Caldara.

Gay, John
1685–1732, ENGLISH

A friend and collaborator of Alexander Pope and Jonathan Swift (1667–1745), John Gay invented the genre of ballad opera with *The Beggar's Opera*. It premiered on 29 January 1728 at Lincoln's Inn Fields, and performed 62 times in its first season. The popular perception that *The Beggar's Opera* was an attack on Italian opera is untrue. It contains a mocking parody of the rivalry between Faustina and Cuzzoni, but Gay had previously contributed to Handel's *Acis and Galatea*, and the success of *The Beggar's Opera* cannot be securely attributed to the same audience that supported Italian operas at the King's Theatre. The target of the satire was intended to be Walpole's government, and censors suppressed the intended sequel *Polly*. Gay never repeated the success of *The Beggar's Opera*, and died one year before his last ballad opera *Achilles* was popularly received at Covent Garden in 1733.

Handel, George Frideric
1685–1759, GERMAN

Handel composed 42 operas between 1704 and 1740, but most of these were neglected and seldom performed after his lifetime. In the twentieth century, Handel's music dramas and in particular his operas underwent a renaissance that has established him as the definitive theatre composer of the late Baroque period. Handel was a maverick composer who pursued his own personal artistic direction, which was at times perceived by some of his London audience as old-fashioned compared to newer Italian composers. His eventual abandonment of Italian opera in favour of composing works in English allowed him to continue using his extraordinary gifts as a musical dramatist while establishing English oratorio as a distinctive and distinguished art form.

ORGAN LOFT TO OPERA HOUSE

Handel was born on 23 February 1685 in the provincial Saxon city of Halle. It is reputed that the Duke of Saxe-Weissenfels persuaded Handel's unsympathetic father to allow the boy to study music with the organist Friedrich Wilhelm Zachow. The young Handel presumably gained a thorough education in counterpoint and theory, but it is likely he yearned to escape Halle's devoutly Pietist atmosphere. In 1703 he arrived in Hamburg, where a chance meeting with **Johann Mattheson** (1681–1764) in an organ loft drew Handel into working his way up through the ranks of opera house orchestra until he composed his first opera, *Almira*, at the age of 19.

PAPAL ORATORIOS AND A PROTESTANT PATRON

Having exhausted his career possibilities in Hamburg, Handel resolved to visit Italy in 1706, where his first major undertaking was *Rodrigo* (1707), for Duke Ferdinando de' Medici at Florence. In Rome, where opera was forbidden by papal decree, Handel produced magnificent church music, dramatic oratorios and cantatas. His massively successful Venetian masterpiece *Agrippina* (1709) is the only opera that Handel set to a libretto written especially for him.

Handel resisted attempts to convert him to Catholicism while in Italy, and preferred to accept the position of *Kapellmeister* at the Protestant court of the Elector of Hanover. Nevertheless, he soon composed *Rinaldo*, which was performed in London. It was enormously popular and he deserted his post in Hanover and relocated permanently to London, where he seems to have overcome any diplomatic problems that might have arisen when his erstwhile employer became George I in 1714.

DIRECTOR OF THE ROYAL ACADEMY OF MUSIC

For a short period Handel provided music for James Brydges, the Earl of Carnarvon, including the masque *Acis and Galatea* that indicated a fertile future in composing English works. However, in 1719 Handel was appointed musical director of the Royal Academy of Music, an aristocratic company that funded performances of Italian opera at the King's Theatre on the Haymarket. This rivalled any opera house in Europe, starring the famous singers Cuzzoni and Senesino, for whom Handel created *Giulio Cesare in Egitto*. The following season, the arrival of the tenor Francesco Borosini influenced *Tamerlano* (1724) and *Rodelinda* (1725). The addition of a second prima donna, the soprano Faustina, heralded the Royal Academy's last phase – known as the 'Rival Queens' era – and in operas such as *Admeto* (1727) and *Tolomeo* (1728), Handel was careful to feature two equally prominent female characters.

CONFLICTING OPERA TRENDS AND TENSIONS

Italian opera became increasingly difficult to sustain on the London stage. In 1729, Handel took over management in partnership with the King's Theatre impresario Heidegger. During the next five years, this semi-independent company (sometimes called the 'Second Academy') allowed Handel to pursue a flexible choice of libretti that reveal a greater degree of variety than the conventional heroic subjects that the Royal Academy had preferred. In 1732, Handel introduced English works into his theatre seasons. For the 1734–35 season, Handel established an independent opera company at John Rich's new Covent Garden Theatre, but, despite the successes of *Ariodante* (1735) and *Alcina* (1735), Handel struggled against competition from the 'Opera of the Nobility', which had replaced him at the King's Theatre. The rivalry did not benefit either faction, and by the end of the 1736–37 season Handel suffered a massive stroke, signalling the end of his most active years as an opera composer. Thereafter he produced *Serse* (1738) and *Imeneo* (1740), which present wittier subject matter, and reveal a more concise economical musical style. After nearly 30 years trying to make a success of Italian opera in London, Handel dedicated the rest of his career to non-staged theatrical works set to English texts, although *Semele* (1743), *Hercules* (1744) and even some biblical oratorios are fundamentally operatic in nature.

Rinaldo

A small number of Handel's dramatic works are known as the 'magic operas', including *Rinaldo*, *Teseo* (1712), *Amadigi* (1715), *Orlando* (1733) and *Alcina*. These operas feature protagonists who use sorcery to manipulate love, usually for evil ends. Most common among these operas is the prima-donna sorceress figure, who attempts to compel a castrato hero away from his true love and military duty. The wicked woman's plans to entice the hero are always doomed to failure: in these operas, the hero's eventual disillusionment and disenchantment are considered in literal and favourable terms. *Rinaldo* was Handel's first Italian opera composed for London, and is notable for its flamboyant music and exotically devised libretto. It is not generally thought to be among Handel's best dramas, but seems to have impressed the London public by combining technically demanding arias with lavish spectacle.

The glories of Handel's score include the heroic aria 'Or la tromba' (featuring four trumpets) and the lament 'Cara sposa', both composed for the castrato Nicolini (1673–1732). However, the dominant character is the villainous enchantress Armida, whose conclusion to Act II, 'Vo far guerra', afforded Handel an opportunity to dazzle his audiences with stunningly intricate harpsichord solos.

Rinaldo

by George Frideric Handel
Composed: 1711
Premiered: 1711, London
Libretto by Aaron Hill and Giacomo Rossi, after Torquato Tasso

ACT I

During the first crusade, in the Christian camp, Goffredo delivers words of encouragement. To the young knight Rinaldo he promises his daughter Almirena's hand in marriage, if the army is successful in capturing Jerusalem. The Saracen king Argante appears and demands a three-day truce, to which Goffredo agrees. Argante then consults his lover, the sorceress Armida, who reveals that without Rinaldo the Christians will never succeed. Rinaldo and Almirena are in a garden exchanging lovers' vows when Armida, using her magic powers, abducts Almirena. Rinaldo runs to Goffredo and his brother Eustazio for advice; they suggest paying a visit to a Christian sorcerer. Rinaldo calls on the elements to assist him in retrieving his love.

ACT II

On their way to visit the sorcerer, Goffredo, Eustazio and Rinaldo arrive at the seashore, where sirens, sent by Armida, are singing to them. Despite the efforts of the others, Rinaldo is enchanted by the sirens; he goes to join them and sails off aboard a magic boat. Rinaldo is taken to Armida's palace, where Almirena is also being held prisoner. Argante has fallen in love with Almirena and is forcing his unwanted attentions on her. Likewise, Armida falls for Rinaldo; after he rejects her she uses her magic to make herself look like Almirena, and tries again to seduce him. Rinaldo sees through her disguise, but Argante fails to and continues his wooing of 'Almirena'. Armida, discovering Argante's treachery, swears she will have vengeance.

ACT III

Goffredo and Eustazio reach the home of the sorcerer, who lives at the base of the mountain on which Armida's palace is situated. They try to climb the mountain but are forced back by evil spirits; the sorcerer provides them with magic wands and they make a successful ascent. As Armida attempts to kill Almirena, Goffredo and Eustazio use their wands to destroy the palace and the setting once again becomes the countryside near Jerusalem. The Christian soldiers, led by Rinaldo, storm the city and capture Argante; Eustazio captures Armida. Rinaldo and Almirena are reunited amidst much joy and celebration, while Argante and Armida agree to convert to the Christian faith.

Recommended Recording:

Rinaldo, Academy of Ancient Music; Christopher Hogwood, conductor; Decca 467 087-2OHO3; Soloists: L. Orgonasova (Armida), Cecilia Bartoli (Almirena), Bernarda Fink (Goffredo), David Daniels (Rinaldo), Gerald Finley (Argante)

Acis and Galatea

While composing for the Earl of Carnarvon at Cannons, Handel was the musical contributor to a distinguished literary circle including the poets John Gay, Alexander Pope (1688–1744) and John Hughes (1677–1720). It is believed that all three authors contributed to the libretto of Acis and Galatea, which was given a private staged performance that probably required only a dozen performers. One observer noted in his diary that it was 'a little opera'. Its pastoral subject and chamber scoring are far removed from the spectacle and high drama of opera seria.

Acis and Galatea

by George Frideric Handel
Composed: 1718
Premiered: 1718, Edgware
Libretto by John Gay and others, after Ovid

ACT I

In an idyllic, pastoral setting, Galatea, a semi-divine sea-nymph, has fallen in love with Acis, a shepherd. She appeals to another shepherd, Damon, for assistance; with his help the two lovers are united and sing of their love for one another, accompanied by various nymphs and shepherds.

ACT II

Act II begins with a more sinister atmosphere, as the chorus warns Acis and Galatea of the approach of Polyphemus, a sea monster. Inflamed by jealousy, Polyphemus threatens to force his love upon Galatea. Acis, ignoring Damon's warnings, prepares to do battle with the fearsome monster. Acis and Galatea swear their eternal love, but their duet becomes a trio as they are interrupted by Polyphemus, who kills Acis. Galatea is heartbroken, but at this point is reminded by the chorus of her divine powers. She then transforms Acis into a beautiful fountain; everyone mourns Acis and sings of his immortality.

Giulio Cesare in Egitto

Handel's operas usually revolve around the voices and particular gifts of the singers that were available to him. *Giulio Cesare* was created in 1724 as a vehicle for Senesino and Cuzzoni, although the characteristic trademark of Handel's best operas is that the emotions and experience of the characters are not sacrificed to the virtuosity of the singers. Although Handel's arias are an opportunity for the singer to impress his audience, they also function as engaging indications of the character's dramatic motivation and thoughts. Handel's ability to portray character often results in an organically evolving personality. In Act I of Giulio Cesare, the title-hero's arias show progress from pompous arrogance ('Presti omai l'egizia terra'), anger ('Empio, dirò tu sei') to a realization of his own mortality ('Alma del gran Pompeo'). Likewise, Cleopatra is transformed from a flirtatious stereotype into a genuinely seductive lover in 'V'adoro pupille', which features a lush onstage continuo band, before her sincere hopelessness demands our pity in 'Piangerò la sorte mia'. The secondary roles of the grieving Cornelia and her vengeful son Sesto are also compellingly brought to life, especially in their sublime duet 'Son nata a lagrimar'.

Giulio Cesare in Egitto ('Julius Cesar in Egypt')

by George Frideric Handel
Composed: 1724
Premiered: 1724, London
Libretto by Nicola Francesco Haym, after Giacomo Francesco Bussani

ACT I

Giulio Cesare is in Egypt and has promised a reconciliation with his old enemy Pompeo, if Pompeo shows himself personally. Achilla, commander of the Egyptian army under King Tolomeo, arrives with Pompeo's head; Cesare is angered by this. Pompeo's wife Cornelia and son Sesto are also present; they are distraught and Sesto swears vengeance. Cleopatra, who rules Egypt jointly with her brother, decides to seduce Cesare, while Achilla tells Tolomeo that he will murder Cesare in return for Cornelia's hand. Cesare, in his camp, is introduced to 'Lidia', who is in fact Cleopatra in disguise. Cesare falls in love with her. Cornelia enters and tries to kill herself, but Sesto prevents her. 'Lydia' offers the services of Nireno, an Egyptian courtier, to help them find Tolomeo, Pompeo's murderer. Cesare arrives at Tolomeo's palace, avoiding ambush. Tolomeo falls for Cornelia when they are introduced, but continues to pretend that Achilla can expect to win her. Cornelia spurns Achilla's advances towards her; Achilla in his anger imprisons Sesto.

ACT II

Cleopatra, as 'Lidia', summons Cesare to her rooms; with the assistance of Nireno, he arrives. Meanwhile, both Achilla and Tolomeo try unsuccessfully to woo Cornelia. Guards approach 'Lydia' and Cesare; Cleopatra reveals her true identity and prays for Cesare as he leaves to face the enemy. Cornelia sits among the people in Tolomeo's harem. Sesto rushes in and attempts to kill the king but is prevented by Achilla, who reveals that Cesare has leapt from a castle window into the sea and cannot have survived. He requests his prize, i.e. Cornelia, but Tolomeo refuses. Sesto now tries to commit suicide but Cornelia stops him. The angry Achilla changes sides, joining the Romans and Cleopatra.

ACT III

A fierce battle rages on the shores of the Mediterranean. Tolomeo's army triumphs and he takes Cleopatra prisoner. Cesare is still alive and rises from the sea. Meanwhile Sesto and Nireno go in search of Tolomeo, but come across Achilla, who is dying. He gives Sesto a seal, which will give him command over a number of soldiers nearby. As Achilla dies, Cesare enters and takes the seal, vowing to save Cleopatra and Cornelia. Cesare saves Cleopatra from where she is being held prisoner. Sesto finds Tolomeo, who is still trying to court Cornelia, and slays him. They are all reunited; Cesare and Cleopatra declare their love for each other and the people rejoice that their land is at peace.

Recommended Recording:

Giulio Cesare in Egitto, Concerto Köln;René Jacobs, conductor; HMC901385.87; Soloists: Barbara Schlick (Cleopatra), Marianne Rorholm (Sesto), Jennifer Larmore (Giulio Cesare), Bernarda Fink (Cornelia), Derek Lee Ragin (Tolomeo), Furio Zanasi (Achilla), Olivier Lalouette (Curio), Dominique Visse (Nireno)

Rodelinda

Composed in 1725, *Rodelinda* is remarkable for its quality. Handel composed many exceptional accompanied recitatives for Senesino throughout their collaborations, and in this opera the dethroned King Bertarido, believed dead by his steadfast wife, laments his misfortune in an accompanied recitative and aria, 'Pompe vane di morte! ... Dove sei amato bene', which shows Handel as a supreme master of his craft. Bertarido's eventual confrontation with his usurper Grimoaldo, in 'Vivi tiranno!', is a thrilling example of how Handel's arias can be both technically spectacular and emotionally astute: the *coloratura* is bright and ferocious, but the sentimental tone of the aria brilliantly captures Bertarido's indignant defiance, giving him a full characterization.

Rodelinda

by George Frideric Handel
Composed: 1725
Premiered: 1725, London
Libretto by Nicola Francesco Haym, after Antonio Salvi and Pierre Corneille

BACKGROUND

The kingdom of Lombardy was split between two brothers, Bertarido and Gundeberto, who then fought over the inheritance. Gundeberto called upon Duke Grimoaldo to help him, offering his sister Eduige's hand in return. Gundeberto met his death, probably through Grimoaldo's doing. Grimoaldo, while betrothed to Eduige, fell in love with Bertarido's wife, Rodelinda, and seized the Milanese throne. Bertarido fled to Hungary, spreading the news of his death.

ACT I

As Rodelinda weeps for Bertarido, Grimoaldo offers to marry her; she rejects him. Duke Garibaldo persuades Grimoaldo to break his engagement to Eduige. Garibaldo then proposes to Eduige himself. Garibaldo, when alone, reveals that he does not love Eduige but hopes to gain the throne. Bertarido has returned and is visiting his tomb. Unulfo, a courtier who has retained his loyalty to Bertarido, advises him to hide. Rodelinda and Flavio arrive, followed by Garibaldo, who threatens to kill Flavio unless Rodelinda marries Grimoaldo. She agrees, stipulating that her first act as queen will be to execute Garibaldo. Bertarido is dismayed at Rodelinda's willingness·to marry Grimoaldo.

ACT II

Eduige agrees to marry Garibaldo. Rodelinda asks Grimoaldo to murder Flavio in front of her, as she cannot marry a usurper and be the mother of the rightful king. Garibaldo encourages Grimoaldo to do just this; both Unulfo and Grimoaldo are horrified by the idea. As Bertarido laments his fate, Eduige hears him and is reunited with her brother. Bertarido admits that he is not interested in the throne and only wishes to be with his family; this pleases Eduige, who still hopes for power. Unulfo arrives and reassures Bertarido of Rodelinda's continuing fidelity; he then brings her to him and the lovers are reunited. Grimoaldo finds them together and declares that he will kill Bertarido.

ACT III

Eduige, remorseful for coveting the throne, gives Unulfo the key to a secret passage through which Bertarido can escape. Garibaldo tries to persuade Grimoaldo to kill Bertarido. In the dungeon, Bertarido is thrown a sword. He uses it to attack the intruder, who turns out to be Unulfo. They hear footsteps approaching and exit, leaving behind a bloodied cloak. Eduige, Rodelinda and Flavio enter, find the garment and believe Bertarido to be dead. Unulfo leaves to fetch the others, while Bertarido conceals himself. Grimoaldo arrives, tortured by guilt, jealousy and love, and falls asleep. Garibaldo attempts to kill him, but is instead killed himself by Bertarido. Grateful for his life, Grimoaldo returns the kingdom of Milan to Bertarido, declaring that he will marry Eduige and they will rule Pavia together.

Orlando

The mid-1730s operas *Orlando*, *Ariodante* and *Alcina* represent the artistic peak of Handel's operatic career. Their stories all originate in the epic poem *Orlando Furioso* by the playwright and poet Ariosto, who was born and bred at the Ferrara court in the late fifteenth century.

Orlando portrays the destructive insanity of its title-hero, who ignores his destiny by pursuing the love of the unkind Angelica rather than glory in war. The climax of this madness, at the end of Act II, was brilliantly conveyed by Handel's use of eccentric time signatures within striking accompanied recitatives, paradoxically followed by the lyrical yet slightly disturbed aria 'Vaghe pupille'. Orlando's magnificent arias also include 'Non fu già men forte Alcide', featuring Handel's typically robust yet melodic use of horns, in which the deluded warrior compares himself to Hercules. This was the last role Handel ever composed for his star castrato Senesino, and it is the most astonishing and innovative. Handel's music for Angelica, the shepherdess

Dorinda and the Prince Medoro is also superb, and their trio 'Consolati o bella', which concludes Act I, confirms that Handel's dramatic ensembles exploring the emotions of different characters can hold their own alongside Mozart's. The wise magician Zoroastro, composed for the remarkably agile bass Antonio Montagnana, is an antecedent of Mozart and **Emmanuel Schikaneder**'s (1751–1812) Sarastro, and is the only magical character in Handel's operas who uses his power for good rather than evil.

Orlando

by George Frideric Handel
Composed: 1732
Premiered: 1733, London
Libretto unknown, after Carlo Sigismondo and Lodovico Ariosto

BACKGROUND

Prince Medoro has been wounded in battle and is being nursed back to health by Dorinda, a shepherdess, and Angelica, Queen of Cathay, who is being courted by Orlando, a knight. Dorinda and Angelica have both fallen in love with Medoro.

ACT I

Zoroastro, a magician, consults the stars and, seeing that Orlando has strayed from his destiny in his pursuit of Angelica, tries to persuade him to abandon his love and dedicate himself to noble deeds. Orlando says that he can reconcile his destiny and his love for Angelica. At Dorinda's house, the shepherdess muses on love, while Angelica and Medoro declare their feelings for each other. Dorinda sees Angelica leaving, but Medoro pretends that she is a relative.

Zoroastro warns Angelica that if Orlando learns of her love for Medoro, the knight will wreak his revenge. To confirm that Orlando loves her, Angelica taunts him by accusing him of loving another. Orlando denies it and offers to prove his love for her by killing fearsome monsters. Angelica then joins Medoro and the two embrace; Dorinda enters and is inconsolable at discovering Medoro does not return her affections. Angelica gives her a jewel.

ACT II

Orlando bursts in upon the grieving Dorinda and accuses her of telling Angelica that he has been unfaithful. Dorinda reveals the truth about Angelica and Medoro, showing Orlando the jewel, which, it turns out, was given to Angelica by Orlando. Consumed by rage, Orlando swears revenge and leaves. Zoroastro, scolding Angelica and Medoro for incurring Orlando's wrath, advises them to flee. They pause in the woods, where Medoro declares his love for Angelica, carving their names on a tree. Orlando finds this evidence and, eventually reaching the lovers, attempts to kill them. Zoroastro protects them and Orlando, tormented by love, fury, grief and his inner conflict, loses his mind.

ACT III

Medoro, who has lost Angelica in the pursuit, returns to Dorinda's house and confesses his love for Angelica. Orlando arrives and declares his love for Dorinda, but he is obviously mad and leaves, guided by his raving fantasies. Dorinda tells Angelica that Orlando has killed Medoro. Orlando confronts Angelica and she defies him; he throws her in a cave. Zoroastro now decides to return Orlando's sanity. Dorinda tells him that he has killed Medoro and he attempts to kill himself, but is prevented by Angelica. With the help of Zoroastro, Orlando accepts Angelica and Medoro's love for each other and rejoices in his own destiny and triumph over love and his own madness.

Recommended Recording:

Orlando, Les Arts Florissants; William Christie, conductor' Erato CD 0630–14636–2; Soloists: Rosemary Joshua (Angelica), Rosa Mannion (Dorinda), Patricia Bardon (Orlando), Hilary Summers (Medoro), Harry van der Kamp (Zoroastro)

Ariodante

Ariodante also derives from Ariosto, but it is a serious opera. Thanks to a fine text, adapted from an old Italian libretto by Antonio Salvi, Handel was able to explore potent tragic situations, such as the King of Scotland being forced to contemplate executing his much-loved daughter Ginvera. The opera is best known for 'Scherza infida', an aria composed for Carestini that explores the anguish of a broken heart. Ariodante also featured a full chorus and several fine dances for Marie Sallé's ballet company.

Ariodante

by George Frideric Handel
Composed: 1735
Premiered: 1735, London
Libretto unknown, after Antonio Salvi and Lodovico Ariosto

ACT I

Ginevra, daughter of the Scottish king, is in her chamber preparing to meet her betrothed. She reveals to her confidante Dalinda that her father approves of her engagement. Duke Polinesso enters, declaring his love for Ginevra. She rejects him harshly. Dalinda, herself in love with Polinesso, explains to him that Ginevra is betrothed to Ariodante, a knight. Polinesso then devises a plot by which he can use Dalinda's love for him to win Ginevra's heart. In the garden, Ginevra and Ariodante sing of their love for each other. The king gives them his blessing and orders Odoardo to begin the wedding preparations. Meanwhile, Polinesso appeals to Dalinda to help him by dressing up as Ginevra and inviting him into Ginevra's room. He offers her his love in return. Flattered, Dalinda agrees. When Polinesso has left, Ariodante's brother, Lurcanio, enters and declares his love for Dalinda; she rejects him. Alone, she sings that she will always love Polinesso. There is a dance, in which Ginevra and Ariodante mingle with shepherds and shepherdesses.

ACT II

Polinesso encounters Ariodante and feigns surprise at the news he is to be married to Ginevra, explaining that he and Ginevra are in love. Ariodante demands proof, upon which Dalinda, dressed as Ginevra, welcomes Polinesso into Ginevra's chamber. Ariodante is shocked and tries to kill himself, but is stopped by Lurcanio. Polinesso continues to pretend that he loves Dalinda. The king is informed that Ariodante has leapt into the sea and is drowned. Ginevra faints at the news. Lurcanio explains Ginevra's apparent treachery to her father, who disowns her. There is a dance in which we see Ginevra's feverish dreams.

ACT III

Contrary to the rumours, Ariodante is alive, and alone in the woods. He hears the frightened cries of Dalinda; she is running from Polinesso, who wants to kill her to ensure her silence. Ariodante saves Dalinda, who then confesses the deception. Back at the palace, the king asks for a knight to defend Ginevra's honour in a jousting match against Lurcanio. Polinesso, hoping to win favour with the king, accepts. The jousting begins and Polinesso is mortally wounded. Lurcanio offers to fight anyone else who will defend Ginevra; an unknown knight responds. It is revealed to be Ariodante, who offers to tell all if Dalinda receives a Royal pardon. Odoardo enters with the news that Polinesso has confessed to his crimes. Dalinda agrees to marry Lurcanio, while Ginevra, in her cell, is reunited with both her father and Ariodante. The opera closes with a courtly dance involving all the couples.

Alcina

Alcina (composed in 1735) is the most celebrated of Handel's 'magic' operas. Its dynamic situations are compelling and poignant: Handel's portrayal of an enchanted hero, his brave true love and

their evil enemy inspired him to create a particularly fine score that examines intense emotional experiences such as loss, guilt, lust, nostalgia and the restoration of memory.

Handel's version is based on an anonymous adaptation of *Ariosto* that had been set to music by Riccardo Broschi, Farinelli's brother, for Rome in 1728. The title role, composed for **Anna Maria Strada del Pó** (active 1719–40), is an especially fascinating and complex woman, although all the characters in the opera reveal complicated emotions and relationships that are examined by some of Handel's finest operatic music.

Alcina
by George Frideric Handel
Composed: 1735
Premiered: 1735, London
Libretto unknown, after Antonio Fanzaglia and Lodovico Ariosto

ACT I

Bradamante, disguised as her brother Ricciardo, has arrived with her confidant Melisso in the realm of Alcina, an enchantress. They hope to rescue Bradamante's lover Ruggiero, who has been bewitched by Alcina. Pretending to have lost their way, the pair are welcomed by Alcina's sister, Morgana, who falls in love with 'Ricciardo' (Bradamante). Alcina, who is in love with Ruggiero, welcomes 'Ricciardo' and Melisso to her palace. Bradamante and Melisso try to rescue Ruggiero, but he does not recognize them. Oronte, betrothed to Morgana, challenges 'Ricciardo' to a duel; Morgana protects 'Ricciardo'. Oronte tells Ruggiero that Alcina loves 'Ricciardo'. Ruggiero confronts Alcina and she denies it. Alcina vows to turn 'Ricciardo' into a wild beast to prove her love for Ruggiero; Morgana urges 'him' to flee. 'He' asks her to tell Alcina that 'his' heart belongs to another; Morgana is overjoyed.

ACT II

Disguised as Ruggiero's old tutor, Melisso manages to persuade Ruggiero of his true identity. He advises Ruggiero to tell Alcina he is going out hunting and then escape. Ruggiero again meets Bradamante, but is mistrustful in case it is Alcina in disguise. As Alcina prepares to turn 'Ricciardo' into a beast, Morgana enters, followed by Ruggiero. He persuades Alcina that she does not need to perform the spell in order to prove her love for him, and tells her that he is going out hunting. Oronte reveals that Melisso, 'Ricciardo' and Ruggiero are preparing to flee and mocks Morgana for believing that 'Ricciardo' loves her. Bradamante reassures Oberto that they will find his father. Bradamante and Ruggiero are finally reunited but are overheard by Morgana, who now knows about Bradamante's disguise and Ruggiero's betrayal. Alcina summons spirits to impede the lovers' escape, but her powers are weakening.

ACT III

Morgana and Oronte are reunited. Ruggiero encounters Alcina and explains that he is betrothed to Bradamante; Alcina swears vengeance. Melisso and Ruggiero prepare to destroy Alcina's powers, with the help of the magic ring; Oronte reveals to Alcina that her powers are no longer working properly. Ruggiero and Bradamante destroy the source of Alcina's powers, despite her protestations that she has no evil intentions. Alcina and Morgana lament their fate; their powers have been removed and the spell has been lifted from the land; the castle lies in ruins and Alcina's captives turn back into humans. Everyone rejoices in love and freedom.

Serse

Although popular now, *Serse* was one of Handel's worst failures during his own time. It was only performed five times in its first run and Handel never revived it. Unusually among his operas, its libretto by **Silvio Stampiglia** (1664–1725) is warmly

---

---

light-hearted and does not seriously concern itself with tragic events or heroic actions. The most famous aria, 'Ombra mai fù', portrays the King of Persia eloquently expressing love to a tree. The opera's arias feature imaginative use of limited resources. The score shows that Handel's genius remained vibrant even towards the unhappy end of his operatic career.

Serse

by George Frideric Handel
Composed: 1738
Premiered: 1738, London
Libretto unknown, after Silvio Stampiglia and Nicolò Minato

ACT I

Serse, King of Persia, sings in his garden, watched by his brother Arsemene and his servant, Elviro. Romilda, Arsemene's secret lover, sings nearby; Serse is enchanted. He orders Arsemene to tell Romilda of his love. This interests Romilda's sister, Atlanta, who loves Arsemene. Romilda rejects Serse's love; Serse banishes Arsemene. Serse's abandoned fiancée Amastre arrives in disguise and swearing vengeance. Ariodate, Romilda's father, brings news of victory; Serse promises him that his daughter will marry a royal. Arsemene gives Elviro a letter for Romilda, describing his grief. Atlanta taunts Romilda and says that Arsemene has been unfaithful.

ACT II

In disguise, Elviro tries to deliver Arsemene's letter. He meets Amastre and reveals that Serse is to marry Romilda. Atlanta intercepts Elviro and takes the letter to Serse, claiming that it was intended for her. Serse shows it to Romilda, who continues to reject his advances. Alone, Romilda confesses her jealousy, while Amastre attempts suicide; Elviro prevents her. Elviro relates all to Arsemene. By their new bridge, Serse and Ariodate sing of conquests. Arsemene arrives; Serse pardons him and gives him permission to marry Atlanta, but he explains that he loves Romilda. Serse encourages Atlanta to forget Arsemene. A storm destroys the bridge. Amastre, calling Serse a traitor, is arrested; Romilda secures her release and then sings of her love for Arsemene.

ACT III

Reunited, Romilda and Arsemene extract the truth from Atlanta. Romilda consents to marry Serse, if her father agrees, but she reveals that she will kill herself should the union go ahead. Serse asks Ariodate if he will allow Romilda to marry a royal man equal in status to Serse. Ariodate, assuming that he means Arsemene, consents. Romilda suggests to Serse that she and Arsemene have consummated their love; he orders Arsemene's execution. Serse is given a letter supposedly from Romilda (written by Amastre) chiding him for his betrayal. He orders Arsemene to kill Romilda, but Amastre reveals her identity and declares that if the treacherous must die, the sword should turn on Serse. Serse pleads for forgiveness and offers Romilda and Arsemene his blessing.

Semele

Semele was first performed at Covent Garden on 10 February 1744 in the manner of an oratorio, without action or scenery. Nevertheless, Handel's occasional collaborator Charles Jennens

regarded it as 'a bawdy opera'. Congreve's libretto, based on a story from Ovid, had originally been set as an opera by John Eccles in 1707, but it was never performed. However the libretto came to Handel's attention, it inspired him to compose a rich work in which the foolish and gullible Semele steals the show with her florid songs 'Endless pleasure' and 'Myself I shall adore'. Handel's music fits each character perfectly, whether it is the malicious venom of the jealous Juno, or the sweet and simple Athamus. The Arcadian music, especially that for Jupiter ('Where'er you walk') and a sleep scene for Somnus, ranks among his finest achievements, but, despite its quality, Semele was not a success: it was performed only six times during Handel's lifetime. Several recent productions have proved that his secular 'oratorio' is ideal for the modern opera house.

Semele

by George Frideric Handel
Composed: 1743
Premiered: 1744, London
Libretto by William Congreve, after Ovid

ACT I

In the temple of Juno, the people of Thebes celebrate the marriage of Semele, daughter of Cadmus, King of Thebes, to Athamas. The goddess is seen to approve of the match. Semele is unwilling to go ahead with the wedding and prays to Jupiter, whom she is in love with, for guidance. Semele's sister Ino is also in a state of distress, for she loves Athamas. Jupiter expresses his disapproval of the marriage with a clap of thunder. The flame on the altar is extinguished and the people, with the exception of Athamas and Ino, flee. Ino tries to express her love for Athamas but he misconstrues her words. Cadmus returns and relates that Semele has been borne up to the heavens by a giant eagle. The priests return, not mourning but celebrating Semele's departure, as she can be heard in the distance singing of endless pleasure and love.

ACT II

Juno, wife of Jupiter, is enraged when Iris tells her of the house that Jupiter has built for Semele, and swears vengeance. Iris warns her of the dragons that guard the gates, and Juno decides to employ Somnus, god of sleep, to help her. Semele sleeps in her new home. On awakening, she feels lonely and ignored by Jupiter and wishes for sleep to reclaim her. Jupiter tries to reassure her but she maintains that while she remains mortal she cannot help but be dissatisfied. Jupiter is concerned that Semele has aspirations to immortality and attempts to distract her. He sends for Ino and transforms the surroundings into Arcadia, encouraging Semele to enjoy the pleasures of nature. Ino arrives, telling excitedly of her journey to the heavens and the beautiful music she has heard. Everyone celebrates the joy of music.

ACT III

Juno tries to persuade Somnus to help her carry out her plans. He is unenthusiastic until she promises him his favourite nymph, Pasithea. Somnus is to bring sleep upon Ino and the dragons at the palace, so that Juno can disguise herself as Ino and reach Semele's room. He is also instructed to send Jupiter an erotic dream, so that when he awakes he will be willing to do anything Semele asks of him. Semele is unhappy and alone when Juno, disguised as Ino, enters her room. Juno asks Semele about her hopes for immortality and shows her a mirror, in which Semele appears to have the perfection of a goddess. Juno then advises Semele that when Jupiter comes to her, she should insist on him appearing in his unmasked, godlike form instead of appearing as a man. In this way, Juno assures her, Semele will become immortal. Semele thanks Juno, who retires.

Jupiter, inflamed by desire following his dream, enters Semele's chamber and goes to embrace her. Semele hesitates, so Jupiter swears to give her anything she desires. She asks to see him in his godlike form. Jupiter, knowing that the force of this will kill Semele, is angry with himself for having sworn to grant her wish. He tries to warn her against it, but Semele assumes that he simply wants to deny her immortality. Juno revels in her victory. Jupiter then descends in a cloud with thunder and lightning. Semele is consumed by his fire and dies. Ino is returned to Thebes and, along with Athamas, Cadmus and the priests, witnesses Semele's death as a storm of fire.

Ino eventually reveals that Jupiter has commanded that she and Athamas wed. Apollo descends with the news that from Semele's ashes will rise Bacchus, god of wine. Everyone celebrates the joyful news.

OPERAS	
1705	Almira; Nero (lost)
1707	Florindo e Dafne (lost); Rodrigo
1709	Agrippina
1711	Rinaldo
1712	Il pastor fido; Teseo
1713	Silla
1715	Amadigi di Gaula
1718	Acis and Galatea
1720	Radamisto
1721	Muzio Scevola; Floridante
1722	Ottone
1723	Flavio
1724	Giulio Cesare in Egitto; Tamerlano
1725	Rodelinda
1726	Admeto; Riccardo I
1728	Siroe; Tolomeo
1729	Lotario
1730	Partenope
1731	Poro
1732	Ezio; Sosarme
1733	Orlando
1734	Arianna
1735	Ariodante; Alcina
1736	Atalanta
1737	Arminio; Giustino; Berenice
1738	Faramondo; Serse
1740	Imeneo; Deidamia
1743	Semele (oratorio)

in 1701. Although he died in 1729, it has been supposed that traces of his unfinished work could be evident in some of Handel's later operas.

Leo, Leonardo
1694–1744, ITALIAN

Leo was born near Brindisi, studied music in Naples at the Conservatorio San Maria della Pietà dei Turchini, and spent most of the rest of his life in the city. He held various organist and church music positions, and his first opera, *Il pisistrato* (1714), was staged before he was 20 years old. In 1723, he composed his first opera for Venice, but soon started to develop the new genre of Neapolitan comic opera. He was promoted to organist of the vice-regal chapel at Naples in 1725, but it was only after the death of Vinci and departure of Hasse from Naples that Leo became a leading opera composer.

In addition to Naples, Leo provided operas for Turin, Milan and Bologna, and acquired a reputation as an oratorio composer. Leo's music was considered to be cerebral and more grounded in counterpoint than that of his more liberal Neapolitan contemporaries, and his operatic style was more conservative than Hasse, Vinci and Porpora. In 1737, Leo set Metastasio's *L'Olimpiade*, but he mostly devoted his talents towards comic opera, and was one of the first to establish it as a respected art form.

Haym, Nicola Francesco
1678–1729, ITALIAN

Haym was the skilful literary adaptor who prepared several of Handel's best opera libretti, including *Radamisto*, *Giulio Cesare*, *Tamerlano* and *Rodelinda*. Rather than writing new texts for Handel, Haym's talent was reorganizing old Italian texts so that they were adequately dramatic and balanced while also reducing the amount of simple recitative for the English-speaking audience. He also adapted the French dramas *Teseo* and *Amadigi* into Italian for Handel.

Haym was an antiquarian and book-collector, but was also Handel's continuo cellist, and had been a member of Cardinal Ottoboni's orchestra in Rome for six years before coming to London

Mattheson, Johann
1681–1764, GERMAN

Born into a wealthy family, Mattheson received a gentleman's education in languages and the arts, and studied law before becoming immersed in Hamburg's operatic scene. He made his debut as a soprano in 1696, but his voice broke soon after and he sang tenor roles until 1705. He took part in more than 60 new operas, including some composed by Keiser, and soon began to compose and conduct his own. Mattheson is best remembered for his friendship with the young Handel, who arrived in Hamburg in 1703 and was encouraged by Mattheson to pursue a career in opera. Their friendship suffered when Handel refused to relinquish the harpsichord to Mattheson during a performance of the latter's *Cleopatra* (1704), and only a button saved Handel's life during the ensuing duel.

Mattheson was a respected organist, but instead preferred to continue composing for the Hamburg opera house. In 1715, he became director of music at the city's cathedral, but by 1728 he was increasingly afflicted with deafness and gave up the post. Mattheson continued to compose until the last years of his life, but today he is less well known for his operas than for his several scholarly treatises about music theory and his relationship with Handel.

Nicolini or Nicolo Grimaldi
1673–1732, ITALIAN

Nicolo Grimaldi, known as 'Nicolini', studied singing in Naples with the composer Francesco Provenzale (1624–1704), and made his debut at the age of 12. Nicolini sang in the cathedral and royal chapel as a soprano, but soon became associated with operas by Scarlatti. He also sang for Bononcini, Lotti, Leo, Porpora and Vinci. Nicolini visited London in 1708, and received great acclaim for performances of Scarlatti's *Pirro e Demetrio* (1708). With the theatre manager Owen Swiney, Nicolini made Italian opera fashionable with adaptations of works such as Bononcini's *Camilla* (1709). He created the title roles in Handel's *Rinaldo and Amadigi*. Nicolini left London in 1717, although during the mid-1720s Swiney repeatedly attempted to influence the Royal Academy into engaging him once more. He remained active until his death, which occurred in Naples during the rehearsals of Pergolesi's first opera *La Salustia* (1732).

Pariati, Pietro
1665–1733, ITALIAN

Pariati was born in Reggio Emilia, and was secretary to the Duke of Modena. He spent time in Madrid, wrote works for Barcelona and spent three years in an Italian prison. He lived in Venice for 15 years, until he was appointed a court poet at Vienna in 1714. While in Venice he worked with Zeno on several libretti, specialized in adapting recent tragedies into opera libretti and updated old seventeenth-century libretti. He gained celebrity for writing comic scenes and *intermezzi*, and drew on influences such as Moliére and Cervantes.

Pariati wrote texts for 13 oratorios and 14 theatrical dramas for the imperial family in Vienna, the most famous of which was *Costanza e Fortezza*, set to music by Fux (1723). Pariati developed a new style of comic fantasy in his libretti, and used his texts as opportunities to provoke satire, not least against conventional *opera seria*.

Pellegrin, Simon-Joseph
1663–1745, FRENCH

Simon-Joseph Pellegrin was a monk who sailed twice with the French fleet to the Orient, and who put into verse Biblical texts that were sung to music by Lully and Campra at the royal convent at St Cyr. Pellegrin provided libretti for many composers, including Campra and Desmarets, but his best-known works are *Jephté*, set to music by Montéclair in 1732, and *Hippolyte et Aricie*, composed by Jean-Philippe Rameau in 1733.

Pellegrin seemed content to mingle the domestic benefits of religious life with the pleasures of the theatre, and was granted a papal dispensation to continue living at the Cluny Monastery while providing texts for the comedies and tragedies that were performed in Paris, until he was eventually excommunicated.

Pergolesi, Giovanni Battista
1710–36, ITALIAN

Pergolesi died at a tragically young age, but he produced a substantial corpus of works during his brief yet intense six-year career. In the 1720s he studied in Naples with teachers including Francesco Durante (1684–1755) and Vinci, but his first opera, *La Salustia* (1732), was a failure due to the death of the star castrato Nicolini. Undeterred, Pergolesi produced his first comic opera *Lo frate 'nnamorato* ('The Brother in Love', 1732), which was enthusiastically received at Naples. Pergolesi specialized in comic works, although *Adriano in Siria* (1734) and *L'Olimpiade* were both serious operas that featured libretti by Metastasio. Pergolesi's last stage work, *Il flaminio* ('Flaminio', 1735), was a very popular *opera buffa* that was still performed in Naples in 1750. However, success came too late for Pergolesi, whose international reputation was rapidly formed posthumously. Pergolesi is best known today for his *Stabat mater*, composed while he was suffering from the illness that eventually killed him, but his historical significance derives from the comic *intermezzo La serva padrona* ('The Maid as Boss', 1734), which was intended to be merely a short companion piece to his full opera *Il prigionier superbo* ('The Haughty Prisoner', 1733).

La serva padrona ('The Maid as Boss')
by Giovanni Battista Pergolesi
Composed: 1734
Premiered: 1734, Naples
Libretto by Gennarantonio Federico

INTERMEZZO I

Uberto, a rich bachelor, is at his wits' end regarding his servant, Serpina. She acts as though she is the mistress of the house and is disobedient, indecisive and opinionated. He decides to extricate himself from Serpina's tyranny by taking a wife who will suppress her capricious nature. He expresses this idea to his mute valet, Vespone. Serpina, who knows that Uberto, deep down, has a soft spot for her, decides that she should be his bride and sets about persuading Uberto to marry her.

INTERMEZZO II

The cunning Serpina, along with Vespone, devises a plan to trick Uberto. She announces that she is to be married to a certain Capitan Tempesta and gives a terrifying description of him that causes Uberto to fear for her future. He demands to meet Capitan Tempesta, who arrives (in fact, it is Vespone in disguise). Serpina explains to Uberto that the capitan has demanded an enormous sum of money as her dowry. Uberto is horrified by the sinister capitan and his threats. Serpina then tells him that the capitan has explained that if he does not receive the dowry immediately, he will refuse to marry Serpina and Uberto must marry her instead. Uberto is not altogether displeased at this suggestion. Serpina reveals the capitan's true identity and the couple thank Vespone for his help in bringing them together. The happy couple then rejoice.

Porpora, Nicola Antonio
1686–1768, ITALIAN

Porpora was born and trained in Naples, where he also taught and worked for much of his career. His first opera was *Agrippina* (1708), and a few years later he composed *Arianna e Teseo* (1714) using a new libretto by Pariati. Between 1715 and 1721 Porpora worked at the Conservatorio di St Onofrio, where he became a widely respected singing teacher. His pupils included Farinelli and Caffarelli, and he also taught Hasse composition. Porpora was one of Metastasio's first musical collaborators, resulting in *Angelica* (1720), and his operas were performed in Vienna and Rome. In 1726 he moved to Venice, but in 1733 he became the music director of the 'Opera of the Nobility' in London, which opened with his *Arianna in Nasso* (1733). Some of Porpora's finest works, including five operas, were composed for London before the company ceased its activities in 1737. Porpora returned to providing operas for Venice and Naples, and in the late 1740s was employed at the Dresden court, where his *Filandro* (1747) was performed under the direction of Hasse. He retired to Vienna, where he met the young Haydn, before spending his final years back at Naples but in poverty.

Rameau, Jean-Philippe

1683–1764, FRENCH

A respected theorist and composer of keyboard music, Rameau did not compose his first opera until he was 50 years old. Consistently adventurous in his operas, he equally inspired passionate admiration and hostility from Parisian audiences and was a comparably powerful figure between the 1730s and 1750s.

THE WANDERLUST YEARS

Rameau was born at Dijon in 1683. Little is known about his early life, but he was presumably taught music by his organist father, and attended a Jesuit college in his teens. He visited northern Italy when he was about 18 years old. Rameau's first musical job was as a violinist with a theatrical troupe that performed throughout Provence and Languedoc. In January 1702, he was appointed temporary *maître de musique* at the Cathedral of Notre Dame des Doms in Avignon, but he quickly found a longer-term job at Clermont Cathedral. Rameau's wanderlust continued, and by 1706 he arrived in Paris, where his *Premier livre de pieces de clavecin* was published in the same year.

Rameau succeeded his father as organist at Dijon's Notre Dame in 1709, but probably moved to Lyons before 1713, where he provided church music for several establishments. In 1715, Rameau returned to his old job at Clermont Cathedral, where he stayed for seven years before settling in Paris in the summer of 1722. Rameau was at first unknown in Paris, but, when he was almost 40 years old, he won acclaim as a writer due to his *Traité de l'harmonie* ('Treatise on Harmony', 1722). This was followed by *Nouveau systéme de musique théorique* ('New System of Music Theory', 1726), and more controversially received theoretical writings about music throughout his life.

FIRST OPERA IN HIS FIFTIES

By the late 1720s, Rameau had provided incidental music for several Parisian plays, although most of his notable compositional activities up to this point were devoted to keyboard music. From at least 1727 it was Rameau's expressed ambition to compose operas. Performances of *Michel Pignolet de Montéclair's Jepthé* (1732) had a profound effect on him, and he was subsequently spurred into creating *Hippolyte et Aricie* (1733) when he was 50 years old. Rameau's first opera caused a controversial storm, with reactions sharply divided between excited admiration and conservative disgust. For decades, French opera had remained firmly under the influence of the late Lully, and *Hippolyte et Aricie* generated a passionate public dispute between the so-called Lullistes and Ramistes. The debate was heightened by Rameau's masterpieces *Les indes galantes* ('The Gallant Indians', 1735), *Castor et Pollux* (1737) and *Dardanus* (1739). Nevertheless, most of Rameau's operas during this period were tremendously successful.

A CONTROVERSIAL CAREER

Voltaire claimed that Rameau said, 'Lully needs actors but I need singers', and this emphasis on the musical content in his operas was ably supported by fine singers including his wife Marie-Louise Mangot, the high-tenor Pierre de Jélyotte and soprano Marie Fel. While

Rameau concentrated increasingly on his operatic career, he worked less on writing theoretical works, but controversy surrounded this aspect of his career in 1735, when his former pupil Louis-Bertrand Castel published a letter in the Jesuit Journal de Trévoux accusing Rameau of failing to acknowledge his indebtedness to previous scholars. Rameau's response was sufficiently sarcastic and devastating that the journal refused to print it, so it was instead published independently. Rameau was not prolific during the early 1740s, but a flurry of activity in 1745 produced *La princesse de Navarre* ('The Princess of Navarre') and *Le temple de la gloire* ('The Temple of Glory'), both of which were collaborations with Voltaire, and the comic opera *Platée*.

BLOSSOMING POPULARITY

Despite the hostility of enemies including Jean-Jacques Rousseau, Rameau's popularity blossomed to the extent that the Marquis D'Argenson forbade the theatre management to stage more than two of Rameau's operas in any one year. But Rameau's newest operas frequently confused his audience, and were often more popular when revised and revived in later years. *Zoroastre* (1749) and *Les boréades* ('The Sons of Boreas', 1763) were both astonishingly original, although the latter was abandoned after rehearsals and not staged until the twentieth century. Rameau died at his home on 12 September 1764; nearly 180 musicians performed in his honour at his funeral.

Hippolyte et Aricie

Rameau's magnificent *Hippolyte et Aricie* is a rare example of a major composer's first attempt at opera also being one of his greatest achievements. However, Rameau was nearly 50 years old and already a respected and experienced musician when he composed it, and had evidently been contemplating the project

for several years. The impressive literary quality of Pellegrin's libretto possesses a plot derived from Euripides, Seneca and Racine. The tragic figures Thésée and Phèdre, whose fatal errors of judgement inspired Rameau to tremendous musical achievements, overshadow the youthful lovers Hippolyte and Aricie. In particular, Phèdre's remorse over the apparent death of her stepson is one of the outstanding soliloquies in Baroque opera. Rameau's music retains its ability to astonish and impress audiences today, not least due to many intense accompanied recitatives and dynamic choruses. In this opera more than any other, Rameau depicts pastoral beauty, emotional pathos and brutal cruelty with unfailing genius. Although the opera created controversy and acclaim alike for its composer, it was heavily abridged prior to its premiere in 1733, and was not considered one of Rameau's finest works during his own lifetime.

Hippolyte et Aricie

by Jean-Philippe Rameau
Composed: 1733
Premiered: 1733, Paris
Libretto by Simon-Joseph Pellegrin

PROLOGUE

Diane and l'Amour dispute who holds more power over the forest's inhabitants. Jupiter explains that l'Amour is supported by le Destin (Fate). Diane resolves to protect Hippolyte and Aricie.

ACT I

Thésée, King of Athens, has vanquished his rivals, with the exception of Aricie. She has been ordered to make a vow of chastity but is in love with Hippolyte, the king's son. The king's second wife, Phèdre, also loves Hippolyte. Aricie prepares to make her vows. Hippolyte enters and they call on Diane for protection. During a procession, Phèdre accuses Aricie of not making her vows; she is defiant and the priestesses protect her. Diane confirms she will look after the lovers. The news arrives that Thésée has descended to the underworld and can therefore be considered dead. Phèdre is convinced that this means she is free to pursue Hippolyte.

ACT II

Thésée was promised three favours from his father, Neptune. His descent to the underworld is the first of these; he wishes to rescue his friend Pirithoüs, who is attempting to abduct Proserpine, wife of Pluton who rules the underworld. Thésée tries to persuade Pluton to let him join his friend. Eventually, a tribunal is called, but Thésée's wish to be reunited with Pirithoüs is not granted. Thésée calls upon his second favour from Neptune: to be released from the underworld. The gods tell him that it is not easy to leave the underworld, but Mercure intervenes and saves him. Thésée is told by spirits that he will find a similar hell at his home when he returns.

ACT III

Phèdre is trying to make Hippolyte return her affections. She offers him power and the crown as well as her love. Hippolyte is appalled and calls on the gods to punish her. Phèdre, ashamed, asks Hippolyte to kill her; he refuses and prevents her from killing herself. Thésée returns from the underworld and is led to believe that Hippolyte has been forcing his affections on Phèdre. A group of townsfolk come to welcome Thésée home. He dismisses them and requests his third favour from Neptune: the punishment of Hippolyte.

ACT IV

Hippolyte laments his fate and is joined by Aricie, who vows she will follow him into exile. A storm breaks out and a sea monster attacks Hippolyte. They fight. Hippolyte is consumed by the creature's flames and disappears. Phèdre arrives and accepts the blame for Hippolyte's death. She prays for his innocence to be revealed to Thésée.

ACT V

Phèdre tells Thésée the truth and he resolves to throw himself in the sea. Neptune prevents him, delivering the news that Hippolyte, saved by Diane, is alive. The king's joy, however, is short-lived; Neptune informs him that his lack of trust in Hippolyte means that he will never see him again. Diane tells Aricie that Hippolyte is alive. The lovers are reunited and everyone rejoices.

Les indes galantes

Composed in 1735, *Les indes galantes* is an *opéra-ballet* in which each act has its own setting and self-contained plot. Its four **entrées** include a scene set in a Turkish garden, Incas worshipping the sun in a Peruvian desert, a flower festival at a Persian market and a village ceremony in a North American forest. The librettist Louis Fuzelier used these exotic elements to draw comparisons between 'savage' rituals and European culture, often to the detriment of the latter. Rameau's witty music made this one of his most popular theatre works, and he revived it during every decade until his death.

Les indes galantes ('The Gallant Indians')
by Jean-Philippe Rameau
Composed: 1735
Premiered: 1735, Paris
Libretto by Louis Fuzelier

BACKGROUND

Hébé, goddess of youth, calls upon the young people of Europe to sing, but the goddess of war, Bellone, convinces them to fight for glory instead. Hébé calls upon l'Amour, who descends from the heavens; they decide to concentrate on other parts of the world.

FIRST ENTRÉE

Osman, the pasha of a Turkish island, is in love with Emilie, who arrived on his shores after being kidnapped by pirates. She rejects his advances, explaining that she remains faithful to the naval officer Valère. After a violent storm, a ship is wrecked on the coast of the island and Valère is on board. As the lovers are reunited, Osman interrupts them. He recognizes Valère and confesses that he himself was once a slave but was liberated by Valère. He gives the two lovers his blessing.

SECOND ENTRÉE

A young Inca woman, Phani, and Don Carlos, a Spanish conquistador, are in love. The high priest of the Sun, Huascar, is also in love with Phani. He tells her that the gods have ordered him to find her a husband, and proposes himself as a suitable match. During a festival, there is a volcanic eruption. Huascar tells Phani that she has caused this by angering the gods, and that she must marry him. Don Carlos intervenes and reveals that Huascar caused the eruption by throwing rocks into the volcano. The volcano erupts again and kills Huascar.

THIRD ENTRÉE

Prince Tacmas loves Zaïre, the slave of Ali, a courtesan. On the day of the flower festival, in Ali's garden, he prepares to win her love. Meanwhile, Tacmas's slave Fatima is in love with Ali. Disguised as a man, she too enters the garden. Tacmas, taking Fatima for a rival, goes to attack her, but recognizes her in time. In a joyous conclusion, the masters swap their slaves and join the flower festival.

FOURTH ENTRÉE

In a North American forest, Ardario, an Indian chief, hides as he prepares to make peace with Damon, a Frenchman and Don Alvar, a Spaniard. Damon and Don Alvar are both in love with Zima, a young Indian woman. When she arrives, they try to make her choose between them by outlining how each will love her. Zima replies that the Spaniard is too fiery, the Frenchman too cold. Ardario appears and Zima reveals that she prefers him to either of the others. The two are united, along with the European and North American cultures, at a feast of peace.

Castor et Pollux

Castor et Pollux was considered Rameau's greatest achievement after he revised it in 1754. The storyline revolves around the generosity of one twin brother willing to forsake his unique immortality so that the other may live, but their complex situation creates strong portraits of inner conflict and tension between other characters, Rameau conveys the magical forces of Hades, the Elysian fields and the tempting celestial pleasures Pollux must forsake if he takes Castor's place in death. The famous lament 'Que tout gémisse', a chorus in which the Spartans mourn at Castor's tomb, was performed at Rameau's own funeral in 1764.

Castor et Pollux

by Jean-Philippe Rameau
Composed: 1737; revised 1754
Premiered: 1737, Paris
Libretto by Pierre-Joseph Bernard (Gentil-Bernard)

BACKGROUND

Minèrve and l'Amour persuade Venus to seduce Mars, bringing peace to the world.

ACT I

In Sparte, the people are mourning the death of their king Castor, mortal twin of the immortal Pollux. Télaïre, Castor's lover, is consoled by Phébé. Pollux offers his love to Télaïre, but she resolves to remain faithful to Castor. She requests that Pollux convince Jupiter to let him descend to the underworld and retrieve Castor.

ACT II

Upset at being rejected by Télaïre and grieving for his brother, Pollux asks Jupiter whether he may do as Télaïre requested. Jupiter agrees, but only on the condition that Pollux takes Castor's place in the underworld. Hébé, the goddess of youth, reminds Pollux of what he will be deprived of if he goes ahead, but Pollux remains determined.

Senesino (Francesco Bernardi)

c. *1680*–c. *1759*, ITALIAN

Francesco Bernardi was nicknamed 'Senesino' after his birthplace, Siena. His first known performance was at Venice in 1707–08, and he sang for Caldara at Bologna in 1709. He was dismissed from Dresden in 1720 because he refused to sing an aria during rehearsals for Johan David Heinichen's (1683–1729) *Flavio Crespo* (1720). He joined the Royal Academy of Music in London in 1720, and remained with the company until its dissolution in 1728, during which time he sang in operas by Bononcini, Ariosti and Handel. Senesino was popular in London, which

explains why Handel re-engaged him in 1730 despite their often-troubled working relationship. Senesino defected to the 'Opera of the Nobility' in 1733. After he left London in 1736 he sang at Florence and Naples, but his singing had fallen out of fashion by the end of the decade.

Silvani, Francesco

c. *1660*–c. *1728–44*, ITALIAN

Little is known about Silvani's life, but he was an abbot who issued his earliest works under the anagram Frencasco Valsini. Silvani regularly produced libretti for Venice between 1691 and 1716, and the title pages of the printed wordbooks state that he served the Duke of Mantua between 1699 and 1705. Silvani identified with the 'reform' librettists such as Zeno and Pariati, and his texts feature clearly motivated plots, elevated language and extensive recitatives. He occasionally based his libretti on literary sources such as Tasso, Seneca and Corneille. Silvani was sensitive to accusations of plagiarism, and he did not include his name on the title page of libretti that had been collaborations with other writers. During an age when the literary credibility of librettists was often questioned, Silvani was esteemed enough to have a collection of 24 libretti published posthumously.

Stampiglia, Silvio

1664–1725, ITALIAN

Stampiglia was one of the 14 founding members of the Accademia dell'Arcadia (The Arcadian Academy). Although a Roman by birth, for many years Stampiglia was associated with operas in Naples, and did not always conform to Arcadian ideals despite being part of their circle. Stampiglia's libretti are often ironic comedies in which conventional heroism is regarded with more affection than sincerity, and the ludicrous behaviour of aristocratic characters is often regarded with disbelief by comparatively sensible servants. *Il trionfo di Camilla* and *La partenope* were his most popular libretti, and were set many times during the early eighteenth century. Stampiglia's final work was the *serenata Imeneo*, set to music by Porpora in 1723. His lively and witty examinations of courtly love inspired Handel to great artistic heights in his settings of *Il partenope*, Serse and *Imeneo*, although none of these was successful in London.

Strada del Pò, Anna Maria
active 1719–40, ITALIAN

The exceptional soprano Strada is known to have sung in Vivaldi's *La verità in cimento* ('The Truth Tested', 1720) in Venice in 1721. Between 1724 and 1726 she sang for Vinci, Porpora and Leo at Naples, where she also married the theatre manager Aurelio del Pò. She arrived in London in 1729, where she was Handel's prima donna in all his opera performances until 1737. Handel's arias for Strada in *Il partenope*, *Poro* and *Sosarme* indicate a superbly talented singer who had a high range, remarkable agility and dramatic conviction. Strada was the only member of Handel's company who did not defect to the 'Opera of the Nobility' in 1733, and was amply rewarded by the roles Ginevra, in *Ariodante*, and *Alcina*. She returned to Italy in 1738, and retired two years later.

Telemann, Georg Philipp
1681–1767, GERMAN

Telemann was born in Magdeburg, and created his first opera at the age of 12, in which he sang the title role and organized its informal performance in the street. Telemann was influenced by the operas he heard at the Brunswick court and Berlin. He attended university in Leipzig, and became the director of the local opera house, while he also provided several operas for the court at Weissenfels. Telemann claimed to have composed more than 50 operas, but only nine of these are extant. The earliest of these is *Die Satyren in Arcadien* ('The Satyrs of Arcadia', 1719, revised for Hamburg 1724). After holding various positions in Sorau, Eisenach and Frankfurt, Telemann became director of music at Hamburg's five principal churches in 1721. The following year he became musical director at the Gänsemarkt opera house (where Handel and Mattheson had worked in the early years of the century). Seven of Telemann's alleged 35 Hamburg operas have survived. Most of these date from the 1720s, and demonstrate the bizarre mixture of German and Italian texts that was popular in Hamburg. By default this makes Telemann an innovative pioneer of German opera, although his musical style was essentially Italianate, and he also adapted operas by Handel, Porpora and Campra for the Hamburg stage.

Vinci, Leonardo
c. 1696–1730, ITALIAN

Vinci studied at the Conservatorio dei Poveri di Gesù Cristo in Naples between 1708 and 1718, and afterwards made his operatic debut with *Lo cecato fauzo* ('The False Blind Man', 1719). He proceeded to dominate operatic life in Naples, and his *Li zite 'ngalera* ('The Lovers on the Galley', 1722) is the earliest extant comic opera of its kind. However, after the enormous success of *Publio Cornelio Scipione* ('Scipio', 1722), Vinci turned his attention primarily to *opera seria*. One of Vinci's greatest triumphs was *Farnace* (1724), which initiated a busy period of activity in Rome and Venice. *Didone abbandonata* ('Dido Abandoned' Rome, 1726) and *Siroe* (Venice, 1726) were both highly acclaimed collaborations with Metastasio. Vinci composed two operas every remaining year of his life, and his partnership with Metastasio produced *Alessandro dell'Indie* ('Alexander in India') and *Artaserse* (both 1730). Vinci's music was a great influence on the new generation of composers including Pergolesi and Hasse. Vinci's work also influenced Handel's later operas, and the older composer appreciated Vinci's operas enough to adapt several into *pasticcios* for London. It was rumoured that Vinci was poisoned as an act of revenge for an illicit love affair.

Vivaldi, Antonio

1678–1741, **ITALIAN**

Vivaldi's father was a talented violinist who was employed at St Mark's in Venice, and it is likely that his father was also involved in managing operas in that city during the late seventeenth century. Although Vivaldi was nominally a Catholic priest by profession, he did not have to say Mass for most of his life, and he followed his father's example by becoming a professional musician. Vivaldi enjoyed a fine reputation as a composer of orchestral concertos, and taught music at the Pio Ospedale della Pietà (an orphanage for musically talented girls). Vivaldi's first known opera, *Ottone in villa* (1713), was swiftly followed by *Orlando finto pazzo* ('Orlando Plays Mad', 1714), and he subsequently attempted to cultivate a dual career as an opera composer and impresario for most of the rest of his life. Vivaldi's endeavours were directed towards Venice, although he also produced operas for Mantua, *Teuzzone* and *Tito Manlio* (both 1719); Rome, *Giustino* (1724); Verona, *Bajazet* (1735) and *Catone in Utica* (1737); and Florence, *Ginevra* (1736). In 1739, Vivaldi claimed to have written 94 operas, but this was probably an exaggeration: over 50 printed libretti and about 20 musical scores have survived, although several exist only in an incomplete form.

Zeno, Apostolo

1669–1750, **ITALIAN**

The Venetian librettist Zeno was a librarian and historian, who sought to establish opera libretti as a recognized literary form. His first opera libretto,

Lucio Vero, was a huge success at Venice in 1695. Zeno continued to write more libretti, although he had reservations about it affecting his scholarly credibility. In 1718, Zeno replaced Stampiglia as imperial poet to the Viennese court of Emperor Charles VI, where he was also appointed imperial historiographer.

Zeno wrote 35 opera libretti, including many in collaboration with Pariati, and he was especially proud of his 17 oratorio texts produced for Vienna. Zeno is credited with introducing historical subjects into opera, and he sought to represent the idealistic code of honour for real sovereigns in uncompromisingly serious operas influenced by the French dramatist Racine. Composers including Tomaso Albinoni (1671–1751), Caldara and Gasparini set his libretti to music. Scarlatti and Handel both set versions of Zeno's libretti that were adapted for them by other authors. Zeno was a major influence on the young Metastasio, who in turn supplanted his predecessor as both court poet in Vienna and the most respected librettist of his generation.

⊛ COMPOSERS AND THEIR LIBRETTISTS ～ p. 78

During the early eighteenth century a few composers enjoyed regular close collaboration with a favourite librettist, such as Fux with Pariati, or both Vinci and Porpora with the young Metastasio. However, such examples were rare, and instead it was common for a popular libretto created for one major Italian opera centre to be adapted for the needs of other composers working all over Europe. Some texts were consequently used many times across several decades, such as the Florentine librettist Antonio Salvi's *Arminio*, which was first set by Scarlatti (1703), but it was also set by Caldara (1705), Hasse (1730), Handel (1737) and Galuppi (1747). In fact, all of Handel's London opera libretti were adapted from

Italian sources. Although some were recent revisions of relatively new texts by Metastasio, most were surprisingly old during an era that craved newness in its fashionable entertainments, and several were modelled on operas that Handel probably encountered while he was in Italy, either during his youth or on his later travels recruiting singers for London. Many composers set the same opera, each with their own variations in arias and alterations to recitative, and often even with the same title!

● THE ARCADIAN ACADEMY
∾ p. 78

Literary clubs that were established in seventeenth-century Italy were commonly known as 'academies', taking their name from the Athenian garden where Plato was thought to have met with his followers. One of the most important such groups in the early eighteenth century was the Roman 'Arcadian Academy'. It was formally established in 1690 to honour the late Queen Christina of Sweden, who had been a keen supporter of the literary arts and was composer Arcangelo Corelli's (1653–1713) first patron.

The 'Arcadian Academy' principally constituted the artistic circle that had already regularly met under the patronage of the queen, although it expanded into a network that spread across Europe. All of the Academy's members adopted nicknames suitable for shepherds and nymphs, in an attempt to recreate the fabled pastoral paradise Arcadia, described in Greek mythology. Founder members included the librettist Silvio Stampiglia and Gian Vincenzo Gravina (the adoptive father of Metastasio). The Marcello brothers, Corelli and Scarlatti were also granted membership, and Zeno was the founder of an affiliated group in Venice. Handel's patrons Cardinal Ottoboni, Cardinal Pamphili and Prince Ruspoli were all members, but although Handel composed some chamber cantatas and duets using Arcadian texts and was closely involved with the Academy's circle of members, he never became a member himself.

● THE LULLISTES V. THE RAMISTES
∾ p. 85

The extended polemic between Lullistes and Ramistes was provoked by the former group's disgust for the Italianate elements in Rameau's *Hippolyte et Aricie*, and their arising concern that the repertoire and tradition established by Lully was under threat. In contrast, Rameau's supporters championed his innovative music that included more elaborate solo songs and increasingly complex use of the orchestra. One venomous Lulliste complained that he was racked, flayed and dislocated by Rameau's *Les indes galantes*.

Similar divisions between opposing opera-loving factions were common during the eighteenth century, and Handel and the 'Opera of the Nobility' had distinct camps of supporters in London during the mid-1730s. However, Parisian opera audiences took such matters to unusually passionate extremes. The derogatory attitude towards Rameau's pioneering work extended to jealous composers, librettists and disgruntled performers at the Paris Opéra, and at one point Rameau was involved in a physical brawl with one of his main detractors, after which friends advised him to stop wearing a sword. Each new Rameau opera during the 1730s intensified the feelings of both sides, but Rameau had considerable support when 1,000 Ramistes pledged to support every performance of *Dardanus*. They did not quite live up to that pledge, but afterwards the Lulliste dissent diminished.

⑨ THE TRAINING OF THE CASTRATI ∾ p. 167

Castration was only the first ordeal that boys with musical potential endured. The brutal operation did not guarantee that the boy would develop a pleasing musical voice, and must have brought only misery to those whose singing ability was insufficient to allow them to study at prestigious music conservatoires such as the four major schools at Naples. For the luckier boys, conditions were often harsh and far removed from the glamorous career they hoped for. The life of a student castrato was almost monastic, arising early in the morning, and attending to religious and strict secular learning with equal fervour throughout the entire day. Teachers at the Neapolitan schools included Francesco Durante, Francesco Provenzale, Porpora, Leo and Scarlatti, several of whom had been educated in the same system. Music lessons with the most famous masters were only given a few times each week, and lasted between two and three hours. Conditions were cramped and noisy, and young castrati spent between six and ten years working principally on breathing techniques. Porpora is alleged to have instructed his students to sing an entire page of exercises every day for six years. This intense yet thorough training brought about incredible technique and vocal longevity.

✖ HANDEL AND HIS SINGERS
✎ p. 79

Handel was notoriously tough on singers who caused him problems. While rehearsing *Flavio* (1723), the tenor Alexander Gordon became exasperated with Handel's method of continuo accompaniment, and threatened to jump on the composer's harpsichord. It is said that Handel retorted 'Oh! Let me know when you will do that, and I will advertise it. For I am sure more people will come to see you jump, than to hear you sing.' Handel was required to discipline petulant singers who wanted to sacrifice the drama in order to have something flashier to sing. There is also the apocryphal tale of the soprano Cuzzoni refusing to sing

the aria 'Falsa imagine' in *Ottone* (1722), perhaps because she did not care for its simplicity. Handel's first biographer, John Mainwaring, reports that the outraged composer exclaimed, in French, 'Madam, I know you are a veritable devil, but I would have you know that I am Beelzebub, chief of the Devils.' Without warning, it is said that Handel grasped her around the waist and threatened to fling her out of the window.

✖ THE FIRST PERFORMANCES
OF *RINALDO* ✎ p. 167

The elaborate attempt to stage *Rinaldo* in London aroused interest from satirists Joseph Addison and Richard Steele in the *Spectator*. Addison, after examining the printed wordbook, reported:

The Opera of Rinaldo is filled with Thunder and Lightning, Illuminations, and Fireworks; which the Audience may look upon without catching Cold, and indeed without much danger of being burnt; for there are several Engines filled with Water, and ready to play at a Minute's Warning, in case any such Accident should happen. However, as I have a very great Friendship for the Owner of this Theatre, I hope that he has been wise enough to insure his House before he would let this Opera be acted in it.

After seeing the opera, Steele said:

The Undertakers of the Hay-Market, having raised too great an Expectation in their printed Opera, very much disappoint their Audience on the stage. The King of Jerusalem is obliged to come from the City on foot, instead of being drawn in a triumphant Chariot by white Horses, as my Opera-Book had promised me; ... We had also but a very short Allowance of Thunder and Lightning; th' I cannot in this Place omit doing Justice to the Boy who had the Direction of the Two painted Dragons, and made them spit Fire and Smoke ... I saw indeed but Two things wanting to render his whole Action compleat, I mean the keeping his Head a little lower, and hiding his Candle.

CLASSICAL

The Enlightenment was a natural, if late, consequence of the sixteenth-century Renaissance and Reformation. Also known as the Age of Reason, the Enlightenment advanced to be recognized in the late seventeenth and early eighteenth centuries and brought with it new, controversial beliefs that upended the absolutisms on which European society had long been based.

Absolute monarchy, with its reliance on the Divine Right of Kings, and the Church, with its demand for unthinking obedience to doctrine, were major casualties of this great intellectual upheaval. In Enlightenment terms, their supremacy now belonged to the power of reason and a sense of individual worth. These new imperatives would promote social progress and education as a means of freeing the masses from ignorance and superstition. If Martin Luther opened the door to the Reformation as a challenge to the status quo, the Enlightenment flung it wide open.

An important effect of Enlightenment ideas was to promote the public as a force in its own right, with its own tastes and preferences. This involved profound changes in opera and music generally. Until now, composers and performers, who were essentially servants to royal or noble employers, had been required to cater for the demands and whims of a privileged elite at the royal, ducal and other noble courts. Now, in the Age of Reason, a well-to-do middle class that could afford the price of tickets was flocking to public concerts and opera houses, where the music was tailored to catch and hold their attention. For the 'old guard' in music, this looked very much like what today would be called the 'dumbing-down' of opera. To adherents of the Enlightenment, the new style meant that opera acquired a wider appeal and mirrored the concerns of real people in the real, everyday world.

KEY EVENTS

1750	Johann Stamitz appointed leader of Europe's finest orchestra – the Mannheim
1755	Samuel Johnson publishes his dictionary
1756	The Seven Years' War begins
1762	Catherine the Great becomes ruler of Russia
1770	Captain Cook claims New Zealand and Eastern Australia for Great Britain
1772	Poland is split between Russia and Prussia
1775	The American Revolution against the British begins
1776	The Declaration of Independence announces the birth of the United States of America; Adam Smith publishes his ecoomic treatise *The Wealth of Nations*
1785	*The Oath of the Horatii* is painted by Jacques-Louis David and becomes a landmark neoclassical painting
1789	The French Revolution begins; the Bastille is stormed; George Washington becomes the first president of America
1791	Mozart dies, leaving his *Requiem* unfinished
1793	Louis XVI and his wife Marie Antionette are beheaded
1801	Richard Trevithick develops his steam engine
1804	Napoleon Bonaparte crowns himself emperor, to Beethoven's disapproval; the philosopher Emmanuel Kant dies; Francis II becomes Emperor of Austria
1805	Lord Horatio Nelson defeats Napoleon in the Battle of Trafalgar; the poet Friedrich von Schiller dies
1810	Simon Bolivar leads an uprising in Venezuela
1811	Luddite riots in Britain against new technologies
1812	Napoleon's army retreats from Moscow
1814	The Congress of Vienna restores a balance of power between the European powers of France, Britain, Russia, Austria and Prussia

Classical
INTRODUCTION

The humanist principles of the Enlightenment removed opera from the extravagant world of baroque and landed it in entirely new territory. After 1720, Baroque became a target for changes initiated by the scholar Gian Vincenzo Gravina of the Arcadian Academy in Rome. Baroque operas based on classical myths had developed exaggerated and ultimately ludicrous forms. Under the Enlightenment principles that influenced Gravina and the Arcadians, these fripperies – the convoluted plots, the outlandish characterization – were all pared away. In their place, operas assumed the spare, ascetic features of ancient Greek theatre and the stark human drama of its tragedies. The result was *opera seria* – serious opera.

METASTASIO AND OPERA SERIA

The protagonists of *opera seria* were not composers, but two Italian librettists – **Apostolo Zeno** (1668–1750) and **Pietro Metastasio** (1698–1782). Metastasio was Italy's most famous poet and, among composers, soon became its most popular librettist. This was how opera **libretti** acquired a new adjective – Metastasian. *Opera seria* with the Metastasian libretto, which became the main operatic genre of the early eighteenth century, was certainly a great stride away from the intricacies of baroque. This, though, was not good enough for the German composer **Christoph Willibald von Gluck** (1714–87), who spied too much clutter even in this new, slenderized form of opera.

GLUCK AND THE REFORM OF OPERA

Gluck thought *opera seria* was too formal, its plots overly restrictive and its structure excessively regulated. In his prologue to

Alceste (1767), which he may have written with the help of his librettist, **Raniero de'Calzabigi** (1714–95), Gluck poured particular scorn on the prominence of **arias** and the chances they gave singers to show off: 'I do not wish to arrest an actor in the greatest heat of dialogue in order to wait for a tiresome *ritornello* [repeat], nor make display of the agility of his fine voice in some long-drawn passage, nor wait until the orchestra gives him time to recover his breath for a cadenza. I did not think it my duty to pass quickly over the second section of an aria of which the words are perhaps the most impassioned and important, in order to repeat regularly four times over those of the first part … for the convenience of the singer who wishes to show that he can capriciously vary a passage in a number of guises.'

Like his *Orfeo ed Euridice* ('Orpheus and Eurydice', 1762), *Alceste* exemplified the 'beautiful simplicity' Gluck believed opera should have. It also planted the seeds of the *Gesamtkunstwerk*, the 'total work of art' later championed by **Richard Wagner** (1813–83) that merged all elements in opera – singing, acting, orchestration, drama, poetry, lighting and stage design. Gluck's reforms never went that far, but they did exert strong influence, for instance on **Wolfgang Amadeus Mozart**'s (1756–91) *Idomeneo* (1781) or *L'anima del filosofo* ('The Soul of Philosophy', 1791) by **Joseph Haydn** (1732–1809). In the event, *opera seria* was overtaken less by Gluck's reforms and more by two other developments that replaced *seria* and brought its eminence to an end. One was the German *Singspiel* ('song-play'), which evolved after about 1750 into comic opera with spoken dialogue. The other was the Italian *opera buffa*, a slightly different type of comic opera that began a separate life on stage after comic roles were deemed contrary to the solemn nature of *opera seria* and were eliminated from the main action.

CLASSICAL: INTRODUCTION

THE RISE OF *OPERA BUFFA*

Instead, after around 1740, comic characters were consigned to the one-act *intermezzi* – interludes staged between the acts of *opera seria*. Comedy was not relegated for long. The *intermezzo* developed as a genre in its own right – the *opera buffa*, which in time proved more vivacious and more expressive and emotionally appealing than *opera seria*. When popular taste demanded more substance than comic opera provided on its own, **Carlo Goldoni** (1707–93), originator of the *opera buffa* libretto, introduced *parte serie* – serious roles – to give the genre the required mixture of comedy and tragedy. *Seria* and *buffa* were effectively reunited in a new genre, *dramma giocoso* ('jocular drama'), and reached their finest joint expression in Mozart's *Le nozze di Figaro* ('The Marriage of Figaro', 1786).

THE *FIGARO* CONTROVERSY

Figaro was much more than another stage in the evolution of opera. By the time it was first performed, both opera and theatre had become highly politicized as Enlightenment philosophy made itself felt onstage. Opera, in fact, already tended to replace the pulpit as a place where new and radical ideas were expressed and new beliefs fortified. As early as 1735, *Les indes galantes* ('The Gallant Indians', 1735) by **Jean-Philippe Rameau** (1683–1764) had mirrored the rejection of class divisions and religious and racial prejudice and the promotion of the 'Brotherhood of Man' by French philosophers such as **Jean-Jacques Rousseau** (1712–78). Mozart's *Figaro* was much closer to the French Revolution of 1789, which expressed the ideals of the Enlightenment in bloodthirsty violence. Consequently, it was controversial, even though Mozart's librettist, **Lorenzo Da Ponte** (1749–1838) had foreseen the problems and removed the inflammatory politics contained in the original play by the French dramatist Pierre Beaumarchais (1732–99). However, neutering the libretto in this way did not quieten fears that it encouraged social upheaval. For the reactionary powers-that-be, *Figaro* was alarming because a servant was given the central role while his master, Count Almaviva, was sidelined. Servants had previously occupied their 'proper' place in the social hierarchy of opera when they appeared as stupid, clumsy or comic characters. It was, therefore, subversive for Mozart and Da Ponte to make one of them the centre of attention.

❧ *PASTICCIO* OPERA ∾ p. 85

The eighteenth-century *pasticcio*, a rather uncomplimentary term meaning 'hotch-potch', was an opera written by several composers. One example was *Muzio Scevola* (1721), which was based on the story of an early Roman hero who burned his hand to ashes in a fire rather than assist the Etruscan enemies of Rome. Filippo Amadei, **Giovanni Bononcini** (1670–1747) and **George Frideric Handel** (1685–1759) composed one act each, in that order. Normally, though, the *pasticcio* did not result from such a neat division of labour. It was more of an assembly of choruses, airs, dances and other music taken from various composers. A *pasticcio* could start out as a conventional opera but then acquire extra text or music or arias grafted onto it from other works by other composers. Although this appears to justify the description of 'hotch-potch', the additions were carefully selected from items that had already proved their popularity in performance, so that the pasticcio could be said to represent an eighteenth-century version of a modern music show. The pasticcio proved extremely popular, especially in mid-eighteenth century London, and some highly respected operas, including Gluck's *Orfeo ed Euridice* were first seen there as *pasticcios* rather than in their proper form.

Classical
GENRES AND STYLES

There was a certain mathematical precision about *opera seria*, which was very much in keeping with the ethos of the Enlightenment, in which the most startling advances were made in the sciences. 'Mathematical' also applied to the Metastasian libretto, which firmly reinforced *seria*'s somewhat inflexible and predictable principles. Almost invariably, the story of an *opera seria* was told in three acts. Each act was structured around alternating arias and recitatives, with occasional, though rare, duets and ensembles. Where ensembles occurred they were often placed at the end of the opera. There were generally six main characters, and the plot had to contain an element of tragedy or heroism.

THE METASTASIAN LIBRETTO
The first aim of the Metastasian libretto in *opera seria* was to provide elegant verse along lines that followed the doctrine of affections, such as hope, hate, love, despair. The other was to showcase the gifts of solo singers, especially **castrati**, who were by now developing into star performers with a fanatical following. It was for them that the ***da capo* aria** was developed to display the splendours of the individual voice and also to provide a means by which a character could confide his innermost feelings to the audience. The *da capo* form of the aria eventually became indispensable to the *opera seria* and virtually synonymous with it. Metastasian texts were so arranged that an aria normally ended most of the scenes.

In the musical division of labour built into *opera seria*, arias and recitatives took the stage turn by turn, and it fell to the recitatives to deal with the workings of the plot and serve as the chief point of contact between the various characters. These recitatives were most often in *secco* form – that is, with continuo rather than orchestral accompaniment, although the full orchestra could step in to reinforce particularly dramatic moments. The dialogue of the recitative in *opera seria* was generally written to the strict pattern known as *versi sciolti*, or blank verse, comprising a mixture of seven- and 11-syllable lines, without rhyme.

THE VIRTUES OF *OPERA SERIA*
Although *opera seria* eschewed the excessive decoration and complexities that Baroque opera had acquired over the years, the source used for its plots – ancient classical myth and legend – remained the same. The difference was, however, that in *opera seria*, the plots were made to serve Enlightenment purposes. Characters were more credibly human, the music was less cluttered and better able to express emotion, and audiences had a greater chance to identify and sympathize with the sufferings being depicted onstage.

SERIA V. BUFFA
Even so, by its very nature – stereotyped, restrictive, and with scant or no outlet for the odd amusing moment – *opera seria* could not appeal to audiences in the same warm way as its opposite, the *opera buffa*. *Opera buffa* did several things that *opera seria* did not do. The genre promoted the **bass** voice, where *seria* gave the best parts and the best music to castrati. In *opera buffa* – unlike in *Singspiel* – there was no spoken dialogue, which made for greater musical continuity than the straitjacket structure of *opera seria* allowed. The aria was retained in ***buffa***, but it was no longer the same star turn it was in *seria*. *Buffa*, which was a more 'democratic' form of opera than *seria*, majored instead in

duets, trios, quartets and **ensembles**. This helped to create onstage an atmosphere of sociability that had the effect of drawing the audience into the action. This was particularly true of the *buffa* finale which, once again, was basically different from its equivalent in *opera seria*. In *seria*, the last act normally finished with a simple ensemble in which all the principal singers took part. In the ensemble finale of *opera buffa*, the last act went out with much more punch. All or the greater part of the cast was on stage for the occasion, and as each new figure entered, the music typified the character by a change of mood or style. In effect, the *buffa* finale resembled a synopsis in music of the plot and the characters featured in it.

GOLDONI AND THE *BUFFA* PLOT

Buffa plots played a major role in popularizing the genre. They were simpler and bore greater resemblance to real life, while emphasizing its more amusing elements. There were stereotyped characters but they were easily recognizable, coming as they did from the real rather than the legendary world: one was Il dottore, a stuffy lawyer from Bologna, another was Pantalone, a womanizer, and there were any number of comic servants, most notably Figaro. Like *opera seria*, the creation of *opera buffa* revolved around a dominant Italian librettist, in this case Goldoni. The earthiness and realism of his texts, their witty dialogue and touches of sentimentality were not only in complete contrast to the artificiality of *opera seria*, but allowed room for the genre to evolve. This was why it proved comparatively easy for Goldoni to respond to the change in public taste that demanded more serious content. In response, Goldoni introduced dramatic characters into *buffa* alongside the established comic roles and the resultant works were renamed *opera semiseria* ('semi-serious opera') and later, *dramma giocoso*.

OPERA SEMISERIA AND OTHER DRAMAS

The sentimentality and melodrama implicit in *opera semiseria* or *dramma giocoso* had originated in the French *comédie larmoyante* ('tearful comedy') and later filtered into *semiseria* through works classified as *dramma disentimento* ('sentimental drama'), *dramma eroicomico* ('heroic-comic drama') and *drama tragicomico* ('tragicomic drama'). The term *opera semiseria* was apparently first used to describe the opera *Nina* (1789) by **Giovanni Paisiello** (1740–1816), which illustrated how a happy ending was essential to this form of opera, no matter what had gone before. In *Nina*, the eponymous heroine goes mad after her lover, Lindoro, is shot in a duel with a rival. All ends happily, however. Lindoro recovers, Nina regains her sanity and the two are married. It seems, though, that *semiseria* arose somewhat earlier than 1789, when *Nina* received its first performance at the royal palace in Caserta, near Naples. After 1748, for example, Goldoni was already describing his works as *dramma giocoso*. In addition, *La buona figliuola* ('The Good-Natured Girl') by **Niccolò Piccinni** (1728–1800), which was given its first performance in Rome in 1760, later came to be regarded as the first *opera semiseria*.

THE RONDO ARIA

Like Goldoni, his librettist for *La buona figliuola*, Piccinni was himself an innovator – as an important exponent of the rondo aria. This was a straightforward form, related to the instrumental or keyboard rondos used, for instance, in symphonies, sonatas and concertos. Quite simple, but appealing in structure, the rondo aria featured one slow section and one fast section, each of them repeated twice. The rondo became a very popular form of aria in the eighteenth century, replacing the more elaborate, more showy *da capo* form of aria that was abandoned in *buffa* in about 1750. The rondo also had its own part to play in the evolution of the ensemble finale. Initially, the finale was somewhat atrophied by too great a devotion to established but inflexible musical forms. What was needed was a looser, freeform musical structure that allowed for rapid changes of tempo and simple melodies, and it was on this last count that the rondo made its contribution.

❊ SINGSPIEL ∾ p. 119

The *Singspiel* was a German form of opera in which songs and other music alternated with dialogue. Although the *Singspiel* originated in the seventeenth century, the term was not generally used until the eighteenth. *Croesus* (1711) by **Reinhard Keiser** (1674–1739) was an early example of *Singspiel*. Towards the middle of the eighteenth century, other forms of opera – the French *opéra comique* and the English ballad opera – exerted their influence on *Singspiel* so that it developed into a type of comic opera with spoken words.

One of the most eminent *Singspiel* composers was **Johann Adam Hiller** (1728–1804), who helped establish the German national form of the genre, and another was the Czech **Georg Benda** (1722–95), who was based in Berlin. *Opéra comique* provided *Singspiel* with its lyrical, comic and sentimental content and promoted its use of folk harmonies and rhythms. By contrast, in Vienna, the *Singspiel* developed in a rather different way, absorbing the lively melodies of *opera buffa*, with plenty of sharp wit and farce to spice up the action. For example, Mozart's *Die Entführung aus dem Serail* ('The Abduction from the Seraglio', 1782) was written as a Viennese-style Singspiel with the folk element represented by its Turkish flavour.

◉ GUERRE DES BOUFFONS ∾ p. 121

Opposing tastes in opera have often provoked minor wars. One of them was the *guerre des bouffons*, which took place in Paris between 1752 and 1754 and ranged the supporters of French serious opera against the advocates of Italian *opera buffa*. On the French side were King Louis, his influential mistress Madame de Pompadour, his court and the aristocracy. Louis' Polish queen, Mary, the philosopher Denis Diderot and other French intellectuals and connoisseurs of opera were ranged against them on the 'Italian' side.

Within the opera houses, battle lines were drawn by the 'French' supporters who gathered around the king's box, and the 'Italians' who were deployed before the queen's. The confrontation was originally sparked off in 1752 when the *intermezzo La serva padrona* by **Giovanni Battista Pergolesi** (1710–36) was performed in Paris by Italian comic actors, or *bouffons*. Ultimately, though, there was no clear victory for either side. French serious opera appeared to have won, but before long, French musicians began to play music in the Italian *buffa* style. This prompted the introduction of the *comédie mêlée d'ariettes*, a kind of comic miscellany, which took its cue more from the Italian than the French side of the argument.

Classical
PERSONALITIES

Bach, Johann Christian
1735–82, GERMAN

Johann Christian Bach, the youngest son of **J. S. Bach** (1685–1750), acquired a more thorough training in opera than most contemporary composers, studying first in Germany and afterwards in Italy. Consequently, his operas combined both styles. As a composer, Johann Christian concentrated initially on church music, but he soon transferred his talents to writing for the opera stage. He was 25 when he wrote his first opera, *Artaserse* (1760), for a Turin opera house. *Catone in Utica* ('Cato in Utica', 1761), written for opera audiences in Naples, followed the next year and *Alessandro nell'Indie* ('Alexander (the Great) in India', 1762) the year after that. Also in 1762, Johann Christian travelled to London, where in the following year, his opera *Orione* thrilled audiences, which included King George III and Queen Charlotte, with its delicate orchestration. Subsequently, Johann Christian was appointed music master to the queen. However, he continued to write for European opera houses, in Mannheim, Germany and Paris, which staged his last opera *Amadis de Gaule* (1779). His final London opera was *La clemenza di Scipione* ('Scipio's Mercy'), which was staged in 1778. While in London in 1764, Johann Christian met the eight-year-old prodigy Mozart, and his influence was later evident in Mozart's own operas *Idomeneo* and *La clemenza di Tito*.

Beaumarchais, Pierre-Augustin Caron de
1732–99, FRENCH

Pierre Beaumarchais, best known for two plays on the theme of 'Figaro', was an amateur musician as well as a playwright. His first Figaro play, *Le barbier de Séville*

('The Barber of Seville', 1775), was produced at the Comédie-Française and his second, *La folle journée, ou Le Mariage de Figaro* ('The Mad Day, or the Marriage of Figaro') was completed in 1781 and performed in 1784. The character of Figaro is said to have been a type of self-portrait of the playwright, who shared a colourful personality with the barber. At the time, just before the French Revolution, these plays were considered seditious, since they depicted an equality between servant and master. As operas, the music for the Figaro stories was written by Rossini and Mozart respectively. As a librettist, Beaumarchais was best known for the five-act opera *Tarare* (1787), produced in Paris. Gluck turned it down, and it was subsequently set to music by **Antonio Salieri** (1750–1825).

Benda, Georg
1722–95, CZECH

Georg Benda was a Czech composer who produced several stage dramas for the ducal court at Gotha, where he was *Kapellmeister*. His first – and only – Italian opera was *Xindo riconosciuto* ('Xindo Remembered', 1765). Subsequent works were distinctly innovative. In this phase of his career, Benda turned first to German 'duodramas', also known as 'melodramas'. He wrote three on ancient Greek themes – *Ariadne auf Naxos* ('Ariadne on Naxos', 1775), *Medea* (1775) and *Pygmalion* (1779), in which the music provided background accompaniment to dialogue spoken by two actors. Between *Medea* and *Pygmalion*, Benda composed *Singspiels*: these featured a different arrangement in which the music alternated with the dialogue. Benda's three *Singspiels* – *Der Dorfjahrmarkt* ('The Annual Village Market', 1775), *Romeo und Julie* ('Romeo and Juliet', 1776) and *Walder* (1776) – were markedly different from previous examples of the genre, which comprised comedy, ballads or fantasy. By contrast,

Benda's experience with melodrama developed his dramatic musical skills and this enabled him to give much more serious plots the *Singspiel* treatment for the first time. Benda's music reflected the tense and heightened atmosphere of these stories and, in doing so, created a much more dramatic musical language. This was done by Benda's frequent changes of tempo and rhythm, and his vivid orchestration.

Benucci, Francesco
c. *1745–1824,* ITALIAN
Francesco Benucci, an Italian bass, created the role of Figaro in Mozart's *Le nozze di Figaro* in 1786. Benucci spent the first 13 years of his career as an opera singer (1769–82) in Italy, before joining the renowned Italian company in Vienna. Benucci remained in Vienna until 1795, with a short break in London in 1789. The London visit, which he made with the English soprano **Nancy Storace** (1765–1817) – reputedly his mistress – was important for English opera audiences. Benucci and Storace introduced them to their first piece from a Mozart opera – 'Crudel! perchè?' from *Le nozze de Figaro*. Mozart himself admired Benucci's voice, calling it 'especially good'. It was deep, rounded and full, and despite the 'weight' of the bass voice, Benucci was able to use it with delicacy.

Bernacchi, Antonio Maria
1690–1756, ITALIAN
The Italian **mezzo-soprano** castrato Antonio Maria Bernacchi earned fame throughout Europe for his impressive technical virtuosity. Bernacchi performed in operas by most of the important composers of his time, including Handel. In 1716 and 1717, Bernacchi sang at the Haymarket, London, in parts previously sung by women, including Goffredo in Handel's *Rinaldo*. However, Bernacchi was not popular with English audiences; the

writer Charles Burney thought his singing 'artificial'. Bernucchi performed for the Elector of Bavaria in Munich between 1720 and 1735. During this period, he won a singing contest in 1727 with the castrato **Farinelli** (1705–82), even though Farinelli was 20 years his junior and is now considered the most famous castrato. Nevertheless, Bernacchi was close to the end of his career and by 1736, when he founded a singing school in his native city, Bologna, his voice was in decline.

Bernasconi, Antonia
c. *1741–c. 1803,* GERMAN
The soprano Antonia Bernasconi was the step-daughter of the Italian composer Andrea Bernasconi, *Kapellmeister* at the Munich court, and created the title role in Gluck's *Alceste* at its first performance in Vienna in 1767. Her father was in the service of the Duke of Württemberg, but after his death and her mother's remarriage, Antonia took her stepfather's name. She made her operatic debut in 1762, but seems to have had a somewhat 'small' voice. Nevertheless, Antonia Bernasconi became prominent in Vienna in tragic roles. In 1770, she left Vienna for Milan, where she sang Aspasia in Mozart's *Mitridate*. Usually described as a 'German' singer, Antonia Bernasconi became known for interpreting German-language roles in such operas as Gluck's *Iphigenie auf Tauris*, in which she sang in Vienna in 1781.

Calzabigi, Raniero de'
1714–95, ITALIAN
Calzabigi was best known for three libretti for Gluck – *Orfeo ed Euridice*, *Alceste* and *Paride ed Elena*, the last taking its eponymous characters, Paris and Helen, from the ancient Greek story of the Trojan War. In these libretti, Calzabigi moved away from the artificiality and limited conventions of *opera seria*, preferring simplicity and realistic drama. Calzabigi

avoided stereotyping his characters. Rather, he drew them as real-life human beings and, although he gave them poetic words to sing, he made sure they followed natural speech patterns. In complete contrast to the intensive business of writing opera libretti, Calzabigi had his scallywag side. While in Paris, he and his brother opened a lottery and took as a partner the adventurer and infamous lover Giacomo Casanova (1725–98). Although they enjoyed the protection of Mme de Pompadour, King Louis XV's powerful mistress, the partners were eventually expelled and their lottery collapsed.

Cavalieri, Katharina
1760–1801, **AUSTRIAN**

Katharina Cavalieri, the Austrian soprano, was both the student and the mistress of the court composer Antonio Salieri. In 1775, when she was 15, she made her debut in Vienna in the role of Sandrina in *La finta giardiniera* by Pasquale Anfossi (1727–97). Her voice was expressive and 'full', and she possessed a first-class singing technique. Though not beautiful, Cavalieri was graceful, and Mozart was much impressed with her. He wrote for her the role of Konstanze in *Die Entführung aus dem Serail*, and Elvira's aria 'Mi tradi' in the Vienna revival of *Don Giovanni*. Cavalieri complained that Elvira did not have sufficient music to sing and the special aria was Mozart's answer. In 1789, Cavalieri sang the role of the Countess Almaviva in a revival of *Le nozze di Figaro*. Considered one of the best among the very gifted singers in Vienna in the late eighteenth century, Cavalieri retired from the opera stage in 1793.

Cimarosa, Domenico
1749–1801, **ITALIAN**

The prolific Italian composer Domenico Cimarosa, who was born near Naples, first attracted attention with his opera *Le*

stravaganze del conte ('The Eccentricity of the Count', 1772). By 1787, Cimarosa had produced one success after another, with 15 operas written for opera houses in Rome and Naples. In 1787, however, Cimarosa accepted a post as *maestro di cappella* at St Petersburg. There he scored further success with *La vergine del sole* ('The Virgin of the Sun' 1788) and *Cleopatra* (1789) but he now had a dazzling international reputation and this made him constantly in demand outside Russia. In 1791, he became *Kapellmeister* to the imperial court in Vienna and, the following year, produced yet another success, *Il matrimonio segreto* ('The Secret Marriage', 1792). The same year, though, the Austrian emperor died and Cimarosa's appointment in Vienna came to an end. He returned home to Naples and a post as *maestro di cappella* to the royal court. Then, in 1799, Cimarosa was imprisoned after King Ferdinand fled in the face of invasion by the armies of Revolutionary France. On his release, Cimarosa headed back to St Petersburg, but died in Venice on the way. His output of more than 60 operas (nearly all of which survive) are noted for their melodic warmth, sparkle and vivacity.

Il matrimonio segreto ('The Secret Marriage')
by Domenico Cimarosa
Composed: 1792
Premiered: 1792, Vienna
Libretto by Giovanni Bertati, after George Colman and David Garrick

ACT I
Carolina, Geronimo's daughter, is secretly married to Paolino, her father's clerk. The couple are trying to find a way to tell Geronimo of their marriage; he would not approve of such a lowly match. Paolino comes up with a plan. In order to win Geronimo's favour, while also addressing his social aspirations, Paolino will arrange

a marriage between nobleman Count Robinson and Carolina's elder sister Elisetta. Paolino tells Geronimo of his idea; Geronimo is overjoyed at the prospect of the wedding. When the Count arrives, he first assumes Carolina is to be his wife, and then turns his attentions to Fidalma, the sister's widowed aunt. He is unimpressed with Elisetta and asks Carolina to marry him instead; Elisetta is enraged. The act ends in confusion, as the deaf Geronimo struggles to make sense of the situation.

ACT II

The Count explains to Geronimo that he wishes to marry Carolina instead of Elisetta. Geronimo hesitates, but the Count offers to take a smaller dowry; this appeals to Geronimo's greed and he consents. Paolino hears about the change of plan. He goes to Fidalma, hoping to confide in her, but she reveals that she is in love with him. Carolina then happens upon the pair and assumes the worst; a heated discussion ensues. Paolino suggests to Carolina that they run away together. Elisetta and Fidalma are furious with Carolina for ruining their hopes of love. They ask Geronimo to send Carolina to a convent; he agrees. Carolina laments her fate and the Count, unaware of her true dilemma, comforts her.

As Carolina and Paolino prepare to escape, Elisetta intervenes and they withdraw into Carolina's room. Elisetta is convinced that the man Carolina is with is the Count. She brings everyone to the door of the room; the couple are forced to show themselves and reveal that they are married. All ends happily as the Count agrees to marry Elisetta, and Geronimo, pleased that everything has turned out well, forgives Carolina and Paolino.

Da Ponte, Lorenzo
1749–1838, ITALIAN
Young Lorenzo Da Ponte's career as a priest came to an abrupt end when he was thrown out of his seminary for adultery.

After settling in Vienna, he became poet to the imperial theatres without having written a single libretto. Nevertheless, Da Ponte produced an impressive adaptation of *Iphigénie en Tauride* (1783) by Nicolas-François Guillard (1752–1814). *Il rico d'un giorno* ('A Rich Man for a Day', 1784), which Da Ponte wrote for Salieri, was his first original libretto. Da Ponte was soon in demand in Vienna and of his total of 46 libretti, his most famous, written for Mozart, were *Le nozze di Figaro*, *Don Giovanni* and *Così fan tutte*. In 1791, Da Ponte fell out of favour in Vienna and left for London. Pursued by creditors, he moved on to the United States, where he established the Italian Opera House in New York in 1833.

Dibdin, Charles
1745–1814, ENGLISH
In the late eighteenth century, Charles Dibdin – composer, actor and singer – catered for the English taste for *Singspiels* and afterpieces, which were short operas or pantomimes provided as extra entertainment after the main work had finished. Initially, Dibdin favoured the Italianate style, but after *The Waterman* (1774), he turned to a more English ballad kind of composition. Dibdin did not entirely abandon European influences. He was among the first to introduce English audiences to the ensemble finale in which the entire cast of an *opera buffa* gradually gathered on the stage in the last scene of an act.

Dibdin's life was crammed with difficulties, including severe financial problems and an inability to work amicably with others. Debts forced him to flee to France in 1776. After his quarrel with the manager of Covent Garden theatre in 1778, no other London management would employ him. He opened his own theatre, but mishandled it and ended up in debtors' prison. His plan to emigrate to India foundered because he was seasick and unable to make the journey. Eventually, Dibdin built a small theatre, ironically named the Sans Souci – 'without care' – where he gave shows called table entertainments.

Favart, Charles Simon
1710–92, **FRENCH**

Charles Favart became director of the Comédie-Italienne in Paris in 1758. His 11-year term as director was evidently important in the theatre's history, for in 1871 it was renamed Salle Favart. As a librettist, Favart's output was prodigious: he wrote 150 libretti for composers such as Gluck, Philidor and Grétry. Favart's forte was the comic libretto, and he was the first really important writer in this genre. His early libretti were, among others, vaudevilles and *drames forains*, which were pieces meant to be performed at trade fairs. In the mid-eighteenth century Favart developed the comédie *mêlée d'ariettes*, a form of the libretto as a continuous story into which songs could be fitted. Favart also became known for his depictions of peasants, normally seen as lumpish oafs, but in his libretti they were treated more realistically and with greater respect. The realism of the later *opéra comique* owed much to Favart's writing.

Ferrarese, Adriana
c. 1759–c. 1803, **ITALIAN**

Adriana Ferrarese was known as 'La Ferrarese' from her birthplace, Ferrara. In 1785, in London, she sang in *Demetrio* by Luigi Cherubini (1760–1842). Da Ponte, her mentor, wrote libretti for operas by **Vincente Martín y Soler** (1754–1806) and Salieri in which she took part. However, Mozart was not particularly impressed when she sang Susanna in a Vienna revival of *Le nozze di Figaro* in 1789: she failed to perform two arias he had specially written for her in the required 'artless manner'. Ferrarese was a difficult woman, described even by the faithful Da Ponte as a 'troublemaker'. The pair became the focus of scandals and they were made to leave Vienna in 1791. They went to Trieste, where Ferrarese sang in Mozart's *Così fan tutte* in 1797, having created the role in Vienna in 1790.

Galuppi, Baldassare
1706–85, **ITALIAN**

Baldassare Galuppi wrote his first opera, *La fede nell'incostanza* ('Faith in Inconstancy', 1722), when he was 16. It failed. Undeterred, Galuppi studied with Antonio Lotti (1667–1740) to improve his technique. Eventually, in 1729, he achieved his first big success, in Venice, with *Dorinda*. This opened the door to a brilliant career in which Galuppi produced some 100 works. In 1741, he began writing operas for London, including *Scipione in Cartagine* ('Scipio (Africanus) in Carthage', 1742) and *Sirbace* (1743), which were regularly performed in subsequent years. Fanny Burney (1752–1840), the diarist and novelist, believed that, of all Italian composers, Galuppi had the most influence on English music.

After returning to Venice in 1743, Galuppi divided his output between opera and church music and in 1762 was appointed *maestro di cappella* at St Mark's. He had already made a seminal contribution to opera in 1749 when he wrote the first full-length *opera buffa*, *L'Arcadia in Brenta*: he later gave this genre an expanded version of the 'chain finale' where successive sections in different rhythm, tempo and texture respond to the dramatic situation and convey the flux of emotions which are portrayed. Galuppi preceded Cimarosa as *maestro di cappella* at St Petersburg, where his *Ifigenia in Tauride* ('Iphigenia in Tauris', 1768) was performed. Galuppi wrote his last opera, *La serva per amore* ('The Servant for Love') in 1773.

Gluck, Christoph Willibald von
1714–87, GERMAN

Famous above all as the composer of *Orfeo ed Euridice,* Christoph Willibald von Gluck was, more than anyone, responsible for purging opera of what he dubbed the 'abuses' of *opera seria* in favour of 'beautiful simplicity', emotional directness and dramatic truth.

FROM BOHEMIA TO VIENNA

Born in the small town of Erasbach in the Upper Palatinate on 2 July 1714, Gluck was determined to become a musician despite opposition from his father, a forester. In his early twenties he went to Milan, where he played in the orchestra of Prince Melzi and composed his earliest opera, *Artaserse* (1741). Its success led to several more works in the then-fashionable genre of *opera seria.* After visiting London, where he met Handel, in 1745, and directing performances of his operas in other European centres, Gluck settled in Vienna in 1752. That year he composed his most boldly inventive *opera seria* to date, *La clemenza di Tito* ('Titus' Clemency', 1752), to a libretto by Metastasio, which Mozart was to use nearly 40 years later.

NEW DIRECTIONS

During the 1750s and early 1760s Gluck wrote, besides *opera seria,* celebratory works on mythological themes for the imperial court (such as *L'innocenza giustificata,* 'Innocence Vindicated', 1755) and several light, tuneful *opéras comiques* – a genre that became popular after the Viennese imperial chancellor Count Kaunitz brought a French troupe to the court. These culminated in *La rencontre imprévue* ('The Unforeseen Meeting', 1764), a delightful work whose plot and Turkish harem setting (then all the rage in Vienna) were reused by Haydn in *L'incontro improvviso* ('The Unforeseen Meeting', 1775) and influenced Mozart's *Die Entführung aus dem Serail.* However,

the two decisive events of these years were the revolutionary dramatic ballet *Don Juan* (1761) and the first of Gluck's so-called 'reform' operas, *Orfeo ed Euridice,* on which he collaborated with the poet and librettist Calzabigi.

THE FRENCH CONNECTION

Orfeo's success prompted two further operas whose simple classical plots and close integration of solos, chorus and ballet consolidated Gluck's and Calzabigi's new dramatic principles: *Alceste,* and the less well-received *Paride ed Elena* ('Paris and Helen', 1770). Two years later Gluck was given an adaptation of Racine's tragedy *Iphigénie en Aulide* ('Iphigenia in Aulis', 1774) by the attaché to the French embassy in Vienna. Between 1774, when this new opera was successfully premiered at the Académie Royale in Paris, and 1779 Gluck applied his revolutionary principles of music drama – themselves influenced by French opera, especially Rameau's **tragédies lyriques** – to further works for the Parisian stage: an expanded version of *Orfeo* as *Orphée et Euridice* (1774), and an even more radical reworking of *Alceste* (1776). This was followed by the romantically coloured *Armide* (1777), which Gluck pronounced 'perhaps the best of all my works', and then by the opera many regard as his supreme masterpiece, *Iphigénie en Tauride* ('Iphigenia in Tauris', 1779).

Gluck's final French opera, the pastoral *Echo et Narcisse* ('Echo and Narcissus', 1779), was a failure. This was partly because of squabbling Parisian claques; a dispute had long raged between supporters of Gluck and those of rival composer Piccinni. It was also partly because the composer's French operas had accustomed his audiences to sterner stuff. Gluck left Paris for the last time in October 1779 and spent his remaining years enjoying his wealth and fame in Vienna. He died, aged 73, on 15 November 1787.

Orfeo ed Euridice

When the Emperor Franz I and his retinue attended the premiere of *Orfeo ed Euridice* at the Burgtheater in Vienna on 5 October 1762, they were doubtless expecting a lightweight pastoral entertainment. The occasion – the emperor's name day – and the opera's billing as an *azione teatrale* (literally 'theatrical action') promised as much. What they got was a work of startling originality that integrated chorus, soloists and ballet in dramatic complexes, abandoned the strict *da capo* aria, and broke down the clear-cut division between **recitative** and aria. Calzabigi, the librettist, was a disciple of the French Enlightenment, and a passionate opponent of the artifices and excesses of Italian opera. He took the archetypal story of Orpheus's descent to Hades to rescue his wife Eurydice and pared it down to essentials. And from the solemn opening chorus of mourning, through the elementally moving contrast between Stygian darkness and dazzling light in Act II, to Orpheus's famous climactic lament, 'Che farò' ('What shall I do without Eurydice?'), Gluck's music makes its effects with swift, shattering economy. In 1774, he revised the opera as *Orphée et Euridice*, adding new arias and ballet numbers for dance-mad Paris, but diffusing the dramatic force of the original. In Vienna the hero had been sung by the castrato Gaetano Guadagni. The French deemed castrati an offence against nature, and Gluck duly reworked the role for the celebrated *haute-contre* (high **tenor**) Joseph Legros.

Orfeo ed Euridice ('Orpheus and Eurydice')

by Christoph Willibald von Gluck

Composed: 1762; revised 1774

Premiered: 1762, Vienna (revised version 1774, Paris)

Libretto by Raniero de' Calzabigi (revised version Pierre-Louis Moline)

ACT I

Orpheus mourns the death of his beloved wife Eurydice, who suffered a deadly snakebite. As he pleads with the gods either to bring her back to life or let him die so that he can be with her, Cupid descends from the heavens. He brings news that the gods have been moved by Orpheus's pleas and have agreed that he can descend to the underworld to try to retrieve Eurydice. To succeed, he must placate first the Furies and then Pluto with the power of his music. There is also one condition that he must observe: he must not look back towards Eurydice as she follows him out of the underworld, and he may not explain his reasons. Realizing that this may make Eurydice doubt his love and doom his quest to failure, Orpheus puts his trust into Cupid and the power of his love for Eurydice.

ACT II

At the entrance to the underworld, Orpheus encounters the terrifying Furies. He pleads with them to be allowed entry but is repeatedly rebuffed as they try to frighten him into returning to the land of the living. Eventually, he charms them with his beautiful singing and they let him pass. Guided by his love for Eurydice, he reaches the Elysian Fields and finds her among other blessed spirits. The lovers are reunited.

ACT III

Orpheus tries to persuade Eurydice to follow him out of the underworld but she is bewildered and is at first reluctant to leave. She grows more concerned when Orpheus refuses to look at her, crying out that he is cold and unfeeling, and that she would rather die if he no longer loves her. Unable to ignore her words, Orpheus turns around and embraces Eurydice, who dies. Orpheus is inconsolable and resolves to kill himself, but he is stopped by Cupid, who is moved by Orpheus's determination and enduring love for Eurydice. He then returns Eurydice to life. The lovers are reunited once again and everyone rejoices.

Recommended Recording:
Orfeo ed Euridice, Freiburg Baroque Orchestra; René Jacobs, conductor; Harmonia Mundi HMC 901742; Soloists: Bernarda Fink (Orfeo), Veronica Cangemi (Euridice), Maria Cristina Kiehr (Amore)

Alceste

Triumphantly premiered in Vienna's Burgtheater on 26 December 1767, *Alceste* was the second of the three collaborations between Gluck and Calzabigi. Today it is probably more famous for the reforming manifesto of its preface than for its magnificent music. Like *Orfeo*, *Alceste* cultivates Gluck's ideal of noble simplicity, with the whole opera based essentially on a single situation – Alcestis's sacrifice for her dying husband. From the powerful **overture** – which, as Gluck said in the preface, should 'apprise the spectators of the action to be represented' – *Alceste* is the most monumental and unrelievedly sombre of all eighteenth-century operas. In the defiant, self-sacrificing heroine, whose music includes the awesome invocation to the underworld 'Ombre, larve', or, in the French version, 'Divinités du Styx', Gluck surely created his greatest soprano role.

Although the opera excited the composer 'to frenzy', he acknowledged its monolithic nature when he reworked it for Paris. The French *Alceste* is in effect a different opera: musically richer, dramatically tauter and more human than the Italian original, with a touch of comedy in the *deus ex machina* figure of Hercules. The librettist Roullet summed up the enthusiasm Alceste aroused when he described it as 'the most passionate, the most energetic, the most theatrical music ever heard in Europe'.

Alceste

by Christoph Willibald von Gluck
Composed: 1767 (revised 1776)
Premiered: 1767, Vienna (revised version 1776)

Libretto by Raniero de' Calzabigi (French version by François Louis Gand Leblanc Roullet)

ACT I

A herald tells the grieving crowd gathered in the square next to the palace of Admetus, King of Thessaly, that the king is near to death. His queen, Alcestis, enters and beseeches the gods to relent and have pity on her and her children. She then invites the crowd to join her in the temple of Apollo and offer a sacrifice to the god. Inside the temple Alcestis asks Apollo to accept the offerings.

The High Priest urges them all to listen to the words of the Oracle, which pronounces that Admetus can only live if another dies in his place. The terrified people flee from the temple, leaving Alcestis alone. Believing that the good of the people is more important than her own life, she offers herself in her husband's place, even if it means leaving her children. Life without Admetus would be meaningless. The High Priest tells her that Apollo has accepted her sacrifice and that the messengers of death will be waiting for her at the gates of Hades by sunset.

ACT II

Admetus has recovered and the people are celebrating in the palace. Barely able to believe his recovery, he announces that he would have given his own life for any of his subjects, but he does not ask to whom he owes his life. Admetus and Alcestis are reunited as the people continue their celebrations. Alcestis, however, cannot hide her tears of sorrow for what is to come. At first Admetus urges her to be happy for his good fortune, but he eventually becomes disturbed and asks why she turns her eyes away from him. She says that she would willingly lay down her life for him a hundred times, but it is only under repeated questioning that she finally confesses what she has done. Admetus is horrified and cannot understand why she should choose to leave him, subjecting him to far greater pains than his own death could bring. The gods must reclaim their original victim. Alcestis calls on the gods to acknowledge that it is her duty to carry out the vow. She must abandon all she loves and be strong in the face of death.

ACT III

In the palace courtyard the people are preparing for the deaths of Alcestis and Admetus, who does not intend to live without her. The hero Hercules arrives to see his friend Admetus. On hearing the news, he declares that he will go to Hades and bring back Alcestis.

Alcestis arrives at the gates of Hades, terrified but determined to go forward. The gods of the underworld call to her and she asks them to hasten her end. Admetus has followed her, seeking his own death, but Alcestis orders him to remember his children and his people. Both of them call on the gods, demanding the right to be the only one to be taken. Thanatos, a god of the underworld, replies that the choice is Alcestis's. As she moves towards the gates, and her death, Admetus tries to follow but is stopped as Hercules bursts in. He attacks the gods and brings Alcestis back from Hades. Apollo appears and grants Hercules immortality for his deeds.

As the gates of Hades disappear, the scene returns to the palace, where Apollo calls on the people to renew their vows of loyalty to Admetus and Alcestis, now restored to life.

Recommended Recording:

Alceste, English Baroque Soloists; John Eliot Gardiner, conductor; Philips 470 293–2PH2; Soloists: Anne Sofie von Otter (Alceste), Paul Groves (Admète), Yann Beuron (Evandre), Ludovic Tézier (Herald, Apollon), Dietrich Henschel (High Priest, Hercule), Nicolas Testé (Oracle, Thanatos)

Iphigénie en Tauride

Gluck's final *tragédie* for Paris, *Iphigénie en Tauride*, was his greatest success and is arguably his supreme achievement. With a tautly constructed libretto (by Nicolas-François Guillard, drawing on the play by Euripides), it represents the climax of Gluck's efforts to 'purify' opera of dramatically superfluous decoration and display. The action moves forward swiftly and remorselessly. Not a note is wasted. In addition, the flexible musical structures, with many ensembles and a fluid intermingling of recitative and **arioso**, powerfully enhance the development of the drama.

Iphigénie and her tormented brother Oreste drew from Gluck some of his most intense and anguished music – the heroine's grieving aria 'O malheureuse Iphigénie', with its forlorn oboe solo and agitated syncopated accompaniment (a favourite Gluckian combination); or the scene for Oreste in Act II culminating in the haunting arioso 'Le calme rentre dans mon coeur', where his imagined peace is disturbingly contradicted by the orchestra. There are raucously barbaric numbers, in the fashionable 'Turkish style', for King Thoas and his Scythian followers, while the serene, luminous choruses for Iphigénie's priestesses are the quintessence of Gluck's 'beautiful simplicity' and left their mark on Mozart's *Idomeneo* (1781) and *Die Zauberflöte* (1791).

Iphigénie en Tauride ('Iphigenia in Tauris')

by Christoph Willibald von Gluck
Composed: 1779
Premiered: 1779, Paris
Libretto by Nicolas-François Guillard, after Guymond de la Touche and Euripides

BACKGROUND

Iphigénie, daughter of Agamemnon and Clytemnestre, is a priestess of Diana on the island of Tauride. Clytemnestre killed

Agamemnon and was killed in turn by Iphigénie's brother, Oreste. Oreste has travelled to Tauride with his friend Pylade.

ACT I

A storm rages on Tauride. Iphigénie and the priestesses appeal to the gods to calm the elements. Iphigénie tells of a terrible dream she has had, in which she was about to kill her brother Oreste. Desperate, Iphigénie prays for Diana to end her life. Thoas, King of Tauride, enters. He announces that Iphigénie must sacrifice every foreigner that arrives in Tauride; otherwise, say the oracles, he will die. He tells her of the capture of two young Greeks – in fact Oreste and Pylade – and orders their deaths.

ACT II

In a cellar, Oreste laments his responsibility for his friend's death and calls upon the gods to end his life. The loyal Pylade reassures him, telling him that he is happy to die if they are together. Pylade is then taken away. Oreste prays again for death and falls asleep, but is tormented by the Furies over his matricide. Iphigénie enters to find out more about the prisoners. They do not recognize one another, and although Oreste tells her of Agamemnon and Clytemnestre's fates, he does not reveal his own identity and claims Oreste to be dead. Iphigénie mourns the deaths of her parents and brother.

ACT III

Iphigénie tells the priestesses of her decision to save one of the prisoners. She has difficulty choosing, but eventually selects Oreste, as she feels an inexplicable tenderness towards him. When she tells the prisoners, however, Oreste will not accept the decision. He was hoping for death to release him from his torments and declares that if he is freed, he will kill himself. Iphigénie reluctantly sets Pylade free instead, entrusting him with a letter to deliver to her sister Electre. Pylade and Oreste bid each other farewell; Pylade resolves to save Oreste.

ACT IV

Iphigénie prepares to sacrifice Oreste, praying to Diana for strength. Oreste offers words of encouragement; he wants to die. However, just as Iphigénie is about to plunge the dagger into Oreste, he cries out that his sister, Iphigénie, died in the same way. Finally realizing each other's true identities, the joyful siblings are reunited. A woman enters with the news that Thoas is approaching, enraged by the liberation of Pylade.

When Thoas arrives, he orders the sacrifice of Oreste and, when Iphigénie refuses, attempts to carry it out himself. He also wants to kill Iphigénie, but at that moment Pylade arrives and kills Thoas. A battle follows but is halted by Diana, who frees Oreste from his torments and announces that he will rule Greece. Everyone celebrates the gods and the restoration of peace throughout the land.

OPERAS

1762	Orfeo ed Euridice (revised 1774 as Orphée)
1767	Alceste (revised 1776)
1770	Paride ed Elena
1774	Iphigénie en Aulide
1777	Armide
1779	Iphigénie en Tauride
1779	Echo et Narcisse

TIMELINE

1714	Born in Erasbach
1745–46	Travels to London
1750	Marries 18-year-old daughter of a Viennese merchant, Maria Anna Bergin
1752	Settles in Vienna
1759	Holds salaried position at court theatre in Vienna
1762	Premiere of Orfeo ed Euridice, Vienna
1767	Premiere of Alceste, Vienna
1770	Premiere of Paride ed Elena, Vienna
1774	Premieres of Iphigénie en Aulide and revised Orphée, Paris
1776	Premiere of revised version of Alceste, Paris
1777	Premiere of Armide, Paris
1779	Premieres of Iphigénie en Tauride and Echo et Narcisse, Paris, the latter unsuccessful; Gluck returns to Vienna
1787	Dies in Vienna

Goldoni, Carlo
1707–93, **ITALIAN**

By profession a lawyer in Pisa, Carlo Goldoni became resident poet at several Venetian opera houses. There he devised and specialized in the *opera buffa* libretto and wrote over 100, using pseudonyms for some of them. Goldoni left Venice for Paris in 1762 and for some years became well known and much admired for his work at the Comédie-Italienne. Goldoni's libretti had a seminal importance and exercised an influence over several major opera composers, including Mozart, Rossini and **Gaetano Donizetti** (1797–1848). Goldoni's influence was felt, too, in the peculiarly Italian genre, the **commedia dell'arte**, some of whose features found their way into comic opera. To these Goldoni added earthy characters and everyday situations that greatly humanized the genre and made it very popular in Italy. Goldoni himself classified his libretti as *drammi giocosi*, and was particularly known and appreciated for the opportunities he created for ensemble singing.

Grétry, André-Ernest-Modeste
1741–1813, **FRENCH**

Grétry, who was born in Liège, composed two *intermezzi* before he headed for Paris and his preferred genre, the *opera comique*. His first success, *Le Huron* (1768), came a year after his arrival and was followed in 1769 by the equally well received *Lucile* and *Le tableau parlant* ('The Talking Picture'). Grétry charmed French audiences with his elegant, expressive melodies and their distinctly Italian grace. A string of successes encouraged Grétry to spread his musical wings with his composition of *Andromaque* ('Andromache', 1780), which was based on Racine's play about the Trojan War. This was a big, dramatic subject, with rather too much tragedy for Grétry's particular talent, which was somewhat overstretched by it. However, the opera considered to be Grétry's masterpiece, *Richard Coeur-de-Lion* ('Richard the Lionheart', 1784) lay ahead of him and received its first performance in Paris. This opera in three acts was based on the thirteenth-century fable telling the story of King Richard and his faithful minstrel Blondel. Blondel's air 'Une fèvre brûlante' was an early example of the reminiscence motif, which is repeated throughout the opera as a reminder of a place, a person or other feature of the story.

Richard Coeur-de-Lion ('Richard the Lionheart')
by André-Ernest-Modeste Grétry
Composed: 1784
Premiered: 1784, Paris
Libretto by Michel-Jean Sedaine

PROLOGUE
Richard I has disappeared on his way home to England from the Third Crusade. Blondel, his squire and a troubadour, is trying to find his master.

ACT I
Peasants are returning in the evening to their homes near Linz Castle. A local boy, Antonio, leads on a blind man and tells him about the girl he will be seeing at a wedding tomorrow, before going to find lodgings for the night. When left alone the man, who is indeed Blondel, reveals that he is only pretending to be blind and that he believes Richard is a prisoner in the castle. Florestan, the castle governor, sends a love letter to Laurette, daughter of the Welsh knight Williams, who intercepts the letter. Blondel asks Antonio to read it aloud, including a reference to a very important prisoner. Laurette declares her love for Florestan, but Blondel warns her that Cupid wears a blindfold. Marguerite of Flanders, Richard's beloved, arrives with her entourage. Blondel plays a tune the king had written for her and, when questioned, says he learned it from a crusader. He then leads the servants in a drinking song.

ACT II

On the castle terrace, Richard despairs of his life as a prisoner. Blondel and Antonio appear below the wall. Richard recognizes Blondel's voice and joins in the song. The soldiers threaten to arrest Blondel, who pretends to have a message from Laurette, inviting Florestan to a party tomorrow.

ACT III

In Williams' house, Blondel reveals his true identity to Marguerite and tells her about Richard. He outlines a plot he has formed in order to capture Florestan when he comes to visit Laurette. During the dancing Florestan is seized. Blondel leads the assault on the castle and Marguerite and Richard are reunited.

Guadagni, Gaetano
1725–92, ITALIAN

The castrato Gaetano Guadagni first sang as a **contralto**, but later retrained as a soprano. Although he had no early training, Handel hired him to sing in his **oratorios** Messiah and Samson. In 1754–55, Guadagni made up for his lack of training by studying with Gioacchino Gizziello (1714–61) in Lisbon and with the English actor David Garrick (1717–79) in London. After returning to mainland Europe in 1757 Guidagni sang in operas by Hasse and Traetta, and created the title roles in Gluck's Orfeo ed Euridice and Telemaco. In later years, Guadagni performed in Munich and Potsdam before retiring to Padua in 1776. Charles Burney was a great admirer of Guadagni, praising him as an actor 'without equal' on stage and as an 'impassioned and exquisite' singer.

Hasse, Johann Adolf
1699–1783, GERMAN

At the age of 22, Johann Adolf Hasse had his first opera, Antioco (1721), produced before being sent to Italy to study under **Alessandro Scarlatti** (1660–1725). In Naples, Hasse's 'dialect comedies' Sesostrate

(1726) and La sorella amante ('The Loving Sister', 1729) made him something of a local celebrity. Hasse's Artaserse (1730), staged in Venice, proved to be a milestone in the development of opera. His music gave the stylized conventions of contemporary opera a new slant, with greater contrast and expression and more chances for the singers to demonstrate the beauty and agility of their voices. Another opera in the same vein – Dalisa – appeared that year. In this same brilliant year of his career, Hasse was invited to the court of Saxony, where the heir to the electorate, Prince Frederick Augustus II, was keen to establish an Italian opera company in Dresden. The company, with Hasse as its director, was established in 1733, after Frederick Augustus succeeded to the electorate. Subsequently Dresden became a centre of opera in Germany that was second only to Berlin. Hasse himself was recognized as an important influence on the development of opera seria, which acquired a new depth, a greater dramatic sweep and emotional appeal for audiences.

Haydn, Joseph
1732–1809, AUSTRIAN

The operatic career of Joseph Haydn spanned four decades, from his lost German Singspiel Der krumme Teufel ('The Crooked Devil', 1753) to his Orpheus opera L'anima del filosofo ('The Philosopher's

Soul'), composed for London in 1791 but not performed there (or anywhere else) during the composer's lifetime. In between, he composed some 20 operas (several lost) for the Esterházy court, ranging from comedies like *Il mondo della luna* ('The World on the Moon', 1777) through 'mixed-genre' works like *La fedeltà premiata* ('Fidelity Rewarded', 1780) and *Orlando paladino* ('Knight Roland', 1782) to the 'heroic drama' *Armida* (1783). Haydn himself valued his operas highly. Yet while most have been recorded, none has entered the regular repertoire.

In his operas, more than anywhere, Haydn has suffered for not being Mozart. Criticisms of far-fetched, slow-moving plots (Haydn never had a Da Ponte at his disposal) and fallible dramatic instinct cannot be dismissed out of hand. Where Mozart would have propelled things forward in an ensemble, Haydn was too often content to write an elegant, static aria in full sonata form. Nevertheless, his operas abound in richly worked, vividly characterized music, sometimes of a sensuous beauty not readily associated with Haydn – for example, the ravishing 'dream' trio in the oriental opera *L'incontro improvviso* ('The Unexpected Meeting', 1775). In addition, among the stock-in-trade characters, there are memorable individual portraits: the 'sentimental' heroine Rosina in *La vera costanza* ('True Constancy', 1778–89); the irrepressible, fast-talking Pasquale in *Orlando paladino*, first cousin to Mozart's Leporello; or, most richly imagined of all, the impassioned, vengeful, ultimately tragic sorceress Armida in Haydn's final opera for the Esterhazy court.

La fedeltà premiata ('Fidelity Rewarded')

by Joseph Haydn
Composed: 1780
Premiered: 1781, Eszterháza
Libretto by Giambattista Lorenzi

ACT I

Amaranta reads an inscription in the Temple of Diana describing how two lovers are to be offered to a sea monster every year until a hero sacrifices himself. Melibeo, the High Priest, chooses the victims and everyone has to be careful not to cross him. On his advice, Lindoro abandons the nymph Nerina for Celia, but Amaranta makes the mistake of preferring Count Perrucchetto to Melibeo. Fileno believes his beloved Fillide is dead, unaware that she is actually Celia. When she sees Fileno, Celia tries to maintain the deception or give herself away to Melibeo. The Count's fleeting interest in Nerina makes Amaranta furious. Melibeo tells Celia she must either marry Lindoro or face the monster with Fileno; before she is forced to accept, she is abducted by satyrs.

ACT II

Melibeo plans to win Amaranta's love by pairing off Celia and the Count, and he persuades Nerina to seduce Fileno. Fileno succeeds in killing a wild boar that is chasing Amaranta, but the Count claims the kill. Fileno contemplates suicide, but manages to break his arrow while carving his story on a tree. Celia finds the carving and the arrow and believes he is dead. On Melibeo's instructions the Count enters a cave where Celia is hiding. When the pair emerges Melibeo announces that they are to be this year's sacrifice.

ACT III

Fileno refuses to accept Celia's protestations of innocence. Fileno declares that, to save Celia, he will be the single sacrificial victim and hurls himself in front of the sea monster, which turns into a grotto from which Diana appears. She brings together Celia and Fileno, Nerina and Lindoro, and Amaranta and the Count. As a punishment for his scheming, Melibeo is taken as her victim, but the curse on Cumae has been lifted.

Hiller, Johann Adam
1728–1804, GERMAN

The German composer and writer Johann Adam Hiller was a keen admirer of Hasse. Although already an established songwriter, Hiller wanted to move into more operatic mode, with Hasse's style as his yardstick. Hiller joined forces with the librettist Daniel Schiebeler (1741–71) and together they produced a romantic comedy-opera *Lisuart und Dariolette* ('Lisart and Darioletta', 1766). A second opera, *Die Muse* ('The Muse', 1767), followed a year later, but neither was much of a success. Subsequently Hiller reverted to the rustic, sentimental pieces he had previously produced with another librettist, Christian Felix Weisse (1726–1804). The first three results of their renewed collaboration were important in establishing *Singspiel* as a popular form in opera. Hiller has been cited as the founder of *Singspiel*, and, in his lifetime, this new style of musical writing was widely emulated. Hiller's work with Weisse mixed together a number of influences – the French *opéras comiques*, German song traditions, the **bel canto** technique used in *opera seria*, or the chatty staccato style used in *opera buffa*. Hiller helped to popularize his own work by publishing scores of his music in simplified versions so that amateur singers could perform them. An added purpose was to encourage German singers to improve their standards.

Jommelli, Niccolò
1714–74, ITALIAN

Jommelli scored successes with his first operas, *L'errore amoroso* ('The Loving Mistake', 1737) and *Ricimero* (1740) and *Astianatte* (1741), and before long these and other operas had won him recognition as an eminent composer. Jommelli's services were eagerly sought and he wrote operas for Rome, where he was appointed *maestro di cappella* at St Peter's in 1749, and that same year composed works for Vienna. Four years later, Jommelli was appointed *Kapellmeister* to the Duke of Württemberg in Stuttgart, where he composed some 33 operas – some of them for other German courts or for Italian opera houses. However, his experience in Stuttgart marked his style so that by the time he returned to Italy, two new operas he produced were judged too German for Italian tastes. Jommelli had more success with four operas written for Portuguese audiences, but Italian audiences seemed to have turned against him. So many of the operas he wrote for the Italians were failures that the stress caused a fatal fit of apoplexy. Nevertheless, Jomelli's contribution to the development of opera was not in doubt: his *opera seria* style was more realistic and less stereotyped than that found in contemporary works.

Legros, Joseph
1739–93, FRENCH

The French tenor and composer Joseph Legros made his debut at the Opéra in Paris, singing Titon in *Titon et Aurore* by Jean-Joseph Mondonville (1711–72). Subsequently he built up a considerable repertoire of roles in operas by Lully, Rameau, Grétry and Gluck, among others. One of his greatest roles was as Gluck's *Orpheus* – a role in which he was considered 'a true to life actor, full of passion'. Legros appeared in several other of Gluck's works, including roles as Achille in *Iphigénie en Aulide*, Cynire in *Echo et Narcisse* and Pylade in *Iphigénie en Tauride*.

Legros's voice was flexible, with a brilliant high register, but on stage he was ungainly and awkward. He fought a running battle with his weight, but it eventually caught up with him. Legros became so fat that by 1783 he could not function properly on stage and had to retire.

Levasseur, Rosalie
1749–1826, **FRENCH**

For 10 years, between 1766 and 1775, Rosalie Levasseur, who appeared in cast lists as Mlle Rosalie, played minor roles, starting with Zäide in *L'Europe galante* by André Campra (1660–1744). In 1775, however, she caught the eye and the interest of the Austrian ambassador to Paris, Count Florimond Claude de Mercy-Argenteau, who decided to promote her talents. Mercy-Argenteau also made Rosalie Levasseur, as she once more became, his latest mistress. The ambassador's efforts on her behalf were brilliantly successful. Levasseur became principal soprano at the Opéra and sang the title role in the first Paris performance of Gluck's *Alceste*. In addition, she created leading roles in *Armide* and in *Iphigénie en Aulide*. Levasseur had a powerful, but somewhat inflexible, voice, although it certainly suited the music of Gluck, who was both her teacher and her friend. As an actress, however, Rosalie Levasseur was considered the most outstanding of her time.

Martín y Soler, Vincente
1754–1806, **SPANISH**

The Spanish composer Martín y Soler wrote his first opera, entitled *La Madrilena* ('The Girl from Madrid', 1776), which was probably a *zarzuela*. Afterwards, Martín went to Italy, where he gained a reputation for writing both serious and comic operas that were performed in Lucca, Parma, Turin, Venice and Naples. Soon his gifts for beautiful melody, striking orchestration and diverting characterization were widely recognized and he was encouraged to visit Vienna. There, together with the renowned librettist Da Ponte, he produced three operas, *Il burbero di buon cuore* ('The Moaner with the Heart of Gold', 1786), *L'arbore di Diana* ('Diana's Tree', 1787) and *Una cosa rara* ('A Rare Thing', 1786), the most successful of the trio. It displaced

---

SOUNDS FAMILIAR

'O QUANTO UN SI BEL GIUBILO!'

Mozart reacted sardonically to the fact that *Una cosa rara* by Martín y Soler replaced his own opera *Figaro* in Vienna in 1786. When writing his *Don Giovanni*, he quoted an aria from *Una cosa rara*, 'O quanto un si bel giubilo!', in the banquet scene that preceded the hero's descent into hell.

Mozart's *La nozze di Figaro*, which had been played for the first time earlier the same year. In 1787, Martín y Soler received an invitation to St Petersburg, where he became court composer to the Empress Catherine II (the Great). In St Petersburg, Martín wrote two operas, directed several opera productions and, most significantly, helped lay the foundations of native Russian opera.

Metastasio, Pietro
1698–1782, **ITALIAN**

The Italian poet Metastasio wrote 27 large-scale opera libretti, some of which were set to music up to 100 times. He created a genre of opera – Metastasian opera – that not only bore his name, but set new patterns for libretti during the 50 years he spent in Vienna. Invited to the imperial court in 1729, Metastasio created a sensation the following year when Hasse used Metastasio's libretto for his *opera seria Artaserse* (1730). This introduced a new elegance into opera, which increased the prominence of solo singers. Metastasio became a particular favourite of performers, whose voices he allowed to be put on very effective display. Metastasio's libretti were faithful to the 'doctrine of the affections', the dominant aesthetic theory of eighteenth-century opera. Although it restricted characterization and expression, his use of the 'doctrine' was tempered by his elegant verse, his vivid imagery and the sheer charm of his writing.

Mozart, Wolfgang Amadeus
1756–91, AUSTRIAN

Alone of the great Viennese classical 'trinity' – Haydn, Mozart and Beethoven – Mozart (1756–91) was a born theatre animal. From boyhood, opera was his greatest passion and he built on existing conventions to enrich and deepen three distinct types of opera: *opera seria, opera buffa* and German *Singspiel.*

THE CHILD PRODIGY

Wolfgang Amadeus Mozart was born in Salzburg on 27 January 1756, the son of Leopold Mozart, violinist and composer at the Salzburg court. From early childhood Wolfgang displayed what one contemporary called 'premature and almost supernatural talents', and Leopold was quick to promote his son's gifts in a series of concert tours. On a visit to London, Wolfgang astonished the philosopher Daines Barrington by improvising recitatives. At nine he had already absorbed the language of *opera seria.* His own earliest operas, though, were both comedies: the ingenuous *La finta semplice* ('The Feigned Simpleton', 1768); and the little pastoral *Singspiel Bastien und Bastienne* (1768), performed at the home of Franz Anton Mesmer, the famous Viennese experimenter in magnetism.

THE CONQUEST OF ITALY

Two years later, on his first trip to Italy, Mozart landed his first major commission: an *opera seria* for the Milan carnival season of 1770–71. He plunged himself excitedly into the new work, *Mitridate, rè di Ponto* ('Mithridates, King of Pontus', 1770). Although preparations were dogged by malevolent intrigue, Leopold Mozart wrote that the first night 'met with unanimous approval'. The *Wunderkind* had 'arrived' as an international operatic

composer with a work whose brilliance and mastery prompted a commission for another *opera seria.* Premiered in Milan, *Lucio Silla* (1772) is, if anything, an even finer work, with strong Gluckian resonances, especially in the darkly coloured music for *Junia.*

In the meantime Mozart had composed two more allegorical works: for Milan, *Ascanio in Alba* ('Ascanius in Alba', 1771), and for Salzburg, *Il sogno di Scipione* ('Scipio's Dream', 1772). Then, after a two-year hiatus, came the *opera buffa La finta giardiniera* ('The Pretend Gardener Girl', 1774–75), staged at the Munich carnival in January 1775. Lavish in its invention, *La finta giardiniera* foreshadows *Figaro* in the multi-movement ensembles of chaos and bewilderment that end the first two acts. Three months later, a royal visit prompted the last opera Mozart completed in Salzburg: *Il rè pastore* ('The Shepherd King', 1775), a static, serenata-type piece in the pastoral tradition.

TRIUMPH IN MUNICH

After his fateful journey to Mannheim and Paris in 1777–78, Mozart began a *Singspiel* with a fashionable oriental setting – *Zaide* (unfinished, 1779). Its many beauties include a glorious quartet and, uniquely in Mozart's works, passages of melodrama – declamation accompanied by highly charged orchestral music. However, there was no opportunity of performing *Zaide* in opera-starved Salzburg, and Mozart abandoned the score just before the final *denouement.* In the summer of 1780, however, his frustrated operatic ambitions were finally fulfilled when he received a commission to write an *opera seria* for Munich. The opera in question, *Idomeneo,* was a work of unique power and splendour, and Mozart's first unqualified stage masterpiece.

Following his dismissal from the Archbishop of Salzburg's service in 1781, Mozart quickly became absorbed in another *Singspiel* on a Turkish theme: *Die Entführung aus dem Serail*, whose composition, like that of *Idomeneo*, is vividly documented in a series of letters between Mozart and his father.

ENTER DA PONTE

After the triumphant premiere of *Die Entführung* in 1782, Mozart flirted with two more operatic projects: *L'oca del Cairo* ('The Goose of Cairo', 1783) and *Lo sposo deluso* ('The Deceived Husband', also 1783), the former to a libretto by the maverick poet and man of the theatre Lorenzo Da Ponte. Both remained fragments. Then, in 1785, Mozart suggested that Da Ponte base a libretto on Beaumarchais' *succès de scandale* of the previous year, *Le mariage de Figaro*. Da Ponte duly obliged, purging the play of much of its subversive political sentiment. The result was *Le nozze di Figaro*, an *opera buffa* of revolutionary complexity and human insight. *Figaro* was a qualified success in Vienna but caused a sensation in Prague, where the *impresario* Pasquale Bondini commissioned a second Mozart–Da Ponte collaboration, *Don Giovanni* (1787). This was still a comedy but one with unprecedented sombre, demonic overtones. The libretto for Mozart's third Da Ponte opera, *Così fan tutte* ('That's Women For You', 1790) has a brittle, typically eighteenth-century cynicism – a quality transmuted by the sensuous beauty and tenderness of Mozart's music.

THE FINAL YEAR

Mozart's fortunes were at a low ebb in 1790, the year of *Così fan tutte*'s premiere. However, they picked up in 1791, when he worked on two very different operatic projects. The first was *Die Zauberflöte* – a seemingly improbable mix of fairy tale, Viennese slapstick and high-minded Masonic allegory composed for a Viennese suburban theatre. Before rehearsals of *Die Zauberflöte* had begun, Mozart received a lucrative commission for an *opera seria* for the coronation of Leopold II as King of Bohemia. The upshot was the hastily composed *La clemenza di Tito* ('Tito's Clemency', 1791), long considered 'cold' and old-fashioned, but now valued for its distinctive elegiac beauty.

Mozart lived just long enough to witness the ever-growing success of *Die Zauberflöte*. A week or so after its premiere, on 30 September, he began work on the *Requiem*. On 20 November he took to his bed and on 5 December he died, aged 35, of acute rheumatic fever. His greatest operas soon became central to the European repertoire, touchstones of grace, humanity and dramatic truth. Their influence on later composers, from **Ludwig van Beethoven** (1770–1827) to **Richard Strauss** (1864–1949) and **Igor Stravinsky** (1882–1971), remains incalculable.

Idomeneo

Mozart had long admired the inspired synthesis of French and Italian opera in Gluck's 'reform' works. His greatest *opera seria*, *Idomeneo*, premiered in Munich on 29 January 1781, draws much from Gluck, especially the hieratic scenes of *Alceste* (another opera concerned with human sacrifice). Yet its harmonic daring, orchestral richness and lyrical expansiveness are entirely Mozart's own. Combining the sophistication of maturity with the reckless abundance of youth, *Idomeneo* constantly challenges and expands the boundaries of *opera seria*. Its prodigious musical invention throws up problems in performance – something Mozart himself acknowledged when at the last minute he drastically pruned the recitatives and cut several arias. Even so, none of Mozart's other operas has such a grand, heroic sweep, or explores emotional extremes so searchingly as this allegory of the passage of power from age to youth.

The characters are drawn with subtlety and compassion, especially the tormented king, played in Munich by the 66-year-old tenor Anton Raaff; the raging, ultimately unhinged Electra; and the Trojan Princess Ilia. They grow from sorrow, in a piercing G-minor lament, through acceptance to radiance. In addition, the writing for the chorus – inextricably bound up in the fate of King Idomeneus and his son Idamantes – has a unique magnificence and dramatic force, above all in the thrilling storm scene that forms the climax of the second act.

Idomeneo

by Wolfgang Amadeus Mozart
Composed: 1780–81
Premiered: 1781, Munich
Libretto by Gianbattista Varesco, after Antoine Danchet and Crébillon

ACT I

In the royal dungeons, Ilia, daughter of King Priam of Troy, is being held prisoner. Her hatred of the enemy is confused by her growing love for Idamantes, Idomeneus's son, who frees the prisoners and declares his love for her. Thinking that he is being courted by Electra, Ilia hides her feelings. The news arrives that Idomeneus has been killed at sea; Electra laments that he can now not bless her wedding to Idamantes and is perturbed to witness Idamantes and Ilia's feelings for each other. Meanwhile, Idomeneus arrives on the shore of Crete while Idamantes searches for his body among the wreckage. The two men meet but do not at first know each other, but as the truth of their identities dawns, Idomeneus is horrified to realize that the sacrifice he must make to Neptune is his only son. He rejects the bewildered Idamantes and runs off.

ACT II

Back at the palace, Idomeneus explains his predicament to Arbaces, his confidant, who feels that Neptune is more likely to spare Idamantes if he is exiled. The two plan for Idamantes to escort Electra back to Argos, her homeland, and stay there until the arrangement with Neptune has been resolved. Ilia encounters Idomeneus; the king, while reassuring and comforting her, realizes that she is in love with Idamantes and laments the fact that she too will suffer if he is exiled. Electra is pleased at the prospect of leaving with Idamantes, certain that she can win his love.

At the port, Idomeneus waits to see off Idamantes and Electra, but before the ship can sail a terrible storm brews up and a giant serpent rises from the sea. Taking this as a symbol of Neptune's anger, the people of Crete are terrified. Idomeneus admits that it is his fault, but does not reveal the dreadful bargain he has made.

ACT III

Idamantes goes to Ilia and announces that he is going to fight the serpent, which is wreaking havoc on the island. Finally, Ilia confesses her love for him. Idomeneo and Electra interrupt them and Idamante asks his father why he is so cold towards him. Idomeneus cannot explain and urges him to leave. Arbaces arrives, bringing news that there has been an uprising and the Cretans are clamouring for the king. Idomeneus faces the people and is told by the High Priest that the serpent is killing the citizens and destroying the island. The High Priest demands to know the intended victim of the sacrifice and everyone is horrified when the king reveals that it is Idamantes. Idomeneus and the priests pray to Neptune at the temple, where they are preparing for the sacrificial ceremony. Arbaces arrives with the news that Idamantes has succeeded in killing the serpent and then Idamantes himself enters. Having discovered that his father was merely trying to protect him, he now offers himself gladly to be sacrificed in order to placate Neptune. As a despairing Idomeneus raises his weapon to strike the fatal blow, Ilia intervenes and offers to die in Idamantes' place. Suddenly, Neptune's great voice is heard, declaring that love has triumphed and that Idomeneus must now give up his throne to Idamantes, who will rule along with Ilia. Everyone rejoices, with the exception of Electra, and Idomeneus gives a farewell speech to the jubilant people of Crete.

Recommended Recording:

Idomeneo, Scottish Chamber Orchestra; Charles Mackerras, conductor; EMI Classics 5 57260 2; Soloists: Lisa Milne (Ilia), Barbara Frittoli (Elettra), Lorraine Hunt Lieberson (Idamante), Ian Bostridge (Idomeneo), Anthony Rolfe Johnson (Arbace)

Die Entführung aus dem Serail

Premiered on 16 July 1782, *Die Entführung* quickly became his most popular work and sealed the composer's operatic reputation in German-speaking lands. The Viennese expected plenty of laughs from a *Singspiel*. Mozart obliged with his first great comic creation: the 'foolish, coarse and spiteful' (Mozart's words) harem overseer Osmin, a larger-than-life compound of sullen irascibility, prejudice, lechery and (in his show-stopping final aria 'Ha, wie will ich triumphieren') gloating sadism. Mozart exploited, to wonderfully grotesque effect, the subterranean notes of the original Osmin, Johann Ludwig Fischer. Through his music, the jangling, crashing Turkish style of the overture becomes a unifying feature of the whole opera, not least in the rollicking drinking duet 'Vivat Bacchus' – an instant hit in Vienna.

Die Entführung, though, is no mere oriental romp, and the music for Belmonte and Konstanze has a power, poignancy and lyrical beauty unprecedented in a *Singspiel*. As in *Idomeneo*, the sheer richness of musical invention occasionally threatens the drama, above all in the gargantuan introduction to Konstanze's aria of heroic defiance, 'Martern aller Arten' – magnificent as music, but famous as a producer's nightmare.

Die Entführung aus dem Serail ('The Abduction from the Seraglio')

by Wolfgang Amadeus Mozart
Composed: 1781–82
Premiered: 1782, Vienna
Libretto by Johann Gottlieb Stephanie the younger, after Christoph Friedrich Bretzner

ACT I

The beautiful Konstanze, her maid Blonde and Pedrillo, the servant of Belmonte, Konstanze's betrothed, have been bought by Pasha Selim from pirates. Konstanze lives in the Pasha's palace as his favourite and Pedrillo works as his gardener, while Blonde has been given as a gift to Osmin, the Pasha's overseer.

Belmonte has arrived at the seaside near the palace in search of Konstanze and the others. He encounters Osmin, who confirms that he is in the right place but becomes angry when Belmonte mentions Pedrillo; Osmin is in love with Blonde and Pedrillo is his rival for her affections. Belmonte then meets Pedrillo, who tells him that he is one of the Pasha's favourites and that, although the Pasha loves Konstanze, he will not force his affections on her. The two men devise a plan to rescue their loves and escape.

There is a chorus of Turkish guards and Belmonte, concealed, watches as Konstanze arrives with the Pasha. He asks her why she cannot accept his love and she explains to him that she is still in love with Belmonte. She then leaves, and Pedrillo takes the opportunity to introduce Belmonte to the Pasha, as a visiting architect. The Pasha is welcoming but then Osmin tries to deny the two men access to the castle; outwitting him, they go inside.

ACT II

In the garden, Blonde rejects Osmin's advances, confusing him with her fiery intelligence and promising him pain and violence if he does not leave her alone.

Meanwhile, Konstanze laments her fate. Why has Belmonte not come to rescue her? The Pasha, beginning to grow impatient, tries to convince Konstanze to marry him. She refuses and, when threatened with torture, says that she would rather die than marry him. Pedrillo then tells Blonde the good news of Belmonte's arrival and reveals that they will rescue the two women from the seraglio (the area in the palace where the women reside) that evening, before escaping by boat. They plan to keep Osmin out of the way by plying him with alcohol.

Later on, Pedrillo takes his chance and does not have much trouble persuading Osmin to partake of some wine, even though it is against Osmin's religion. He falls asleep and is dragged out of the way. Belmonte and Konstanze are reunited and are joined by Pedrillo and Blonde; the men are at first unsure of the women's fidelity, but they are quickly reassured and the four sing of their love.

ACT III

Belmonte and Pedrillo arrive at the walls of the seraglio with ladders and the rescue operation begins. Belmonte rescues Konstanze, but before Pedrillo and Blonde can escape, the jealous and evil Osmin awakes and intercepts them. Palace guards bring the four lovers before the angry Pasha. When Belmonte suggests that the Pasha take a ransom from his family, the Pasha realizes that Belmonte's father is an old enemy, who instigated the Pasha's exile. As he considers the lovers' fate, Belmonte and Konstanze sing of their love for each other. Surprisingly though, the Pasha decides to be merciful rather than vengeful and releases the two couples, giving them his blessing and allowing them to set sail for Spain. Osmin is enraged, but the Pasha promises him rewards to make up for his losing Blonde. As the joyful lovers leave, the chorus praises the Pasha's generosity.

SOUNDS FAMILIAR

'MARTERN ALLER ARTEN'
This is the soprano aria from Act II of Mozart's opera Die Entführung aus dem Serail, which is set in Turkey. The aria is sung by the heroine Konstanze, who declares that nothing, not even torture and the threat of death is going to make her give herself to her captor, Pasha Selim.

Recommended Recording:
Die Entführung aus dem Serail, Orchestra del Maggio Musicale Fiorentino; Zubin Mehta, conductor; TDK DV–OPEADS (DVD Region 0); Soloists: Eva Mei (Konstanze), Patrizia Ciofi (Blonde), Rainer Trost (Belmonte), Mehrzad Montazeri (Pedrillo), Kurt Rydl (Osmin), Markus John (Pasha)

Le nozze di Figaro
The librettist Lorenzo Da Ponte wrote that Le nozze di Figaro offered 'a new kind of spectacle ... to a public of such assured taste and refined understanding', and it would be fair to say that after Figaro's premiere on 1 May 1786, opera buffa was never quite the same again. There were precedents, of course, for the opera's social and sexual tensions, and for its extended 'chain' finales – not least in Paisiello's recent 'Figaro' opera, Il barbiere di Siviglia ('The Barber of Seville', 1782) and Mozart's own La finta giardiniera. Still, Figaro far eclipses all predecessors in its structural mastery, owing much to Da Ponte's ingenious adaptation of Beaumarchais' play, as well as its mingled comic brio and profound human insight, and the way Mozart's music simultaneously illuminates character and sweeps the drama forward. No opera unfolds at such a pace – indeed, the Countess's lament that opens Act II is all the more moving for being the first slow music in the work.

In this funniest and most humane of musical comedies, each of the characters is brilliantly drawn in their arias, with the servant pair Figaro and Susanna revealing a growing depth as the opera proceeds. But *Figaro*'s greatest glories are its many ensembles, far more intricate than anything the Viennese had heard before. Here Mozart uses his symphonic and contrapuntal mastery to weave together contrasted musical lines for dramatic ends, as in the 'recognition' sextet in Act III, the composer's own favourite number.

Le nozze di Figaro ('The Marriage of Figaro')

by Wolfgang Amadeus Mozart
Composed: 1786
Premiered: 1786, Vienna
Libretto by Lorenzo Da Ponte, after Pierre-Augustin Caron de Beaumarchais

ACT I

Figaro, the Count's valet, and Susanna, the Countess's maid, prepare for their wedding. Susanna reveals that the Count has designs on her; Figaro angrily resolves to outwit his master. Dr Bartolo enters with his housekeeper Marcellina. They plan to force Figaro to marry Marcellina to pay a debt he owes her. The Count's page, Cherubino, arrives and announces that the Count has caught him with Barbarina, the gardener's daughter. He professes his love for the Countess, and all the other women in the palace, but then hears the Count approaching and hides behind a chair. The Count makes advances towards Susanna, but also hides when Don Basilio, the music master, enters. Don Basilio mentions Cherubino's love for the Countess, at which the Count reveals himself, discovering Cherubino at the same time. The Count is furious, and orders Cherubino to join his regiment. Figaro returns with other servants; they praise the Count for renouncing the old right of the master to replace his valet on his wedding night. Figaro then advises Cherubino on military life.

ACT II

In her bedroom, the Countess laments her husband's waning affection. Together with Susanna and Figaro, she hatches a plot to trick the Count: they will send Cherubino, dressed as Susanna, to meet the Count in the garden and then denounce his infidelity. Cherubino enters and the others begin to dress him. Susanna leaves to fetch a ribbon and suddenly the Count enters; Cherubino hides in the dressing room. Suspicious, the Count leaves with the Countess to fetch some tools, with which to open the dressing room door. Susanna returns and takes Cherubino's place, while he jumps out of the window. The Count and Countess open the door to reveal Susanna. Figaro enters to announce that everything is ready for the wedding. Antonio, the gardener, arrives, furious that someone has jumped into his flowerbed beneath the window. Faking a limp, Figaro pretends that it was he who jumped. Bartolo, Marcellina and Basilio arrive to tell Figaro he must marry Marcellina to cancel his debt.

ACT III

Susanna offers to meet the Count in the garden that evening if he gives her the dowry he promised. However, the Count then sees her talking to Figaro and is suspicious. As Figaro tries to avoid marrying Marcellina by protesting that his parents are not present, it transpires that he is the son of

Marcellina and Bartolo. Susanna enters and misconstrues Figaro and Marcellina's embrace, but all is explained. Susanna, with the help of the Countess, composes a note inviting the Count to meet her. The wedding ceremony begins and Susanna slips the note to the Count. Figaro sees him.

ACT IV

Figaro and Marcellina encounter Barbarina, who unwittingly reveals that Susanna sent the note to the Count. Ignoring Marcellina's reassurances, Figaro plans to get revenge on his new wife for her supposed infidelity, and invites Basilio and Bartolo along as witnesses. Susanna and the Countess have swapped clothes. Susanna sings of her love for Figaro but he, overhearing, thinks she is referring to the Count. Cherubino arrives and begins to court the Countess – thinking she is Susanna – until the Count intervenes and begins seducing 'Susanna' himself. Figaro tells the 'Countess' (actually Susanna) about their respective partners' infidelities, but is quick to recognize Susanna's voice and joins in the joke. Figaro and the 'Countess' loudly declare their love for one another; the Count arrives and is horrified. He calls everyone to the garden and denounces his unfaithful wife. The real Countess then reveals herself and the deception is explained. The Count begs forgiveness, the Countess relents and everyone rejoices.

Recommended Recording:
Le nozze di Figaro, MusicAeterna; Teodor Currentzis, conductor; Sony 37092; Soloists: Simone Kermes (Contessa di Almaviva), Fanie Antonelou (Susanna), Mary-Ellen Nesi (Cherubino), Christian van Horn (Figaro), Andrei Bondarenko (Conte di Almaviva)

Don Giovanni

Composed in 1787 and triumphantly premiered in Prague on 29 October that year, Don Giovanni reworks the old legend of the serial seducer, drawing on the

Spanish play by Tirso de Molina (1630) and Molière's Don Juan (1665). The opera revolves around the tensions of class and sex that were so central to Figaro. Ensembles and propulsive 'chain' finales remain crucial, although the structure is more episodic than Figaro's. The roles are likewise a mixture of the serious and the comic, with the chameleon Don Giovanni and the scorned but devoted Donna Elvira of so-called 'mixed type' (mezzo carattere).

Mozart called Don Giovanni an opera buffa. However, from the awesome D minor introduction of the overture – foreshadowing the chilling appearance of the 'stone guest' who drags the hero to his doom – it is a very different work from Figaro. The main section of the overture is a tense, brilliant D major allegro, leading directly to a wry buffo aria for the comic servant Leporello. Typically, though, comedy is immediately juxtaposed with tragedy as Don Giovanni emerges from Donna Anna's bedroom, fights a duel with her father and kills him. In the second-act finale, tragedy and comedy are superimposed, with the terrifying statue commanding Don Giovanni to repent, while Leporello provides a chattering counterpoint. The demonic, supernatural elements of Don Giovanni and the enduring fascination of its convention-flouting hero made Don Giovanni beloved by the Romantics, at a time when much of Mozart's music was patronized for its supposed Dresden china prettiness.

Don Giovanni
by Wolfgang Amadeus Mozart
Composed: 1787
Premiered: 1787, Prague
Libretto by Lorenzo Da Ponte, after Giovanni Bertati

ACT I

Leporello awaits his master outside the Commendatore's house, where Don Giovanni is in Donna Anna's room. He comes out, pursued by Anna. Anna's father, the Commendatore, challenges Giovanni; they fight and the Commendatore falls, mortally wounded. Anna demands that her betrothed, Don Ottavio, avenge the murder. Giovanni scents a woman. Donna Elvira enters, seeking the man (Giovanni) who seduced her. He steps out to 'comfort' her, then recognizes her and slips away, leaving Leporello to explain that she is but one entry in his catalogue of conquests. Country folk are celebrating the wedding of Zerlina and Masetto. Giovanni, attracted by the bride, sends everyone else off to be wined and dined. Telling Zerlina she is too good for that peasant, he promises marriage and invites her to his villa. As she agrees, Elvira enters, denounces Giovanni and sends Zerlina off. Anna and Ottavio enter, and greet their neighbour Giovanni. Elvira claims that Giovanni is a betrayer but Giovanni assures them that she is mad. Anna recognizes Giovanni as the man who invaded her room and tells Don Ottario that after a struggle she freed herself. She again demands vengeance. Ottavio determines to bring her comfort.

Giovanni hopes for a successful party that evening. Zerlina tries to calm Masetto and they go off to the ball. Anna, Elvira and Ottavio enter, masked, solemnly stating their intention of confronting Giovanni. The music starts, with different dances for the different social groups. Giovanni manoeuvres Zerlina to an anteroom; she screams and all make to rescue her. Giovanni re-enters, and the act ends in general confusion and confrontation.

ACT II

Giovanni has noticed Elvira's maid and, to improve his chances with her, exchanges cloaks with Leporello. Leporello is deputed to get Elvira out of the way: on her balcony, she hears Giovanni singing of love and repentance, descends and goes off – with the disguised Leporello. Giovanni serenades the maid, but Masetto arrives, armed, with friends. Giovanni (disguised as Leporello) greets them, offers to help and sends them off

in different directions, then giving Masetto a beating. Zerlina finds Masetto and offers the ultimate in comforts. Leporello wants to free himself from Elvira. Anna and Ottavio arrive, then Zerlina and Masetto; they take him for Giovanni. He discards his disguise and slips off. Ottavio sings lovingly of Anna.

Giovanni and Leporello meet in the cemetery. A solemn voice is heard saying that Giovanni's laughter will be silent by dawn. It was the statue of the slain Commendatore. Invite him to supper, Giovanni commands, and the terrified Leporello does so. The statue nods its head in acceptance.

In Anna's house, Ottavio offers to marry her immediately. She asks for a period of mourning. Giovanni, in his banqueting hall, awaits a meal. Leporello serves, with a band in attendance. Elvira bursts in and begs Giovanni to mend his ways. She emits a piercing scream as she leaves. When Giovanni sends Leporello to investigate he too screams and tells Giovanni that the statue is there. The stone guest enters. Giovanni commands that another place is set for dinner. But the statue refuses and asks Giovanni to be his guest instead; Giovanni accepts. The statue seizes his hand in his chill grasp and demands repentance; Giovanni, refusing, is consigned to the flames of hell.

Leporello emerges from hiding and Elvira, Anna, Ottavio, Zerlina and Masetto enter, with police, for Giovanni. When Leporello describes what has happened they announce their plans for the future, and recite the moral – that evildoers come to a sticky end.

Recommended Recording:

Don Giovanni, Philharmonia Orchestra; Carlo Maria Giulini, conductor; EMI Classics CDS 7 47260 8; Soloists: Joan Sutherland (Donna Anna), Elisabeth Schwarzkopf (Donna Elvira), Graziella Sciutti (Zerlina), Luigi Alva (Don Ottavio), Eberhard Wächter (Don Giovanni), Giuseppe Taddei (Leporello), Piero Cappuccilli (Masetto), Gottlob Frick (Commendatore)

Così fan tutte

While *Don Giovanni* was the nineteenth century's favourite Mozart opera, *Così fan tutte*, premiered on 26 January 1790, was widely considered frivolous, immoral and (not least by Beethoven) an insult to women. Today we can see it as perhaps the most ambivalent and disturbing of Mozart's three Da Ponte comedies. In the composer's hands the 'laboratory experiment' of the elegant, geometrically structured libretto becomes an unsettling commentary on the unpredictability and alarming power of human feelings, and on the need for mature self-knowledge, cloaked in the most sensuously beautiful music Mozart ever wrote.

Of the quartet of lovers it is Fiordiligi who makes the most far-reaching journey to self-discovery. Both her arias exploit the virtuosity of the original singer of the role, Adriana Ferrarese. 'Come scoglio' in the first act is at once serious and parodistic in its extravagant leaps and heroic posturing. But her Act II rondò 'Per pietà' uses wide vocal leaps and the singer's rich low register to express the deep disquiet of a woman torn between her passion for the 'Albanian' and the mingled guilt and tenderness she feels towards her fiancé Guglielmo.

Fiordiligi then reveals a newly awakened understanding of her sexuality in her duet with Ferrando. Convention demanded that the original pairings should be restored. However, the emotional journeys undertaken by Fiordiligi and, to a lesser degree, Ferrando make this an unconvincing 'happy end', a feeling reinforced by the finale's hollow burst of C major.

Così fan tutte ('That's Women for You')

by Wolfgang Amadeus Mozart
Composed: 1789–90
Premiered: 1790, Vienna
Libretto by Lorenzo Da Ponte

ACT I

Don Alfonso discusses women with his two friends, the young officers Ferrando and Guglielmo. The young men profess the virtue and constancy of their sweethearts, but Don Alfonso maintains that all women are fickle. He lays a wager that if the officers do everything he asks of them, he can prove it to them by the end of the day. Meanwhile, their sweethearts, the sisters Dorabella and Fiordiligi, proclaim their love for Ferrando and Guglielmo as they gaze upon their portraits. Alfonso enters, with the news that the young men must leave to join their regiment. Sure enough, the officers arrive and the lovers sing a heartfelt farewell. Alfonso remains sure of his impending victory.

The sisters' maid, Despina, tells them that all men are fickle and suggests that they find solace in courting others; she is scolded by the indignant sisters. Alfonso then persuades Despina to introduce the sisters to his two 'Albanian' acquaintances; she does not realize that they are in fact Ferrando and Guglielmo in disguise. The two 'foreigners' attempt to woo the sisters, each taking the other's sweetheart, but Fiordiligi and Dorabella declare their fidelity to their lovers and leave. The officers boast of their lovers' constancy but Alfonso warns them that there is still plenty of time. Ferrando sings of his love for Dorabella while Despina helps Alfonso devise a plan to make the sisters fall for the 'strangers'.

Fiordiligi and Dorabella mourn Ferrando and Guglielmo's absence when the 'foreigners' stagger in, declaring that they have poisoned themselves in despair. Fiordiligi and Dorabella begin to soften towards the unfortunate men; Alfonso and Despina go to find a doctor who then appears – it is actually Despina in disguise. The 'doctor' draws the poison from the men with a special magnet and bids Fiordiligi and Dorabella to nurse then back to health. As the men 'recover', their passion for the sisters is renewed but they are again rejected.

ACT II

Despina scolds Fiordiligi and Dorabella for their stubbornness and advises them on dealing with men. She persuades them to indulge in a little harmless flirtation and the sisters decide which of the men to court, each choosing the other's original lover. A serenade is arranged in the garden. Guglielmo successfully courts Dorabella, persuading her to relinquish her portrait of Ferrando. Meanwhile, Ferrando courts Fiordiligi with less success, although when alone she confesses that she has feelings for him.

The young men compare their progress. Guglielmo, relieved that Fiordiligi appears to be faithful, reluctantly shows Ferrando his portrait that Dorabella has surrendered and sings of the fickle nature of women. Ferrando laments Dorabella's betrayal and reveals that he still loves her. Guglielmo, thinking that he has won the wager, has to be reminded again by Alfonso that the day is not yet over.

Fiordiligi scolds Dorabella for her infidelity but eventually admits that she too has fallen for her 'foreigner'. Alone, Fiordiligi plans to run away and join Guglielmo, but Ferrando enters and manages to seduce her. Alfonso explains to a furious Guglielmo that this is the way of women.

A double wedding is arranged. As the sisters, at the instigation of the notary – Despina in another disguise – sign the marriage contracts, fanfares are heard in the distance signalling the return of the regiment. Fiordiligi and Dorabella panic and force their new husbands out of the room, who then return as Ferrando and Guglielmo. When they find out about the wedding, the officers appear enraged, but go on to reveal the true identities of the 'foreigners'. Alfonso then explains the deception and encourages everyone to learn from the experience.

Recommended Recording:

Così fan tutte, English Baroque Soloists; John Eliot Gardiner, conductor; Deutsche Grammophon 073 026–9AH2; Soloists: Amanda Roocroft (Fiordiligi), Rosa

Mannion (Dorabella), Eirian James (Despina), Rainer Trost (Ferrando), Rodney Gilfry (Guglielmo), Claudio Nicolai (Don Alfonso)

Die Zauberflöte

The librettist of *Die Zauberflöte*, Emanuel Schikaneder, Mozart's old friend and fellow freemason, drew on an eclectic variety of sources, including a French novel, *Sethos*, Paul Wranitzky's magic opera *Oberon* (1789) and the oriental fairy tale *Lulu*. In the bird catcher Papageno, Schikaneder created for himself a character that could exploit his talent for milking an audience; and in early performances he predictably stole the show, abetted by Mozart's own antics on the glockenspiel.

Stylistically *Die Zauberflöte* is the most heterogeneous opera in the repertoire, juxtaposing pantomime and grave masonic ritual, solemn fairy tale and earthy Viennese humour. Yet the power of Mozart's music ensures that there is no sense of incongruity. Among the 'low' characters, the children of nature, Papageno and Papagena, contrast with the Moor Monostatos, who sings in a frenetic *buffo* style. The hard glitter of the Queen of Night's music is set against the grave nobility of the numbers for Sarastro and the priests. At the centre are the two lovers, Pamina and Tamino, and it is they who, in the two extended finales, dominate the opera's crucial scenes. The spiritual climax is the trial scene in the second finale, beginning with the Lutheran chorale of the two Armed Men and culminating in the lovers' final union. Pamina's 'Tamino mein!' is the most sublime moment in the work, and the inspiring embodiment of its central message of human enlightenment and redemption.

Die Zauberflöte ('The Magic Flute')
by Wolfgang Amadeus Mozart
Composed: 1791
Premiered: 1791, Vienna
Libretto by Emanuel Schikaneder

ACT I

Prince Tamino, trying to escape a serpent, faints. Three ladies-in-waiting to the Queen of Night, in whose realm the action takes place, appear, kill the serpent and then leave. Papageno, the Queen's feathered bird catcher, arrives and tells Tamino, who has regained consciousness, that it was he who saved him. The ladies then reappear, padlocking Papageno's mouth and showing Tamino a portrait of Pamina, the Queen of Night's daughter. Tamino falls in love with Pamina and is told that she has been imprisoned by the evil Sarastro. The Queen of Night appears, lamenting the loss of her daughter. She promises Pamina to Tamino if he and Papageno will rescue her. The ladies remove the padlock from Papageno's mouth and issue him with some magic chimes to ensure his safety; to Tamino they give a magic flute. They are also to be accompanied by three Genii.

In Sarastro's palace, the Moor Monostatos is forcing his attentions upon Pamina. Papageno appears, frightening Monostatos away. He recognizes Pamina, and tells her of Tamino's love for her and her imminent rescue. The three Genii lead Tamino to three temples. He enters one and encounters a High Priest, who reveals that Sarastro is not evil, but a wise and noble man. Tamino

plays the magic flute and charms the wild animals. He hears Papageno's panpipes and goes to find him.

Papageno enters with Pamina. They are almost captured by Monostatos, but Papageno uses his magic chimes to overcome the Moor. As Pamina and Papageno celebrate their escape, a chorus is heard in praise of Sarastro, who then enters in a procession. Pamina explains that they were running away from Monostatos. The Moor then appears with Tamino, expecting to be rewarded by Sarastro, but is instead punished. Pamina falls in love with Tamino. Papageno and Tamino are then taken into the temple to learn how to qualify for higher happiness.

ACT II

Sarastro announces his intentions. Papageno and Tamino are to undergo the initiation process in order to gain admission to the Temple of Light and thereby overpower the Queen of Night. Tamino is then free to wed Pamina, who is to be held in Sarastro's protection for the time being. At the temple, Papageno and Tamino are preparing to undergo their first ordeal: a vow of silence. The ladies-in-waiting try unsuccessfully to trick them into speaking.

In the garden, Monostatos creeps up on the sleeping Pamina. The Queen of Night appears, giving her daughter a dagger with which to kill Sarastro. Monostatos threatens Pamina, but Sarastro arrives and dismisses him. Tamino is still trying to keep his vow of silence. Papageno talks to himself, before entering into conversation with an old lady who claims to be a lover he has yet to meet. She vanishes and the Genii appear, arranging a feast. Pamina arrives and, not knowing of Tamino's vow of silence, is hurt by his apparent coldness.

Sarastro comforts Pamina. Papageno is visited again by the old lady, who makes him swear to be faithful to her. When he swears, she turns into Papagena, a beautiful young feathered woman, but Papageno is told that *he is not yet ready. Pamina considers suicide, but is prevented by the Genii. Tamino enters for the final ordeals of his initiation: those of fire and water. Pamina accompanies him as he undergoes the tests; he can now speak again. In a parody of the previous events, Papageno too contemplates suicide, but changes his mind when Papagena is brought to him. At the Temple of Light, the Queen of Night, her ladies-in-waiting and Monostatos try to wreak revenge on Sarastro, but are destroyed. Tamino and Pamina, who have passed the ordeals, are accepted into the community.*

Recommended Recording:
Die Zauberflöte, Ludwigsburg Festival; Wolfgang Gönnenwein, conductor; ArtHaus Musik 100 188 and 189; Soloists: Ulrike Sonntag (Pamina), Andrea Frei (Queen of Night), Deon van der Walt (Tamino), Thomas Mohr (Papageno), Cornelius Hauptmann (Sarastro)

La clemenza di Tito

Premiered in Prague on 6 September 1791, Mozart's last opera is based on an old Metastasio libretto, updated (with added ensembles and choruses) for contemporary taste. Popular in the early nineteenth century, it then went into eclipse. Nowadays, though, *La clemenza di Tito* is valued on its own terms rather than as a pale successor to the much more expansive *Idomeneo*. While the music for the enlightened Emperor Tito has a certain chilly formality, that for the vacillating Sesto and, especially, the manipulative, ultimately remorseful Vitellia is richly expressive. Two other highlights, in a score characterized by a neo-classical purity, economy and restraint, are the exquisite farewell duet for Annio and Servilia 'Ah perdona' ('Ah, forgive') and the moving finale to the first act. This does the opposite of what we expect from an operatic finale, beginning in turmoil and ending with an elegiac andante.

La clemenza di Tito
('Titus' Clemency')
by Wolfgang Mozart
Composed: 1791
Premiered: 1791, Prague
Libretto by Caterino Tommaso Mazzolà, after Pietro Metastasio

ACT I
Vitellia, daughter of the deposed Roman emperor Vitellius, wants to become empress. She persuades Sesto, who loves her, to assassinate the emperor, Tito, if he marries Berenice, whom he loves. News comes that Tito is sending Berenice away because he must marry a true Roman, and her hopes are revived. Sesto's friend Annio asks for his sister Servilia's hand. Sesto agrees and they swear eternal friendship.

Tito enters and the people pay homage. He declares his determination to rule by kindness and to reward virtue. He then tells Annio that he has decided to marry Servilia; Annio, crestfallen, goes to tell her and bid farewell to her and to his hopes. However, Servilia does not accept the situation and courageously goes to tell Tito of her and Annio's love; he commends her candour and releases her. Vitellia, learning that Tito has selected Servilia, is enraged. She despatches Sesto to set the assassination in train. Reluctantly, but blindly obedient to her wishes, he agrees. Then Annio arrives with Publio, head of the Praetorian Guard: they tell Vitellia that she is the chosen empress. She is shocked and bewildered but cannot now call off the plot. The Capitol is on fire: Sesto and his friends have set the plot in motion. He returns, believing Tito dead, and wracked by guilt. All gather to mourn the emperor's death; Sesto makes to confess his role but Vitellia silences him.

ACT II
Annio tells Sesto that Tito has survived. Sesto admits he initiated the plot but will not explain why; Annio urges him to confess to Tito. It is too late however: Publio comes to

arrest him. Sesto bids Vitellia farewell. The people assemble to give thanks for Tito's survival. Tito learns that Sesto is implicated and has been arrested and condemned to death by the Senate. Annio pleads for him. Tito summons him: surely there must be some rational explanation. Sesto cannot face his former friend (and cannot betray Vitellia); before his dismissal, he begs Tito to remember their friendship. Tito ponders: should he be merciful? Servilia pleads to Vitellia to intercede. Vitellia faces up to her dilemma: can she wed Tito, and let Sesto die? No, she must confess her role. The people acclaim the emperor. Tito intends to spare Sesto, but Vitellia steps forward and owns her responsibility. The magnanimous Tito spares everyone, and all join to praise his clemency.

OPERAS

1770	Mitridate, rè di Ponto K87/74a
1772	Lucio Silla K135
1775	La finta giardiniera K196
1775	Il rè pastore K208
1780–81	Idomeneo K366, revised 1786
1781–82	Die Entführung aus dem Serail K384
1786	Le nozze di Figaro K492
1787	Don Giovanni K527
1789–90	Così fan tutte K588
1791	Die Zauberflöte K620
1791	La clemenza di Tito K621

TIMELINE

1756	Wolfgang Amadeus Mozart born in Salzburg
1762	Performs at the Vienna court
1763	Tour of western Europe begins,
1770	Mitridate, rè di Ponto commissioned, written and premiered in Milan
1772	Premiere of Lucio Silla, Milan
1778	Visits to Mannheim and Paris
1781	Premiere of Idomeneo, Munich
1782	Premiere of Die Entführung aus dem Serail, Vienna; marries Constanze Weber
1784	Joins the Freemasons, which influenced his writing, most notably in Die Zauberflöte
1786	Premiere of Le nozze di Figaro, Vienna; Idomeneo revived, Vienna
1787	Premiere of Don Giovanni, Prague; becomes Chamber Composer to the court at Vienna
1789	Travels to Dresden, Leipzig and Berlin
1790	Premiere of Così fan tutte, Vienna
1791	Premieres of Die Zauberflöte, Vienna and La clemenza di Tito, Prague (allegedly written in just 18 days); Requiem composed; death of Mozart

Pacchierotti, Gasparo
1740–1821, ITALIAN

The Italian soprano castrato Gasparo Pacchierotti made his debut in Venice in 1766 in *Achille in Sciro* by Gassmann. He had joined the Teatro San Giovanni Grisostomo the previous year and after another six years he moved to the Teatro San Carlo in Naples. Pacchierotti made his first appearance at the King's Theatre, London in 1778, where he created a sensation. His triumphs in London were considered unparalleled. Also in 1778, he sang at the inauguration of the Teatro alla Scala in Milan. Pacchierotti's repertoire included Orpheus in Gluck's opera, and roles in operas by Jommelli. Haydn was impressed by Pacchierotti's beautiful voice, wide range, virtuosity and acting ability, and picked him to sing in his cantata *Arianna a Naxos*. Two years later, Pacchierotti sang at the inauguration of the Teatro la Fenice in Venice, but soon afterwards he retired to Padua.

Paisiello, Giovanni
1740–1816, ITALIAN

Giovanni Paisiello scored his first successes in *opera buffa*. Compositions such as *L'idolo cinese* ('The Chinese Idol', 1767) were performed to enthusiastic audiences all over Italy. Paisiello's talents rivalled those of other prominent composers, such as Cimarosa. Like Cimarosa and others, he caught the interest of Empress Catherine of Russia, who invited Paisiello to St Petersburg in 1776. Paisiello established the Italian opera tradition at Catherine's court and wrote two operas in the same year – *Lucinda ed Armidoro* and *Nitteti* (both 1777). He also wrote his own 'Figaro' opera, *Il barbiere di Siviglia*. Opera audiences loved it, so much so that Rossini had considerable trouble breaking down popular prejudice against his own *Il barbiere*, written in 1816 – the year Paisiello died.

Paisiello returned to Italy in 1784 and while on the way, in Vienna, he composed *Il re Teodoro in Venezia* ('King Theodore in Venice', 1784). Paisiello was appointed *maestro di cappella* to King Ferdinand IV in Naples in 1783, and it was here that he wrote one of his best-loved operas, *Nina* (1789). Paisiello wrote more than 80 operas, including several in the *opera buffa* genre that he converted from light, somewhat inconsequential entertainment into something far more dramatic and emotional.

Il barbiere di Siviglia ('The Barber of Seville')

by Giovanni Paisiello
Composed: 1782
Premiered: 1782, St Petersburg
Libretto by Giuseppe Petrosellini, after Pierre-Augustin Caron de Beaumarchais

ACT I

Count Almaviva stands below the window of Rosina, ward of Dr Bartolo, serenading her. Figaro, a self-important barber, arrives. Rosina appears at the window and drops a note for the Count, asking him to introduce himself in song. Figaro tells the Count to gain entry to the house by disguising himself as a drunken soldier. Learning that Rosina will be forced to marry Bartolo the following day, the Count presents himself to her as 'Lindoro'. He offers Figaro money in exchange for his help.

ACT II

Figaro tells Rosina of Lindoro's love. She gives him a letter for Lindoro. Bartolo tries to obtain information from his servants, Lo Svegliato and Giovinetto, but Figaro has drugged them. Bartolo's friend Don Basilio enters with news that Count Almaviva is pursuing Rosina and suggests that they slander him. Figaro warns Rosina of Bartolo's intentions. Bartolo and Basilio find Rosina's letter and forbid her to leave the house. The Count, disguised as a soldier,

arrives demanding lodgings, but Bartolo refuses. In the confusion, the Count passes a note to Rosina; Bartolo sees this and demands to read it but Rosina hands him another paper.

ACT III

The disguised Count arrives, claiming to be a music teacher sent by Don Basilio, and gives Rosina her music lesson. Figaro enters and the lovers plan their escape; Don Basilio arrives, but leaves with a hefty bribe. Figaro decides to distract Bartolo, but the doctor then recognizes the fake music teacher as Rosina's lover.

ACT IV

Bartolo tells Rosina that her lover is merely an agent for Count Almaviva. Distraught, she agrees to marry Bartolo; he sends Basilio to fetch a notary. Figaro and the Count arrive, ready to flee through the window with Rosina. She refuses until the Count reveals his true identity. Bartolo steals their ladder, trapping them. Basilio enters with the notary and, after some bribery, Rosina and the Count are married. Bartolo arrives too late and is forced to accept the situation.

Philidor, François-André Danican

1726–95, FRENCH

Philidor was more or less forced into writing *opéras comiques* once his earlier, Italian, style got him banned from the Paris Opéra in 1756. Philidor adapted splendidly. He soon became a successful composer in this typically French genre, producing *Blaise le savetier* ('Blaise the Cobbler', 1759) and *Le Sorcier* ('The Sorcerer', 1764). At a performance of *Le Sorcier*, Philidor became the first composer to take a curtain call. However, like his later opera *Ernelinde, princesse de Norvège* ('Ernelinde, Princess of Norway', 1767), *Le Sorcier* sailed perhaps too close to plagiarism due to the influence exerted by the work of Gluck, whom Philidor greatly admired. Nevertheless, Philidor's contribution to *opéra comique* was impressive: melodies acquired greater character and his deft use of modulation coloured the musical harmonies to significant effect. Philidor was innovative too, though this was not always welcome to audiences. The unaccompanied canon quartet for his opera *Tom Jones* (1765), taken from Henry Fielding's story of the same name, was at first too much of a novelty for audiences and it was booed. Later the opera was recognized as Philidor's masterpiece. Philidor also included everyday sounds in his scores – a hammer striking metal or a donkey braying.

Ernelinde, princesse de Norvège ('Ernelinde, Princess of Norway')

by François-André Danican Philidor
Composed: 1767
Premiered: 1767, Paris
Libretto by Antonine Alexandre Henri Poinsinet after Francesco Silvani's libretto *La fede tradita, e vendicata*

PROLOGUE

The brother of Ricimer, King of the Goths (Sweden), has been killed by Rodoald, King of Norway. In revenge, Ricimer has attacked Rodoald's capital at Nidaros (now Trondheim). Sandomir, Prince of Denmark, is in alliance with Ricimer, even though he is betrothed to Rodoald's daughter Ernelinde.

ACT I

Nidaros has fallen and Ernelinde is found as the town is being sacked. Sandomir promises to defend her against any harm. The victorious Ricimer, who also wants to marry Ernelinde, enters and has a violent quarrel with Sandomir. Even though he has been taken prisoner, Rodoald forbids Ernelinde to have anything to do with Ricimer.

ACT II

In order to get rid of his rival, Ricimer orders Sandomir's arrest. He then tells Ernelinde that either her father or her lover must die: the choice is hers. Ernelinde is in torment, but eventually decides that she must save her father. After she has told Ricimer her decision and Rodoald has been released, however, she is stricken with remorse and sees a vision of her lover reproaching her for abandoning him to his fate.

ACT III

Ernelinde visits Sandomir in prison and they resolve to die together before the altars of Odin and Frigga. Rodoald, meanwhile, has rallied his troops and the Danes loyal to Sandomir. He arrives just in time to prevent the double suicide. Ricimer is overthrown, but Sandomir spares his life. Through his marriage with Ernelinde, Sandomir will now inherit the kingdoms of Denmark, Norway and Sweden.

Piccinni, Niccolò
1728–1800, ITALIAN

Le donne dispettose ('The Spiteful Women', 1754) was Piccinni's first opera and was received with great enthusiasm. The eventual composer of some 120 works, he went on as he had begun, scoring several successes that climaxed with his masterpiece, *La buona figliuola*. Receiving its premiere in Naples, another of Piccinni's operas, *I viaggiatori* ('The Travellers', 1775) was particularly well liked. At around this time there was resistance in France to the reforms promulgated by Gluck, who had introduced a mixture of music, dance and mime into opera among other 'unwelcome' innovations. Unfortunately, Piccinni became the stick with which this faction sought to beat Gluck. The Italian was invited to Paris in 1776, where he was obliged to enter a contest with Gluck, in which both of them wrote an opera, *Iphigénie en Tauride*. Piccinni lost out, and Gluck's 1779 version eclipsed Piccinni's, which was produced in 1781. After Gluck, another rival for Piccinni – Antonio Sacchini (1730–86) – arrived in Paris. Although the success of Piccinni's *Didon* (1783) masked the truth, as a composer he was in decline. He has been mainly remembered for his *opera buffa*, his beautiful melodies and harmonies, and his skilful orchestration.

La buona figliuola ('The Good-Natured Girl')
by Niccolò Piccinni
Composed: 1760
Premiered: 1760, Rome
Libretto by Carlo Goldoni, after Samuel Richardson's novel *Pamela*

ACT I
Cecchina, a servant girl, is secretly in love with the Marchese della Conchiglia. Believing that her dream will never come true, she runs away when he confesses his own affections for her. He asks one of the maids, Sandrina, to assure Cecchina of his intentions, but she also once had hopes of the Marchese and is now jealous that the servant Mengotto also loves Cecchina. Sandrina warns the Cavaliere Armidoro, who is engaged to the Marchese's sister Lucinda, that the Marchese is to marry a common gardener with no known parents, and a foreigner. To prevent this spoiling her own coming marriage, Lucinda arranges for Cecchina to leave the household. The Marchese discovers her in tears and declares his love. Mengotto offers Cecchina his love again, but the Marchese surprises them together and rejects Cecchina.

ACT II
The Marchese regrets his jealousy, but by now Cecchina has been arrested on Armidoro's orders. Mengotto rescues her from the armed escort, but the Marchese arrives and takes her away, leaving Mengotto ready to commit suicide. He is stopped by Tagliaferro, a

German soldier looking for Mariandel, his colonel's daughter, who was lost there 20 years ago. Lucinda is made to believe that the worst is happening, but in fact Cecchina still refuses the Marchese. Tagliaferro tells the Marchese that Cecchina is indeed Mariandel. Together they come across Cecchina asleep, dreaming of her father.

ACT III
To the satisfaction of Armidoro and Lucinda, the Marchese announces that he is to marry a German noblewoman and persuades Cecchina of her true identity, confirmed by a blue mark on her breast. Mengotto consoles himself with Sandrina.

Raaff, Anton
1714–97, GERMAN
The German tenor Anton Raaff studied in both Germany and Italy and made his debut in Munich in 1736. There followed performances in Italy in 1739, Bonn and Frankfurt in 1742 and in Vienna in 1749, where, according to Metastasio, he 'sang like an angel'. Raaff went on to perform in Madrid in 1755 and Naples in 1759. In 1770, he entered the service of Carl Theodor, the Elector Palatine. When Mozart first heard Raaff he was not impressed, but changed his mind and wrote an aria especially for him. Raaff returned the compliment and asked the elector to commission *Idomeneo* from Mozart. *Idomeneo* was produced in Munich in 1781, and Mozart wrote the title role with Raaff's vocal qualities in mind. One rare quality Raaff's voice possessed was longevity: it was still in top condition in 1787, when he was 73.

Rousseau, Jean-Jacques
1712–78, SWISS
Best known as the Swiss political philosopher with a crucial influence on Romanticism and the French Revolution, Jean-Jacques Rousseau was also a composer, author and musicologist. In his most famous work, *Le devin du village*

('The Village Soothsayer', 1752), Rousseau's small talent confined him to simple melodies with simple accompaniments. What was really important was the way his liberal outlook in politics coloured his plot and its characters. *Le devin du village* demonstrated how simple, honest, virtuous, country folk overcame the corrupt, cynical aristocracy – an idealized, sentimental but recognizable metaphor for the revolution of 1789. In addition to Rousseau's influence on the cast list of operas, in which simple folk were given more prominence, he was partly responsible for the increasing importance of the orchestra in early Romantic opera, where the instrumentalists were able to depict natural events – storm, rain, wind – when they were part of the plot.

Salieri, Antonio
1750–1825, **ITALIAN**

When he was 16, Antonio Salieri was the protégé of the Bohemian composer Florian Gassmann (1729–74), who brought him to Vienna in 1766. Gassmann was influential at the imperial court and, as well as teaching Salieri composition, introduced him to some very high-ranking contacts. Salieri's first surviving opera, written when he was 20, was *Le donne letterate* ('The Cultured Ladies', 1770). It was a success, so much so that only four years later, Salieri – still only 24 – was appointed court composer to the Austrian Emperor Joseph II.

In 1784, he succeeded Gluck at the Paris Opéra, where he was regarded as Gluck's true successor. His exalted, original and rather austere post-Gluckian operas, *Les Danaïdes* ('The Danaids', 1784) and *Tarare* (1787), were his greatest accomplishments while in Paris. In 1788, he became *Kapellmeister* to the Austrian court, and in this post Salieri was in charge of Italian opera. Salieri's life and work was now centred on Vienna, where he wrote some 30 operas, including both

opera seria and *opera buffa*, including *La fiera di Venezia* ('The Fair of Venice', 1772) and *Falstaff* (1799), although he was interested in combining both elements in a single work. Most Salieri operas were produced in Vienna, but he also scored much success in Milan, Venice and Rome. Salieri's output observed the musical conventions of his era and show Gluck's influence, with accompanied recitative, dramatic choral writing and careful declamation. His popularity, considerable in his lifetime, failed to endure once that era was past.

Les Danaïdes ('The Danaids')
by Antonio Salieri
Composed: 1784
Premiered: 1784, Paris
Libretto by François Louis Gand Leblanc Roullet, after Raniero de' Calzabigi

The opera is based on a Greek myth. Under the guise of an act of reconciliation, the daughters of Danaus (the Danaids) have been betrothed to the sons of Danaus's brother and enemy, Aegyptus, who is now dead. They swear an oath of friendship. Hypermnestra, the eldest daughter, loves Lynceus, the eldest son. However, Danaus tells his daughters that the marriages are a trick and part of his scheme to secure revenge. They must kill their husbands on their wedding night and, at his command, they take an oath to Nemesis, goddess of vengeance. All must conform or, the oracle has foretold, he himself will die. Hypermnestra does not take the oath, but her father demands that she too kill her husband. In her dilemma she prays for guidance and for death.

The wedding is celebrated with singing and dancing. Hypermnestra comes close to warning Lynceus of the plot. She pleads vainly to her father for mercy for Lynceus. After the wedding celebrations she tells Lynceus that they must part. Then they hear his brothers' cries, off stage, as they are attacked by their brides. Danaus tells them to pursue Lynceus, but he has fled: he returns to attack the palace and he slays the Danaids, finishing by burning down the palace. Hypermnestra faints. In the final scene the Danaids are seen in the underworld, with the Furies promising them eternal torment; Danaus is chained to a rock and a vulture attacks his entrails.

Schikaneder, Emanuel
1751–1812, **AUSTRIAN**

Emanuel Schikaneder spent his early years as a nomadic musician, until he encountered a travelling theatrical troupe in Augsburg. He married the director's daughter and eventually took over the management of the troupe. However, Schikaneder was not just an opportunist with an eye for the boss's daughter and the boss's job. The eventual author of 50 libretti, including Mozart's last opera, *Die Zauberflöte*, Schikaneder ranked among the most talented comic singer-actors of his day. His meeting with Mozart, which took place in Salzburg in 1780 while the troupe was on tour, proved fortuitous. Some years later, Schikaneder was in all sorts of trouble while running theatres in Regensburg and Vienna. He sank deep in debt, but was saved from financial ruin by the success of *Die Zauberflöte*. Subsequently, Schikaneder returned to theatrical management, but in 1806 he suddenly went mad and had to leave Vienna.

Shield, William
1748–1829, **ENGLISH**

William Shield, who was both composer and librettist, belonged to a trio of musicians (with Charles Dibdin and Stephen Storace) who dominated the English comic opera stage in the late eighteenth century. Shield started out as an apprentice boat builder, but moved on to become a violinist. In 1772, he arrived in London from the north of England to take up a position of leader of the viola section of the Haymarket theatre orchestra.

Shield's first work was an 'afterpiece' called *The Flitch of Bacon* (1778). *The Flitch* was very successful and set up him as a popular composer, much-liked and admired by London audiences. Shield's output included more than 50 works, both full-length operas and afterpieces. Most of these were written for performance at Covent Garden, where Shield was the house composer for 13 years. As their titles indicate – *The Magic Cavern* (1784), *The Enchanted Castle* (1786) and *The Crusade* (1790) – a fair number of Shield's pieces dealt with exotic or magical themes and catered for the contemporary English taste for fantasy. In addition to writing his own works, Shield made adaptations of Grétry's *Richard Coeur-de-Lion*.

Storace, Nancy
1766–1817, **ENGLISH**

The English soprano Nancy Storace was the sister of the composer Stephen Storace and sang in his operas at Drury Lane, London, from 1789 until his death in 1796. Nancy was only 10 years old when she made her debut as Cupid in *Le ali d'amore* by Venanzio Rauzzini (1746–1810). Five years later, in Florence, Nancy outmatched the castrato soprano Luigi Marchesi (1755–1829). Marchesi was one of the greatest contemporary castrati, with a sizeable ego to match, and Storace had to go. In 1783, Storace's gift for comedy was earning her great popularity in Vienna, where Mozart was impressed by her. He started to write a part for her, as Emilia in *Lo sposo deluso* ('The Deceived Bridegroom') but the opera was unfinished. However, Susanna in Mozart's *Le nozze di Figaro* was also written for Storace and was one of her greatest successes.

Storace, Stephen
1762–96, **ENGLISH**

The English composer Stephen Storace wrote his first two operas – *Gli sposi malcontenti* ('The Discontented

Newlyweds', 1785) and *Gli equivoci* ('The Misunderstandings', 1786) – for Vienna. His next two works, written for London after 1787, were not particularly successful, and subsequently Storace concentrated on English dialogue operas, either full-length or in the form of short afterpieces. Storace's normal practice was to borrow music from other operas and sometimes from his own. Another of his methods was to rework operas written by other composers. This is what he did with, for example, *Doktor und Apotheker* ('Doctor and Apothecary', 1788) by Karl Ditters von Dittersdorf (1739–99).

Success arrived at last with Storace's full-length opera *The Haunted Tower* (1789), which packed Drury Lane with enthusiastic audiences and counted among the most popular operas staged during the entire eighteenth century. This opera alone earned Storace a reputation as a leading theatre composer and the standard-bearer for a practice he considered vital to the success of an opera: close collaboration between composer and librettist. This, though, was no democratic arrangement: as Storace's own opera *The Pirates* (1792) indicates, the effect in practice was to increase the importance of the music, while the words were of lesser standing.

Traetta, Tommaso
1727–79, **ITALIAN**

The Italian composer Tommaso Traetta reflected Gluck's ideals for opera, in which orchestration, choral scenes, dance and solo arias were combined. One example of these principles was Traetta's setting of an Italian translation of the text Rameau had used in his own *Hippolyte et Aricie* ('Hippolytus and Aricia', 1759), which married the French and Italian opera styles. However, Traetta was much more than a copyist. He had a gift for impressive chorus work, as shown in his *Ifigenia in Tauride* (1763). Just as admirable was his

symphonic treatment of operatic themes and his ability to write graceful melody; this last was admirably displayed in his short solo songs known as cavatinas and in his *da capo* arias. Traetta's early operas were written in the main for Naples and Parma, but in 1765 he moved to Venice, where his output included two comic operas. In 1768, Traetta became another composer to be tempted from Western Europe to Russia, where Catherine the Great appointed him director of opera. For the Russian court, Traetta wrote *Antigona* (1772), based on an ancient Greek tragedy. However, life in Russia had a bad effect on his health and he departed in 1775. He died four years later in Venice.

Verazi, Mattia
c. 1730–94, **ITALIAN**

Mattia Verazi was the author of around 20 libretti, most of them written for performance in Italy. Among the first was *Ifigenia in Aulide* (1751), which was set to music by Jommelli. Some 10 years later, Verazi was at the court in Mannheim, which later moved to Munich. Verazi went too. The most important libretti that he wrote while in Munich included *Sofonisba* (1762), written for music by Traetta, and an ancient Roman subject, *Lucio Silla* (1775), which Verazi wrote for Johann Christian Bach. Verazi did not confine himself to the Munich court, but wrote for other noble patrons, including *Fetonte* (1768) for the Duke of Württemberg. This, too, was set by Jommelli, who used it to write one of his most inventive scores. Verazi and Jommelli frequently worked as a team and between them created several dramatic French-style operas for the ducal court at Stuttgart.

❈ **THE SONATA PRINCIPLE** ∾ **p. 120**

One of Mozart's most brilliant achievements in his mature operas is the way he harnesses the symphonic energies and key structures of the Classical sonata style to reveal character and propel the action forward. The sextet from *Figaro* is a famous example: here the sonata design is a perfect musical equivalent of the stage action as the initial situation spawns confusion, discord (in the central 'development') and, with the restoration of the original key of F major, eventual reconciliation.

Another sextet, in Act II of *Don Giovanni*, is an equally inspired manipulation of the sonata principle. It begins in E flat as Elvira and Leporello (disguised as Don Giovanni) grope their way in the darkness, and modulates to the 'tensing' dominant, B flat, as Leporello becomes ever more agitated. Then, with a breathtaking shift to D major (enhanced by the solemn new sonority of trumpets and drums), Donna Anna and Don Ottavio enter. The tonality darkens to D minor (the opera's key of death and retribution) when Anna remembers her dead father; and a far-ranging development culminates in the glorious comic-dramatic moment of Leporello's 'unmasking'. Confusion yields to unanimous denunciation of Don Giovanni. The accumulated harmonic tensions are released in a long E flat molto allegro that emphasizes the basic chords of tonic and dominant.

❈ RECONCILIATION AND REDEMPTION ∾ p. 120

All Mozart's operas, from *Idomeneo* to *La clemenza di Tito*, are touched by a Shakespearean wisdom and compassion. In the spirit of the eighteenth-century Enlightenment, tolerance, forgiveness and reconciliation lie at the heart of each of these works, sometimes encapsulated in music of sublime, transfiguring stillness. The hushed reflections on forgiveness in the two finales of *Die Entführung auf dem Serail*, and the Countess's pardon of her errant husband at the climax of *Figaro* are all the more poignant for the animation that surrounds them. Equally, the final

union of Pamina and Tamino in *Die Zauberflöte*, initiated by a magical change of key, is a moment of rarefied loveliness that confirms the depth and truth of the opera's central message. In the outwardly cynical, worldly *Così fan tutte*, such numbers as the 'farewell' quintet and trio in Act I transform the potentially ridiculous into transcendent beauty. Donna Elvira in *Don Giovanni* begins as an object of mockery. But Mozart infuses her music in the second act, above all in the trio 'Ah taci, ingiusto core' ('Be still, unjust heart'), with profound tenderness. His characters may be frail, self-centred and absurd, but through Mozart's music they are ennobled and redeemed.

❈ VAUDEVILLE ∾ p. 165

Vaudevilles, which took melodies from well-known operas, were popular tunes incorporated into works performed at venues such as the Comédie-Italienne in Paris. The vaudeville – taken from *voix de ville*, 'voice of the town', had its own identifiable pattern. Its title was the same as the first line of the melody: this, in turn, was the first line as it appeared in the original opera. In the sixteenth century, 'vaudeville' described a short song, usually on the subject of love. The melody was simple and repeated rhythms were a regular feature of the vaudeville. These tunes were sometimes called *fredons*, from the French verb *fredonner*, to hum, or *Pont du Neuf* melodies, after the broad bridge over the River Seine where minstrels gathered. When incorporated into opera, the mix of music and drama greatly influenced the development of *opéra comique*, which included parodied versions of serious opera and other satirical material, some of it political. The vaudeville itself could be backed up by a vaudeville finale, in which the stanzas are shared out between each character and are then performed, ensemble-style, by the whole cast singing together.

◉ A ROYAL PATRON OF OPERA
～ p. 125

A composer, librettist or other musician who attracted a royal patron acquired personal influence as a result. In Germany, this great good fortune devolved on anyone favoured by King Frederick II ('The Great') of Prussia. Frederick was an immensely powerful and able ruler and a rigid disciplinarian and it was inevitable that he approached his great interest, *opera seria*, as a demanding martinet. His control over operas performed in Berlin was unprecedented, even in an age of royal despotism. No libretto could reach Frederick's composers, Hasse or Graun,unless the king had seen and approved it first. He also composed his own plots for operas and insisted on supervising the design of the stage sets and costumes. He was a constant – and daunting – presence at rehearsals, where he halted proceedings if one of the singers deviated even slightly from the agreed score. However, Frederick's 'reign' as master of Berlin opera was relatively brief. After the outbreak of the Seven Years' War in 1756, all opera staff were dismissed and Berlin's influence on *opera seria* came to an end.

ℰ DOCTRINE OF THE AFFECTIONS
～ p. 121

The 'doctrine of the affections' was the main theory for the design of opera in the eighteenth century. Its name was not coined until the twentieth century, but the ideas behind it were discussed in the writings of theorists such as Johann Mattheson (1681–1764). These ideas were put into practice on stage by the famous librettists Zeno and, in the following generation, Metastasio. The doctrine defined specific 'affections' or emotions, such as love, hate, sorrow, despair or hope. Each of these 'affections' was given exclusive rights to its own musical feature – a movement, aria or choral passage, for example. The arrangement may strike modern listeners as artificial and repetitive. However, the set pattern made it easy to identify which feelings were going to be explored and prepared audiences for what they were about to hear. The 'doctrine of the affections' also enabled arias to be easily moved from one work to the next where the actual music would change, but the mood and the emotion would remain the same.

ℰ THE PURSUIT OF DRAMATIC TRUTH ～ p. 125

Two crucial figures in Gluck's operatic career were the controller of the Viennese theatres Count Durazzo and the Francophile poet and librettist Raniero de' Calzabigi. Both were intent on the reform and revitalization of Italian opera. In Gluck they found their perfect musical collaborator.

Some of Gluck's Italian stage works had already begun to integrate solos and chorus, but it was in his three Italian 'reform' operas – *Orfeo*, *Alceste* and *Paride ed Elena* – that broke most boldly with tradition. In the famous preface to *Alceste*, probably co-written with Calzabigi, the composer resolved to divest music of 'all those abuses, introduced by the misguided vanity of singers or the excessive complaisance of composers that have so long disfigured Italian opera'. The Byzantine plots and sub-plots and 'useless superfluity of ornaments' of *opera seria* were ditched in favour of concentration, classical simplicity and the direct expression of profound emotion.

Gluck could, however, occasionally backslide. The Italian *Alceste* contains dramatically dispensable roles for two confidants (Evandro and Ismene) and stretches of 'dry' recitative, while for the French *Orphée* he pandered to the 'misguided vanity' of the star tenor, Joseph Legros, and gave him a brilliant **coloratura** showpiece to end the first act.

EARLY ROMANTIC

The early nineteenth century was a period of insurgence in Europe, beginning with the French Revolution in 1789 to the uprisings in 1848. The Industrial Revolution, which began in Britain before spreading south to the rest of Europe, was also making its mark. These two strands of revolution caused transformations in society: growing awareness of national identity, social development, growth of cities and important technological advances – all of which were reflected in the arts.

The first two decades of the nineteenth century also marked a rejection of the scientific certainty that had defined the Enlightenment: symmetry, classical balance and simplicity were replaced gradually by Romantic expressivity, individualism and grand gestures. Distinctive traits – many of which derived from French philosopher Jean-Jacques Rousseau's writings – included an interest in nature, the supernatural, the relatively recent past (the Middle Ages in particular) and individual and national identity. Closer links were forged between the arts and social and political reality. In literature, Goethe's Faust and Walter Scott's chivalric novels were seen as an embodiment of the age. Of all the arts, it was music that came to be seen as the ideal means of expression, partly because of its ambiguous, indefinable quality.

Classical structures were retained in music throughout this period, but were expanded upon, and new ways to shock or move were sought. Opera increasingly used realistic settings and historical events for its subjects; orchestral music

was inspired by historical or literary themes, and virtuoso concertos and intimate mood pieces focused on the expression of the individual. The most influential developments in opera took place in Italy and France, and instrumental music flourished in German-speaking lands.

KEY EVENTS

1808	Part I of Goethe's *Faust* published
1812	French invasion of Russia
1815	French defeated at Waterloo; Napoleon is exiled and Bourbon monarchy restored in France and the Vienna Peace Settlement is signed; Johann Nepomuk Maelzel patents his metronome
1820	Revolts crushed in Naples, Spain and Portugal
1822	Greek War of Independence begins following an uprising against the Turks the previous year
1824	Death of Lord Byron at Missolonghi, fighting for the Greeks
1827	Ludwig van Beethoven dies
1829	Stephenson builds the locomotive *Rocket*
1830	July Revolution in France; Belgian revolt reputedly sparked by a performance of Auber's *la muette de Portici*
1831	Michael Faraday discovers electromagnetic induction; circumnavigation by Charles Darwin
1832	Reform Bill passed in Britain; Metternich issues repressive decrees in Germany; Giuseppe Mazzini founds La Giovane Italia with the aim of achieving national independence for Italy; completion of the first continental railway
1837	Death of William IV; Queen Victoria accedes to the British throne; Louis Daguerre invents the daguerrotype, the first practicable process of photography
1840	Death of Friedrich Wilhelm III of Prussia and succession of Friedrich Wilhelm IV
1842	*Gazzetta musicale di Milano* first published in Italy; Verdi's *Nabucco* performed – the choris 'Va pensiero' later becomes the provisional national anthem in Italy
1845	Wagner's *Tannhauser* performed in Dresden

Early Romantic
INTRODUCTION

The **Romantic period in opera, music, literature and art lasted more than a century overall, from around 1790 – the year after the French Revolution – to 1910, four years before the outbreak of the First World War. In this context, the meaning of 'romantic' went far beyond the usual amorous connotations: it stood for the imaginative, the exotic, the fantastic, even the occult. This new ethos drew a line under the Classical era, which emphasized restraint and discipline, balance, good taste and expressiveness, but not the sort that spilled over into sentimentality or blurred too far the edges of musical convention.**

NEW SOCIAL AND POLITICAL IDEAS

In time, Romantic music was revealed as a quantum leap away from the set-piece formulae of Baroque. It was, in its way, a metaphor for the French Revolution that caused a fundamental and ultimately fatal crack in the armour of absolute kingship in Europe. It was not simply a matter of exchanging a monarchy for a republic. The Revolution let loose new social and political ideas, which included the notion that a country belonged not to its king, but to its people. The slogan of the Revolution, 'liberté, egalité, fraternité', and its defiant nationalistic anthem the 'Marseillaise' were only the start of an upheaval that made once-seditious ideas mainstream and one-time heresies respectable.

IDEOLOGY AND MYTHOLOGY

Opera reflected the new situation, in which a particular *bête-noire* was the privilege once reserved for royalty and aristocracy. The ancient Greek and Roman myths, which now lost favour, had been the staple of Baroque opera plots; they were now identified with the unfair social advantages monarchs and nobles had once enjoyed and the exploitation of the peasantry for which their supremacy stood. Kings, queens, emperors and princes ceased to be the heroes or heroines of opera. Their place was taken by stories featuring ordinary people, mainly young men who had sacrificed themselves during the Revolution.

THE ORDINARY HEROES OF 'RESCUE OPERA'

Several such men became the subjects of operas, such as *Le siège de Lille* ('The Siege of Lille', 1792) by Rodolphe Kreutzer (1766–1831), which was staged a month after the siege in question was lifted in October of that year. The new heroes also included victims of political and other persecution and this produced a new genre, the 'rescue opera'. In rescue opera, the plot included the saving of a hero, heroine or a persecuted group from prison or some other dangerous threat. The composer Henri-Monton Berton (1767–1844), for one, lost no time in getting the first of these rescue operas into production, with his *Les rigeurs du cloître* ('The Rigours of the Cloister', 1790). The victims in this opera were monks persecuted by a vengeful authority bent on destroying their way of life.

OPERA AS ENTERTAINMENT

All this meant that opera was in danger of being politicized. If this trend went unchecked, opera could cease to be entertainment and become propaganda. However, the didactic approach did not prove popular even with the patriotic, nationalist audiences in France. They, at least, had not forgotten the role of opera as entertainment, and fortunately there were more subtle ways to inject into the action the social and psychological changes initiated by the Revolution. Four operas by **Etienne-Nicolas Méhul**

(1763–1817) typified this less blatant approach: *Euphrosine* 1790), *Stratonice* (1792), *Mélidore et Phrosine* (1794) and *Ariodant* (1799). These featured characters marooned in isolation by problems of jealousy, frustration or anger – problems they were unable to resolve. Far from being secure, if limited, in the assigned social place as they existed pre-Revolution, these characters were cast adrift in the storm of their own emotions.

This was the essence of Romanticism and the new ethos was reflected in Méhul's music. Unlike some Baroque composers, such as **Antonio Salieri** (1750–1825), Méhul was not afraid to experiment. He believed that expression in music did 'not dwell in melody alone ... everything concurs either to create or destroy it – melody, harmony, modulation, rhythm, instrumentation, the choice of deep or high registers ... a quick or slow tempo'.

DEATH OPERAS

Around this time, at the dawn of Romantic music, Italian as well as French opera was affected by the more realistic, more sober atmosphere that prevailed after the Revolution. This, after all, had been an appallingly bloodthirsty event, in which the fury of the disadvantaged had let loose a tide of manic vengeance, and Madame Guillotine made severed heads rolling into baskets a popular entertainment. As a mirror of its time – at least in the 1790s – opera could no longer countenance the regulation happy ending of *opera seria*. *Opera seria* had been welcomed in 1772 by the critic Antonio Planelli as a sign of society's 'gentility, urbanity and clemency'. However, these were qualities well and truly buried by the Revolution and from the last decade of the eighteenth century, a long series of *morte* or death operas was performed.

GOTHIC THEMES

This was not an entirely new genre, but had been prefigured by operas such as Alessio Prati's *La vendetta di Nino* ('Nino's Revenge', 1786), in which a son murdered his mother on stage, watched by the ghost of the husband whose death she had caused. Under the impetus of the Revolution and its fearful events, the death opera caught the imagination of audiences and began to create a new, somewhat morbid, taste in entertainment. In 1796, this development was praised in a review written after a performance at La Scala, Milan, of *Giulietta e Romeo*, composed by Niccolo Zingarelli (1752–1837) and based on William Shakespeare's tragedy *Romeo and Juliet*:

'The gloominess of the story ... appears somewhat weighty to those who ... are used to going to the theatre to be entertained and not distressed. But if the action demands, if the music responds to the text, one cannot but praise the poetry and the composer who has dressed it with such beautiful and expressive notes.'

A REPERTOIRE IS DEVELOPED

As soon became clear, the action did demand, the music did respond, and suitable stories were salted to provide opera plots. In this context, the writings of the prolific Scots novelist, Sir Walter Scott (1771–1832) proved a gold mine for librettists on the hunt for material. Scott was so successful in giving them what they were looking for that 19 of his novels were turned into a total of 63 operas; *Ivanhoe* (1819) was used 10 times and another novel, *Kenilworth* (1821), 11 times. The Scott operas were written by several composers, notably **Gioachino Rossini** (1792–1868), **Gaetano Donizetti** (1797–1848) and **Vincenzo Bellini** (1801–35), whose work scaled the pinnacle of the *bel canto* singing style.

EXOTIC INFLUENCE OF NOVELS

Some of Scott's novels, such as *Ivanhoe*, *Quentin Durward* (1823), or *The Talisman* (1825) catered for another new preference among opera audiences – their interest in operas with exotic locales, gothic story lines and medieval settings.

Others, such as *The Bride of Lammermoor* (1819), on which Donizetti based his opera *Lucia di Lammermoor* (1835), amply fulfilled the requirements of the death opera; Walter Scott provided the chance for Donizetti to depict the heroine, Lucia, wandering the stage overtaken by madness and soaked in the blood of the husband she had just married – and murdered. As a genre, the death opera had a long-term effect: throughout the nineteenth century and into the twentieth, the majority of operatic heroes and heroines routinely died on stage before the final curtain came down.

⊚ OPÉRA-COMIQUE ∾ p. 166

The Opéra-Comique company was established in 1714 to offer French opera as an alternative to the Italian opera that dominated the continent at the time. After several misadventures, which included a bankruptcy, the Opéra-Comique settled at the Salle Feydeau in 1805. Here, its essentially radical approach to opera soon became clear.

At this time, composers such as Méhul, François-Adrien Boieldieu (1775–1834) and Nicolo Isouard (1775–1818) were pioneering a new genre, the *opéra comique*, which was not yet acceptable to the rather hidebound Paris Opéra. The Opéra-Comique, by contrast, gladly embraced the genre and its early practitioners, and its stage was the scene of sensational premieres that became the talk of Paris opera-goers all season long. The Opéra-Comique, which moved to the Salle Favart in 1840, continued in the same vein, featuring unconventional, new or foreign works that were turned down by the more conservative management of the Paris Opéra. Unlike its rival, where spoken dialogue on stage was banned, the Opéra-Comique made itself a home for works that used this technique and included in its repertory operas by the 'new wave' of composers such as **Daniel-Francois-Esprit Auber** (1782–1871), **Adolphe Adam** (1803–56) and, much later, **Jules Massenet** (1842–1912).

𝄞 MASTERY OF STAGE DESIGN: PIERRE-LUC-CHARLES CICÉRI
∾ p. 167

The artistry, ingenuity and creativity of Pierre Cicéri (1782–1868), the greatest designer in early nineteenth-century France, made him an almost legendary figure in the world of Romantic opera. Originally, Cicéri trained as a singer, but turned to painting and became an assistant at the Paris Opéra in 1806. When he graduated to stage design, he made use of the latest technological innovations, for example using gaslight for Isouard's *Aladin, ou La lampe merveilleuse* ('Aladdin, or the Marvellous Lamp', 1822). Cicéri's instinctive appreciation of architecture and sense of history enabled him to create on-stage panoramas wonderfully keyed into the grandiose drama of French *grand opéra*. For Auber's *La muette de Portici* ('The Dumb Girl of Portici', 1828) he constructed a view of Vesuvius and its surrounding countryside and used carefully controlled fireworks to simulate a volcanic eruption. Cicéri devised a mobile panorama, in which a backcloth was turned on a revolving drum, gradually unwinding a scene so that a boat, static on stage, looked as though it was sailing along a river. The same device, when used in Auber's *Le lac des fées* ('The Lake of Fairies', 1839) simulated a descent from the sky down to Earth.

Early Romantic
PERSONALITIES

Auber, Daniel-François-Esprit
1782–1871, FRENCH

The French composer Daniel Auber made a favourable impression on his teacher, **Luigi Cherubini** (1760–1842) with his first opera, *L'erreur du moment* ('The Mistake of the Moment', 1805). However, he had to wait 15 years for popular appreciation until he established himself with two works: *La bergère châtelaine* ('The Lady Shepherdess', 1820) and *Emma* (1821). In 1823, Auber teamed up with the French playwright Eugene Scribe, his librettist for the Italian-style operas *Leicester* (1823) and *La neige* ('The Snow', 1823) and then the French-style *Léocadie* (1824). Auber was soon establishing himself as a master of *opéra comique* and confirmed this status with *Le Maçon* (1825), again with a **libretto** by Scribe. Three years later, Auber changed course again and, with his *La muette de Portici*, produced a work that helped establish French *grand opéra* as a new and imposing genre. In this seminal work, Auber injected more power into the leading roles and the choruses, reflected in his music the vivid scenic effects produced on stage and increased the role of the orchestra in building up the drama. Auber's music was an important influence on the works of other composers, including **Richard Wagner**'s (1813–83) *Lohengrin* (1850).

Beethoven, Ludwig van
1770–1827, GERMAN

Ludwig van Beethoven was born in Bonn to a musical family, on 16 December 1770. He started composing at the age of 11 and experienced opera from the inside when he joined the Bonn court orchestra as a viola player in 1789. His letters reveal that from his early years in Vienna, where he moved in 1792, he was eager to compose music for the stage. In the event, though, it was to be over a decade before he completed the first version of *Fidelio*.

AN ABORTED ROMAN OPERA

In 1803, Beethoven got as far as writing the first scene of a *grand opéra*, *Vestas Feuer*, to a libretto by **Emanuel Schikaneder** (1751–1812), **Wolfgang Amadeus Mozart**'s (1756–91) collaborator on *Die Zauberflöte* ('The Magic Flute', 1791). But the project foundered on the incongruity between the ancient Roman setting and what the composer called 'language and verses that could only have come out of the mouths of our Viennese apple-women'. Beethoven was, though, to rework a G major duet from the abandoned opera as the climactic love duet for Leonore and Florestan in *Fidelio*.

A TRUE STORY

Much more to Beethoven's taste was Jean-Nicholas Bouilly's *Léonore, ou L'amour conjugale* ('Leonore, or Conjugal love'), based on a true incident in the author's native Tours. Beethoven came across this libretto at the end of 1803 and gave it to the Viennese court secretary Joseph Sonnleithner to rework in German. *Fidelio* – the title was changed, apparently against Beethoven's wishes, to avoid confusion with operas by Pierre Gaveaux (1798) and Ferdinando Paer (1804) – finally saw the stage on 20 November 1805. It lasted for only three performances, partly because Beethoven's supporters had fled Vienna as Napoleon's troops advanced, and partly because it was deemed too repetitious and undramatic. Beethoven tightened the score for a revival in 1806, but this, too, failed. It was only in 1814, after wholesale revisions, that *Fidelio* finally triumphed.

SEARCH FOR LIBRETTI

In 1807, Beethoven had offered to compose an opera each year in exchange for a fixed income. He continued to cast around for suitable libretti, making sketches for an opera on a German adaptation of *Macbeth* (1808–11) and around 1823–24, he was seriously contemplating a 'fairy-tale' opera, *Melusine*, to a libretto by the Austrian poet Franz Grillparzer. But *Fidelio* remained Beethoven's sole opera, and the work he cherished above all others, yet of which he said shortly before his death: 'Of all my children, this is the one that caused me the most painful birth-pangs and the most sorrows.'

Fidelio

Premiered at Vienna's Kärntnertor Theater on 23 May 1814, the final version of *Fidelio* is a fundamentally different opera from the 1805 original. There is now much less emphasis on the gaoler's daughter Marzelline and her world of *Singspiel* domesticity. Although the fate of Florestan and Leonore remains central, the individual characterization becomes more idealized and stereotyped. The human element is now subordinate to the opera's moral message; and the prisoners, released from darkness into daylight, become archetypes of oppressed humanity. *Fidelio* in its final form is above all a celebration of abstract ideals dear to Beethoven: freedom, heroic courage in the face of tyranny, perfect womanhood and the brotherhood of man.

The insistent, emphatic tone of *Fidelio*'s choral finale, drawing its power from massed forces and sheer reiteration, shows Beethoven's debt to Cherubini and the composers of the so-called French Revolutionary School. A more pervasive influence on the opera is Mozart, though a movement like the quartet in Act II has a dynamic force unique to Beethoven. The quartet encapsulates the opera's movement from oppression to liberation, and contains its most thrilling coups, above all the offstage trumpet call that heralds the final denouement. It is strokes like this, together with such moments

as Leonore's aria of hope and resolve 'Komm, Hoffnung' ('Come, Hope'), and the dazed emergence of the prisoners into daylight in the first-act finale, that can make Fidelio the most elementally moving of all operas.

Fidelio

by Ludwig Van Beethoven
Composed: 1805; rev. 1806, 1814
Premiered: 1805, Vienna (early version)/ 1814, Vienna (final version)
Libretto by Joseph Sonnleithner (early version)/Friedrich Treitschke (final version), after Jean-Nicolas Bouilly

ACT I

In a Seville prison, Marzelline, daughter of Rocco the jailer, rejects the advances of Jacquino, her father's assistant and porter, whom she had previously agreed to marry. Although feeling pity for Jacquino, Marzelline is smitten by the conscientious new assistant, Fidelio. Fidelio is in reality the noblewoman Leonore; she has disguised herself as a boy and gained employment at the prison in the hope of finding her husband, Florestan, who disappeared two years previously under suspicious circumstances. Knowing that Pizarro, the prison governor, was an enemy of Florestan, she has high hopes of finding him here. Fidelio is understandably disturbed by Marzelline's affections, especially when Rocco blesses their union, but Leonore sees that she can use it to her advantage.

Leonore asks Rocco whether she can accompany him to the deepest dungeons, where the most closely guarded prisoners are kept. She learns of one prisoner that only Rocco is allowed to see; he has been there for about two years, is near death and is treated harshly by Pizarro. Believing it to be Florestan, Leonore again pleads to assist Rocco on his rounds; the jailer agrees to ask Pizarro.

Pizarro receives news that Don Fernando, the Minister for Justice, is coming to inspect the prison, after hearing reports of unjust imprisonment. Panicking, Pizarro organizes a watch and, paying Rocco, orders him to murder the prisoner. Rocco refuses, but is nevertheless charged with the task of digging the prisoner's grave. Pizarro resolves to kill the prisoner himself.

Leonore arranges for the prisoners to walk in the courtyard. They enjoy their brief moments of freedom before Pizarro orders them back to their cells. Rocco, having persuaded Pizarro to allow Fidelio in the deepest dungeons, asks Fidelio to help him dig the grave. Leonore is horrified, but follows him as he descends.

ACT II

In the deepest dungeon, Florestan languishes in chains. He has a vision of Leonore, in the form of an angel, coming to rescue him, and lies down in exhaustion. Rocco and Fidelio enter and begin to dig the grave. It is too dark for Leonore to distinguish Florestan in the cell, but when he speaks she knows it is indeed her husband. Florestan asks Rocco who is keeping him prisoner and, when told it is Pizarro, asks for a message to be sent to his wife. Rocco is afraid to tackle Pizarro, but he and Fidelio defy his orders by offering bread and water to the grateful prisoner.

Rocco signals to Pizarro that the grave is ready and the governor rushes in to kill Florestan. But as he raises the dagger Leonore, revealing her true identity, throws herself between them and threatens Pizarro with a pistol. A trumpet sounds in the distance, signalling the arrival of Don Fernando. Pizarro, furious at realizing it is too late for him to kill Florestan, is led away by Rocco. Leonore and Florestan enjoy an ecstatic reunion.

Outside the prison, Don Fernando announces that he has been sent to end Pizarro's tyranny and release all the prisoners that are being held unjustly. He is surprised and overjoyed to find his old friend Florestan alive; Rocco relates the fantastic events that have taken place. Marzelline realizes her misplaced love and Pizarro

is arrested, while Leonore is given the keys for Florestan's chains. She releases him and everyone celebrates the virtues of love and fidelity.

OPERAS

1805	*Fidelio* (rev. 1806; 1814)

TIMELINE

1770	Ludwig van Beethoven born Bonn, Germany
1795	First public appearance in Vienna
1798	First signs of deafness appear
1803	Writes first scene of *Vestas Feuer*, but later abandons it; discovers the libretto that will later become *Fidelio*
1805	*Fidelio* (originally called *Leonore*) premieres in Vienna, but is withdrawn after three performances
1806	Beethoven revises *Fidelio*
1808	Begins work on another opera, a German adaptation of *Macbeth*
1812	Meets writer Goethe in Bohemia
1814	Revised version of *Fidelio* is performed in Vienna to great acclaim
1819	Beethoven forced to use notebook for communication due to deafness
1827	Beethoven dies, Vienna

Bellini, Vincenzo
1801–35, ITALIAN

The musical abilities of Vincenzo Bellini were already well known in his home city of Catania in Sicily before he went to Naples at age 18 to study at the conservatory under Zingarelli. A competent pianist at age five, composer of his sacred music at six, the youthful Bellini's **ariettes** and instrumental works were performed in aristocratic salons and provided anthems for the churches in Catania.

A SUCCESSFUL STUDENT

Like Rossini, whose admiring disciple he was, Bellini scored success while still a student. His *opera semiseria Adelson e Salvini* (1925), which was staged at the conservatory, showed such promise that both the Teatro San Carlo, Naples, and La Scala, Milan, commissioned work from him. For Naples, Bellini composed

Bianca e Fernando (1826). He was obliged to change the latter name to Gernando, because Ferdinand I, the autocratic king of the Two Sicilies (Naples and Sicily) claimed a monopoly of his own name and any other too closely resembling it. The original name of the opera was restored, though, after Ferdinand died later in 1825.

THE OPERA THAT MADE HIS NAME

The opera that made Bellini's name was his work for Milan, *Il pirata* ('The Pirate', 1827) which had its first performance at La Scala on 27 October 1827. Though still only 26 at the time, Bellini had already demonstrated the basic elements of his personal style – creamy melody, graceful ornamentation, dramatic orchestration and touching, heartfelt sentiment. This was a winning combination that he carefully honed to reflect the emotions of his characters and the drama of their plight. Bellini soon revealed himself as the master of *bel canto*, a style that had connotations beyond the world of opera: the nocturnes, preludes and other melodies of the Polish pianist and composer Frederic Chopin (1810–49) reproduced on the keyboard the long, lyrical musical lines Bellini wrote for the voice.

A FAVOURITE WITH THE LADIES

Like Chopin, whom he met when he visited London in 1833, Bellini had a strong appeal for women, with his slim figure, aristocratic looks and the delicate aspect that marked so many nineteenth-century musicians destined for short lives. While in Milan, where he remained for six years after the success of *Il pirata*, Bellini caught the eye of Giuditta Cantu, who was married to a wealthy landowner and silk manufacturer. The two embarked on a passionate love affair, which was later romanticized in literature, but caused a considerable scandal at the time.

Gossip about it was all the more vigorous because in 1831, Bellini had become internationally famous after writing two more operas *La sonnambula* ('The Sleepwalker', 1830) and *Norma* (1833). Bellini's visit to London in 1833 removed him from the scene of scandal not long after the affair became public and divorce proceedings began.

AN EARLY END

Bellini disliked London, its audiences and its climate, although *La sonnambula* was a great success there. In August 1833, Bellini travelled to Paris, which was much more to his liking and where Rossini, now retired, was on hand to encourage him. In Paris Bellini wrote his tenth and last opera, *I puritani* ('The Puritans', 1835), which received its first performance on 25 January 1835. It was a tremendous success and Bellini was the toast of Paris. He was, however, exhausted and later that year, he fell ill, first with dysentery and then with an inflamed intestine, complicated by a liver abscess. Years earlier, it was said, Bellini had heard the *Stabat mater* by **Giovanni Battista Pergolesi** (1710–36) and afterwards remarked: 'If I could write one melody as beautiful as that, I would not mind dying young like Pergolesi.' He did write melodies as beautiful as that, and he did die young, aged 34.

La sonnambula

Vincenzo Bellini's two-act opera *La sonnambula*, which had a pastoral background, was first produced at the Teatro Carcano in Milan on 6 March 1831. The story derived from a comédie-vaudeville of 1819 and a ballet-pantomime of 1827, both part-written by the French dramatist Eugene Scribe. The title role, Amina, was created by Giuditta Pasta (1797–1865) who, though essentially a **mezzo-soprano**, performed brilliantly in the soprano range. Pasta was regarded as the greatest tragic singing actress of her day. Subsequently, Her Majesty's Theatre in London, where the opera was performed in 1833, was the scene of one of the most talked-about stage effects of the early nineteenth century: a virtual high-wire act in which the sleepwalking Amina crossed the eaves of the mill-house roof, several feet above the characters watching in horror on the stage below. The bridge, it seems, was the idea of the Swedish soprano **Jenny Lind** (1820–87) who sang the role of Amina at Her Majesty's. When *La sonnambula* premiered in New York in 1835, the role was sung by the Scottish soprano Mary Ann Paton, a beautiful singer, but one who acted her parts 'like an inspired idiot', as one observer put it.

La sonnambula
('The Sleepwalker')

by Vincenzo Bellini
Composed: 1831
Premiered: 1831, Milan
Libretto by Felice Romani, after Eugene Scribe

ACT I

The villagers celebrate the approaching wedding of Amina and Elvino, with the exception of Lisa, the innkeeper and Elvino's former lover. Consumed by jealousy, she rejects the advances of her new admirer, Alessio. Amina gives thanks to all of her friends, in particular Teresa, who owns the mill and who raised the orphaned Amina as her own child. Elvino returns from praying at his mother's grave and presents Amina with a ring, which belonged to his mother.

A stranger arrives in the village, with a curiously detailed knowledge of the local area. Unbeknownst to the villagers, he is in fact Count Rodolfo, the long-lost son of the recently deceased count, returning home. He shows a marked interest in Amina, much to Elvino's displeasure. Teresa and the villagers warn the stranger

of a phantom who haunts the village by night. Realizing that the castle is a long way off, he agrees to stay at Lisa's inn. Amina assures a piqued Elvino that he has no need to be jealous.

Lisa is now aware of Rodolfo's true identity and flirts with him in his room. Amina then enters, sleepwalking and talking about Elvino. Lisa leaves, dropping a handkerchief as she does so, and goes to fetch Elvino. Rodolfo is tempted to take advantage of the vulnerable Amina, but is touched by her innocence and restrains himself. Rodolfo leaves as the villagers, who have learned of the stranger's identity, arrive to welcome their new lord. They find only a sleeping woman. Lisa and Elvino return, and the woman is revealed to be Amina; Elvino is furious and breaks off the engagement. Only Teresa remains to comfort Amina.

ACT II

The villagers remain fond of Amina and set off for the castle to ask Rodolfo for confirmation of her innocence. Amina and Teresa are also on their way to the castle, but Amina can go no further than Elvino's farm. Elvino continues to reject her, even when the villagers return with the joyful news that the count has declared Amina's innocence. Elvino takes back his mother's ring.

Alessio learns that Elvino has decided to marry Lisa instead of Amina. Rodolfo tries in vain to explain to Elvino that Amina is a sleepwalker and was unaware of her actions, but Elvino will not be persuaded. Teresa, meanwhile, bids the villagers remain quiet to let Amina sleep. She confronts Lisa with the handkerchief, proving that she too spent time alone with Rodolfo in his room. Elvino laments the fickleness of women. Rodolfo continues to plead Amina's innocence, when she appears, sleepwalking along the roof of the mill and mourning the loss of Elvino's love. Elvino goes to her and replaces the ring and she awakes in his arms. Everyone rejoices and the wedding plans resume.

Recommended Recording:
La sonnambula, Orchestra del Maggio Musicale Fiorentino; Richard Bonynge, conductor; Decca 448 996-2DMO2; Soloists: Joan Sutherland (Amina), Sylvia Stahlman (Lisa), Margreta Elkins (Teresa),Nicola Monti (Elvino), Giovanni Foiani (Alessio), Fernando Corena (Rodolfo)

Norma

Norma, Bellini's eighth opera and his masterpiece, followed hard on the heels of his *La sonnambula* when its first performance was given at La Scala less than four months later, on 26 December 1831. Once again, Giuditta Pasta created the title role, although this time she had parts of the opera transposed down to the key of F where it catered more comfortably for her mezzo-soprano voice. The role has remained scored in F ever since. Pasta's problems – and Bellini's – did not end there, however. The singer declared that 'Casta diva' was 'ill-adapted to her vocal abilities' – in other words, the aria was to blame for being 'impossible' to sing. Bellini deployed all his diplomatic gifts and told Pasta to practice the aria every morning for a week. Then, if she was still dissatisfied, he would change it. A week later, the composer received a gift from the singer and a confession of shame that she had been 'little suited to performing your sublime harmonies'. *Norma* was coolly received at first – 'the audience was harsh' Bellini wrote in despair – but they gradually warmed to it. During the 1831–32 season, *Norma* was performed 39 times and was received with great enthusiasm.

Norma

by Vincenzo Bellini
Composed: 1831
Premiered: 1831, Milan
Libretto by Felice Romani, after Alexandre Soumet

SOUNDS FAMILIAR

'CASTA DIVA' ('CHASTE GODDESS')
'Casta diva' is sung by the Druid priestess *Norma* in Act I of the opera, which is set in the first century BC, during the conquest of Gaul by Rome. Addressing the goddess of the Moon, she prays for peace between her war-torn homeland, Gaul (France), and the Roman invaders.

ACT I
The high priest Oroveso leads the druids to worship at the altar of Irminsul. They are preparing for moonrise, when Oroveso's daughter, Norma, will lead them in an uprising against the Romans. The Roman pro-consul Pollione enters with his friend Flavio and confesses that he no longer loves Norma, but has discovered a new passion for Adalgisa, a novice priestess. He plans to take her back to Rome and marry her. The druids return; Norma prays to the moon and laments the loss of Pollione's love. Adalgisa, meanwhile, prays to be released from the bonds of Pollione's ardour, but he eventually persuades her to flee to Rome with him.

Norma learns that Pollione must return to Rome and she is concerned for the future of the two children she has borne him. She confides in her companion Clotilde that Pollione has another lover, although she does not know her identity. Adalgisa enters, declaring that she is in love and asking Norma for guidance. Norma, bearing in mind her own conduct, is about to allow Adalgisa to revoke her chastity vows when Pollione enters and Norma, realizing he is the object of Adalgisa's affections, flies into a rage. Adalgisa is equally horrified to learn that Pollione is Norma's former lover and declares that she would rather die than take him from Norma. The temple gong sounds and Pollione is warned that his death is imminent.

ACT II

Norma watches over her sleeping children with a dagger in her hand, tormented by the choice of either killing them or letting Pollione take them to Rome as slaves. She cannot bring herself to carry out the murder and asks Adalgisa to take them to their father. Adalgisa pleads with Norma to pity her children, swearing that she will renounce Pollione's love and bring him back to Norma.

Oroveso announces to the druids that Pollione is departing, only to be replaced by an even crueller pro-consul. He laments the hardships of living under Roman rule, but promises that, with patience, the time will come to revolt.

At the temple of Irminsul, Clotilde informs Norma that Adalgisa's protestations to Pollione have made no difference to the pro-consul's plans. Enraged, Norma announces that the moment of revolution has arrived. Oroveso demands a victim to sacrifice to the gods and Pollione is brought in, having been arrested for breaking into the virgins' sanctuary. In private, Norma offers him his freedom if he will leave Adalgisa and return to her, but Pollione refuses. Norma then orders the druids to prepare a funeral pyre, confesses her affair and offers herself as the human sacrifice. Pollione, moved by her nobility, resolves to die with her. Oroveso is deeply ashamed by Norma's confessions, but she eventually persuades him to look after her children, following which Norma and Pollione are led to their deaths among the flames.

OPERAS

1825	Adelson e Salvini
1826	Bianca e Fernando
1827	Il pirata
1829	La straniera
1829	Zaira
1830	I Capuleti e i Montecchi
1831	La sonnambula
1831	Norma
1833	Beatrice di Tenda
1835	I puritani

TIMELINE

1801	Vincenzo Bellini born, Sicily
1819	Moves to Naples to study at San Sebastiano Conservatory
1822	Begins to study under Conservatory's director, Niccolo Zingarelli
1824	Attends the Naples performance of Rossini's Semiramide
1825	Premiere of first opera Adelson e Salvini leads to commission from Teatro San Carlo, Naples
1827	Begins partnership with librettist Felice Romani on Il pirata; produced at La Scala, Milan, it lays foundation for his career
1829	Zaira is inaugural opera at Parma's new Teatro Ducale
1830	I Capuleti e i Montecchi premieres in Venice, with soprano Giuditta Pasta
1831	Premiere of La sonnambula in Milan; Norma is greeted coolly at its premiere in Milan, but soon becomes a hallmark of the bel canto style
1833	Bellini visits London; four of his operas are performed
1835	Commissioned to write I puritani for Théâtre Italien, Paris; appointed Chevalier de la Légion d'honneur after I puritani's success; Bellini dies, Paris

Berlioz, Hector
1803–69, FRENCH

The French composer Hector Berlioz, who once wrote that the opera houses of his time were too large, did a splendid job of filling their auditoria with the mighty sound of epic opera. His opera output was small, consisting of only five completed works, but their impact transcended mere numbers. Berlioz's first surviving opera, *Benvenuto Cellini* (1837) based on the life of the famous goldsmith and engraver of Renaissance Italy, was a failure. However, a later work, the two-part *Les troyens* ('The Trojans', 1856–58 and 1860–63), for which Berlioz wrote both words and music, was an epic fully worthy of the name. *Les troyens*, set during the Trojan War in the twelfth century BC, combined impressive spectacle, lyricism and classical grandeur with heroic tragedy on the most monumental scale possible. Berlioz had a fascination for the ancient Roman poet Virgil (70–19 BC), whose account of the

Trojan War in his *Aeneid* was used as the basis for *Les troyens*. Berlioz, however, was also capable of the delicate touch and demonstrated this in an opera that he himself described as 'a caprice written with the point of a needle' – his *Béatrice et Bénédict* (1862), based on Shakespeare's *Much Ado About Nothing*.

Benvenuto Cellini

by Hector Berlioz
Composed: 1834–37
Premiered: 1838, Paris
Libretto by Léon de Wailly and Auguste Barbier, after Cellini

ACT I

The Pope has commissioned Cellini to make a statue of Perseus. Balducci, the treasurer, is annoyed; he wants the commission to go to Fieramosca, who he also wants to marry his daughter Teresa; she is in love with Cellini.

Masked revellers, Cellini among them, mock Balducci. Teresa watches, hoping to see her lover. Cellini and Teresa meet and he outlines a plan for their elopement: he and his apprentice Ascanio, dressed as monks, will abduct Teresa at the theatre. Fieramosca overhears the plan but is discovered by a furious Balducci.

Cellini and the metalworkers drink and praise their art. Balducci's meagre payment for the statue arrives; they arrange for him to be mocked in a play. Fieramosca tells Pompeo of Cellini's plan; they decide to steal the idea.

At the theatre, Balducci is enraged by the play. He attacks the actors and the four 'monks' make for Teresa. A fight breaks out, in which Cellini kills Pompeo. Cellini escapes, while Fieramosca is arrested.

ACT II

Teresa and Ascanio pray for Cellini, who appears. They rejoice, until an angry Balducci arrives with Fieramosca. The Pope enters, demanding his statue. After being persuaded not to re-commission the work,

the Pope promises Cellini a pardon and Teresa's hand if the statue is finished in a day; if not, Cellini will hang.

Cellini wishes for an easy life as he works on the statue. Fieramosca enters, challenging Cellini to a duel, and bribes the workers to leave. Teresa intervenes and Fieramosca is forced to join in the workforce.

The Pope and Balducci arrive to watch the casting. The metal runs out; Cellini orders his previous works to be melted down. The casting is successful. The Pope is pleased and Balducci allows Teresa to marry Cellini. Everyone rejoices in the triumph of the arts.

Les troyens ('The Trojans')

by Hector Berlioz
Composed: 1856–58
Premiered: 1890, Karlsröhe
Libretto by the composer, after the *Aeneid* by Virgil

ACT I

The Trojans celebrate peace and admire the wooden horse left by the Greeks after the siege. Cassandre (Cassandra), King Priam's daughter, forsees the fall of Troy. Her husband Chorèbe (Coroebus) urges her to join the celebrations, but she begs him to flee. Énée (Aeneas) reveals that sea serpents have killed the priest Laocöon, after he suggested destroying the horse. Fearing the fury of the gods, the Trojans bring the horse into the city.

ACT II

Hector's ghost tells Énée to leave for Italy to found a new Troy. Panthée, Énée's friend, enters with the news that Greeks have burst out of the horse and are sacking the city. In the palace, Cassandre tells the Trojan women of Énée's quest. She prepares to kill herself, urging the others to do the same to save themselves from the Greeks. Some refuse and are driven away; the others declare their right to die free. The Greeks enter in search of the treasure, which Énée has taken; they are greeted by a mass suicide.

ACT III

In her palace, Didon (Dido) celebrates the anniversary of the founding of Carthage. Her sister Anna assures her she will find love again. The poet Iopas brings news of the shipwrecked Trojans and Didon welcomes them. Énée, hearing that Carthage is to be attacked by Numidians, offers to assist in battle; Didon falls in love with him.

ACT IV

The royal hunt is halted by a storm. Didon and Énée seek shelter in a cave. Didon's advisor, Narbal, complains to Anna that since the Numidian battle the queen is neglecting her duties. He is also uneasy of Didon's affair, since Énée has to leave for Italy. Didon enters with Énée, requesting tales of Troy and finding comfort in his words. They declare their love for each other until interrupted by Mercury, who reminds Énée of his destiny.

ACT V

The Trojans are besieged by omens and ghosts, urging them to leave for Italy. Énée reluctantly tells Didon that he must leave. She entreats him not to go, but he is resolved, especially when the Trojan ghosts appear. Didon curses him. Later she asks Anna to persuade Énée to stay, but the Trojans have set sail. Furious, she orders a pyre to be built. Didon burns the relics of Énée's visit. A vision of the glory of Rome appears. Predicting that Hannibal will avenge her, Didon stabs herself. The Carthaginians swear vengeance on Énée and his race.

Recommended Recording:

Les troyens, London Symphony Orchestra; Colin Davis, conductor; LSO Live LSO0010; Soloists: Petra Lang (Cassandre), Michelle DeYoung (Didon), Sara Mingardo (Anna), Ben Heppner (Énée), Kenneth Tarver (Iopas), Toby Spence (Hylas), Peter Mattei (Chorèbe), Stephen Milling (Narbal)

Boieldieu, François-Adrien
1775–1834, FRENCH

Adrien Boieldieu wrote his first opera, *La fille coupable* ('The Guilty Girl', 1793), when he was 18. Shortly afterwards, he left his home town of Rouen and settled in Paris. He scored quick success with his *opéras comiques*, but his talent did not stop at the standard ingredients of the genre. He was also capable of writing, for example, the exotically oriental *Le calife de Bagdad* ('The Caliph of Baghdad', 1800). After five years as court composer in St Petersburg, Boieldieu returned to France in 1812, where his *Jean de Paris* ('John of Paris', 1812) was admired by **Carl Maria von Weber** (1786–1826) for the 'freedom and elegance of his vocal line … and … his careful and excellent use of the orchestra.' Boieldieu's masterpiece, *La dame blanche* ('The White Lady', 1825), was judged one of the most important French Romantic operas written in the 1820s. By this time Boieldieu had spent the last 10 years as court composer to King Louis XVIII, who was restored to the throne after the downfall of Napoleon in 1815. However, his career effectively ended with the revolution of 1830, which swept away the old Bourbon monarchy – and everyone, even musicians, who had served it.

Cammarano, Salvadore
1801–52, ITALIAN

Salvadore Cammarano wrote several plays before producing his first libretto in 1834. This so impressed the management at the Teatro San Carlo in Naples that Cammarano was appointed house poet in 1835. That same year, he wrote the libretto for Lucia di Lammermoor, composed by his friend Gaetano Donizetti. Cammarano and Donizetti worked on many more operas together, notably *Roberto Devereux, ossia Il Conte d'Essex*. In 1845, **Giuseppe Verdi** (1813–1901) asked Cammarano for a libretto for Alzira, a two-act opera based on a tragedy by Voltaire. This, unfortunately, was one of Verdi's – and Cammarano's – few failures. Disappointment did not deter Verdi from again working with Cammarano, who had an unusual talent for writing libretti acceptable to everyone – audience, composer, even the censor. Cammarano wrote the text for Verdi's *Luisa Miller* (1849) and *Il trovatore* but died six months before the latter premiered in Rome on 19 January 1853.

Cherubini, Luigi

1760–1842, ITALIAN

The Italian composer Luigi Cherubini studied in Florence, Bologna and Milan, first writing church music, and then, in 1779, producing his first operas. By 1787, when he settled in Paris, he had written 13 operas, but nothing, as yet, that was innovatory. This changed when his *Démophon* (1788) signalled a new direction, towards the pioneering of *opéra comique* and *grand opéra*. With his *Loidoïska* (1791), Cherubini introduced richer orchestration, more powerful **ensemble** music, stronger, more compelling drama, more realistic characters and a new ingredient – the contribution to the action made by natural forces, in this case a fire.

Gradually, as more operas followed, Cherubini displayed more of the early symptoms of Romantic opera, with arias for subordinate characters or peasants depicted as simple but virtuous in accordance with the social principles of Rousseau. *Musique d'effet* – effect music – entered the equation, with Cherubini increasing the importance of the orchestra and accompanying the voice with horn or clarinet *obbligati*. These Romantic elements were poignantly on display in Cherubini's *Médée* ('Medea', 1797) – a tragedy of elemental passion based on Greek legend. However, Cherubini was just as sure-handed with the simpler characters of *opéra comique* and the suspense of 'rescue operas', such as the work *Faniska* (1806).

Médée ('Medea')

by Luigi Cherubini
Composed: 1797
Premiered: 1797, Paris
Libretto by François Benoit Hoffman, after Pierre Corneille

ACT I

At the palace of Corinth, Glaucé, daughter of King Créon, prepares for her approaching marriage to Jason. She fears the wrath of Médée, a sorceress who helped Jason to steal the Golden Fleece from Cholcis. Médée betrayed her family to help Jason and later bore him two children, who are now in Jason's care. Créon and Jason reassure Glaucé. Médée arrives and orders Jason not to marry Glaucé, but he defies her, warning her against incurring Créon's wrath. She curses him and swears vengeance.

ACT II

Créon has banished Médée from the city, but she insists on seeing her children; he allows her to remain for one more day. She asks Jason to see them but he refuses. Realizing how much he loves the children, she resolves to kill them in order to spite him. He eventually allows Médée to look after the children until she leaves the city. Médée admits to her servant Néris that she considers the children to belong only to Jason, and that she does not love them. She gives Néris a cloak and diadem to deliver to Glaucé as wedding gifts and then gleefully looks on as the wedding guests arrive.

ACT III

Néris brings the children to Médée. Momentarily recovering her maternal instincts, she embraces them. Cries from the temple signify that Glaucé has been killed by Médée's gifts, which were steeped in poison. Remembering Jason's treachery, Médée resumes her path of revenge and takes the children into the temple. Jason arrives with an angry crowd; Néris tries to tell him of Médée's plans but it is too late. Médée, having slaughtered her sons, emerges from the temple covered in blood and surrounded by Furies. As the temple burns, Médée vanishes into the air with the Furies, promising to meet Jason in the underworld.

Cinti-Damoreau, Laure
1801–63, FRENCH

The French **soprano** Laure Cinti-Damoreau was only 15 when she made her debut at the Théâtre Italien in 1816 in **Vicente Martín y Soler**'s (1754–1806) 30-year-old opera *Una cosa rara* ('A Rare Thing', 1786). Ten years later, Cinti-Damoreau created several leading roles at the Paris Opéra, for example in Rossini's *La siège de Corinthe* ('The Siege of Corinth') and in his last opera, *Guillaume Tell* ('William Tell'). Cinti-Damoreau's voice was classed as 'exceptionally pure'. She had the clear, controlled mastery of ornamentation that led the Belgian scholar, critic and composer François-Joseph Fétis (1784–1871) to write of her *beau talent* – 'beautiful talent'. The French writer Stendhal (1783–1842) apparently referring to her diminutive stature, wrote of Cinti-Damoreau as 'that charming little singer'. The soprano was certainly versatile, able to encompass both *grand opéra* and roles in Auber's works that were performed at the Opéra-Comique between 1837 and 1841.

Colbran, Isabella
1785–1845, SPANISH

Isabella Colbran, the Spanish soprano, married Gioachino Rossini in 1822 after a seven-year relationship, and sang a series of leading roles that he wrote for her. Colbran specialized in dramatic, tragic roles and having her on hand, as it were, enabled Rossini to write roles in this more serious genre. They included Elisabetta in *Elisabetta, regina d'Inghilterra*, Desdemona, the doomed wife in *Otello*, and Elena in *La donna del lago* ('The Lady of the Lake', 1819), based

on a poem by Sir Walter Scott. Colbran, who was famous throughout Europe, was among the first operatic 'divas', with a fiery temperament, an imposing physical presence on stage, impressive acting talent and a big, dramatic voice that had a range of some three octaves. Although her voice was already past its best in 1815, Colbran continued to sing for another nine years before she retired.

Davide, Giovanni
1790–1864, ITALIAN

The tenor Giovanni Davide, son of another Italian tenor, Giacomo Davide (1750–1830), made his debut at 18 in Milan, in Simon Mayr's (1763–1845) *Adelaide di Guesclino* (1799) and 15 years later created the role of Narciso in Rossini's *Il turco in Italia*. Rossini was impressed enough to write other parts for Davide in *Otello* and *La donna del lago*, among others. Davide was also in demand by Mayr, Donizetti and Giovanni Pacini the Sicilian composer; the tenor created roles in operas by all of them. Davide's voice was described as 'full-toned and extremely flexible'; he was able to cover three octaves by skilful use of falsetto, in which the normal range of the tenor voice was extended upwards by partial use of the vocal chords. Davide retired from the opera stage in 1839, and then travelled to Russia, where he took up a position as manager of the St Petersburg Opera.

Donizetti, Gaetano
1797–1848, ITALIAN

Gaetano Donizetti, who was born in Bergamo, wrote seven operas, some of them while still a student in Bologna, and several of them unproduced, before he scored his first success with *Zoraide di Grenata* ('Zoraide of Granada', 1822), which was performed in Rome. *Zoraide* attracted the attention of *impresario* Domenico Barbaia, who offered Donizetti a contract to write for the Naples theatres.

The result was a series of comic works, which, though successful, were clearly influenced by the compositional styles of Rossini and Bellini.

ARRIVAL OF INTERNATIONAL FAME

Then Donizetti wrote *Anna Bolena* ('Anne Boleyn', 1830), an opera set in sixteenth-century England, dealing with the life and death of Anne Boleyn, the second wife of King Henry VIII. *Anna Bolena*, which revealed Donizetti's individual style for the first time, brought international fame that enabled him to branch out beyond the confines of Naples and write for other opera houses. One of the first fruits of Donizetti's new artistic freedom was *L'elisir d'amore* ('The Elixir of Love', 1832) a sentimental comedy produced at the Teatro della Canobbiana in Milan.

A SINISTER AND SOMBRE OPERA

After the great success of *L'elisir d'amore*, Donizetti turned in a new direction. He was anxious to explore the high emotion of tragic opera and found his ideal plot in the story of Lucrezia Borgia (1480–1519), the incestuous poisoner of lurid, though fanciful, popular history. The opera, based on a play by the French writer Victor Hugo (1802–85), was strong stuff, so much so that it was not staged for two years, until 1833, when it was produced at La Scala, Milan, and ran for 33 performances. *Lucrezia Borgia* included several innovations, among them a sombre melody played by the orchestra as a sinister comment that reflected the plotting of two conspirators on stage.

INFLUENCE ON VERDI

The dramatic effect was not lost on the 20-year-old Verdi, who was studying in Milan in 1833. Eighteen years later, Verdi used a similar device in his *Rigoletto* (1851), as musical background to the furtive meeting between Rigoletto and the assassin Sparafucile. In this and other ways, Donizetti was an important forerunner of Verdi, pioneering greater dramatic expression, richer orchestration and new combinations of voices for ensemble singing – and all of it without losing the beautiful melodic lines and harmonies that were his hallmarks.

GRAND OPÉRA

In 1835 Donizetti returned to high-operatic drama, this time fortified by viewing French *grand opéra* during a visit to Paris. The result was his most famous opera, *Lucia di Lammermoor*, based on the novel *The Bride of Lammermoor* by Sir Walter Scott. *Lucia* was followed in 1837 by one of Donizetti's many ventures into English history, for another sinister tale of betrayal, despair and death in high, royal places with *Roberto Devereux, ossia Il conte d'Essex* ('Robert Devereux, or The Count (Earl) of Essex', 1837). Robert Devereux (c. 1566–1601), the last favourite of Queen Elizabeth I, was executed for plotting against her.

A SLIGHTLY DISMAL END

After *Roberto Devereux* premiered in Naples on 29 October 1837, Donizetti left for Paris, where he returned to his former, light-hearted vein with *La fille du régiment* ('The Daughter of the Regiment', 1840). This was his first French opera and was well received, running for 44 performances in 1840. However, his time in Paris was not entirely successful. Audiences reacted coolly to his *grand opéra La favorite* ('The Favourite', 1840). Victor Hugo objected to changes in his plot for *Lucrezia Borgia*, which had to be withdrawn, and there were censorship problems in Milan. Worse was Donizetti's declining health, but even as his syphilis advanced, he produced his comic masterpiece, *Don Pasquale* (1843). Eventually, syphilis paralysed him and he died, aged 50, on 8 April 1848.

L'elisir d'amore

Donizetti's prolific output owed a great deal to the speed with which he was able to compose. He could compose operas at the rate of three or four a year. However, even this rate of production was overtaken by the mere fortnight it took him to write the music for *L'elisir d'amore*. This pastoral comedy was his forty-first opera in 16 years, and premiered at the Teatro della Canobbiana in Milan on 12 May 1832. *L'elisir* owes much of its enduring popularity to 'Una furtiva lagrima' ('One Furtive Tear'), the exceptionally beautiful tenor aria in Act II sung by the opera's hero, Nemorino.

L'elisir d'amore ('The Elixir of Love')

by Gaetano Donizetti
Composed: 1832
Premiered: 1832, Milan
Libretto by Felice Romani, after Eugène Scribe

ACT I

The wealthy Adina relaxes with her friend Giannetta and peasants, while Nemorino, her admirer, looks on. He is a poor villager and laments that he can offer her nothing but his love. Adina relates the story of Tristan, who drank a love potion to make Isolde return his love. A drum roll announces the arrival of Sergeant Belcore, who asks Adina to marry him. She refuses, but says she will consider it. Nemorino, wishing he had Belcore's confidence, shyly declares his love to Adina. She answers that she is fickle and enjoys her freedom, and that he would do better to leave for the city and tend to his rich, ailing uncle.

The travelling quack Dr Dulcamara arrives in the town square, selling his new medicine. Nemorido asks whether he has a love potion like the one in Adina's story. Dulcamara produces a bottle – which contains cheap wine – and tells Nemorino that it is just what he is looking for. Nemorino

'UNA FURTIVA LAGRIMA' ('ONE FURTIVE TEAR')

Nemorino tries to win Adina with a love potion. In this tenor aria from Act II, he sings of a tear in her eye, showing she loves him, and believes the potion has worked; in fact Adina was jealous of the other girls.

drinks the 'love elixir' and ignores Adina when she arrives, trusting in the magic of the elixir to win her heart. Adina is annoyed by his coldness and flirts with Belcore, who announces that he must leave and that she should marry him immediately; she accepts. Nemorino begs for the wedding to be postponed, worried that it will be over before the elixir starts to take effect. Adina ignores his pleas and invites everyone to her wedding.

ACT II

Everyone, with the exception of Nemorino, celebrates the approaching marriage. Dr Dulcamara suggests that Adina and Belcore sing a duet about a girl who chooses a poor man over a rich suitor. The couple prepare to sign the marriage contract, but to Adina's annoyance Nemorino is not present; she postpones the wedding until nightfall. Nemorino pleads with Dulcamara for another bottle of the magic elixir, but he is refused as he has no money. Belcore intervenes, revealing that if Nemorino signs up to the army immediately he will be rewarded in cash. Nemorino agrees and leaves to sign up.

Giannetta spreads the news among the women that Nemorino's rich uncle has died, leaving him a fortune. Nemorino, dizzy after drinking another bottle of 'elixir', does not yet know this. As the girls flock around him, he believes that the magic potion has finally taken effect. Adina sees Nemorino surrounded by girls and is enraged that he no longer loves her. Dulcamara explains that Nemorino's newfound popularity is a result of the love elixir and attempts to sell Adina a bottle; she refuses, saying that she will use her own charms. Nemorino sees tears in Adina's eyes and knows that she will soon be his, so he feigns indifference when they meet. Adina restores his enlistment papers to him, declaring her love. Belcore takes the rejection well, assuming that many other women await him. Dr Dulcamara alerts the villagers to the success of his love elixir and sells as many bottles as he can.

Lucia di Lammermoor

While writing *Lucia di Lammermoor*, Donizetti observed a common custom of the 1830s; tailoring his music to the voices of the original cast. For example, **Fanny Tacchinardi-Persiani** (1812–67), who created the role of Lucia, was technically brilliant and Donizetti's writing reflected her outstanding abilities. Matching music to performers was a shrewd move: the formula increased the popularity of operas. In the case of Lucia, the effect on the first-night audience at the Teatro San Carlo, Naples on 26 September 1835 was startling. They became so caught up in the drama and in the plight of the lovers that many of them wept openly during Lucia's mad scene preceding her death and Edgardo's suicide. There was a French as well as an Italian version of Lucia, first performed at the Théâtre de la Renaissance in Paris on 6 August 1839. Lucia was given in opera houses all over Europe and in Cuba, Mexico, the United States and even Indonesia and Trinidad; *Lucia* was the first opera to be seen on the Caribbean island in 1844.

Lucia di Lammermoor

by Gaetano Donizetti
Composed: 1835
Premiered: 1835, Naples
Libretto by Salvatore Cammarano, after Sir Walter Scott

ACT I

In the grounds of Lammermoor Castle, Normanno leads a group of guards searching for an intruder. Enrico enters and laments his sister Lucia's refusal to marry Arturo, a match that would save him from his impending political and financial ruin. Normanno reveals that she has been secretly meeting a lover who saved her from a wild bull. After further questioning, Normanno confesses that the man in question is Edgardo, Enrico's bitter enemy, and he swears vengeance.

Near a ruined fountain, Lucia and her confidante Alisa await Edgardo. Lucia tells Alisa of a female ghost who haunts the fountain, and who has warned her that her secret affair will end in tragedy. Alisa pleads in vain with Lucia to end the relationship. Edgardo arrives and announces that he must depart for France on a political matter. He suggests that they tell Enrico of their affair and try to make amends, but Lucia, knowing Enrico will never allow it, begs him to keep it secret. Edgardo eventually relents. The lovers exchange rings and vows, and bid each other farewell.

ACT II

In the months since Edgardo's departure, Enrico and Normanno have continued to plan how to persuade Lucia to marry Arturo. They have been intercepting the lovers' letters and forge a letter to Lucia from Edgardo, declaring that he loves another. Enrico shows Lucia the forged letter and, distraught, she hopes for death. Enrico reminds her of the benefits to be gained from her marrying Arturo. Lucia's elderly tutor Raimondo, unaware of the deception and believing Edgardo to be faithless, gently persuades her to agree to the match.

At the wedding ceremony, Enrico explains to Arturo that their mother's recent death is the cause of his sister's melancholy demeanour. As soon as the *bride and groom have signed the contract, Edgardo bursts in. He challenges his rival to a duel, but Raimondo dissuades them. Edgardo is shown Lucia's signature on the marriage contract and, cursing her faithlessness, removes his ring and leaves. Lucia, overcome by emotion and confusion, collapses.*

ACT III

As a storm rages, Edgardo sits alone pondering on the day's events. Enrico enters and challenges him to a duel at dawn. Meanwhile, Raimondo interrupts the wedding celebrations to inform the guests that Lucia has gone mad and has stabbed and killed Arturo. Lucia enters, deranged and covered in blood, believing herself to be married to Edgardo. Enrico rushes in to berate her, but is filled with pity and remorse when he sees her condition. Lucia dies in Alisa's arms. By the tombs of his ancestors, Edgardo awaits Enrico and prepares for the duel. Filled with anger at Lucia's betrayal, he hopes to die. As the wedding guests leave, they inform him that the dying Lucia spoke of him. He rushes to be with her but it is too late; Raimondo brings news of her death. Realizing he has misjudged her, Edgardo stabs himself and dies.

La fille du régiment

Donizetti's *opéra comique La fille du régiment* acquired its French title because of its French librettists, Jules-Henri Vernoy, Marquis de Saint-Georges (1799–1875) and Jean-François-Alfred Bayard (1796–1853), and its first night was at the Opéra-Comique in Paris on 11 February 1840. *La fille*, which was set in the Tirol, in Austria during the Napoleonic Wars was Donizetti's first French opera and one of his greatest successes. In 1840 it ran for 44 performances. The opera's Italian premiere took place at La Scala, Milan on 3 October, followed by New Orleans in 1843 and London in 1847.

La fille du régiment ('The Daughter of the Regiment')

by Gaetano Donizetti
Composed: 1840
Premiered: 1840, Paris
Libretto by J. F. A. Bayard and Jules-Henri Vernoy de Saint-Georges

ACT I

As villagers pray for protection from the Napoleonic forces, the Marquise of Berkenfield, forced to take a detour on her way home, arrives at the village. Sergeant Sulpice of the 21st Regiment enters, with Marie, their vivandière. She was found on the battlefield as a baby and had been raised by the regiment. Sulpice questions her about a young man she has been seen with. She explains that the man, Tonio, saved her from falling off a cliff. Just then, soldiers enter with Tonio; he has been discovered in the camp and arrested as a spy. Marie explains that he is her rescuer and saves him from execution. Tonio is taken away, but manages to return and he and Marie sing of their love for each other.

The marquise asks Suplice to ensure her safe conduct to Berkenfield. The name Berkenfield reminds Suplice of Captain Robert, a former officer; it also appeared on the birth papers found with Marie. The marquise declares that her sister was married to Captain Robert and that Marie is her niece. She insists on taking her back to Berkenfield, to live a more ladylike existence. Tonio has joined the regiment to be near Marie. The other soldiers accept him, having learned that she returns his love. However, Suplice enters with Marie and announces that she is to leave with the marquise. Marie is pleased that Tonio has joined the regiment. The soldiers express their sorrow at her departure and bid her farewell.

ACT II

The marquise has arranged for Marie to marry the Duke of Crakentorp, to which

Marie has reluctantly agreed. The marquise summons Sulpice to encourage Marie; together they sing the regimental song, to the marquise's distaste. Although Marie has tried to please the marquise, she misses the military life to which she is accustomed and still loves Tonio. Suplice reminds her that she is the marquise's niece and must do as she says. Marie hears the sound of marching in the distance and the 21st Regiment appears, including Tonio, whose bravery has earned him the post of officer. He tells the marquise of his love for Marie, but she will not change her plans. She confesses to Sulpice that Marie is in fact her illegitimate daughter; marrying the duke will provide Marie with the wealth and nobility that the marquise cannot offer her. As the wedding guests arrive, the marquise reveals her real identity to Marie, who resigns herself to the proposed match. Tonio and the regiment enter and declare that Marie was their vivandière. The wedding guests are shocked, but are moved as Marie tells them of the regiment's kindness towards her. The marquise relents and allows her to marry Tonio.

Don Pasquale

Donizetti's three-act comic opera, Don Pasquale, full of fun and infectious humour, was first performed at the Théâtre Italien in Paris on 3 January 1843. There was no hint here of Donizetti's failing health, but as time proved, Don Pasquale was among the last of his remarkable total of 67 operas. The first performance was a tremendous success. Donizetti was there and, to judge from a letter he afterwards wrote to his music publisher, Giovanni Ricordi (1785–1853), he was lionized by the audience: 'I was called out at the end of the second and third acts,' he wrote, 'and there was not one piece, from the overture on, that was not applauded to a greater or lesser extent. I am very happy.' Donizetti was not the only one to score a brilliant success. Luigi Lablache (1794–1858), who created the title role, sang at

the London premiere at the Haymarket Theatre on 29 June 1843. Afterwards, a contemporary journal, The Musical World of London, raved about Lablache, calling him 'one of the greatest ornaments of the Italian opera in this or any other age'. Queen Victoria, the reigning monarch, was certainly impressed with him: she appointed Lablache as her singing teacher.

Don Pasquale
by Gaetano Donizetti
Composed: 1842–43
Premiered: 1843, Paris
Libretto by Giovanni Ruffini, after Angelo Anelli

ACT I
Don Pasquale, a bachelor, is angry with his nephew Ernesto for refusing to marry the woman of his choice. Ernesto is in love with the widow Norina, who is far from wealthy, and Don Pasquale has decided to punish him by taking a bride himself and disinheriting his nephew. His friend Dr Malatesta arrives to announce that he has found a suitable bride – his sister Sofronia, a shy convent girl. Don Pasquale is delighted.

Don Pasquale offers Ernesto one more chance to agree to the match, but Ernesto, declaring his love for Norina, refuses. His uncle then tells Ernesto about his own coming wedding. Ernesto is dismayed, realizing he will never marry Norina, and begs his uncle to talk it over with Malatesta. When Don Pasquale reveals that not only does Malatesta approve of the idea, but has offered his own sister as the bride, Ernesto feels betrayed.

Norina laughs over a romantic novel, declaring that she is more capable of manipulating men. She receives a letter from Ernesto, which she later shows to Malatesta; it explains that Malatesta has betrayed them by arranging Don Pasquale's marriage, and that Ernesto, disinherited, is leaving Europe. Malatesta reassures

Norina and explains his plan: she is to be Sofronia and a phoney notary will perform the marriage ceremony. As soon as she becomes Don Pasquale's bride, Sofronia will transform into the caricature of a nagging, extravagant wife.

ACT II

A dejected Ernesto prepares for his departure. Malatesta arrives with 'Sofronia' – Norina in disguise – who is as shy and innocent as Malatesta promised. She admits that her only real pleasure lies in sewing. When she is unveiled, Don Pasquale demands that they marry immediately. Malatesta fetches the 'notary', who provides a pretend marriage contract. As they sign the contract, Ernesto is called in as a witness and is appalled to see that the bride is Norina. Malatesta takes him aside and explains the plan.

Sofronia, now that she is married to Don Pasquale, changes completely. She refuses to kiss her new husband and declares that nothing in the household is good enough – they must order new servants, furniture, and carriages. Poor Don Pasquale is in despair. Amid the confusion, Norina reassures Ernesto that everything is going to plan.

ACT III

Don Pasquale laments the mounting bills, as servants deliver Sofronia's extravagant purchases. Sofronia enters, announcing that she is going to the opera. She slaps Don Pasquale when he tries to stop her, telling him that old men should be in bed. She drops a note as she leaves and Don Pasquale is enraged when he reads it – it is a letter from a mystery lover arranging a rendezvous in the garden. Malatesta feigns incredulity at Sofronia's dreadful conduct and advises Don Pasquale to go along to the garden and catch his wife red-handed.

In the garden Ernesto and Norina meet and sing a romantic duet. Ernesto then leaves, as Don Pasquale and Malatesta

arrive. Sofronia feigns horror at being caught, but defiantly defends her right to meet people in her own garden. Malatesta suggests that he take control of the situation and tells Sofronia that, provided Don Pasquale approves, Ernesto is to marry Norina, so that her power in the household will be diminished. Sofronia objects, causing Don Pasquale to approve the match and promise Ernesto a generous allowance. Ernesto then shows himself, and Norina reveals her identity, while Malatesta explains the deception. Don Pasquale is furious at first, but his relief at not being married to Sofronia is greater and he gives the couple his blessing.

Recommended Recording:

Don Pasquale, Opéra de Lyon; Gabriele Ferro, conductor; Erato 2292-45487-2; Soloists: Barbara Hendricks (Norina), Luca Canonici (Ernesto), Gino Quilico (Malatesta), Gabriel Bacquier (Don Pasquale)

TIMELINE

1797	Gaetano Donizetti born, Bergamo, Italy
1806	Begins to study music with Mayr at Bergamo
1816	Composes opera, *Il pigmalione*
1818	While in Austrian Army, Donizetti writes *Enrico di Borgogna*
1822	*Zoraida di Granata* premieres in Rome; obtains release from army
1822	Establishes himself at Naples Conservatory with *La zingara*
1830	*Anna Bolena* premieres, bringing composer international fame
1832	Milan premiere of *L'elisir d'amore*
1835	*Lucia di Lammermoor* opens in Naples, including tenor Gilbert-Louis Duprez
1837	Becomes director of Naples Conservatory
1838	Moves to Paris
1840	*La fille du régiment* and *La favorite* premiere in Paris
1842	Conducts Rossini's *Stabat mater* in Bologna
1842	Becomes *Kapellmeister* to the Austrian court, Vienna
1843	Comic masterpiece *Don Pasquale* premieres in Paris
1844	Premiere of *Caterina Cornaro* in Naples
1844	Becomes paralysed and mentally unbalanced due to syphilis
1848	Donizetti dies, Bergamo

OPERAS

1816	*Il pigmalione* (comp.)
1817	*L'ira d'Achille*
1818	*Enrico di Borgogna; Una follia*
1819	*Il falegname di Livonia; Le nozze in villa*
1822	*Zoraida di Granata; La zingara; La lettera anonima; Chiara e Serafina*
1823	*Il fortunato inganno; Alfredo il Grande*
1824	*L'ajo nell'imbarazzo; Emilia di Liverpool*
1826	*Alahor in Granata; Gabriella di Vergy* (comp.; 2nd version 1838); *Elvida*
1827	*Otto mesi in due ore*
1828	*Alina, regina di Golconda; Gianni di Calais; L'esule di Roma*
1829	*Il giovedi grasso; Il paria; Elisabetta al castello di Kenilworth*
1830	*Il diluvio universale; I pazzi per progetto; Imelda de' Lambertazzi; Anna Bolena*
1831	*Olivo e Pasquale; Il borgomastro di Saardam; Le convenienze teatrali; Le convenienze ed inconvenienze teatrali*
1831	*Gianni di Parigi; Francesca di Foix; La romanziera e l'uomo nero*
1832	*Fausta; Ugo, conte di Parigi; L'elisir d'amore; Sancia di Castiglia*
1833	*Il furioso nell'isola di San Domingo; Parisina; Torquato Tasso; Lucrezia Borgia*
1834	*Rosmonda d'Inghilterra; Gemma di Vergy*
1835	*Marin Faliero; Lucia di Lammermoor; Maria Stuarda*
1836	*Belisario; Il campanello di notte; L'assedio di Calais; Betly*
1837	*Roberto Devereux; Pia de' Tolomei*
1838	*Poliuto* (comp.; 2nd version, *Les martyrs*, 1840); *Maria de Rudenz; Elisabetta di Siberia*
1839	*Le duc d'Albe* (incomplete)
1840	*La fille du regiment; La favorite*
1841	*Adelia; Rita, ou Le mari batt* (comp.); *Maria Padilla*
1842	*Linda di Chamounix*
1843	*Don Pasquale; Maria di Rohan; Dom Sébastien, roi de Portugal*
1844	*Caterina Cornaro*

Duprez, Gilbert
1806–96, FRENCH

Gilbert Duprez, the French tenor, made his debut aged 19 as Count Almaviva in Rossini's *Il barbiere di Siviglia*. He went to Italy in 1829 to further his operatic studies, and remained there for six years. During this time, Duprez created the role of Edgardo in Donizetti's *Lucia di Lammermoor*. He had arrived as a youth with a beautiful, but small, light voice. By the time he returned to Paris, he was a mature 29 with much more vocal power. This enabled Duprez to become the leading tenor at the Paris Opéra where he performed for 12 years between 1837 and 1849. Duprez created the title role in Berlioz's *Benvenuto Cellini* among others. Duprez created something of a sensation in Paris when he became the first tenor to produce a 'chest voice' top C, an extraordinarily high note beyond the range of many tenors before and since.

Falcon, Cornélie
1814–97, FRENCH

Cornélie Falcon's singing career was brief. At 18 she made her debut at the Paris Opéra in 1832, singing the role of Alice in **Giacomo Meyerbeer's** (1791–1864) *Robert le diable*. However, Falcon was a mezzo-soprano who wanted to be a soprano and ruined her full, resonant voice by forcing it too high. By 1838 her career was over and an attempt to return in 1840 was an embarrassing failure. Nevertheless, despite her few years on stage, Falcon achieved a great deal. She created Rachel, the tragic heroine of **Jacques-Francois-Fromental Halévy's** (1799–1862) *La juive* and Valentine in Meyerbeer's *Les Huguenots* among other important roles. Falcon was a fine actress, and together with the French tenor **Adolphe Nourrit** (1802–39) raised the artistic status of the Paris Opéra. Her voice came to typify the dramatic soprano roles in which she specialized, and its type is today called 'Falcon soprano'.

Flotow, Friedrich von
1813–83, GERMAN

Though German-born, Friedrich von Flotow studied in Paris and became largely identified with French opera. His first operas in the French style were written for private salon performances. *Alessandro Stradella* (1844), his first international success, revealed his penchant for building a work around one 'hit tune', in this case 'Jungfrau Maria'. After leaving Paris for Vienna, von Flotow scored his greatest and most enduring triumph with *Martha* (1847), which included the popular song 'The Last Rose of Summer'. Sadly, von Flotow never scaled these heights again, despite the charm of his *La veuve Grapin* ('The Widow Grapin', 1859). Nevertheless, von Flotow ensured his place in the development of opera with his cosmopolitan approach; he combined the influence of French *opéra comique* with the Italian lyricism of his vocal writing and the orchestral style favoured in German Romantic opera. Though his light touch made his music less suited to the more weighty operatic subjects, it was ideal for comic arias, with just the right fluency, grace and charm. One secret of von Flotow's success in Paris was his skill in adapting the somewhat florid sentimental style of German Romantic opera to please the more cerebral French taste.

Garcia, Manuel
1775–1832, SPANISH

The Spanish tenor, composer and teacher Manuel Garcia founded a remarkable family of eight singers in four generations. He was best known for interpretations of Rossini – notably Otello – and created the part of Norfolk in *Elisabetta, regina d'Inghilterra*. The role of Count Almaviva in *Il barbiere* was written for Garcia. After some six years performing in Paris and London between 1819 and 1825, Garcia went to New York, where he introduced American audiences to Italian opera. Performances of Rossini's *Il barbiere*, *La Cenerentola* and *Otello* and Mozart's *Don Giovanni* were Garcia family affairs, with casts that included Manuel's wife, son and 16-year-old daughter Maria, later the famous Malibran. Later, while touring Mexico, the scores of *Il barbiere*, *Otello* and *Giovanni* were stolen by bandits, but Garcia saved the day by rewriting them from memory. A handsome man of great vitality, Garcia wrote several *zarzuelas* and popular Spanish songs.

Glinka, Mikhail Ivanovich
1804–57, RUSSIAN

As the composer of *A Life for the Tsar* (1836), Glinka became the founder of Russian historical opera. *A Life for the Tsar* told the story of Ivan Susanin, a popular Russian hero who, in 1612, saved the life of the future tsar and founder of the Romanov dynasty, Michael Romanov. Although French and Italian influences were present, Glinka's music was unmistakably Russian in its use of folk songs, balalaika music and **recitative** that conformed to the inflections of the Russian language.

The opera made Glinka an overnight success and Russia's leading composer at its first performance in St Petersburg on 9 December 1836. He was already planning his next work, *Ruslan i Lyudmila* ('Ruslan and Ludmilla', 1842), but suffered problems with the text after Alexander. Pushkin (1799–1837), who had written the poem on which the opera was based, was killed in a duel. Glinka had to make do with a less than satisfactory libretto, written by several people. His music, however, transcended this problem with its original rhythms, strong harmonies, oriental content and dazzling orchestration. Like *A Life for the Tsar*, *Ruslan* was a seminal work, this time founding the genre of Russian magic opera.

A Life for the Tsar

by Mikhail Ivanovich Glinka
Composed: 1836
Premiered: 1836, St Petersburg
Libretto by Baron Yegor Fyodorovich Rozen and others

BACKGROUND

The years of turmoil following the death of Tsar Fyodor I in 1598 might finally be coming to an end. The revolt of the 'False Dmitri' in 1605 has led to Polish intervention. In 1613, after an interregnum of nearly three years, Mikhail Fyodorovich Romanov has been elected tsar, but has been forced to go into hiding in a monastery near Kostroma.

ACT I

In the village of Domnino the peasants are affirming their devotion to the tsar. Antonida, daughter of the peasant Ivan Susanin, is preparing for her marriage to Sobinin, who arrives with news of Prince Pozharsky's victories against the Poles. He asks permission to marry Antonida, but Susanin says they must wait until there is a lawful Russian tsar on the throne. When told of Mikhail Romanov's election Susanin withdraws all objections to the marriage.

ACT II

At the Polish court the nobility are celebrating their successes against the Russians in a series of national dances. A messenger brings news of the election of a Russian tsar, to challenge their own claimant. Some soldiers set off to capture the new tsar before his coronation.

ACT III

Susanin assures Vanya, his ward, that no one would betray the tsar. They are joined by Antonida and Sobinin, and Susanin blesses the couple. Polish soldiers burst into the hut and demand to know where the tsar is hiding. Susanin eventually agrees to show them the way, but whispers to Vanya that he will take them in the wrong direction, giving Vanya time to raise the alarm. Antonida begs him not to go, knowing the Poles will kill him. After they have left, Sobinin and the peasants swear vengeance.

ACT IV

In the forest, Sobinin's men have lost their way. Vanya arrives at the monastery and warns them that the Poles are on their way. The Poles suspect that they have been tricked and pitch camp. While they sleep Susanin takes leave of his life. When they awake, he tells the Poles how he deliberately misled them. As they beat him to death he sees the first light of day. Sobinin and the peasants fall on the Poles.

EPILOGUE

Among the crowds celebrating the tsar's coronation are Antonida, Sobinin and Vanya, who are told that the tsar will never forget Susanin's sacrifice.

Ruslan i Lyudmila ('Ruslan and Ludmilla')

by Mikhail Ivanovich Glinka
Composed: 1837–42
Premiered: 1842, St Petersburg
Libretto by Konstantin Bakhturin, Valerina Shirov and various others, after Alexander Pushkin

ACT I

Everyone celebrates the marriage of Lyudmila to the knight Ruslan. Her rejected admirers Farlaf and Ratmir are also present. As Lyudmila's father Svyetozar blesses the couple, a thunderbolt is heard and darkness falls. When the light returns, Lyudmila has vanished. Her father offers half his kingdom and Lyudmila's hand in marriage to whoever saves her. Farlaf, Ratmir and Ruslan all pledge to find her.

ACT II

Ruslan meets Finn, a magician, who informs him that Lyudmila has been abducted by Chernomor, an evil dwarf. Finn warns him *of Naina, a wicked sorceress. Meanwhile, Farlaf encounters Naina, who says she will help him to find Lyudmila. Ruslan arrives at a battlefield. He encounters an enormous head, which belongs to a sleeping giant. The giant, revealing a magic sword, explains that he is Chernomor's brother. This sword is the only weapon that can overcome the evil dwarf, whose strength lies in his beard.*

ACT III

Naina arranges for her servants to seduce Ratmir, much to the distress of his companion and admirer, Gorislava. Ruslan is also drawn to the maidens, but is saved from temptation by Finn, who also frees Ratmir from the spell and makes him return Gorislava's love. Ratmir resolves to help Ruslan.

ACT IV

Lyudmila considers suicide and is not amused by the dwarf's attendants. Chernomor arrives, hoping to seduce her, and performs a dance. Ruslan challenges Chernomor to a duel. The dwarf sends Lyudmila to sleep and then consents. Ruslan cuts off Chernomor's beard, rendering him powerless, and sets off with the slumbering Lyudmila.

ACT V

Farlaf abducts Lyudmila, but Finn gives Ratmir a magic ring for Ruslan, which will awaken her. Farlaf arrives at the palace with Lyudmila to claim his reward, but cannot awaken her. The others arrive with the ring and Ruslan rouses Lyudmila. The wedding celebrations resume and everyone rejoices.

Goethe, Johann Wolfgang von
1749–1832, GERMAN
Johann von Goethe, greatest of all German poets and dramatists, created what became almost a genre in its own right with his *Faust* (1808). The theme captured the imaginations of numerous composers and among the 122 operas based on Goethe's writings, the Faustian

legend formed the plot for 20 of them. Goethe did more than provide texts for composers, however. He had a passion for music and wrote the libretti for eight *Singspiel* compositions. He was a great admirer of Mozart's *Die Zauberflöte* and, being a Freemason, recognized and appreciated its masonic content. Goethe wrote part of a sequel to *Die Zauberflöte*, but unfortunately it was never set to music. Between 1791 and 1817, when Goethe was director of the Weimar Theater, the repertoire included several operas, and Mozart's music featured in 280 of the performances.

Grisi, Giulia
1811–69, ITALIAN
The Italian soprano Giulia Grisi made her debut at age 17 in Bologna, singing in Rossini's Zelmira. Three years later, in Milan in 1831, Grisi created the role of the priestess Adalgisa in Bellini's *Norma* – a part he wrote especially for her. Her Paris debut followed in 1832, when she sang the title role in Rossini's *Semiramide* at the Théâtre Italien. Grisi remained in Paris for the next 14 years. In the role of Elvira in Bellini's *I puritani*, which she created, the composer remarked that 'she sang like an angel'. Her subsequent career was peripatetic. Grisi sang at Covent Garden, London (1847–51), toured the United States (1854–55) and made a series of 'final' performances (1854–66). These constant shifts meant that she had a far-flung – and adoring – public, who appreciated her beauty as much as her rich, flexible voice and acting ability. Queen Victoria was among her many admirers.

Halévy, Jacques-François-Fromental
1799–1862, FRENCH
Jacques-François-Fromental Halévy, who was born in Paris, studied there with several composers – of whom the most influential was Cherubini. Success at the

opera house was rather long in coming, however, and Halévy had to endure rejections and failures before scoring his first success with *Clari* (1828), which was written for the Spanish mezzo-soprano **Maria Malibran** (1808–36). Halévy's next significant work did not appear for another seven years, but when it did, it was his masterpiece. The opera, *La juive* ('The Jewess', 1835) took its place among the fundamental works of French *grand opéra* and was praised at several levels by other composers. Berlioz admired its vivid orchestration, while Wagner lauded the 'pathos of (its) high lyric tragedy' and Halévy's skill at recreating the fifteenth-century background of religious persecution with a minimum of detail. Halévy went on to show remarkable versatility as a composer, moving easily between *opéra comique* with *L'éclair* ('The Brief Meeting', 1835) or *Le lazzarone* ('The Vagabond', 1844) and *grand opéra* with *Guido et Ginevra* (1838) or *Charles VI* (1844). Although Berlioz believed that he was at his best in light opera, Halévy was one of the most important proponents of French *grand opéra*.

Lablache, Luigi
1794–1858, **ITALIAN**

The Italian bass Luigi Lablache enjoyed a career lasting over 40 years. He possessed a magnificent, sonorous voice with a wide range, impressive stage presence and the ability to sing both comic and tragic roles, many of which he created. His repertoire was vast and included Figaro in Rossini's *Il barbiere di Siviglia*, King Henry VIII in Donizetti's *Anna Bolena* and the title role in Donizetti's *Don Pasquale*. Lablache also sang leading roles in works by Bellini, Mercadante and Pacini, among others. The English opera house manager Benjamin Lumley described Lablache as 'the greatest dramatic singer of our time'. Despite growing hugely fat, Lablache was physically strong and

'RACHEL'

In this tenor aria from Act IV of Halévy's *La juive*, the Jewish goldsmith Eléazar sings of his fearful dilemma: should he let his daughter Rachel die at the hands of her persecutor Cardinal de Brogni, or should he save her by revealing that she is, in reality, de Brogni's daughter?

robust, and his voice was still fresh and powerful when he was 60. Royalty figured among Lablache's numerous admirers, including Tsar Alexander I of Russia and Queen Victoria, and **Franz Schubert** (1797–1828) dedicated three Italian songs to him.

Lind, Jenny
1820–87, **SWEDISH**

The soprano Jenny Lind was nicknamed 'the Swedish nightingale' because of her fresh, pure voice. She sang as a child performer before making her operatic debut in Stockholm in 1838 as Agathe in Weber's *Der Freischütz*. In the next three years, Lind sang several demanding roles, including Lucia di Lammermoor and Norma, and her voice began showing signs of strain. She retrained in Paris and returned to Stockholm in 1842, her voice restored. Her Norma in Bellini's masterpiece was highly praised, as was her Vielke in Meyerbeer's *Ein Feldlager in Schlesien* ('A Field Camp in Silesia', 1844) – a part that had been written for her. Jenny Lind went on to become a sensation in Germany, Austria and in England where she created the role of Amalia in Verdi's *I masnadieri* (1847). In 1850 she travelled to New York, where she made her name immortal. She remains one of the nineteenth century's most famous prima donnas.

Malibran, Maria
1808–36, SPANISH

Mezzo-soprano Maria Malibran was the elder daughter of Manuel Garcia and made her debut at age 17 singing in the chorus of the King's Theatre in London. Shortly afterwards, she replaced the indisposed Giuditta Pasta as Rosina in *Il barbiere*. Malibran was a brilliant, charismatic performer and was so successful as Rosina that she sang the part for the remainder of the season. In 1825, when the Garcia family was in America, Malibran sang the lead in eight operas performed over nine months. After returning to Europe in 1827, Malibran sang in London, Bologna, Naples and Milan, excelling in *Norma*, *La Cenerentola* and as Desdemona in Rossini's *Otello*. She appeared in London, Bologna, Naples and Milan, where she took the title role in Donizetti's *Maria Stuarda*. She died at the age of just 28 from injuries sustained in a riding accident.

Mario, Giovanni
1810–83, ITALIAN

The Italian tenor and one-time army officer Giovanni Mario played the title role in Meyerbeer's *Robert le diable* at the Paris Opéra in 1838 and in 1843 was the first to sing Ernesto in Donizetti's *Don Pasquale* at the Théâtre Italien. Mario Cavaliere di Candia, to use his real, aristocratic, name, had good looks, elegance, an attractive stage presence and a voice of great sweetness and expressiveness. After his debut, Mario travelled the opera world receiving great acclaim for his extensive repertoire of roles: these included Rossini's Otello, Count Almaviva in Rossini's *Il barbiere* and Manrico in Verdi's *Il trovatore*. Mario sang in London at the Haymarket (1839–46) and Covent Garden (1847–71), in St Petersburg (1849–63 and 1858–70), in New York in 1854 and in Madrid in 1859 and 1864. His voice lasted and lasted, despite his fondness for cigars, and he did not retire until he was over 60.

Marschner, Heinrich
1795–1861, GERMAN

Heinrich Marschner, the German composer, had the best possible backer for his first opera, *Heinrich IV und d'Aubigné* (1817–18), which was set around the turn of the seventeenth century. It featured King Henri IV of France and his follower the Huguenot poet Théodore d'Aubigné. Carl Maria von Weber, no less, staged the opera in Dresden, where Marschner became his assistant in 1824. However, their friendship faded when Weber became convinced that Marschner was imitating his style and using it, not for the advancement of German opera, but for his own commercial purposes. After Weber's death in 1826, Marschner was passed over as his successor and left Dresden. For a time Marschner's fortunes faltered, as he failed as music director in Danzig. However, after moving to Leipzig, Marschner began to work on *Der Vampyr* ('The Vampire', 1828), which scored a welcome success despite its resemblance to Weber's *Der Freischütz*. This was followed by his third and last success, *Hans Heiling* (1833). Although his work was uneven – none of his five other operas reached the same heights as his successful trio – Marschner pioneered the hero torn between good and evil, the real and supernatural worlds and showed how music could typify melodrama and emphasize its emotional effects.

Hans Heiling
by Heinrich Marschner
Composed: 1832
Premiered: 1833, Berlin
Libretto by Eduard Devrient, after a Bohemian legend

PROLOGUE
Hans Heiling, the King of the Gnomes, announces that he wishes to marry Anna, a mortal. His mother tries to dissuade him, since he would lose his powers.

ACT I

Anna and her mother Gertrude come to Heiling's house above ground. While Anna still dreams of her lover Conrad, Gertrude insists on the match with Heiling. Anna makes Heiling burn the magic book that gives him his powers. He declares his love for Anna and agrees to go to the village festival with her, but forbids her to dance.

At the festival Conrad tells his friends that anyone who marries an earth spirit will meet with disaster. Heiling is jealous of the attention Anna pays to Conrad. She still wants to dance, saying that she will do as she pleases until she is married. Heiling storms out, realizing that she never loved him.

ACT II

Anna is alone in the forest. The Queen of the Gnomes appears and tells her of Heiling's true identity. Before sinking into the ground she urges Anna to send him back to his home. Conrad is surprised to find Anna here. On hearing that she will never marry Heiling, Conrad offers his protection.

As a storm rages, Conrad brings Anna to Gertrude's hut. Heiling appears and offers her a casket of jewels. Anna still refuses him and in a fight Conrad is wounded.

ACT III

Heiling resolves to return to his underground kingdom. The villagers process to the church for the wedding of Anna and Conrad. Heiling enters during the ceremony. Conrad challenges him, but his sword is shattered. As gnomes burst in and threaten the villagers, the queen appears to recall Heiling to his kingdom, never to be seen again.

Martin, Jean-Blaise
1768–1837, FRENCH

The French baritone Jean-Blaise Martin gave his name to the voice type termed baryton-Martin, through his ability to extend his voice range into falsetto mode by an extra octave. This sort of voice, in which the baritone's normal top notes shade into the falsetto, is classed as a 'high baritone' and enables singers to take on part of the tenor repertoire. Subsequently, these roles became a regular feature of *opéra comique*. Martin made his debut at the Théâtre de Monsieur in Paris at age 20 in 1788. Subsequently, he performed in *opéras comiques* at La Salle Favart between 1794 and 1801 and its successor theatre in Paris, the Opéra-Comique, from 1801 to 1823. He returned to the Opéra-Comique in 1826 and 1833. Jean-Blaise Martin created numerous roles for several composers, including Méhul, Boieldieu and Halévy. Martin simultaneously taught at the Paris Conservatoire.

Mayr, Simon
1763–1845, GERMAN

The German-born composer Johannes Simon Mayr was studying in Italy when the patron who supported him died and he faced an uncertain future. Piccini encouraged him to write opera and Mayr took his advice. Mayr's first opera, *Saffo* (1794), attracted several commissions, but his great breakthrough came when *Ginevra di Scozia* ('Ginevra of Scotland', 1801) was performed at the Teatro Nuovo in Trieste. It made his name known all over Italy. Subsequently Mayr wrote operas for Naples, Rome, Milan and Venice and his work was performed internationally in Germany, London, St Petersburg, New York and several other places. Mayr's masterpiece, *Medea in Corinto* ('Medea in Corinth', 1813), was first performed in Naples in 1813, a year in which he wrote two other operas, but after that he produced no more. In his last years, he was blind. Mayr's output, however, made a significant mark on the evolution of opera, which influenced Rossini and his generation of Italian composers. Mayr increased the role of the chorus, characters acquired a greater range of expression, the orchestra was able to emulate storms and earthquakes, among other natural happenings, and in *Medea in Corinto* there was greater continuity between the arias.

Méhul, Etienne-Nicolas
1763–1817, FRENCH

Euphrosine (1790), the second opera composed by Méhul, was an *opéra comique* containing a duet that not only became instantly popular, but also used a comparatively new musical device, the reminiscence motif. In *Gardez-vous, la jalousie* ('Beware of Jealousy') Méhul wrote alternating thirds to represent 'jealousy' and repeated it throughout the opera. This was only one way in which Méhul made his name as an innovative composer. In typical Romantic fashion, he made imaginative use of the orchestra, giving it a greater share in the drama on stage. In *Ariodant* (1799), set in the world of knightly adventures, Méhul provided dark, moody orchestration to add expressiveness to the music. Méhul's career coincided with the French Revolution and its aftermath and some of his work inevitably reflected contemporary politics. For example, he was commissioned, possibly by Napoleon, to write an opera – *La prise du pont de Lodi* ('The Capture of the Bridge at Lodi', 1797) – celebrating Napoleon's victory over the Austrians in Italy in 1796. Four years later, Méhul embarked on a series of comedies, but reverted to a biblical theme for his last successful opera *Joseph* (1807), which contained the graceful melody and realistic atmosphere that were his trademarks.

Meyerbeer, Giacomo
1791–1864, GERMAN

Neither Giacomo Meyerbeer's first oratorio, nor his first opera, written in 1812 and 1813, was successful and his *Singspiel Das Brandenburger Tor* (1814) came too late to achieve its purpose – to celebrate the return home of the victorious Prussian army. It was a poor start for Meyerbeer but his fortunes changed dramatically after he left his native Germany for Italy, where he wrote six operas. These were so successful that Meyerbeer was touted as the new Rossini. More success awaited in France with his *Robert le diable* ('Robert the Devil', 1831) – a *grand opéra* set in thirteenth-century Sicily when it was under the rule of the demi-devil Robert, Duke of Normandy. In this and his next, even more successful work – *Les Huguenots* ('The Huguenots', 1836) – Meyerbeer showed keen understanding of how to cope with the vast size and lavish staging of *grand opéra*. *Les Huguenots*, based on the history of the massacre suffered by the Protestants of France in the sixteenth century, established Meyerbeer as, arguably, the most important composer of *grand opéra*. In this context, he deployed many brilliant talents – his inventive orchestration, dazzling vocal music and his unerring ability to match imposing themes to major historical events.

Les Huguenots
('The Huguenots')

by Giacomo Meyerbeer
Composed: 1836
Premiered: 1836, Paris
Libretto by Eugène Scribe, Emile Deschamps and Gaetano Rossi

ACT I

Nevers, a Catholic, has invited the Huguenot Raoul to a feast, as the king desires peace between the two factions. The guests describe their experiences of love. Raoul has fallen for a lady whom he saved from some students. Marcel, Raoul's servant, arrives and sings a Huguenot song.

Nevers' page announces the arrival of a woman to see Nevers. The guests watch the encounter; Raoul is incensed to see it is the woman he loves. She is Valentine, Nevers' fiancée, and has come to break off the engagement as she now loves another. Urbain, a page, enters with a note for Raoul inviting him to a rendezvous, and to come blindfolded. The guests notice the seal of Marguérite de Valois.

ACT II

Marguérite is arranging for Raoul to marry Valentine, uniting the Catholics and Huguenots. Raoul is led in and his blindfold removed; he pledges loyalty to Marguérite. He agrees to the match, but when Valentine is brought in he recognizes her as his 'faithless' lover and rejects her. Her father, Saint-Bris, is furious; the Catholics swear vengeance.

ACT III

The wedding of Nevers and Valentine begins. Marcel delivers Raoul's challenge of a duel to Saint-Bris, who plots an ambush. Valentine overhears and warns Marcel. Raoul rallies his companions but Marguérite intervenes and prevents the fight. Raoul learns the truth about Nevers and Valentine, but they are now married.

ACT IV

As Valentine laments losing Raoul, he appears. He hides as Saint-Bris enters and overhears the Catholics' plans for a slaughter of Huguenots that evening. He leaves to warn the others.

ACT V

As the Huguenots celebrate Marguérite's marriage to Henri de Navarre, a badly injured Raoul enters with news of the conflict. Raoul, Marcel and Valentine find each other among the fighting. Nevers is dead and they are free to marry. Saint-Bris and Catholics shoot at the Huguenots, realizing too late that they have killed Valentine.

Milder-Hauptmann, Pauline Anna
1785–1838, AUSTRIAN

This Austrian soprano studied in Vienna with Antonio Salieri. In 1803, she made her debut in Vienna as Juno in Der Spiegel von Arkadien ('The Mirror of Arcadia',

1794) by Franz Xaver Süssmayr (1766–1803), a one-time pupil of Mozart. In 1805 Milder-Hauptmann created the role of Leonore in Beethoven's Fidelio. She was, however, dissatisfied with certain 'unbeautiful, unsingable' passages in Leonore's aria and persuaded Beethoven to rewrite them in the later, 1814 version of his opera. Beethoven hoped to write another opera for Milder-Hauptmann, but it never transpired. Milder-Hauptmann, whose powerful voice was 'like a house' according to the composer **Joseph Haydn** (1732–1809), became identified with the role of Leonore. She sang in Berlin in 1812 and 1816–29 before appearing in Vienna. Milder-Hauptmann evinced great nobility on stage and her emotional intensity brought her acclaim in several roles, notably in **Christophe Willibald von Gluck**'s (1714–87) operas, Iphigénie en Aulide (1774) and Iphigénie en Tauride.

Nicolai, Carl Otto Ehrenfried
1810–49, GERMAN

Although Otto Nicolai was born in Kaliningrad, northwest of Moscow, he is classed as a German composer. Between 1833 and 1836, Nicolai was organist at the Prussian Chapel in Rome where he became fascinated with opera. His first work for the opera stage, Enrico II ('Henry II', 1839) was enthusiastically received in Trieste. Best known as a conductor, Nicolai cleverly combined this career with the opera by becoming principal conductor at the Vienna Hofoper in 1841. One of his first tasks was to introduce the 'Leonora No. 3' **overture** as an **entr'acte** at a performance of Beethoven's opera, Fidelio. After six years in Vienna, Nicolai moved to Berlin, where he became opera Kapellmeister and cathedral choir director in 1848. In Berlin, Nicolai wrote his Romantic comic opera Die lüstigen Weiber von Windsor ('The Merry Wives of Windsor', 1849), which was based on Shakespeare's comedy of that name.

In this work, which marked the apogee of German comic opera, Nicolai skilfully married German musical traditions with the fluent melodic grace of the style he imbibed in Italy. *Die lüstigen*, Nicolai's masterpiece, premiered in Berlin on 9 March 1849 and only just in time. Two months later, Nicolai was dead.

Nourrit, Adolphe
1802–39, FRENCH

Adolphe Nourrit, the French tenor, made his debut at the Paris Opéra in 1821, singing Pylade in Gluck's *Iphigénie en Tauride*. Nourrit remained at the Opéra until 1837, singing, among other roles, Mozart's *Don Giovanni* and Rossini's *Otello*. Nourrit was a brilliant all-round performer, charming his audiences with his subtle, expressive voice and riveting them with his acting talent. Berlioz, for one, found Nourrit 'electrifying'. In addition, Nourrit was a gifted writer; Meyerbeer found his help invaluable while composing *Les Huguenots*, calling him the 'second father' of the opera. After leaving the Paris Opéra in 1837, Nourrit successfully toured Belgium and France. Tragically, one asset Nourrit did not possess was mental stability, which left him vulnerable to melancholia. Problems with his voice, perhaps through over-use, exacerbated the problem and in Naples, in 1839, Nourrit, 37, committed suicide in a fit of depression.

Nozzari, Andrea
1775–1832, ITALIAN

Andrea Nozzari was one of the greatest tenors to sing in Rossini's operas, creating, among many others, the roles of the Earl of Leicester in *Elisabetta, regina d'Inghilterra* and the title role in *Otello*. Nozzari was the complete opera singer, with a strong voice and graceful stage presence. He probably made his debut at Pavia, Italy in 1794, afterwards moving on to La Scala, Milan where he

performed in 1796–97, 1800 and 1811–12. Meanwhile, Nozzari performed at the Théâtre Italien in Paris in 1803 and 1804. His final berth was at the Teatro San Carlo in Naples (1811–25) where he was one of a group of tenors who set new standards of singing, including great technical facility, wide voice range and the ability to sing top notes in falsetto. Another member of the group was **Giovanni Battista Rubini** (1794–1854), a one-time pupil of Nozzari's.

Pasta, Giuditta
1797–1865, ITALIAN

Giuditta Pasta, who created the title role in Bellini's *Norma*, was classed as a soprano, but was probably closer to a mezzo-soprano. On stage, she was majestic, and her acting was so powerful that, according to Stendhal, she 'electrified the soul'. However, success did not come her way all that quickly. After her debut in Milan in 1815, she performed in Venice, Padua, Rome, Brescia and Turin before scoring her first substantial success at the Théâtre Italien in Paris in 1821. Three years later, Pasta appeared at London's Haymarket Theatre and continued to sing in both of these capital cities until 1837. She also appeared at the Teatro San Carlo, Naples (1826), in Vienna (1829), at La Scala, Milan (1831) and in St Petersburg (1840). In addition to Norma, Giuditta Pasta created many other title roles such as Donizetti's Anna Bolena and Amina in Bellini's *La sonnambula*.

Romani, Felice
1788–1865, ITALIAN

Felice Romani was greatly admired by around 100 Italian composers who sought to enlist his instinct for operatic drama and his ability to write elegant verse. Among them were Rossini, for whom Romani wrote *Il turco in Italia* ('A Turk in Italy', 1814) and Verdi, whom he provided with the libretto for *Un giorno di regno* ('King for a Day', 1840). However, the name of

Romani is most closely associated with Bellini and Donizetti. Romani supplied Donizetti with the libretti for *Anna Bolena* and *L'elisir d'amore*. For Bellini, Romani wrote the text for *La sonnambula* and *Norma*. Romani's collaboration with Bellini began with the opera that first made the composer's name – *Il pirata* – and included a third member, the tenor Rubini, who created the title role at La Scala, Milan on 27 October 1827.

Rossini, Gioachino
1792–1868, **ITALIAN**

By the age of 14, Gioachino Rossini could play the violin, cello, harpsichord and horn, and had written a ***buffo*-**style cavatina, a short solo song. In 1806, Rossini was studying at the Bologna Conservatory and wrote his first opera, *Demetrio e Polibio*. The next year he produced his first professional work – *La cambiale di matrimonio* ('The Bill of Marriage').

A RUNAWAY SUCCESS

The lyrical charm of Rossini's music soon made him a runaway success. His *L'inganno felice* ('The Happy Deception', 1812) and a commission from La Scala, Milan, *La pietra del paragone* ('The Touchstone', 1812) entranced opera audiences, who loved their graceful melodies, amusing characters and ingenious plots. At barely 20 years of age, Gioachino Rossini was made.

A PROFUSION OF OPERAS

In the next 17 years, until he retired, a profusion of operas flowed from Rossini's pen. He produced four in the six months between November 1812 and May 1813. One of these, the darkly dramatic *Tancredi* (1813), made Rossini internationally famous. The opera's appeal owed much to his sensitive handling of heroic virtues, and innovative orchestration, most particularly his use of woodwind instruments to track the vocal line and give it added expressiveness. For Rossini, *Tancredi* was a venture into sombre territory, but with his next work, *L'italiana in Algeri* ('The Italian Girl in Algiers', 1813) he returned to the operatic romp, full of subterfuge, false identities and impudent ruses.

A LIVELY MASTERPIECE

Rossini was now in great demand not only by audiences, but also by opera-house managements. In around 1814 the composer accepted a six-year contract from Domenico Barbaia (1778–1841) as music director of the Teatro San Carlo and the Teatro del Fondo in Naples. It was in Naples that Rossini unveiled his great masterpiece, *Il barbiere di Siviglia* ('The Barber of Seville', 1816). This was Rossini at his witty, vivacious best, in an opera full of fun, lively, inventive orchestration and catchy melodies.

A TRAGIC ALTERNATIVE

Yet this same year, Rossini unveiled a total contrast – his *Otello* (1816), a dark tale of love, jealousy and betrayal based on one of Shakespeare's great tragedies. The part of the doomed heroine, Desdemona, was written for Rossini's wife, Isabella Colbran, who specialized in tragic roles. The violent ending of *Otello*, in which Otello murders Desdemona was considered too disturbing for audiences, who preferred problems solved and happiness ever after. As a result, Rossini had to concoct a happy ending when *Otello* was premiered in Rome.

A PROLIFIC AND POPULAR COMPOSER

Nevertheless, Rossini was all the rage – the most popular opera composer of his day and the most prolific, with 25 operas to his credit in the 10 years since *Tancredi* won him international fame. He was still only 31 when he left Italy to take up a post in Paris as director of the Théâtre

Italien. At this time, in the early 1820s, *grand opéra* was beginning to make an impact on French audiences. It was a change of mood that was going to upstage the charm and the light touch of which Rossini was such a consummate master. Ironically, Rossini himself helped to set the new-style opera on its way with his *Guillaume Tell* ('William Tell', 1829). This had a length and scope that made it one of the masterpieces of early French *grand opéra*, but it was the last of Rossini's 40 works for the opera stage.

Though his retirement lasted nearly 40 years, he was not forgotten and some 6,000 mourners attended his funeral at Santa Croce Church in Florence in 1868. A chorus 300-strong sang the prayer from his opera *Mosè in Egitto* ('Moses in Egypt', 1818). The performance was so compelling that the audience outside the church demanded an encore.

L'italiana in Algeri

Despite its North African setting, Rossini's *L'italiana in Algeri* was a resolutely Italian opera. Unlike *Aida* (1871), in which Verdi took care to evoke the mysterious atmosphere of ancient Egypt, Rossini made no particular attempt to reflect the exotic nature of Algiers. However, given the good-natured harum-scarum fun of this two-act comic opera and the inventiveness of Rossini's music, none of this mattered a great deal to the audience at the opera's premiere at the Teatro San Benedetto in Venice on 22 May 1813. What mattered was Rossini's mastery of comedy in this first of what were to become his three masterpieces of **opera buffa**.

L'italiana in Algeri ('The Italian Girl in Algiers')

by Gioachino Rossini
Composed: 1813
Premiered: 1813, Venice
Libretto by Angelo Anelli

ACT I

Elvira, wife of Mustafa, Bey (governor) of Algiers, is lamenting her husband's waning affection to her confidante, Zulma. Mustafa reveals to Captain Haly that he is tired of Elvira and wishes her to marry Lindoro, his Italian slave. He asks Haly to find him an Italian woman for his harem. Lindoro does not wish to marry Elvira; he still loves his lost Italian sweetheart Isabella.

Haly's pirates return with their captives – Isabella, who is searching for Lindoro, and Taddeo, her admirer. The pirates try to separate them, but they claim that Taddeo is her uncle and they must stay together. Haly rejoices in having found an Italian woman for Mustafa's harem. Isabella is annoyed by Taddeo's jealousy, but they stick together.

Lindoro and Elvira eventually agree to marry, although neither is keen. Lindoro will be allowed to leave for Italy, but Elvira still loves Mustafa and has no desire to go. Mustafa meets Isabella and falls in love with her. She realizes that she can outwit him and plays along. Elvira, Lindoro and Zulma come to bid farewell to Mustafa; Lindoro and Isabella recognize each other. Isabella persuades Mustafa not to send his wife away, and insists on keeping Lindoro as her slave.

ACT II

Elvira still hopes to regain Mustafa's love. Isabella scolds Lindoro for agreeing to marry Elvira; he assures her of his fidelity and they decide to escape. Mustafa, meanwhile, employs Taddeo as his Kaimakan, to help gain Isabella's affection. Isabella advises Elvira on how to handle Mustafa. She then leaves and Isabella keeps Mustafa waiting outside. She eventually invites him in, along with Taddeo, whom Mustafa has instructed to leave when the Bey sneezes. Taddeo refuses to leave and Mustafa is further frustrated when Isabella invites Elvira to join them for coffee.

As Lindoro and Taddeo plan their escape, Mustafa enters. Lindoro reassures him that

Isabella is in love with him, to the extent that she wants him to join the exclusive Italian order of Pappataci. Mustafa is pleased at this honour; Lindoro and Taddeo explain that he must only eat, drink and sleep, oblivious to the world around him. Isabella prepares a ceremony of initiation. Mustafa is pronounced a Pappataci and is presented with food, while Isabella and Lindoro loudly declare their love, as a test. As Mustafa concentrates on remaining oblivious, the Italians prepare their ship for departure. By the time he realizes what is happening, they have set sail. Mustafa has learned his lesson and begs Elvira for forgiveness.

Il barbiere di Siviglia

Rossini's opera was given its first performance, in Rome, on 20 February 1816, but not under the name by which it is now known. The reason was that Rossini's *Il barbiere* was faced with a rival – an opera on the same subject by Giovanni Paisiello, that had first been produced in St Petersburg in 1782. More than 30 years later, when the first performance of Rossini's opera was about to take place, Paisiello's *Il barbiere* was still enjoying great popularity among Italian opera audiences. Rossini was therefore obliged to resort to subterfuge: he changed his title to *Almaviva, ossia L'inutile precauzione* ('Almaviva or The Useless Precaution'). The title *Il barbiere di Siviglia* was not used until it was performed in Bologna later on in 1816.

However, the opera illustrated Rossini's use of a common practice among nineteenth-century opera composers – borrowing from their own works as long as the reused music was not first performed in the town that had heard the original. This was how Rossini's overture for *Il barbiere* was the third run of this music: he had already used the overture in his *Aureliano in Palmira* (1813) and *Elisabetta, regina d'Inghilterra* ('Elizabeth, Queen of England', 1815).

Il barbiere di Siviglia ('The Barber of Seville')

by Gioachino Rossini
Composed: 1816
Premiered: 1816, Rome
Libretto by Cesare Sterbini, after Pierre-Augustin Caron de Beaumarchais

ACT I

The beautiful Rosina, ward of Dr Bartolo, is confined in the doctor's house. Count Almaviva, disguised as a poor student, Lindoro, stands below her window with a group of musicians and serenades her. She does not come to the window, so the musicians, receiving payment from the count, depart. Figaro, the town barber, approaches, boasting of his skills and importance. The count offers him a reward, if he will assist the count in gaining entry to Bartolo's house and wooing Rosina. The count, as Lindoro, sings again to Rosina, who is entranced by his voice and drops him a note as Bartolo pulls her away from the window. Figaro suggests than the count should go to the house disguised as a drunken soldier and say that he has been billeted there.

Rosina recalls Lindoro's voice and decides to try and outwit Bartolo. Meanwhile Bartolo is warned by Don Basilio, the music master, that Count Almaviva has designs on Rosina. Bartolo hopes to marry Rosina himself and Basilio suggests slandering the count, to which Bartolo agrees. Figaro overhears and relates to Rosina that Bartolo plans to marry her the next day; she entrusts him with a note for Lindoro. The housekeeper, Berta, opens the door to a drunken soldier – the count in disguise – who is demanding lodging; Bartolo refuses him entry. The count manages to pass Rosina a love letter, but Bartolo is watching. When he demands to see it, Rosina hands him a laundry list. Figaro enters with the news that a crowd has gathered outside to see what the commotion is about. The police arrive and arrest the count, but he quietly informs them of his identity and is released.

ACT II

A young music teacher, Don Alonso – in fact the count in another disguise – arrives at the house, claiming to have been sent by Don Basilio, who is unwell. Rosina enters for her music lesson and recognizes Don Alonso as 'Lindoro'. As Bartolo sleeps in a chair, Rosina and Don Alonso sing of their love for one another. As a further distraction, Figaro arrives to shave Bartolo and manages to procure the key for the balcony window. Basilio arrives, in full health; he is bribed to become 'ill' and leaves. As the lovers plan their escape, Bartolo becomes aware of the conspiracy and sends Figaro and Lindoro away. Bartolo sends Basilio to fetch a notary and tells Rosina that Lindoro is probably working for Count Almaviva, who is known to be in pursuit of her.

Following a storm, Figaro and the count climb into the house through the balcony window. Rosina at first rejects Lindoro, believing what Bartolo has told her, but succumbs when the count reveals that he and Lindoro are one and the same. As they leave they realize that the cunning Bartolo has removed the ladder. Basilio enters with the notary and, after some bribery, the marriage ceremony is instead performed between Rosina and the count. Bartolo arrives too late and is forced to accept the new married couple. The count suggests that he keep Rosina's dowry in compensation for his loss.

Recommended Recording:

Il barbiere di Siviglia, Failoni Chamber Orchestra; Will Humburg, conductor; Naxos 8 660027/9; Soloists: Sonia Ganassi (Rosina), Ingrid Kertesi (Berta), Ramón Vargas (Almaviva), Roberto Servile (Figaro), Angelo Romero (Dr Bartolo), Franco de Grandis (Don Basilio)

La Cenerentola

Rossini's two-act version of the Cinderella story, his twentieth opera and last Italian comic opera, received its first

---

SOUNDS FAMILIAR

'LARGO AL FACTOTUM' ('ROOM FOR THE FACTOTUM')

In Act I, Figaro, the barber of Seville, introduces himself to the audience by singing, rather ruefully, a catalogue of the many different tasks he must perform. He confides how hard it is to have to try and please everyone.

---

performance at the Teatro Valle in Rome on 25 January 1817. This was followed by performances in London (1820), Vienna (1822) and New York (1826). The Teatro Valle, which had commissioned Rossini to write the opera for the carnival in Rome, gave him a deadline of 26 December 1816. However, by 23 December, no subject had yet been decided. The librettist, Jacopo Ferretti (1784–1852) suggested 20 possibilities to Rossini. The composer rejected them all. At last, though, Rossini agreed to the Cinderella theme. Ferretti stayed up all night, writing an outline. Just over three weeks later, the libretto was complete and Rossini composed the music for it in another 24 days. When the premiere of *La Cenerentola* ('Cinderella', 1817) took place, just over six weeks separated the initial idea from the first performance. Unfortunately, the opera was not well received and Ferretti became depressed. Rossini, however, assured him that audiences would eventually 'fall in love' with *La Cenerentola*. He was right. In the last few days of the Rome Carnival, the opera was being applauded frenziedly by its audiences.

La Cenerentola

by Gioachino Rossini
Composed: 1816–17
Premiered: 1817, Rome
Libretto by Jacopo Ferretti, after Charles Perraut

ACT I

Don Magnifico's daughters Clorinda and Tisbe pamper themselves while his stepdaughter Cenerentola completes her chores. A beggar – in fact Prince Ramiro's tutor, Alidoro – comes to the door. The sisters send him away, but Cenerentola gives him food. He says her goodness will be rewarded. Prince Ramiro, who is holding a ball to find a bride, arrives. Don Magnifico hopes that he will marry one of his daughters.

Prince Ramiro arrives, disguised as his valet, Dandini. Alidoro has told him that one of Don Magnifico's daughters is a suitable bride. He meets Cenerentola and they fall in love. Ramiro announces the arrival of the 'prince' – a disguised Dandini. Cenerentola pleads in vain to be allowed to attend the ball. Alidoro asks the whereabouts of Don Magnifico's third daughter and he declares that she is dead. Everyone leaves for the ball. Cenerentola encounters the 'beggar', who reveals his identity and asks her to accompany him to the ball.

The 'prince' escorts the sisters into the palace and offers Don Magnifico the position of court vintner. Dandini tells Ramiro that the sisters are awful. Dandini offers his 'valet' – Ramiro – to the sister he does not choose; they are unimpressed. Alidoro introduces a lady; all are struck by her resemblance to Cenerentola.

ACT II

Don Magnifico is worried and Ramiro bewildered by the mysterious guest. Ramiro hides as she enters with Dandini. She tells the 'prince' that she is in love with his valet; Ramiro reveals himself. Cenerentola tells him that he must seek her out, and gives him one of two matching bracelets. She leaves; Ramiro and Dandini resume their identities.

Don Magnifico demands to know which daughter Dandini is to marry; the valet admits the truth. He orders Don Magnifico and the sisters to leave. Cenerentola tends the fire. The others return and demand their supper. A storm breaks out. Alidoro causes

Prince Ramiro's carriage to break down outside Don Magnifico's castle. The prince and Dandini enter and the truth slowly dawns on Cenerentola. She begs Ramiro to forgive Don Magnifico and his daughters; eventually everyone is reconciled.

Le Comte Ory

Le Comte Ory (1828) was another of Rossini's bright, brilliant operas buffa. This one, based on an old Picardy legend, premiered at the Paris Opèra on 20 August 1828. The first performance in London took place at the Haymarket on 28 February 1829, and was possibly intended as a celebration for Rossini's thirty-seventh birthday, the best the theatre could do for a celebrity born on 29 February. However, Le Comte Ory was not entirely an original piece of work. Rossini had already used much of the music, including the overture, in his Il viaggo a Reims ('A Journey to Rheims', 1825).

Le Comte Ory

by Gioachino Rossini
Composed: 1828
Premiered: 1828, Paris
Libretto by Eugène Scribe and Charles Gaspard Delestre-Poirson

ACT I

While the men are away on a crusade, Countess Adèle renounces love. Count Ory has disguised himself as a hermit who gives the villagers potions for matters of the heart. He hopes to court the countess. The countess's confidante Ragonde arrives and informs the hermit that her mistress wishes to see him; he consents. The count's tutor and his page Isolier arrive in search of the count, and also hope to find the countess, whom Isolier loves. The tutor realizes the hermit's true identity. Isolier asks the hermit for advice and reveals his plan to gain entry to the castle by dressing up as a nun; the count resolves to use this idea himself. The countess arrives to consult *the hermit, who tells her that falling in love will ease her pain. She admits that she is in love with Isolier, but the hermit advises her against the match. The tutor then reveals the count's deception. News arrives that the men are returning. The count resolves to enter the castle.*

ACT II

While the women await the men's return, a storm breaks out. Hearing cries, the women discover several nuns (in fact the count, his tutor, Raimbaud, and associates), who plead for protection. They are admitted and the count insists on embracing the countess. The 'nuns' celebrate. Isolier announces that the men will return that night, and reveals the true identities of the 'nuns'. The count insists on joining the countess in her bedroom, not realizing that Isolier is also there. In the darkness, he takes Isolier's hand. Trumpets announce the return of the crusaders and the count realizes that Isolier has tricked him. The count and his associates flee and the household rejoices in love's victory.

Guillaume Tell

Rossini called the first performance of his *grand opéra Guillaume Tell* a 'quasi-fiasco'. The overture, he said, was fine, the first act had some interesting effects, and the second was a triumph, but the third and fourth were disappointing. However, the theatre director was more concerned with audience reaction at the Théâtre de l'Académie Royale de Musique in Paris, where the premiere took place on 3 August 1829; the reception had been distinctly cool. As a result, he told Rossini, he was going to cancel his contract for future works. Rossini, unfazed, offered to withdraw the contract himself, adding that he would never write another opera. He kept his word.

In time, though, *Guillaume Tell* came to be appreciated for the colour and variety of its music and its brilliant special effects, such as the thunderstorm in the overture. However, the opera was immensely long, spreading its four acts over three hours and 45 minutes. Soon after the first performance, the theatre management began performing it one act at a time. Even this did not solve the problem, as Rossini was well aware. On being told that the second act was to be performed, he remarked, sardonically: 'What, the whole of it?'

Guillaume Tell ('William Tell')
by Gioachino Rossini
Composed: 1829
Premiered: 1829, Paris
Libretto by Etienne de Jouy and Hippolyte Louis-Florent Blis, after Johann Christoph Friedrich von Schiller

ACT I

As the villagers on the shores of Lake Lucerne celebrate the impending marriage celebrations, Guillaume Tell laments the rule of Gesler, an Austrian oppressor. The respected patriarch Melchthal advises his son Arnold to marry, but the youth is in love with Gesler's daughter Mathilde. The sound of horns signal that Gesler's hunt is near and Arnold prepares to meet Mathilde. Guillaume Tell tries to recruit him to his patriotic cause and Arnold agrees, but he is torn between loyalty to his country and love for Mathilde.

Melchthal blesses the wedding couples and the festivities continue, with Tell's son Jemmy winning an archery contest. The celebrations are interrupted by the arrival of Leuthold, a shepherd. He announces that he has killed an Austrian soldier, who was attempting to rape his daughter. Tell ferries him to safety across the lake, much to the anger of the Austrian soldiers. Gesler's henchman Rodolphe demands to know the identity of the rescuer but the villagers remain silent in their loyalty towards Tell. Infuriated, Rodolphe takes Melchthal hostage.

ACT II

Mathilde is contemplating her love for Arnold when he appears and the couple sing a duet. Mathilde hears Guillaume Tell and Walter approaching and leaves, promising to meet Arnold the next day. Tell and Walter break the news to Arnold that Melchthal has been murdered. Arnold swears vengeance, allying himself to Tell's cause. Foresters join them and together the Swiss revolutionaries, with Tell as their leader, plan to overthrow the tyrannical Austrian rule.

ACT III

Arnold and Mathilde rendezvous in a ruined chapel. Arnold explains about the death of his father and the plans for an uprising. The lovers bid each other farewell, assuming they will not meet again. Meanwhile, in the town square, Gesler has ordered a celebration marking 100 years of Austrian rule. The Austrian soldiers force the Swiss to dance, sing and bow down before their ruler. Guillaume Tell is alone in refusing to bow, enraging Gesler, and his fate is further sealed when Rodolphe recognizes him as the accomplice in Leuthold's escape. Gesler decrees that Tell can live only if he successfully shoots an apple from Jemmy's head. Thankfully, Tell's shot is accurate, but he then drops a second arrow which was meant for Gesler should he have failed in his task. To the horror of the Swiss people, Tell is sentenced to death and taken away by boat. Mathilde announces that she will protect Jemmy.

ACT IV

Arnold has returned to his family home. He is informed that Guillaume Tell has been taken prisoner and resolves to lead the uprising himself, showing his companions where Tell and Melchthal concealed the weapons in preparation for the revolt. Mathilde restores Jemmy to his mother, Tell's wife Hedwige, and offers herself as a hostage to ensure Tell's safety.

A storm breaks out and Tell, a skilful oarsman, is released from his chains to be given control of the boat. Tell steers back to the shore and escapes. Gesler follows, but Jemmy hands Tell a bow and arrow, with which he shoots the Austrian ruler dead. As the storm passes, Arnold and the other patriots capture the castle and everyone rejoices that peace and liberation have been restored to their country.

OPERAS

1809	Demetrio e Polibio
1810	La cambiale di matrimonio
1811	L'equivoco stravagante
1812	L'inganno felice; **Ciro in Babilonia**; La scala di seta; La pietra del paragone; L'occasione fa il ladro
1813	L'italiana in Algeri; Aureliano in Palmira; Il Signor Bruschino; Tancredi
1814	Il turco in Italia; Sigismondo
1815	Elisabetta, regina d'Inghilterra; Torvaldo e Dorliska
1816	Il barbiere di Siviglia; La gazzetta; Otello
1817	La gazza ladra; Armida; Adelaide di Borgogna; La Cenerentola
1818	Mosè in Egitto; rev. 1827 as Moïse et Pharaon; Adina; Ricciardo e Zoraide
1819	Ermione; Eduardo e Cristina; La donna del lago; Bianca e Falliero
1820	Maometto II
1821	Matilde di Shabran
1822	Zelmira
1823	Semiramide
1825	Il viaggio a Reims
1826	Le Siège de Corinthe (rev. of Maometto II)
1828	Le Comte Ory
1829	Guillaume Tell

TIMELINE

1792	Gioacchino Rossini born, Pasaro, Italy
1796	Moves with mother to Bologna
1805	Only appearance as singer in Ferdinando Paer's Camilla at Bologna's Teatro del Corso
1806	Enters Bologna Academy and writes fist opera, Demetrio e polibio
1810	First commission for opera, La cambiale di matrimonio
1812	La pietra del paragone produced at La Scala, Milan
1813	Has first international successes with opera seria Tancredi and opera buffa L'italiana in Algeri
1815	Moves to Naples as director of Teatro San Carlo and Teatro del Fondo
1815	Premiere of Elisabetta, regina d'Inghilterra; leading part taken by Rossini's future wife Isabella Colbran

1816	*Otello* produced, and admired by composers including Verdi
1816	Writes *opera buffa Il barbiere di Siviglia*, reputedly in two weeks
1818	Premiere of *Mosè in Egitto*
1822	Marries Isabella Colbran
1823	Travels to London and meets Beethoven
1823	*Semiramide*, last of Italian operas, premieres in Venice
1824	Becomes director of Théâtre Italien, Paris
1825	Appointed composer to King Charles X
1828	New opera *Le Comte Ory* written for the Opéra
1829	Writes last opera, *grand opéra Guillame Tell*
1832	Begins work on his *Stabat mater*
1837	Returns to Italy; suffers from long illness
1845	Isabella dies
1846	Marries Olympe Pelissier and then leaves Bologna
1855	Settles in Paris
1857	Begins *Péchés de viellesse*
1863	*Petite messe solennelle* completed
1868	Rossini dies, Paris

Rubini, Giovanni Battista
1794–1854, **ITALIAN**

The Italian tenor Giovanni Battista Rubini was said to 'enchant' listeners with his powerful yet sweet and subtle voice. He was also able to move his audiences to tears with his famous musical 'sob'. Bellini created several roles for Rubini, including Gualtieri in Il pirata, Elvino in *La sonnambula* and Arturo in I puritani. The qualities of Rubini's voice greatly influenced Italian Romantic opera, especially when it was showcased in Bellini's supremely smooth and tuneful operas. Rubini made his debut at 20 in 1814 in Pavia when he sang in *Lagrime di una vedova* ('A Widow's Tears', 1808) by Pietro Generali (1773–1832). He performed in Naples for 13 years, 1816–29, and also at La Scala, Milan in 1818 and 1825–31, the Théâtre Italien in Paris in 1825 and 1831–43, London 1831–43, and St Petersburg in 1843 and 1844.

Schröder-Devrient, Wilhelmine
1804–60, **GERMAN**

Wilhelmine Schröder-Devrient was born into 'show business'. Her father was Friedrich Schröder (1744–1816), the first German Don Giovanni in Mozart's opera of that name, and her mother was the 'Mrs Siddons of Germany', the actress Sophie Bürger (1781–1868). Wilhelmine was a child actress and ballet dancer before making her debut at the Kärnterthortheater in Vienna as Pamina in Mozart's *Die Zauberflöte* in 1821. She sang in Dresden for 25 years (1822–47), with excursions to Berlin (1828), Paris (1831–32), and the London Haymarket in 1832–33 and 1837. She retired in 1847. Schröder-Devrient was a highly emotional singer and actress who became known as the 'Queen of Tears' for weeping on stage while performing the many powerful and tragic parts in her repertoire. She sang Bellini's Norma, Valentine in Meyerbeer's *Les Huguenots*, and, in what was termed the greatest interpretation of the role, Leonore in Beethoven's *Fidelio*.

Schubert, Franz
1797–1828, **AUSTRIAN**

Celebrated for his instrumental works and over 600 songs, Franz Schubert knew that musical fame and fortune in Vienna lay above all in the opera house. In his teens he completed several one-act comedies and the 'magic opera', *Des Teufels Lustschloss* ('The Devil's Pleasure Palace', 1814). Thanks to his friend, the baritone Johann Michael Vogl, his operetta *Die Zwillingsbrüder* ('The Twin Brothers', 1818–19) was professionally staged in Vienna in June 1820. Though only a moderate success, it was followed by the melodrama *Die Zauberharfe* ('The Magic Harp', 1820). Though its often-delightful music did not go unnoticed, *Die Zauberharfe*'s preposterous plot doomed it to failure, setting the pattern for most of Schubert's stage works over the next few years. In any case, German opera had little chance in a Vienna intoxicated by Rossini. Schubert's grandest, most ambitious operas, *Alfonso und Estrella* (1821–22) and *Fierrabras* (1823) were rejected by the Court Theatre, and remained unperformed in his lifetime.

Both *Alfonso* and *Fierrabras* contain much beautiful and characteristic music, especially in nature descriptions such as the exquisite duet 'Weit über Glanz und Erdenschimmer' ('Far Above the Shimmering Earth') from *Fierrabras*. Yet both suffer from creaky, diffuse plots and unsure dramatic timing. Probably Schubert's most successful opera in the theatre is the ebullient one-act comedy *Die Verschworenen* ('The Conspirators', 1823), a nineteenth-century take on Aristophanes' *Lysistrata*.

Schiller, Friedrich von
1759–1805, GERMAN

Friedrich von Schiller, the great German poet, playwright and historian, trained for the Church, the army, the law and military medicine before he finally found his niche. It happened when, at his own expense, Schiller published his revolutionary drama *Die Raüber* ('The Robbers', 1781). When the play was staged in Mannheim in 1782, it was an encouraging success, but the playwright, who was still in the army, was arrested for attending the first night without the permission of his commanding officer. Over 50 years later, in 1836, the Italian composer Saverio Mercadante (1795–1870) wrote an opera based on Schiller's first play.

As an opera it was the first of an ultimate total of 56 by a variety of composers. Among the most famous examples were Verdi, who used Schiller's work as a basis for *Luisa Miller* and *Don Carlos* (1867), Donizetti for his *Maria Stuarda* and Rossini for his *Guillaume Tell* (1829).

Scribe, Eugene
1791–1861, FRENCH

Eugene Scribe, the French librettist, scored his first success with Auber's *opéra comique La dame blanche* ('The White Lady', 1825). However, Scribe concentrated mainly on French *grand opéra*, with libretti that matched the genre's visual and musical grandeur and the dramatic on-stage action. Scribe formed a partnership with Auber, who set no less than 38 of his libretti to music. The central figures of French *grand opéra*, such as Halévy and Meyerbeer also recognized in Scribe an artist whose verse was capable of equalling the 'size' of their music. A situation in which composer and librettist 'thought big' was essential in *grand opéra* for which Scribe drew his plots from history at its most dramatic: he specialized in the clash of religions, as in Meyerbeer's *Les Huguenots*, or in political and national rivalries in which real life was entwined with the fate of characters caught up in epoch-making events.

Sontag, Henriette
1806–54, GERMAN

The German soprano Henriette Sontag made her debut in 1821 as the princess in Boieldieu's *Jean de Paris* (1812). In 1823, in Vienna, Weber asked Sontag to create the title role in his *Euryanthe* (1822–23) after seeing her in Rossini's *La donna del lago*. He was justified when her appearance in Berlin in 1825 caused an outbreak of 'Sontag-fever'. Sontag's voice was sweet, flexible, and she possessed a 'brilliant, inventive and pleasing' freshness. She sang many top roles – Rossini's Semiramide, Donizetti's Lucrezia Borgia and Weber's Agathe in *Der Freischütz* among them. Sontag retired in 1830 after marrying a diplomat whose career might have been compromised by her fame, but returned to the opera stage after he retired. She was still at the peak of her powers and her fame when she died of cholera in 1854.

Spontini, Gaspare
1774–1851, ITALIAN

Gaspare Spontini's early career was blighted by insecurity after the French, under Napoleon Bonaparte, invaded Italy in 1796. Spontini, it seems, decided that his future lay in France, but after arriving in Paris in 1800 he found his musical style was unsuited to the prevailing genre, opéra comique. Spontini turned instead to serious themes and produced *Milton* (1804), which dealt with the English Puritan poet John Milton in old age. *Milton* was a success but *La vestale* ('The Vestal Virgin', 1807) took success a step further and marked out Spontini as one of the leading composers of opera in his time. Subsequently Spontini played a crucial role in founding French *grand opéra*, pioneering the genre's most imposing features – rituals, processions, large choruses, stage bands and other grandiose effects. These ingredients came together in their greatest splendour in *Fernand Cortez* (1809), Spontini's historical pageant on the sixteenth-century Spanish conqueror of Aztec Mexico. Among its sensational effects was a full-scale cavalry charge on stage. Unfortunately, Spontini was haughty and overbearing, and his later career was marked by quarrels with colleagues in Paris and Berlin, where his later work, *Agnes von Hohentaufen*, was performed in 1827.

Tacchinardi-Persiani, Fanny
1812–67, ITALIAN

The angelic-looking soprano Fanny Tacchinardi-Persiani was made to play the delicate, suffering heroines of early Romantic opera. Fanny Tacchinardi – as she was before marrying the composer Giuseppe Persiani in 1830 – made her debut in 1832 at Livorno and went on to great success in Venice, Naples and Milan. She sang at the Théâtre Italien in Paris (1837–48), in London at the Haymarket Theatre (1838–46) and Covent Garden (1847–49), in Vienna in 1837 and 1844, and St Petersburg (1850–52). Tacchinardi-Persiani created the title roles in Donizetti's *Rosmonda d'Inghilterra*, *Lucia di Lammermoor* and *Pia de'Tolomei*

('Pia of Tolomei', 1837). She was widely acclaimed for her Linda of Chamonix and Lucrezia Borgia. Giuseppe Persiani's operas benefited from his marriage to such a brilliant and popular singer. So did the London opera world, for in 1847, husband and wife helped establish the Royal Italian Opera at Covent Garden.

Tamburini, Antonio
1800–76, ITALIAN

Antonio Tamburini, the Italian baritone, was 18 when he made his debut in *Cento in Contessa di colle erboso* ('Countess of the Grassy Hill', 1814) by Pietro Generali. Tamburini went on to appear at La Scala, Milan in 1822 and 1827–30, in Naples in 1824 and 1828–32), the London Haymarket (1832–51) and Covent Garden (1847). He sang regularly at the Théâtre Italien in Paris between 1832 and 1854 and also appeared in Vienna, Genoa and St Petersburg. The handsome, popular Tamburini was personable, with a 'rich, sweet and equal' voice, splendid **coloratura** technique and 'sensational' falsetto. When he failed to appear at the Haymarket Theatre, London in 1840, the disappointed audience staged a riot. Tamburini performed in Mozart and Rossini operas and created roles in Bellini's *Il pirata* and *I puritani*. He sang in 10 operas by Donizetti, including *Lucia di Lammermoor* and *Don Pasquale*, in which he appeared as the doctor Malatesta.

Velluti, Giovanni Battista
1780–1861, ITALIAN

Giovanni Battista Velluti, the Italian soprano **castrato**, created Rossini's only castrato role, as Arsace in his *Aureliano in Palmira* (1813), but infuriated the composer with his pretentious and showy ornamentation. After that Rossini wrote his own ornamentation. Velluti also created the role of Armando in Meyerbeer's *Crociato in Egitto* ('The Crusader in Egypt', 1824); Meyerbeer wrote the opera especially for him. Velluti made his debut at Forli in 1800. He went on to perform at the Teatro San Carlo, Naples (1803), Rome (1805–07), La Scala, Milan for most years between 1808 and 1814 and later in Vienna, St Petersburg and the Haymarket, London. Despite his good looks and what Stendhal called his 'prodigious gifts', Velluti shocked London audiences who were no longer familiar with castrati or their voices. However, women found Velluti fascinating and he had numerous mistresses. Velluti, the last great castrato, retired in 1830, and became a farmer.

Weber, Carl Maria von
1786–1826, GERMAN

Carl Maria von Weber was a teenage prodigy who wrote his first opera aged 14. By 1804 Weber, still only 18, was musical director in Breslau. By the time he had moved on to Stuttgart, Weber had reworked his first opera, *Das Waldmädchen* ('The Forest Girl', 1810), and gave it the new title of *Silvana*. With *Silvana*, first performed in Frankfurt in 1810, Weber's music prefigured his masterpiece, *Der Freischütz* ('The Free-Shooter', 1821) and revealed an impressive sense of theatre.

INGENIOUS IDEAS

The composer made life difficult for himself by creating a heroine who was unable to talk, much less sing. Even so, he met the challenge with some ingenuity, making his orchestration 'speak' for her and speak lyrically, too. Weber first came across the story of *Der Freischütz* in 1810, but his first attempt at writing an opera on the subject foundered when his librettist deserted him. Eleven years passed before the opera finally triumphed in Berlin. By that time, Weber had occupied posts at Prague and Dresden and in both cities set about reforming the management of opera. He hired performers as ensemble singers rather than as opera 'stars'.

RADICAL REHEARSALS

He formulated a new, radical schedule of rehearsals that began with the performers absorbing the drama of the opera before tackling the music. He rearranged both the chorus and the seating of the orchestra and, in Dresden, brought German opera to the fore as his answer to the rival Italian opera performing there. Weber was influential in promoting what Wagner later termed *Gesamtkunstwerk* – 'the total work of art' – in which all related arts are blended into a new creation. Tragically, time was short for the consumptive Weber, who died aged 39 in 1826.

Der Freischütz

The Faustian theme, with its connotations of the black arts, was not new to opera when Weber wrote *Der Freischütz*. Since 1796 there had already been eight operas based on the sixteenth-century legend as composers responded to one of the most seductive themes of the early Romantic era: a pact with the devil for personal gain or, in the influential drama by Goethe, for the chance of immortality. Among these early Romantic operas, Weber's achieved much greater impact than most, as well as far greater popularity. His treatment of the theme was imaginative and his melodies were inspired by well-known German folk songs. There were echoes of the *Singspiel* tradition that originated in the sixteenth century, and a skilful recreation in music of the mysteries and supernatural feel of the forest. In this, *Der Freischütz* was the embodiment of German Romanticism, familiar in its traditional musical forms, yet eerie in its occult atmosphere. However, *Der Freischütz* was not just a work for German consumption. It had universal and international appeal and was among the most popular and successful operas ever written. The libretto, by Friedrich Kind (1768–1843) was translated into no less than 25 languages.

Der Freischütz
('The Free-shooter')

by Carl Maria von Weber
Composed: 1817–21
Premiered: 1821, Berlin
Libretto by Friedrich Kind, after Johann August Apel and Friedrich Laun

ACT I

Max, a forest ranger, is in love with Agathe, daughter of the head ranger Kuno. Her father agrees to the match, on the condition that Max passes a test of marksmanship. Max's shooting skills get worse as the day of the test draws near. A peasant, Kilian, beats him in a competition and the people mock him. Caspar, who also loves Agathe, offers to help Max win Prince Ottaker's shooting competition the next day. He reveals that seven magic bullets can be cast, which will automatically reach the marksman's intended target. Unbeknownst to Max, Caspar has sold his soul to the devil, represented by Samiel, the 'Dark Huntsman', and is due to forfeit his life. Caspar hopes that he can arrange for another human life to be sacrificed in his place. To prove to Max the power of the bullets, Caspar hands him a loaded rifle. Max, discharging it in into the air, manages to shoot an eagle flying high above. Impressed, Max agrees to accompany Caspar to Wolf's Glen at midnight, in order to cast the magic bullets.

ACT II

In her room, Agathe is feeling uneasy. She tells her relative Aennchen that she has encountered a hermit, who warned her of danger and gave her flowers to offer her protection. A picture of one of Agathe's ancestors has also fallen from the wall, injuring her; she sees this as a bad omen; Aennchen tries to amuse her.

Agathe and Aennchen are horrified when Max arrives and tells them that he has shot a deer near Wolf's Glen and is going to retrieve it. They plead with him not to go, telling him the glen is haunted, but he is resolute.

At Wolf's Glen, Caspar summons up Samiel and they prepare to forge the magic bullets. Samiel agrees to allow Caspar three more years of life in exchange for a substitute human life. Samiel will be in control of the seventh bullet; Caspar suggests that it be aimed at Agathe. Max arrives and they begin to cast the bullets. Various fantastic and terrible visions appear to Max, including the ghost of his mother, who warns him of the danger he will face. There is also a ghostly hunt with fire-breathing animals, and a vision of Agathe dying.

ACT III

During the next day's hunt Max is, unsurprisingly, rather successful. He only has one magic bullet remaining – the one controlled by the 'Dark Huntsman' – for the prince's shooting contest. Meanwhile, Agathe is filled with a sense of foreboding. She has had a bad dream, in which she took the form of a dove and was shot by Max. Aennchen again seeks to comfort her. The bridesmaids then arrive with her bridal wreath in a box, but she opens it to reveal a funeral wreath. Everyone is shocked. Agathe fashions a new bridal wreath from the flowers given to her by the hermit.

At the contest, a dove is selected as Max's target. Agathe, distraught, tries to stop him, crying out that she is the dove, but Max fires his gun. Both Agathe and Caspar fall to the ground. However, Agathe, protected by the hermit, survives; the bullet was deflected by the bridal wreath and she has merely fainted. Samiel chooses to take Caspar's life rather than Max's; Caspar dies, cursing the world. Max offers an explanation of the events to Prince Ottaker, who at first decides to exile him. However, the hermit declares that shooting contests should be abolished and Max given another chance. The prince agrees to give Max a year to prove himself; after that time he is free to marry Agathe. Everyone rejoices in God's mercy.

OPERAS

1800	Das Waldmädchen
1801–02	Peter Schmoll und seine Nachbarn
1804–05	Rübezahl
1808–10	Silvana
1810–11	Abu Hassan
1817–21	Der Freischütz
1820–21	Die drei Pintos
1822–23	Euryanthe
1825–26	Oberon

TIMELINE

1786	Carl Maria Weber born, Oldenburg, Germany
1798	Taught by Michael Haydn in Salzburg
1800	Moves to Freiburg and composes first opera, Das Waldmädchen
1803	Returns to Salzburg and completes Peter Schmoll und seine Nachbarn
1803	Begins to study under Abbé Vogler
1804	Appointed Kappellmeister at Breslau; begins work on Rübezahl
1806	Quits Breslau for Karlsruhe
1807	Offered court secretarial post at Stuttgart
1808	Begins work on new version of Das Waldmädchen, called Silvana
1810	Moves to Darmstadt and takes lessons from Vogler; writes Abu Hassan
1810	Premiere of Silvana, Frankfurt
1813	Appointed director of Prague Opera
1817	Becomes Court Kappellmeister at Dresden, briefed to establish German national opera
1820	Begins work on Die drei Pintos, a comic opera that he never completes
1821	Completes Der Freischütz, which premieres in Berlin with great success
1822	Begins work on Euryanthe for Kärntnerthor Theatre, Vienna
1823	Euryanthe is produced, Vienna
1824	Commissioned by manager of Covent Garden to write an opera, Oberon
1826	Moves to London, Oberon premieres at Covent Garden
1826	Weber dies, London

❅ BEETHOVEN AND MOZART
∾ p. 165

Mozart was, with Handel, the composer Beethoven revered above all others. And Fidelio could hardly have been written without the example of Mozart's mature operas. Yet with his strongly ethical, idealistic outlook, even to the point of priggishness, Beethoven regarded works such as Don Giovanni (1787) and, especially, Così fan tutte (1790) as flippant and immoral. His favourite Mozart opera by far was Die Zauberflöte, though we can guess that he valued it more for its Masonic solemnity and portrayal of ideal love than for the Viennese pantomime antics of Papageno.

Beethoven may have been repelled by the 'La donna è mobile' sentiments of Così fan tutte, but at least two of its numbers left their mark on Fidelio: the 'canon' quartet in the second-act finale of Così surely lies behind the sublime quartet 'Mir ist so wunderbar' ('I Feel so Strange') in Act I, where the four characters voice their contrasting emotions in turn; and the opening of Leonore's 'Komm, Hoffnung', with its elaborate obbligato for three horns, recalls Fiordiligi's second-act aria in the same key. Other numbers, including the trio 'Gut, Söhnchen gut' ('Good, My Son, Good'), look back to Die Zauberflöte; while the quintet of transfigured stillness at the heart of the second finale, with its ethereal oboe melody, evokes such transcendent Mozartian moments as the final union of Pamina and Tamino and the Countess's forgiveness of her errant husband in Figaro.

❅ CABALETTA ∾ p. 166

The cabaletta or cavaletta came from the Italian word for 'grasshopper'. Originally, the cabaletta was a short popular aria with a simple, repetitive rhythm. However, by the nineteenth century the cabaletta had a more specialized meaning; now, it described the final, lively section of an aria or a duet, which followed a 'smoothly sung' cantabile and so ignited the enthusiasm of the audience with an exciting ending. Unfortunately, the cabaletta – and especially its repeats – provided opportunities for singers prone to show off with a bravura vocal display and much ornamentation. This prolonged an aria or duet and held up the action of the opera. Both Rossini and Donizetti wrote cabalettas for their operas and so did Bellini, in the 'sleepwalking aria' he wrote for Amina in Act III of his *La sonnambula*. However, the real master of the technique was Giovanni Pacini (1796–1867). Pacini, composer of some 40 operas, produced very energetic melodies with all the fire that made the cabaletta so rousing. Giuseppe Verdi also wrote cabalettas for arias in some of his operas, notably *La traviata* ('The Fallen Woman', 1853) and *Il trovatore* ('The Troubador', 1853). Even so, Verdi did not really approve of the cabaletta, and, under his influence, it eventually disappeared.

❋ FRENCH *GRAND OPÉRA* ∽ p. 170

In France audiences had a taste for imposing grandeur and the big canvas of elemental events that manifest itself in opera after about 1820 as French *grand opéra*. Everything about *grand opéra* was supersized and deliberately made so by its chief architects, the artist and set designer Pierre-Luc-Charles Cicéri (1782–1868), the lighting expert Louis Daguerre, the librettist Eugene Scribe and the co-ordinator of all their efforts Louis Véron (1798–1867), manager of the Paris Opéra. French *grand opéra* normally comprised four or five acts and included performances of ballet. Great care was taken to use only historically and geographically accurate sets that were changed for each act, and sometimes for each scene. Scenery was usually three-dimensional and was subtly varied by the use of lighting effects and moving backcloths. Stage machinery came into operation for the finale to depict some cataclysmic event such as an earthquake, volcanic eruption, avalanche, shipwreck or other disaster. The cast list for *grand opéra* could be extensive, since the performers had to 'populate' processions, battles, festivals, riots and other crowd scenes. The orchestra, too, increased in size and there were also on-stage bands, which played unusual instruments such as saxhorns, tuned bells and even anvils.

◉ FRENCH VERSUS ITALIAN OPERA
∽ p. 170

At the start of the Romantic era, French and Italian opera were fighting it out for possession of the opera stage in Paris. However, in attempting to turn back the tide of Italian taste and vocal technique, which had 'invaded' the opera in France, the French were at a severe disadvantage. As one contemporary English guidebook to the Paris opera commented: 'Nothing can be worse than the style of singing which characterizes the French School.' Worse still, the French style was fighting a losing battle when the Italian had the keen support of no less a personage than Napoleon Bonaparte, the effective ruler of France. Napoleon and his wife Josephine were enthusiastic patrons of the new Théâtre Italien, which opened in Paris in 1801. Here, Italian operas virtually monopolized the repertoire and the great stars of the show were Italian singers – the **contralto** Giuseppina Grassini (1773–1850) and the castrato Girolamo Crescentini (1752–1846). Subsequently, the Italians grasped the management of the Théâtre Italien. Rossini was musical director from 1824 to 1826 and was officially named 'Inspector General of Singing in France' by the government. Eventually, even the more chauvinistic Paris Opéra and Opéra-Comique had to bow to the vogue for Italian opera.

✦ VOCAL POWER IN ROMANTIC OPERA ∾ p. 239

The greater drama and intensity, the expanding orchestras and the trend for larger opera houses that marked the early Romantic era placed pressure on singers to increase their voice power to match. A larger opera house, seating more people and employing more orchestral musicians than before, meant a bigger space for voices to fill and greater competition from the accompaniment. The *bel canto* singing style of the eighteenth century, while undoubtedly beautiful and never out of fashion, even today, had neglected the 'resonances' that could reinforce and prolong the sound of a voice. Jenny Lind, the Swedish soprano who made her operatic debut in Stockholm in 1838, was one *bel canto* soprano who was able to project her voice sufficiently to make it fill a concert hall. However, this ability was not all that common. Singers, therefore, had to go into new, special training in order to acquire weightier timbre, more sonorous low notes and more brilliant top notes so as to cope with the more demanding requirements of Romantic opera. The result was the advent of new types of voice that underlined greater strength and volume, among them the tenor robusto, tenor di forza and dramatic soprano.

✦ FIRST PERFORMANCE OF LES TROYENS ∾ p. 240

Les troyens was such a monumental proposition that even Berlioz was daunted by it. An entry for 1854 in his memoirs read: 'For the last three years I have been tormented by the idea of a vast opera for which I would write both the words and the music ... I am resisting the temptation of carrying out this project, and I hope I will resist to the end (Footnote: Alas, no, I have not been able to resist) ... The subject seems to me elevated, magnificent and deeply moving – sure proof that the Parisians will find it dull and boring.'

Les troyens certainly made too many demands on performers and audience for a continuous performance, which is why it was divided into two parts. The first was entitled *La prise de Troie* ('The Capture of Troy'). The second, *Les Troyens à Carthage* ('The Trojans in Carthage') premiered at the Théâtre Lyrique in Paris on 4 November 1863. La prise de Troie, however, had to wait almost 30 years for its first performance, until 1890, when it was reunited with *Les troyens à Carthage* and both were played together at Karlsruhe in Germany on 6 December 1890.

✦ STAGE EFFECTS IN ROMANTIC OPERA ∾ p. 241

Spectacle and optical illusion were involved in opera stage settings from the start. Even the comparatively intimate Baroque operas, while musically 'balanced' and 'restrained', relied heavily on visuals. In Romantic opera, the music itself acquired more drama and more atmosphere so that stage settings had to increase their impact to match. In Italy, for example, cunning use of backdrops and receding arches made the stage appear deeper than it really was. In Paris, popular theatres were quick to modernize, with more elaborate lighting, scenery and stage effects, together with historically accurate costumes. Except for the introduction of gas lamps for stage and front-of-house lighting in 1822, the conservative Paris Opéra held back. Eventually, in 1827, a committee was formed to look into new ways of staging opera. Before long, the Opéra acquired extra changes of scenery, correctly dressed choruses and non-singing performers to fill out processions on stage. One important innovation was the method of double-painting scenery devised by the pioneer of photography, Louis Jacques Mandé Daguerre (1789–1851). This made it possible to transform scenery as the audience watched, by lighting it from different angles.

HIGH ROMANTIC

In 1891, when the Irish playwright Oscar Wilde (1854–1900) wrotehis famous words 'Life imitates art far more than art imitates life', he had somehow managed to overlook the artistic realities of the late nineteenth century. By that time, after some 50 years of the High Romantic era, music and opera had brought real life on stage and had presented it in the raw, with all its disappointments, tragedies, insecurities, injustice and grief.

In a foretaste of the Italian *verismo*, or 'reality' opera, that crystallized after 1880, opera audiences were confronted with uncomfortable truths as they affected characters not unlike themselves. There were the agonies of jealousy endured by Verdi's Otello or by Canio, the betrayed husband, in *I pagliacci* ('Clowns', 1892) by Leoncavallo. Verdi's *Rigoletto* struggled to preserve his daughter from would-be rapists, the consumptive Violetta in Verdi's *La traviata* ('The Fallen Woman', 1853) was doomed to early death from a then-incurable disease. In *Carmen* by Georges Bizet, the soldier, Don José, was ruined by a fascinating but promiscuous gypsy.

In real life, these situations were nothing new. They and many others like them had been there for the suffering for hundreds, if not thousands, of years. What was new was a fundamental change of emphasis that was set in train by the French Revolution of 1789 and reverberated through the nineteenth century. The focus of attention shifted to ordinary people of no particular eminence or achievement, wealth or favoured status. Previously, their

concerns had been subsumed in the priorities of their privileged rulers. Now, they had been brought to the fore by unprecedented events and, through those events, had recast the action on the opera stage.

KEY EVENTS

1846	Irish potato famine
1848	Uprisings throughout Europe; abdication of Ferdinand I of Austria and succession of Franz Joseph; abdication of Louis Philippe in France and French Republic proclaimed with Louis-Napoleon as president
1861	Friedrich Wilhelm I becomes Prussian Kaiser
1862	Bismarck made prime minister of Prussia
1865	American Civil War ends with the surrender of the Confederate Army
1868	The Trades Union Congress (TUC) is founded in Britain
1869	Tolstoy finishes *War and Peace*
1871	France loses the Franco–Prussian War; riots and commune follow in Paris
1874	First Impressionist exhibition is held in Paris, including Monet's *Impression: Sunrise*
1876	The Bayreuth Festspielhaus opens with the first performance of Wagner's *Ring*
1881	Tsar Alexander II is assassinated; Dostoyevsky completes *The Brothers Karamazov*
1886	German philosopher Karl Marx finishes *Das Kapital*
1887	First performance of Verdi's *Otello*

High Romantic
INTRODUCTION

On the face of it, the French Revolution failed when the House of Bourbon returned to rule France after the defeat of Napoleon in 1815. The face of it, however, was deceptive. The forces of liberalism unleashed by the Revolution had simply made a strategic withdrawal. In France, liberals, socialists and republicans remained opposed to extreme right-wing royalists, a situation duplicated throughout Europe where the ruling elites and the formerly powerless masses were set for collision.

CONDUCTORS, COMPOSERS AND POLITICS

Richard Wagner (1813–83) was conductor of opera in Dresden when revolution broke out in the city in May of 1849. He joined in public demonstrations and was present when the street barricades went up. Twice, he opened his house for meetings designed to organize the distribution of arms to the citizens of Dresden, and, it appears, participated in the manufacture of hand-grenades. This was sedition and treason, punishable by death. A warrant was issued for Wagner's arrest but by then he had managed to escape to Switzerland.

In Italy, Wagner's close contemporary **Giuseppe Verdi** (1813–1901) was less inclined to go to extremes. Nevertheless, there was little doubt about his liberal leanings and the way he identified himself with the man in the street. When King Victor Emmanuel offered him a noble title, Verdi declined. He told the monarch: 'o son un paesano' – 'I am a peasant'. Strictly speaking, this was not true – Verdi's parents were village innkeepers and shop owners – but he certainly looked for his audiences among ordinary people rather than the intellectual elite.

POLITICAL OPERATIC PRODUCTIONS

Even before the revolutions of 1848, Verdi made what was taken as a political statement in support of the downtrodden masses: the Jews in exile in Babylon in his *Nabucco* were regarded by the people of Milan as a metaphor for their own servitude under the harsh rule of the Austrians. The following year Verdi was in trouble over the fiery, patriotic choruses in *I Lombardi alla prima Crociata* ('The Lombards at the First Crusade', 1843), which were considered politically dangerous and in 1851, his *Rigoletto* was initially banned because of its unflattering portrait of a ruler, the licentious Duke of Mantua.

CENSORSHIP AND FEAR

These were not the only occasions when Verdi fell foul of the opera censorship, but they certainly established his progressive credentials. It has been suggested that Verdi's identity as a symbol of the *Risorgimento* – the movement to free and unite the states of Italy under the rule of Victor Emmanuel – may have reflected the view of later generations. However, Verdi's liberal contemporaries seemed to regard the composer as one of their own, so much so that the letters of his surname became a symbol of their struggle. V-e-r-d-i, by unusual coincidence, stood for 'Vittorio Emmanuele re d'Italia'– 'Victor Emmanuel, King of Italy' – and since it was seditious to proclaim the monarch's name in public, the cry of *Viva Verdi!* ('Long live Verdi!') was substituted.

The *Risorgimento* achieved its objective and acquired its king in 1870. This, and the unification of the German states in 1871, symbolized a new pride in the state's culture and its traditions. This influence also made itself felt in opera, notably in the works of Wagner, with their mighty Teutonic heroes and elements taken from German and Norse Viking myths.

NATIONAL PRIDE AND NATIONALISTIC COMPOSERS

Similar influences were at work elsewhere. For example, in Russia, **Nikolai Rimsky-Korsakov** (1844–1908) devoted all but two of his 15 operas to Russian themes, infusing many of his scores with the seductive oriental harmonies that typified the Eurasian character of his vast country. In Czechoslovakia, **Zdeněk Fibich** (1850–1900) promoted a Czech idiom in opera, and his work was furthered by the first of the country's great nationalist composers, **Bedřich Smetana** (1824–84). Traditions, national heroes and historical themes also marked the operas of Polish composer **Stanislaw Moniuszko** (1819–72) and the Hungarian **Ferenc Erkel** (1810–91). In the nineteenth century, Czechoslovakia and Hungary were under Austrian rule – although the latter had some autonomy – and Poland was part of Russia.

❋ END OF THE ARIA? ～ p. 173

The demise of the **aria**, as suggested by Wagner and to a lesser extent by Verdi, never really happened. The aria, of course, had its disadvantages. To start with, it encouraged performers to show off and hog the stage for much longer than was justified. This was a real possibility as the fame of individual singers increased, and their egos expanded to match. However, even if this did not occur, arias interrupted the story and held up the action. There were, however, equally cogent arguments in favour of the aria. A well-written aria was a memorable melody that stuck easily in the minds of audiences and so prolonged their enjoyment long after they had left the theatre. An opera's popularity, therefore, depended principally on its arias. Secondly, the aria served a dramatic purpose that nothing else in opera could do. Like the soliloquy in Shakespeare's plays, it provided a niche for a character's personal musings, fears or anxieties. It also acted like the theatrical 'aside', enabling characters to confide to the audience thoughts or information kept secret from the rest of the cast. Ultimately, the aria survived – albeit with a lesser prominence – and in the twentieth century arias featured in the works of neo-classical composers.

◉ LA SCALA, MILAN
～ p. 173

The Teatro alla Scala – known outside Italy as La Scala, Milan – is one of the world's most famous opera houses and originally opened in the sixteenth century as the Salone Margherita in the Palazzo Ducale. Both this theatre and another built on its site, the Teatro Regio Ducale, burned down, in 1708 and 1776 respectively. After an appeal by 96 box holders to the Austrian Empress Maria Theresa, La Scala was built to replace the Ducale in 1778. The new opera house, which could hold an audience numbering 2,800, opened on 3 August 1778 with the premiere of Antonio Salieri's (1750–1825) *L'Europa riconosciuta* ('Europe Recognized').

The worldwide reputation of La Scala was established in the early nineteenth century, when it staged important premieres of works by **Gioachino Rossini** (1792–1868), **Gaetano Donizetti** (1797–1848), **Giacomo Meyerbeer** (1791–1864) and others. In two years alone – 1824 to 1826 – operas by Rossini were given some 250 performances at La Scala. Works were commissioned from **Vincenzo Bellini** (1801–35) and from Verdi, including his *Oberto, conte di San Bonifacio* ('Oberto, count of Saint Boniface', 1839) and *Nabucco* (1842). Towards the end of the High Romantic era, in 1898, the despotic but charismatic conductor Arturo Toscanini (1867–1957) became director of La Scala, and later attracted many of the world's greatest singers to its stage.

High Romantic
GENRES AND STYLES

The Italian **Giuseppe Verdi** and the German **Richard Wagner**, the dominant composers of the High Romantic period, were very different personalities who shared the same operatic aim. Both saw opera as **Gesamtkunstwerk**, the total work of art in which all elements – singing, acting, orchestration, drama, poetry, stage design – merged into a single homogeneous entity. This music-drama meant continuous on-stage action, in which none of the component parts was preponderant. In particular, there would be no arias to hold up the story or provide a platform for bravura displays by individual performers.

EMERGENCE OF MUSIC DRAMA

In the event, the total revolution in music and opera, which these changes implied, never fully transpired. The aria survived but the 'democratic' concept of equal partners in performance foundered, as opera, including Wagner's total works of art, continued to be identified by its music. Nevertheless, neither Verdi nor Wagner left opera as they found it: music drama, or at least its most powerful elements, had seminal effects.

EARLY ROMANTIC LEGACY

Of the two composers, Verdi was much more the heir of his early Romantic predecessors than Wagner. Verdi retained the **bel canto** style of singing and lavished it on a long series of memorable melodies. Inevitably, this meant the show-stopping aria figured in most Verdi operas. Verdi's first two works – *Oberto* and the unsuccessful *Un giorno di regno*

('King for a Day', 1840) – were clearly influenced by the music of Rossini. However, with *Nabucco* Verdi's sense of drama, particularly human drama, had greatly heightened, and after *Rigoletto* he was giving Italian opera a much darker aura, with more incisive characterization and dramatic atmosphere than before. By the time Verdi reached old age, his *Otello* and his last work, the comic opera *Falstaff* (1893), were much closer than his early work to Wagner's idea of a unified work of art.

EPIC IDEAS

For Wagner, however, it was not close enough. Compared to what he had in mind, *Otello* and *Falstaff*, which both depict the vagaries of human behaviour, were too earthbound. Wagner's vision was of epic proportions, involving myths, gods and goddesses, ancient legends, heroic sagas, death and sacrifice – all of it on an unprecedented scale. The music drama, he planned, would grow out of the **libretti** he himself wrote, and would undercut established ways of composing and using music. For example, Wagner eschewed the tonality and predictable harmony, which 'told' an audience what the music was going to do next. Instead, he intended to write music that ebbed and flowed like the current of a river: it was much more continuous, with one melody barely finishing, or not finishing at all, before it melted into the next.

THE *LEITMOTIF*

The orchestra in the Wagner music drama did much more than accompany the singers on stage: it was an equal partner, so much louder than orchestras had ever been before that singers needed to undergo special training to acquire the lung-power to compete with it. This was the origin of the Wagnerian **soprano** and the **Heldentenor**, the heroic or Wagnerian **tenor**. Harmonies were richer and denser. Characters, events or ideas were associated with their own *leitmotif* (leading motive) which was played by the orchestra throughout the drama as a reminder to the audience. This was opera as *tour de force* and, like its composer, it towered over the music of its time.

WAGNER'S INFLUENCE IN FRANCE

The influences that radiated from Wagner's music were immense, even in France where Germans were regarded as politically dangerous and the Teutonic intensity of Wagner's work jarred on aesthetic French tastes. Nevertheless, several French composers took cues from Wagner. For instance, in his *Faust* (1859), **Charles Gounod** (1818–93) emulated him by greatly enhancing the role of the orchestra and scoring recurring motifs for the instruments to play. Gounod adopted Wagnerian harmonies for his love music in *Roméo et Juliette* ('Romeo and Juliet', 1867) and the Wagnerian *leitmotif* was used by **Georges Bizet** (1838–75) in his *Carmen*. In all three of these operas, both composers provided opportunities for musical scene-painting and exploration of the public 'outer' and secret 'inner' life of the characters. **Camille Saint-Saëns** (1835–1921) wrote Wagnerian love music for Act II of his *Samson et Dalila* (1877). In 1884, Ernest Reyer (1823–1909) ventured even further into Wagner territory with his *Sigurd*, a French version of the same Nordic sagas and legends Wagner used for his *Ring* cycle.

AN ON-STAGE SLICE OF LIFE

Although the monumentally egotistical, Wagner regarded his music dramas as the ultimate truth in opera, his concepts were not the only ones at work in the High Romantic era. Italian *verismo*, which first emerged with *Cavalleria rusticana* ('Rustic Chivalry', 1890) by **Pietro**

Mascagni (1863–1945), brought the brutal 'slice of life' to the opera stage, with particular emphasis on the crime of passion. *Verismo* also made principle characters out of villains once avoided by composers for fear of offending audience sensibilities – pimps, prostitutes, criminals, murderers and other squalid, violent, low-life characters.

OPERETTA – JUST FOR FUN

However, this emphasis on brutal reality, tragedy, death and larger-than-life legends did nothing to dent – and probably increased – the popularity of an established genre of a different kind: operetta, the escapist 'little opera' which majored in fun, fantasy and romantic high jinks. Operetta evolved in the mid-nineteenth century from the French *opéra comique*. The genre enjoyed a very long – and still continuing – life, changing its name on the way to musical comedy or simply, the musical. Subsequently, operetta spread from France to Vienna and on to England, where it appeared in a delightful and quintessentially English version known as the 'Savoy operas' by the librettist **William Gilbert** (1836–1911), a well-known wit, and playwright and the composer, **Arthur Sullivan** (1842–1900).

SATIRE AND SHOCK TACTICS

The 'father' of French operetta was **Jacques Offenbach** (1819–80), a French composer of German origins, whose declared aim was to take the pretensions and seriousness out of *opéra comique* and inject it with fun and satire. In 1857, Offenbach announced a competition for new operettas, which was won jointly by the 19-year-old Bizet with his *Le Docteur Miracle* ('Doctor Miracle') and **Charles Lecocq** (1832–1918). The following year, Offenbach produced his own satirical operetta – *Orphée aux enfers* ('Orpheus in the Underworld'), which was premiered at his theatre, the Bouffes-Parisiens, on 21 October 1858. Offenbach's *Orphée* shocked critics rigid by poking fun at ancient Greek gods and goddesses, the hallowed heroes and heroines of Baroque and later opera, and by debunking **Christoph Willibald von Gluck**'s (1714–87) work on the same subject. Offenbach was unfazed: he took a second swipe at ancient Greece with *La belle Hélène* ('Beautiful Helen', 1864).

Meanwhile, in Vienna, Franz von Suppé (1819–95) produced several light-hearted one-act operettas that prepared the ground for *Indigo und die vierzig Räuber* ('Indigo and the Forty Robbers', 1871) by **Johann Strauss II** (1825–99). This ended Offenbach's virtual monopoly of full-length operetta productions. Strauss, the eventual composer of 16 operettas, was the son and namesake of the so-scalled 'Waltz King', **Johann Strauss I** (1804–49) and recast operetta as a vehicle for exotic settings and dances. Strauss's best-known and most enduring operetta, *Die Fledermaus* ('The Bat', 1874) was full of comic intrigue, mistaken identities, flirtations and, of course, a generous helping of the Strauss family hallmark – the waltz.

※ THE *BANDA* ∿ p. 237

The *banda* was an onstage band, which originated in the eighteenth century and by the nineteenth comprised around 20 brass and woodwind players. Although essentially a military band, the *banda* was used for ballroom scenes or on-stage parades or processions. The on-stage band was not part of the regular orchestra, but was recruited by the theatre *impresario*. Consequently, its musicianship was not always expert. The *banda* appeared occasionally at first, but after Rossini used it in his *Ricciardo e Zoraide* ('Ricciardo and Zoraide', 1818), it became a regular feature of Italian opera performances. The *banda* was later taken up by Verdi, and in his operas it assumed various guises depending on the on-stage action. It was raucous and somewhat vulgar in *Nabucco* and in *I Lombardi*, very much in keeping with the mood of patriotic fervour that gripped Italy during the *Risorgimento* (1820–70). Verdi's music for the *banda* in the ballroom scenes of *Rigoletto* and *Un ballo in maschera* ('A Masked Ball', 1859) was much more subtle. However, in the *auto-da-fé* – act of faith – scene in *Don Carlos* (1867), depicting the burning of heretics, the *banda*'s music acquired a strident urgency that matched this particularly horrific spectacle.

❂ PARIS OPÉRA ∿ p. 238

The Académie Royale de Musique (now known as the Paris Académie de Musique or the Paris Opéra), has had many homes. The Académie opened in 1671, and from 1672–87 was largely controlled by **Jean-Baptiste Lully** (1632–87). In 1763, the building was destroyed by fire, as was the next building in 1781. The Opéra moved to rue de Richelieu as Theatre des Arts in 1794, to the rue Favart in 1821, and then to rue Lepeletier in 1822 where it experienced a golden age in its history. Operas by Meyerbeer and **Daniel Auber** (1782–1871) were performed, as well as specially commissioned works by Rossini (*Guillaume Tell*, 1829) and Verdi (*Don Carlos*, 1867 and *Les vêpres siciliennes*, 1855).

The Palais Garnier, or Salle Garnier, designed by architect Charles Garnier, opened in 1875 and could seat 2,600. This fairy-tale venue, with its myriad underground vaults and passages, inspired Gaston Leroux's novel *The Phantom of the Opera* (1910), and also showcases the famous Chagall ceiling. The new house, Opéra Bastille, opened in 1990 and able to seat 2,700, is located at the Place de la Bastille.

High Romantic
PERSONALITIES

Balfe, Michael
1808–70, IRISH

Michael Balfe was an Irish-born composer, singer and violinist and wrote some 29 operas. His debut as a violinist took place when he was only 15. Balfe went on to sing Figaro in Rossini's *Il barbiere di Siviglia* in Paris in 1827. Subsequently, he was principle baritone in Palermo, where he made his debut as an opera composer with *I rivali di se stessi* ('Their Own Rivals', 1830). Five years later, he returned to England and launched his career as a composer of English operas. Balfe had a fine talent for charming ballads and his first two operas – *The Siege of La Rochelle* (1835) and *The Maid of Artois* (1836), which he wrote for Maria Malibran – were very successful. In 1841, Balfe tried, unsuccessfully, to establish English opera at the Lyceum Theatre in London. Later, though, his *The Bohemian Girl* (1843) was enthusiastically acclaimed at the Drury Lane Theatre, London. Balfe went on to devote himself to the cause of English national opera.

Betz, Franz
1835–1900, GERMAN

The German baritone Franz Betz made his debut in Hanover in 1856, singing the part of Heinrich in Wagner's *Lohengrin.* Three years later, he was at the Hofoper in Berlin as Don Carlo in Verdi's *Ernani.* He also sang Don Giovanni in Mozart's opera, Amonasro in Verdi's *Aida* and the title roles in *Hans Heiling* by **Heinrich Marschner** (1795–1861) and Verdi's Falstaff. Betz created the role of Hans Sachs in Wagner's *Die Meistersinger von Nürnberg,* singing it again at Bayreuth in 1889, and took the roles of the Wanderer and Wotan in the first performance of Wagner's complete *Der Ring des Nibelungen.*

Bizet, Georges
1838–75, FRENCH

Out of 30 projected operas, Bizet only completed six but would no doubt have left more had his life not been cut short at the age of 36. Born in Paris into a musical family, he was prodigiously gifted and started lessons at the Conservatoire before he was 10. He was taught composition by Fromental Halévy, the uncle of **Ludovic Halévy** (1834–1908), who was the co-librettist both of his first performed work for the stage, the operetta *Le Docteur Miracle*, and of his last: *Carmen* itself.

OPERATIC BEGINNINGS

Le Docteur Miracle, written when the composer was 20, had been preceded by a one-act *opéra comique, La maison du docteur.* Both show the influence not only of his teacher Halévy, but also of the leading French opera composer of the day, Charles Gounod. After winning the coveted prix de Rome in 1857, Bizet stayed almost three years in Italy and came under the influence of Italian opera. It was a comic Italian libretto by Carlo Cambiaggio that he set as his next stage work, the **opera buffa** *Don Procopio* (1859), but this was not performed in his lifetime. Bizet seemed to lack direction.

A TASTE FOR THE EXOTIC

While a lost one-act *opéra comique, La guzla de l'Emir* (1863) was set in Turkey, *Les pêcheurs de perles* ('The Pearl Fishers', 1863) used Ceylon (Sri Lanka) as its setting and possibly drew its famous Act I duet 'Oui c'est elle, c'est la déesse' ('Yes it is she, it is the goddess'), with its harp and flute accompaniment, from this earlier opera. Here at last was a proper commission for Bizet. Written quickly in 1863, it enjoyed an initial run of 18 performances. It was not revived during the composer's lifetime but has since entered the repertoire. The director of the Théâtre Lyrique continued to champion Bizet by commissioning a setting of a libretto dropped by Gounod, *Ivan IV* (1862–65), a work unperformed until 1946. His next exploration of the exotic followed the French fashion for the novels of Walter Scott, in this case *The Fair Maid of Perth*. *La jolie fille de Perth* was first given at the Théâtre Lyrique in 1867 and suffered a similar fate to *Les pêcheurs de perles*, although it has been revived less.

TOWARDS CARMEN

The Paris commune interrupted Bizet's enterprises, but in 1871 the Opéra-Comique offered him a commission for a one-act opera, *Djamileh*, having rejected his Grisélidis (1870–71). Adapted from Alfred de Musset's *Namouna*, *Djamileh* is set in Cairo. This work established the composer's reputation at the Opéra-Comique after its premiere in 1872, and he was offered a full-length commission, on condition he used the established librettists **Henri Meilhac** (1831–97) and Halévy. Much to the dismay of the directorate of the Opéra-Comique, Bizet put forward the idea of an opera based on Prosper Mérimée's *Carmen*. Compromises were reached between the librettists, Bizet and the administrators whose clientele were unused to murders, gypsy whores and brigands. At one point a happy ending was even suggested.

A few other projects were on the drawing board before it was eventually staged, including the popular *L'Arlésienne* (1872), which consisted of melodramas and **incidental music**. After a lukewarm first run, when the work was admired by many critics but did not attract audiences, Carmen eventually became Bizet's masterpiece and one of the greatest operas of the repertoire. Bizet died three months later, not from despair at the opera's relatively lukewarm reception (as early biographers maintained) but from swimming in the Seine from his house in Bougival, now a suburb of Paris, even though he was suffering

from poor breathing and rheumatism. He was never to witness the immense popularity of *Carmen*, which rose to fame after its revivals in the 1880s and its performances worldwide.

Les pêcheurs de perles

While the success of *Carmen* overshadows his other operas, Bizet's first lasting success was with *Les pêcheurs de perles*, written when he was only 24. Set in Ceylon (Sri Lanka), it uses gently oriental inflections to portray the priestess Leïla torn between love and her sacred vows, and a more romantic and dramatic style for the conflict between two pearl fishers who are both in love with her. Memorable for its duet in Act I and its overall dramatic continuity, it was revived posthumously after the eventual success of Carmen.

Les pêcheurs de perles ('The Pearl Fishers')

by George Bizet
Composed: 1863
Premiered: 1863, Paris
Libretto by Eugène Cormon and Michel Carré

ACT I

Fishermen are gathered in Ceylon to prepare for their annual pearl-fishing expedition. Zurga reminds them that they need to appoint a leader and at once they swear loyalty to him. He recognizes a new arrival as Nadir, and asks if he has been faithful to the vow they swore years before, when they fell in love with the same priestess. Rather than risk their friendship, they had sworn to renounce her. They then reaffirm their friendship.

A boat arrives carrying Leïla, a veiled priestess selected for her purity, whose singing is intended to ward off any evil that might befall the divers. She takes an oath of chastity on pain of death. Nadir recognizes the voice of the priestess. Zurga notices that she is troubled, but she confirms that she will do her duty. As she takes her vigil, Nadir recalls how he had broken his vow by trying to see her again. He falls asleep and wakens to the sound of her incantation. He calls out and she answers, drawing aside her veil.

ACT II

All the fishermen have returned safely. When reminded of her vow, Leïla tells Nourabad, the high priest, a story to illustrate how she can keep her word. When she was a girl she had protected a fugitive to save his life. By way of thanks he gave her a necklace, which she still wears. As she lies down to sleep, she hears Nadir approaching and they are rapturously reunited. He promises to return, but is captured as he slips away. Both Leïla and Nadir are accused of sacrilege. When her veil is torn away, Zurga finally recognizes the priestess he loved and demands that both must die.

ACT III

Zurga reflects on Nadir's fate. Begging mercy for Nadir, Leïla claims it was her fault alone. Zurga briefly relents but then orders her to be taken to the pyre. As she goes he notices her necklace. Nadir and Leïla are facing death together. At the last moment Zurga breaks in with news that the camp is on fire. Zurga frees the captives and tells them that he was the fugitive she had saved, and has done this to give them a chance to escape. They embrace and then Nadir and Leïla run off together.

Carmen

Carmen is the opera that has ensured Bizet's lasting fame but which, somewhat uniquely, was partly fashioned by pressures from the directorate of the commissioning theatre, the Opéra-Comique. The revenue from this theatre was largely dependent on attracting the bourgeoisie, providing an evening out for chaperoned couples with an eye on marriage. Thus a setting including a cigar factory, a murder outside a bullring

and a tavern inhabited by gypsies somewhat contravened the norm. Bowing to administrative pressure to soften the tone, the character of Micaëla, the good Catholic girl, was introduced to counterbalance the free-living Carmen and her compatriots. The opera was ahead of its time in its introduction of real popular music: the *Habanera* in Act I where Carmen advocates free love was taken from a book of Spanish-language **cabaret** songs and the *Chanson Bohème* and the *Seguidilla*, among other movements, employ Spanish modes and dance rhythms. The theme which introduces Carmen and accompanies the fateful card scene and her death imitates a gypsy scale. Originally conforming to the Opéra-Comique norm of a mix of spoken dialogue and operatic numbers, it was for a long time preferred in its posthumous adaptation, in which the dialogue was replaced by recitatives. More recently, productions prefer its richer version with the details of the full dialogue retained.

Carmen

by Georges Bizet
Composed: 1873–74
Premiered: 1875, Paris
Libretto by Henri Meilhac and Ludovic Halévy after Prosper Mérimée's novel

ACT I

Micaëla, a country girl, approaches a corporal, Moralès, in Seville and asks where she may find another corporal named Don José. Moralès tells her to wait for the guard to change, but she declines. At midday the girls come out of the nearby cigarette factory for a rest and a smoke. The last to appear is Carmen, a gypsy, who warns her admirers that they are playing with fire. Only José ignores her and she throws a flower to him and the girls return to work.

Micaëla gives José a letter from his mother, together with a symbolic kiss, and then leaves him to read the letter, in which his mother urges him to marry Micaëla. Girls run out screaming with news of a fight in the factory, which spills out into the square. Zuniga orders José to investigate and he returns with Carmen, who refuses to answer any questions. José is ordered to tie her up and take her to prison. Carmen entices him to go dancing at Lillas Pastia's tavern outside the walls of Seville. Mesmerized, José agrees to help her escape. He unties the rope and, as they leave for prison, Carmen slips away. Don José is arrested.

ACT II

The gypsy girls are entertaining the officers in the tavern. Zuniga tells Carmen that José has spent the last month in prison. The great toreador Escamillo arrives with his supporters and replies to a toast with tales of his dangerous profession. Carmen gently brushes off Escamillo's advances. After he has left, Le Dancaïre and Le Remendado appear and attempt to persuade Carmen, Frasquita and Mercédès to join them in a smuggling plot. Carmen declines and explains that she is in love: nothing can change her mind.

José is heard approaching and the others leave Carmen alone. José is jealous that she danced for the officers, since she should dance only for him. As she dances they hear the bugle calling the soldiers back to barracks. She is furious when he starts to go and he tries to calm her by telling how he cherished her flower when in prison. If he loved her, she insists, he would desert. He refuses, but as he is leaving Zuniga returns, looking for Carmen. The smugglers arrive to break up a fight between José and Zuniga. José now has no choice but to join the smugglers' band.

ACT III

The smugglers rest on their way through the mountains. Carmen taunts the jealous José that it would be better if he left. As they

SOUNDS FAMILIAR

'HABANERA'

It might have simply been the *Habanera* from *Carmen* were it not for the mobile phone, but the chirpy first tune of the overture is now inescapable thanks to ring tones. Bizet based the aria on 'El Arreglito', a song written by Spanish composer Sebastián de Yradier, who had spent time in Cuba.

read their fortunes in the cards, Frasquita and Mercédès can only see happiness, but Carmen sees death. The girls demonstrate how they will distract the customs guards. José is left to guard the contraband, but he does not see Micaëla arrive. Frightened, she hides when José fires at an intruder. It is Escamillo, who is looking for Carmen. José challenges him to a knife-fight and the smugglers rush on and separate them. Wooing Carmen, Escamillo invites them all to his next fight in Seville. He leaves and Micaëla is discovered. José still declares that he will never leave Carmen, but Micaëla's news that his mother is dying changes his mind.

ACT IV

The crowds watch the bullfighters' procession. Escamillo publicly declares his love for Carmen. She is warned that José has been seen nearby, but she waits to confront him. She mocks his protestations of love, asserting that she now loves Escamillo, and throws down José's ring. In his desperation he stabs her.

OPERAS

1832	Le Docteur Miracle
1859	Don Procopio
1802–05	Ivan IV
1863	Les pêcheurs de perles
1867	La jolie fille de Perth
1871–72	Djamileh
1873–74	Carmen

TIMELINE

1813	Georges Bizet born, Paris
1848	Accepted into the Paris Conservatiore of Music, where he is influenced by Gounod
1850	Writes one-act operetta *Le Docteur Miracle*
1857	*Le Docteur Miracle* wins first prize in a competition organized by Jaques Offenbach; Bizet wins the Prix de Rome, allowing him to spend three years in Italy
1859	Writes *Don Procopio* while living in Rome
1862	Work begins on *Ivan IV*, but the opera is not staged
1863	Writes *Les pêcheurs de perles*, which premières at the Théâtre-Lyrique as commissioned by director Léon Carvalho
1867	Writes *La jolie fille de Perth*, which premières at the Théâtre-Lyrique
1869	Marries Geneviève Halévy, daughter of composer Fromental Halévy
1870	Outbreak of Franco–Prussian war, closing all Paris theatres; Bizet joins National Guard
1871	Work begins on *Djamileh*
1872	Premiere of *Djamileh* at the prestigious Opéra-Comique, Paris, to little success
1873	Abandons work on an opera called *Don Rodrigue*, due to a fire at the Paris Opéra and the theatre's decision to stage a different work
1875	Premiere of *Carmen*, Paris, to shocked audiences and scathing critics; Bizet dies three months later, unaware that *Carmen* will go on to become one of the world's most popular operas

Boito, Arrigo

1842–1918, ITALIAN

Although best known as a librettist, Arrigo Boito was also a composer in his own right. He studied music in Milan with Alberto Mazzucato (1813–77). Later he went to Paris, where he met Verdi and began to think about subjects for operas. The choice was between Nero, the Roman Emperor, and Faust – a subject that fascinated numerous writers, artists and composers during the nineteenth century. In the event Boito chose both subjects, but Faust came first, when he composed his *Mefistofele* ('Mephistopheles', 1868). Sadly, the opera failed at La Scala, Milan. Boito became depressed and turned instead to a much greater talent, his ability to write powerful, meaningful libretti. Boito was also adept at languages and translated into Italian the libretti of several operas

– **Carl Maria von Weber**'s (1786–1826) *Der Freischütz* and Wagner's *Rienzi* (1842) from German and, from Russian, Glinka's *Ruslan i Lyudmila* (1842). Meanwhile, with Verdi's encouragement, Boito tried again with *Mefistofele* and after revisions, the opera was successfully performed in 1875. Boito began another opera, *Nerone* ('Nero') in 1877, but it was still unfinished when he died some 40 years later. *Nerone* was completed by Vincenzo Tommasini (1878–1950) and Arturo Toscanini and premiered at La Scala, Milan on 1 May 1924.

Mefistofele ('Mephistopheles')

by Arrigo Boito
Composed: 1866–67
Premiered: 1867, Venice
Libretto by the composer after Goethe's *Faust*

PROLOGUE

Mefistofele wagers with God that he can win Faust's soul.

ACT I

Crowds celebrate Easter Sunday in Frankfurt. The aged Faust is bored and watches a mysterious friar, who follows him back to his study. When Faust opens his bible the friar reveals himself as Mefistofele, who agrees to Faust's yearning for one perfect moment in exchange for his soul. The contract is signed.

ACT II

In Marta's garden Faust, now rejuvenated, courts Margherita while Mefistofele entertains Marta. Faust declares his love and, wishing to see her alone, offers Margherita something to make her mother sleep more deeply. Mefistofele and Faust watch witches gathering for their Sabbath in the Harz Mountains. The witches hail Mefistofele as their king and present him with a glass globe, in which he sees the vileness of the world before smashing it. Faust sees a vision of Margherita in chains.

ACT III

Margherita is in prison, having drowned her baby and unintentionally poisoned her mother. Mefistofele brings Faust to her cell to urge her to escape with him. Margherita confesses her crimes and says that they might be happy together far away. She recognizes Mefistofele as the devil, prays for forgiveness and dies rejecting Faust, while a celestial choir announces her salvation.

ACT IV

Mefistofele has taken Faust back to classical Greece, where they encounter Elena (Helen of Troy) obsessed with the burning of the city. Faust is entranced by the surroundings, but it is not to Mefistofele's taste. Faust and Elena pledge their love for each other.

EPILOGUE

Faust is old once more. Wearying of his life he seizes his bible, praying for salvation. Mefistofele offers more adventures, but Faust dies. Mefistofele has lost his wager.

Borodin, Alexander

1833–87, RUSSIAN

Alexander Borodin was the illegitimate son of the Georgian Prince Luka Gedianov. As was customary in nineteenth-century Russia, his irregular birth was concealed by registering him under the name of a serf owned by the prince. Borodin was in no way deprived by this lowly status, and his talent for music was actively encouraged. Even so, he followed the usual path of Russian composers of his time by taking up a profession and studying and working on his music in his spare time. This was why Borodin called himself 'a Sunday composer'. He distinguished himself in his profession and, after 1862, lectured in chemistry at the St Petersburg School of Medicine for Women. The work was very demanding, and consequently Borodin's musical output was small. Most of it consisted of orchestral works and chamber music of stunning melodic

beauty and though his operas were few, this was a quality they shared. Like his friend **Modest Mussorgsky** (1839–81), Borodin completed only one opera project – *The Bogatyrs* (1867) – a pastiche first performed in Moscow. Also like Mussorgsky, Borodin left his masterpiece, *Prince Igor*, unfinished, partly due to delays and difficulties with the libretto, which he wrote himself.

Prince Igor

by Alexander Borodin
Composed: 1869–70, completed 1874–87
Premiered: 1890, St Petersburg
Libretto by the composer, after Vladimir Vasil'yevich Stasov

PROLOGUE

Ignoring an eclipse of the sun, Prince Igor prepares to leave Putivl' for a campaign against the pagan Polovtsï, accompanied by his son Vladimir. Skula and Yeroshka, two musicians, decide to desert. Igor refuses to listen to the appeals of the people and his wife, Yaroslavna, and entrusts her in his absence to her brother, Prince Galitsky.

ACT I

Skula and Yeroshka lead Galitsky's followers in praising their master's profligacy. He has abducted a local girl and now describes the life his men would lead if he ruled the city. Women rush in, protesting against the abduction, but they are driven away when Galitsky refuses to hand her back. Singing his praises again, the men decide that Igor should be deposed.

Yaroslavna, lamenting her loneliness, has been having troubled dreams. The women arrive, asking for her help in winning back the girl. At first Galitsky laughs off the charges, but Yaroslavna orders him to release the girl and he gives in. Boyars bring news that Igor and Vladimir have been defeated and taken prisoner. The alarm bell sounds as the Polovtsï attack and burn the city.

ACT II

Khan Konchak's daughter, Konchakovna, who has fallen in love with Vladimir, orders food to be given to the Russian prisoners. Vladimir and Konchakovna declare their love for each other, but Vladimir knows that his father will not consent to a marriage while still a prisoner. Ivan enters and agonizes over his longing for freedom and his separation from Yaroslavna. Ovlur, a Christian Polovtsian, offers to help him escape, but Igor refuses. Igor also rejects Konchak's magnanimous offer to free him so that they might join forces and conquer the world. Konchak orders his slaves to entertain them.

ACT III

Konchak celebrates the victory at Putivl! Stories of Polovtsian cruelty persuade Igor and Vladimir to escape on horses provided by Ovlur. Konchakovna begs Vladimir to stay and raises the alarm to stop him. Igor escapes but Vladimir is captured. Konchak pardons him and gives his blessing to their marriage.

ACT IV

Yaroslavna laments what has befallen her husband and her people. Horsemen are seen on the horizon and she fears another attack, but she recognizes Igor and they are reunited. Skula and Yeroshka ring the bells and the people gather to greet their ruler.

Recommended Recording:

Prince Igor, Kirov Opera; Valery Gergiev, conductor; Philips 442 537–2PH3; Soloists: Galina Gorchakova (Yaroslavna), Olga Borodina (Konchakovna), Gegam Grigorian (Vladimir), Mikhail Kit (Igor), Vladimir Ognovienko (Prince Galitsky), Bulat Minzhilkiev (Khan Konchak)

Cornelius, Peter
1824–74, GERMAN

The German composer Peter Cornelius first intended to be an actor, but instead chose music after studying in Mainz, his home town, and Berlin. In 1852, Cornelius went to Weimar, where he encountered Liszt, then *Kapellmeister* to the grand duke. While admiring him, Cornelius was wary of the influence of Wagner, the giant of contemporary German opera, and instead chose to go his own musical way. His objective was to make German comic opera more substantial than the light, frothy offerings then being composed. He found the story he wanted in the classic collection of Arabian fairy tales, the *1001 Nights*. The result was *The Barber of Baghdad* (1858), with libretto as well as music by Cornelius, which was first performed at Weimar. Liszt conducted. Unfortunately, opponents of the 'New German School' led by Liszt sabotaged the premiere and the opera failed. Cornelius' historical drama, *Der Cid* ('The Lord', 1865), was based on the life of the medieval Spanish hero Roderigo Diaz de Vivar and the *Gunlöd* (completed 1891) was based on Norse legend.

Dargomïzhsky, Alexander
1813–69, RUSSIAN

Alexander Dargomïzhsky belonged to an aristocratic family in St Petersburg. He entered government service, but resigned his post in 1843. The musical training he received in his youth enabled him to build a reputation as a pianist and his acquaintance with during the winter of 1833–34 with **Mikhail Glinka** (1804–57) involved him in the movement to establish national opera based on the Russian folksong tradition. Dargomïzhsky's first foray into opera was *Lucrèce Borgia*, based on a play by the French writer **Victor Hugo** (1802–85). However, he abandoned this and turned instead to another Hugo novel, *The Hunchback of Notre Dame* (1831), for his second opera, *Esmeralda* (1840), which was staged in Moscow in 1847. By this time Dargomïzhsky had become a well-known singing teacher and had embarked on writing songs that were keyed in to Russian speech patterns. Here he found his own niche, with lyrical as well as dramatic and declamatory melodies. His opera *Rusalka*, produced in St Petersburg in 1856, was in a similar genre, with its colourful folk setting. Sadly Dargomïzhsky died before completing his last opera, *The Stone Guest* (1866–69). The opera was completed by Cui and Rimsky-Korsakov in 1870, and premiered in St Petersburg in 1872.

The Stone Guest
by Alexander Dargomïzhsky
Composed: 1866–69, completed by Cui and Rimsky-Korsakov 1870
Premiered: 1872, St Petersburg
Libretto set directly to Alexander Sergeyevich Pushkin's verse tragedy

ACT I
Don Juan has been exiled from Madrid for murdering Don Alvaro, the commander. He has now returned in secret, accompanied by his servant Leporello, to see an old flame, the actress Laura. While he is standing outside a monastery, an old monk tells him that the commander's beautiful widow, Donna Anna, visits her husband's grave there every evening. He waits to catch a glimpse of her, hidden behind her veil, and vows to woo her. Laura is entertaining her admirers with songs. One of them is Don Carlos, the commander's brother, who reminds her of Don Juan. After she has dismissed the other guests to be alone with Don Carlos, Don Juan himself enters. Don Carlos challenges him to a duel and is killed, leaving Don Juan to seduce Laura.

ACT II
Don Juan disguises himself as a monk and waits for Donna Anna in the monastery beside the statue of the commander. When she appears he woos her with protestations of love, until she finally agrees to an assignation at her house the following evening. After

she has left Don Juan instructs Leporello to invite the statue to guard the door of the house while he is there. The statue nods in assent and they flee in terror.

ACT III
Next evening Don Juan reveals his identity to Donna Anna and swears he loves her. Even though this is her husband's murderer, she cannot resist. She kisses him as a token of forgiveness and they agree to meet tomorrow. The statue appears at the doorway, as invited. It seizes Don Juan by the hand and drags him down to hell.

de Reszke, Jean
1850–1925, POLISH
Jean de Reszke was a Polish tenor whose handsome face and fine physique suited him for romantic roles. He made his debut at the Teatro La Fenice in Venice in 1874, not as a tenor, but in the baritone part of Alfonso in Donizetti's *La favorite*. He continued to sing baritone roles until he re-trained and made his tenor debut in Madrid in 1879, in Meyerbeer's *Robert le diable*. This was not particularly successful, but later, in 1884, de Reske triumphed as John the Baptist in **Jules Massenet's** (1842–1912) *Hérodiade*. He continued to sing tenor roles at the Opéra in Paris (1885–1902), Covent Garden, London (1888–1900) and the Metropolitan Opera House, New York (1891–1901). Unfortunately, the versatility that enabled him to sing demanding parts within a few days of each other – Lohengrin and Faust, for example – overstrained his voice and forced him to retire in 1902.

Erkel, Ferenc
1810–93, HUNGARIAN
Ferenc Erkel, known as the 'father' of Hungarian national opera, was principally a pianist and conductor. In 1838, he became chief conductor of the National Theatre in Pest, and in 1853 founded the Budapest Philharmonic. He was also

active as a composer, and his first opera, *Bátori Mária* (1840), was successfully staged in Pest, followed by Hunyadi László in 1844. In his efforts to establish a distinctively Hungarian opera, Erkel employed the inflections of Hungarian speech in his recitatives and also incorporated national dances into his works. These were, most notably, the vigorously rhythmic *csárdás* and the *verbunko*, which was used by recruiting sergeants to persuade young Hungarians to enlist in the army. Erkel was not immune, however, to foreign influences and included both Viennese and Italian elements in his operas. He also gave the English ballad opera a new, Hungarian guise. In 1861, he produced his greatest success, *Bánk bán*, making its content much more typically Hungarian and underlining this by using the cimbalom, the Hungarian box zither. This was the first opera in which this instrument was used and the work achieved considerable success. Erkel's later operas never reached this peak, although his *Brankovics György* (1874) was considered to be his masterpiece in his lifetime.

Bánk bán

by Ferenc Erkel
Composed: 1844–53
Premiered: 1861, Pest
Libretto by Béni Egressy after József Katona's play

PROLOGUE

King Endre of Hungary is away at war and his wife Gertrud and her corrupt followers have taken control at court.

ACT I

At Gertrud's instigation, her brother Otto intends to seduce Bánk's wife Melinda. Rebels opposed to Gertrud have sent a message to Bánk seeking his help. Word arrives of Endre's victory. Bánk arrives and is told that Melinda is in danger. He promises to help
the rebels. *Bánk observes Otto's advances to Melinda and is tormented by jealousy, even though he believes she remains devoted to him. Biberach, who has his own plans for revenge, helps to turn Bánk against Gertrud and gives Otto a powder with which he is to drug the unfortunate Melinda.*

ACT II

Bánk fears for the country's future. Biberach brings news that Otto has raped Melinda, who pleads with Bánk to kill her but to spare their child. Bánk asks Tiborc, an old peasant, to escort them to his castle. Bánk confronts Gertrud in her room, accusing her of encouraging her brother's depravity and ruining the country. When she draws a dagger he stabs her.

ACT III

Tiborc tries to persuade Melinda to cross the River Tisza before the storm breaks. By now she is raving and uncomprehending of her situation. Picking up the child, she throws herself in the river and drowns. Endre has returned and the court is in mourning. The nobles try to convince him of Gertrud's crimes. Bánk admits that he killed Gertrud and justifies his action. As Endre prepares to fight him in a duel, Tiborc appears with peasants carrying the bodies of Melinda and the child. Stricken with grief, Bánk begs to be buried alongside them. Endre pardons him, since this is punishment enough.

Faure, Jean-Baptiste
1830–1914, FRENCH

The French baritone Jean-Baptiste Faure – impressive on stage, with fine vocal discipline and strong dramatic sense – made his debut at the Opéra-Comique in Paris in 1852, singing Pygmalion in *Galathée* by Victor Massé (1822–84). Faure continued singing at the Opéra-Comique until 1859. Meanwhile, he taught singing at the Paris Conservatoire 1857–60. He performed at Covent Garden, London (1860–76), and at the Paris Opéra (1861–

69/1872–76) where he created the part of Nélusko in Meyerbeer's L'africaine ('The African Woman', 1865). Faure was also the first to sing the part of Rodrigo in Verdi's *Don Carlos* and the title role in Thomas's *Hamlet*. Other opera houses in which Faure sang were in Vienna, Brussels, Berlin and Monte Carlo. His last public appearances were in Marseilles and Vichy in 1886, the year he published *La voix et le chant* ('The Voice and Singing'), his treatise on the art of performing opera.

Gounod, Charles
1818–93, FRENCH

Charles Gounod almost became a priest, and his first works comprised church music. However, the **mezzo-soprano** Pauline Viardot (1821–1910), a member of the Garcia operatic family, perceived Gounod's potential and persuaded him compose opera. Eventually, he wrote 12 of them. Gounod composed *Sapho* (1851) for Viardot, but it did not make a distinctive 'French' mark on opera, as the composer had hoped, and neither did his *grand opéra*, also written for Viardot, *La nonne sanglante* ('The Bleeding Nun', 1854).

Gounod appears to have come to the conclusion that *grand opéra* was not his style. He turned instead to *opéra comique*, choosing first one of the witty comedies of the French playwright Molière, *Le médecin malgré lui* ('A Doctor in Spite of Himself', 1666). Gounod's opera, first performed in 1858, was not only his first *opéra comique*, but also his first substantial success. It was soon followed by another, even greater achievement, his *Faust*. Gounod's reputation as an operatic composer has tended to rest on this one outstanding success. He never quite attained the same peak again, but *Mireille* (1864) was notable for its colourful score and *Roméo et Juliette* (1867) for its beautiful love music.

Faust
by Charles Gounod
Composed: 1858
Premiered: 1859, Paris
Libretto by Jules Barbier and Michel Carré

ACT I
Faust's search for knowledge has been futile and he calls on the devil. Méphistophélès offers wealth, fame or power, but all Faust wants is youth. He is shown a vision of Marguerite and signs his soul away, being transformed into a young man.

ACT II
The townspeople mill around at the Kermesse. Valentin is leaving for war and asks Siébel to look after his sister, Marguerite. He then calls on heaven to protect her. Méphistophélès offers a drinking song and then tells fortunes, including that Valentin will die in a duel and that any flowers Siébel touches will wither. Valentin takes Méphistophélès' toast to Marguerite as an insult, but his sword shatters. Méphistophélès is driven back with the sign of the cross. Faust appears, asking for the girl from his vision. Marguerite enters, but declines his arm and leaves.

ACT III
Siébel's flowers for Marguerite have withered. He dips his fingers in holy water and the spell is broken. Faust is moved by the innocence of Marguerite's house. Méphistophélès returns with a casket of jewels. Marguerite is still thinking about the stranger in the marketplace when she discovers the jewels and tries them on. Faust then begins to woo her, while Méphistophélès flirts with her neighbour Marthe. Marguerite succumbs, but at the first kiss she runs into the house. From her window she confesses that she loves Faust, and he follows her inside.

ACT IV
Faust has deserted Marguerite, now pregnant. Siébel attempts to raise her spirits. The soldiers have returned.

Siébel fails to stop Valentin going into his house. Méphistophélès sings a mock serenade beneath the window. Valentin demands satisfaction from the seducer and is mortally wounded, thanks to Méphistophélès' intervention. As he dies he curses Marguerite. Méphistophélès comes to Marguerite in church as she prays and tells her she is damned.

ACT V

Méphistophélès and Faust attend the witches' Sabbath. Faust is distracted by history's most beautiful women, but demands to be taken to Marguerite. She is now in prison for infanticide and has gone insane. When she sees Faust she recalls their past meetings. At the sight of Méphistophélès, however, she calls for divine protection and rejects Faust. As she dies Méphistophélès claims her soul, but celestial voices announce that she is saved.

Halévy, Ludovic
1834–1908, FRENCH

Ludovic Halévy was the nephew of the French composer **Fromental Halévy** (1799–1862) and first made his name as a novelist and playwright. Halévy worked as a civil servant until 1865, when he retired to write full time. By then he had already become friendly with Jacques Offenbach and in 1858, together with Hector Crémieux (1828–92), he wrote the libretto for Offenbach's *Orphée aux enfers*. Another even more fruitful partnership, with Meilhac, began in 1860. Their witty, provocative and irreverent writing as displayed in *La belle Hélène* and *La grande duchesse de Gérolstein* ('The Grand Duchess of Gérolstein', 1867) – among others – was ideally suited to Offenbach's operetta style. Meilhac and Halévy also provided the libretto for Bizet's *Carmen*. In 1884, Ludovic Halévy was elected a member of the French Academy but after 1892, when his *Kari Kari* appeared, he virtually ceased writing.

Hoffmann, Ernst Theodor Amadeus
1776–1822, GERMAN

E. T. A. Hoffmann, the German novelist, critic, composer and conductor was among the most influential literary figures of the Romantic movement. He was the first to suggest that Mozart's *Don Giovanni* was a Romantic rather than a Classical opera because of its strong associations between love and death. Hoffmann wrote several operas with dialogue, notably *Undine* (1816), as well as important critical works on Romanticism and numerous stories, many of which were used as a basis for over two dozen operas by various composers. Among them was Adolphe Adam (1803–56), who took his *La poupée de Nuremberg* ('The Doll of Nuremberg', 1852) from Hoffmann's *Der Sandmann* ('The Sandman', 1816). *Der Sandmann*, together with two other Hoffmann stories, with the German author himself as the central character, were used by Offenbach for his last opera, *Les contes d'Hoffmann*. Hoffmann also featured as a character in three twentieth-century operas.

Hugo, Victor
1802–85, FRENCH

Like the Scots novelist Sir Walter Scott, the French writer Victor Hugo had the happy facility for writing fiction that naturally lent itself to opera. Apart from his genius as a story-teller, Hugo's secret lay in his vigorous attachment to Romantic principles, which exercised profound influence over librettists and composers of Romantic opera. Hugo himself made one attempt at writing a libretto, *Esmeralda* (1836). This text, written for the French composer Louise-Angélique Bertin (1805–77) was an adaptation of his own famous novel, *Notre-Dame de Paris*. This was the first of at least 21 operas subsequently based on this novel. Many more Hugo stories were turned into operas, notably by Verdi, who used Hugo's

Hernani (1830) for his opera *Ernani*, which he composed in 1844, and his *Le roi s'amuse* for *Rigoletto*.

Materna, Amalie
1844–1918, AUSTRIAN

Amalie Materna, the Austrian soprano, sang Brünnhilde at the first performance of the complete *Der Ring des Nibelungen* at Bayreuth in 1876. Wagner was deeply impressed by her performance – so much so that he declared Materna the only woman truly capable of singing the exceptionally demanding role. Materna, a singer of great stamina, made her debut at age 20 at Graz, in Austria, in the rather less exhausting *Leichte Kavallerie* by Franz von Suppé. She moved to Vienna in 1869, where she sang at the Hofoper until 1894. During that time, she also appeared at the Metropolitan Opera, House New York in 1885, and gained a reputation as a leading Wagnerian soprano of her time. After her first Brünnhilde at Bayreuth in 1876, she also created the role of Kundry, the wild woman and temptress in Wagner's last opera Parsifal (1882).

Meilhac, Henri
1831–97, FRENCH

Henri Meilhac, the French dramatist and librettist, wrote most of his texts for operas in collaboration with other writers. Meilhac's most renowned partnership, which began after a chance meeting outside a Paris theatre in 1860, was with Ludovic Halévy. They produced libretti for Bizet, **Léo Delibes** (1836–91) and most famously for Offenbach. Meilhac and Halévy had great talent for depicting and satirizing the foibles and shortcomings of human nature. The Meilhac-Halévy libretto for Bizet's dramatic and tragic *Carmen* was something of a departure for them, since their forte lay in operetta. The genre gave them plenty of chances to make fun of ancient myths and parody some of the more stuffy conventions of

opera. Meilhac collaborated with Albert Millaud (1844–92) on the libretto for *Mlle Nitouche* (1882) by Hervé (Florimond Ronger) (1825–92) and with Philippe-Emile-François Gille (1831–1901) for *Manon* (1884) by Massenet.

Melnikov, Ivan
1832–1906, RUSSIAN

Ivan Melnikov, the Russian baritone, was best known for creating the role of Boris Godunov in Mussorgsky's opera in 1869. Trained in Russia and Italy, Melnikov had made his debut at the Maryinsky Imperial Theatre in St Petersburg only two years earlier, as Riccardo in Bellini's *I puritani*. Melnikov continued to sing at the Maryinsky until 1890. Other parts created by Melnikov included the title role in *The Demon* by Anton Rubinstein (1829–94) and Prince Igor in Borodin's opera of 1890. Melnikov was a friend of Mussorgsky and **Pyotr Ilyich Tchaikovsky**'s (1840–93) favourite baritone. He sang in Tchaikovsky's operas, including roles in *The Oprichnik*, *Vakula the Smith*, *Eugene Onegin* and *The Queen of Spades*. The critic Vladimir Stasov praised Melnikov's dramatic interpretations of his roles, and his legato singing was greatly admired by Modeste Tchaikovsky, brother of the composer.

Moniuszko, Stanisław
1819–72, POLISH

Stanisław Moniuszko began by writing a series of operettas before producing *Halka* (1846–47), his best-known work, and the first of his three operas. After a revised version was given its first performance in Warsaw in 1858, *Halka* was hailed as the first important Polish national opera and Moniuszko acquired a place at the forefront of Polish composers. Moniuszko received his musical training in Berlin and, on his return to Poland, was appointed organist at St John's, Vilnius. He also began teaching piano and conducted the theatre orchestra. Moniuszko came to opera by way of an interest in dramatic music, which was sparked off by contact with Polish writers. Nationalist composers had particular value at a time when Poland was under foreign, Russian, rule. Most of his operas depicted the world of the Polish nobility, and, as in *Halka*, showed the ordinary people as victims of cruel masters. The Polish atmosphere in Moniuszko's operas derived from his use of folk-dance rhythms, such as the *mazurka* or the *polonaise*. However, the restrictions under which he worked – namely that large-scale public performances were not possible – were revealed in his 12 *Songbooks for Home Use*, comprising over three hundred songs published in the years 1843–59 and 1877–1910.

Halka
by Stanisław Moniuszko
Composed: 1846–47
Premiered: 1858, Warsaw
Libretto by Włodzimierz Wolski

ACT I
Guests are celebrating the betrothal of Janusz, a nobleman, to Stolnik's daughter Zofia. They are interrupted by the voice of Halka, a serf whom Janusz promised to marry. She is now pregnant and yearns to be near him. Janusz fears that this news would ruin his prospects. Still claiming that he loves her, he arranges another meeting and persuades Halka to leave.

ACT II
While the party continues, Halka comes back to the garden where she meets Jontek, another of Janusz's serfs, who has long loved her. He unsuccessfully tries to convince her that Janusz cannot be trusted. They hear the guests wishing the couple eternal happiness. Halka throws herself against the door, demanding to see the father of her child. Janusz tells them to go and Jontek turns on him. Janusz promises him a reward if he

takes Halka away and then tells everyone that she is mad.

ACT III
In the village the peasants are celebrating Sunday and discussing the wedding. Jontek leads in Halka, who has now lost her reason, and they recount the events at the manor house. The villagers are sympathetic and one of them sees a black crow, a sign of ill omen. The wedding procession is heard approaching.

ACT IV
Jontek still wishes to help Halka and asks the piper to play a lament. Halka waits outside the village church for the procession to arrive. She tells Zofia that she has lost Jasko, her falcon, and Janusz hurries them into the church. Halka imagines her child dying of hunger and is about to set the church on fire when she hears prayers within. Calling on Janusz to pardon her, she hurls herself from the cliff into the river.

Mussorgsky, Modest
1839–81, RUSSIAN
Modest Mussorgsky was born in to a family of aristocratic landowners – a status in life that afforded him both luxury and leisure. His musical talent was evident from an early age. Taught at first by his mother and his governess, Mussorgsky could play concertos by John Field (1782–1837) at the age of nine. At age 10, his parents engaged the pianist Anton Herke as his music teacher.

ARMY LIFE
It was not intended, though, that this should lead to a musical career. Patronage of the arts barely existed in Russia and composers, even those of aristocratic birth, usually followed other careers, with music as a sideline. César Cui studied engineering. Rimsky-Korsakov was a naval officer and Borodin was a medical army officer. Mussorgsky was destined for

the military and at 13 entered the School of Guards in St Petersburg as a cadet. It was here that he began writing music.

In 1856, Mussorgsky received an officer's commission in the crack Preobrajzensky Regiment. Around this time he met Borodin, who was impressed by Mussorgsky s talent and creativity. In 1857 Mussorgsky also encountered Cui, Rimsky-Korsakov and another Russian composer, Mily Alexeyevich Balakirev (1837–1910). Together with Borodin, these four made up what the champion of Russian national music, Vladimir Stasov (1824–1906), called the 'Mighty Handful' of composers (or 'The Five'), who were destined to give Russian music its own identity. All were amateurs, all were patriots and they all longed to represent the history and people of Russia in music.

ALCOHOLISM AND BANKRUPTCY

However, for Mussorgsky, disaster intervened. By 1858, when he abandoned his military career in favour of a musical one, he was well on the way to becoming an alcoholic. In 1861, the tsar's emancipation of the Russian serfs drove his family into bankruptcy and Mussorgsky was obliged to take a lowly job as a government clerk. Despite these tribulations, Mussorgsky continued to compose, but he was hampered by his lack of musical education. He started several works, only to leave them unfinished. One of them, *Oedipus in Athens* (1858–60) survived as only one scene. Another, *The Marriage* (1868) never got beyond its first act.

COMPLETED MASTERPIECE

Shortly after *The Marriage* was abandoned, however, Mussorgsky produced his masterpiece, *Boris Godunov*, which was based on a play written in 1825 by Alexander Pushkin (1799–1837). This illustrated the life of Tsar Boris Godunov, whose reign cast Russia into chaos. The opera employed Mussorgsky's radical declamatory style based on everyday speech patterns, and Boris's soliloquies and choruses show concern for the Russian masses. Mussorgsky completed the work in 1869, but came under fire from other members of 'The Five'. Cui, for instance, attacked the opera as immature and lacking in technique. Several revisions were required before Boris was accepted by the opera house in St Petersburg, where it was performed in 1874.

DISSOLUTE DEMISE

In 1872 Mussorgsky, who eked out a bare existence through occasional engagements as a pianist, had begun work on another opera, *Khovanshchina* ('The Khovansky Affair'). This, too, took its subject from Russian history, but the work was abandoned and was eventually completed by Rimsky-Korsakov. Similarly, Mussorgsky's comedy *Sorochintsy Fair* (1876–81) was left for other composers to finish. By this time, drink, poverty, mental instability and depression were disintegrating Mussorgsky's life and mind. Delirium tremens and epileptic fits developed, and Mussorgsky died in the Military Hospital at St Petersburg on 28 March 1881, a week after his forty-second birthday.

Boris Godunov

Boris Godunov, the only project out of nine that Mussorgsky completed himself, has been cited as the great masterpiece of nineteenth-century Russian opera – with its thrilling crowd scenes, historic panorama and the chilling power of its principal character. *Boris* was unusual in having its chief male role written for a **bass** voice and for the 'sung prose' used instead of verse for the inn scene in Act I, Scene Two. The opera was also a prime example of realism in music. Boris's death scene, for instance, tracked the tsar's fading strength; just as would happen in real life, his vocal line fragments and dims away to nothing as he dies. Many problems had to be overcome before *Boris* could take the stage. Mussorgsky's first, 'raw', version was rejected by the St Petersburg opera house. Songs and duets were added, the third act was recast and eventually the opera was lengthened to almost three hours. The first performance took place at last on 8 February 1874 but ran for only 25 performances. *Boris* was then given in Moscow, before the first of Rimsky-Korsakov's two revised versions was performed at St Petersburg on 10 December 1896.

Boris Godunov

by Modeste Mussorgsky
Composed: 1868–69; rev. 1871–72; rev. 1873
Premiered: 1874, St Petersburg (rev. version)
Libretto by the composer, after Alexander Sergeyevich Pushkin

PROLOGUE

Boris Godunov, regent of Muscovy, has instigated the murder of Tsar Fyodor's brother Dmitry. In 1598, after Fyodor's death and the withdrawal to a monastery of his widow Irina (Boris's sister), the people turn to Boris as their tsar. The crowds in Moscow are told that Boris is still reluctant to take the throne and call on him to save them from anarchy. When he relents they acclaim him, but he is full of foreboding and prays that he may reign justly.

ACT I

Five years later Pimen, a monk, is in his cell completing his chronicle of Russia. His novice, Grigory, awakes from a nightmare that suggests high ambition and a sudden fall. He envies Pimen's memories of war and the court. Pimen describes the murder of Dmitry, who would have been the same age as Grigory, and tells how Boris has usurped the throne. Dmitry plans to impersonate the murdered tsarevich. He arrives at an inn on the Lithuanian border with two dissolute

monks, Varlaam and Missail. Varlaam sings a drinking song while Grigory learns from the hostess that sentries are looking for a fugitive. The guards cannot read their orders and Grigory pretends to read a description of Varlaam, giving himself time to escape.

ACT II

In his rooms in the Kremlin, Boris consoles his daughter Xenia and tells his son Fyodor that soon all Muscovy might be his. He reflects that his rule has brought only unhappiness. At night he sees a vision of a bloodstained child. Boris warns Fyodor not to trust Prince Shuysky, who comes with news of a pretender gathering support in Poland. When questioned, Shuysky relates how the dead tsarevich's body had appeared unspoilt and smiling. As the clock strikes Boris is haunted by the dead child.

ACT III

Grigory has been accepted by the Poles as Dmitry and is preparing to invade Muscovy. He has fallen in love with the Voyevoda of Sandomierz's daughter, Marina Mniszek, who has ambitions to be tsarina. Rangoni, a Jesuit, tells her that she should pretend to return his love and use her influence to convert Muscovy to Roman Catholicism.

In the castle gardens, Dmitry responds enthusiastically to Rangoni's reports of Marina's passion for him. His distrust of Rangoni, however, appears to be confirmed when he sees Marina with a group of nobles anticipating a Polish victory. It is soon obvious that all she wants is the throne itself, calling him a serf. Regally he declares himself tsarevich and describes how soon she will grovel at his feet. Shocked, she claims that she was only trying to increase his passion. Rangoni foresees his success.

ACT IV

News has reached Moscow of Dmitry's approach. Urchins steal a coin from a holy fool, who stops Boris on the steps of St Basil's Cathedral and asks him to kill them as he murdered the young Dmitry. He refuses to pray for Boris, 'Tsar Herod', and prophesies tears. Boris has been wracked by guilt. He tells his councillors that the child is still alive and that Shuysky should be punished for saying otherwise. Shuysky introduces Pimen, who recounts a miracle at the tsarevich's grave. Boris asks his son to uphold the Orthodox faith. He then begs God's forgiveness and dies. The peasants, led by Varlaam and Missail, head towards Moscow in support of Dmitry. In a forest near Kromï they seize two Jesuits. Dmitry arrives and all acclaim him. The holy fool is left to bewail the fate of Russia.

Recommended Recording:
Boris Godunov (1869 and 1872 versions), Kirov Opera; Valery Gergiev, conductor; Philips 462 230-2; Soloists: 1869: Viktor Lutsuk (Grigory), Konstantin Pluzhnikov (Shuysky), Nikolai Putilin (Boris Godunov); 1872: Olga Borodina (Marina), Vladimir Galusin (Grigory), Konstantin Pluzhnikov (Shuysky), Yevgeny Nikitin (Rangoni), Vladimir Vaneev (Boris Godunov)

Khovanshchina

Khovanshchina ('The Khovansky Affair'), a dark opera, full of conspiracy, gloom and imminent violence, was based on a historical event. In 1682, the future modernizing tsar Peter the Great (1672–1725) was made co-ruler of Russia with his mentally retarded half-brother Ivan V (1666–96). At this time, introducing Greek and Latin practices into the Russian Church was bitterly opposed by the 'Old Believers', a sect led by the 'archpriest' Avvakum. Avvakum was burned at the stake in 1682, and groups of Old Believers, up to 2,500 at a time, committed suicide by fire rather than compromise their faith. Some productions of *Khovanshchina* have reproduced this mass burning by means of flickering tongues of light. Mussorgsky

left the opera unfinished and there was no orchestration for the vocal score. It was completed by Rimsky-Korsakov and in 1886 the first performance was given at the Kononov Hall in St Petersburg, by an amateur musical drama group. The first professional production was not staged until 1911, when it was performed at the Maryinsky Theatre.

Khovanshchina
by Modest Mussorgsky
Composed: 1872–80; 5th act unfinished
Premiered: 1886, St Petersburg
Libretto by the composer, compiled with Vladimir Vasil'yevich Stasov

PROLOGUE
When Tsar Fyodor III died in 1682, his brother Ivan and half-brother Peter were made co-tsars, with Ivan's sister Sophia as regent. Their mothers' families fought for power. Ivan's faction was backed by Prince Ivan Khovansky, leader of the strel'tsï (musketeers), and his son Andrey.

ACT I
Strel'tsï are on guard in Red Square. Boyar Shaklovity, the regent's agent, dictates a letter to a scribe denouncing the Khovansky faction. Ivan Khovansky enters and vows to crush opposition to the royal family. Emma, a German girl, enters, trying to escape from Andrey Khovansky, who is stopped by his former lover Marfa, now a member of the Old Believers sect. His father demands Emma for himself but Andrey refuses to let her go. They are interrupted by Dosifei, leader of the Old Believers. The strel'tsï are ordered back to the Kremlin and Dosifei broods on the preservation of the faith.

ACT II
In his study Prince Golitsïn, Sophia's principal minister, is reading a love-letter from her and wondering whether she is to be trusted. A Lutheran pastor comes to complain about Emma's treatment by the

Khovanskys. Marfa is brought in to read Golitsïn's fortune. She foresees his disgrace and exile and he gives secret orders to drown her. Ivan Khovansky enters and accuses Golitsïn of attacking the boyars' hereditary rights. Dosifei urges them both to join him in restoring the traditional faith. Marfa bursts in and describes how Golitsïn's men tried to kill her and how she was rescued by Tsar Peter's guards. Shaklovity informs them that, acting on a letter of denunciation, Peter has vowed to destroy the Khovanskys' power.

ACT III

On the other side of the river, Marfa recalls her unrequited love for Andrey and is denounced by Susanna as a servant of the devil. Dosifei tries to comfort Marfa, but she exultantly predicts that soon she and Andrey will burn together. She begs Dosifei to punish her with death, but he tells her she must never stop loving Andrey. Alone, Shaklovity prays that someone will save Russia from her enemies. The strel'tsï return, still drunk from the night before, and they are harangued by their wives. The scribe arrives with news that mercenaries loyal to Tsar Peter have sacked their homes. They call on Ivan Khovansky for guidance and he advises them to disperse: the new tsar has taken power and their dominance is finished.

ACT IV

Ivan Khovansky is being entertained by his serving girls. He ignores a warning sent by Golitsïn and calls for his Persian slave girls. Shaklovity enters to announce that Sophia has summoned him to a grand council. Khovansky puts on his ceremonial robes and is assassinated as he reaches the doorway.

ACT V

Golitsïn is escorted through Red Square on his way to exile. Dosifei laments the fall of Khovansky and Golitsïn. Marfa tells him that Peter's troops are hunting down the Old Believers, and together they decide on immolation. Andrey enters, calling for Emma, but Marfa tells him she has returned to her own country. The strel'tsï enter in chains, ready for execution, and Marfa drags Andrey away. A boyar announces that the strel'tsï have been pardoned.

ACT VI

Gathered in a forest, Dosifei and the Old Believers prepare for death. Marfa tells Andrey that they are to die together. He tries to break away, still calling for Emma, but Marfa pulls him back into the flames as Peter's troops look on in horror.

Recommended Recording:

Khovanshchina, Vienna State Opera; Claudio Abbado, conductor; Image Entertainment IMG9243DVD (DVD Region 1); ArtHaus Musik 100 310 (DVD Region 2); Soloists: Joanna Borowska (Emma), Ludmila Semtschuk (Marfa), Vladimir Atlantov (Andrey Khovansky), Yuri Marusin (Golitsïn), Anatoly Kocherga (Shaklovity), Nicolai Ghiaurov (Ivan Khovansky), Paata Burchuladze (Dosifei)

OPERAS

1868–69	Boris Godunov; rev. 1871–72
1872–80	Khovanshchina
1876–81	Sorochintsy Fair

TIMELINE

1838	Modest Mussorgsky born, Karevo
1856	Joins the army, where he meets Alexander Borodin and César Cui
1858	Resigns from army to pursue musical career
1861	Joins civil service and composes in his spare time
1868	Work begins on Boris Godunov
1872	Work begins on Khovanshchina
1874	Premiere of Boris Godunov, St Petersburg
1876	Work begins on Sorochintsy Fair
1881	Mussorgsky dies, St Petersburg
1886	Premiere of Rimsky-Korsakov's completion of Khovanshchina, St Petersburg
1013	Premiere of Lyadov's completion of Sorochintsy Fair, Moscow

Offenbach, Jacques

1819–80, **FRENCH**

Jacques Offenbach had an acute sense of theatre and an incisive understanding of how to cater for French tastes. He was 14 when his father sent him to Paris, where Jews were freer than they were in Germany. Offenbach became a cellist, performing in fashionable salons, and finally, in 1855, became famous. He rented the Théâtre Marigny, named it Les Bouffes-Parisiens and staged a series of successful operettas. In 1858 he scored his greatest triumph with his own *Orphée aux enfers* ('Orpheus in the Underworld'). This irreverent exposé of naughty goings-on among the ancient Greek gods scandalized classicists, delighted audiences and made Offenbach world-renowned. A series of successful operettas followed, including *La belle Hélène* ('Fair Helen', 1864) and *La vie Parisienne* ('Paris Life', 1866), all satirical and full of fun. It was said that the sound of laughter could be heard in Offenbach's music. His last work, *Les contes d'Hoffmann* ('The Tales of Hoffmann', 1881), was an attempt at something more serious, but sadly he died during rehearsals.

La belle Hélène ('Fair Helen')

by Jacques Offenbach
Composed: 1864
Premiered: 1864, Paris
Libretto by Henri Meilhac and Ludovic Halévy

ACT I

Since Pâris awarded Vénus the golden apple, her cult has become more popular than Jupiter's. Hélène, wife of King Ménélas of Sparta, is waiting for Pâris to come and claim her. Disguised as a shepherd, Pâris enlists the help of Calchas, High Priest of Jupiter, and it is soon apparent that Hélène is interested. The Kings of Greece enter for a ceremonial intelligence test, which the shepherd wins easily. Hélène is flustered and thrilled when Pâris announces his true identity. Calchas arranges for a divine thunderstorm to occur and, speaking as the oracle, instructs Ménélas to go to Crete for four weeks.

ACT II

After consulting a statue of her parents, Hélène receives Pâris in her apartments. He insists that she shall be his, by trickery if necessary. The kings arrive to play the Game of Goose. Hélène excuses herself and prepares for bed, asking Calchas to send her a beautiful dream of Pâris, who has disguised himself as a guard. He slips into her room. When she awakes she thinks it is all part of the promised dream. Ménélas returns unexpectedly and summons the kings to witness his dishonour. Pâris is ordered to leave.

ACT III

The court has moved to Nauplia. Hélène insists that it was not her fault. The kings tell Ménélas that it was due to the immoral cult of Vénus sweeping the country. Calchas and Agamemnon advise him to appease the goddess. The High Priest of Vénus arrives and demands that Hélène accompanies him to Cythera. As they sail away he throws off his disguise. It is Pâris, who announces that they are off to Troy.

Orphée aux enfers ('Orpheus in the Underworld')

by Jacques Offenbach
Composed: 1858; rev. 1874
Premiered: 1874, Paris
Libretto by Crémieux and Halévy

ACT I

Eurydice cannot abide her violin virtuoso husband Orphée. She would rather die than be bored to death. Jealous that she is seeing too much of the beekeeper Aristée, he tells her about the snakes in Aristée's cornfield. She goes to warn him and is bitten. Aristée reveals that he is Pluton and whisks her off to Hades. Orphée's freedom is cut short when Opinion Publique orders him to appeal to the gods on Olympus.

ACT II

The gods are woken by Diane's angry account of Jupiter's interference in her love life. Pluton has been summoned to answer for his actions. As Jupiter reprimands him they are interrupted when the lesser deities rebel against Jupiter's own hypocrisy. Orphée reluctantly puts his case and all the gods demand an adventure in Hades to ensure Pluton returns Eurydice.

ACT III

Eurydice had expected endless infernal orgies, but instead she is locked away in the care of John Styx, who tries to forget his past with Lethe water. Eurydice is hidden when Pluton arrives with Jupiter, but Cupidon sees her next door and helps Jupiter to return as a fly. Jupiter allows himself to be caught, reveals his true identity and arranges to take her away.

ACT IV

The party builds up from stately dancing to a wild gallop. Pluton prevents Jupiter from escaping with Eurydice. Cupidon suggests making Orphée's return to earth with Eurydice conditional on him not looking back. As they leave, Jupiter throws a thunderbolt and Orphée turns. Eurydice chooses to become a bacchante. Only Opinion Publique is unhappy.

Les contes d'Hoffman ('The Tales of Hoffmann')

by Jacques Offenbach
Premiered: 1881, Paris
Libretto by Jules Barbier after the play by Barbier and Michel Carré

ACT I

Hoffmann has neglected poetry in his search for love. His muse is transformed into a companion named Nicklausse in order to protect him. Hoffmann's latest love, Stella, an opera singer, is also admired by Counsellor Lindorf. Luther's tavern fills up during the interval of Don Giovanni. Hoffmann tells the story of Kleinzack, but his mind keeps wandering to a lost love. He recognizes Lindorf and claims that something evil always happens when he is there. Hoffmann announces that Stella embodies three former loves: an artist, a young girl and a courtesan. He begins three fantastical tales of his loves.

ACT II

Spalanzani has invented a mechanical doll that he will introduce as his daughter Olympia. He hopes to make his fortune, but still owes money to Coppélius. Hoffmann is unaware that she is a doll and Coppélius gives him spectacles that make her appear human. Olympia is introduced to the guests with great success and Hoffmann declares his love. Coppélius discovers that Spalanzani has cheated him and destroys the doll. The guests mock Hoffmann's infatuation.

ACT II

Crespel's wife, an opera singer, suffered from a fatal chest disease and he has forbidden his daughter Antonia to overtax herself by singing or seeing Hoffmann. Frantz, their deaf servant, admits Hoffmann and Nicklausse. Although Nicklausse tries to stop them, Antonia insists on singing with Hoffmann. Crespel returns with Dr Miracle, whom he believes was responsible for his wife's death, but who claims that only he can cure Antonia. Miracle contrasts humdrum married life with Antonia's dreams of the stage and calls on her to sing with an apparition of her mother. She collapses with the strain and dies as Crespel blames Hoffmann.

ACT IV

Hoffmann and Nicklausse attend a party held by the Venetian courtesan Giulietta. Dapertutto bribes Giulietta to seduce Hoffmann and steal his reflection as she *has taken Schlemil's shadow. She tells Hoffmann that Schlemil has the key to her boudoir. He kills Schlemil in a duel and takes the key. Giulietta urges Hoffmann to flee and promises to join him later. She asks for a keepsake and his reflection becomes imprisoned in a mirror. Schlemil's body has been found. Hoffmann curses Giulietta and tries to stab her but instead kills her servant Pitichinaccio.*

ACT V
Back at the tavern Hoffmann is drunk and contemplating suicide. He insults Stella and she bids him farewell. Now that his passion can once again be directed towards poetry, his muse returns.

Recommended Recording:

Les contes d'Hoffmann, Royal Opera, Covent Garden; Georges Prêtre, conductor Warner Music Vision 0630-19392-2 (DVD Region 0, NTSC); Soloists: Luciana Serra (Olympia), Ileana Cotrubas (Antonia), Agnes Baltsa (Giulietta), Claire Powell (Muse/Nicklausse), Phyllis Cannan (Voice), Placido Domingo (Hoffmann), Robert Tear (Spalanzani), Robert Lloyd (Lindorf), Geraint Evans (Coppelius)

Patti, Adelina
1843–1919, ITALIAN

The Italian soprano Adelina Patti was among the greatest of all prima donnas. As such, she enjoyed special privileges. One was exemption from rehearsals. Another was top pay for her time, amounting to $5,000 (£2,725) a performance after 1882. Patti made her singing debut at age seven, and first appeared on stage at the Academy of Music, New York in 1859, in the title role of Donizetti's Lucia di Lammermoor. After 1860, Patti travelled worldwide, singing in New Orleans (1860–61) and Covent Garden, London (1861–95), as well as Berlin, Paris, Vienna, Moscow, St Petersburg, Milan, Madrid and South America. She was 63 when she retired in 1906, but made occasional comebacks until 1914. Some of Patti's best roles included Desdemona in Rossini's *Otello*, Violetta in Verdi's *La traviata*, Marguerite in Gounod's *Faust* and the title role in Delibes' *Lakmé*.

Petrov, Osip
1806–78, RUSSIAN

Osip Petrov, a Russian bass with a rich, dark voice and strong dramatic instincts, made his debut in 1826 and sang regularly at St Petersburg from 1830 until his death. He soon established himself as the first great Russian bass. His arrival on the Russian opera scene was fortuitous. Nationalist composers sought him out to create important bass parts in their operas, and he performed this function at St Petersburg for almost a half century. Petrov took the parts of Ivan Susanin in Glinka's *A Life for the Tsar*, Ruslan in the same composer's *Ruslan i Lyudmila*, Leporello in Dargomïzhsky's *The Stone Guest*, Ivan the Terrible in Rimsky-Korsakov's *Maid of Pskov* and Varlaam, the vagabond friar, in Mussorgsky's *Boris Godunov*. Mussorgsky called Petrov his 'Grandpa' and at his funeral in 1878 mourned the 'irreplaceable instructor ... who inspired me to creativity'.

Piave, Francesco Maria
1810–76, ITALIAN

Although Francesco Piave's fame rests on his libretti written for Verdi, he produced texts for several other composers of the Romantic era. These included Michael Balfe, Antonio Cagnoni (1828–96), **Saverio Mercadante** (1795–1870) and **Giovanni Pacini** (1796–1867): Piave supplied Pacini with the libretto for his *Lorenzino de' Medici* (1845), which was first performed in Venice. By this time Verdi was beginning to dominate the opera world and Pacini found himself eclipsed. Piave, too, was aware of the change at the top, and had already written his first libretto for Verdi, *Ernani*, which premiered at the Teatro La Fenice in Venice in 1844. This was followed by *I due Foscari*, *Macbeth*, *Il corsaro*, *Stiffelio* (plus its revision as Aroldo, 1857), *Rigoletto*, *La traviata*, the first version of *Simon Boccanegra* (1857) and *La forza del destino*.

Ponchielli, Amilcare

1834–86, ITALIAN

Amilcare Ponchielli, composer of nine operas, became famous for only one of them – *La gioconda* ('The Joyful Girl', 1876). Ponchielli was born at what was, for him, an unfortunate time. Verdi dominated the opera scene and Ponchielli was later overshadowed by one of his own pupils – **Giacomo Puccini** (1858–1924). Ponchielli's first venture into composition was a joint effort with his fellow students in Milan – *Il sindaco babbeo* ('The Simpleton Mayor', 1851). His own first opera, *I promessi sposi* ('The Betrothed', 1856) was performed in Cremona but scored better success when revived in Milan in 1872. Two years later, *I lituani* ('The Lithuanians', 1874), which was commissioned from Ponchielli by Ricordi, the music publishers, was well received in Milan. Ponchielli had a great fondness for the exotic in music. In *I lituani*, he employed a Slavonic style, for *Il figliuol prodigo* ('The Prodigal Son', 1880) he opted for oriental harmonies, and for his last opera, *Marion Delorme* (1885), he came close to the style of *opéra comique*. Ponchielli married the soprano Teresina Brambilla (1845–1921), who belonged to a renowned family of Italian musicians and she sang in the revised version of *I promessi sposi*.

La gioconda ('The Joyful Girl')

by Amilcare Ponchielli
Composed: 1876
Premiered: 1876, Milan
Libretto by Tobia Gorrio, after Victor Hugo

ACT I

Gioconda leaves her blind mother, La Cieca, surrounded by revellers outside the Doge's Palace while she looks for her betrothed, Enzo Grimaldi. When Gioconda refuses Barnaba's advances, he has La Cieca accused of witchcraft. Laura, the wife of Alvise, a Venetian state official, intercedes and is given a rosary in thanks. She also recognizes Enzo as a former love. Barnaba tells Enzo that he could have him arrested as a Genoese prince, but instead he will arrange an assignation with Laura. Gioconda overhears Barnaba dictating a letter of denunciation, with details of the meeting.

ACT II

Enzo is waiting on his brigantine. Barnaba escorts Laura on board. Enzo goes below. Laura's prayers are interrupted by Gioconda, who is about to stab her when she sees the rosary. She pushes Laura into a boat and tells her to escape. When told of Barnaba's treachery Enzo sets fire to the brigantine and dives into the sea.

ACT III

Alvise orders Laura to take poison, which Gioconda exchanges for a powerful sleeping draught. When Alvise returns he thinks Laura is dead. At a ball Barnaba accuses La Cieca of witchcraft and then tells Enzo that Laura is dead. Enzo denounces Alvise and is arrested. Gioconda tries to save him by submitting to Barnaba.

ACT IV

The sleeping Laura is carried into Gioconda's home. At first Gioconda wants to kill her rival, but then she considers suicide. Enzo, who has been freed, is about to murder Gioconda when she tells him that Laura's tomb is empty, but Laura wakes and describes how Gioconda saved her. Laura and Enzo escape by boat. Barnaba confronts Gioconda. She pretends to keep their bargain, but instead stabs herself and dies as Barnaba claims to have drowned La Cieca.

Pushkin, Alexander Sergeyevich
1799–1837, RUSSIAN

Russian composers of the High Romantic era were able to enjoy a ready-made source of stories for operas in the works of Alexander Pushkin. His first success was the romantic poem *Ruslan i Lyudmila* (1820), which Glinka used for his opera of the same name, first performed in 1842. Pushkin produced not only poetry, but essays, blank-verse historical dramas, such as *Boris Godunov*, and novels in verse like *Eugene Onegin* (1830). Both *Boris* and *Onegin* were used as the basis for operas, by Mussorgsky and Tchaikovsky respectively, but these were only two among a long list of Pushkin stories to be given this treatment. In all, 109 operas of the nineteenth and twentieth centuries were based on stories by Pushkin. The poet himself became the subject of operas dealing with his exile in 1820, his liberal politics and his death in a duel in 1837.

Saint-Saëns, Camille
1835–1921, FRENCH

Camille Saint-Saëns was a child prodigy as both pianist and composer. He began composing when he was six. At 10, he gave his first piano recital, and entered the Paris Conservatory aged 13. At 17, in 1852, Saint-Saëns wrote his prizewinning *Ode à Sainte-Cécile* ('Ode to Saint Cecilia') and at 18, he produced his first symphony. Gounod, Rossini, Liszt and Berlioz were all mightily impressed with Saint-Saëns, as was Wagner, who called him 'the greatest musical mind of our time'. Saint-Saëns, in his turn, greatly admired Wagner. A prolific composer, he wrote orchestral, piano and vocal music, as well as 13 operas, including most notably *La princesse jaune* ('The Yellow Princess', 1872), his masterpiece and chief contribution to the present-day operatic repertoire, *Samson et Dalila*, and *Henri VIII* (1883). *La princesse jaune* was an operetta, a style Saint-Saëns did not subsequently pursue. *Henri VIII*, which dealt with the second, fated, marriage of the English King Henry VIII to Anne Boleyn, was a *grand opéra*, perhaps rather too lavish for Saint-Saëns, whose natural style was quintessentially French – neatly proportioned, polished, elegant, disciplined.

Samson et Dalila
by Camille Saint-Saëns
Composed: 1867–68; 1873–77
Premiered: 1877, Weimar
Libretto by Ferdinand Lemaire

ACT I
Outside the temple of Dagon, the Hebrews fear that God has deserted them. The Philistine satrap, Abimélech, mocks them, saying that they should worship Dagon. When Samson speaks out Abimélech attacks him and is slain. The gates of the temple open, revealing the high priest – who curses the Hebrews. The beautiful Dalila enters with a group of priestesses. She declares that Samson has conquered her heart, not for the first time, and asks him to visit her again. An old Hebrew warns Samson against her. While Dalila sings and the priestesses dance, Samson is unable to resist watching her.

ACT II
Dalila revels in her power over Samson. The high priest tells her that it is even more important that she discovers the secret of Samson's power now that the Hebrews have captured the city. Samson must die. She refuses the gold he offers, saying that revenge for Samson's earlier treatment of her will be enough. Samson enters to say farewell, but Dalila invokes the power of love. As Samson declares his love Dalila demands total surrender, saying that he must reveal the secret. Samson eventually follows her into the house and Dalila gives a signal to the Philistine soldiers.

ACT III

Blinded, and with his hair shorn, Samson turns a treadmill while the Hebrews are heard lamenting his betrayal. The Philistines are celebrating in the temple. Samson is led in and mocked by the high priest. Dalila tells how she betrayed him out of hatred. As the Philistines make offerings to Dagon, the high priest orders Samson to be brought forward. Standing between the two pillars that support the temple, he calls on God to restore his strength and brings the roof crashing down.

SOUNDS FAMILIAR

'MON COEUR S'OUVRE À TA VOIX'

In this aria from Act II of *Samson et Dalila*, Dalila attempts to seduce Samson, hoping to weaken his resolve not to reveal the secret of his strength. If she succeeds, she can deprive him of it and so enable the high priest of Dagon to capture him. Samson tries to refuse her but eventually succumbs.

Schnorr von Carolsfeld, Ludwig
1836–65, GERMAN

After making his debut at Karlsruhe in 1854, playing small roles, Ludwig Schnorr von Carolsfeld attracted Wagner's attention, who considered his dramatically powerful voice ideal for tenor roles in his operas. Schnorr von Carolsfeld created a sensation as Lohengrin and another as Tannhäuser. When *Tristan und Isolde* premiered in Munich on 10 June 1865, Schnorr von Carolsfeld created the role of Tristan. Six weeks later, on 21 July, the tenor died suddenly in Dresden. Wagner was profoundly upset, as was the tenor's wife, the Danish soprano Malvina Garrigues (1825–1904), who had created the part of Isolde. Garrigues could not face continuing in opera without him, and retired soon after he died.

Smetana, Bedřich
1824–84, CZECH

In 1866, the Czech composer Bedřich Smetana won a national competition with his first of eight operas, *The Brandenburgers in Bohemia*. In this work, written for the National Theatre in Prague where he was conductor, he revealed his skill in writing orchestral music, his strong dramatic sense and his understanding of the cadences of the Czech language. From the start, therefore, Smetana was all set to become the first great nationalist composer of distinctively Czech music. Just how 'nationalist' he was remained in doubt for some critics, who charged him with taking too much of a cue from Wagner's operas. This was an accusation Smetana had to face throughout his career, and it bothered him so much that in the first version of his comic masterpiece, *The Bartered Bride* (1863–66), dialogue was spoken, not sung. The fact was that Smetana was very much a nationalist composer, taking for his model Czech folk dances and rhythms typical of Czech folk songs, all of it laced with Czech lyricism. His use of *leitmotif* and chromatic harmony, both Wagnerian characteristics, did nothing to detract from the Czech character of his music.

The Bartered Bride
by Bedřich Smetana
Composed: 1863–66; rev. 1869–70
Premiered: 1870, Prague
Libretto by Karel Sabina

ACT I

While the villagers enjoy themselves at the fair, Mařenka tells her lover Jeník that she is to be married off against her will to the son of a farmer named Mícha, to whom her own father, Krušina, owes money. She knows little of Jeník's past and he explains that he left home when his mother died and a new stepmother drove him out. They promise to remain faithful to one another. Kecal, the marriage-broker, gives Krušina and his wife Ludmila a glowing description of the intended bridegroom. Krušina wonders which of Mícha's two sons is being offered and is assured that this is the respectable younger son, not the elder scoundrel. Mařenka breaks the news that she already loves another. Kecal decides to get rid of Jeník.

ACT II

Mařenka recognizes Vašek, stuttering and in his Sunday best, as her intended husband. She tells him that the 'Mařenka' he is to marry is a faithless shrew who would probably poison him. When he protests that he is only obeying his mother, she charms him into renouncing the match. He is now devoted to this unnamed girl. Kecal offers Jeník a rich bride if he will go away. Jeník bargains for an additional 300 gulden, finally agreeing on the condition that Mařenka will be allowed to marry no one except Mícha's son and also that Krušina's debt is written off. Krušina is angry when he hears how Jeník has sold his interest in Mařenka. She has had a lucky escape.

ACT III

Varek is enthralled by the colour and excitement of the circus, and especially by the legs of Esmeralda the tightrope walker. Esmeralda and the circus master talk him into appearing as a principal attraction, a dancing bear. Kecal, Mícha and his wife Háta cannot understand when Vašek refuses the match. Mařenka cannot believe what Jeník has done, but would rather remain single than marry Vašek, who returns and sees the girl he would happily marry. Mařenka agrees to reconsider the matter alone. When Jeník appears she tells him to go away. She tells her parents that she will marry Mícha's son and is amazed when Jeník addresses Mícha as his father. There can be no objection to his marriage to Mařenka. There is uproar when it seems that a bear is loose, but it is only Vašek. Háta drags him off as the other parents give their blessing.

Recommended Recording:

The Bartered Bride, Czech Philharmonic Orchestra; Zdeněk Kosler, conductor; Supraphon 10 3511–2; Soloists: Gabriela Benacková (Mařenka), Marie Veselá (Ludmila), Marie Mrázová (Háta), Peter Dvorsky (Jeník), Miroslav Kopp (Varek), Alfred Hampel (Circus Master), Jindrich Jindrák (Krušina), Richard Novák (Kecal), Jaroslav Horácek (Mícha)

Stolz, Teresa
1834–1902, BOHEMIAN

Teresa Stolz made her debut at Tbilisi, Georgia in 1857 and subsequently appeared in Odessa, Constantinople, Bologna, Milan (1865–72), Cairo, Vienna, St Petersburg and Paris. Stolz was a beautiful woman with a powerful voice, 'diamond-like' in its clarity and purity. Her phrasing was extraordinary for she could sustain the breath supply for an unusually long time. Stolz sang Mathilde in Rossini's Guillaume Tell, Alice in Meyerbeer's Robert le diable and the title role in Donizetti's Lucrezia Borgia, but was best known as an incomparable Verdi performer. Her Verdi roles included Amelia in Simon Boccanegra and Leonora in both Il trovatore and La forza del destino. Stolz also created the soprano role in Verdi's Requiem. Verdi, who admired Stolz greatly, thought her the ideal Aida.

Strauss II, Johann
1825–99, AUSTRIAN

The Austrian violinist, conductor and composer Johann Strauss II belonged to what was probably the most widely known of all musical families. His father Johann Strauss I introduced the waltz to Vienna, a tradition continued by the second Johann, the eldest son, and his two composer-conductor brothers. The second Johann was only 19 when he made his first appearance in Vienna with his own orchestra, in competition with his father's. The two orchestras merged after the elder Strauss's early death in 1849. Johann Strauss II quickly became the most eminent composer of light music in the Austrian capital and acquired the nickname of 'The Waltz King'. He did not, however, confine his music to the dance floor. Johann Strauss II was also a substantial composer of operettas for the stage. The first was *Indigo und die vierzig Räuber* ('Indigo and the Forty Thieves'), which premiered at the Theater an der Wien in Vienna in 1871. Indigo was followed by Strauss's greatest success for the stage, *Die Fledermaus*, which featured several examples of the ubiquitous family trademark, the waltz. Of his other 13 operettas, only the exuberant *Der Zigeunerbaron* ('The Gypsy Baron', 1885) achieved a comparable popularity.

Die Fledermaus ('The Bat')

by Johann Strauss
Compose: 1874
Premiered: 1874, Vienna
Libretto by Carl Haffner and Richard Genée after Henri Meilhac and Ludovic Halévy's *Le réveillon*

PROLOGUE

Falke wants revenge for a practical joke when Eisenstein left him sleeping, dressed as a bat, outside the Vienna law courts.

ACT I

Eisenstein's wife, Rosalinde, recognizes the voice serenading her as her lover Alfred. Her maid Adele has been invited to Prince Orlofsky's ball and, pleading her aunt's illness, tries to get the night off, but Rosalinde refuses since Eisenstein is about to go to prison for a few days. Rosalinde gets rid of Alfred by saying he can return when her husband has left for prison. Eisenstein's

sentence has been increased on appeal. Falke persuades him to delay reporting in until the last moment so they can go to the ball. Now looking forward to her assignation with Alfred, Rosalinde tells Adele to go to her sick aunt. Husband, wife and maid sing of their sadness, while looking forward to romantic entanglements. Eisenstein departs, apparently to prison, in full evening dress. Alfred slips in and is wearing Eisenstein's dressing gown when Frank, the prison governor, arrives to collect his new inmate. To save Rosalinde's honour, Alfred pretends to be Eisenstein.

ACT II

At the ball Falke explains to Orlofsky, who is bored by everything, that he has arranged an entertainment, The Revenge of a Bat. The first character is Adele, who indignantly denies that she is a maid when Eisenstein, claiming to be the 'Marquis Renard', recognizes her in Rosalinde's dress. Frank is introduced as the 'Chevalier Chagrin'. Summoned by Falke, Rosalinde arrives as a masked Hungarian countess. Eisenstein proceeds to woo this stranger with his usual bait, a watch, which she pockets. The 'countess' sings of her homeland, Orlofsky proposes a toast to 'King Champagne' and the guests drunkenly promise eternal friendship. As the clock strikes six, Eisenstein and Frank rush out.

ACT III

The drunken jailer Frosch is disturbed by Alfred's singing. Adele has followed Frank, hoping to impress him with her acting talents. Eisenstein finally turns up at the prison, only to find that someone called Eisenstein is already there. He appropriates the gown and wig of his lawyer, Blind, and questions Alfred and Rosalinde about last night's events. When he dramatically reveals himself, Rosalinde produces the watch. Falke announces it was all a trick and everyone blames the champagne.

Recommended Recording:
Die Fledermaus, Bavarian State Opera; Carlos Kleiber, conductor; Deutsche Grammophon 073 007–9GH; Soloists: Pamela Coburn (Rosalinde), Janet Perry (Adele), Brigitte Fassbaender (Prince Orlofsky), Josef Hopferweiser (Alfred), Eberhard Wächter (Eisenstein), Wolfgang Brendel (Falke), Benno Kusche (Frank)

Tamagno, Francesco
1850–1905, **ITALIAN**

The Italian tenor Francesco Tamagno was idolized for his powerful voice and dramatic delivery. Tamagno thrilled his many admirers with his effortless top C, which not all tenors were able to reach, and his passionate on-stage performances. His voice was described as 'enduring brass'. Otello, the eponymous hero of Verdi's penultimate opera, which he created in 1887, was arguably the most demanding tenor role outside the work of Richard Wagner; however, Tamagno was considered incomparable as the tortured Moor, by Verdi himself as well as by many others. After his debut in Turin in 1870, Tamagno scored one success after another in Venice, Milan, Chicago, New York, London, Buenos Aires, Madrid and St Petersburg. Among Tamagno's numerous roles were Radamès in Verdi's *Aida*, Don José in Bizet's *Carmen*, Samson in Saint-Saëns' *Samson et Dalila* and Gabriele Adorno in the revised version of Verdi's *Simon Boccanegra*, in 1881.

Tamberlik, Enrico
1820–89, **ITALIAN**

Enrico Tamberlik, the Italian tenor, made his debut in Naples in 1841, as Enrico Danieli, singing Tebaldo in *I Capuleti e i Montecchi*, Bellini's *Romeo and Juliet* opera. Afterwards, while at the Teatro San Carlo, Naples, he took the surname Tamberlik and retained it for engagements in London, St Petersburg, Paris, Madrid, Buenos Aires and elsewhere. Tamberlik impressed with his strong, ringing tone and dramatic, virile stage presence. Nevertheless, a more lyrical delivery was well within his scope. Tamberlik was a fearless exponent of the high C and the high C-sharp, half a tone higher. Among varied roles, Tamberlik sang Rossini's Otello, Don Ottavio in Mozart's *Don Giovanni*, Florestan, Leonore's imprisoned husband, in Beethoven's *Fidelio* (1814) and the title roles in Berlioz's *Benvenuto Cellini* and Gounod's *Faust*. Tamberlik retired around 1882. Settled in Madrid, he became an arms manufacturer.

Tchaikovsky, Pyotr Ilyich
1840–93, **RUSSIAN**

Tchaikovsky was an intensely emotional, painfully sensitive man, much given to depression and morbid states of mind. He almost went mad with grief when his mother died of cholera in 1854, when he was 14. To compound his melancholy mindset, Tchaikovsky was tortured by his homosexuality, and saw marriage as a possible solution. In 1877 he married one of his pupils, but the strain was so great that to escape it – and his wife – he tried to kill himself. Perhaps these personal tragedies in part explain the broad, arching melodies and his tendency towards the agonized self-expression found in his music.

HIS CHILDHOOD EPIPHANY

From the start his aim was to write opera, but Tchaikovsky did not envisage making his living that way. Instead, he became a minor civil servant at the Ministry of Justice. Fortunately, he was in St Petersburg at exactly the right time – 1862 – for the founding of the city's Music Conservatory by Anton Rubinstein (1829–94). Tchaikovsky enrolled at once, and made such progress that in 1865, he was asked to teach harmony at the new conservatory in Moscow.

STRUGGLE FOR SUCCESS

Success as a composer was elusive at first and it was some time before Tchaikovsky established himself in the opera world. He had planned his first, one-act work *Hyperbole* when he was 14, but the libretto went missing and the opera was never written. Other early compositions included a setting of a scene from Pushkin's play *Boris Godunov* (1863–64) and his first complete opera, *Voyevoda* ('Dream on the Volga', 1867–68). Tchaikovsky, however, was dissatisfied with *Voyevoda* and after its first performance at the Bolshoi in 1869 he abandoned it, although he retained some of the best music for future use. Tchaikovsky's next opera, *Undina*, (1869) fared little better: the composer destroyed it after the imperial theatres in St Petersburg rejected it. However, his own individual style of dramatic music began to emerge with *The Oprichnik* ('The Life Guardsman, 1874), and in *Vakula the Smith* (1876) his lyrical love music and lively dances were impressive.

NATIONAL FOLKLORE AND FLAVOUR

In these, as in all his works, Tchaikovsky was a distinctively Russian composer, with great feeling for Russian folk tunes and for recreating the town and country life of Russia in his music, much of it touched by the oriental harmonies typical of a homeland spanning both Europe and Asia. The Russian flavour of Tchaikovsky's music certainly showed in his great masterpiece *Eugene Onegin* (1879), a tale of frustrated love that he himself described as a series of 'lyrical scenes'.

A RUSSIAN LOOKING WEST

Even so, Tchaikovsky was better known as a westerner among Russian composers and was regarded as an outsider by his more nationalistic contemporaries. Their case against him seemed made with his choice of non-Russian subjects for all but one of his later operas, the exception being *Mazeppa* (1884). *The Maid of Orleans* (1881) was the story the fifteenth-century French national heroine, Joan of Arc. Although taken from a Pushkin story, *The Queen of Spades* (1890) betrayed the influence of Mozart, Wagner, Bizet's *Carmen* and the Gallic elegance of the eighteenth-century Russian court. Likewise, Tchaikovsky's last opera, *Yolanta* (1892), was set far away from Russia, in Provence, southeast France. Less than a year after the premiere of Yolanta in St Petersburg on 18 December 1892, Tchaikovsky was dead. He died, an apparent suicide, on 6 November 1893, four days after drinking water that he knew to be infected with cholera.

Eugene Onegin

Eugene Onegin was written after the disaster of Tchaikovsky's marriage in 1877, and was also influenced by his platonic relationship with his admirer and patron Nadezhda von Meck. Tchaikovsky began *Eugene Onegin* by writing the famous 'letter scene' from Act I, in which the heroine Tat'yana spends the night writing to Onegin, telling him of her love for him. Letter scenes first became a popular device in seventeenth-century opera, but they have been monopolized by this one, which has been called the most moving of them all. As before, Tchaikovsky went to Pushkin for his story and *Onegin* was based on his verse novel, dating from 1830. The first, amateur, performance of *Eugene Onegin* took place at the Maly Theatre in Moscow on 29 March 1879. The first professional performance followed at the Bolshoi Theatre, Moscow on 23 January 1881. The opera was not universally welcomed by those nationalist composers who believed that promoting Russian values and culture was the most important point of Russian art. Tchaikovsky, however, had proceeded from a more eclectic premise;

he intended to produce an intimate opera with the main attention on the characters and their situation.

Eugene Onegin

by Pyotr Ilyich Tchaikovsky
Composed: 1877–78
Premiered: 1879, Moscow
Libretto by the composer and Konstantin Stepanovich Shilovsky after Alexander Sergeyevich Pushkin's novel in verse

ACT I

Seated in the garden of her country estate, Madame Larina listens to her daughters, Tat'yana and Olga, and reflects on the time before her marriage when she loved a cavalry officer. The estate's serfs return from the fields and celebrate the harvest. The two sisters are very different. Tat'yana reads and dreams, which concerns Larina, while Olga would rather spend the day dancing. The serfs leave and Filipp'yevna, the girls' nurse, announces the arrival of Lensky, a poet who has been courting Olga. Lensky enters with Onegin, who has just inherited a nearby estate. Tat'yana at once sees the man of whom she has been dreaming. Onegin and Tat'yana leave together, while Lensky passionately declares his love for Olga. Tat'yana is unable to sleep. She asks Filipp'yevna about her own marriage but, preoccupied, she barely hears her story. At last she bursts out that she is in love. She sends Filipp'yevna away and starts to write a love-letter to Onegin, pouring out her feelings and saying that her life is bound to him for ever. She longs for him to save her. All she needs is one word. It is now morning and Tat'yana asks Filipp'yevna to send the letter to Onegin.

Tat'yana is terrified that she has gone too far. When Onegin arrives he gently warns her against such impetuous behaviour. She has also chosen the wrong man, since he is not one to show affection and certainly not to marry. He will always love her as a brother, but no more.

ACT II

The dance to celebrate Tat'yana's nameday is in full swing. The guests gossip about Onegin's reputation as a gambler and a drunk. Soon he is bored and flirts with Olga, to Lensky's dismay. Monsieur Triquet offers verses in Tat'yana's honour. Lensky is now so jealous that he accuses Onegin of breaking Tat'yana's heart and compromising Olga. Their friendship is ended. Onegin tries to reason with him but Lensky challenges him to a duel. Onegin accepts, but Lensky continues to taunt him and they have to be separated.

At dawn Lensky and his second, Zaretsky, are waiting impatiently for Onegin's arrival. Lensky reflects that the happy days of his childhood seem so far away. What happens next is out of his hands since death will claim him at a moment of her choice. Soon no one will remember his name, except Olga. Although they are both full of remorse, honour is at stake and the duel goes ahead. At the first shot Lensky falls dead in the snow.

ACT III

Onegin arrives at a ball in St Petersburg. He has just returned after years travelling abroad hoping to forget what he has done. His life is aimless and everything is boring. Prince Gremin, a retired general, enters with his wife. Onegin is astonished to recognize Tat'yana: the impetuous young girl has become a dignified lady. Gremin tells Onegin that they have been married for two years and that Tat'yana's devotion has transformed his life. Onegin is introduced to Tat'yana, who hides her emotions and excuses herself, pleading tiredness. As he watches her go, Onegin realizes that he loves her and must declare himself. At Gremin's house Tat'yana is reading a love-letter from Onegin. When he enters she tries to send him away. With growing passion he begs her to leave Gremin and go away with him. Although overcome with emotion, she insists she will honour her marriage vow and bids him farewell.

The Queen of Spades

The Queen of Spades, based on another story by Pushkin, was Tchaikovsky's penultimate opera and one in which western influences were particularly evident. It was first produced at the Maryinsky Theatre in St Petersburg on 19 December 1890. However, 20 years passed before it was staged at the Metropolitan Opera, New York on 5 March 1910 and another five before it was premiered in London on 29 May 1915. In 1876, when Tchaikovsky was visiting Paris, he saw a performance of Bizet's *Carmen* and became entranced by its tuneful, graceful music.

Three years later, echoes of Carmen went into *The Queen of Spades* and so did the style of another composer Tchaikovsky greatly admired – Mozart. Mozart's elegant music was recalled in Tchaikovsky's recreation of St Petersburg in the refined Francophile days of the Empress Catherine the Great. Tchaikovsky was obsessed with the inexorable workings of fate and how helpless mere mortals can be when faced with its inevitability; this was a feature shared by *Carmen* and *The Queen of Spades*. In the closing scenes of *The Queen of Spades*, Tchaikovsky borrowed from Wagner by using chromatics to convey a sense of supernatural horror.

The Queen of Spades

by Pyotr Ilyich Tchaikovsky
Composed: 1890
Premiered: 1890, St Petersburg
Libretto by Modest Il'yich Tchaikovsky and the composer after Alexander Sergeyevich Pushkin's novella

ACT I

While children play in the Summer Garden in St Petersburg, Chekalinsky and Surin describe how Hermann watches them every night but never gambles. Hermann admits to Count Tomsky that he has fallen in love with an unknown, but high-born, beauty. The other officers congratulate Prince Yeletsky on his recent engagement, but Hermann sees only bitterness. He is horrified when Yeletsky's betrothed, Lisa, arrives with her grandmother, the countess. They recognize Hermann as the strange man who has recently been following them. Tomsky tells how the countess came to be known as the 'Queen of Spades'. To recover her gaming losses in Paris she had given herself in exchange for the secret of three winning cards. Both men she revealed the secret to died and a ghost is supposed to have foretold her death at the hands of the third man who tries to take it. Hermann considers the prospect of winning the secret and Lisa.

Lisa accompanies Pauline at the harpsichord. All her friends join in the dancing and a governess breaks up the party. Lisa begs Pauline not to tell Yeletsky that she is unhappy about the engagement. Left alone, Lisa confides to the night that she is obsessed with Hermann's mysterious gaze. Hermann appears at the window and pleads for a moment of happiness with her before his imminent death. Lisa cries but does not draw away her hand. As he kisses it the countess is heard from the next room. Hermann hides when the countess tells Lisa to make less noise. He renews his pleas and Lisa finally falls into his arms.

ACT II

At a masked ball the officers are mocking Hermann's obsession with the cards. Yeletsky begs Lisa to confide in him. Hermann is convinced he must win at cards before he can see Lisa again. The officers tease him that he is to be the 'third man'. The guests watch a masque, The Faithful Shepherdess, whose players include Pauline as Daphnis and Tomsky as Plutus. Lisa slips a key to Hermann enabling him to reach her through the countess's bedroom tomorrow night, but he insists on going tonight. The Master of Ceremonies announces the arrival of Tsarina Catherine.

Hermann is mesmerized by a portrait of the beautiful young countess in her bedroom, convinced that their fates are linked. Servants prepare the countess for bed. Lisa is nervous that Hermann is already there and asks her maid to keep guard. The countess reminisces about her days in Paris and sings to herself an air by Grétry, ordering the servants to leave. Hermann begs her to tell him the secret, but she remains silent. He threatens her with a pistol and she dies. Lisa sees the body and is convinced that all Hermann wanted was the secret.

ACT III

Lisa has written to Hermann, asking him to meet her by the canal at midnight. The countess's ghost appears, telling him to marry Lisa and revealing the secret: three, seven, ace. Lisa is waiting for Hermann. She refuses to go to the gaming house with him and he pushes her away. In despair she throws herself in the canal.

Hermann wins with his first two cards, drawing a three and a seven. Seeking revenge, Yeletsky challenges him to draw again. Hermann declares it is an ace, but Yeletsky corrects him: it is the Queen of Spades. Hermann sees the countess's ghost again and stabs himself, telling her to take his life.

OPERAS

1870–72	The Oprichnik
1874	Vakula the Smith; rev. 1885 as The Slippers
1877–78	Eugene Onegin
1878–79	The Maid of Orleans
1881–83	Mazeppa
1887	The Enchantress
1890	The Queen of Spades
1891	Yolanta

TIMELINE

1840	Pyotr Ilyich Tchaikovsky born, Kamsko-Votkinsk (Vyatka Province)
1844	First composition, the song 'Our Mama in St Petersburg'
1862	Becomes one of the first students at the newly opened St Petersburg Conservatory
1865	Graduates from St Petersburg Conservatory and takes up teaching post at Moscow Conservatory
1874	Premiere of The Oprichnik, St Petersburg
1876	Premiere of Vakula the Smith, St Petersburg
1877	Work begins on Eugene Onegin; long-term patronage of Nadezhda von Meck begins; marries and swiftly separates from Antonina Milyukova
1878	Work begins on The Maid of Orleans in Florence
1879	Premiere of Eugene Onegin, Moscow Conservatory
1881	Premiere of The Maid of Orleans, St Petersburg
1884	Eugene Onegin lavishly staged by Imperial Opera in St Petersburg; premiere of Mazeppa, Moscow
1887	Premiere of The Enchantress, St Petersburg
1890	Premiere of The Queen of Spades, St Petersburg, patronage of Nadezhda von Meck inexplicably withdrawn
1892	Premiere of Iolanthe, in a lavish double-bill with The Nutcracker ballet, St Petersburg; Tchaikovsky impressed by a production of Eugene Onegin conducted by a young Gustav Mahler
1893	Sudden death of Tchaikovsky nine days after the premiere of his Symphony No. 6

Thomas, Ambroise
1811–96, FRENCH

The French composer Ambroise Thomas was a staunch anti-Wagnerian, regarding this and other 'modern' influences as dangerous to French music. Thomas's music, which included nine stage works written between 1837 and 1843, was firmly in the French musical tradition. Of these works, the most successful was

La double échelle ('The Double Ladder', 1837). Thomas also wrote several *opéras comiques*, using Auber as his model, enlivening the genre and making it more Romantic. One *opéra comique*, *Le songe d'une nuit d' été* ('A Midsummer Night's Dream', 1850) had no connection with Shakespeare's play, although Shakespeare appeared in it. *Le songe* was Thomas's passport into the French Academy of Music, where he was elected in 1851 to succeed **Gaspare Spontini** (1774–1851). Appointed professor at the Conservatoire in 1856, he graduated to director in 1871 and remained in the post until his death. Thomas was always susceptible to the influence of other composers and most especially to Charles Gounod. His *Mignon* (1866), imitated Gounod's *Faust* and he repeated the exercise by modelling his *Hamlet* (1868) on Gounod's *Roméo et Juliette*.

Tichatschek, Joseph
1807–86, BOHEMIAN

The Bohemian tenor Joseph Tichatschek made his debut at the Kärntnertor Theatre in Vienna in 1833, as the farmer, Raimbaut, in Meyerbeer's *Robert le diable*. After a year, 1837, at Graz, Tichatschek found a regular berth at Dresden, where he sang between 1838 and 1870. He also performed at the Drury Lane Theatre in London in 1841. Tichatschek was not impressive as an actor, but his impassioned singing, brilliant tone and heroic stage presence made him much admired by Berlioz, Liszt, **Otto Nicolai** (1810–49) and Wagner, who wrote of his 'lively nature, glorious voice and great musical ability'. Tictatschek created two important title roles for Wagner, in *Rienzi* and *Tannhäuser*. In total contrast, Tichatschek was also adept at Mozart roles. He sang the title part in *Idomeneo* and the Javanese prince Tamino in *Die Zauberflöte*.

Giuseppe Verdi
1813–1901, ITALIAN

Giuseppe Verdi was that rarity, a modest, diffident genius. He was so unaware of his powers that he called himself 'the least erudite among past and present composers'. Born in Le Roncole, near Busseto, Parma, Verdi was eight when his talents were noticed by a local merchant and patron of music, Antonio Barezzi. In 1832, Barezzi paid for Verdi to attend the Milan Conservatory, but he failed to be accepted, partly due to 'lack of piano technique and technical knowledge' and 'insufficient' gifts.

A MODEST START

Verdi took private lessons to improve his musical skills and the same year he married Margherita, Barezzi's daughter, he completed his first opera, *Rocester* (1836). It was never staged, but much of its music went into a second opera, *Oberto, Conte di San Bonifacio* (1839). *Oberto* was so well received at La Scala, Milan, that Verdi was contracted to write more.

However, Verdi's first work under contract, the comic opera *Un giorno di regno* ('King for a Day', 1840) was overshadowed by tragedy: both his children had died in infancy, and in 1840, he also lost his young wife. *Un giorno* was a fiasco, withdrawn after only one performance and the grieving Verdi was ready to give up. Fortunately, the *impresario* and librettist Bartolomeo Merelli (1794–1879) perceived his genius and persuaded him to try again. Merelli's faith was more than justified. Verdi's next opera, *Nabucco*, produced at La Scala in 1842, was a splendid success, and also signalled his emergence from the influence of Rossini and Donizetti. From now on, musically speaking, Verdi was his own man.

A POLITICAL TROUBLEMAKER?

Nabucco made Verdi's name known throughout Italy, not only in the opera houses, but also in the political talking shops where the *Risorgimento*, the movement for the unification and independence of Italy, was being brewed. Even though Verdi had no interest in active politics, there is no doubt that he supported the *Risorgimento*. The censors, for their part, marked him down as a potential revolutionary. Verdi's long and fractious involvement in censorship was at least partly the result of these suspicions.

THE CREAM OF HIS CONTEMPORARIES

Verdi's *Ernani* was another brilliant success; he was deluged with commissions and entered what he called his *anni di galera* – his 'galley years', in which he composed 16 operas in 11 years – 1842 to 1853 – half of them produced between 1844 to 1847 alone. Writing under pressure meant mixed results. The 'galley years' produced inspired achievements like *La traviata* and *Il trovatore*, both of which premiered in 1853, but also included *Stiffelio*, which was unloved by audiences despite Verdi's extensive revisions. By the time the 'galley years' ended, Verdi, aged 40, eclipsed all others as the most highly acclaimed living composer of opera. However, he was not sitting on his laurels. In 1871, *Aida*, which was set in ancient Egypt, had its premiere in Cairo and although his *Requiem* (1873), which he wrote after the death of the Italian poet and patriot Alessandro Manzoni (1785–1873), was his last major work for 13 years, there were more achievements to come. In an astoundingly creative old age, Verdi produced two operas based on Shakespeare's plays – the tragedy *Otello* and the comic opera *Falstaff* – and, in 1897, his *Quattro pezzi sacri* ('Four Sacred Pieces') for voices and orchestra. His second wife, the soprano Giuseppina Strepponi (1815–97), had died the same year, and the frail Verdi, with failing eyesight and hearing, did not long survive her. He died on 27 January 1901 in Milan, after donating 2.5 million lire to found a home for infirm musicians. Some 28,000 people lined the streets as his cortege passed by.

Nabucco

Nabucco was originally named *Nabucodonosor*. An opera in four acts set in Jerusalem and Babylon in the sixth century BC, *Nabucodonosor* was first produced at La Scala, Milan on 9 March 1842 with Giuseppina Strepponi, who later became Verdi's second wife, as Abigaille. The opera was not billed as *Nabucco* until 1844. It occasioned Verdi's first serious brush with the censors, who criticized it for its biblical sources. The real message, though, was their concern for the way the opera's theme of a people enslaved by a cruel conqueror could be used to further the *Risorgimento* movement.

Nabucco

by Giuseppe Verdi
Composed: 1841
Premiered: 1842, Milan
Libretto by Temistocle Solera, after Auguste Anicet-Bourgeois, Francis Cornue and Antonio Cortesi

ACT I

The Israelites lament their fate at the hands of Nabucco, King of Babylon. The high priest Zaccaria enters with a hostage: Nabucco's daughter Fenena. She is entrusted to Ismaele, who loves her; she freed him in Babylon and he intends to return the favour. Abigaille, Nabucco's elder daughter, enters and offers to free the Hebrews if Ismaele returns her love; he refuses. Nabucco enters. Zaccaria threatens Fenena but Ismaele saves her. Zaccaria declares him a traitor and Nabucco orders the temple to be destroyed.

ACT II

Abigaille finds out that she is actually a slave's daughter and swears vengeance on Nabucco and Fenena, who is regent during the war. Encouraged by the high priest of

Belo, Abigaille considers killing Fenena and announcing that Nabucco is dead. Zaccaria converts Fenena to the Hebrew faith and Ismaele is pardoned for saving her. Abdallo, a royal advisor, warns Fenena to flee but it is too late; Abigaille arrives. Nabucco returns, declaring himself king and god. Lightning knocks the crown from his head and sends him mad. Abigaille grabs the crown.

ACT III

In Babylon, Abigaille is hailed as queen. She tricks Nabucco into sealing a death warrant for all Hebrews. He realizes too late that Fenena will die. He threatens Abigaille with revealing her lowly birth, but she destroys the documents. Pleading with her to spare Fenena's life, Nabucco is taken away and imprisoned. The Hebrews lament the loss of their homeland. They pray for help and Zaccaria foresees their revenge.

ACT IV

The imprisoned Nabucco tries to escape and begs forgiveness from the Hebrew god, promising to convert the Babylonians. He is released and sets out to rescue Fenena and reclaim the crown. The executioners prepare to kill the Hebrews. Nabucco arrives, ordering the idol of Belo to be destroyed; it shatters of its own accord. Praying to the Hebrew god for forgiveness, Abigaille poisons herself and dies. Nabucco declares his new faith and commands the Hebrews to return to their homeland.

Ernani

Verdi's four-act opera Ernani, which has been called his 'most romantic' work, was first performed at the Teatro La Fenice in Venice on 9 March 1844. An immediate success, it was based on the tragedy Hernani by the French writer Victor Hugo. Politically, the treatment of the subject was far more overt than Nabucco, featuring a revolutionary outlaw as its eponymous hero and the King of Spain as the conniving villain. The fifth of Verdi's

---

SOUNDS FAMILIAR

'VA PENSIERO'

In 'Va pensiero', from Nabucco, the Hebrews exiled in Babylon send thoughts to their faraway homeland. Italians under foreign rule identified with them and the chorus became the anthem of the Risorgimento. It was sung by the crowds at Verdi's funeral in Milan in 1901.

---

total of 28 operas, Ernani was the first of them to be performed in England, at Her Majesty's Theatre, London on 8 March 1845.

Ernani

by Giuseppe Verdi
Composed: 1843
Premiered: 1844, Venice
Libretto by Francesco Maria Piave, after Victor Hugo

ACT I

Ernani, an outlawed nobleman, is leading a group of rebels in a plot to overthrow the king Don Carlo, to avenge his father's death. Ernani is in love with Elvira, but she is being forced to marry Don Ruy Gomez da Silva and is living in his castle where she awaits Ernani. Don Carlo also loves Elvira and arrives at the castle to claim her. Ernani arrives at the same time and da Silva enters Elvira's room to find her two suitors. Furious, he challenges them to a duel, but calms down when he recognizes the king. Don Carlo saves Ernani from da Silva's wrath by introducing him as a royal messenger.

ACT II

Elvira's wedding to da Silva is approaching. Ernani's conspiracy to dethrone Don Carlo has failed. He takes refuge in da Silva's castle. Although displeased to find Ernani with Elvira, da Silva adheres to the rules of hospitality and protects Ernani when the king comes in search of him. The king leaves with Elvira; da Silva and Ernani, realizing that Don Carlo is their common foe, join forces against him. Da Silva agrees to help Ernani on one condition: if he wants Ernani to die, he need only blow his hunting horn and the deed is done.

ACT III

The election of the emperor is imminent. By the tomb of Charlemagne, Don Carlo, having heard rumours of a conspiracy, conceals himself. Ernani and da Silva arrive with the rest of the rebels and Ernani is elected to kill the king. Da Silva promises Ernani his life if he will let him carry out the task instead, but Ernani refuses. Don Carlo is elected emperor and confronts the rebels. Elvira persuades him to spare their lives and, realizing that she will only ever love Ernani, Don Carlo allows the couple to marry and restores Ernani's property and status. Da Silva is furious.

ACT IV

At the palace of Ernani, who is in fact Don Giovanni d'Aragona, wedding guests celebrate his marriage to Elvira. The servants are made uneasy by the presence of a masked man in a black cloak. As Ernani and Elvira declare their love for one another, they hear the sound of a hunting horn. Ernani sends Elvira away; Da Silva reveals his identity and reminds Ernani of their pact. Despite the pleas of Elvira, who has returned, Ernani remains true to his word and kills himself.

Macbeth

Verdi was an enthusiastic admirer of Shakespeare and *Macbeth* was the first opera based on his work. It premiered at the Teatro della Pergola in Florence on 14 March 1847, with Verdi himself conducting. Performances followed throughout Europe, including Madrid (1848), Vienna (1849), and New York (1858). For the premiere in Paris, at the Théâtre Lyrique on 21 April 1865, Verdi revised the opera. This included several additions: an extra aria in Act II for Lady Macbeth, 'La luce langue' ('The Weak Light'), two new choruses, a new duet for the Macbeths, a battle fugue and a ballet.

Macbeth

by Giuseppe Verdi
Composed: 1847–47; rev. 1864–65
Premiered: 1847, Florence
Libretto by Francesco Maria Piave and Andrea Maffei, after William Shakespeare

ACT I

Macbeth and Banquo encounter three witches, who declare that Macbeth will become Thane of Cawdor and then king of Scotland, while Banquo will father many future kings. The news arrives that Macbeth is to succeed the comdemned Thane of Cawdor. Lady Macbeth receives a letter from her husband about the predictions. The king, Duncan, is staying at their castle and she plots his murder. Macbeth returns and his wife reveals her plans. He is persuaded to carry out the murder but is racked with guilt. Lady Macbeth goes to incriminate the guards with the king's blood. Banquo and Macduff arrive and discover Duncan's body. All mourn and swear vengeance.

ACT II

Macbeth feels uneasy as king, although Duncan's son Malcolm has fled to England. Remembering the witches' predictions for Banquo, he schemes with his wife to kill him and his children. Assassins carry out the murder but Banquo's son Fleance escapes. That night the ghost of Banquo appears at a banquet. Only Macbeth can see the apparition. Macduff resolves to join Malcolm's forces.

ACT III

Macbeth revisits the three witches. They tell him to beware Macduff, but that he is safe until Birnam Wood rises against *him. Macbeth enquires about Banquo and his apparition appears, along with royal sons. Lady Macbeth encourages him to murder Banquo's offspring, as well as the family of Macduff.*

ACT IV

Macduff laments the loss of his wife and children. Malcolm arrives from England with a troop of soldiers and encourages Macduff to join him in his plan to kill Macbeth. Macduff joins the troops and, concealing themselves with branches, they approach the castle.

Lady Macbeth is guilt-ridden over her crimes. As she sleepwalks and describes the murders, she is overheard by members of staff. Macbeth, fearing his own death, is unmoved by the news that Lady Macbeth has killed herself. Soldiers inform him that Birnam Wood appears to be approaching the castle.

The English troops storm the castle and Macduff confronts Macbeth. They fight and Macbeth dies, cursing the witches. Malcolm is crowned king.

Recommended Recording:

Macbeth, Zürich Opera; Franz Welser-Möst, conductor; TDK DV-OPMAC (DVD Region 0, PAL); Soloists: Paoletta Marrocu (Lady Macbeth), Luis Lima (Macduff), Thomas Hampson (Macbeth), Roberto Scandiuzzi (Banquo)

Rigoletto

Verdi's three-act opera *Rigoletto*, based on Victor Hugo's play *Le roi s'amuse* ('The King Amuses Himself', 1832), was originally entitled *La maledizione* ('The Malediction') – a reference to the curse placed on the superstitious court jester Rigoletto, which fulfills itself in the final scene. The first performance of *Rigoletto* took place at the Teatro La Fenice in Venice on 11 March 1851. The London premiere followed on 14 May 1853 and the first performance in New York on 19 February 1855.

Rigoletto is a superb example of the integrated opera in which action, music and characterization combined to create dramatic unison. This, even though the opera's five most famous numbers, including the great quartet from the last act, are often detached and performed separately. *Rigoletto* is also an unconventional opera, based on what Verdi called a 'series of duets'. He also used a reminiscence motif, repeating the chilling, doom-laden phrase introduced in the prelude to the opera to represent the jester's terror at the curse laid on him. The motif made its own subtle contribution to the famous aria 'La donna è mobile', which tells Rigoletto that his planned murder of the licentious Duke of Mantua has failed.

Rigoletto

by Giuseppe Verdi
Composed: 1850–51
Premiered: 1851, Venice
Libretto by Francesco Maria Piave, after Victor Hugo

ACT I

In the court of Mantua, the duke tells the courtiers of his success with women. Rigoletto, the duke's jester, taunts Count Ceprano about the duke's interest in his wife. The count plots revenge on Rigoletto with some other courtiers; the jester is believed to keep a mistress at his house and they plan to abduct her. A nobleman, Monterone, enters, intending to denounce the duke for seducing his daughter. Rigoletto mocks him and Monterone is arrested; as he is led away, he curses the horrified jester. The curse worries Rigoletto as he returns home. He is approached by the assassin, Sparafucile, who offers his services, but Rigoletto refuses and muses on how words can be as harmful as a dagger. He is welcomed home by his daughter, Gilda, whom he keeps hidden from the world and, more importantly, the philandering duke. Rigoletto laments the death of his wife and, fearing for Gilda's safety, orders her nurse Giovanna to prevent anyone from entering the garden.

As Rigoletto leaves, the duke, having bribed Giovanna, enters the garden. He introduces himself to Gilda as Gualtier Maldè, an impoverished student, and declares his love for her. She has seen him in church and, after he leaves at the sound of approaching footsteps, dreamily muses over his (false) name.

Ceprano and the courtiers stop Rigoletto and enlist his help in abducting Ceprano's wife. They blindfold him and, confusing him, trick him into putting a ladder up against his own wall. The courtiers then abduct Gilda and make off with her. Hearing her cries for help, Rigoletto removes his blindfold and sees that everyone has vanished. Finding Gilda's scarf, he laments Monterone's curse.

ACT II

The duke is concerned about Gilda's abduction, picturing her crying alone, but cheers up when his courtiers reveal that they have her and that she awaits the duke in his chamber. He rushes off to seduce her. Rigoletto arrives in search of Gilda and the courtiers are surprised to learn that she is in fact his daughter and not his mistress as they had assumed. Despite his pleas, however, they refuse to let him pass. Gilda runs from the duke's room, telling her father of her abduction and explaining that she has been courted by the duke over a long period of time, during their visits to church. As Monterone is led past on his way to the dungeons, Rigoletto swears vengeance on him and the duke, whom Gilda begs him to forgive.

ACT III

Rigoletto and Gilda stand outside the inn owned by Sparafucile and his seductive sister Maddalena. As the duke drinks and flirts with Maddalena, singing of the fickleness of women, Rigoletto comforts Gilda. He sends Gilda away to disguise herself as a boy,

arranging to meet her in Verona where they will be safe. He then pays Sparafucile to murder the duke and departs. Maddalena, who has fallen for the duke, pleads with her brother to kill Rigoletto instead. He refuses, but is eventually persuaded to kill the next person to enter the inn, in the duke's place. Overhearing this, Gilda resolves to sacrifice herself for the duke, whom she still loves despite his infidelity. She enters the inn and Sparafucile stabs her and puts her in a sack. Rigoletto comes to collect the body and takes it to the river to dispose of it. But, suddenly, he is horrified to hear the presumed-dead duke singing in the distance. He opens the sack to reveal his dying daughter, who begs forgiveness. Rigoletto cries that Monterone's curse has been fulfilled.

Recommended Recording:

Rigoletto, Vienna Philharmonic Orchestr; Carlo Maria Giulini, conductor; Deutsche Grammophon 415 288-2GH2; Soloists: Ileana Cotrubas (Gilda), Elena Obraztsova (Maddalena), Placido Domingo (Duke), Piero Cappuccilli (Rigoletto), Nicolai Ghiaurov (Sparafucile), Kurt Moll (Monterone)

Il trovatore

Of all Verdi's operas, *Il trovatore* ('The Troubadour') provides the fullest panorama of melodies, each of them memorable in its own right. *Il trovatore* did not have the subtle characterization of *Rigoletto*, and suffered from an all but impenetrable plot, but nonetheless became as frequently played. The *Miserere* (meaning 'Have Mercy') sung by a chorus of monks in Act IV was for some time the best-loved number in any opera. *Il trovatore* was one of Verdi's speediest creations: he wrote its four acts in only 30 days, between 1 and 29 November 1852. Less than two months later, on 19 January 1853, the premiere took place in at the Teatro Apollo in Rome followed by New York and London in 1855. The menacing mezzo-soprano role of the gypsy Azucena was a new departure for singers in Italian opera and may have been influenced by a similar character in Meyerbeer's *Le prophète* ('The Prophet', 1849), which premiered in Paris.

Il trovatore ('The Troubadour')
by Giuseppe Verdi
Composed: 1851–52
Premiered: 1853, Rome
Libretto by Salvatore Cammarano and Leone Emanuele Bardare, after Antonio García Gutiérrez

ACT I
Count di Luna waits beneath the window of his love Leonora. Meanwhile, Ferrando, the captain of the guard, entertains the soldiers by telling them of how the count's brother was bewitched as a child by a gypsy, who was subsequently burned at the stake. Her daughter, to avenge her death, kidnapped the child and is thought to have killed him. Leonora reveals to her confidante Inez that she has fallen in love with an unknown troubadour, who serenaded her at a tournament. The count arrives to court Leonora and the troubadour, Manrico, also arrives. He serenades Leonora and she confuses him with the count in the darkness. When she realizes her mistake, she declares her love for Manrico. Manrico and the count threaten to kill each other.

ACT II
In a camp, the gypsies go about their work. Azucena, the daughter in the tale related by Ferrando, recalls her mother's dying call for vengeance and laments accidentally throwing her own son into the flames. Manrico, who has been brought up as Azucena's son, overhears. She encourages him to exact revenge on the count, but Manrico relates that, during battle, he was about to kill him in a duel, but something held him back. He agrees to help his 'mother' to avenge her

mother's death. A messenger brings the news that Leonora, thinking Manrico dead, is entering a convent. Ignoring Azucena's pleas, Manrico leaves.

Under the count's orders, Ferrando and his men wait by the convent to abduct Leonora. When she appears, Manrico arrives and a fight breaks out. Leonora and Manrico escape together.

ACT III
In the count's camp, near where Manrico has taken Leonora, the soldiers prepare to besiege the castle; the count laments the loss of his love. Ferrando announces that a gypsy woman has been taken prisoner; Azucena is brought in, explaining that she is looking for her son. On realizing the count's identity, she reveals that she was his brother's abductor. The count orders her burned at the stake. Assuming that Manrico is her true son, he hopes to trick his rival into leaving Leonora, while also avenging his brother. Manrico learns of Azucena's imminent execution; he rushes to her rescue.

ACT IV
Outside the tower where Manrico is being held prisoner, Leonora sings of her love for him. A chorus prays for the condemned Manrico and he bids farewell to Leonora. Leonora offers herself to the count in exchange for Manrico's life; he agrees. She takes a slow-working poison. In the prison, Manrico comforts Azucena. Leonora enters and urges Manrico to flee, but adds that she must remain behind. Manrico, guessing the bargain that she has struck with the count, is further horrified when she reveals that she has poisoned herself and dies in his arms. The count, realizing he has been tricked, is furious and orders Manrico's immediate death. Azucena tries in vain to dissuade the count. As the axe falls on Manrico, Azucena informs him that he has killed his own brother. Her mother's death is finally avenged.

Recommended Recording:

Il trovatore, New Philharmonia Orchestra; Zubin Mehta, conductor; RCA RD86194; Soloists: Leontyne Price (Leonora), Fiorenza Cossotto (Azucena), Placido Domingo (Manrico), Sherrill Milnes (Conte di Luna), Bonaldo Giaiotti (Ferrando)

La traviata

La dame aux camélias ('The Lady of the Camellias') by Alexandre Dumas had barely been staged in 1852 before Verdi took it up for *La traviata*, one of the great operas from his middle period. It premiered at Teatro La Fenice, Venice on 6 March 1853, and the first performance was disastrous. Verdi blamed the singers and the audience burst out laughing in the final scene when the hefty soprano playing the heroine, Violetta, was supposed to be 'wasting away' from consumption.

La traviata managed to salvage success from its unfortunate beginnings, but it was still controversial. Violetta was modelled on the consumptive Parisian courtesan Marie Duplessis (1824–47) who, together with other dubious, immoral characters of the demi-monde, offended the puritan tastes of the nineteenth century. Opera houses reacted by substituting a seventeenth-century setting to place *La traviata* at an acceptable distance. However, in retaining a courtesan as heroine despite the moralists, Verdi was anticipating the *verismo* of later nineteenth-century opera. In addition, Verdi experimented by changing the vocal music as the tragedy developed: the fun-loving Violetta of Act I, for instance, acquired a passionate intensity in Act II and ended in Act III as a fragile, fading shadow of her former self. In 1854, it was restaged at another Venetian theatre, and this time had been thoroughly rehearsed and better cast. It was a resounding success.

La traviata
('The Fallen Woman')

by Giuseppe Verdi
Composed: 1852–53
Premiered: 1853, Venice
Libretto by Francesco Maria Piave, after Alexandre Dumas

ACT I

Violetta, a high-class prostitute, is holding a party in her Parisian home. She indulges in a gay lifestyle, partly to distract herself from the fact that she is in the early stages of consumption. The nobleman Gastone introduces her to his friend Alfredo, who admires her. As the other guests go into another room to dance, Violetta is seized with a coughing fit and stays behind; Alfredo remains with her. He tends to her and expresses his love for her; she is touched. Left alone, she confesses that she has fallen in love for the first time.

ACT II

Violetta has given up her life in Paris and is living with Alfredo in a small house in the country. Annina, a servant, informs Alfredo that they have no money left; in order to pay for the house, Violetta has been selling her jewellery. He leaves immediately for Paris, in order to raise the money to repay her.

Violetta receives an invitation to a party from Flora, a friend from Paris, and reminisces about her life there. Giorgio Germont, Alfredo's father, arrives on a visit. He at first accuses her of dragging his son into poverty, but she explains that she has been supporting them herself. He urges her to break off her relationship with Alfredo, as her sullied reputation is ruining that of his family. Furthermore, Alfredo's sister wishes to marry and the family's link to Violetta might prevent the match from going ahead.

Violetta realizes that leaving Alfredo will be in everyone's best interests. She writes to Flora, accepting the invitation, and then composes a farewell letter to

Alfredo. When he returns, he informs her that his father is coming to persuade him to end their relationship. Violetta, suggesting that the two men be left alone, departs. She sends her farewell letter to Alfredo via a messenger. He is devastated; his father comforts him.

Violetta attends Flora's party with her former lover, Baron Douphol. Alfredo, who discovered Flora's invitation and guessed that Violetta would attend, arrives in search of her. He has won large amounts of money while gambling at the party. On seeing Violetta with Douphol, Alfredo insults her. Douphol challenges him to a game and Alfredo wins. Alone with Alfredo, Violetta pleads with him to leave the party, as she fears a duel between him and Douphol. Alfredo insults her, accusing her of infidelity. Unable to disclose Germont's orders, Violetta confesses that she has sworn to break off their relationship but lets him believe that it was at Douphol's request. Calling the guests in, Alfredo publicly insults Violetta and proclaims her faithlessness. Throwing his winnings at her feet, he declares his debt to her repaid. Germont enters and scolds Alfredo for being so hard on Violetta; however he does not reveal the truth about his involvement.

ACT III

Violetta is now very ill with consumption and is confined to her bed. Her doctor offers her words of encouragement but she knows the end is near. A letter arrives from Germont; he begs forgiveness for his actions. He has revealed the truth of Violetta's sacrifice to Alfredo, who was horrified and is hurrying over to visit her. As she lies in bed, doubting he will arrive in time to see her alive, he enters. Overjoyed to see him, Violetta finds the strength to sit up and they sing ecstatically of their future together. The doctor then enters, accompanied by a regretful Germont. Unfortunately, Violetta's recovery was only temporary and she dies in Alfredo's arms.

Recommended Recording:

La traviata, Royal Opera, Covent Garden; Georg Solti, conductor; Decca 071 431–9 (DVD Region 0, NTSC); Soloists: Angela Gheorghiu (Violetta), Leah-Marian Jones (Flora), Frank Lopardo (Alfredo), Robin Leggate (Gastone), Leo Nucci (Germont)

Les vêpres siciliennes

Verdi inherited the libretto for *Les vêpres siciliennes* ('The Sicilian Vespers') from *Le duc d'Albe* ('The Duke of Alba'), an opera left unfinished when its composer, Donizetti, died. Verdi made it a five-act work and it had its first performance at the Paris Opéra, for which it was commissioned, on 13 June 1855. It was well received, but the Italian censors made difficulties, objecting to Naples as a setting for a massacre. The locale was changed to Sicily, then Portugal. The Italian title, *I vespri siciliani*, was replaced by *Giovanna di Braganza*, *Giovanna de Guzman* and *Batilde di Turenna* before its rightful name was reinstated in 1857.

Les vêpres siciliennes ('The Sicilian Vespers')

by Giuseppe Verdi
Composed: 1854
Premiered: 1855, Paris
Libretto by Eugene Scribe and Charles Duveyrier

ACT I

The Duchesse Hélène laments the execution of her brother, encouraged by Robert, a French soldier, and stirs emotions amongst the crowd. A fight breaks out between the French and the Sicilians. The unpopular governor of Sicily, Guy de Montfort, tries to calm them and interrogates Henri, a Sicilian who wants to speak to Hélène. Suspecting him to be an anarchist, Montfort warns him against involvement with the duchess. Henri ignores his orders.

ACT II

Jean Procida, a returning exile, reveals that there is little support for the Sicilian cause. Henri declares his love to Hélène; she asks him to avenge her brother's death. Henri is arrested for declining a royal invitation. To annoy the Sicilians, Procida persuades French soldiers to abduct some local girls.

ACT III

Guy de Montfort learns that Henri is his son. Neither of them is pleased. Procida tells Henri that they must put their plot to assassinate the governor into action. Wanting to protect his father, Henri prevents the assassination from going ahead. Hélène and Procida are arrested, while the Sicilian people revile Henri's treachery.

ACT IV

Henri visits Hélène and Procida in prison and explains his reasons for defending Montfort. Hélène forgives Henri; he pledges to rejoin the conspirators now that he has saved his father's life. The weapons for the uprising arrive. De Montfort promises to free Hélène and Procida if Henri publicly acknowledges him as his father; Henri agrees. Montfort blesses Henri's marriage to Hélène, which he hopes will unite France with Sicily; Hélène feels uneasy.

ACT V

The marriage celebrations are underway. Procida informs a horrified Hélène that the wedding bells will be the signal for the uprising to begin. Montfort, sensing that something is wrong, rings the bells to start the ceremony. At this signal, the armed Sicilians burst in on the unsuspecting French.

Simon Boccanegra

Verdi's dark, brooding opera *Simon Boccanegra* had a tortuous history before 24 March 1881, when its final version premiered at La Scala, Milan. Verdi composed *Boccanegra* in 1857, but the Venetian audience reacted coolly; an anti-

Verdi claque sabotaged the performance and a false rumour spread, claiming that Verdi had written the libretto and made a mess of it. A quarter of a century passed before the opera reappeared with extensively revised music and libretto. This time, it ran for 10 performances in Milan, but New York had to wait until 1932 and London until 1948.

Simon Boccanegra

by Giuseppe Verdi
Composed: 1856–57; rev. 1880
Premiered: 1857, Venice
Libretto by Francesco Maria Piave and Giuseppe Montanelli, after Antonio García Gutiérrez

PROLOGUE

Paolo and Pietro hope to gain power by electing Boccanegra as doge. He hopes it will enable him to marry Maria, the mother of his child, imprisoned by her father Fiesco. As Fiesco laments Maria's death, Boccanegra arrives to make peace. Fiesco demands his grandchild, but the child is missing. As Boccanegra mourns Maria, he is hailed as doge.

ACT I

25 years later, Amelia Grimaldi awaits her lover, Adorno. Boccanegra arrives; Amelia fears he will force her to marry Paolo. Adorno asks Amelia's guardian Andrea (in fact Fiesco) for her hand; he consents. The doge sees a portrait of Maria and realizes that Amelia is his daughter. He refuses Paolo her hand, so Paolo plots her abduction. Adorno suspects Boccanegra of the attempted kidnap, but Amelia intervenes. Adorno is imprisoned and Paolo forced to curse the kidnappers; he obeys, cursing himself.

ACT II

Paolo sends Pietro to free Adorno and poisons Boccanegra's drink. He tries to persuade Andrea to kill Boccanegra and suggests to Adorno that Amelia and the doge are lovers. Amelia arrives; Adorno berates her, hiding as the doge enters. Boccanegra allows Amelia to marry Adorno and drinks the poison. Adorno goes to stab Boccanegra but Amelia prevents him. Learning that Boccanegra is her father, he pledges his life to him. An uprising is heard; if Adorno calms the people, Amelia will be his.

ACT III

The rebellion is suppressed. The condemned Paolo tells Andrea about the poison; Andrea makes his peace with Boccanegra. The doge blesses Amelia and Adorno, naming the latter his successor before dying.

Un ballo in maschera

In 1857, Verdi was virtually asking for censorship trouble when he chose *Gustavuse III, ou Le bal masqué* ('Gustavus III, or The Masked Ball') for his next work. In 1792 King Gustavusus III of Sweden had been shot dead at a masked ball in Stockholm. Regicide was a taboo subject and the Neapolitan censors immediately demanded radical changes. They objected to the Swedish location because it was too close to home – and shooting the king dead on stage was too much like the real event, although stabbing with a knife would be permitted. Verdi refused the censors' demands and left Naples for Rome, where he accepted a change of locale to Boston in the USA and exchanged 'Riccardo, Count of Warwick' for 'King Gustavus III' for the premiere at the Teatro Apollo on 17 February 1859.

Further alterations were made for the Paris premiere in 1861 – for instance Boston was relocated to Naples. Despite this tinkering, *Un ballo*'s splendidly varied music and mixing of comic and tragic elements, the beautiful love duet in Act II and imaginative effects like the assassins plotting on stage, while a stately court dance is played, combined to make the opera an enduring success.

Un ballo in maschera ('A Masked Ball')

by Giuseppe Verdi
Composed: 1857
Premiered: 1859, Rome
Libretto by Antonio Somma, after Eugene Scribe

This synopsis uses the Swedish character names from the original Scribe libretto. Where necessary, the names used in the revised US version are shown in brackets.

ACT I

Courtiers await the arrival of Gustavus III (Riccardo). Among them are the Counts Horn and Ribbing (Tom and Samuel), who are plotting his downfall. Gustavus arrives; Oscar, his page, hands him a list of guests for a masked ball. Gustavus, seeing the name of Amelia, sings of his concealed love for her; she is the wife of Anckarstroem (Renato), Gustavus's secretary. Anckarstroem enters and warns Gustavus of a conspiracy against him; the king does not heed his words.

A judge brings Gustavus a document to sign, banishing Mademoiselle Arvidson (Ulrica), a fortune-teller. Oscar advises Gustavus against signing the order. The king suggests they pay her a visit. He will disguise himself as a fisherman.

Mlle Arvidson invokes the devil to aid her prophesies. A sailor, Christian (Silvano) hears that he will soon find promotion and wealth, which comes true since Gustavus has slipped some money and a recommendation into his pocket.

Amelia arrives. She reveals to the fortune-teller that she is in love with the king and wishes to calm her feelings. Mlle Arvidson instructs her to pick a herb at midnight. Overhearing, Gustavus is overjoyed to learn that his love is reciprocated and resolves to meet Amelia at midnight. He requests his fortune. Mlle Arvidson recognizes his hand as that of a great man, but is unwilling to disclose what she reads there. Once persuaded, she tells him that his death is imminent. His assassin will be a friend, more specifically, the next person to shake his hand. Unconvinced, Gustavus offers his hand to the assembled crowd, but no one will shake it. Seeing Anckarstroem approaching, Gustavus runs to offer him his hand. This must disprove the fortune-teller's prediction, since Anckarstroem is his best friend. Everyone realizes Gustavus's identity and Mlle Arvidson repeats her warning.

ACT II

As Amelia seeks the magic herb, Gustavus arrives and declares his love for her. She admits that she returns his love but does not want to betray her husband. Anckarstroem enters, fearing for Gustavus's safety; Amelia covers her face with a veil. Gustavus leaves, insisting that Anckarstroem returns the woman to the city without lifting her veil. The conspirators arrive and find Gustavus gone. They mock Anckarstroem, demanding to know the woman's identity; Amelia intervenes and drops her veil. The conspirators are amused but Anckarstroem is furious; he arranges a meeting with the Counts Ribbing and Horn.

ACT III

Anckarstroem has resolved to kill Amelia, who begs to see her child before she dies. She leaves and Anckarstroem addresses Gustavus's portrait, realizing that it is he that should be punished, not Amelia. Horn and Ribbing arrive and Amelia returns; she is asked to draw lots to see which of the men will kill the king. Anckarstroem is pleased when his name is pulled out. Oscar arrives with invitations for a masked ball; the conspirators realize that this is the perfect opportunity for the assassination. Gustavus reluctantly signs a document to send Anckarstroem and Amelia abroad. Oscar enters with an anonymous letter, which warns Gustavus to avoid the ball. Not wanting to appear cowardly and desiring to see Amelia one last time, Gustavus ignores the note.

At the ball, Anckarstroem tricks Oscar into revealing which of the masked figures is Gustavus. Amelia tries to warn Gustavus but he will not listen and tells her that he is sending her away. Anckarstroem stabs Gustavus. As he dies, the king assures Anckarstroem of his wife's innocence, shows him the document he has signed for the couple's emigration and forgives the conspirators. Full of remorse, Anckarstroem and the courtiers lament the death of the magnanimous king.

Recommended Recording:
Un ballo in maschera, Teatro alla Scala; Claudio Abbado, conductor; Deutsche Grammophon 453 148-2; Soloists: Katia Ricciarelli (Amelia), Edita Gruberova (Oscar), Elena Obraztsova (Ulrica), Placido Domingo (Riccardo), Renato Bruson (Renato)

La forza del destino

La forza del destino was commissioned by the Imperial Theatre, St Petersburg where it premiered in 1862. Verdi and considered the opera an 'excellent success' with 'opulent' settings and costumes, although critics thought the tragic, lugubrious love story had a depressing effect on the audience. It was first performed in New York in 1865 and London in 1867. Verdi had composed La forza in only two months, and it represented a 'halfway house' in his development as an opera composer. The music recalled his earlier, lyrical melodies and instrumentation but also contained the rich orchestration and the darker, more intense atmosphere of his later work. In particular, the tense urgency and rising four-note pattern of the overture offered a foretaste of Verdi's later music. Despite its success, La forza had a worrying effect on performers: a superstition arose that it was unlucky to mention the opera's title inside a theatre. In 1869 it was extensively revised for its Milan production.

La forza del destino ('The Force of Destiny')

by Giuseppe Verdi
Composed: 1861–62; rev. 1869
Premiered: 1862, St Petersburg
Libretto by Francesco Maria Piave, after Angel de Saavedra and Friedrich von Schiller

ACT I

Leonora is preparing to elope with Alvaro. Her father, the Marquis of Calatrava, considers Alvaro unworthy. Leonora regrets having to leave her home and family, but when Alvaro arrives she agrees to leave with him. Her father enters and demands an explanation. Alvaro declares that he is abducting Leonora, who is innocent. He then throws down his pistol in a gesture of surrender. The gun goes off, fatally wounding the marquis. He curses Leonora and Alvaro.

ACT II

Leonora is looking for Alvaro. Disguised as a man, she enters an inn, observed by Preziosilla, a gypsy girl. Leonora's brother Carlo also enters the inn, disguised and in search of the couple; he intends to kill them to avenge the death of his father. He questions Trabuco, a muleteer, about the person he has just seen enter the inn. Preziosilla sings of the wars in Italy and pilgrims pass by, on their way to a nearby monastery. Carlo continues to ask Trabuco about the traveller and identifies himself as a student, Pereda, who is helping a friend to track down his sister and her lover who killed their father; the man is thought to have escaped abroad. Leonora overhears and feels betrayed by Alvaro's flight abroad. She goes to the monastery and is admitted by brother Melitone. She begs the Padre Guardiano, to whom she reveals her true identity, for forgiveness. He allows her to live in a nearby cave as a hermit. He summons the monks and bids them respect the new hermit's solitude.

ACT III

In war-torn Italy, Alvaro sings of his wretched life and asks Leonora – whom he assumes is dead – to look down on him from heaven. Hearing a cry, he hurries to help. A quarrel has broken out over a card game and Carlo is in danger. Alvaro saves him and the men introduce themselves – Alvaro as Federico Herreros, and Carlo as Felice de Bornos. The two men swear eternal friendship and go into battle. Alvaro is badly wounded; Carlo fetches the surgeon. Alvaro gives Carlo a package and asks him to destroy it. Carlo wants to open the package; his sense of honour prevents him, but he discovers a portrait of Leonora nearby and the truth dawns. He receives the news that Alvaro will live and is overjoyed, as he can now kill him. When Alvaro returns, Carlo challenges him to a duel and the men fight until a patrol separates them; Alvaro departs to join a monastery. At dawn, the soldiers and vivandières go about their duties. Preziosilla tells fortunes, while Trabuco strikes bargains among the soldiers and brother Melitone sermonizes.

ACT IV

At the monastery, brother Melitone distributes food to the poor. With the Padre Guardiano, he discusses the new monk, brother Rafaello, who is in fact Alvaro in hiding. Carlo has tracked Alvaro down and arrives at the monastery asking to see Rafaello. He announces to Alvaro his intention of killing him. Alvaro tries to avoid conflict, but Carlo remains unmoved by his piety and hurls insults at him. Unable to ignore Carlo's slighting of his family, Alvaro takes the sword Carlo has brought for him and the fight begins.

Leonora, who has been unable to forget Alvaro, emerges from her cave. She hears the sound of fighting and Alvaro arrives, asking her to give Carlo his last rites. The lovers recognize each other and Alvaro reveals that her brother lies dying. Leonora runs to him but Carlo, still intent on revenge, stabs her before he dies. *The Padre Guardiano offers Leonora comfort as she dies and Alvaro laments that he, guilty and alone, must live.*

Don Carlos

Verdi's five-act opera *Don Carlos* was taken from a drama written in 1787 by the German playwright Friedrich von Schiller (1759–1805). Written for the Paris Opéra, *Don Carlos* was first performed there on 11 March 1867. Schiller's play was translated and the libretto written by Joseph Méry, who unfortunately died before it was completed, and Camille du Locle, secretary of the Opéra. The libretto also included elements taken from a contemporary play by Eugène Cormon, which examined the life of King Philip II of Spain. The resulting *Don Carlos* was a highly romanticized version of the brief, tragic life of Don Carlos, son and heir of Philip II, who was nothing like the gallant, ardent hero of the opera, but conspired against his father and died at age 23 in suspicious circumstances. *Don Carlos*, a *grand opera* that juxtaposed political matters of state and church with private relationships, so dissatisfied Verdi in the original that he revised it several times. Sometimes labelled by critics as 'sprawling' and 'flawed', the opera was written with Parisian tastes in mind, which explains its spectacle and high melodrama. Dance sequences had long been a feature of French opera and the ballet in Act III, entitled 'Le ballet de la reine' ('The Queen's Ballet'), lasted a full 15 minutes. For many years *Don Carlos* was rarely performed as Verdi had intended it, although it is now recognized as one of his greatest works.

Don Carlos

by Giuseppe Verdi
Composed: 1866
Premiered: 1867, Paris
Libretto by Joseph Méry and Camille du Locle, after Friedrich von Schiller and Eugene Cormon

ACT I

Don Carlos, son of King Philip II of Spain, is betrothed to Elisabeth de Valois, whom he has never met. In secret, he travels to France to see her. They meet in the forest at Fontainebleau and fall in love; he gives her his portrait. Thibault, a page, arrives with the news that, to settle the peace treaty between France and Spain, Elisabeth must now marry Don Carlos's father. For the sake of peace, she reluctantly agrees.

ACT II

By the tomb of his grandfather, Emperor Charles V, Don Carlos laments his loss. Monks from the nearby monastery pass by and Carlos is struck by the resemblance of one of them to the former emperor. Carlos confides in his friend Rodrigo, who encourages him to assist the Flemish people gain independence from Spanish rule. They swear allegiance to the cause.

Meanwhile, Princess Eboli sings to the ladies of the court. Elisabeth arrives and Rodrigo hands her a note from Carlos, requesting a meeting. Carlos and the queen are left alone; he declares his love for her, but she explains that nothing can be done; he leaves. Philip enters; angry at finding Elisabeth unattended, he dismisses her lady-in-waiting. Rodrigo reveals that he wants peace for Flanders. Philip confides that he suspects a relationship between his wife and his son and asks Rodrigo to investigate.

ACT III

Carlos arrives at a secret meeting with a veiled lady. Assuming it is Elisabeth, he declares his love. She reveals herself as Princess Eboli. Angry at his rejection, she threatens to reveal his love for the queen.

Rodrigo arrives and tries to distract the princess and then kill her, but Carlos prevents him; nevertheless, she swears vengeance. Rodrigo relieves Carlos of any incriminating documents. In the city square, heretics are being burned at the stake. Carlo leads in a group of Flemish deputies, pleading with the king to end the tyranny in Flanders. Philip refuses; Carlos threatens him, but is disarmed by Rodrigo. A heavenly voice comforts the condemned men.

ACT IV
The king laments his wife's indifference. The grand inquisitor enters and declares that Carlos and Rodrigo must be executed as rebels. Elisabeth enters in tears because her jewellery box is missing. The king produces it and finds the portrait of Carlos. Furious, he accuses her of infidelity. Rodrigo and Princess Eboli enter. The princess admits that she stole the jewellery box and delivered it to the king. Elisabeth forgives her, but when Princess Eboli also confesses to being the king's mistress, she is banished to a convent. Rodrigo visits Carlos in his cell and explains that he has allowed the documents to be found on his person, thereby taking the blame. Carlos does not believe him, until a soldier kills him. The king enters and, under pressure from the people, frees Carlos. The grand inquisitor shields the king from the angry mob.

ACT V
Elisabeth prays at the tomb of Charles V, as she prepares to bid Carlos farewell. He arrives, announcing his intention to leave for Flanders. Their farewell is interrupted by the arrival of Philip and the grand inquisitor, who go to arrest Carlos. Suddenly, the tomb opens; the young man's grandfather emerges and saves him.

Aida
Aida, set in Ancient Egypt, was not composed to celebrate the opening of the Suez Canal in 1869, as has often been suggested. Nor was it commissioned by the Khedive of Egypt to mark the opening of the Cairo Opera House that same year. It happened that the French Egyptologist, Auguste Mariette, keeper of monuments to the Egyptian government, suggested the opera to the Khedive as a suitable

'ELLA GIAMMAI M'AMO'
In Act IV of Verdi's *Don Carlos*, King Philip II of Spain grieves over the loneliness he suffers both as a man and as a king. His wife, Queen Elisabeth, has never, and will never, love him nor will his subjects. He will never know peace, he concludes, until he dies.

celebration for the canal, but was thwarted by delays in getting the libretto to Verdi. Written by Antonio Ghislanzoni, from a text by Camille du Locle, the libretto did not reach the composer until 1870 and the Cairo Opera House did not stage *Aida* until 24 December 1871. The opera was a huge success and within a few weeks, on 8 February 1872, it was premiered at La Scala, Milan, followed by New York on 26 November 1873. After triumphing throughout Europe, it had its London premiere on 22 June 1876. *Aida* was the complete opera, containing every feature at Verdi's disposal – spectacle, large-scale choruses, dance, pageantry, memorable arias, incisive characterization – and all of it overlaid with the semi-oriental harmonies that formed an impression in music of its exotic location.

Aida
by Giuseppe Verdi
Composed: 1870
Premiered: 1871, Cairo
Libretto by Antonio Ghislanzoni, after Auguste Mariette and Camille du Locle

ACT I
During the war between Egypt and Ethiopia, Aida, daughter of Amonasro, the Ethiopian king, has been captured and given as a slave to Amneris, daughter of the Egyptian king. Ethiopian forces are invading to reclaim her. Radamès, unaware of Aida's identity,

is in love with her. Ramfis, the high priest, informs him that the gods have decided who is to lead the Egyptian forces; Radamès hopes he has been chosen. Amneris enters; she loves Radamès and, suspecting he loves Aida, attempts to disguise her jealousy towards her slave. The king enters, with the news that Radamès is to lead the troops against the Ethiopians; the people hail Radamès. Aida is torn between her love for him and that for her country. She prays for mercy. In the temple of Vulcan, the priests prepare Radamès for war and give him a sacred sword.

ACT II

The Egyptians have triumphed in the battle and Amneris prepares for the forthcoming celebrations. She tricks Aida into revealing her love for Radamès by declaring him to be dead and observing her reactions. Amneris then discloses the deception and swears vengeance. Aida struggles to prevent herself from revealing her real identity.

Radamès arrives in a triumphal procession and is presented before the king and his daughter. The Ethiopian prisoners, which include Amonasro, are also presented. Amonasro signals to Aida to keep quiet, and then announces that the Ethiopian king died in battle. Radamès requests as his reward that the prisoners be freed. Ramfis advises the king against this as it could lead to a rebellion; a compromise is reached and all will be freed with the exception of Aida and Amonasro. Radamès is also promised Amneris' hand, and is told that he will eventually rule Egypt.

ACT III

Ramfis takes Amneris to the temple to pray for a blessing on her wedding. Aida, waiting nearby to bid farewell to Radamès, longs for her homeland. Amonasro, who has been hiding in the bushes, appears and tries to persuade her to extract information from Ramadès about the route that the Egyptian army plans to take to Ethiopia. She at first refuses, but he torments her with images of her family and country, and she eventually relents. Amonasro conceals himself, as Radamès arrives. Radamès, full of love for Aida, is easily tricked into divulging the information when she suggests the optimum route for their elopement. Amonasro emerges and assures Radamès that the Ethiopian soldiers will be waiting. Radamès is inconsolable as he realizes that he has betrayed his country. Amneris and Ramfis emerge from the temple and Amonasro attempts to kill Amneris. Radamès shields her and gives himself up to Ramfis as a traitor, while Aida and Amonasro make their escape.

ACT IV

Amneris visits Radamès as he awaits his trial and offers to save him if he will renounce his love for Aida. Radamès is prevented from agreeing by his sense of honour and his feelings for Aida; he refuses and declares himself ready to die. He learns that Amonasro has died in battle but Aida's fate is unknown. Amneris listens with increasing anguish to the tribunal and is horrified to hear the priests condemn Radamès to death by burial alive. She pleads with the authorities to have mercy on him, but to no avail.

Beneath the Temple of Vulcan, Radamès is enclosed in the crypt. He faces his approaching doom calmly but regrets that he does not know what has happened to Aida. Suddenly, she appears; she has hidden in the tomb in order to die with Radamès. Reunited, the couple await death, while above them in the temple, Amneris mourns and prays for Radamès.

Otello

Verdi's late masterpiece, Otello, completed when he was 74, was the second of his three operas taken from the plays of Shakespeare. The libretto by Arrigo Boito dispensed with the Shakespeare's opening scene, set in Venice and concentrated the action on Cyprus, giving it an almost claustrophobic intensity. Long considered Verdi's greatest opera and his most outstanding achievement, *Otello* was written at a time when the composer believed he had reached his peak with *Aida* and was being upstaged by Wagner's Teutonic grandeur, which was dominating the European music scene. Verdi was wrong on both counts. His *Otello* fulfilled Wagner's concept of a 'total work of art' in more ways than one. Music fused with drama and each scene with the next, with few set-piece arias or ensembles like those found in Verdi's previous works. The orchestral picture of a storm off the coast of Cyprus has thrilled audiences ever since the opera was first performed at La Scala, Milan on 5 February 1887. Yet there are also intimate moments and sublime expressions of love between Otello and his doomed wife Desdemona that scale great heights of lyricism and melodic beauty.

Otello

by Giuseppe Verdi
Composed: 1884–85
Premiered: 1887, Milan
Libretto by Arrigo Boito, after William Shakespeare

ACT I

The island of Cyprus is under Venetian rule. The people wait at the port for their governor, Otello. The ship arrives and the people rejoice as Otello announces their victory. Iago, Otello's ensign, swears revenge on his master for promoting Cassio to captain. He conspires with Roderigo, who loves Otello's wife Desdemona, to wreak revenge on Cassio and cause Otello's downfall. Iago insinuates to Roderigo that Cassio admires Desdemona and provokes a duel between them. The retiring governor Montano intervenes, while Iago causes a commotion. Otello arrives, angry that Montano has been wounded and Desdemona's sleep disturbed. He retracts Cassio's promotion and bids everyone leave.

ACT II

Iago reveals to Cassio that Desdemona alone can persuade Otello to restore his promotion. Iago muses on his nihilistic view of the world. He sees Cassio approach Desdemona in the garden and suggests to Otello that Cassio has designs on his wife. Desdemona pleads Cassio's innocence but Otello is inflamed by jealousy. Desdemona offers to wipe his brow with a handkerchief – an early love token from Otello. He snatches it and throws it to the ground; Emilia, Iago's wife, retrieves it. A bewildered Desdemona begs forgiveness, while Iago procures the handkerchief with a view to planting it in Cassio's house. Otello asks to be left alone but Iago remains behind to inform him that Cassio has spoken of Desdemona in his sleep. He also mentions having seen Cassio in possession of the handkerchief. Furious, Otello swears vengeance.

ACT III

Iago tells Otello that he can prove Desdemona's infidelity. Desdemona again approaches Otello about pardoning Cassio; he demands to see the handkerchief. When she admits she cannot produce it, he accuses her of infidelity and sends her away. Iago persuades Otello to hide while he speaks to Cassio about Desdemona. Iago then engages Cassio in conversation about a courtesan and manipulates the discussion so that Otello, unable to hear every word, belives them to be discussing Desdemona. A confused Cassio produces the lost handkerchief, further infuriating Otello. Trumpets announce Venetian ambassadors; Otello resolves to kill Desdemona. Lodovico, an ambassador, brings the news that Otello is to return to Venice and Cassio is to become governor. Otello begins to lose his mind and strikes Desdemona, while Iago encourages Roderigo to murder Cassio. Otello orders everyone to leave and curses Desdemona, before collapsing in a fit. Iago exults in his triumph.

ACT IV

Emilia helps Desdemona prepare for bed. Desdemona is upset by Otello's unprovoked anger towards her. She says her prayers and bids farewell to Emilia before going to bed. Otello enters and, kissing her, orders her to repent her sins. He berates her infidelity and, ignoring her protestations of innocence, smothers her. Emilia enters to announce that Cassio has killed Roderigo and is horrified to discover the dying Desdemona. She calls Cassio, Iago and Lodovico to the chamber and reveals the truth to Otello; Iago flees. Realizing that Desdemona was innocent, Otello is distraught. He kisses her and Lodovico seizes his sword but Otello, drawing a dagger, kills himself.

Falstaff

Verdi's last opera, *Falstaff* was the third taken from William Shakespeare, this time from his *Merry Wives of Windsor* and *Henry IV, Parts 1 and 2*. Verdi wrote the opera when he was 79, but it was not his only comic opera, as is often supposed. There was another, *Un giorno di Regno*, which he wrote more than 50 years before, in 1840. *Un giorno* had failed and ever since, Verdi longed to write another comic opera. However, he did not appear to envisage staging it: he wrote *Falstaff*, he told his publisher Ricordi just to amuse himself and pass the time. His librettist, Boito, had other ideas: he nagged Verdi to get on with *Falstaff* and the composer worked on it two hours a day for two years before the finished opera premiered at La Scala, Milan on 9 February 1893.

Falstaff is an opera in which ensemble singing is prominent and in no way did it show Verdi's great age. On the contrary, it is fresh, high-spirited, with schoolboy zest and a mischievous sense of fun, all of it underlined by Verdi's quicksilver music. The first-night audience demanded two encores and the ovations lasted half an hour.

Falstaff

by Giuseppe Verdi
Composed: 1889–92
Premiered: 1893, Milan
Libretto by Arrigo Boito, after William Shakespeare

ACT I

At the Garter Inn, Caius accuses Falstaff and his cronies Pistol and Bardolph of theft, which they deny. The time comes to pay the bill and Falstaff laments his lack of funds. He announces his plans to woo the wives of two wealthy gentlemen and writes love letters to the ladies – Alice Ford and Meg Page – asking Pistol and Bardolph to deliver them. When they refuse, Falstaff chases them from the inn and entrusts the letters to a pageboy.

Alice and Meg, along with Mistress Quickly and Alice's daughter Nanetta, discuss their letters from Falstaff. It transpires that they have received identical letters, and they decide to play a trick on Falstaff. While Nanetta embraces Fenton, her sweetheart, Pistol and Bardolph inform Ford of Falstaff's designs on his wife. Outraged, Ford decides to introduce himself to Falstaff in disguise, so that he can keep an eye on him. The ladies agree that Mrs Quickly should visit Falstaff and put their plan into action.

ACT II

Pistol and Bardolph join Falstaff at the inn and feign regret at having refused to carry out his orders. Mistress Quickly enters and assures Falstaff that both Meg and Alice return his love, adding that Alice will see him that afternoon. Ford enters, as Master Brook, and asks Falstaff to help him court Alice. To his horror, Falstaff boasts that he is meeting her that very day. Mrs Quickly reports back to the other women. Nannetta laments that her father is forcing her to marry Caius, when she loves Fenton; Alice reassures her. Falstaff arrives and Alice is left alone with him. He declares his love for her but is interrupted by Mistress Quickly, who announces the arrival of Meg; she in turn enters to warn them of Ford's approach. Ford arrives, with Fenton, Caius, Bardolph and Pistol, and begins to search for Falstaff by looking in the laundry basket. As they move away to look elsewhere, the women help Falstaff into the basket. Kissing is heard from behind a screen and Ford investigates; he is furious to discover Nannetta and Fenton there. The men leave and Alice orders her servants to empty the laundry basket containing Falstaff into the Thames.

ACT III

Falstaff sits outside the Garter Inn. Mistress Quickly arrives and declares that Alice loves him and regrets the incident. A midnight meeting is arranged in Windsor Park. So Alice will recognize him, he is to dress up as the Black Huntsman. The park is rumoured to be haunted, and the others plan to frighten Falstaff. Ford, who has been assured of his wife's fidelity, takes Caius to one side, instructing him to wear a particular costume so that he can be recognized and married to Nannetta; Mistress Quickly overhears.

In the park, the conspirators don their costumes. Fenton wears an outfit identical to that described to Caius by Ford. Falstaff arrives and declares his love to Alice, but Meg enters, warning them of approaching spirits. Falstaff is set upon by fairies and goblins who prod and torment him until he begs for mercy. Ford then presents himself and forgives Falstaff, and the deception is revealed, much to Falstaff's amusement. There is a marriage ceremony involving two couples in identical costumes. Ford has been tricked into marrying Caius to Bardolph and Nannetta to Fenton. He forgives everyone and Falstaff declares that the world is a joke.

OPERAS

1830	Oberto, conte di San Bonifacio
1840	Un giorno di regno
1842	Nabucco
1843	I Lombardi alla prima Crociata
1844	Ernani; I due Foscari
1845	Giovanna d'Arco; Alzira; Attila
1847	Macbeth; I masnadieri; Jérusalem
1848	Il corsaro
1849	La battaglia di Legnano; Luisa Miller
1850	Stiffelio
1851	Rigoletto
1853	Il trovatore; La traviata
1855	Les vêpres siciliennes
1857	Aroldo; Simon Boccanegra
1859	Un ballo in maschera
1862	La forza del destino
1867	Don Carlos
1871	Aida
1887	Otello
1893	Falstaff

TIMELINE

1813	Giuseppe Verdi is born, Le Roncole
1825	Begins studying music under Ferdinando Provesi
1828	Composes a new overture for a performance of Rossini's Il barbiere di Siviglia
1832	Travels to Milan to study under Vincenzo Lavigna
1836	Marries Margherita Barezzi, the daughter of his patron
1839	Oberto premieres at La Scala in Milan
1840	Death of Margherita sends Verdi into a spiral of despair
1842	Nabucco triumphs at La Scala, with Giuseppina Strepponi singing Abigaille
1847	Verdi and Strepponi become lovers
1848	Donizetti dies and Verdi becomes the leading Italian composer
1851	Rigoletto is a raging success at La Fenice
1854	Verdi and Strepponi move to Paris
1857	Simon Boccanegra and Aroldo receive cool reviews
1859	Verdi marries Strepponi
1861	Stands for parliament in the newly unified Italy, and is elected
1864	Becomes a member of the French Académie des Beaux-Arts
1871	After a delay caused by the Franco–Prussian War, Aida opens in Cairo
1879	Meets Arrigo Boito in Milan
1884	Begins work on Otello
1887	Otello premieres at La Scala to a standing ovation
1893	Falstaff receives a similar reception
1897	Giuseppina Strepponi dies
1901	Verdi dies, Milan

Wagner, Richard

1813–83, GERMAN

If – to quote Mark Twain – Wagner's music 'is not as bad as it sounds', then the composer's life was by no means as turpitudinous as it is generally claimed to be. Idolized by his friends and supporters as a family man who was kind to animals and plagued by self-doubts, he was demonized by his enemies as a cross-dressing womanizer and opportunistic megalomaniac. What is beyond doubt is that he changed the course of music and built a lasting shrine to his art in the northern Bavarian town of Bayreuth.

EARLY SUCCESSES

A myth-maker in life as in art, Wagner sought to portray himself as a natural genius with an inborn aptitude for composition. In fact, his formal lessons extended over a period of three and a half years from the autumn of 1828 to the spring of 1832 and resulted in a large number of vocal, instrumental and orchestral works, at least six of which were performed in public before his twentieth birthday. None of them reveal any great originality, and the same is true of the operas that date from the following decade: *Die Hochzeit* ('The Wedding'), which was abandoned in 1833, *Die Feen* ('The Fairies'), which Wagner completed in 1834 but which was not staged in his lifetime, *Das Liebesverbot* ('The Ban on Love'), which received a single, disastrous performance in 1836, and *Rienzi*, a gargantuan *grand opéra* inspired by Spontini and Meyerbeer that Wagner wrote in Paris, where he eked out a living between 1839 and 1842. Thanks to the help of Meyerbeer, *Rienzi* was accepted for performance in Dresden and proved a spectacular – if local – success, encouraging the company to stage *Der fliegende Holländer* ('The Flying Dutchman') early the following year, 1843, and to appoint its composer *Kapellmeister* to the Royal Court of Saxony.

IN EXILE

Here Wagner spent the next six years, working in his spare time on *Tannhäuser* (1845) and *Lohengrin* (1850), and growing increasingly disenchanted with what he saw as the constraints of his post and the philistinism of his employers. An active member of the Dresden intelligentsia, he became embroiled in the liberal, revolutionary movement of the period and was implicated in the Dresden Uprising of May 1849, when he fled the city with a price on his head. He spent the next nine years living as an exile in Zurich, before embarking on a peripatetic existence that took him all over Europe, including conducting engagements as far afield as Brussels, Vienna and Moscow. Having abandoned his work on the four-part *Ring* and having failed to find a home for *Tristan und Isolde*, which quickly acquired for itself the reputation of being unperformable, he sank further into debt, only to be rescued at the very last moment by the newly enthroned King Ludwig II of Bavaria.

COMPLETING THE RING

Ludwig's intervention allowed Wagner to stage *Tristan und Isolde* (1865) and *Die Meistersinger von Nürnberg* ('The Mastersingers of Nuremberg', 1868) and to complete the *Ring*, which he had begun in 1848 and which he finished in 1874. But Ludwig's contractual insistence on seeing the first two parts of the cycle – *Das Rheingold* ('The Rhinegold') and *Die Walküre* ('The Valkyrie') – staged separately in 1869 and 1870 respectively led to another of the frequent rifts between king and composer, persuading Wagner to build his own theatre at Bayreuth in Upper Franconia. It was here, on 26 July 1882, that his final work, *Parsifal*, was first staged. He died in Venice on 13 February 1883 and was buried at a private ceremony in Bayreuth five days later.

Der Fliegende Holländer

Initially a one-act opera, *Der fliegende Holländer* was later expanded to three. Wagner was anxious to make sure it was performed in the way he wished, and wrote detailed production notes for the directors and singers. He also conducted the first performance at the Hofoper or Court Opera in Dresden on 2 January 1843. Although Wagner regarded *Holländer* as his first 'total work of art', this music drama was too advanced for his audience. However, by the time it premiered at Drury Lane, London on 23 July 1870 – the first Wagner opera to be seen in the capital – taste in opera had moved on in Wagner's direction. *Holländer* became, as it remains, a defining work of Romanticism in opera. It used music to create 'sound pictures' with a new, hightened realism (e.g. the storm in the **overture**). Wagner may have used personal experience for this passage: during a voyage in 1839, his ship was almost wrecked by storms three times before finding safety in a Norwegian harbour.

Der Fliegende Holländer ('The Flying Dutchman')

by Richard Wagner

Composed 1840–41; rev. 1846, 1853

Premiered 1843, Dresden

Libretto by the composer

ACT I

As a violent storm rages, Captain Daland and his crew take refuge offshore for the night. A sinister ship with blood red sails draws up beside them. It belongs to the Flying Dutchman, who has been condemned by the Devil to sail the seas eternally. His only chance of salvation is finding a woman who will love him faithfully until death, and he returns to shore once every seven years in search of such a woman. Lamenting his fate and hoping that death will soon free him from his wretched existence, the Dutchman goes ashore.

Daland awakes and joins the Dutchman, questioning him. Learning that they are only a few miles from Daland's home, the Dutchman asks for hospitality, offering handsome payment. His crew bring forth some treasure and Daland is impressed; he offers the Dutchman not only hospitality but

'SENTA'S BALLAD'

'Senta's Ballad', a soprano aria, occurs in Act II of *Der Fliegende Holländer*, and begins with the arresting cry of 'Johohoe!'. In the ballad, Senta, the heroine, is at her spinning-wheel, recounting the legend of the 'Flying Dutchman' who is condemned to wander the high seas as punishment for blasphemy.

also his daughter Senta's hand in marriage in return for more riches. The Dutchman, although apprehensive, hopes that he may finally be saved from the curse. The ships set sail for Daland's hometown.

ACT II

In Daland's house the nurse Mary and some village girls sit spinning, while Senta gazes dreamily at a portrait on the wall depicting the legendary Flying Dutchman. The girls mock Senta for falling in love with the portrait when she is being courted by the handsome Erik. Senta sings the ballad of the Flying Dutchman and prays for his salvation, hoping herself to be his saviour. Erik overhears and, entering, announces that Daland's ship has been sighted. While the girls rush off to greet their sweethearts, Erik asks Senta to agree to their marriage. Avoiding the question, she suggests that they go and greet Daland. Erik is annoyed by Senta's infatuation with the portrait. He tells of his dream, in which Daland returned from a voyage with a man who resembled the face in the portrait. Senta had then embraced the man and disappeared to sea with him. Realizing that his dream is coming true, Erik leaves.

Daland enters with the sinister Dutchman. Senta, entranced by the stranger, forgets to welcome her father home. He asks Senta to be welcoming to the Dutchman and then broaches the subject of marriage, assuring her that she will be wealthy. Realizing that they only have eyes for each other, he leaves. Senta and the Dutchman gaze at each other; both have seen each other in their dreams and feel that this is their long-awaited destiny. The Dutchman asks if she agrees with her father's decision that they should marry; she promises to be faithful unto death. They tell Daland.

ACT III

The Norwegian sailors and villagers are celebrating Daland's return. Bemused by the deathly silence from the Dutchman's ship, they call to the crew to join them, but to no avail. As they return to their revelry, a storm breaks out around the Dutchman's ship and a flame flares up from the deck. The ghostly crew are revealed and call for their captain to return. They mock the Norwegian sailors, who retreat, terrified, below decks.

Senta appears, followed by Erik who is angry at her betrayal. Overhearing them, the Dutchman fears that Senta will not be capable of fidelity. Lamenting the loss of his freedom, he bids Senta farewell and prepares to set sail. Senta tries to reassure the Dutchman but he declares that she does not know who he is. Replying that she is the only one who can save him, Senta struggles away from her friends as the Dutchman boards his ship. Crying out that she has remained faithful unto death, she throws herself from the cliff. The Dutchman's ship sinks and his spirit, embracing that of Senta, rises into the heavens.

Tannhäuser

The full title of this opera in three acts is Tannhäuser und der Sängerkrieg auf Wartburg ('Tannhäuser and the Song Contest on the Wartburg'). Wagner, who took nearly three years to write the opera, conducted the first performance at the Dresden Hofoper on 19 October 1845. This was the first of two Wagner operas in which a song contest played a part in the action: the other was Die Meistersinger von Nürnberg. The finale of Tannhäuser showed clear traces of the Italian influence that informed his early work. Before Tannhäuser could be performed at the Paris Opéra on 13 March 1861, Wagner's libretto had to be translated into French in accordance with the opera house rules. The French poet Charles Baudelaire (1821–67) raved about Tannhäuser, citing the 'rare joy' it had given him, with its 'vast horizons', 'diffused light' and 'passionate energy of expression'. 'No musician,' Baudelaire concluded, 'excels as Wagner does in depicting space and depth, material and spiritual.' The 1867 Munich production featured spectacular scenery, including dancers playing the Three Graces and cupids who rained down love-arrows in order to defuse a riot. Wagner made many revisions to the score of Tannhäuser but was never entirely satisfied.

Tannhäuser
by Richard Wagner
Composed: 1843–45; rev. 1847–52; after 1861
Premiered: 1845, Dresden
Libretto by the composer

ACT I

In the Venusberg, nymphs and sirens take part in an orgy. Tannhäuser, rising from the lap of Venus, hopes for release from the artificial pleasures of the Venusberg. He longs to return to the simplicity of the outside world, with the earthly pleasures and pains that it brings. Venus chides him and tempts him with promises of endless joy, but Tannhäuser returns each time to his need for freedom and begs to leave her; she curses him. Invoking the Virgin Mary, Tannhäuser escapes Venus' spell.

He finds himself in a valley close to the castle of the Wartburg, where a shepherd sings of the joys of spring. A procession of pilgrims passes by, on its way to Rome, and Tannhäuser falls to his knees in prayer.

He is found by the Landgrave and some knights, who are surprised to recognize their old friend. Although suspicious at first, they greet him warmly, especially Wolfram. Tannhäuser refuses their invitations to join them, until Wolfram reminds him of Elisabeth, the Landgrave's niece, who fell in love with Tannhäuser through their singing contests. He reveals that, since Tannhäuser's departure, Elisabeth has become withdrawn. Tannhäuser agrees to join his companions.

ACT II

Elisabeth has heard of Tannhäuser's return and happily greets the hall where the singing contests took place. Wolfram enters with Tannhäuser and the couple are joyfully reunited, while Wolfram looks on sadly; he too loves Elisabeth. The Landgrave announces a song contest, with the theme of love. Suspecting that Elisabeth has fallen for Tannhäuser and assuming that he will be the winner, the Landgrave suggests that the victor should ask Elisabeth for whatever he desires. The nobles arrive to watch the contest.

Wolfram begins with a song about the refreshing stream of love, from which one should not drink. The second and third contestants also adhere to this image of love. Tannhäuser, still under the influence of Venus, declares that everyone should drink from the sensual stream. Elisabeth applauds, while the spectators look on in silent disapproval. Wolfram sings again of innocent, pure love, but Tannhäuser responds with a frenzied hymn to the sins of the flesh, urging everyone to go to the Venusberg and learn the true meaning of love. Scandalized, the ladies withdraw, while the men draw their swords and threaten Tannhäuser. Elisabeth intervenes and begs the Landgrave to pardon Tannhäuser. He agrees, on the condition that Tannhäuser join the pilgrims and seek forgiveness in Rome. Tannhäuser swiftly departs.

ACT III

It is now autumn, and Elisabeth is praying by a shrine in the valley. The pilgrims are returning but she cannot see Tannhäuser among them. Desperate, she prays to the Virgin Mary for forgiveness and then asks to be received in heaven, where she can pray for Tannhäuser's soul. She then sets off up the mountain; Wolfram begs to be allowed to accompany her but she refuses. He prays to the evening star to watch over her.

An exhausted Tannhäuser staggers by on his way back to the Venusberg. He reveals to Wolfram that despite his long journey to Rome and the penances he endured along the way, the Pope declared that his sins were too great and that he was as likely to be pardoned as the Pope's staff was to blossom. Desperate, Tannhäuser invokes Venus, who appears, only to vanish again when Wolfram brings Tannhäuser to his senses by mentioning Elisabeth. Tannhäuser kneels in despair as Elisabeth's funeral bier is brought past. Begging her to pray for his soul, he dies. Pilgrims enter, bearing the Pope's staff, which has mysteriously blossomed. All praise this miracle as the sun rises.

Recommended Recording:
Tannhäuser, Vienna Philharmonic Orchestra; Georg Solti, conductor; Decca 414 581–2; Soloists: Helga Dernesch (Elisabeth), Christa Ludwig (Venus), René Kollo (Tannhäuser), Victor Braun (Wolfram), Hans Sotin (Herrmann)

Lohengrin

Franz Liszt, the great Hungarian composer whose daughter Cosima married Wagner in 1870, conducted the first performance of the three-act opera *Lohengrin* at the Court Theatre, Weimar on 28 August 1850. Wagner provided a blueprint for productions of *Lohengrin*, just as he did for *Tannhäuser*, and emphasized the duty of the stage manager not to leave stage business to the individual performers, but to 'intervene' for 'the good of the opera'.

Wagner's methods in his later music dramas were already in evidence in *Lohengrin*: for example, the overture was marked by *leitmotifs*. However, French and Italian influences were still present and gave an air of French *grand opéra* to the wedding scene. Wagner's intention to exclude the set-piece arias and other separate melodies was not yet fully in action: the celebrated 'Bridal Chorus' for the heroine, Elsa – 'Here Comes the Bride' in its English version – escaped the opera stage entirely and became a popular feature at wedding ceremonies. It was, however, largely dropped from Jewish wedding ceremonies in favour of the march by Felix Mendelssohn (1809–47) after the Nazi Party in Germany, which shared Wagner's racist and anti-semitic views, made a national hero of him in the 1930s.

Lohengrin
by Richard Wagner
Composed 1846–48
Premiered 1850, Weimar
Libretto by the composer

ACT I
King Heinrich arrives in the Duchy of Brabant to rally troops for an approaching conflict, but finds the land divided by civil war and devoid of a leader. He demands an explanation from Frederick von Telramund, who reveals that the Duke has died, entrusting his two children, Elsa and Gottfried, to Telramund. He then adds that Gottfried has disappeared, thought to have been murdered by Elsa. Telramund, meanwhile, has married the sinister Ortrud and is assuming the role of leader. Heinrich offers to judge the matter himself and summons Elsa, inviting her to answer to Telramund's accusations. She replies that she has had a dream in which an unknown knight appeared to save her. The king rules that the case should be decided by a duel and calls for a contestant to fight for Elsa's honour. As she prays, a knight appears, in a boat pulled by a swan. He reveals that he has been sent to save her and she accepts him as her champion. They also decide to marry, after she has agreed not to enquire about his identity. The knight defeats Telramund in the duel, but spares his life.

ACT II
Telramund berates Ortrud, who claims to have witnessed Elsa's fratricide, but she maintains that the knight used magic to win the duel. She adds that if they can trick the knight into revealing his name, his power will be lost. Failing this, they can defeat him by cutting off one of his limbs, even if it is only the tip of his finger.

Elsa appears on her balcony and Ortrud calls to her. Elsa, pitying Ortrud, lets her in. Ortrud invokes the pagan gods and tries to undermine Elsa's faith in the knight, suggesting that he could disappear as suddenly as he arrived. Elsa is unconvinced.

Telramund has been banished and the mysterious knight proclaimed leader by King Heinrich. Telramund conspires with four noblemen to stage a rebellion. At the wedding, Ortrud advises Elsa to demand that the knight reveals his identity, as he may be a fraud. Telramund warns Elsa that the knight is a sorcerer and offers to steal into their chamber and cut off the tip of his finger to release his powers. Elsa remains steadfast and enters the church with the knight.

ACT III
In the bridal chamber, Elsa and her husband declare their love. However, Elsa is growing uneasy. Fears that he will leave her eventually force her to ask his identity. Telramund suddenly enters and is killed by the knight. He instructs the nobles to carry the body to the king and then assures Elsa that he will answer her question in the king's presence. The knight declares that he cannot lead the troops into battle, as Elsa has broken her vow.

He explains that he is one of the knights of the Holy Grail, who are sent out to perform acts of chivalry but must leave when their identities are revealed. His name is Lohengrin, son of Parsifal. As the swan which drew his boat approaches, Lohengrin tells Elsa that if he could have stayed longer her brother, who is not dead as she thinks, would have been returned to her. Ortrud rushes in, rejoicing in her triumph and revealing that she has bewitched Gottfried and turned him into a swan. Lohengrin kneels in prayer and gradually the swan turns back into Gottfried; Lohengrin crowns him leader of the Duchy. Ortrud's powers are quenched and Elsa falls lifeless to the ground as Lohengrin's boat departs, now drawn by the white dove of the Holy Grail.

Recommended Recording:

Lohengrin, Metropolitan Opera; James Levine, conductor; Pioneer Classics PC-11500D (DVD Region 1); Soloists: Eva Marton (Elsa), Leonie Rysanek (Ortrud), Peter Hofmann (Lohengrin), Leif Roar (Telramund), John Macurdy (Heinrich der Vogler)

Tristan und Isolde

Wagner's music drama *Tristan und Isolde*, written between 1856 and 1859 and first produced at the Hof- und Nationaltheater in Munich on 10 June 1865, broke the established mould of opera and took it to the threshold of 'modern' music. *Tristan* was based on an Arthurian legend, and featured a regular theme in Wagner's operas – the plight of lovers doomed to a cruel, inescapable fate. In *Tristan*, Wagner illustrated the themes of love and death with chromatics, a term describing notes that did not belong to the diatonic scale: this scale comprised only those notes in a given key. Chromatics not only gave a feeling of urgency to the music, they also broke up the tonality which indicated where the music was going next. This did away with the predictability so evident,

for instance, in the operas of Donizetti. Wagner began *Tristan* as he meant to go on: the prelude was a break with musical tradition, so much so that the music could not be pinned down to any definite key. The opera has been described as 'an overwhelming experience'.

Tristan und Isolde

by Richard Wagner
Composed: 1857–59
Premiered: 1865, Munich
Libretto by the composer

ACT I

On a ship bound from Ireland, Isolde is escorted by Tristan, a knight, to marry his uncle, King Marke of Cornwall. Furious at Tristan's lack of consideration for her feelings, Isolde wishes that she had her mother's magic powers, in order to sink the ship. She sends her companion Brangäne to summon Tristan. Brangäne approaches him but he explains that he must steer the ship. His companion Kurwenal sings an insulting song about Tristan's killing of Morold, Isolde's betrothed. Isolde bitterly recalls how the longing in Tristan's eyes forced her to nurse him back to health even after she discovered that he killed Morold. She is furious that he is repaying this kindness by delivering her to his uncle as a bride, and curses Tristan, hoping to also die herself. Brangäne assures her that Tristan is only doing his duty, and reminds her of the love potion her mother has provided for her wedding night. Isolde requests instead the elixir of death.

Land is sighted, but Isolde refuses to leave the ship until Tristan begs forgiveness. He arrives at her quarters and offers her a sword with which to kill him, but Isolde replies that she cannot kill her future husband's nephew. She offers him a drink of friendship; Tristan realises that she means to poison him. They drink the potion, but instead of dying they find themselves falling in love; Brangäne admits she administered the love potion instead of the poison.

ACT II

As Marke leaves with his hunt, Isolde awaits Tristan. Brangäne warns her to be wary of spies, especially Melot, who has been keeping a close eye on Tristan. Isolde declares Melot to be a friend. Brangäne regrets bringing the couple together, but Isolde insists that Love herself was responsible. She puts out the torch, signalling to Tristan that it is safe to approach. He arrives and the lovers embrace, claiming the protective night as their friend. Brangäne warns that day will soon reveal them and they equate the safety of night to the eternal comfort of death. Kurwenal enters, followed by Marke, Melot and courtiers. Marke bewails the fact that Tristan, who he loves so dearly, has betrayed him. Tristan confesses that he cannot explain and, turning to Isolde, asks if she will follow him into death. She agrees and he kisses her; a furious Melot sets upon Tristan with his sword. He falls wounded into Kurwenal's arms.

ACT III

Tristan lies near his Brittany castle, tended by Kurwenal. A shepherd pipes a melancholy tune; he is watching for Isolde's ship. When it arrives, he will play a merry melody. Tristan awakes and relates that he has visited the kingdom of death, but has returned for Isolde. Kurwenal imparts that she has been sent for to heal him and Tristan, hallucinating Isolde's ship, is brought back to reality only by the mournful tune of the shepherd's pipe. It reminds him of the death of his parents and his own wounding during the duel with Morold. He wishes that he had been allowed to die then. Suddenly, the shepherd's tune becomes more cheerful. Kurwenal goes to greet Isolde and Tristan rips the bandages from his wounds. However, as she approaches, he is only able to speak her name before dying. Another ship arrives, bearing King Marke, Melot and Brangäne. Kurwenal kills Melot and is killed in return. Marke laments Tristan's death; Brangäne has revealed all and he has come to forgive the lovers and bless their union. Isolde sees the spirit of Tristan and falls lifeless upon his body, as their spirits unite in death.

Der Ring des Nibelungen

Wagner's Ring cycle is made up of four works – Das Rheingold ('The Rhinegold', 1851–54), Die Walküre ('The Valkyrie', 1851–56), Siegfried (1851–57; 1864–71) and Götterdämmerung ('Twilight of the Gods', 1848–52; 1869–74). Although there have been other, even more ambitious projects in the history of opera – Rutland Boughton's cycle of choral dramas based on the Arthurian legends and **Karlheinz Stockhausen's** (b. 1928) seven-opera Licht cycle, for example – the Ring has proved to be an enduring masterpiece, supremely challenging in the demands that it places on audiences and performers alike and no less rewarding in terms of its infinite fascination and endless ability to engage an audience's emotions on the very deepest level.

ORIGINS OF THE RING

Wagner first became interested in the subject of the Ring in the mid-1840s, at a time when several other composers, including Felix Mendelssohn (1809–47), Robert Schumann (1810–56), Liszt and Niels Gade (1817–1890), were similarly drawn to the theme. All of them were responding to the operatic potential of the early thirteenth-century Nibelungenlied ('Lay of the Nibelungs'), which had been rediscovered after centuries of neglect and which was now seen as a focus of nationalist aspirations, the epitome of an age when the German nation had been powerful and united. But in Wagner's eyes the appeal of the Nibelungenlied began to wane as soon as he developed anarchical leanings and turned away from the narrow historical perspective of the medieval epic and towards the dramatic possibilities of myth as the expression of necessary social change. History could not predict the future. Myth alone could embody the universal struggle between the forces of reaction and a more humane and enlightened regime. It was in order to excavate what he believed was the mythic substratum of the material that he started to delve more deeply into the Scandinavian versions of the legend enshrined in the *Eddas*, versions which, in keeping with the scholarly thinking of his time, he regarded as more archaic and, hence, as more prototypically German than the courtly accretions of the *Nibelungenlied*. Here in the *Eddas*, Wagner also found the alliterative verse form, or *Stabreim*, that constitutes what is perhaps the cycle's most notorious linguistic feature.

A NEW MUSICAL LANGUAGE

The libretto that Wagner drafted in the wake of his *Nibelung* reading was called *Siegfried's Death* and essentially covered the same ground as the work we now know as *Götterdämmerung*: it told of the hero's murder as part of a cycle of death and renewal. But it soon became clear that this drama contained too much narrative and presupposed too much existing knowledge on the audience's part, with the result that Wagner prefaced it first by *Young Siegfried* in 1851 and then by *Das Rheingold* and finally *Die Walküre* in 1852. So vast a project required a new musical language, and it was not until November 1853 that Wagner felt able to make a start on the music, employing the *leitmotif* technique ineluctably bound up with his name. Wagner did not coin this term and did not even sanction it, preferring instead to speak of 'melodic elements' and 'fundamental motifs' to describe the musical ideas that acquire a specific associative meaning in conjunction with a significant moment in the drama or a particular passage in the text. But, far from remaining unchanged, these motifs

are developed along Beethovenian lines, gaining additional layers of significance and at the same time playing a vital role in the work's symphonic structure.

STAGING THE RING

Lack of progress on the score, coupled with the fading prospect of a performance and the distraction afforded by *Tristan und Isolde*, prompted Wagner to lay aside the work from 1857 to 1864 and again from 1865 to 1869. By now he was enjoying the patronage of King Ludwig II of Bavaria and under contract to complete the Ring. Indeed, so eager was the king to hear the work that he issued instructions for the two finished instalments, *Das Rheingold* and *Die Walküre*, to be staged in Munich in 1869 and 1870 respectively. Although Wagner initially fell in with the plan, it soon became clear that *Das Rheingold* – with its swimming Rhinemaidens, giants, dwarfs, magical transformations and rainbow bridge – was going to be a notoriously difficult work to stage; furthermore, the decision to perform the incomplete cycle angered the composer, and he withdrew his support.

He continued to work on the scores of *Siegfried* and *Götterdämmerung*, while giving Ludwig the impression that their completion still lay some distance away in the future and simultaneously casting round for an alternative venue, where he could perform the four-part cycle free from royal interference. He finally settled on Bayreuth and after endless difficulties and delays staged the first complete cycle in his own specially designed Festival Theatre between 13 and 17 August 1876. It had always been his intention to perform the work on four consecutive evenings, but the sudden indisposition of Franz Betz (1835–1900), who was singing Wotan, necessitated a postponement. Since then, the sheer demands of the *Ring*'s leading roles have forced opera-houses to adopt a more leisurely schedule. Unable to reconcile his inner vision of the cycle with the romantic realism of his day, Wagner was unhappy with the production and hoped to revive it the following year in a substantially different form, but the deficit on the first festival meant that his theatre remained closed until 1882, when it reopened its doors for *Parsifal*.

Written over a period of 26 years, the *Ring* reflects its creator's changing and often contradictory thinking, resulting in a complex work that remains perennially enthralling and that admits countless interpretations, whether socialist, Jungian, feminist or ecological. It is a measure of the *Ring*'s greatness as a work of art that it continues to acquire new meanings for each successive generation – a mirror in which we may see ourselves reflected feeling the rawest of raw emotions. We may not necessarily like what we see there.

Recommended Recording:

Der Ring des Nibelungen, Bayreuth Festival Orchestra; Pierre Boulez, conductor; Philips 070 407-9 (DVD Region 0, NTSC); Soloists: Gwyneth Jones (Brünnhilde), Jeannine Altmeyer (Sieglinde, Gutrune), Hanna Schwarz (Fricka), Gwendolyn Killebrew (Waltraute), Ortrun Wenkel (Erda), Peter Hofmann (Siegmund), Manfred Jung (Siegfried), Heinz Zednik (Loge, Mime), Helmut Pampuch (Mime), Donald McIntyre (Wotan), Hermann Becht (Alberich), Franz Mazura (Gunther), Matti Salminen (Fasolt, Hunding), Fritz Hübner (Fafner, Hagen)

Preliminary Evening: Das Rheingold

by Richard Wagner

The Rhinemaidens, who guard the magic gold hidden beneath the waters of the Rhine, are approached by Alberich, a Nibelung dwarf. They tease him mercilessly and, unwisely, reveal that if someone were prepared to renounce love and fashion a ring from the gold, he would acquire the power to dominate the world. Failing to woo the maidens, Alberich curses love and steals the gold.

Wotan, the ruler of the gods, is sleeping near Valhalla, the gods' new home. His wife Fricka wakes him and rebukes him for agreeing to give Valhalla's builders, the giants Fafner and Fasolt, her sister Freia in return for their work. Wotan explains that he has no intention of paying and that Loge, the god of fire, will help him evade the agreement. Freia enters, followed by the giants demanding payment. Wotan says that they must accept an alternative but the giants insist on Freia. Loge appears and admits that he has found no solution, as a beautiful woman is valued above all. However, he has found one exception in Alberich, who has forsworn love to possess the Rhinemaidens' gold. The giants agree to accept the gold instead of Freia, but keep her as a hostage. Wotan and Loge descend to Nibelheim, the home of the Nibelungs.

The Nibelungs, slaves to the magic ring, work ceaselessly mining gold for Alberich. His brother Mime has made a magic cap, the tarnhelm, which allows its wearer to take on any form or to become invisible. Alberich siezes it and leaves. Wotan and Loge arrive and Mime tells of the Nibelungs' plight and the tarnhelm. When Alberich returns, Loge asks him to demonstrate its power. He transforms himself into a dragon and then a toad, which the gods catch. They take Alberich away as a prisoner.

The gods tell Alberich that the price of his freedom is his gold. He agrees, knowing that the ring will maintain his power, and orders the Nibelungs to bring the gold. The tarnhelm is added and Wotan demands the ring as well. Alberich curses the ring. The giants return with Freia and demand that the pile of gold be big enough to conceal her. To achieve this, the tarnhelm is added but there is still a gap, which the giants insist must be plugged with Wotan's ring. He resists but the Earth goddess Erda appears, warning him to relinquish it. The giants quarrel over the treasure. Fafner kills Fasolt and departs with the gold. As the gods enter Valhalla, the Rhinemaidens are heard lamenting the loss of their gold.

First Day: Die Walküre
by Richard Wagner

ACT I
A storm rages. Siegmund enters a forest cottage and collapses. Sieglinde offers him refreshment. She persuades him to stay and meet her husband Hunding, who arrives and is suspicious. Siegmund reveals that his mother and sister were abducted and that he and his father were separated. Earlier that day he fought to rescue a girl from a forced marriage, but he was forced to flee. Hunding reveals that he is related to the groom and challenges Siegmund to a fight the next day.

The couple retire to bed. Siegmund recalls his father's promise to provide him with a sword when most needed. Sieglinde enters; she has drugged Hunding. She tells Siegmund how a stranger came to her wedding and plunged a sword into the tree at the centre of the cottage. She is convinced he is the man to claim it. As they sing of their past and their love for each other, they realise they are brother and sister. Siegmund pulls the sword, which he names Notung, from the tree and they flee into the forest.

ACT II
Fricka tells Wotan that Hunding must win the fight, as Siegmund has broken the laws of hospitality, marriage and incest. Wotan pleads for Siegmund and Sieglinde, who are his children, but eventually agrees. He summons his daughter Brünnhilde – a Valkyrie, who brings fallen heroes to Valhalla – and recalls recent events, including Alberich's curse. Everything must end unless a hero appears and alters the course of destiny. He tells Brünnhilde that Siegmund must die in the fight.

The lovers arrive. Brünnhilde tells Siegmund that he must follow her to Valhalla. As Sieglinde cannot accompany him, he refuses. Brünnhilde is won over by the power of his love for Sieglinde. This, and knowing Wotan's true feelings, persuade her to allow Siegmund to win. Hunding arrives and the fight begins. Wotan returns and breaks Siegmund's sword against his spear, allowing Hunding to win. Brünnhilde escapes with Sieglinde; Wotan kills Hunding, vowing to punish Brünnhilde.

ACT III
Brünnhilde and Sieglinde approach the Valkyries and beg for protection, but they dare not defy Wotan. Sieglinde wishes to die and rejoin Siegmund; Brünnhilde reveals that she is carrying his son and must escape with the broken sword and bear the child, naming him Siegfried. Wotan arrives and banishes Brünnhilde; she is no longer a Valkyrie, and must sleep on the mountain until the first man to find her makes her his wife. The Valkyries depart and Brünnhilde defends herself; by ignoring his orders, imposed by Fricka, she obeyed his true will. She adds that Sieglinde will have Siegmund's child. Wotan is moved. She must be punished, but will be protected by a magic fire that only a hero will brave. He removes her godhead and calls Loge to surround her with fire.

Second Day: Siegfried
by Richard Wagner

ACT I
The act opens in Mime's smithy, in a forest near where Fafner, now a dragon thanks to the tarnhelm, lives in a cave guarding his treasure. Years before, Sieglinde sheltered there and, dying, entrusted her child and the broken sword to Mime's care. He has raised Siegfried as his son, hoping to persuade him to kill Fafner so that he, Mime, can take the gold and the ring. Mime is forging a new sword for Siegfried, who hates him. Siegfried enters, shattering the sword with one blow,

and asks Mime about his mother. Mime explains about his birth and shows him the shards of Notung. Siegfried orders him to re-forge the sword and leaves. The Wanderer (Wotan in disguise) enters, challenging Mime to a riddling contest with his life as the price of failure. The Wanderer answers Mime's questions but Mime is unable to answer his final question – who can remake Notung? Only one who does not know fear can do it and Mime's life is now owed to that man: Siegfried. The Wanderer leaves and Siegfried returns. He finds the sword in pieces, so re-forges it himself. He prepares to leave, but Mime persuades him that he must first know fear, by tackling Fafner.

ACT II

Alberich is outside Fafner's cave, hoping to regain the ring. The Wanderer appears and tells Alberich of Mime's plan. They leave as Mime and Siegfried approach. Mime hides and Siegfried blows his horn to compete with a Woodbird, inadvertently rousing Fafner. Siegfried kills the dragon; his hand is splashed by its blood. As he puts his hand to his mouth and tastes the blood, he realizes he can understand the Woodbird's song. She tells him to take the ring and tarnhelm from Fafner's cave. When Siegfried emerges from the cave, Mime tries to make him drink a sleeping draught so that he can kill him and take the ring. However, Siegfried is able to hear the dwarf's thoughts; he kills him with a blow from Notung. The Woodbird tells him about Brünnhilde, sleeping on a rock surrounded by fire and waiting to be awoken by a hero. He decides to make her his bride and the Woodbird leads him off.

ACT III

Near Brünnhilde's rock, the Wanderer rouses Erda and asks her if there is any way of preventing the approaching end of the gods' supremacy. She cannot help. The Wanderer realizes his power must pass to Siegfried, and waits to greet him. Siegfried arrives but treats the old man with contempt; the Wanderer tries to bar his way. Siegfried shatters the spear, symbolic of the god's power, with Notung; the Wanderer departs. Siegfried enters the fire and finds the sleeping Brünnhilde. He wakes her with a kiss and they sing a passionate love duet.

Third Day: Götterdämmerung
by Richard Wagner

PROLOGUE

Erda's daughters, the Norns, sit on a rock spinning the rope of destiny. They recall recent events but are unable to see the future, since the rope has frayed. The rope beaks and they return under the earth. Siegfried prepares to set off. He gives Brünnhilde the ring and she gives him her horse, Grane.

ACT I

Gunther, lord of the Gibichungs, sits with his sister Gutrune and half-brother Hagen in his hall near the Rhine discussing the honour of the Gibichungs. Hagen declares that they would benefit from powerful marriages. He suggests Brünnhilde as a bride for Gunther. Siegfried, who will help them to win Brünnhilde, could marry Gutrune. Siegfried's horn sounds. Hagen tells Gutrune to prepare an amnesiac for Siegfried; he drinks it and, forgetting Brünnhilde, falls in love with Gutrune. He proposes marriage and agrees to help Gunther marry Brünnhilde. Gunther and Siegfried take an oath of brotherhood and set off to find her. Hagen reveals his intention of seizing the ring. Waltraute visits Brünnhilde and reveals that the gods are in Valhalla awaiting their doom. She begs her to return the ring to the Rhinemaidens. Brünnhilde hears Siegfried's horn but, wearing the tarnhelm, he appears as Gunther. He claims Brünnhilde as his bride, wrenching the ring from her hand.

ACT II

Hagen's father Alberich appears and reminds him to recover the ring. When Hagen awakes, Siegfried appears, *transported by the tarnhelm. He tells Hagen and Gutrune that Brünnhilde and Gunther are returning. Hagen invites the Gibichungs to celebrate the double wedding. Gunther arrives with Brünnhilde, who is bewildered to find Siegfried betrothed to Gutrune. He is wearing the ring. Siegfried, drugged by Gutrune's potion, swears his innocence. He persuades the Gibichungs to join him at the wedding feast. Brünnhilde, Gunther and Hagen remain and agree that Siegfried will be killed the following day.*

ACT III

Siegfried is separated from a hunting party and meets the Rhinemaidens. They beg him to return their ring, warning him about the curse, but he refuses to be intimidated. He rejoins the others and Hagen persuades him to tell his story. Siegfried tells of his life and, as Hagen gives him a drink to undo Gutrune's potion, of how he married Brünnhilde. Hagen claims that Siegfried has lied and plunges his spear into his back. The dying Siegfried sings of his love for Brünnhilde. Hagen demands the ring but Gunther says that it belongs to Gutrune. Hagen kills him but when he tries to take the ring, Siegfried's hand rises, menacingly. Brünnhilde, who realizes what has happened, returns. She orders the Gibichungs to build a funeral pyre where she will join Siegfried, and takes the ring from his finger. She tells ravens to fly to Valhalla and tell Wotan that the end has come. She lights the fire and rides Grane into the flames. The Gibichungs' hall burns and the Rhine overflows. The Rhinemaidens reclaim the ring and drag Hagen under the waves. There is a red light in the heavens as Valhalla and the gods are consumed by fire.

Die Meistersinger von Nürnberg

Die Meistersinger has often been described as a comedy. This, though, is not 'comedy' as found in the operas of Rossini or in Verdi's *Falstaff*: what 'comedy' means in this context is the bitter 'human comedy'. The premiere of *Die Meistersinger* took

place in Munich on 21 June 1868. Wagner based his opera on the real-life members of the Guild of Mastersingers in sixteenth-century Germany. They were the middle-class equivalent of the aristocratic groups whose Song Contest featured in Wagner's *Tannhäuser*. The principal character in *Die Meistersinger*, Hans Sachs (1494–1576) was a poet and composer living in Nuremberg. He wrote a poem 'Die Wittenbergisch Nachtigall' ('The Nightingale of Wittenberg') in support of Martin Luther (1483–1546) and the Protestant Reformation. Wagner included part of Sachs' verses in *Die Meistersinger*. The overture is often played as a separate concert item, as is the 'Prize Song' with which the hero, Walther, wins the contest: despite Wagner's efforts to exclude arias from his operas, this one has become a tenor's favourite.

Die Meistersinger von Nürnberg ('The Mastersingers of Nuremberg')

by Richard Wagner
Composed: 1862–67
Premiered: 1868, Munich
Libretto by the composer

ACT I

Walther von Stolzing has arrived in Nuremberg and fallen in love with Eva Pogner, daughter of a rich mastersinger. She returns his love, but her father has offered her hand to the winner of the forthcoming mastersinger contest. Eva's companion Magdalene asks her lover David, apprentice to the poet and cobbler Hans Sachs, to prepare Walther for the auditions, since only mastersingers may enter. David, knowing that mastersingers endure years of study, introduces Walther to just a few of the rules stipulated by the contest.

The apprentices prepare for the singing trials. Walther begs Pogner and the other mastersingers to let him enter. He makes an enemy in Beckmesser, the clerk, who also hopes to win Eva's hand. Pogner announces his intention to reward the winner of the contest with not only his daughter's hand, but also his fortune, to prove that businessmen appreciate the arts. Sachs suggests that the people and indeed Eva should have some say in the winner. Walter is introduced and sings his freeform trial song. So many of the mastersingers' rules are broken that he fails before the song is even finished. Only Sachs recognizes the true worth of Walther's composition.

ACT II

David informs Magdalene of Walther's failure, which she conveys to Eva. Sachs ponders the beauty of Walther's song and is visited by Eva, who unwittingly betrays her feelings for Walther. Feigning disapproval, Sachs secretly resolves to help the lovers.

Walther persuades Eva to elope. She swaps clothes with Magdalene; Beckmesser is coming to serenade Eva, and Magdalene must take her place. As Walther and Eva make to leave, Sachs shines a light so that they cannot escape. As Beckmesser begins his serenade, Sachs takes up his hammer and starts to sing. Beckmesser asks for silence but Sachs explains that he is working on Beckmesser's new shoes. They arrange that Sachs will hammer only when Beckmesser breaks one of the mastersingers' rules. Beckmesser resumes his singing; the hammering is so frequent that the shoes are finished before the song. David arrives and, seeing Beckmesser serenading Magdalene, attacks him. A riot ensues, during which the lovers are separated. The arrival of the night watchman quells the commotion.

ACT III

Sachs contemplates the previous evening and is visited by Walther, who tells him of a dream he has had. Sachs realizes that it has the potential for a song and helps Walther to apply the mastersingers' rules to the piece. They leave the unfinished song unattended and Beckmesser finds it. Sachs discovers this

and, to Beckmesser's surprise, invites him to keep it. Confident of winning, Beckmesser goes to learn it.

Eva arrives and Walther sings her his song. Sachs declares it a mastersong; Eva and Walther express their gratitude. Sachs calls in Magdalene and David and gives the latter a promotion so that they too may marry. They leave for the contest.

Everyone assembles and dances as the mastersingers file in. Sachs introduces the contest. Beckmesser is the first to sing, but stumbles over Walther's words, failing to fit them to the music and making many mistakes. As the crowd jeers, he tries to blame Sachs, who he claims to be the author of the song. Sachs denies this and introduces Walther as the true composer. Walther gives an enthralling performance of the song and everyone hails him as the winner. The Mastersingers offer him the trophy but he refuses, until persuaded by Sachs to honour the guardians of the arts and accept it. Walther is now mastersinger and may marry Eva.

Recommended Recording:
Die Meistersinger von Nürnberg, Bavarian Radio Symphony Orchestra; Rafael Kubelík, conductor; Calig CAL50971/4; Soloists: Gundula Janowitz (Eva), Brigitte Fassbaender, Sándor Kónya (Walther), Gerhard Unger (David), Thomas Hemsley (Beckmesser), Thomas Stewart (Hans Sachs), Keith Engen (Kothner), Franz Crass (Pogner)

Parsifal

Wagner had first encountered the early thirteenth-century romance Parzivál by Wolfram von Eschenbach (c. 1170–c. 1220) in 1845 and frequently returned to the subject in the course of the decades that followed, completing the libretto in 1877 and the music in 1882. By now his views had changed, and the text and its imagery are permeated by the Aryan Christianity that typified his old age. The work was part of a programme of national and racial regeneration that prompted him to place an embargo on its 'sacred mysteries' and to ban all performances outside Bayreuth for a period of thirty years. Described as a *Bühnenweihfestspiel* (a 'festival play to consecrate the stage'), it was written with the Bayreuth theatre and its sunken orchestra pit in mind, producing a mellow, homogenized sound that no other theatre can match. Stepping back from the chromatic intensity of *Tristan und Isolde*, Wagner created a diaphanous but no less voluptuous score which sounds, in Debussy's apt phrase, to be 'lit from behind' and whose play of light and shade anticipates many of the qualities associated with Impressionism in music. As such, the work had a seminal impact on the Symbolist and Decadent artists of the 1880s and 1890s.

Parsifal

by Richard Wagner
Composed: 1877–82
Premiered: 1882, Bayreuth
Libretto by the composer

ACT I

Gurnemanz, an elderly knight of the Holy Grail, awakens in a forest near the castle of Monsalvat. He arouses two other knights and bids them prepare a bath for the king, Amfortas, who suffers from an incurable wound. Kundry, a wild woman, enters with balsam for the king, who is then carried in by his courtiers. Gurnemanz relates the tale of how the sorcerer Klingsor wished to gain entry to the brotherhood of the Grail, but was denied due to his sinful lust. Even after castrating himself he was not admitted. In revenge, he created a magic garden inhabited by sirens to seduce wandering knights; Amfortas fell under the garden's spell and was seduced by Kundry. Klingsor stole from him the holy spear that pierced Christ's side on the cross and proceeded to wound Amfortas with the relic. The wound can only be healed by a fool who grows wise through compassion. Suddenly, a swan is shot down by an arrow. A youth, Parsifal, is brought in; he appears to know nothing. Kundry fills in the little she knows concerning his name and his dead parents. As Amfortas is borne back to the castle, Gurnemanz wonders if Parsifal may be the fool they require; he takes the boy with him.

In the Hall of the Grail, the knights prepare to celebrate the Last Supper. The Grail is brought before Amfortas and the voice of his father, Titurel, can be heard encouraging him to uncover it. However, while the power of the chalice sustains the elderly Titurel, it prolongs Amfortas' suffering; the king hesitates. The Grail is eventually uncovered and the bread and wine distributed. Parsifal pities Amfortas' obvious pain, but understands nothing. Gurnemanz chases him away.

ACT II

Klingsor orders Kundry to seduce Parsifal, who he realises has the power to save the Grail. In the magic garden, Parsifal is first approached by flower maidens but manages to shake them off. Kundry then appears as a seductive siren and begins to woo him, bewitching him with memories of his childhood and parents. As he goes to kiss her, Parsifal is struck by the sudden realization of how Amfortas received his wound and recoils. Kundry then goes on to describe her pitiful life – she has been cursed since laughing at Christ on the cross – but Parsifal is no longer swayed by her words. She curses him, while Klingsor throws the holy spear to him. Parsifal catches the spear and, making the sign of the cross, causes the castle and garden to crumble and vanish.

ACT III

Gurnemanz, now old and grey, is living as a hermit. He comes across an almost lifeless Kundry in the undergrowth. A knight passes, carrying a spear, and is reproached by Gurnemanz for being armed on Good

Friday. The old man then recognizes Parsifal, who explains that he has been searching for the castle for many years, in order to relieve Amfortas of his wound. He is saddened to hear of Amfortas' refusal to uncover the Grail and Titurel's consequent death. Gurnemanz removes Parsifal's armour and Kundry bathes his feet; he baptizes her in return. Gurnemanz leads Parsifal to the Grail Hall. A group of knights passes, bearing Titurel's coffin, while another carries Amfortas' litter. The people call for Amfortas to uncover the Grail, but he cannot and bids them kill him instead. Parsifal, touching him with the spear, heals his wound and becomes the guardian of the Grail. Holding it aloft, he accepts command of the rejoicing knights. Kundry, released at last from her existence of endless wandering, falls lifeless to the ground.

Recommended Recording:

Parsifal, Bayreuth Festival Orchestra; Hans Knappertsbusch, conductor; Philips 464 756-2PM4; Soloists: Irene Dalis (Kundry), Jess Thomas (Parsifal), George London (Amfortas), Hans Hotter (Gurnemanz), Gustav Neidlinger (Klingsor), Martti Talvela (Titurel)

TIMELINE	
1813	Richard Wagner born, Leipzig
1828	Begins composition lessons
1834	Composes *Die Feen*, his first completed opera, writes his first essay on opera and makes début as an opera conductor
1842	Successful Dresden premiere of *Rienzi*
1843	Accepts *Kappelmeister* post after premiere of *Der fliegende Holländer*
1845	Dresden premiere of *Tannhäuser*
1848	Start of the *Ring*
1850	Premiere of *Lohengrin* under Liszt
1853	Finishes the *Ring* text and starts composing *Das Rheingold*
1854	Plans *Tristan und Isolde* after reading Schopenhauer's philosophy
1857	Stops work on *Siegfried* to start *Tristan*
1859	Finishes *Tristan* and settles in Paris
1861	*Tannhäuser* scandalizes the Paris Opéra
1865	Premiere of *Tristan* under Bülow
1868	Triumphant premiere of *Die Meistersinger von Nürnberg* in Munich
1869	Work on the *Ring* resumes

1872	Foundation stone of Bayreuth Festspielhaus laid
1874	Score of the *Ring* finally completed
1876	First Bayreuth festival and premiere of entire *Ring* cycle
1878	Composition of *Parsifal* begins
1882	Second Bayreuth festival and premiere of *Parsifal*
1883	Wagner dies, Venice

OPERAS

1832	*Die Hochzeit* (incomplete)
1833–34	*Die Feen*
1835–36	*Das Liebesverbot*
1837–40	*Rienzi, der Letzte der Tribunen*
1840–41	*Der fliegende Holländer*
1843–45	*Tannhäuser und der Sängerkrieg auf Wartburg*; rev. 1847, 1860
1845–47	*Lohengrin*
1851–54	*Das Rheingold*
1851–56	*Die Walküre*
1851–57; 1864–71	*Siegfried*
1848–52; 1869–74	*Götterdämmerung*
1856–59	*Tristan und Isolde*
1845; 1862–67	*Die Meistersinger von Nürnberg*
1857; 1865; 1878–81	*Parsifal*

REALISM, NATURALISME AND VERISMO
∾ p. 244

In Italian they called it *verismo*, in French *naturalisme*. Bizet's *Carmen* was the starting point of a movement that increasingly probed the problems of modern life by representing a series of realistic events. *Carmen* was an *opéra comique* where 'realistic' spoken dialogue was essential, communicating more like a play than an opera, and raising more contemporary questions than mythical or historical operas. And there's more local colour too: here are real Spanish dances and gypsy girls singing. Bizet originally wrote Carmen's entry as an operatic aria, with all its clichés. But he replaced it in the staging process, having found a *Habanera* – a dance-song – in a book of South American cabaret songs. Would Carmen have been such a success without this flash of inspiration? Probably not. Suddenly there were real events onstage: not just a heroine singing about herself, but presenting her body, and her ideals of free love, to the characters around her.

Strong stuff for an opera house whose function was basically a marriage bureau for chaperoned females! This was the start of a trend that affected opera profoundly. Suddenly, in tune with literature and painting, it became interested in contemporary life: observation rather than literary research became the source for subject-matter.

⦿ KING LUDWIG AND THE FESTSPIELHAUS ⮑ p. 238

King Ludwig II of Bavaria (1845–86), a homosexual and a strange, obsessive character, came from a royal family, the Wittelsbachs, which had a strong streak of madness in it. Ludwig virtually fell in love with Wagner and his music, calling the composer his 'one true friend whom I shall love until death.... If only, I had the opportunity to die for you' he added. After he succeeded to the Bavarian throne in 1864, Ludwig paid Wagner's debts, installed him in a comfortable villa and ordered the construction of a festival theatre in Munich for performances of the *Ring*. Ludwig's ministers, who suspected Wagner of political interference in Bavarian affairs, halted the building work and forced the composer out of the country. He fled to Switzerland, where the besotted King purchased a villa for him. Ludwig also advanced Wagner 200,000 marks to build the Festspielhaus in Bayreuth, which opened in 1876. After Wagner left Bavaria, King Ludwig became a morbid recluse. He occupied himself constructing fantastic castles like the 'fairytale' Neuschwanstein. Ludwig was certified mad in 1886 and a few days later drowned in the Starnberger Lake at his castle of Berg during a walk with his psychiatrist. The psychiatrist also died.

⦿ ST PETERSBURG THEATRE ⮑ p. 238

The city of St Petersburg was founded in 1703 by Peter the Great as his 'window

on the West' – part of his plan to connect backward Russia to the modern world. A court theatre was included as part of Peter's modernizing policy, but plays were being performed there for more than 30 years before the first opera was staged. This was *La forza dell'amore e dell'odio* ('The Force of Love and Hate', 1736) by the Italian composer Francesco Araia (1709–*c.* 1770). Araia's *Cephalus and Procris* (1755) was the first opera to be performed in Russian. In 1757 St Petersburg's first public theatre opened, and opera shared the repertoire with stage plays. Later, the Bolshoi Kammeny or Grand Stone Theatre (1783) opened, followed by the Maly or Small Theatre. Italian opera was staged at the Bolshoi between 1829 and 1832 and in 1840. For a long time after its premiere there, Glinka's *A Life for the Tsar* (1836) was performed at the start of every season. By the century's end, the opera had been given some 700 times. In 1862 Verdi's *La forza del destino* was premiered at the Maryinsky, one of St Petersburg's three imperial theatres.

⦿ TCHAIKOVSKY'S PATRON ⮑ p. 239

In 1876 Pyotr Tchaikovsky began an extraordinary relationship with a wealthy widow, Nadezhda von Meck (1831–94), which was totally platonic and conducted entirely by letter. The two of them never formally met, but they remained devoted to each other for the rest of their lives. Madame von Meck settled on Tchaikovsky an allowance of 6,000 roubles, which gave the composer much-needed financial security. Tchaikovsky dedicated his Fourth Symphony (1878) to her. They corresponded for the next 13 years, sometimes writing to each other every day. Tchaikovsky confided to her his innermost thoughts, his ideals and aspirations and she replied with encouragement and sympathy.

Madame von Meck had made it a condition of her continuing support that the two of them would never meet, but on one occasion, she dropped her guard and invited Tchaikovsky to visit her while both of them were in Florence. Tchaikovsky demurred, but subsequently, they accidentally came face to face, and were so embarrassed that they fled. After Tchaikovsky died in 1893, Madame von Meck survived him by only two months, dying in Wiessbaden early in 1894.

⚫ THE *CLAQUE* ~ p. 292

The *claque*, a French word for 'slap' or 'clap', was a crowd of supporters hired by composers, *impresarios* or performers to work up enthusiasm for an opera or, alternatively, sabotage the work of rivals. Most professional *claques* were indistinguishable from the rest of the audience and flourished more in France and Italy than they did in Germany and England, but the tradition still existed. It was put on to commercial lines in France in 1820 when a certain entrepreneur named Sauton opened a *claque* agency named L'*assurance des succès dramatiques* – ('Assurance of Dramatic Success'). Monsieur Sauton hired out *chefs de claque* – *claque* directors; *tapageurs*, who clapped energetically; connaisseurs, who specialized in shouts of approval; and *pleurers*, who carried hidden bottles of smelling salts to make themselves cry, apparently with emotion. Rates of pay varied, depending on the response being faked: in the High Romantic era, five francs were paid for ordinary applause, expressions of horror and guffaws, 12.5 francs for groans and 15 francs for renewed applause, murmurs of alarm and cries of amusement. Often, the *chef de claque* was invited to the dress rehearsal of an opera to make sure that his team performed these effects in the right places.

⚓ NEW GERMAN SCHOOL ~ p. 239

The failure of Peter Cornelius's *The Barber of Baghdad* was not due to lack of charm or talent – the opera contained both in plenty – but to a small, vociferous group of reactionary musicians who objected to the influence of Franz Liszt and his 'New German School'. The ethos of the New German School was to foster the work of 'progressive' composers who experimented with new harmonies and regarded music as a means of expressing pictorial or literary ideas. The 'absolutist' opposition, whose greatest supporter was the German composer Johannes Brahms (1833–97), preferred their music 'pure' and non-representational. Intellectual warfare in the arts – whichever art was in dispute – has often turned to violence, and this campaign was no exception. The 'absolutists' mounted a noisy demonstration at the premiere of Barber, creating so much disruption that Liszt chose to resign as *Kapellmeister* and leave Weimar. However, the principles of the New German School survived and were dramatically typified by the pyrotechnics of Liszt's piano and other music. Adherents of the New German School included not only Peter Cornelius, but the pianist and conductor Hans von Bülow (1830–94), composer Felix Draeseke (1835–1913) and Richard Wagner.

⚓ CONVENIENZE ~ p. 240

The term *convenienze* – 'conveniences' – described the hierarchy of singers in nineteenth-century Italian opera and the etiquette surrounding their participation. The three main principals were the soprano or prima donna – first lady – the tenor or primo uomo – first man – and the baritone or basso cantante – lower or bass singer. Under the Code Rossini, the formal structure of opera that applied between around 1815 and 1860, each of the principal singers was given a cavatina, a short solo song, with which to make themselves known to the audience. Each also had a *scena*, a dramatic solo that was less than an aria, but concluded with a short solo section, the cabaletta. This was often used for displays of vocal technique. Secondary roles, such as maids, servants or confidantes, were known as seconda donna – second lady – and secondo uomo – second man. No solo arias were written for them, but they could sing in ensembles where their individual voices were allowed a phrase or two of their own. An intermediate performer, known as comprimario – supporting actor or actress – had a little more latitude: he or she might take part in a duet or even have a short, simple aria to sing alone.

꧁ SINGING IN
THE *RING* ꧁ p. 299

When Wagner broached the *Ring* in earnest in 1848, it was as a single work, a three-act 'grand heroic opera' that he planned to stage with singers familiar to him from the Dresden Court Opera. But as the work continued to grow, so its demands increased, not least in terms of the stamina required to sustain such dramatically challenging roles over four consecutive evenings. Wagner characteristically made the problem worse by falling out with a number of singers who might otherwise have created the cycle's principal roles, adding to its reputation for ruining singers' voices. (Nor was its reputation helped when three of the singers involved in the 1876 production inconsiderately died insane.) Its difficulties have been compounded since Wagner's death by the inexorable rise in pitch, so that Wagner's top C is now more than a semitone higher; by the increased size of opera houses, forcing singers to use a vibrato that Wagner himself intended to be employed only for expressive effect on

individual phrases; and by the desire on the part of conductors to impose their own personality on the score – ironically a development to which Wagner himself contributed. Wagnerian singers are regarded by many as a race apart.

꧂ THE *RING* AT BAYREUTH, 1876
꧁ p. 240

Bayreuth in Bavaria had had an opera house, the Margraves' Opera House, for 130 years before King Ludwig II contributed towards the construction of the Festspielhaus – the Festival Theatre. The foundation stone was laid on 22 May 1872, and the 1,345-seat theatre opened four years later (it has since been repeatedly enlarged and now seats 1,925). The complete *Ring* cycle was performed there on 13, 14, 16, and 17 August 1876. Some 4,000 people came to Bayreuth for the occasion, which was regarded as an event of world-class significance. This historic occasion was attended by the emperors of Germany and Brazil, and some of the greatest contemporary composers, including Tchaikovsky, Gounod, Saint-Saëns, Grieg and Liszt. Innovative technology provided special attractions. For instance, a magic lantern illuminated the 'Ride of the Valkyries' in Act III of *Die Walküre*, the second opera in the *Ring* cycle.

This first Bayreuth festival lost around 98,000 marks (over £220,000/$380,000 in today's prices), and no other took place until the first performance of *Parsifal* in 1882. After Wagner's death in 1883, his second wife, Cosima, took over the direction of the Festspielhaus and made sure that her late husband's style of production continued. Members of the Wagner family have been directors of the Festspielhaus ever since.

꧂ PREMIERE OF *OTELLO* ꧁ p. 293

The opening of *Otello* at La Scala on 5 February 1887 was a major occasion, which musicians and critics attended from all over the world. People's excitement mounted to fever pitch, both inside and outside the opera house. They were not to be disappointed. The seamless continuity of the opera, the lavish costumes, the richness and sophistication of the orchestral settings and the perfect harmony of the poetry and music guaranteed the opera's instant success. The audience was captivated from the opening lines and at the final curtain both Verdi and his librettist Boito received a standing ovation. It is reported that even after Verdi had retired for the night, crowds thronged around his hotel 'shouting and yelling' in appreciation.

Verdi himself was reputed to have been unhappy with the premiere of *Otello*, which is not surprising given the perfectionist stance he had taken with this particular work all along. However, despite the composer's dissatisfaction, the opening of the opera was greeted with worldwide acclaim and was recognized as an event of great significance in the shifting trends of operatic style.

⚷ VERDI AND HIS LIBRETTISTS
∿ p. 241

Throughout his long career, Verdi worked with several librettists and gained a reputation for being something of a tartar. Sometimes he would even write the text himself, only allowing his librettist to put it into verse. The composer had strong ideas about what he wanted from the text to his operas; in the early compositions this was a dramatic series of confrontations, perfectly set by *Temistocle Solera* in *Nabucco*, *I Lombardi*, *Giovanna d'Arco* and *Attila*, and set by Salvatore Cammarano in *Luisa Miller*, the celebrated *Il trovatore* and others.

Verdi worked more comfortably with Francesco Maria Piave (1810–76), a personal friend who was responsible for *Ernani*, *I due Foscari*, *Macbeth*, *Il corsaro*, *Stiffelio*, *Rigoletto*, *La traviata*, *Simon Boccanegra* and *La forza del destino*. Another librettist who did not give in to Verdi's bullying was Eugene Scribe; they clashed on several occasions, but Scribe usually won. A more congenial librettist, Camille du Locle, wrote *Don Carlos* and provided the original libretto of *Aida*, which was translated into Italian by Antonio Ghislanzoni, a former baritone who had sung in Ernani in Paris.

⚷ CENSORSHIP IN OPERA ∿ p. 245

Opera censorship was a fact of life for nineteenth-century composers and librettists. Libretti were minutely picked over for anything that might give offence, encourage sedition or create public disorder. Censors even attended dress rehearsals to make sure there was no 'improper' scenery, costumes or stage business. The Spaniards, Austrians and French who occupied Italy at various times suspected the natives of sedition, rebellion or worse and fancied that they were at their most dangerous en masse. This made the opera house potentially dangerous, since it was virtually the only place in the Italian peninsula where large gatherings were permitted. Censorship came in various forms. Political censorship, which intensified after the revolutions of 1848, forbade operas to depict regicide or any behaviour that put royal personages in a bad or insulting light. Operas could also be censored on moral grounds, for example when the Roman censor allegedly baulked at the crystal shoe in Rossini's *La Cenerentola* because fitting it exposed a naked foot in public. Verdi's *La forza del destino* got into trouble for religious reasons; *forza* could mean 'power' as well as 'force' and, according to the censors, 'destiny' was not a power: the only power was God's will.

TURN OF THE CENTURY

The political structure of Europe changed greatly during the second half of the nineteenth century. Germany and Italy became united countries under supreme rulers. The Habsburgs' Austrian Empire, ruled from Vienna, became fragmented into Austria-Hungary. The borders of this new confederation contained the cauldron of difficulties that eventually developed into the confrontations which culminated in the First World War in 1914.

It was not just the political landscape that was shifting beyond recognition, either. The industrial revolution had slowly but surely altered the day-to-day life of all Europeans. By the middle of the 1800s, there had been dramatic changes in personal circumstances. Increased personal choice, due to improving earning power, co-existed with increases in social control, which were largely a result of the rapidly expanding workforce. On the other hand, the growth of industry brought about by the industrial revolution created a divide between the wealthy and the poor that was exacerbated by problems of sanitization and welfare. It was these unappealing aspects of mid-nineteenth-century society that led to artistic reaction against the opulence and self-indulgence of the Romantics.

Emile Zola began an artistic school of thought known as 'naturalism'. He believed that art, specifically the novel in his case, should examine people and their social environment in scientific detail. His work intentionally tackles social problems such as alcoholism, disease and degeneracy head-on. A zealous social reformer, Zola was convinced in order to solve such problems, we first had to understand them, however unattractive they appeared. Zola's approach ran alongside a similar belief system known as 'realism'. The two concepts often converge, but the realist school did not hold to such rigidly scientific methods. Writers such as Gustave Flaubert (1821–80) and George Eliot (1819–80) aimed to describe life as they saw it, without idealization. In their work, a character's environment is often an integral part of the dramatic canvas.

KEY EVENTS

1894	Alfred Dreyfuss is tried for treason and imprisoned on Devil's Island
1898	Pierre and Marie Curie discover radium and polonium
1899	Boer War begins between Britain and the Boers in South Africa
1900	Italian King Umberto I is assassinated; Sigmund Freud publishes *The Interpretation of Dreams*
1902	Edward VII becomes King of Britain
1903	The Wright brothers make the first powered flight in America
1904	The Russo–Japanese War begins; work starts on the Panama Canal
1905	Bloody Sunday in Russia, storming of the Winter Palace; Fauvism is introduced by artists Henri Matisse
1907	Birth of the Cubist style in art
1908	The Model-T Ford is launched
1909	Robert Peary becomes the first man to reach the North Pole
1911	Ernest Rutherford discovers the structure of the atom
1912	The *Titanic* sinks on its maiden voyage
1914	Assassination of the heir to the throne of Austria-Hungary leads to world war

Turn of the Century
INTRODUCTION

The schools of naturalism and realism had an immediate effect in Italy. With scant literary tradition to draw on from this period, Italian writers in the second half of the nineteenth century seized upon Zola's beliefs as a potent dramatic source. The style they developed came to be known as *verismo* and was exemplified by writers such as Giovanni Verga and Luigi Capuana. The characteristically veristic traits of strong local colour, down-to-earth language and – to the audiences – familiar and often personally resonant plots, made the style immediately popular. Opera was quick to latch on to the possibilities offered by *verismo*. Giordano's *Mala vita* ('The Miserable Life', 1892) recreates in careful detail the squalid environment of an inner city prostitute without pulling any punches. It reveals without flinching the quotidian torments of inner-city Neapolitans.

EXCITING, SENSATIONAL OPERA

Perhaps unsurprisingly, opera audiences did flinch from the extremes of *verismo* and the style quickly moved away from its didactic origins. What did grasp the imagination of audiences across Italy and Europe were sensational, technicolour texts set to viscerally powerful music. These were tremendously exciting for audiences, and operas with veristic traits – though perhaps lacking a truly veristic ideology, like Pietro Mascagni's (1863–1945) *Cavalleria rusticana* (1890) and Ruggiero Leoncavallo's (1858–1919) *Pagliacci* (1892) – spread like wildfire across Italy and Europe.

The influence of naturalism was soon seen in the approach to staging as well as in the artwork itself. André Antoine formed his Théâtre Libre in Paris in 1887 – in opposition to all he had been taught at the capital's Verismo – with the aim of presenting the works of naturalist authors. Antoine wanted to achieve a more intimate style of acting and a realistic use of stage space, eliminating grand gestures. Antoine's work inspired the German director Otto Brahm who, in 1889, established the Freie Bühne in Berlin. Like Antoine, Brahm wanted to divest German theatre of its old production methods and bring a new realism to the stage. In 1894, Brahm's theatre merged with the large Deutsches Theater and Brahm became director. Under his leadership, the theatre mounted productions of Molière, Shakespeare and Sophocles as well as naturalist works by Ibsen and Hauptmann.

THE SEEDS OF MODERN STAGE PRODUCTION

Brahm's successor at the Deutsches Theater was Max Reinhardt, whom Brahm had directed in several productions prior to his succession. Reinhardt was keen to move on from his realist inheritance and was particularly interested in the ideas of Adolphe Appia and Edward Gordon Craig. Appia was a Swiss theorist who had a strong interest in **Richard Wagner**'s (1813–83) ideas on stage design. He espoused the use of three-dimensional sets in order to make the actors a part of the stage rather than simply being on it. Appia was also interested in the use of light to create atmosphere, a trait that he shared with his English contemporary Craig. Craig's work had led him to reject some of the realist theories then fashionable and turn to a more suggestive style of set design.

Reinhardt, along with many of his German colleagues, quickly latched on to these theories. His work was instrumental in establishing one of the most vital partnerships in opera: that of **Richard Strauss** (1864–1949) and **Hugo von Hofmannsthal** (1874–1929). Appia's ideas also influenced the Austrian designer Alfred Roller who, with Max Reinhardt as director, had worked on the premiere of Strauss's opera *Der Rosenkavalier* ('The Knight of the Rose', 1911) in Dresden, written to a Hofmannsthal libretto. Roller's work with Gustav Mahler (1860–1911), during his time as director of the Vienna Hofoper, was revolutionary. Using intense lighting and sparse but powerfully suggestive sets, he focused the audience's attention on the drama. This was in marked contrast with the norm of visually stunning designs that often overshadowed the unfolding story. It is these men who, along with others such as Stanislavsky, Nemirovich-Danchenko and Sir Henry Irving, created stage production as we know it today. They were interventionist in the sense of trying to make the action and design match, even amplify, what we hear from both the music and the text. They were also the first to receive criticism for using their role to further their own ideals as opposed to simply presenting opera in its best light.

THE BIRTH OF EXPRESSIONISM

The realist and naturalist aesthetics became increasingly extreme as the nineteenth century progressed. The Swedish writer Johan August Strindberg was strongly influenced by Ibsen's naturalism. By the late 1880s, however, he had developed a more strident style that retained naturalist subject matter, but departed from its objective narrative techniques for a more overtly emotive tone. This was the birth of Expressionism. The Expressionists felt that too much emphasis was laid on external realities at the expense of a more powerful, internal truth. It is particularly associated with the German dramatists Ernst Toller (1893–1939), Frank Wedekind (1864–1918) (two of whose plays were adapted by the composer as the basis to **Alban Berg**'s (1885–1935) *Lulu* and Georg Kaiser (1878–1945), as well as with the writing of Franz Kafka (1883–1924) and James Joyce (1882–1941).

Expressionism focused increasingly on psychological relationships and states. It also reflected changes in perception of the function of art. From its eighteenth-century position as bourgeois-sponsored, sophisticated entertainment, art had become a vital means of self-expression. It had become less about skill and style and more about the unquenchable need to say something. 'Art', said **Arnold Schoenberg** (1874–1951), 'comes not from ability but from necessity.' It was here that the West reached a crisis point. The industrialization process had altered the entire social fabric of Europe and had effects that no one had envisioned or seemed able to control. Art was quick to respond to these changes and in its increasing anxiety we can see mirrored the social and political tensions of the time. By the time Schoenberg came to utter those words, there was already a chain of events in motion that would rip Europe apart.

❧ ORCHESTRATION ∿ p. 245

Developing instrumental technologies and increased expressive demands ensured that the orchestra grew in both size and variety during the nineteenth century. Italian opera, perhaps unexpectedly, given its devotion to the beauty of the voice, showed considerable imagination with composers such as **Giacomo Meyerbeer** (1791–1864) and **Serverio Mercadante** (1795–1870) making use of saxhorns, bass clarinets and the viola d'amore.

By **Giacomo Puccini**'s (1858–1924) time, the orchestra had become a vast force that could be used to achieve a huge variety of colouristic and dramatic effects. Puccini's operas use striking orchestral colours to point up dramatic moments, such as the snow in Paris in the third act of *La bohème* ('Bohemian Life', 1896). Strauss mastered the orchestra to a degree perhaps not matched by anyone. He was able to characterize anything through his inventive instrumentation. In *Salome*, for example, he uses the extremes of register to create viscerally terrifying sounds and in no time he softens the timbres to be gentle and caressing. No less impressive, but of an entirely different character, are the carefully crafted sonorities of **Claude Debussy's** (1862–1918) *Pelléas et Melisande* (1902). By considered blending of timbres he achieves gossamer textures that defy gravity.

❊ VERISMO ❧ p. 247

The term has been liberally applied to a range of musical styles but, properly, it refers to a movement in Italian literature of which the main exponent was Giovanni Verga. The major influence on the veristic writers was Emile Zola who believed that reality could be best understood by objective observation. For instance, a character would be placed in a situation and his reactions observed. The generating influence behind Zola's ideology was the rapid industrialization of France. Italy was not undergoing such rapid changes, but the essential idea remained an attractive one. The Italian veristi tended to concentrate their work on the lower social classes. The language used is always that of the subject – Verga, for example, obsessively collected short phrases and idioms that he would incorporate into his work. The result is that we hear the words of the subjects themselves, not polished verse given to them by the author. The associated traits of verismo – stark emotions,

brutal violence and strong regional colour – are also part of the desire to give a true reflection of real life. As a result of these characteristics, however, the term verismo came to imply vulgar sensationalism and it rapidly lost its essential meaning. Properly speaking the term is applied to a certain literary style and not to music at all. The fervour with which operas with veristic texts, such as Mascagni's setting of Verga's Cavalleria rusticana, were taken up meant that the term verismo quickly became associated with any kind of high-octane opera.

❧ GUSTAV MAHLER ❧ p. 366

No discussion of this period in opera's history would be complete without looking at Gustav Mahler (1860–1911). Although he is known primarily for his expansive, neurotically tinged symphonies and orchestral song cycles, he contributed hugely to the development of opera through his work as a conductor.

Mahler was born in 1860 and he began his conducting career at Bad Hall, Austria in 1880. Moving between posts in places such as Laibach (Ljubljana), Kassel, Prague and Leipzig, he finally achieved his dream when appointed director of the Hofoper in Vienna in 1897. Mahler spent the next decade at the theatre performing a wide variety of operas, including works by Wagner, Puccini, Tchaikovsky, Smetana, Mozart and Gluck. He was determined to achieve the best possible performances and his insistence on the highest standards often led him into confrontation. He wanted to make the opera house a place of serious performance as opposed to a social meeting place where the music and drama were secondary to displays of fashion and wealth. Mahler's work in Vienna with the designer Alfred Roller was of particular importance in defining staging techniques as being integral to the drama and meaning of opera.

Turn of the Century
GENRES AND STYLES

Richard Wagner (1813–83) and Giuseppe Verdi (1813–1901) were the dominant figures as opera moved from the nineteenth into the twentieth century, and it was the great German whose influence was most pervasive. His particular use of mythical subjects, symphonic conceptions, compositional techniques, philosophy and psychology left an indelible mark on all composers who came after him. On Wagner's death, in 1883, Verdi wrote to his friend, the music publisher Giulio Ricordi: 'It is ... a name that leaves a powerful imprint on the history of art.' Before sending the letter he crossed out 'powerful' and replaced it with 'the most powerful' – such was Wagner's stature.

WAGNER'S LEGACY

It is Wagner more than anyone who can be heard in almost every score written around the turn of the century. Even in Debussy's symbolist opera *Pelléas et Mélisande*, Wagner is present in the compositional techniques on both macro and micro levels. Verdi permeated musical consciousness far less. Puccini, for whom Verdi was so vital in his youth, showed more interest in French opera and, of course, Wagner, than the grand old man of Italy. The influence of French opera, and of **Jules Massenet** (1842–1912) in particular, should not be underestimated. Although the composer of *Manon* (1884) and *Werther* (1893) is not today held in such high regard as his contemporaries and immediate successors, Puccini and Debussy, among others, would not have been the same without him.

USE OF *LEITMOTIF*

In terms of subject matter, the strongest trend was for exotic locations. The counter-fashion for strong local colour, begun by the veristic writings of Giovanni Verga and then Mascagni and Leoncavallo, provided a welcome sideline but *La fanciulla del West* (1910), *Madama Butterfly* (1904), *Salome* (1905), *Elektra* (1909) and even *Der Rosenkavalier* (1911) testify to the continued allure of unfamiliar worlds. This was allied with increasing fluidity in the form taken by opera. By the dawn of the twentieth century it was taken for granted that an opera would be conceived as a symphonic entity – composed as a complete piece, rather than as a series of discrete sections, with internal structures generated in particular through the use of *leitmotifs*. **Recitative** had effectively ceased to exist: there was no longer a boundary between moments of action and moments of reflection. Indeed, it became common for operas to have very little real action and focus instead on a character's psychological state – *Salome* and *Pelléas* are just two examples.

SCHOENBERG'S ATONALITY

This change of focus went hand-in-hand with dramatic changes to the musical language of opera. The solid ground of diatonic harmony became increasingly shaky as the turn of the century approached. By the first decade of the twentieth century, it had been violently shaken and the full force of an harmonic 'meltdown' took hold. Puccini stepped gradually closer to the tonal precipice throughout his life, but perhaps died too soon to step off. Strauss looked directly over the edge – for dramatic reasons as much as personal ones – straightened up and walked in a very different direction. It was Schoenberg who took the plunge. With *Erwartung*, which he completed in 17 days of white-hot composition in 1909, opera found new territory.

The score more resembles a musical psychoanalysis than an unfolding drama, and it smashed any notions that opera could not function without sweet diatonic melody.

AN INNOVATIVE ERA

This was an era rich in tradition and innovation. The massive influence of Wagner and the resulting developments in compositional technique and stagecraft were added to an already highly developed corpus of operatic work. The form, language and subject matter – opera's tools of expression – were pushed to their limits. As one century handed over to another, the question was clearly formed: was opera's great frame able to withstand the pressure?

❋ OPERETTA ∾ p. 247

Operetta, from its beginnings with **Jacques Offenbach** (1819–80) in France during the 1850s, had reached a high point by the turn of the century. When **Johann Strauss** (1825–99) moved from the dance hall to the opera theatre, the Austrians had found an equal to the famous Frenchman. The English played their part with the inseparable (if often tempestuous) partnership between **W. S. Gilbert** (1836–1911) and **Sir Arthur Sullivan** (1842–1900). In Spain, too, the revival of the *zarzuela* brought local colour to the genre.

In contrast to the increasing proportions of opera, operetta was a light bite, a sometimes spicy and always fashionable snack. Its subjects were topical, reflecting contemporary tastes and fashions but as willing to satirize as to glamorize. Operetta rapidly grew from its origins as speech with a few songs to a form that rivalled full-blown opera. **Franz Lehár** (1870–1948) showed clear awareness of Puccini in his scores, and the latter repaid the compliment in the composition of his operetta *La rondine* (1917). By the first decade of the twentieth century, operetta had become a subtle, flexible form, capable of grasping and manipulating the audience's emotional responses. At the same time, it remained true to its roots and was always light in tone, full of melodic vitality and sparklingly inventive.

❋ THE SECOND VIENNESE SCHOOL ∾ p. 291

Spearheaded by Arnold Schoenberg, the Second Viennese School included composers such as Alban Berg and **Anton Webern** (1883–1945) and formulated a new approach to music and composition that proved at once radically innovative and deeply controversial.

Schoenberg considered the work of composers such as Wagner and Mahler to have become over-complicated and harmonically cluttered, and felt that a new system of musical composition was needed in order to restore the clarity of expression evident in the works of the Classical-era composers. The new musical language – known as the twelve-tone technique – that Schoenberg developed as a solution to these issues was described by the composer as a 'method of composing with 12 notes which are related only to one another'. In this system the 12 notes of the chromatic scale are treated with equal importance, with no particular notes having the emphasis enforced upon them by classical harmonic conventions. Schoenberg's departure from tonal music was intended to create a more simple and unified means of musical expression, but in reality the mostly atonal compositions that resulted from using the twelve-tone technique were not always well received. Early performances of twelve-tone works by Schoenberg, Berg and Webern reputedly ended in verbal abuse and fighting, and critical opinion remains divided to this day.

Turn of the Century
PERSONALITIES

Adami, Giuseppe
1878–1946, ITALIAN

Adami worked as a playwright and journalist as well as a librettist. He found most success with lighter plays such as *Una capanna e il tuo cuore* (1913) and also wrote a number of ballet scenarios. His is best known operatically for his collaborations with Puccini. The publisher Giulio Ricordi brought the two together, and their first project was *La rondine,* an operetta commissioned by the directors of the Karltheater. The work was not a great success but Puccini felt encouraged enough to continue using Adami for *Il tabarro* and *Turandot,* which Adami completed in collaboration with Renato Simoni. Adami retained his link with the Ricordi house, acting as their publicist, as well as writing music criticism for two Italian journals.

Battistini, Mattia
1856–1928, ITALIAN

Battistini was gifted with a beautiful baritone voice and after only a short period of study was given the opportunity to take on the leading role in **Gaetano Donizetti**'s (1797–1848) *La favorite* in 1878. Such was his success that Battistini embarked immediately on a busy schedule. His liquid, agile, high voice was ideally suited for the gymnastic requirements of the ***bel canto*** repertoire. Indeed, he fitted into a vocal category popular in the nineteenth century termed baritenore. Battistini's voice was also capable of a darkness and edge that made him ideally suited to his most famous roles including Rigoletto, Germont and Eugene Onegin.

Caruso, Enrico
1873–1921, ITALIAN

Tenor Caruso's first singing experiences came in local churches. Through mixed experiences of public performance, Caruso slowly came to master his voice and from his debut at the Metropolitan Opera in New York in 1903, his fame was assured. Caruso's voice mixed the burnished colour of a baritone with the sheen of a tenor. He developed an impressive flexibility of tone that enabled him to sing a wide variety of roles. Caruso's enthusiasm for recording ensured that he left a valuable legacy, and one that has ensured his fame continues long after his death.

Chabrier, Emmanuel
1841–94, FRENCH

Chabrier's father was determined that his son should enter the legal profession, even to the extent of moving the entire family to Paris in order that he could prepare for law school. In 1858, Chabrier entered law school and was soon employed in the Ministry of the Interior. His interest in music remained potent, however, and during the 1860s he began a number of projects, including two operettas to libretti by Paul Verlaine, all of which remained incomplete. Like many of his contemporaries, Chabrier was fascinated with Wagner and it was attending a performance of *Tristan und Isolde* that finally committed him to a path in music.

Chabrier had a gift for light, comic music and his biggest hit was *Le roi malgré lui* (1887). Despite an initial lack of public interest, the work's sure touch and sympathetic characterization has ensured it continues to retain interest. Chabrier completed little else of great interest, though fragments of works show that he lost neither his wit nor his technical facility. He became rapidly disillusioned with what he regarded as a paucity of success which, coupled with financial insecurities, took its toll on his health and he died in 1894.

Chaliapin, Fyodor Ivanovich
1873–1938, **RUSSIAN**

Almost entirely self-taught as a singer, Chaliapin began singing in Tbilisi and St Petersburg. He made a name for himself singing both Boris and Valaam from **Modest Mussorgsky**'s (1839–81) *Boris Godunov* (1874). Although best known for singing the Russian repertoire, Chaliapin performed in a wide range of operas, including those by **Gioachino Rossini** (1792–1868) and **Vincenzo Bellini** (1801–35). He possessed a flexible voice that enabled him to take on baritone roles, such as Eugene Onegin, as well as true bass roles like Philip II in **Giuseppe Verdi**'s (1813–1901) *Don Carlos* (1867). Chaliapin was regarded as a great singing actor and constantly demanded perfection in small details of staging, make-up and costume.

Charpentier, Gustave
1860–1956, **FRENCH**

Born in 1860, Charpentier studied the violin at the Lille Conservatory and subsequently entered the Paris Conservatoire where he studied both violin and composition. Having begun composition studies with Hector Pessard, he later studied under Massenet, whose advice contributed to Charpentier's victory in the Prix de Rome in 1887. Part of the prize involved a trip to Rome itself and it was there that he began his best-known opera, *Louise*.

Charpentier was naturally inclined towards the prevailing trend for starkly realistic settings and, although he took advice from friends to tone down the work's rougher edges, it was a success when premiered in 1900 at the Opéra-Comique. Another opera, *Julien*, was completed in 1913 and met with considerable acclaim. After this, however, projects were mooted and sometimes started but never brought to completion.

Louise

by Gustave Charpentier
Composed: 1889–96
Premiered: 1900, Paris
Libretto by the composer or Saint-Pol-Roux

ACT I

From the balcony of her parents' house in Montmartre, Louise can see Julien, a poet. He has written two letters to her father, asking to marry her, although she says she loves her parents too much to elope. Her mother drags her away and they quarrel. After supper her father suggests that they have been too strict, but her mother threatens to walk out if Julien enters the house. Louise slaps her. Her father tells her to forget Julien.

ACT II

Street life in Montmartre awakens. Julien shows his friends where Louise works. She arrives, escorted by her mother. Once her mother has gone, Julien tries to persuade Louise she must not allow her parents to stifle her happiness. Despite her love for her father she agrees to see Julien later. Inside the workshop the seamstresses tease Louise about being in love. Julien and his friends are heard serenading Louise. The seamstresses mock his words. Increasingly agitated, Louise runs out to join Julien.

ACT III

In their garden overlooking the lights of Paris, Louise and Julien declare their love for each other and the city that brought them together. Their neighbours are preparing for a carnival. Louise is crowned 'Muse of Montmartre'. Her mother brings news that her father is ill. She promises Julien that Louise will be allowed to return after a few days.

ACT IV

Her father curses Julien for taking Louise away. He suggests she should remain with her parents, but she declares they will never win her back by denying her freedom. She calls on Paris to help her. He opens the door and tells her to go. She briefly hesitates and then runs out. He calls her back, but she has gone.

Cilea, Francesco
1866–1950, ITALIAN

It was the intention of Francesco Cilea's father that his son should enter the legal profession. It was not to be, however, and under the tutelage of Paolo Serrao, Beniamino Cesi and Giuseppe Martucci at the Naples Conservatory, he quickly made a name for himself. His first opera, *Gina* (1889), was performed during his final year at the conservatory and attracted the attention of the publisher Sonzogno, who commissioned *La tilda* (1892) from him. Another opera, *L'arlesiana* (1897), followed, the premiere of which starred none other than Enrico Caruso. This led to Cilea's greatest success – *Adriana Lecouvreur*. Written to a libretto by Arturo Colautti, the opera is a pleasing mixture of comedy and tragedy with attractive if largely unremarkable music. Particularly noteworthy is Cilea's use of normal, unsung, speech at the end of the third act. The opera's longevity can in part be attributed to its vocally unchallenging title role, which gives ample chance for a prima donna to display her talents. Although a handful more works followed, none met with the same success and Cilea gradually focused his attention on teaching.

Adriana Lecouvreur
by Francesco Cilea
Composed: 1902
Premiered: 1902, Milan
Libretto by Arturo Colautti, after Eugene Scribe and Ernest Legouvé's play *Adrienne Lecouvreur*

ACT I
Backstage at the Comédie-Française, the stage manager Michonnet tries to propose to the actress Adriana Lecouvreur, but she loves Maurizio, who is the Count of Saxony in disguise. She gives Maurizio some violets. An intercepted letter of assignation, believed to be from another actress, is actually with Maurizio's former lover, the Principessa di Bouillon. Her husband plans to surprise them and invites Adriana after Maurizio has broken an earlier assignation.

ACT II
To allay her suspicions, Maurizio gives the violets to the Principessa, who hides when her husband arrives. Adriana is told of Maurizio's identity. He admits that there is another woman in the next room, but their relationship is political, not romantic. He asks her to help the unknown woman to escape. From the few words they exchange in the dark, it is evident that both love Maurizio. As the Principessa escapes, Adriana acquires her bracelet.

ACT III
Maurizio has been arrested on the Principessa's orders, but Adriana has pawned her jewels to release him. The Principessa recognizes Adriana's voice and tells her that Maurizio has been fatally wounded in a duel. He enters, very much alive. The two women snipe at each other. The Principe identifies his wife's bracelet. Adriana recites a speech from Phèdre that makes the Principessa furious.

ACT IV
Four actors and Michonnet, who has redeemed her jewels, try to persuade Adriana to return to the stage. The violets, now withered, arrive in a casket labelled 'from Maurizio'. Believing their love is over, she kisses them and throws them on the fire. She is overjoyed when Maurizio asks her to marry him. Suddenly she is taken ill. The Principessa has had the violets sprinkled with poison. Delirious, Adriana dies.

D'Albert, Eugen
1864–1932, GERMAN

Born in Glasgow, d'Albert's parents were German, with French blood. D'Albert eventually took Swiss nationality but not before he had studied with Arthur Sullivan in London, Hans Richter in Vienna and Liszt in Weimar. D'Albert was a prolific composer and completed some 20 operas of widely differing styles and subjects. His most publicly successful work is *Tiefland* (1903). Written using many of the traits and techniques of the Italian veristic tradition, it is a strong work that was quickly taken up by opera houses across Europe following its premiere in Prague's Neues Deutsches Theater in 1903. The main focus of d'Albert's musical life was a career as a pianist and teacher. Although he composed many other works following *Tiefland*, none was to meet with the same success.

D'Annunzio, Gabriele
1863–1938, FRENCH

D'Annunzio's most famous influence on music was Debussy's elaborate incidental music for his extraordinarily long play *The Martyrdom of Saint Sebastian* (1911). In fact, his connections with music were far wider. He was an extravagant eccentric and continually sought the company of musicians. The French pianist Raoul Pugno and the composer Nadia Boulanger collaborated on a setting of his *La ville morte (La città morta)*, and various Italian composers including Ildebrando Pizzetti (1880–1968) and Gian Francesco Malipiero (1882–1973) set his works for the stage. Most interesting is his *Parisina* (1913), which was intended for Puccini but was instead taken up by Mascagni.

Debussy, Claude
1862–1918, FRENCH

Debussy wrote only one opera that has entered the repertoire, but there were many other compositions without which this masterpiece among masterpieces may never have come into being. His lover, the singer Marie-Blanche Vasnier, some years his elder, had deepened his understanding of literature in his early twenties, and his interest in poetry and painting was at the root of *Pelléas et Mélisande*.

PRE-RAPHAELITE SYMPATHIES

In the late 1880s, Debussy became fascinated by the English Pre-Raphaelites and composed a cantata, *La damoiselle élue*, to a text of Dante Gabriel Rossetti. At the same time the Belgian playwright Maurice Maeterlinck was similarly fascinated by the Pre-Raphaelites, which somehow probed modern life through a return to images from Medieval times: literally 'before the time of Raphael'. Artistically, the two were destined to meet, and Debussy's encounter with Maeterlinck's play, performed at one single matinee, changed his career. He had found the text for which he was searching: one 'which only said things by half, and which left him the room to add'.

A LIFELONG LOVE OF LITERATURE

Before *Pelléas*, Debussy had almost completed a setting of a libretto on the subject of Le Cid entitled *Rodrigue et Chimène*, which has some ravishing moments. He learnt a lot from his struggle with this libretto, which turned out to be too concrete to interest him, but techniques were forged and he came to *Pelléas* more mature. He had also wrestled with a couple of Edgar Allan Poe (1809–49) settings, which would have come to naught were it not for subsequent musicologists, but which confirmed his lifelong engagement with literature. He was never really a composer of absolute music, somehow relying on the 'mysterious correspondences between nature and the imagination', as he put it. A composer with only one real opera: but what an opera!

Pelléas et Mélisande

Pelléas survives because it challenges its interpreters to peel away layers and discover new depths. Its story can be written on the back of a postage stamp: brother marries girl; other brother falls in love with her; brother kills brother; girl dies. But of what? Her wound would not have killed a sparrow, we are told. It is the question marks in Maeterlinck's play – and this is a play not a libretto – which are so striking in this piece. Several performance traditions have emerged. Is it a love story in which we sympathize with the eponymous couple: a love too great for the world? Or are there deeper scenarios? Mélisande the abuse victim – at first by Bluebeard (we learn this from a subsequent Maeterlinck play, *Ariane et Barbe-bleu*) and then by Golaud – has been an angle recently explored. The first approach plays up the beauty of the music, the second its potential for terror. Whichever way it is performed, it is strong and unforgettable. Here is an opera that moves because of what it does not explain rather than what it does. That is the essence of its symbolism, relying for the most part on the contrast between light and darkness.

Pelléas et Mélisande

by Claude Debussy
Composed: 1893–85; 1901–02
Premiered: 1902, Paris
Libretto after Maurice Maeterlinck's play

ACT I

Golaud, grandson of King Arkel of Allemonde, discovers Mélisande weeping by a pool. She will not let him retrieve a crown sparkling in the water. He persuades her to follow him, although they are both lost. Geneviève reads to the near-blind Arkel a letter from her son Golaud to his half-brother Pelléas. Golaud has been married to Mélisande for six months but still knows little about her. He asks Pelléas to display a

light if Arkel will receive Mélisande. Arkel had hoped that an arranged marriage might end years of strife, but he accepts Golaud's choice. Arkel reminds Pelléas that his father is gravely ill. Geneviève tells him to place the light in the turret. Pelléas joins Geneviève and Mélisande in the gardens. A storm is brewing. Mélisande fears for the safety of a departing ship. She does not understand when he tells her he is going away.

ACT II

Pelléas has brought Mélisande to a well. Her long hair falls down to the water. He asks how she met Golaud. As she plays with her wedding ring it falls into the well. Asked what she should tell Golaud, Pelléas replies 'the truth'. Mélisande is unhappy living in the gloomy castle and fears that she will not live long. Golaud notices that the ring is missing. She replies that she must have lost it while looking for shells with his son, Yniold. He tells her to look for it with Pelléas. They go to the grotto together, even though they know the ring is not there. Inside they see three sleeping beggars. Pelléas says they will return one day.

ACT III

Mélisande is combing her hair at a window. Pelléas asks her to lean out and her hair tumbles down. He kisses it and will not let go until Golaud appears, telling them they are like children. Pelléas cannot breathe in the vaults beneath the castle. Golaud warns Pelléas that Mélisande is to be a mother and must avoid excitement. He should see less of her. Golaud is asking Yniold about Mélisande's behaviour with Pelléas. He lifts up Yniold so he can see into her room. Pelléas and Mélisande are standing apart, looking into a light. Yniold is frightened.

ACT IV

Pelléas's father, now recovering, has told him he must leave. Pelléas arranges to meet Mélisande beside the well. Tomorrow he will depart for ever. Arkel hopes that Mélisande's presence will bring new happiness to the castle. Golaud is distraught at Pelléas's departure. Overwhelmed with jealousy, he seizes her hair and forces her to her knees. Yniold is trying to move a boulder to reach his ball. A flock of sheep passes. Pelleas reaches the well. He must look into her eyes and tell her all he has left unsaid. He calls Mélisande into the shadows. The castle gate will soon be locked. They declare their love for each other. She says that she never lies, except to Golaud. They hear the gate being locked and sense Golaud's presence. Pelléas urges her to go, but she clings to him. Golaud strikes Pelléas with his sword.

ACT V

Mélisande has given birth, but she is dying. Arkel brings forward a repentant Golaud, who claims all the blame. Asked about her love for Pelléas, Mélisande insists she is telling the truth when she says they were not guilty. He continues to press her until Arkel intervenes. She is too weak to hold her daughter. The serving-women enter, waiting for her to die. Silently she drifts away. The daughter will take her place in the world.

Recommended Recording:

Pelléas et Mélisande, Orchestre National de France; Bernard Haitink, conductor; Naïve V 4923; Soloists: Anne Sofie von Otter (Mélisande), Hanna Schaer (Geneviève), Wolfgang Holzmair (Pelléas), Laurent Naouri (Golaud), Alain Vernhes (Arkel)

OPERAS

1893–85; 1901–02 Pelléas et Mélisande

TIMELINE

1862	Achille-Claude Debussy born, St Germain-en-Laye
1872	Enters the Paris Conservatoire
1880	Debussy and soprano Marie-Blance Vasnier become lovers
1884	L'enfant prodigue ('The Prodigal Son') wins the Prix de Rome 1885 Goes to Villa Medici, Rome
1888	Visits Bayreuth Festival
1889	Hearing Javanese gamelan music at Paris Exposition has profound effect on him
1891	Becomes friends with Erik Satie
1893	Sees Maurice Maeterlink's play Pelléas et Mélisande; begins work on his opera Pelléas et Mélisande
1894	Préludes à l'aprés-midi d'un faune is not well-received by some critics
1899	Marries Rosalie (Lily) Texier; completes work on his three Nocturnes
1902	Pelléas completed and first performed at the Opéra-Comique
1905	Premiere of La mer; composition of the Images begins
1908	Marries singer Emma Bardac
1910	Diagnosed with cancer; first volume of Préludes published
1913	Ballet Jeux for Diaghilev completed
1915	Final volume of Etudes completed
1918	Dies from cancer, Paris

Delibes, Léo
1836–91, FRENCH

Delibes was initially taught by his mother and uncle before entering the Paris Conservatoire. He worked as an accompanist and chorus master at the Théâtre Lyrique as well as writing occasional music. Delibes soon completed his first full stage work, Deux sous de charbon (1855), which was produced in 1856. His second work, Deux vieilles gardes, which was produced only a few months later, was a great success. Delibes was soon garnering praise for his wit and melodic facility. His natural medium was the operetta, and he developed a style that also lent itself easily to ballet. Delibes' appointment in 1864 as chorus master at the Paris Opéra extended his opportunities and two ballets, Coppélia (1870) and

Sylvia (1876), made his name, as well as remaining in the repertoire today.

Delibes harboured a desire for a grander, more serious work and his admiration for both Meyerbeer and Bizet resulted in his masterwork. *Lakmé* is set in colonial India and follows two lovers whose attempts to be together are thwarted and who die with tragic beauty for each other's love. In its exoticism and careful reserve, *Lakmé* is very much of its time. The strength of the music and the opportunities it affords the prima donna, however, have ensured that it remains a popular work. Following the triumphant premiere of *Lakmé* at the Opéra-Comique in 1883, Delibes was assured of a solid future. However, he suffered from a lack of self-belief and wrote very little in the ensuing years.

Destinn, Emmy
1878–1933, CZECH

Born in Prague as Ema Kittl, Destinn studied with Marie Loewe-Destinn, whose name she adopted out of gratitude. She made her debut at the Hofoper in Berlin with the role of Santuzza from Mascagni's *Cavalleria rusticana*. Her most famous performances are those of Minnie in the premiere of Puccini's *La fanciulla del West* at the Metropolitan Opera in New York and the title role in Richard Strauss' *Salome* in Berlin. Destinn developed a reputation as a femme fatale and her love affairs were always hot gossip. In addition to singing, Destinn also wrote novels, essays and plays. She also composed and a romance was recorded by the Victor record company.

Dvořák, Antonín
1841–1904, CZECH

While Dvořák is best known for his contribution to the symphonic repertoire, opera was a vital part of his musical make-up and he produced 10 stage works during his life. His musical education was

THE 'BELL SONG' AND 'FLOWER DUET'

Léo Delibes' music has been particularly fashionable with transport advertisements. P&O Stena Line used the 'Bell Song' from *Lakmé* (1883) but the most popular has been the 'Flower Duet' from the same opera. Originally used by British Airways in 1998, it later advertised the Ford Galaxy before being re-appropriated by BA.

traditional: at the Prague Organ School he studied harmony, counterpoint, fugue and chorales. On graduating, he joined the Provisional Theatre orchestra as a violist. Over the following nine years, he performed a catholic mix of repertoire from Italy, Germany and France as well as his native land.

Bedřich Smetana (1824–84) had already blazed a trail with. *The Bartered Bride* (1883–86) by the time Dvořák began serious operatic work. Both shared a fascination with the use of characteristic national melodies and Dvořák's early comic operas share many elements with his compatriot. *The Cunning Peasant* (1877), a comic opera written to a libretto by Veselý premiered in 1878, was his first major success and capped an intense period of operatic activity. Dvořák spent much of the 1880s travelling, in particular to England, to oversee performances of his orchestral music. He sustained a steady output of theatrical music but this was cut further by the invitation to direct the National Conservatory of Music of America in New York from 1892. His return to Europe in 1895 coincided with an increased interest in dramatic music, chiefly opera and the symphonic poem. The new operatic fashion for raw, starkly emotional subjects was not for Dvořák, and for his most successful theatre work he took on a folk story by Jaroslav Kvapil. Unlike many operas written at the time, *Rusalka* is not a high-octane drama but rather a bewitching, lyrical love story told at a distance.

Rusalka

by Antonín Dvořák
Composed: 1900
Première: 1901, Prague
Libretto by Jaroslav Kvapil after Friedrich de la Motte Fouqué's Undine

ACT I

Rusalka, a water nymph, has fallen in love with a prince. She longs to leave the water and acquire human form. Vodník, a water spirit, tells her that Ježibaba the witch can grant her every human power except speech. If the prince rejects her, however, she will be forever an outcast between earth and water, and he will be damned. Ježibaba casts the spell. The prince is drawn to the water and sees Rusalka. Although she cannot speak he falls in love.

ACT II

Preparations are made for the wedding. A gamekeeper and a kitchen boy fear that the mysterious girl has bewitched the prince. He has grown tired of Rusalka's silence and timidity and is increasingly interested in the foreign princess, who taunts Rusalka. In despair she calls on Vodník, who urges her to try to win him back. Seeing the prince embrace the foreign princess, she breaks in but is thrust away. Vodník drags Rusalka back to the water and the princess rejects the prince.

ACT III

Even Rusalka's sisters reject her. Ježibaba tells her she can break the spell by killing the prince. The gamekeeper and kitchen boy ask Ježibaba to heal the prince, who has fallen ill. Vodník declares he will have vengeance on mankind and tells the wood

nymphs of Rusalka's fate. The prince comes looking for Rusalka and recognizes where he first saw her. She warns him, although she still loves him, that he would die if he were to kiss her now that she is once more a water spirit. He begs her to take his life away with a kiss. He dies contented in her love and she returns to the waters.

Farrar, Geraldine
1882–1967, **AMERICAN**

Farrar made her debut in *Faust* at the Berlin Königliches Opernhaus. She rapidly acquired a strongly devoted audience who were as enamoured with her looks and stage presence as with her voice. She remained in Berlin until 1906, when she made a successful debut at the Metropolitan Opera in New York. Farrar retired from the operatic stage in 1922 but continued to make silent films and appear in recitals. Her voice was not to everyone's taste. Puccini, during the New York premiere of *Madama Butterfly*, was not the only one to express serious concerns.

Fibich, Zdeněk
1850–1900, **CZECH**

Although little known today, during his lifetime Fibich was fêted as the successor to Smetana and certainly commanded operatic attention equal to Dvořák. He studied initially with his mother in Prague, then in Leipzig, Paris and Mannheim. His early adult life was far from easy, with the death of his wife less than a year after their marriage. He subsequently married his first wife's sister, and earned a good living from operetta and chorus conducting while continuing to compose prolifically. Fibich searched wider than Dvořák and Smetana for his inspiration. His theatrical works draw on subjects as diverse as Greek mythology (*Hippodamia*, 1888–91), Czech mythology (*Šárka*, 1896–97) and writers including Schiller, Lord Byron and Shakespeare. As was the case for most stage composers of the time, the influence of Wagner was unavoidable. Fibich was also indebted to **Carl Maria von Weber** (1786–1826) and Schumann as well as to the folk music of his native country for helping to develop his style.

Forzano, Giovacchino
1884–1970, **ITALIAN**

Librettist Forzano found his métier in writing and was a follower of Arrigo Boito. Forzano also worked with several other leading Italian composers, particularly those representative of *verismo* such as Mascagni and Leoncavallo. Forzano also worked as a stage director, producing Puccini's *Turandot* in 1926.

Garden, Mary
1874–1967, **AMERICAN**

Born in Aberdeen, Scotland, Garden moved to America when she was six. She studied in Chicago and then Paris, where she debuted as Charpentier's *Louise* at the Opéra-Comique. Perhaps her most historically significant role was creating Mélisande in Debussy's *Pelléas et Mélisande* in 1902. It was in this part that she made her American debut at the Chicago Lyric Opera in 1910. She spent 20 years there, as leading soprano. Garden herself was equivocal about her vocal abilities but she was regarded as a consummate actress who possessed great variety in colouration. Harold Schonberg, long-time music critic of the *New York Times*, described her as, 'lively, indomitable, glamorous, witty, imperious, publicity-minded, capricious and a great artist on top of all that'.

Giacosa, Giuseppe
1847–1906, **ITALIAN**

Under Arrigo Boito's influence, Giacosa developed into the leading Italian playwright of the time. His most striking operatic work was made in conjunction with Puccini. Initially brought in by Giulio Ricordi to smooth the troubled relationship between Puccini and Luigi Illica, Giacosa soon became indispensable. It was Giacosa's responsibility to take the detailed scenario worked out by Illica and turn it into refined verse. The three men produced the three best-loved of Puccini's operas: *La bohème*, *Tosca* and *Madama Butterfly*. Giacosa supported himself through teaching until the 1890s when his growing success enabled him to concentrate purely on writing. Even before this, though, he was regarded as a literary heavyweight and for Ricordi to win his services was a significant feat.

Gilbert, William Schwenk
1836–1911, **ENGLISH**

It was Gilbert's dry, satirical wit that first gained him literary attention when, in the early 1860s, he began contributing to the comic journal *Fun*. Thereafter he acquired a name for himself through a succession of caustic plays before being introduced to Arthur Sullivan. The combination of Gilbert's acerbic verse and Sullivan's felicitous music made the pair into national stars. Their often tempestuous relationship lasted for 25 years, during which time they produced many works that remain popular today. Gilbert continued to write after taking official retirement and died, gallantly, rescuing a woman from drowning.

Giordano, Umberto
1867–1948, **ITALIAN**

Having successfully avoided the career of fencing master intended for him by his father, Giordano studied at the Naples Conservatory and entered a one-act opera, *Marina*, in the Sonzogno competition in 1889. This was the year in which Mascagni blew away the competition with *Cavalleria rusticana* and Giordano came a respectable sixth.

Even so, Sonzogno (a music publisher and rival of Ricordi) was sufficiently taken with the work to commission a full opera from its composer. The resulting work was *Mala vita* (1892). Sonzogno's next commission, *Regina Diaz*, was given in Naples in 1894 but failed to capture anybody's imagination. Sonzogno, who had been providing a monthly stipend for Giordano, was beginning to lose patience when another of his composers, Alberto Franchetti, gave up the libretto to Andrea Chénier. Giordano seized on the chance to set this strong, veristic text by Luigi Illica and was rewarded with a triumphant premiere, which propelled him fame. His next opera, *Fedora*, was also a great success and, like its immediate predecessor, has remained in the repertoire. There followed a series of undistinguished works until *La cena delle beffe* ('The Supper of Jests'), which, with its macabre conclusion, made a strong impression. Although not a repertoire piece, many regard it as Giordano's best work and it has enjoyed a number of successful revivals.

Andrea Chénier
by Umberto Giordano
Composed: 1896
Premiered: 1896, Milan
Libretto by Luigi Illica

ACT I
During the early days of the French Revolution, Gérard, a servant, is secretly in love with Maddalena, daughter of the Contessa de Coigny. Among the guests at the contessa's soirée is the poet Andrea Chénier. The other guests are offended by his call for liberty, but Maddalena is intrigued. The soirée is broken up by a mob of peasants led by Gérard, who tears off his livery. The contessa orders them to leave and the dancing begins again.

ACT II
Chénier has become disillusioned by the years of the Terror. He is recognized by Bersi, Maddalena's maid, who joins the crowd following condemned prisoners. Roucher brings him a passport and advises him to leave France, but he is anxious to learn the identity of someone signing herself 'Hope' who wishes to see him tonight. Gérard, now a sans-culotte, still wants Maddalena. She reveals herself to Chénier as 'Hope' and begs for his protection. Gérard tries to abduct Maddalena and is wounded by Chénier. Maddalena escapes with Roucher. Gérard has recognized Chénier but claims he does not know his assailant.

ACT III
Chénier has been arrested. Gérard reflects that he is now a slave to his passion for Maddalena. She comes to Gérard and tells him how her mother died and her home was destroyed. She offers to give herself to Gérard if he will save Chénier. At Chénier's trial, Gérard attempts to withdraw all the charges against him, but he is still condemned to execution.

ACT IV
Chénier is in the St Lazare prison. Gérard brings in Maddalena, who bribes the gaoler to substitute her for another of the prisoners. Gérard leaves them to make a final appeal to Robespierre. They are taken to the guillotine together.

Hofmannsthal, Hugo von
1874–1929, AUSTRIAN

Hofmannsthal was a precocious talent. His first published poem appeared when he was just 16 and he rapidly made the acquaintance of some of the leading literary figures of the day. Most important was a paternalistic relationship with the German poet Stefan George (1868–1933). Hofmannsthal's youthful ability led to a creative crisis in his mid-twenties from which he emerged with a renewed belief in the value of drama. He believed in the reformatory power of writing; this principle lay behind his foundation of the Salzburg Festival. It was with his long relationship with Richard Strauss that Hofmannsthal's contribution to opera was made. An initial approach made by the writer with a scenario for a ballet was rejected, but Strauss suggested a few years later that Hofmannsthal make a libretto from his adaptation of Sophocles' *Electra*. The partnership produced *Der Rosenkavalier*, *Ariadne auf Naxos*, *Die Frau ohne Schatten*, *Die ägyptische Helena* and *Arabella*. Hofmannsthal also collaborated with Edgard Varèse (1885–1965) on *Oedipus und die Sphinx* (1909–13).

Humperdinck, Engelbert
1854–1921, **GERMAN**

Humperdinck showed an aptitude for vocal composition from an early age and, despite the concerns of his family, entered the Cologne Conservatory in 1872. He was a high achiever, winning multiple prizes for his Schumann-influenced compositions. Wagner soon came to dominate the young composer's artistic thoughts and, following a short visit to him, in January 1881 Humperdinck was invited to Bayreuth to help Wagner with preparation for the first production of *Parsifal*.

Wagner's musical ideals were antithetical to Humperdinck's naturally simple and ingenuous style, and they caused a long creative hiatus. This difficulty was compounded by the contemporary vogue for baldly realistic subjects. Humperdinck's natural instincts, however, were largely responsible for the success of his first and most famous opera, *Hänsel und Gretel*. Humperdinck began by writing a handful of songs for his sister based on the Brothers' Grimm fairy-tale. These grew into a small work and finally into the full opera we know today. The work's inventiveness and melodic felicity were largely responsible for its overwhelming popularity. The immediate success of *Hänsel und Gretel* – it was performed in over 72 theatres within a year of being premiered –

encouraged Humperdinck to undertake a second Grimm fairy-tale. *Die sieben Geislein* (1898), though, suffered from a clumsy libretto and music that was ill-fitted to the subject's needs. Several other projects foundered for similar reasons until the success of *Königskinder* (1910), which revealed more fully Humperdinck's admiration for Wagner.

Illica, Luigi
1857–1919, **ITALIAN**

At the beginning of the 1890s, librettist Illica began an association with the Ricordi publishing house that resulted in collaborations with the most prominent Italian opera composers over the next 20 years. Most significant was his work with Puccini. Although they had a tempestuous relationship, it resulted in *Manon Lescaut* and, in collaboration with Giuseppe Giacosa, *La bohème*, *Tosca* and *Madama Butterfly*. Illica's work, though perhaps not of the highest literary order, shows great awareness of theatre and its needs. His ability to shape action and character were invaluable to his collaborators, as was his catholic taste.

Lehár, Franz
1870–1948, **AUSTRO–HUNGARIAN**

Lehár's father worked as a bandmaster as well as composing dances and marches. Lehár himself played in the theatre orchestra at Barmen-Elberfeld before playing in a band for his military service. He left the military having arrived in Vienna, where he took up a position as conductor at the Theater an der Wien. Lehár's youth and early adult life had given him great exposure to lighter music and his inventive, charming and witty music is abundantly present in his first major successes, *Wiener Frauen* (1902) and *Der Rastelbinder* (1902). In 1905, *Die lustige Witwe* ('The Merry Widow') was premiered in Vienna to an extraordinary reception. The work is remarkable for its energy and inventiveness, its subtlety in character portrayal and its imaginative orchestration. The premiere heralded a new dawn for operetta, paving the way for other composers and whetting the public appetite.

Lehár was unwilling to remain static and in his ensuing work, he pushed back the barriers of operetta in terms of both style and subject matter. A vital partnership developed with Richard Tauber during the 1920s, for whom Lehár wrote many of his leading roles. So strong was their association that the particular style of vocal writing used for the tenor became known as the Tauber-Lied. Lehár also spent time writing original film music and making versions of his operettas for film. Perhaps his most satisfying stage work after *Die lustige Witwe* is *Giuditta* (1934) in which the seriousness of the subject and its treatment take operetta very close to opera. Lehár marked himself apart from his contemporaries by completing his own orchestrations, often showing his interest in Puccini and Strauss as well as the French Impressionists.

Die lustige Witwe
('The Merry Widow')

by Franz Lehár
Composed: 1905
Premiered: 1905, Vienna
Libretto by Victor Léon and Leo Stein, after Henri Meilhac's *L'attaché d'ambassade*

ACT I

Baron Zeta, the Pontevedrin ambassador in Paris, must ensure that only a Pontevedrin marries Hanna Glawari, a rich, glamorous widow. All the French guests swoon over her at an embassy reception. Zeta thinks that his attaché, Count Danilo Danilowitsch, would be a suitable match. He is summoned from his usual haunt, Maxim's. Hanna wakes him. They used to be lovers, until his family interfered. Now he
cannot declare his love without appearing to be just another person after her money. Valencienne, Zeta's wife, suggests Camille de Rosillon, her own excessively ardent admirer, as Hanna's dance partner. Hanna offers the dance to Danilo, who scandalizes everyone by putting it up for sale. The price is too high. Hanna and Danilo are left to dance together.

ACT II

Hanna entertains her guests. She accuses Danilo of avoiding her. Camille is still pursuing Valencienne. Zeta is told that Camille is in the summerhouse with an unknown lady. Hoping to find evidence to make a marriage with Hanna impossible, he is shocked to see Valencienne through the keyhole. Camille comes out with Hanna and declares his love to her. Danilo tells the tale of a prince who kept silent and so lost his princess. He leaves to forget everything at Maxim's.

ACT III

Hanna's house has been transformed into Maxim's. Valencienne performs with a troupe of grisettes. Hanna explains to Danilo that she was in the summerhouse only to protect a married woman's honour. They can now declare their love. Valencienne's fan is found in the summerhouse, but the words 'I am a respectable wife' written on it are enough to calm Zeta.

Leoncavallo, Ruggero
1857–1919, ITALIAN

Leoncavallo was born and studied in Naples. His first opera, *Chatterton* (1876), written to a libretto by himself, did not initially procure any performances and, in spite of encouragement from his family, Leoncavallo did not appear to be going far in the world of opera. However, with the support of the baritone Victor Maurel he received a commission from the leading Italian publisher of the time, Giulio Ricordi. The project Leoncavallo embarked on was an ambitious trilogy, intended as the Italian equivalent to Wagner's Ring cycle. His work became increasingly erratic and it was never completed.

Leoncavallo earned his keep mostly through writing (it is possible that he was a co-author of the libretto to Puccini's *Manon Lescaut*), and it was not until the sensational premiere of Mascagni's *Cavalleria rusticana* in 1890 that Leoncavallo found a true sense of direction. With an instinct for a marketable idea, Leoncavallo was swift to present the publisher Sonzogno with an outline for a powerful story of jealously obsessive love, similar in broad outline and ethos to Mascagni's work. The resulting one-act opera *Pagliacci*, written again to his own libretto, was a smash hit. Its fast pace and robust music ensure that the audience is pulled right into the drama. Like Mascagni, Leoncavallo was unable to repeat the triumph of *Pagliacci*. His work focused increasingly on the lighter side but he suffered from his unwillingness or inability to develop with the times.

Pagliacci ('The Players')
by Ruggero Leoncavallo
Composed: 1892
Premiered: 1892, Milan
Libretto by the composer, based on a newspaper crime report

PROLOGUE
Tonio addresses the audience. The author has sent him to explain that they are to see real people and real passions.

ACT I
A troupe of four travelling players arrives in a Calabrian village. They are led by Canio, with his wife Nedda, Tonio and Beppe. The crowd greets them enthusiastically. Canio promises a splendid entertainment at 11 o'clock. Canio and Beppe accept the offer of a drink at the tavern. Tonio says he will stay to

groom the donkey. Canio reacts to a villager's joke by saying that the stage and real life are different. If Nedda were to cheat on him he would not react as his stage character Pagliaccio does. Nedda fears Canio's anger. She envies the freedom of the birds. Tonio is watching her. He tries to explain that he has fallen under her spell. She laughs at him. As he advances she strikes him with a whip. He leaves, threatening revenge.

Nedda's lover, Silvio, urges her to elope with him at midnight. His increasing passion breaks down her defences until she admits she loves him. Tonio has returned. She declares that she gives herself wholly to Silvio. As they kiss passionately and Silvio leaves, Tonio brings on Canio to watch. Canio demands to know her lover's name and threatens her with a knife. Beppe rushes on and seizes the knife. It is time to get dressed for the performance. Canio tells himself he has to become Pagliaccio and make the audience laugh, even if his heart is breaking.

ACT II
The villagers are fighting for the best places beside the stage. Nedda sees Silvio arrive. At last the audience is quiet. Nedda, dressed as Columbine, hears Harlequin (Beppe) serenading her. She rejects the attentions of the servant Taddeo (Tonio). Harlequin throws him out and gives Columbine a drug to make Pagliaccio sleep so they can elope. Harlequin escapes as Pagliaccio enters. As Nedda tries to keep the play on course, Canio is unable to separate the play from real life. The crowd cheers his acting, but he is now out of control, demanding her lover's name or her life. She refuses to tell him and Canio stabs her. She calls for Silvio, who rushes to the stage and is also killed. Canio announces that 'the comedy is over'.

Maeterlinck, Maurice
1862–1949, BELGIAN
Maeterlinck is best known for his play *Pelléas et Mélisande* set verbatim but with

cuts by Debussy. It has become one of the pinnacles of French opera. Maeterlinck was one of the main founders of symbolist theatre. Thoroughly Belgian in his dark mysticism, he took Paris by storm in the early 1890s and was suddenly proclaimed the 'Belgian Shakespeare' after the single matinee of *Pelléas* in Paris. An admirer of the English Pre-Raphaelites, his symbolism operates at all levels: in the structure of the early plays, in their development and in their local symbols. Much of it is Christian: doves, rings, water etc. Some of it is Poeian: stagnant water, clocks chiming. Other operas were also based on his plays, most notably Paul Dukas' *Ariane et Barbe-bleu*, the very play in which we learn that Mélisande was once a wife of Bluebeard.

Mascagni, Pietro

1863–1945, **ITALIAN**

Mascagni was a precocious talent and surprised nobody by disobeying his father's wishes and pursuing musical studies at the Milan Conservatory. There he shared a room with Puccini, to whom he would remain close throughout his life, but he was not inclined to study and soon left to tour Italy as a conductor with various companies. He settled in Cerignola, Apulia, in 1886. He began work on a number of projects but abandoned them all to enter the Sonzogno competition in 1888. The work entered was *Cavalleria rusticana*. Not only did it win the competition, but within a few months of its premiere at the Teatro Costanzi in Rome it had been heard in almost every major European city. In setting the work in a scene familiar to all Italians rather than the fashionable orient, and in creating characters distinguished by their lack of material wealth in comparison to their powerful emotional states, Mascagni established a precedent that was to carry Italian opera to new heights. *Cavalleria rusticana*'s prime virtues are its strong

SOUNDS FAMILIAR

INTERMEZZO:
CAVALLERIA RUSTICANA

Mascagni's *Cavalleria rusticana* proved particularly popular in films about American-Italians. The *intermezzo* is used to great effect in Martin Scorsese's *Raging Bull* and the prelude is used in Francis Ford Coppola's *Godfather III*.

melodic vitality and its fluid dramatic and musical canvas that enables the raw and often violent emotions of its protagonists to be laid bare.

Mascagni, in spite of his wide-ranging skills, never managed to repeat the success of *Cavalleria rusticana*. He lacked the innovative instinct of his Milan classmate Puccini and was unwilling to grasp the radical musical transformations taking place in his later life. The flicker of fame was momentarily fanned during the Fascist regime but Mascagni ultimately died a quiet death in 1945.

Cavalleria rusticana ('Rustic Chivalry')

by Pietro Mascagni
Composed: 1888
Premiered: 1890, Rome
Libretto by Giovanni Targioni-Tozzetti and Guido Menasci after Giovanni Verga's play

Early on Easter Day, Turiddu is heard offstage serenading Lola. The villagers start arriving for church. Santuzza stops Mamma Lucia, Turiddu's mother, and asks where she may find him. He is supposed to have gone to another village to buy wine, but Santuzza has heard that he is still here. Alfio enters, extolling his life as a carter and his faithful wife Lola. Earlier that morning he had seen Turiddu near his house. The villagers are heard singing in church, but Santuzza, believing herself to be excommunicated, cannot enter it and leads the Easter hymn from outside. She reminds Mamma Lucia that Turiddu had been betrothed to Lola before he left for military service, but in his absence she had married Alfio. He had turned instead to Santuzza. Lola has now lured him back, leaving Santuzza pregnant and alone. She asks Mamma Lucia to pray for her in church. Santuzza confronts Turiddu and tells him Alfio has seen him. As he tries to get away, she demands that he confesses he loves Lola. She will love and forgive him, even if he beats her. Lola enters and teases Santuzza that she is hearing Mass in the square. Santuzza replies that only those who have not sinned may enter the church. Lola goes inside. Turiddu tears into Santuzza, accusing her of spying on him, and follows Lola. Santuzza tells Alfio that Lola is betraying him with Turiddu. He swears to have vengeance that day.

The villagers leave church after Mass. Lola intends to go home to see Alfio, but Turiddu urges her to stay. Some villagers join Turiddu in a drinking song. Alfio refuses to join him in a toast. Lola leaves, worried by what is to come. Following tradition, Turiddu and Alfio embrace. In a gross insult, Turiddu bites Alfio's right ear. Turiddu knows he is in the wrong, but if he were to let Alfio kill him Santuzza would be left alone. It is his duty to kill Alfio, who leaves to prepare for the coming fight. Turiddu asks Mamma Lucia to bless him, as she did when he left to be a soldier, and to look after Santuzza as her own if he does not return. He rushes off. Soon a voice screams that Turiddu has been killed.

Massenet, Jules
1842–1912, FRENCH

The son of a businessman, Jules Massenet had a musical mother and was admitted to the Paris Conservatoire at the age of 11. He had a prolific career with varying degrees of success, but above all he became reputed for his orientalist excursions,

his brilliant musical projection of the female character, and the ability to write supremely curvaceous melodies.

EARLY YEARS OF TOIL

The family moved to Chambéry, much to Massenet's chagrin: having tried to run away once, he was allowed to return to the capital with an older sister. Here he earned his keep as a pianist and percussionist in theatre orchestras, and at the age of 18 began to study composition and harmony at the Verismo. Most important among his teachers was **Ambroise Thomas** (1811–96) whose success with *Mignon* (1866) and *Hamlet* (1868) clearly influenced Massenet, not least in their use of the saxophone. In 1863 he won the Prix de Rome at the second attempt and had some success with the oratorios *Marie-Magdeleine* (1873) and *Eve* (1875). It was not until his triumph with *Le roi de Lahore* that he gained a foothold in the opera house, in this case the prestigious Paris Opéra itself. Massenet never looked back: operas poured out until the end of his life, some successful, others less so.

SUCCESS AT LAST

In 1878, Ambroise Thomas secured him a professorship of composition at the Conservatoire, a post whose duties he diligently fulfilled for 18 years. *Le roi de Lahore* was soon to be withdrawn from the repertoire of the Opéra, but already the composer had contacts elsewhere. Maybe something of his father's business acumen had rubbed off on him; certainly Massenet became one of the richest musicians of his time. He was courted by the opera-house in Brussels as well as by the Opéra-Comique in Paris where his first great success centred on a female character was given in 1884. *Manon* was based, like Puccini's *Manon Lescaut*, on the novel by Abbé Prévost. In the same year, *Hérodiade* was given a Paris airing and he had another commission in hand for the Opéra, this time for an epic whose eponymous hero Le Cid was the teenage warrior destined to murder his lover's father. It was a subject of an opera already attempted by **Georges Bizet** (1838–75), but curtailed by his untimely death. Certainly Massenet's career might have been different had Bizet lived on.

A PERIOD OF DOUBT

Massenet met the Californian soprano Sybil Sanderson in 1887 and promptly revised *Manon* and wrote the title role in *Esclarmonde* for her. The early 1890s produced only failures and unfinished works, but his next durable success was to be premiered in Vienna in 1892: *Werther*, a setting of a libretto based on Goethe. This has become one of his most popular works and was quickly followed by the oriental *Thaïs*, whose 'Meditation' has become a party-piece for violinists. *La Navarraise* was a realist score including cannon effects that had considerable success in London.

AN UNCERTAIN REPUTATION

The rest of his operas require reassessment. It is hard to label them successes or failures, largely because they have been rarely revived and the composer himself, and his works, insufficiently studied. The biennial Massenet festival at his home town of Saint-Etienne has courageously staged his lesser-known works to great effect. *Sapho*, for example, given in 2003, has considerable strengths and adds to his reputation as a psychoanalyst of the disturbed female, while managing to grip his audience. *Chérubin*, *Don Quichotte* and *Cendrillon* have again found favour with recording companies and major opera houses alike. Massenet's reputation after the war was at an all-time low, but it has risen dramatically: no longer can that awful jibe be aimed at him: that he was merely 'la fille de Gounod'.

Manon

Manon and *Werther* have become Massenet's most frequently performed operas, but several others are gaining ground, among them *Hérodiade*, *Thaïs*, *Sapho*, *Cendrillon*, *Grisélidis*, *Chérubin* and *Don Quichotte*, all recently revived. Both *Manon* and *Werther* – and the other operas as well – are about relationships. The tale of *Manon* explores a theme that fascinated Massenet: the conflict between religion and passion. The opera culminates in a scene in the church of Saint-Sulpice in Paris. Both Manon, at the beginning of the opera, and Des Grieux, who fell in love with her and provided her with an escape route from the convent, at times turn to the church. But physical love, it seems, is more powerful than the love of God. It is in the church that the lovers reunite. A gambling episode makes the opera, resulting in terrible consequences for Manon, the female victim whom opera lovers in the late nineteenth century seemed to adore. Lumps in the throat are legion as we see her preparing for deportation to the colonies, musically heightened by the device of recalling earlier times. Massenet intensifies the moment by having Manon lose her singing voice: she speaks the words above highly emotional music from the orchestra.

Manon

by Jules Massenet
Composed: 1882–83; rev. 1884
Premiered: 1884, Paris
Libretto by Henri Meilhac and Philippe Gille after Abbé Prévost's novel

ACT I

Guillot, an elderly roué, and Brétigny, a tax collector, are entertaining three actresses at an inn in Amiens. Lescaut meets his cousin Manon, so dizzy with excitement after her coach journey that she almost forgets she is on her way to a convent. Guillot propositions her but she laughs at him. He tries again, telling her that his carriage is waiting. Lescaut reminds her of their family honour. She sees the elegantly dressed actresses and reflects on how marvellous endless pleasure would be. The Chevalier Des Grieux sees Manon and is immediately smitten. She explains that she is being sent to the convent because she is considered too fond of pleasure. He declares he would do anything to stop her. Seeing Guillot's carriage, she suggests running off to Paris together. Lescaut returns with Guillot to find they have gone.

ACT II

In their Paris apartment, Manon reads aloud the letter Des Grieux has written asking his father's permission to marry. He is curious about some flowers that she claims were thrown through the window. The maid announces Lescaut and, she whispers, the tax collector who loves her. Lescaut angrily demands to know if Des Grieux plans to marry Manon and is shown the letter. Brétigny warns Manon of a plan to abduct Des Grieux on his father's orders. It would be to her advantage to say nothing. Left alone, Manon hesitates. She still loves Des Grieux but yearns for luxuries. She bids farewell to their humble surroundings. He describes his dream of their future rural life together. There is a knock, which she begs him not to answer. He is abducted.

ACT III

Amid the hubbub on the Cours-la-Reine the three actresses snub Guillot, who has heard that Manon's extravagances might be too much for Brétigny. Manon, revelling in her youth and beauty, enters with Brétigny. The Count Des Grieux, the Chevalier's father, tells Brétigny that his son is to take holy orders. Brétigny points out Manon. She has overheard some of this conversation but is unaware of the count's identity. She asks after Des Grieux and is told that he has forgotten her. Guillot returns with the opera ballet to please Manon. During the

performance she calls for her carriage to take her to Des Grieux at St-Sulpice. In the church, the count tells his son it is not too late to marry. Des Grieux cannot be dissuaded and the count agrees to give him his inheritance. Des Grieux tries to banish his memories. Manon enters and prays for God's mercy. Des Grieux orders her to go, but she begs for forgiveness, calling on him to remember their former love. Her presence is too strong for him to resist.

ACT IV

Manon has brought Des Grieux to the gaming tables at the Hôtel de Transylvanie to recover his dwindling inheritance. Challenged by Guillot, he hits a winning streak. The actresses agree with Manon that all they want is pleasure and money. Lescaut loses everything. Guillot accuses Des Grieux and Manon of cheating and they are arrested. The count appears to announce that he will soon be freed, but Manon is taken away.

ACT V

Manon has been sent for deportation from Le Havre. Lescaut bribes a guard to let her see Des Grieux. Dying, she begs his forgiveness for destroying their love. He declares that heaven has also forgiven her. As she slips away she recalls their happy days together. With a final kiss she dies in his arms.

Werther

In comparison to Manon, Werther is the romantic dreamer, totally lost as he sees his beloved Charlotte marry another man. But his music – a seductive, rocking melody where he and Charlotte at once express the strength of their love and the necessity to deny it in the face of social pressure – etches itself on the audience's heart. Here is the core of the opera, and the reason for its immortality. All the elements of unfulfilled love in the context of a loveless but socially acceptable marriage are explored, with Werther's jealousy of the marriage bed and Charlotte's tearful re-reading of his youthful love-letters. The setting of all this at Christmas brilliantly intensifies the emotional pitch, as does Massenet's use of the saxophone, one of many ways in which he knows how to wring the heartstrings to maximum effect. Another is the way in which the scene with the dying Werther is framed, having committed suicide. It is Christmas day, turning full circle in the opera that began with the rehearsal of the same Christmas carol with which the opera ends: children's voices are heard as he dies. This is crisis at Christmas. By now, Massenet had learnt to manipulate all the stock-in-trades to maximum effect, and was particularly brilliant at the heart-rending aria.

Werther

by Jules Massenet
Composed: 1885–87
Premiered: 1892, Vienna
Libretto by Edouard Blau, Paul Milliet and Georges Hartmann, after Goethe's novel *Die Leiden des jungen Werthers*

ACT I

Le Bailli is rehearsing a carol in his garden with his six younger children. His friends Johann and Schmidt tease him that it is July. Nearly everyone, including Werther, a somewhat melancholy young poet, is going to a dance at Wetzlar. Sophie, Le Bailli's second daughter, will be staying at home, but the eldest, Charlotte, is getting ready. Werther appears, hymning the simple joys of nature, and listens to the carol. Charlotte gives the children their tea. Le Bailli introduces Werther to Charlotte, who has looked after the household since his wife died. Werther is enchanted as Charlotte kisses the children goodbye. They leave for the dance. Albert, Charlotte's fiancé, returns unexpectedly after six months away and asks Sophie not to tell anyone until the morning. Later Charlotte returns with Werther. While the poet rhapsodizes, Charlotte insists that he

knows nothing about her. She greatly misses her mother and hopes she has kept her promise to look after the others. He declares his love for her. Le Bailli tells them of Albert's return. Under Werther's spell she had almost forgotten she had promised her mother to marry him. Werther tells her to keep the promise, even if it means his death.

ACT II

It is a Sunday afternoon in September in Wetzlar. Johann and Schmidt are drinking. Charlotte and Albert are now married, and he asks if she has any regrets. Werther watches as she reassures Albert and they enter the church. Furiously he declares that Charlotte should have been his. Albert tries to console him, since he understands Werther may have loved Charlotte before her marriage. Sophie bursts in, brightly looking forward to dancing at a party. Albert quietly suggests that Werther might consider Sophie. She asks Werther for the first minuet and goes off with Albert. Werther knows he should leave, but seeing Charlotte again brings everything back. She asks whether no other woman is worthy of his love, since she belongs to Albert. He should go away for some time, say until Christmas. Werther's thoughts turn to suicide. He leaves Sophie in tears when he bids her farewell, for ever. From Charlotte's reaction Albert knows Werther still loves her.

ACT III

Charlotte can think only of Werther and cannot destroy his letters, the last of which says she should weep if she does not hear from him by Christmas. It is Christmas Eve. Sophie comes to cheer her up and invite her to join Le Bailli and the children. Charlotte prays for strength to do her duty. Werther appears, claiming that until today he would rather have died than return, but now he cannot stay away. She points out that the room is just as it was before. Even the pistols, however, remind him of his love for her; she must admit that she loves him. She struggles to control herself and breaks away from his arms, bidding him farewell for the last time. He leaves in search of death. Albert watches her agitated reaction to a letter from Werther asking to borrow his pistols, since he is leaving on a lengthy journey. He orders her to give the pistols to the servant herself, but when Albert has gone she rushes off, praying to reach Werther in time.

ACT IV

Werther has shot himself. Charlotte finds him dying. She declares her love and they kiss for the first time. Hearing the children singing, he thinks they are angels. He dies, hoping that one woman at least will remember his grave.

OPERAS

1865	Esmeralda
1866	La coupe du roi de Thulé
1867	La Grand' tante
1872	Don César de Bazan
1874	L'adorable bel'-boul'
1877	Le roi de Lahore
1878–81	Hérodiade (rev. 1883)
1882–83	Manon (rev. 1884)
1884–85	Le Cid
1889	Esclarmonde
1891	Le Mage
1880–90; 1910–11	Amadis
1891	Werther
1894	Thaïs (rev. 1897); Le Portrait de Manon; La Navarraise; Grisélidis (rev. 1898)
1899	Cendrillon
1897	Sapho; rev. 1909
1902	Le jongleur de Notre-Dame; Roma (rev. 1909)
1905	Chérubin
1906	Ariane
1907	Thérèse
1908–09	Don Quichotte
1909	Bacchus
1912	Roma
1913	Panurge
1914	Cléopâtre

TIMELINE

1842	Jules Massenet born, St Étienne, France
1848	Massenet family moves to Paris
1853	Enters the Paris Conservatoire
1859	Wins first prize for piano
1863	Cantata David Rizzio wins Prix de Rome
1863	Moves to Rome where he meets Franz Liszt
1866	Returns to Paris; composes La Grand' tante;
	marries Louise-Constance de Gressy
1869	Joins the Paris Conservatoire
1871	Completes Scènes pittoresques for orchestra; founds Société Nationale de Musique with Saint-Saëns
1872	Begins work on Le roi de Lahore
1875	First performance of the Scènes dramatiques at the Paris Conservatoire
1877	Premiere of Le roi de Lahore
1878	Becomes professor of composition at the Paris Conservatoire; work begins on Hérodiade
1884	Manon has its premiere at the Opéra-Comique
1885	Works on Le Cid and Werther
1887	Meets soprano Sybil Sanderson
1889	Meets Tchaikovsky in Paris
1892	Composes his first ballet Le Carillon; first performance of Werther in Paris
1894	Premiere of Thaïs
1908	100th performance of Le jongleur de Notre-Dame
1910	First performance of Don Quichotte is a triumph
1912	Massenet dies in Paris

Maurel, Victor
1848–1923, FRENCH

Maurel studied in Paris and made his debut in Marseilles in Rossini's *Guillaume Tell* in 1867. He appeared in Paris shortly afterwards and steadily expanded his international career by appearing in Cairo, Venice and St Petersburg. Maurel was much admired by Verdi, who chose him to create the first Iago in 1887 and the first Falstaff in 1893. Maurel was also instrumental in the career of Ruggero Leoncavallo, introducing the young composer to the publisher Ricordi. He created the role of Tonio for Leoncavallo's *Pagliacci* in 1892. Maurel also worked as a director, teacher and designer.

Mayr, Richard
1877–1935, AUSTRIAN

Mayr was persuaded to consider singing by Mahler. He studied in Vienna before making his debut in Bayreuth. Immediately afterwards, Mahler engaged him to sing at the Vienna Hofoper, where he worked for over 30 years. He was admired by Strauss, who wanted him to take on the creation of Baron Ochs in *Der*

Rosenkavalier. In spite of his inability to undertake the premiere, his performance in the role a few months later proved how well suited he was for the part. Mayr was able to take on a wide range of roles, from Wotan to Figaro, and he was admired for his spontaneity. Mayr possessed a full, rich voice and was able to perform with great virtuosity.

Melba, Nellie
1861–1931, **AUSTRALIAN**

Melba made her debut in Brussels in 1887 at the Théâtre de la Monnaie and the following season sang at Covent Garden and the Paris Opéra. She sang Lucia at the Metropolitan Opera in New York in 1893, which began an intermittent relationship that lasted until 1910. Her musical mainstay, however, was Covent Garden. Melba was admired particularly for her consistent beauty of tone in all registers of her voice and for her virtuosity. It is said that two dishes are named after her: peach Melba, created for a party in her honour at the Savoy in London in 1892, and Melba toast, a particularly thin, dry toast she requested when ill in 1897.

Muzio, Claudia
1889–1936, **ITALIAN**

The daughter of a stage director and a chorus member, soprano Muzio debuted in Arezzo in 1910 before making a number of appearances in Turin. She appeared at La Scala, Milan in 1913 and then Covent Garden in 1914. It is often said of Muzio that she had very little private life, choosing instead to devote herself completely to her art. Contemporary reports speak of her impressive presence, most of all in tragic roles. Although she was particularly associated with the veristic repertoire, she sang with a subtle intensity. She was able to move rapidly between colours, making her ideally suited for Verdi and Puccini.

Prévost, Abbé
1697–1763, **FRENCH**

Prévost has a place in operatic history quite simply because two major nineteenth-century composers made lasting operas out of his work: Massenet's *Manon* and Puccini's *Manon Lescaut* both derive from Prévost's most famous novel, *L'histoire du Chevalier des Grieux et de Manon Lescaut*. Its exploration of the tribulations of a passionate woman made ideal material for operatic exploration. Puccini's and Massenet's settings make an interesting contrast, both in the slant of their libretti and in the emphasis of their musical responses. In fact, operatic interest in Prévost's work had started far earlier. Daniel Auber had composed a *Manon Lescaut* in 1856 and the English composer Michael Balfe's opera *Maid of Artois* (1836), written for Maria Malibran, was based on the same text. More recently, Hans Werner Henze's *Boulevard Solitude* of 1952 used Prévost as its source.

Puccini, Giacomo
1858–1924, **ITALIAN**

Puccini's unerring instinct for strong melody and evocative harmony, coupled with his ability to bring to life passionate and sensual relationships, has made him one of the most popular of opera composers. Puccini brought Italian opera into the twentieth century, synthesizing music and drama in a symphonic idiom, but retaining the voice as the focal point.

EARLY LIFE IN LUCCA

Puccini was born on 22 December 1858 in Lucca, in the north-west of Italy. He was the fifth generation of a family of composers. Michele Puccini, Giacomo's father, was held in such esteem that Pacini and Mercadante, two of Italy's leading composers, spoke at his funeral. Puccini studied music first with his uncle in Lucca and then, with support from both a bachelor relation and a royal bursary from Queen Margherita, at the conservatory in Milan. There, he was taught by Antonio Bazzini and Amilcare Ponchielli, who regarded him as an able, though not particularly diligent, student. In 1883 Puccini entered a competition run by the publishing firm Sonzogno. *Le villi* ('The Willis'), written to a libretto by Ferdinando Fontana, was neither selected nor deemed worthy of mention – officially due to its near-illegibility. Fontana, however, was not prepared to give up on the work and raised funds for a performance at the Teatro dal Verme.

The production was a great success and encouraged Giulio Ricordi, the third generation of the famous publishing dynasty, to sign up the young composer. Puccini's pleasure at this accomplishment was shattered by the death of his mother in July. Albina had been an untiring support to her son and he felt her loss keenly.

THE FIGHT FOR FAME AND FORTUNE

Ricordi was quick to commission a new work from Puccini and Fontana, but they did not respond with such alacrity. Fontana's work on the libretto faltered and Puccini had responsibilities towards his family and had begun an affair with a married woman, Elvira Gemignani. It was not until April 1889 that *Edgar* was premiered at La Scala – and it was a disaster.

The essential problem of *Edgar* was that Puccini's dramatic and musical nature was out of sympathy with Fontana's text. There seemed to be no easy solution, however, and the genesis of Puccini's next work, *Manon Lescaut*, was tortuous. When the opera finally reached completion it was a sensation, catapulting Puccini to fame and fortune after its 1893 premiere. The doubts that had persisted about his future were now completely resolved and he became a man of comfort and leisure, disinclined to work except when it completely suited him. Ricordi had several potential subjects

lined up for the new toast of Italy: a scenario along the lines of *Cavalleria rusticana* with Giovanni Verga and several ideas with Luigi Illica, including the germs of *Tosca*. Illica had been involved in *Manon Lescaut*, but his relationship with Puccini was not an easy one.

MATURITY AND MASTERY

Ricordi showed his perspicacity by engaging Giuseppe Giacosa as co-librettist. A law graduate, he had come to be seen as Italy's pre-eminent playwright and his presence smoothed the way between Puccini and Illica. The results of this collaboration were Puccini's most cherished operas: *La bohème* ('The Bohemian Life'), *Tosca* and *Madama Butterfly*. With Giacosa's death in 1906, Puccini's work – which was never fast at the best of times – foundered. A subject was eventually found and *La fanciulla del West* was premiered at the Metropolitan Opera in New York in 1910. In 1912, Puccini was devastated by the death of Giulio Ricordi. Ricordi's son, Tito, took over the publishing firm, but Puccini never felt able to trust him as he done his father. This uneasy relationship led to him accepting a commission from the Vienna Karltheater for the operetta *La rondine*.

AN UNFINISHED MASTERPIECE

Puccini's mastery was now such that he searched for a greater challenge. In *Il trittico* ('The Triptych') he gave himself the problem of creating a coherent evening from three separate operas: *Il tabarro* ('The Cloak'), *Suor Angelica* ('Sister Angelica') and *Gianni Schicchi*. In 1920, Puccini, who by now was in his sixties, began what was to be his final opera, *Turandot*. It is a work that combines all of his great traits: synthesis of drama with music, a symphonic view of the music and powerful flesh-and-blood characters. The great tragedy is that he never completed the work. Despite apparently successful treatment for cancer of the throat, Puccini died of a heart attack on 29 November 1924, leaving the finale incomplete. Several completions exist, most recently that of **Luciano Berio** (b. 1925), but we will always be left wondering what might have been.

Manon Lescaut

With *Manon Lescaut*, Puccini took his place at the head of the Italian operatic table. Ricordi worked hard to persuade Puccini of the dangers inherent in setting a story that had already received successful treatment by Massenet, but the young composer was not to be swayed. Puccini's determination proved well-founded, for the opera received an ecstatic reception after its premiere in the Teatro Regio, Turin on 1 February 1893. Although it remains an unsatisfactory work in many ways, the level of musical invention is extremely high, betraying in particular Puccini's strong interest in Wagner.

Manon Lescaut

by Giacomo Puccini
Composed: 1890–92
Premiered: 1893, Turin
Libretto by Domenico Oliva and Luigi Illica, after Abbé Prévost's novel

ACT I

Townspeople and students are gathered outside an inn in Amiens. The Chevalier des Grieux addresses some girls with a mocking serenade. A coach arrives bearing the wealthy, elderly, Geronte, and Lescaut and his sister Manon. Geronte has designs upon Manon and Lescaut sees the advantage in helping him. Left alone, Manon tells Des Grieux that she is on her way to a convent. He reflects on her beauty. Edmondo, a student, warns Des Grieux that Geronte plans to abduct Manon. Des Grieux persuades her to leave for Paris with him in the carriage. Finding them gone, Lescaut observes that it will not be long before Des Grieux's money runs out and she is back with Geronte.

ACT II

Manon is now Geronte's mistress. Despite the luxury that surrounds her she is nostalgic for the humble lodgings she shared with Des Grieux. Lescaut tells her that Des Grieux has turned to gambling to be able to support her again. Geronte arrives with his cronies and watches as a dancing master teaches her the minuet. Lescaut goes to fetch Des Grieux. When everyone has gone Des Grieux enters. He reproaches her for deserting him, but soon he is overcome by her beauty once more. Geronte discovers them together and threatens that they will meet again. Lescaut urges them to escape, but Manon is reluctant to abandon all her jewels and starts gathering them up. Des Grieux tells her that her love of luxury can only lead to unhappiness. It is too late. Geronte enters with the guards and she is arrested for theft.

ACT III

Manon has been taken to Le Havre for deportation to Louisiana. Lescaut plans to bribe a guard to help her escape. Des Grieux stands below her window at the barracks and warns her, but Lescaut's plan fails. Manon is taken with the prostitutes to the ship. Des Grieux pleads with the captain to be allowed to go with her.

ACT IV

Manon and Des Grieux are escaping across a vast plain near New Orleans, but she is exhausted and begs him to go so she can die alone. He leaves to find shelter, but when he returns she is dying.

Recommended Recording:
Manon Lescaut, New York Metropolitan Opera Chorus/New York Metropolitan Opera Orchestra; James Levine, conductor; Decca 4402002; Soloists: Mirella Freni (Manon Lescaut), Luciano Pavarotti (Il Cavaliere des Grieux), Dwayne Croft (Lescaut), Giuseppe Taddei (Geronte di Ravoir), Ramón Vargas (Edmondo), Cecilia Bartoli (Un Musico)

La bohème

Puccini's first work following the overwhelming triumph of *Manon Lescaut* was immediately beset by problems. Leoncavallo had already begun preparations on the same scenario and, on hearing of Puccini's choice of subject, publicly berated his rival and friend and claimed priority over the project. Puccini responded calmly by declaring that both composers should go to work and allow the public to be the final arbiters.

In dealing with characters from the lower social strata and in its attempts to portray the drama in as realistic a manner as possible, the opera belongs in part to the so-called *verismo* tradition that began with Mascagni's *Cavalleria rusticana*. Puccini's use of artisans enables him to bridge the gap smoothly between the stark hardship of the characters' lives and the heightened emotions of their relationships. His music moves seamlessly from the conversational – even including unpitched spoken interventions – to the soaringly melodic. *La bohème* is probably Puccini's most popular opera. Its blend of passion, tragedy and humour, tied together with a colourful, sensual score, is supremely alluring. The opera rarely fails to draw the listener entirely into its world.

La bohème
('The Bohemian Life')

by Giacomo Puccini
Composed: 1894–95
Premiered: 1896, Turin
Libretto by Giuseppe Giacosa and Luigi Illica, after Henry Murger's novel *Scènes de la vie de bohème*

ACT I

Marcello, a painter, and Rodolfo, a poet, are shivering in their Parisian garret and cannot work for the cold. Rodolfo's play is burning on the stove when the philosopher Colline enters. The musician Schaunard arrives with food, wine and wood bought with money from a curious commission to play to a parrot. Since it is Christmas Eve, he says they ought to eat out. They are disturbed by Benoît, who comes to collect the overdue rent. They ply him with drink, flatter him and throw him out when he drunkenly confesses that he cannot abide his wife. Rodolfo stays behind to finish an article while the others wait downstairs. Mimì knocks at the door, asking for a light for her candle. As Rodolfo helps her to a chair, since she is clearly unwell, she drops the candle and her key. He lights her candle, but it goes out again when she cannot find the key. He soon finds it, but pretends to carry on searching until they touch hands in the dark. He introduces himself and she tells of her lonely life as a seamstress. His friends call on him to hurry and he asks them to save two places at the Café Momus. Turning, he sees her framed in the moonlight and they realize they are in love.

ACT II

On the way to the Café Momus, Rodolfo buys Mimì a bonnet. The others find a table and settle down. Rodolfo introduces Mimì and they order food and wine. Parpignol pushes his cart of toys past them, chased by children. As the friends are about to drink a toast they hear Musetta, Marcello's on-off lover, who enters in a spectacular outfit, followed by her latest admirer, Alcindoro. Marcello tries to ignore her, but she makes a scene to get his attention, smashing a plate and flaunting herself. She sends Alcindoro to buy more shoes and then falls into Marcello's arms. A military parade passes. The bohemians cannot pay for their meal and Musetta says to put it on Alcindoro's bill.

ACT III

A few weeks later, Marcello and Musetta are living at a tavern near the tollgate. It is dawn. Mimì, weak and coughing, describes to Marcello how Rodolfo's jealousy is driving them apart. She overhears Rodolfo telling

Marcello that he is leaving her because he cannot support her as she dies of consumption. She is overcome by coughing and Rodolfo runs to help her. Marcello dashes inside when he hears Musetta laughing. Mimì says she is leaving and tells Rodolfo to keep the bonnet, but they eventually agree to remain together until April. Marcello noisily quarrels with Musetta and they separate.

ACT IV
Marcello and Rodolfo can only think of their lost loves. Colline and Schaunard return to the garret with food. The four friends fool about dancing and fighting a mock duel. Musetta interrupts them with the news that Mimì is too weak to climb the stairs. They carry Mimì to a bed and Musetta describes how she found her dying in the street, asking to be with Rodolfo. Musetta offers to sell her earrings for medicine and a muff, while Colline pawns his prized overcoat. Mimì and Rodolfo recall their love and how they met. The others gradually return as Mimì falls asleep. Schaunard whispers to Marcello that Mimì is dead. Rodolfo is the last to realize that she has gone.

Recommended Recording:
La bohème, Berlin Philharmonic Orchestra; Herbert von Karajan, conductor; Decca 421 049-2; Soloists: Mirella Freni (Mimì), Elizabeth Harwood (Musetta), Luciano Pavarotti (Rodolfo), Rolando Panerai (Marcello), Gianni Maffeo (Schaunard), Nicolai Ghiaurov (Colline)

Tosca
In *Tosca*, Puccini created his most complex and challenging of female roles and it is partly for this reason that the work has gained such a central place in the public consciousness. The role has been a magnet to sopranos wishing to demonstrate not only their vocal abilities, but also their acting skills. Victorien Sardou's play *La Tosca* first caught Puccini's attention as early as 1889 and

gave him a fast-paced drama that cried out for the kind of musical description at which he excelled. It is a brutal work, full of strong dissonances and twisting harmonies. Scarpia, the barbaric, scheming chief of police, pervades the work both musically and dramatically. Puccini's use of the Wagnerian technique of *leitmotif* allowed him to introduce Scarpia's threatening presence before he is seen on stage. Amongst the darkness, though, are moments of levity and great beauty, such as Tosca's aria 'Vissi d'arte' ('I Live for Art').

Tosca
by Giacomo Puccini
Composed: 1898–99
Premiered: 1900, Teatro Costanzi, Rome
Libretto by Giuseppe Giacosa and Luigi Illica, after Victorien Sardou's play *La Tosca*

BACKGROUND
In 1800 Rome has been taken by an Austro-Neapolitan army. Power lies with Baron Scarpia, the police chief. Angelotti, a former consul of the republic, has escaped from his custody.

ACT I
Angelotti runs into Sant'Andrea della Valle, finds a hidden key and slips into the Attavanti family chapel. Cavaradossi enters to finish his painting of St Mary Magdalen, which, the sacristan points out, resembles a strange blonde lady often seen here. Cavaradossi reflects that his only inspiration is his beloved Floria Tosca, the singer. Angelotti greets Cavaradossi. Tosca is heard outside. Cavaradossi thrusts a basket of food at Angelotti and tells him to hide. Tosca enters with flowers for the statue of the Madonna, suspicious that she has heard voices. He agrees to take her to his villa that evening. She recognizes the Magdalen's blue eyes as those of the Marchesa Attavanti, Angelotti's sister, but

he calms her by declaring that none could compare with hers. She accepts his eternal love, but, as she leaves, asks him to paint them black. Angelotti describes how his sister left the key and some women's clothes as a disguise. Cavaradossi tells him to go to his villa after dark. They leave when they hear a cannon announcing the escape. The sacristan returns, surrounded by altar boys celebrating the rumour of Napoleon's defeat. Scarpia enters with his henchmen, who find the key, the empty basket and a fan with the Attavanti crest. After praising Tosca's piety, Scarpia uses the fan to arouse her jealousy and orders Spoletta to follow when she rushes off to the villa. As the choir and congregation sing the Te Deum, Scarpia looks forward to a double prize, Angelotti and Tosca.

ACT II

Scarpia is dining at the Palazzo Farnese, anticipating that Tosca will submit out of love for Cavaradossi. Spoletta reports that Angelotti was not at the villa, but he has brought back Cavaradossi for interrogation. Tosca is heard outside singing a cantata before the Queen of Naples. Hearing Cavaradossi's agony as he is tortured, Tosca breaks down and reveals where Angelotti is hiding. Cavaradossi curses her for betraying him, but he is exultant when news comes that Napoleon has won. Scarpia orders him to be shot at dawn. Tosca asks the price of his freedom, but Scarpia makes it clear that he wants her, not money. It is her passion he desires, whether hatred or love. Tosca calls on God to tell her why her piety should be repaid in this manner. She gives in. Spoletta announces that Angelotti has killed himself. Scarpia instructs him to arrange a fake execution, 'just like Count Palmieri'. Tosca demands a safe-conduct to Civitavecchia. When he has sealed it he advances towards her, arms wide open. She stabs him with a knife she has concealed. She then places candles beside his body and a crucifix on his chest.

ACT III

A shepherd boy is heard as dawn breaks at the Castel Sant'Angelo. Cavaradossi bribes the gaoler to deliver a farewell letter. Spoletta brings on Tosca. When they are alone she tells Cavaradossi how she acquired the safe-conduct. The firing squad will use blanks and he must fall at the first shot. They will then escape far from Rome. Scarpia, however, has tricked them. The muskets are loaded with shot and Tosca thinks Cavaradossi is acting. When the soldiers have gone she turns over the body and finds he is dead. Scarpia's body has been found. Spoletta rushes on to seize Tosca, but she jumps from the parapet.

Madama Butterfly

Madama Butterfly is the last opera to be written by the trio of Puccini, Illica and Giacosa. It was, as usual, beset by difficulties in the preparation and approval of the libretto. Puccini was as opposed to one particular scene as Giacosa was for it. Puccini, of course, won, but Giacosa remained so convinced that he demanded that the excised text remain in the printed libretto – a request that was not granted.

Madama Butterfly was famously heckled at its premiere but has gone on to achieve a similar level of popularity to its two immediate predecessors. Those who disliked it, including Ricordi, pointed to its superficiality and facile emotiveness. However, others remarked on the work's great tonal range and colour, its integration of oriental inflections into Puccini's harmonic language and the skill with which the character of Cio-Cio-San is developed. This last point is perhaps most pertinent since Cio-Cio-San is Puccini's first character to grow and change as we watch her. The contempt with which *Madama Butterfly* was greeted caused Puccini to make several revisions and there is no consensus as to which version is ideal.

Madama Butterfly

by Giacomo Puccini
Composed: 1901–04; rev. 1906
Premiered: 1904 La Scala, Milan; rev. version 1904, Brescia
Libretto by Giuseppe Giacosa and Luigi Illica, after David Belasco's play *Madame Butterfly*

ACT I

Goro, a marriage broker, shows Lieutenant F. B. Pinkerton the house he has rented on the hill overlooking Nagasaki. He then presents the servants, including the maid Suzuki, and lists all the wedding guests. Pinkerton explains to Sharpless, the American consul, that he is taking a wife on similar terms to the house, a contract he can cancel at a month's notice. Sharpless hopes she will come to no harm. Goro announces the wedding party, and Cio-Cio-San (Butterfly) is heard approaching. All the guests bow to Pinkerton. Cio-Cio-San explains to Sharpless that her family has fallen on hard times and she shyly admits to being 15. Pinkerton smiles when she shows him her few possessions, including a sheath, which Goro explains contains the dagger with which her father committed suicide. She offers to throw away the figures of her family gods and bow before Pinkerton's god. The marriage contract is signed and Sharpless leaves. Butterfly's uncle, the Bonze, curses her for renouncing her religion. Amid the uproar, Pinkerton orders the guests to leave and comforts Butterfly. As darkness falls, Suzuki helps Butterfly change out of her wedding dress. Left together, Butterfly confesses her doubts about marrying a barbarian, but she loved Pinkerton at first sight. She fears that in his country butterflies are often mounted on a pin, but he promises to keep her safe. They pledge their love under the stars.

ACT II

Three years later, Butterfly cannot understand that Pinkerton has abandoned her. If he did not mean to return why did he ask Sharpless to provide for her? She threatens to kill Suzuki for suggesting that every foreign husband leaves his Japanese wife. She knows he will return in the spring, 'when robins nest', and imagines how it will be, from the first sign of smoke on the horizon. When Sharpless enters she makes a show of western manners and asks if American robins are different, since Japanese ones have already nested three times.

Goro has been urging her to marry Prince Yamadori, but she refuses Yamadori's offer of riches and claims that under American law she is still married. Goro whispers to Sharpless that Pinkerton's ship has been sighted. Sharpless, who already knows that Pinkerton does not wish to see Butterfly, cannot bear to finish reading Pinkerton's letter to her. When he urges her to marry Yamadori she asks him to leave. Changing her mind, she fetches her child, of whom both Pinkerton and Sharpless are unaware. Sharpless promises to tell Pinkerton and leaves. Suzuki attacks Goro for spreading stories about the boy's parentage. Hearing a cannon-shot, Butterfly sees Pinkerton's ship arriving in the harbour. Suzuki helps her deck the house with flowers and then dresses her in her wedding clothes. They wait together, as the light fades.

The next morning, Suzuki persuades Butterfly to rest. Sharpless returns with Pinkerton, and his new wife, Kate. Sharpless tries to explain to Suzuki that, in the child's best interests, Butterfly should give him up. Despite his remorse, Pinkerton cannot bring himself to see Butterfly again and leaves. Kate assures Suzuki that she will treat the boy as though he were her own. Butterfly finds Suzuki weeping and guesses Sharpless's news. Seeing Kate, she agrees to hand over the boy to Pinkerton in half an hour and orders the faithful Suzuki to leave. Unsheathing her father's dagger, she bids a last farewell to her child and stabs herself. As she dies Pinkerton is heard calling her name.

La fanciulla del West

Puccini visited the Metropolitan Opera in New York during 1907 to see the US premieres of *Manon Lescaut* and Madama Butterfly. While there he saw David Belasco's play *The Girl of the Golden West* and his next opera began to take shape. *La fanciulla del West* is notable particularly for the vital part the vast orchestra plays in depicting the characters' emotions. As well as having Wagnerian traits, the opera demonstrates the interest Puccini had in Strauss, and in *Salome* in particular.

La fanciulla del West

by Giacomo Puccini
Composed: 1908–10
Premiered: 1910, Metropolitan Opera, New York
Libretto by Guelfo Civinini and Carlo Zangarini, after David Belasco's play *The Girl of the Golden West*

ACT I

Sheriff Jack Rance stops miners at the Polka Saloon lynching a card cheat. Ashby, the Wells Fargo agent, reports the imminent capture of the bandit Ramerrez. Rance and Sonora quarrel over Minnie, the camp's only woman. Sonora gives Minnie his gold for safe-keeping. She begins to take a Bible class. Rance declares his love, but Minnie knows he is married. Rance is suspicious of Dick Johnson, a stranger, but Minnie remembers she has seen him before. Ashby brings in Castro, who offers to betray Ramerrez and whispers to Johnson that his gang is waiting: Johnson is Ramerrez. Minnie is entranced by his words. She tells him a robber would have to kill her before stealing the gold and he does nothing when he hears a whistle. She invites him to her cabin.

ACT II

Minnie evades Johnson's kiss when he arrives. They talk politely about the cabin and reading. He asks for a kiss and she cannot resist. He declares he loved her at
first sight. It is snowing. He offers to leave, but she tells him to stay the night. He hides when Rance and Ashby arrive to tell her Johnson's true identity. When they have gone she berates him for planning to rob her, but he claims he longs to renounce his life as a bandit. She cannot forgive him stealing her first kiss. As he leaves he is shot, and Minnie hides him in the loft. Assured that Johnson is not there, Rance is about to leave when a drop of blood lands on his hand. She challenges Rance to a game of poker with herself as the prize if Rance wins. If he loses, however, Johnson is hers. She switches the cards and wins.

ACT III

The men are beside a campfire in a forest clearing. Rance wants revenge. Various miners narrate Johnson's capture, and he is brought in to be lynched. He asks them never to tell Minnie how he died, but to say he went far away. At the last moment she enters and threatens to kill Johnson and herself. She reminds the miners of what she has done for them and Sonora persuades them to release Johnson. Minnie and Johnson ride off to a new future.

Il trittico

In constructing an operatic triple-bill, Puccini followed no precedent. He had nursed the idea for some time, to the despair of Giulio Ricordi, who felt it would be a box-office disaster. With the publisher's death in 1912, Puccini soon felt able to work on the project. His librettist for *La rondine*, Giuseppe Adami, provided Puccini with the text for the first one-acter, *Il tabarro*. As usual, though, Puccini did not make life easy and Adami did not stay the course. It was Giovacchino Forzano, a medicine and law graduate who had begun work as a baritone, who brought the remaining two pieces to fruition. It became clear that some sort of unifying theme would be needed and Forzano found the thread in the subject of death. Il tabarro, which begins the set, concerns a disintegrating love affair and ends with a tragic, unintended death. In *Suor Angelica* we follow the grief of the nun Angelica who, on hearing that her child has died, takes her own life. Finally, in *Gianni Schicchi*, we are treated to a greedy family that cannot wait to be shot of a wealthy relative.

From the outset, Puccini had viewed *Il trittico* as a group of contrasts. The idea of tragedy in *Il tabarro* and comedy in *Gianni Schicchi* had quickly taken shape, but the spiritual tone of *Suor Angelica* was slower to arrive. The triple-bill was premiered in December 1918 at the Metropolitan Opera in New York. It was not received to any great acclaim – generally it was felt to be too long and to be weakened by *Suor Angelica*. This second criticism particularly stung Puccini, who felt the middle opera to be the strongest. *Gianni Schicchi*, with its slick, dark comedy, quickly became a favourite and entered the repertoire as a genuine equal to Verdi's *Falstaff*. The first of the sequence, *Il tabarro*, was slower to gain widespread appeal. In dealing with characters from the Parisian slums, the work is very much a part of the veristic tradition and was compared (not always favourably) with *Cavalleria rusticana* and Pagliacci. *Suor Angelica* was quickly excised from *Il trittico* and, although the outer two works are often performed, the triple-bill is rarely heard in its entirety.

Il trittico ('The Triptych')

by Giacomo Puccini
Composed: 1913–18
Premiered: 1918, Metropolitan Opera, New York
Libretto by Giuseppe Adami after Didier Gold's play *La houppelande*

IL TABARRO ('THE CLOAK')

Michele, the owner of a barge on the Seine, is watching the sunset. His wife Giorgetta, half his age, suggests that the stevedores deserve a drink. He agrees, but is disappointed when she does not return his affection. Luigi, Il Tinca ('tench') and Il Talpa ('mole') come onboard. Giorgetta passes out the glasses. Luigi calls over a passing organ-grinder and they dance until Michele appears and signals the stevedores to go below. Giorgetta asks whether they will be leaving soon and whether Luigi will be going with them. While a ballad-seller entertains the passers-by, she tells Michele that she would rather be beaten than have to suffer his moody silences. La Frugola ('lively') comes looking for her husband, Il Talpa. She shows Giorgetta the day's pickings and gives her the best, a new comb. She has even found a treat for her cat. Il Tinca heads off to a tavern. Luigi rages against their working life, which turns every happiness to misery. La Frugola has always dreamed of a little place in the country, but Giorgetta shares with Luigi a love of Paris since they both come from Belleville. She is unhappy cooped up on a barge.

Luigi tries to embrace Giorgetta, but she pushes him away, worried that Michele will find them together. They recall last night's kisses. Luigi asks Michele to put him ashore at Rouen, but Michele refuses since there would be nothing there for him. Michele goes to fix the lanterns. Mad with jealousy, Luigi declares that he would rather stab her than lose her to another. They arrange for him to return when he sees the usual signal, a lighted match. She denies Michele's accusation that she no longer loves him, but says she is unable to sleep below. He reminds her of their dead child and how he used to wrap them in his cloak. He pleads with her to stay with him and love him as before, but she says they have both changed. As she goes he murmurs 'Slut'. He wonders who she is waiting for and lights his pipe. Luigi crosses the gang-plank. Michele seizes him and begins to throttle him, repeatedly telling him to confess. He wraps Luigi's body in his cloak. Giorgetta returns to ask for his forgiveness. As he opens the cloak the body falls at her feet.

SUOR ANGELICA
('SISTER ANGELICA')

The nuns are heard singing the 'Ave Maria' at Vespers. They leave the church and the monitress punishes two latecomers. The mistress of novices describes to Sister Genovieffa how the waters of the fountain appear to turn gold in the setting sun on just three days a year. Genovieffa, who used to be a shepherdess, wishes to see a lamb again after five years in the convent. Sister Angelica, who is skilled in making medicines from flowers and herbs, denies she has any special desires, but the other nuns all know that she was a princess and has been there for seven years waiting for news of her family. Word comes of a grand visitor in a carriage. The Abbess summons Angelica to see her aunt, a formidable princess.

The princess explains that Angelica's parents had entrusted her with the disposal of their estate. She wants Angelica to sign over her inheritance so that her younger sister can marry someone prepared to overlook the shame Angelica has brought to the family. Angelica answers that she has done everything possible to atone, but she cannot forget the baby who was taken from her. At first the princess stays silent when asked about the boy, but when she says he was taken ill two years ago Angelica knows he is dead and she collapses. The princess starts to help, but stops when she sees her sobbing. Angelica slowly recovers enough to sign the document and the princess leaves.

It is growing dark. Angelica addresses her dead child, who never knew a mother's love. She asks how long it will be before they can be together. The other sisters tell her that the Virgin has answered her prayer. They all go to their cells. Angelica returns alone and begins making a potion from herbs and flowers. She bids her sisters farewell, saying that her son is calling her. She embraces and kisses a cross, and then drinks the potion. Suddenly she realizes she has committed a mortal sin and calls on the Virgin to save her from damnation. Light floods from the church, which is miraculously full of angels. In the doorway stands the Virgin, holding Angelica's child. He takes three steps towards his mother, while choirs praise the Virgin. Angelica falls back and dies.

GIANNI SCHICCHI

Buoso Donati, a wealthy Florentine merchant, has just died. A rumour spreads around his sobbing relations beside the bed that he has left everything to a monastery. At Simone's suggestion they ransack the room looking for the will. Rinuccio finds it and hands it to Zita, his aunt, on condition that he is allowed to marry Lauretta, Gianni Schicchi's daughter. Zita replies that if the will is favourable he can marry anyone. Rinuccio sends for Lauretta and Schicchi. All the relations anticipate inheriting the house, the mills at Signa and the mule, but the will confirms that everything goes to the monks. Rinuccio advises them to consult Schicchi, but Zita will have nothing to do with a peasant. Rinuccio declares that new blood from the country makes Florence great. Schicchi arrives with Lauretta. The family's apparent grief is soon explained by the lost inheritance. To the lovers' dismay, Zita refuses to allow Rinuccio to marry without a dowry. Rinuccio appeals for Schicchi's help, but he remains unmoved until Lauretta declares that, if she cannot marry Rinuccio, she will drown herself in the Arno. All watch expectantly as Schicchi examines the will. He sends Lauretta away and confirms that no one else knows about the death.

When the doctor enters Schicchi hides behind the bed curtains and, imitating Buoso, tells him that he feels much better. Schicchi reveals a plan to dress in Buoso's nightgown and dictate a fresh will. All the relations put in a word for what they want. Simone proposes that they leave the division to Schicchi's judgement. As they hand him his disguise the senior relatives offer bribes for the house, the mills and the mule. He warns them that the penalty for falsifying *a will is to have your hand cut off and be banished from Florence. Before a lawyer and two witnesses, Schicchi dictates the will. Everyone praises his choices, especially the five lire left to the monastery, but there is consternation when the house, the mills and the mule are left to Schicchi. He stifles any interruptions by repeating 'Farewell, Florence'. When the lawyer and witnesses have gone the family scream at Schicchi, who drives them from what is now his house. Lauretta has a dowry and there can be no obstacle to her marriage. Schicchi asks the audience, if they have enjoyed themselves, to pardon him.*

Recommended Recording:
Il trittico, Philharmonia Orchestra; Antonio Pappano, conductor; EMI Classics 556587-2; Soloists: Il tabarro: Maria Guleghina (Giorgetta), Elena Zilio (La Frugola), Neil Shicoff (Luigi), Carlo Guelfi (Michele) Suor Angelica: Cristina Gallardo-Domâs (Suor Angelica), Dorothea Röschmann (Suor Genovieffa), Bernadette Manca di Nissa (Princess), Felicity Palmer (Abbess), Gianni Schicchi: Angela Gheorghiu (Lauretta), Patrizia Ciofi (Zita), Felicity Palmer (Zita), Roberto Alagna (Rinuccio), José van Dam (Gianni Schicchi)

Turandot

Puccini spent the last five years of his life working on *Turandot*. He patched up his differences with Adami who, together with Renato Simoni, got to work on creating a libretto from Carlo Gozzi's fairy-tale.

Through the usual prevarications, doubts and rows, Puccini slowly worked on the score. At the beginning of 1924, he began to complain of a sore throat. He retired to a spa town for recuperation but no improvement came and in late autumn came the news that he was suffering from cancer. Treatment proceeded and was thought to be successful until suddenly, on 29 November, Puccini died.

The task of completing *Turandot* fell to Franco Alfano, whose version is most often heard today. The premiere was conducted by Toscanini who, at the point where Puccini's music came to an end, turned to the audience and quietly announced the fact. There followed a hushed silence into which someone cried 'Viva Puccini!' and the entire audience burst into shouts and applause.

Without doubt, *Turandot* is an extraordinary work. Its harmony demonstrates Puccini's continued desire to expand his expressive palette and the construction of large-scale blocks of music shows an astonishing dramatic and musical mastery.

Turandot
by Giacomo Puccini
Composed: 1920–26
Premiered: 1926, La Scala, Milan
Libretto by Giuseppe Adami and Renato Simoni, after Carlo Gozzi's fairy-tale

ACT I
Within the Imperial City in Peking, a Mandarin announces that the Prince of Persia is to be executed. He is the latest royal suitor to fail to answer the three riddles that would win the Princess Turandot in marriage. The crowd rushes forward, knocking over a blind old man. Liù, a slave girl, calls for help and a man appears, who recognizes the blind man as his father, Timur, the exiled King of Tartary. They are both in disguise. Timur describes how Liù has helped him, all because the prince once smiled at her. The people are waiting for the next execution. When they see the victim, however, they call on Turandot for mercy, but she silently signals the execution. The prince, intending to curse her, has been smitten by her beauty. Timur urges him to stop, but he rushes towards the great gong in the courtyard. He is intercepted by the emperor's ministers, Ping, Pang and Pong, who graphically describe the fate of failed suitors.

Still enraptured at Turandot's beauty, the prince sees their ghosts on the ramparts. Liù pleads with him and he asks her to look after Timur, whatever happens. Nothing can hold him back. He strikes the gong three times, announcing that he is the next suitor.

ACT II

The ministers are preparing for a wedding or a funeral. Each describes the country home he hopes to see again, if only a suitor were to solve the riddles. This is the twenty-seventh prince to try. Perhaps he may be the one to bring the slaughter to an end. Emperor Altoum, enthroned high above the square, tries to dissuade the prince. Turandot, resplendent and icy, explains how a distant ancestress, Lo-u-Ling, was carried off and ravished by a foreigner. The trial of the three riddles is her revenge. No one will ever possess her. The prince solves each riddle in turn with the answers 'hope', 'blood' and 'Turandot'. The crowd is exultant at the final answer, but Turandot is shattered. She pleads with her father not to give her away like a slave girl, but he tells her the oath is sacred. She asks the prince whether he means to take her by force. He replies that he wants her love. He will ask only one riddle in return: if she can discover his name by dawn he will die.

ACT III

Turandot has ordered everyone to stay awake in the search for his name. The prince is confident of success. The ministers offer him women, jewels and fame if he will go away. They fear what new tortures Turandot may devise to punish them. Soldiers drag on Timur and Liù. They must know the secret. As Ping tells Turandot that the tools of torture are ready, she notices the prince's first sign of indecision. Timur remains silent and Liù pushes forward, claiming that she alone knows his name. Love gives her the power to resist torture and love will overcome even Turandot. She seizes a dagger and stabs herself. Timur declares that her spirit will

have vengeance and the people call on her forgiveness. Liù's body is carried off. Alone with Turandot, the prince tears away her veil. As she protests her purity he seizes and kisses her. For the first time in her life she weeps, admitting that she fears and loves him. He tells her his name, Calaf. Outside the imperial palace Turandot announces to the emperor that she knows the prince's name: love.

OPERAS

1883–84	Le villi
1884–85	Edgar; rev. 1901 & 1905
1893	Manon Lescaut
1896	La bohème
1900	Tosca
1904	Madama Butterfly; rev. 1906
1910	La fanciulla del West
1917	La rondine; rev. 1918–19
1918	Il trittico: Il tabarro, Suor Angelica, Gianni Schicchi
1920–26	Turandot, last scene completed by Franco Alfano

TIMELINE

1858	Giacomo Puccini born, Lucca, Italy
1876	First contact with opera after hearing *Aida*
1880	Goes to study at Milan Conservatory
1883	Enters his first opera *Le villi* in competition, does not win
1884	Two-act version of *Le villi* performed at Teatro dal Verne, Milan
1889	*Edgar* premieres at La Scala, Milan
1893	*Manon Lescaut* performed, Turin; Puccini becomes star overnight
1896	Premiere of *La bohème*, Turin, conducted by Toscanini
1900	Tosca performed, Teatro Costanzi, Rome;

	Covent Garden premiere of *Tosca*
1904	*Madama Butterfly*'s premiere, La Scala, is a fiasco; revised *Madama Butterfly* performed at Bresica; Puccini marries Elvira Gemignani
1907	Puccini travels to New York
1910	*La fanciulla del West* premieres at the Metropolitan Opera, New York
1912	Death of Giulio Ricordi, Puccini's publisher
1914	Starts work on an operetta, *La rondine*
1917	Premiere of *La rondine*, Monte Carlo
1918	*Il trittico* produced at the Metropolitan Opera, New York
1920	Begins work on *Turandot*
1924	Puccini dies of throat cancer before *Turandot* is completed
1926	Premiere of *Turandot* after completion by Franco Alfano, La Scala, Milan

Rimsky-Korsakov, Nikolay Andreyevich

1844–1908, RUSSIAN

In spite of being the most prolific of contributors to Russian opera, Rimsky-Korsakov's stage works have never found a solid place in the mainstream international repertoire. As a youth, Rimsky-Korsakov was encouraged and taught by Mily Alekseyevich Balakirev (1837–1910). The young composer displayed an undoubted mastery of orchestration and a keen ear for evocative harmony, which makes it all the more strange that his operas were never fully embraced in the West. Only his final opera achieved lasting popularity, and this was perhaps partly due to the glitzy showmanship of the impresario Diaghilev. *The Golden Cockerel* is based on an imitation folk tale by Pushkin that was turned into a libretto by Vladimir Nikolayevich Bel'sky. The fantastic nature of the subject was a good match for Rimsky-Korsakov's exotic music and its visually enticing, though posthumous, premiere ensured a lasting appeal.

The Golden Cockerel

by Nikolay Andreyevich Rimsky-Korsakov
Composed: 1907–09
Premiered: 1909, Moscow
Libretto by Vladimir Nikolayevich Bel'sky
after Alexander Pushkin

PROLOGUE

An astrologer warns the audience that the story has a moral.

ACT I

King Dodon's country is surrounded by enemies. He is not satisfied by the advice offered by his sons, Guidon and Afron, or by General Polkan. The astrologer offers a magic golden cockerel that can warn of approaching danger. In exchange he wants a written promise to pay whatever he asks for at a later date. Although delighted, Dodon refuses to put anything in writing. The astrologer is displeased. Dodon dreams about a beautiful maiden. The cockerel sounds the alarm. Dodon has to be woken by General Polkan. Guidon and Afron are sent to attack the enemy in a pincer movement. He returns to his dreams. Again the cockerel crows a warning. Dodon sets off to war.

ACT II

His sons' armies have killed each other. A tent appears on the battlefield. The Queen of Shemakha, the beauty of Dodon's dream, emerges singing a hymn to the Sun. She will not use force to overcome him, but instead use her wiles. Dodon succumbs to her dancing and descriptions of what she has in store for him. He begs her to be his queen and orders Polkan to be executed.

ACT III

Dodon returns to his palace with his new bride. The astrologer appears and names his reward: he wants to marry the queen. Dodon refuses and strikes him dead with his sceptre. The queen finds this funny. She rejects Dodon's advances. The cockerel crows another warning, swoops down, pecks Dodon on the head and kills him. The queen vanishes, laughing.

EPILOGUE

The astrologer reassures the audience it was all an illusion, apart from the queen and himself.

Schumann, Elisabeth

1888–1952, GERMAN

Soprano Schumann made her debut in the Neues Stadt-Theater in Hamburg in 1909 and stayed there until 1919. Richard Strauss persuaded her to join the Vienna Staatsoper where she remained until 1938. She made her Covent Garden debut in 1924 as Sophie in *Der Rosenkavalier*. From 1938 she took up residence in New York where she had already performed many times. Schumann had a high, delicate soprano voice which was particularly well-suited to Strauss and **Wolfgang Amadeus Mozart** (1756–91), and she also became known for performing in Wagner's operas; having debuted in *Tannhäuser* she also won acclaim for the role of Eva in *Die Meistersinger von Nürnberg*.

Strauss, Richard

1864–1949, GERMAN

Often regarded as the best composer never to have achieved greatness, Strauss succeeded Wagner and Johannes Brahms (1833–97) as the most important living German composer. At his most impressive, Strauss commands complete control over the orchestra and possesses striking harmonic inventiveness.

CHILDHOOD AND FAMILY

Strauss was born in Munich on 11 June 1864. His father, Franz, was an outstanding horn player, a member of the Munich court orchestra and much admired by the conductor Hans von Bülow. Strauss was a precocious child: he began piano lessons aged four, composed his first music aged six and took up the violin aged eight. By the time he was 13 years old, he was playing in the back desks of his father's semi-professional orchestra and regularly attended rehearsals for the Munich court orchestra. In spite of his father's attempts to 'protect' his son, Strauss had already heard Wagner's *Tannhäuser* (1845) aged 10. *Lohengrin* (1850) *Siegfried* (1876) and

Tristan und Isolde (1865) soon followed. Interestingly, however, Strauss betrayed no sign of Wagner's influence at the time. His father was his greatest musical influence and Strauss's music follows established classical patterns, with the figures Schumann and Brahms looming particularly large.

FINDING A VOICE

In 1885, Bülow took Strauss on as assistant conductor in Meiningen, where the young composer met Alexander Ritter, a first violinist in the orchestra. Ritter filled Strauss with enthusiasm for Wagner and **Franz Lizst** (1811–86), and their capacity to take music into the future. The result was a sea change in Strauss's outlook, first heard in the tone-poem *Macbeth* (1887–88). From this point onwards, Strauss began to find his true voice and the acclaim that greeted *Don Juan* in 1889 signalled the arrival of a significant artist. Ritter had challenged Strauss to complete an opera along the same lines as Wagner – including writing his own libretto.

FIRST OPERATIC STEPS

The premiere of *Guntram* in 1894 was a disaster; it won over neither the critics nor the public. For all his success with the dramatic music of his tone-poems, it was not until the premiere of *Salome* in 1905 that Strauss gained a firm hold on opera. Oscar Wilde's (1854–1900) play had attracted fury and outrage in England, but Hedwig Lachmann's German translation was triumphantly staged in Berlin. Strauss swiftly got to work and, inspired by the charged eroticism and the powerful psychological conflicts of the text, created a sensation. The relative shortness of *Salome* enabled Strauss to stay close to the kind of writing he had developed in his tone-poems. For his next opera he again chose a short play as his basis, this time by the great Austrian playwright Hugo von Hofmannsthal.

HOFMANNSTHAL

Hofmannsthal had written to Strauss in 1900 suggesting a scenario for a ballet, which had been rejected. Strauss, though, did not forget their correspondence and they began an extraordinarily productive relationship with *Elektra*. The premiere of *Elektra* in 1909 was again a great success and the pair moved on with increased conviction. Strauss had been anxious to write a lighter, comic work even before beginning *Elektra* and the result was *Der Rosenkavalier*: his greatest operatic success. Hofmannsthal and Strauss rarely met in person and their collaborative work was carried out mostly by letter. They were ideally matched: the composer's instincts for theatrical sweep were refined by the librettist's care for detail of character and place. The pair also created *Ariadne auf Naxos*, *Die Frau ohne Schatten*, *Die ägyptische Helena* and, finally, *Arabella*. Hofmannsthal died in 1929, before a final version of the second and third acts to *Arabella* could be created and Strauss, who was distraught, resolved to set the text as it stood, out of respect.

TOWARDS AN INDIAN SUMMER

Strauss subsequently collaborated with Stefan Zweig on *Die schweigsame Frau*. The partnership boded well, but it was cut short by the Nazi regime in 1935. There followed an unsatisfactory relationship with Joseph Gregor, producing *Freidenstag*, *Daphne* and *Die Liebe der Danae*, but Strauss was never entirely happy. Gregor began work on Strauss's final operatic project, *Capriccio*, but it was Strauss himself and Clemens Krauss who eventually completed it. The post-Hofmannsthal period was incredibly productive for Strauss, but it was also marred by difficulties on all fronts of his life. None of his operatic work of this time has gained a strong foothold in the repertory and it was not until the end of the Second World War that Strauss rediscovered his musical feet.

Salome

Strauss saw Hedwig Lachmann's German version of Oscar Wilde's play in Berlin in 1903. Directed by Max Reinhardt, it made an immediate impression on the composer and he decided to set Lachmann's text himself. The relatively short length of *Salome* allowed Strauss to approach the composition as though it were another of the tone-poems with which he had established his reputation. The work is symphonically conceived and the giant orchestra is used with great deftness to create a wide range of colours. It was the perfect find for Strauss. A strong drama, inviting a powerful score and benefitting from grand theatrical effects; it also presented a psychological introversion that invited a more lyrical, chamber-music style. Harmonically, the work is forward-looking. Although the essential language is diatonic, there are moments of bitonality as well as a number of unprepared dissonances, designed for theatrical shock effect.

Salome

by Richard Strauss
Composed: 1904–05
Premiered: 1905, Dresden
Libretto by the composer to Hedwig Lachmann's German translation of Oscar Wilde's play

Jochanaan the prophet has been imprisoned in a cistern at the palace of the Tetrarch Herodes for foretelling a new kingdom of God and denouncing Herodias, formerly the wife of Herodes' murdered brother and now of Herodes himself. Narraboth is watching Herodias's daughter Salome, who is disgusted at the way Herodes has been looking at her. She demands to see Jochanaan, even though Herodes has forbidden the cistern lid to be raised. Aware that Narraboth is obsessed with her, she persuades him to bring out Jochanaan. She is fascinated by the prophet's pale and wild appearance and declares she will kiss him. Narraboth cannot bear this and kills himself. Jochanaan announces that only the One who is to come can save her. Herodes enters with Herodias. The body is taken away. Herodes is disturbed by a sound of beating wings. Herodias rebukes him for staring at her daughter. Salome rejects his offers of wine and fruit and refuses to sit next to him. Herodias demands that Jochanaan is silenced.

Herodes' belief that Jochanaan is a holy man who has seen God prompts a discussion by five Jews, while two Nazarenes assert that the Messiah has come and is working miracles, including raising the dead. Herodias is still more disturbed by Jochanaan's pronouncements. Herodes asks Salome to dance for him. Herodias objects and again Salome refuses to obey Herodes. He offers her anything she desires, even half his kingdom. He hears the beating wings once more and can barely breathe. Salome agrees to dance, to Herodias's fury. Herodes is so overcome by her dance that he agrees to keep his oath. Her demand for Jochanaan's head on a silver charger brings Herodias's delighted approval but fills Herodes with horror. He offers priceless jewels and even the veil of the Tabernacle, but Salome remains adamant. Herodias takes the death-ring from Herodes' finger and gives it to the executioner, who goes down into the cistern. Salome leans over the side, listening for the sound of the execution. She seizes the severed head as it is lifted up and declares how she longs to kiss him. She knows that, if he had looked at her, he would have loved her. She kisses his lips and tastes the bitterness of death. Herodes orders the soldiers to crush her with their shields.

Elektra

Following *Salome* was no easy task, and Strauss felt strongly that he needed to tackle an entirely different subject – by preference a light, comic work. He had been in correspondence with the playwright Hofmannsthal and the

approached him with an idea for such a work. Hofmannsthal had other ideas, and was insistent that Strauss should take up his adaptation of Sophocles' play *Electra*. Like *Salome*, *Elektra* has a one-act structure and its central figure is an obsessive, destructive woman. Also like *Salome*, Strauss's enthusiasm for the subject stemmed from watching a Max Reinhardt production of Hofmannsthal's play. *Elektra* continues along the harmonic path of *Salome*, venturing further into dissonance and, at times, veering towards complete atonality, which is all at the service of the drama.

It is the psychological examination of character that makes both *Elektra* and *Salome* so compelling. Strauss's taught, colourful and incisive score draws us into the fractured world on stage. He creates a world of raw emotion that smashes its way into our consciousness. Strauss was equivocal about *Elektra*, even to the extent of issuing a press statement to the effect that the work did not represent a break with tonality. Later in his life, he was often faced with accusations of backing away from a modernist path by not continuing in the same vein. It is probably fair to say, though, that the music fulfils the demands of the text. Strauss had always looked to extra-musical sources for inspiration and produced music that matched the subject.

Elektra

by Richard Strauss
Composed: 1906–08
Premiered: 1909, Dresden
Libretto by Hugo von Hofmannsthal, after Sophocles' *Electra*

After the Trojan War, Agamemnon has been murdered by his wife Klytemnästra and her lover Aegisth. Agamemnon's son Orest has been sent into exile. The elder daughter, Elektra, cannot forgive her mother. She is treated worse than the servants and lives only to take revenge.

The maids drawing water from the well in the palace courtyard at Mycenae show their contempt for Elektra. Only the fifth maid speaks up for her, and she is beaten by the overseer. Elektra duly appears and calls on the spirit of Agamemnon to show itself. She graphically describes his murder and prophesies how his murderers' blood will pour into his grave, while Orest and their sister Chrysothemis dance with her in triumph. Chrysothemis has overheard Klytemnästra and Aegisth planning to imprison Elektra in a tower. She blames Elektra's hatred of their mother for her own imprisonment in the palace. Why can she not accept that their father is dead and Orest will not return? She yearns for children and would prefer death itself to this living death. She pleads with Elektra to stay away from Klytemnästra, who is said to have dreamt about Orest.

Klytemnästra enters, raddled and covered with jewels and charms. Leaning on a stick, she wonders why she does not have the strength to rid herself of Elektra. Her confidantes try to dissuade her from speaking to Elektra, but she rejects their malign whisperings. She asks Elektra how she can banish her dreams and is told she will dream no more when the appointed victim, a woman, falls under the axe. Klytemnästra does not comprehend that she herself is the intended sacrifice and enquires about the rites to be observed. Elektra asks whether Orest may be allowed home and accuses her mother of paying someone to strangle him. From Klytemnästra's reaction she knows that he must still be alive and that she fears him.

Elektra turns on Klytemnästra and delivers a horrifying prophecy of Orest's revenge as he chases her screaming through the palace. Her dreams will be no more and those who live will rejoice. A confidante whispers to Klytemnästra. Suddenly everything changes. Klytemnästra laughs and leaves. Elektra is bewildered, but Chrysothemis appears with news that Orest is dead. Aegisth is sent for. Elektra tells Chrysothemis that it is now up to them. She has hidden the axe that killed Agamemnon, but the deed will take two people and she needs her help. Extravagantly she praises her womanly strength and promises to be more than a sister, her slave. Chrysothemis rushes away. Elektra starts to dig for the axe. A stranger appears, claiming to know how Orest died. At first he takes her for a servant and is shocked when he realizes this is Elektra. She refuses to listen. It is only when servants come to kiss his hand that she recognizes Orest. Overjoyed, she describes how she has waited for his return.

Hearing that there is no man in the house, Orest enters the palace. Suddenly Elektra realizes she has not given him the axe. Klytemnästra's screams are heard. Elektra meets Aegisth, who cannot understand why she is dancing, and shows him towards the door. He is seen at the window shouting for help and is then dragged away. Chrysothemis describes the rejoicing inside the palace. She is thrilled at the new life awaiting them. At last she will know love. Elektra is overwhelmed. She breaks into a wild dance and calls on Chrysothemis to join her. At its height she falls dead.

Recommended Recording:

Elektra, Vienna Philharmonic Orchestra; Georg Solti, conductor; Decca 417 345-2; Soloists: Birgit Nilsson (Elektra), Marie Collier (Chrysothemis), Regina Resnik (Klytämnestra), Gerhard Stolze (Aegisth), Tom Krause (Orest)

Der Rosenkavalier

For the follow-up to *Elektra*, Strauss declared he wanted to write a Mozart opera. Despite Hofmannsthal's protests about a light, Renaissance subject set in the past, the librettist soon came up with a scenario that delighted Strauss. The correspondence between librettist and composer was good-natured and respectful. Each made suggestions to the other and the work gradually took shape between 1908 and 1910. The result was a bitter-sweet comedy of social observation. Hofmannsthal's detailed text enabled Strauss to create a ravishingly detailed musical world, remarkable for its detail as much as for its symphonic sweep.

Even this work was not without its problems in rehearsal. Showing Octavian and the Marschallin in bed was thought to be obscene and Hofmannsthal was forced come up with alternatives. What seemed to cause no problems was the now-famous musical orgasm that opens the work before revealing Octavian and the Marschallin luxuriating in each other's company. The premiere in Dresden in 1911 was an astonishing success. Fifty more performances took place in Dresden alone and the opera had flashed across Germany in weeks. It remains Strauss's best-loved opera; its vitality, wit and beauty never fail to entice the listener into its seductive world.

Der Rosenkavalier ('The Knight of the Rose')
by Richard Strauss
Composed: 1909–10
Premiered: 1911, Dresden
Libretto by Hugo von Hofmannsthal

ACT I
After an active night, the Marschallin is relaxing in bed with her young lover, Count Octavian Rofrano. She has been dreaming that she heard her husband coming home. Now there are noises outside. It is her cousin Baron Ochs auf Lerchenau. Octavian emerges from hiding dressed as a maid. Ochs greets the Marschallin as graciously as his manners allow, but is distracted by the pretty maid. He is to marry Sophie, the daughter of Faninal, a wealthy merchant newly ennobled, and wants the Marschallin to recommend a nobleman to act as the 'Knight of the Rose' and deliver the ceremonial silver rose to his betrothed. She suggests

Octavian and shows him a miniature that looks remarkably like 'Mariandel', the maid he has been trying to proposition. He naturally supposes that she is an illegitimate Rofrano, much like his own bastard servant, Leopold. Petitioners and trades-people enter for the Marschallin's levee. Ochs interrupts a tenor's singing and the Marschallin dismisses everyone. Valzacchi and Annina, two scheming Italians, offer to discover more about 'Mariandel' for Ochs. His boorish behaviour has upset the Marschallin, who recalls how she was forced into an arranged marriage. Octavian reappears in his own clothes. She is feeling the passage of time and describes how she sometimes stops all the clocks. She gently tries to tell him that one day he will leave her for a girl of his own age. Too late she realizes she has not kissed him goodbye and sends her page Mohammed to deliver the rose to him.

ACT II
Sophie is excitedly waiting for the Knight of the Rose to arrive. Octavian appears, richly dressed, and makes the presentation. They are immediately attracted. She knows all the gossip about him. She promises to be faithful to her future husband, but she has never seen anyone as handsome as Octavian. Sophie is horrified by Ochs' manners when Faninal introduces him. In his silent anger Octavian crushes a wineglass. Ochs' servants start molesting Faninal's maids. Sophie pleads for Octavian's help in freeing her from the marriage. As they declare their love they are seized by Valzacchi and Annina, who call for Ochs. He seems unconcerned as Octavian falteringly speaks up for Sophie. When Ochs threatens to have Sophie dragged away to sign the contract, Octavian draws his sword. Ochs is slightly wounded and screams for a doctor. Faninal frantically apologizes. If she refuses to marry Ochs, she will be sent to a convent for life. Annina brings Ochs a letter from 'Mariandel' asking for a rendezvous. He sings his favourite song in anticipation of tomorrow evening.

ACT III

'Mariandel' is approving the unpleasant surprises Valzacchi has prepared in an inn's private room. Ochs demands to be left alone with her. Feigning shyness, she is greatly surprised by the hidden bed. He tries to kiss her and is unpleasantly struck by her likeness to Octavian. As he starts to loosen 'her' bodice, faces stare at him from the walls and Annina bursts in, dressed as his long-lost wife with her four children. There is uproar. Ochs tells a police inspector that 'Mariandel' is his fiancée. Faninal is horrified.

To the inspector's amusement Mariandel's clothes are handed out from behind a curtain. The Marschallin enters, followed by Sophie, who announces that the engagement is over. The Marschallin advises Ochs to go while some dignity remains and he leaves, pursued by creditors. The Marschallin tells Octavian to go to Sophie. He hesitates. She sadly renounces his love and blesses them. Octavian and Sophie can scarcely believe what has happened. The Marschallin shows the couple to Faninal. As they leave Sophie accidentally drops her handkerchief. Mohammed runs on to find it as the curtain falls.

Recommended Recording:

Der Rosenkavalier, Vienna State Opera; Carlos Kleiber, conductor; Deutsche Grammophon 073 008-9; Soloists: Felicity Lott (Feldmarschallin), Barbara Bonney (Sophie), Anne Sofie von Otter (Octavian), Anna Gonda (Annina), Keith Ikaia-Purdy (Singer), Heinz Zednik (Valzacchi), Gottfried Hornik (Faninal), Kurt Moll (Baron Ochs)

Ariadne auf Naxos

Strauss may not have been the out-and-out modernist many have wanted him to be, but neither was he one to sit back and reproduce carbon copies of past successes. Strauss and Hofmannsthal decided to follow up Der Rosenkavalier with an altogether different proposition. Ariadne auf Naxos, in its original version, is a curious amalgam of play and opera. Its conception was troubled and led the two collaborators into their first serious disagreement. After discussing numerous ideas, they finally settled on a scenario that mixed **commedia dell'arte** characters with eighteenth-century operatic stereotypes.

Strauss was initially curious, but not moved to any great enthusiasm. As his work on the project progressed, though, it grew so far beyond Hofmannsthal's original conception that the librettist felt compelled to write to Strauss explaining exactly what he had meant. The work was finally finished in 1912 and lasted about an hour and a half, compared to the original conception of half an hour. The premiere was a let-down, with neither audience nor critics grasping the work, and Strauss and Hofmannsthal immediately set about revising it. The tone of the piece is knowing in a similar way to Der Rosenkavalier, but its sending up of every kind of theatrical convention and musical style was a surprise. It remains a difficult piece to stage and is regarded by many as extravagant and over-written, both musically and dramatically.

Ariadne auf Naxos ('Ariadne on Naxos')

by Richard Strauss
Composed: 1911–12; rev. 1916
Premiered: 1912, Stuttgart
Libretto by Hugo von Hofmannsthal

PROLOGUE

A large drawing room belonging to the richest man in Vienna has been turned into a theatre. He has commissioned varied entertainment to follow dinner: an **opera seria**, an **opera buffa** and fireworks. Crew, performers and admirers bustle backstage. The music master is unhappy that his pupil's opera is to be followed by a low comedy. Zerbinetta, leader of the commedia dell'arte troupe, tells the dancing master it will be difficult to entertain the audience after a boring opera. Disgusted at having to mix with such low people, the prima donna is assured by the music master that everyone will remember her in the title role. The major-domo announces a change of plan: both pieces are to be performed together. The composer is about to walk out when the music master observes that he would lose six months' pay. The dancing master believes no one would mind if the opera were cut, and the prima donna and the tenor vie to make sure the other loses out. When the opera's plot is explained to her, Zerbinetta says that Ariadne is waiting for another lover, not death. The composer defends his heroine but is overcome by Zerbinetta's flirtation. Enchanted, he rhapsodizes to the music master about the power of music. He realizes too late what the performance will be and leaves in despair.

OPERA

Ariadne, abandoned by Theseus on the island of Naxos, sleeps in her cave, watched by three nymphs. She awakes to lament that she is still alive. Without Theseus she is alone, waiting for Death. Four comedians decide to cheer her up with a song. Ariadne meditates on the pure land of the dead to which Hermes will take her. The quartet breaks in with a noisy song-and-dance routine. When this has no effect, Zerbinetta agrees that men are faithless and relates how each of her many lovers seemed like the love of her life.

Arlecchino begins to woo Zerbinetta; she dances off with him. The nymphs announce the arrival of Bacchus, who is heard proclaiming how he escaped from Circe. At first Ariadne thinks this is Theseus, but then she calls him the herald of Death. She has been waiting for him to take her away so she can find peace. As she waits to be transformed, he declares that the stars will perish before he allows death to take her. Through her he feels his divine powers becoming stronger. While they continue to

declare their passion, Zerbinetta observes that 'When a new god comes to woo us we are dumb!'

Die Frau ohne Schatten

Like *Ariadne auf Naxos*, *Die Frau ohne Schatten* had a tempestuous genesis. The idea itself stemmed from the period immediately after the premiere of *Der Rosenkavalier*, but Hofmannsthal's continual flood of ideas compounded by Strauss's curmudgeonliness ensured the project stalled regularly. The start of the First World War did nothing to help, and it was not until 1917 that the opera was completed and 1919 before it premiered in Vienna. It was poorly received – viewed as evidence that Strauss belonged to a bygone age and did not possess the tools or temperament to write music relevant to the time.

Die Frau ohne Schatten ('The Woman Without a Shadow')

by Richard Strauss
Composed: 1914–17
Premiered: 1919, Vienna
Libretto by Hugo von Hofmannsthal

BACKGROUND

Keikobad, ruler of the spirit world, gave his daughter a talisman to transform herself into an animal. Hunted by the emperor's falcon, she changed from a gazelle into a beautiful woman with whom the emperor fell in love, but the falcon flew off with the talisman.

ACT I

Every month a messenger enquires whether the new empress casts a shadow (can have children). The twelfth messenger announces that, unless she has one within three days, she will return to Keikobad and the emperor will turn to stone. The empress and her nurse, who despises mortals, descend to the mortal world. Barak, a dyer, and his bitter wife are childless. The nurse tempts her with riches and lovers, with the empress *and herself as her servants for three days, if she will sell her shadow. The wife hears the voices of her unborn children, but refuses to sleep with Barak.*

ACT II

Although the empress has doubts, the nurse summons up a lover for the wife. Barak returns unexpectedly with his three brothers. His wife will not eat, but the ever-generous Barak distributes food to beggars and neighbours. The emperor smells the human world on the empress and the nurse as they return to the falcon house. He cannot bring himself to kill her.

The nurse drugs Barak and brings back the vision. Pulling back at the last moment, the wife pours water over Barak and cruelly rejects him. The empress knows she has wronged Barak and dreams of her husband turning to stone. The wife tells Barak she has sold her shadow. The empress, however, sees blood on it and refuses to touch it. The nurse conjures up a sword for Barak. The wife desperately tries to retract her words, telling him to kill her quickly. The house collapses and waters pour through it.

ACT III

Barak and his wife, separated, yearn for one another. A voice calls them up into the light. The nurse begs the empress not to enter the Spirit Temple, but she insists on finding the waters of life for her husband. The nurse curses mankind. The Spirit Messenger sends her screaming back to the mortal world. The empress refuses to drink the golden waters, even when she sees the emperor turned to stone. Her shadow appears. Reunited, they hear their unborn children. The two couples, and their shadows, rejoice.

Capriccio

Strauss's final opera marked a belated return to form. He had suffered since the end of his collaboration with Hofmannsthal and jettisoned his original librettist, Joseph Gregor, in favour of the conductor Clemens Krauss. The conception was a simple but subtle one in which the characters in the piece decide to write an opera. Only at the end is it finally clear that we have been listening to their own work. Strauss and Krauss used the idea to examine the creative process and ceaseless discussion as to whether the words or the music should have primacy in opera. In spite of Strauss's reservations about the work, it was enthusiastically received at its premiere in 1942 under Krauss. It has since become one his most-performed works.

Capriccio

by Richard Strauss
Composed: 1940–41
Premiered: 1942, Munich
Libretto by the composer and Clemens Krauss

Preparations are underway for a play for Countess Madeleine's birthday. Flamand and Olivier, rivals and respectively a composer and a poet, are discussing which comes first, words or music. La Roche, a theatre director, extols his craft. The countess is passionate about both music and drama. Her brother, the count, is to appear in Olivier's play with the famous actress Clairon. Their newly written love-scene ends with a sonnet that Olivier confesses should be addressed to the countess. Flamand seizes the manuscript and rushes off to set it to music. Olivier asks the countess to choose between her suitors. Flamand returns and sings the finished setting, which Olivier thinks has ruined his poetry. The countess, however, believes that music has heightened the words. She claims the song for herself. Olivier is needed in the theatre, leaving Flamand alone with the countess. He describes how music overwhelmed him when he fell in love with her in the library. He begs her to choose between them and meet him there at 11 o'clock the next morning.

Everyone gathers in the salon for chocolate. The count is much taken with Clairon, who was once involved with Olivier. A performance by La Roche's latest discovery, a dancer, leads to renewed argument about words and music, now extended to a contrast between opéra seria and Gluck's reform operas, championed by the countess. Two Italian singers perform an old-fashioned florid duet. La Roche's description of the two halves of the birthday entertainment, 'The Birth of Pallas Athene' followed by 'The Fall of Carthage', with elaborate scenery and effects, is greeted with general laughter that develops into Olivier and Flamand's scorn. La Roche defends the dignity of the stage and challenges them to help him 'people the stage with beings like us who speak our language'. The countess proposes that they should collaborate with La Roche. Subjects suggested include Daphne, Ariadne and the Trojan War. The count suggests a faithful presentation of the day's events. All are intrigued. The guests return to Paris with the count. No one has woken Monsieur Taupe, the prompter. The countess is told that Olivier will be in the library at 11 o'clock. She must decide between words and music, but they are now bound together. She asks her reflection to help her find an ending.

TIMELINE

1864	Richard Strauss born Munich, Germany
1887	Composes first tone poem, *Macbeth*
1887	Completes first opera, *Guntram*
1889	Premiere of *Don Juan* causes sensation
1894	Debut as conductor at Beyreuth Festival; *Guntram* unsuccessful at Weimar
1896	Tone-poem *Don Quixote* completed; becomes chief conductor of Munich Opera
1898	Becomes conductor of Berlin Royal Opera
1905	*Salome* condemned as being blasphemous
1906	Strauss first collaborates with Hofmannsthal on *Elektra*
1912	Premiere of *Ariadne auf Naxos*, Stuttgart
1919	Becomes joint director of Vienna Opera
1920	Co-founds Salzburg Festival
1935	*Die schweigsame Frau* banned by Nazis
1936	Visits London and conducts at Covent Garden
1947	Starts work on *Vier letzte Lieder*
1949	Strauss dies at Garmisch

TURN OF THE CENTURY: PERSONALITIES

OPERAS

1887–93	*Guntram*; rev. 1934–39
1900–01	*Feuersnot*
1904–05	*Salome*
1906–08	*Elektra*
1909–10	*Der Rosenkavalier*
1911–12	*Ariadne auf Naxos*; rev. 1916
1914–17	*Die Frau ohne Schatten*
1917–23	*Intermezzo*
1923–27	*Die ägyptische Helena*
1930–32	*Arabella*
1933–34	*Die schweigsame Frau*
1935–36	*Friedenstag*
1936–37	*Daphne*
1938–40	*Die Liebe der Danae*
1940–41	*Capriccio*

Sullivan, Arthur
1842–1900, ENGLISH

Sullivan's name is synonymous with that of librettist W. S. Gilbert in England. It is their association with Richard D'Oyly Carte and the succession of operettas written for the Savoy Theatre that continue to ensure that Gilbert and Sullivan remain household names. Sullivan's aim, however, after education at the Royal Academy of Music in London and the Leipzig Conservatory, was to write serious music on serious subjects. The collaboration between Gilbert and Sullivan began with *Thespis* in 1871 and continued into the 1870s when D'Oyly Carte requested a piece for the Royalty Theatre. The resulting work, *Trial by Jury* (1875), was a great success and set the seal on their partnership.

The combination of Gilbert's wit and Sullivan's lightness of touch and melodic facility proved irresistible and the pair had countless successes. Difficulties were never far from the surface, however. The first serious rift was repaired to produce what many regard as their finest work, *The Mikado*, and they continued to collaborate well until *The Gondoliers*. Another row followed and, though there was further collaboration, nothing compared with their earlier work. It remained for Sullivan to fulfil his desire and, in 1891, *Ivanhoe*, to a libretto by

Julian Sturgis after the Walter Scott novel, was premiered at the Royal Opera House in London. It proved a sturdy piece and received 161 performances. However, its dramatic weaknesses stand against it and it has achieved no longevity.

The Mikado
by Arthur Sullivan
Composed: 1884–85
Premiered: 1885, London
Libretto by W. S. Gilbert

ACT I

The Mikado's son, Nanki-Poo, has fled from court to avoid marrying Katisha and is now wandering Japan as a second trombone. He has returned to Titipu on hearing that Ko-Ko, his rival for Yum-Yum, has been condemned to death for flirting. Ko-Ko, however, has been reprieved and appointed Lord High Executioner. Nanki-Poo and Yum-Yum declare their love for each other, so far as the law allows. Word arrives from the Mikado that unless someone is beheaded within a month the city will be reduced to a village. The only person on the death-list is Ko-Ko. He must find a substitute, an honour that Pooh-Bah, who holds every other official post, declines. Nanki-Poo agrees on condition that he marries Yum-Yum for a month, after which she may marry Ko-Ko. The celebrations are interrupted by Katisha, who claims her perjured lover.

ACT II

Nanki-Poo tries to brighten Yum-Yum's spirits when she realizes she will be a widow within a month. Ko-Ko discovers that, by law, when a married man is beheaded his wife is buried alive. They plot a fake execution. The Mikado arrives, accompanied by Katisha. After exaggerated accounts of the beheading, Katisha sees Nanki-Poo's name on the death certificate. Ko-Ko, Pooh-Bah and Pitti-Sing are to be executed after lunch for slaying the heir apparent. Yum-Yum and Nanki-Poo, now married, persuade Ko-Ko to woo the monstrous, bloodthirsty Katisha. She is won over by Ko-Ko's tale of a bird pining away for love. Everything is ready for the triple execution. Katisha pleads for mercy for her new husband. Nanki-Poo enters with Yum-Yum. Ko-Ko claims that the Mikado's word is law. If he orders a man to be killed he is as good as dead. The Mikado finds this very satisfactory.

The Gondoliers
by Arthur Sullivan
Composed: 1889
Premiered: 1889, London
Libretto by W. S. Gilbert

ACT I

Marco and Giuseppe, two gondoliers of proud republican descent, choose Gianetta and Tessa as their brides. The Duke and Duchess of Plaza-Toro arrive in Venice with their daughter Casilda and their servant Luiz. Casilda is told that she was married when a baby to the infant son of the King of Barataria. Don Alhambra, the Grand Inquisitor, abducted her husband when the King became a Wesleyan Methodist. After a coup she is now Queen. Luiz, whose mother was the prince's nurse, and Casilda sadly renounce their secret love. Don Alhambra explains that her husband is one of two gondoliers. The wedding party is interrupted by Don Alhambra's news that one of them is a king. Gianetta and Tessa are excited at the prospect of being a queen, but they are told they must stay in Venice while Marco and Giuseppe sail to Barataria to rule jointly until their old nurse can identify the rightful king.

ACT II

Marco and Giuseppe are happy enough, insisting on doing their share of housework, but miss their wives. They are amazed when Gianetta and Tessa burst in, having grown tired of waiting for them to write. Don Alhambra breaks up their celebratory dance and tells them to behave like kings.

He explains that one of them is married to Casilda. The wives are devastated. The Duke's finances have been transformed by cashing in on commoners' fascination with aristocracy. He teaches Marco and Giuseppe to dance a gavotte. Left alone with Casilda they confess their love for their wives, who join them in reflecting on an unprecedented quandary. The nurse reveals that, as a precaution, she had swapped over the infant prince and her own son. Luiz is the rightful King of Barataria.

Wolf-Ferrari, Ermanno
1876–1948, ITALIAN

Born as Ermanno Wolf, Wolf-Ferrari added his mother's maiden name to his own when he was 19. He showed ability as both an artist and a musician and initially studied at the Accademia dei Belle Arti in Rome. By the late 1890s, however, he had become a student of Arrigo Boito in Milan and unsuccessfully tried to encourage Giulio Ricordi to publish his scores. He was an unsettled person, moving around a great deal and seemingly unable to settle into a personal style of composition. His operas are variously comic, serious and veristic; none have been consistently taken into the repertoire.

Verga, Giovanni
1840–1922, ITALIAN

Librettist Verga came relatively late to serious writing but his contribution, when it came, was forceful. In 1884, he had a volume of short stories published of which one was entitled *Cavalleria rusticana*. The story was expanded into a play shortly afterwards and it was this version that was adapted for Mascagni's eponymous opera. Verga's strident passion and simmering violence were to prove a powerful catalyst for Mascagni and the resulting work signalled the birth of a new style in Italian opera. In many ways, Mascagni's music underplays the violence of the play, which, both in that

respect and in its unrestrained depiction of the poorest classes, was shocking in its brutality. Verga found considerable success with his other plays and founded the brand of realism that swept through Italy in the late nineteenth century. His impersonal, colourful prose style (he made extensive use of the vernacular) acted as a catalyst for the regeneration of Italian literature.

Zenatello, Giovanni
1876–1949, ITALIAN

Zenatello studied as a baritone at Verona and debuted at Belluno in 1898 as Silvio in *Pagliacci*. He sang Canio in the same opera the following year in Naples. His La Scala debut in 1902 was a success and he regularly appeared there in the years immediately afterwards. He worked extensively in South America and appeared occasionally at Covent Garden. He retired from operatic performance in the late 1920s, devoting his energies to teaching and directing. Zenatello's particular vocal qualities included a rich, dark timbre coupled with an ability to easily reach the higher register.

Zola, Émile
1840–1902, FRENCH

Zola's influence on French opera extended beyond his libretti for the composer Alfred Bruneau as his realist credo became known not only through his novels but also through public exposure. While Bizet's *Carmen* began the trend for realistic events, Zola's ideas confirmed it. Charpentier's *Louise* is notable, and there are also works by Gabriel Dupont, Camille Erlanger, Xavier Leroux and Charles-Marie Widor – not to mention Massenet – which display elements of the realist approach. Bruneau himself first set *Le rêve*, rather an exception to Zola's usual realism, in 1891, in a version by Gallet, a professional librettist whose adaptation of Zola was also the formula for Bruneau's next work, *L'attaque du moulin* ('The attack on the mill') of 1893. With Messidor (1897), *L'ouragan* ('The hurricane', 1901) and *L'enfant roi* (1905) collaboration was direct with no intermediary. After Zola's death, a couple more adaptations were made before Bruneau turned his attentions elsewhere.

A GOLDEN AGE ~ p. 291

Taken as a whole, the period from the mid-nineteenth century to the early years of the twentieth can be seen as golden age for opera. With Verdi and Wagner looking on from their vastly different perspectives, there was a commonality of language and purpose that made opera an attractive and highly expressive form of music. The increasing influence of symphonic elements in opera – whereby the music was increasingly conceived as one large, dramatic structure as opposed to a musically discrete series of songs and choruses – gave composers the technical means to write powerfully affective music. In partnership with the growing technological capabilities in theatres, audiences were given productions as stunning visually as they were aurally.

That opera was so beholden to fashion is just one indication of the central position it occupied socially and culturally. It is perhaps difficult to believe now that figures such as Schoenberg and Webern, who are often viewed as radical destroyers of their musical inheritance, were fulsome in their admiration of the great opera composers. The turn of the century brought particular musical as well as social difficulties for opera. The rapid developments in harmonic and rhythmic language coupled with the development of technologies such as cinema – and, later, the physical and psychological devastation of the two world wars – removed many of the elements that had enabled opera to take up such a strong position.

PUCCINI AND WAGNER ~ p. 291

Puccini's lifelong interest in Wagner began when he was a student. In spite of infrequent stage productions of his operas, Wagner aroused strong sentiments in Italy. Both Puccini's teachers were determined anti-Wagnerians and, to make life even more difficult for Puccini, so was Giulio Ricordi. Some have even given Puccini's love of Wagner as a reason for him not winning the Sonzogno prize for *Le villi*.

It is in the Wagnerian system of *leitmotifs*, where particular phrases or colours are given specific associations, that Puccini found the greatest inspiration. It was a technique that appealed to many Italian composers since it enabled the music to be put in direct service of the drama. Puccini, though, was alone amongst his contemporaries in using the technique as a means of enhancing the narrative. In *Tosca*, for example, Scarpia's theme continually threatens to break the gentle bickering of the two lovers, Tosca and Cavaradossi, in the opening scenes. We do not see Scarpia, but his threatening presence is all too clear. By creating a specific association with a small, but memorable, section of music, Puccini was able to voice his character's unspoken thoughts or reveal to his audience something that his characters could not yet know. Unlike Wagner, though, Puccini never allowed the *leitmotif* to dominate his textures; to do so ran the risk of threatening the voice as the true centre of all his music. Puccini's operas also make use of the aria to good effect – a technique that Wagner avoided in his works.

HAREMS, DESPOTS AND SEX-SLAVES ~ p. 292

Massenet delighted in the nineteenth-century penchant for the oriental more than any other operatic composer. Following Meyerbeer in *L'africaine*, Berlioz in *Les Troyens* and the little-known Ferdinand David, who plundered

Eastern techniques and themes in several of his works, Massenet first began to use pastiches of oriental musical techniques by imitating the inflections of North African and Arabic music, although ultimately remaining within the confines of Western music.

Massenet's first opera on an oriental theme was *Le roi de Lahore*, first staged in 1877. It employs large-scale scenes in the style of Meyerbeer, which, musically, use slightly odd Western techniques to evoke the Indian setting. But it does have a *mélodie hindoue* for flute, using an oriental scale and free-rhythmic, improvisatory gestures. It foreshadows the style of the incantation from Act II of Delibes' *Lakmé*, which would be premiered in 1883, although as yet Massenet does not go as far as Delibes in invoking the orient through pastiche. *Hérodiade*, first given in 1881, goes much further, and was fuelled by the international success of *Le roi de Lahore*. Here there are exotic touches of orchestration throughout and pastiche oriental dances are introduced several times with great effect. A religious scene uses the music of a Jewish cantor. Contrasted with all this is his sensual, curvaceous and lushly harmonized music of seduction. A remarkable scene occurs where sex-slaves comfort the despotic Herod with a drink-drugs cocktail.

Similar oriental music occurs in *Thaïs*, an opera that directly opposes Christian renunciation with oriental excess. Thaïs, a courtesan in love with Athanaël, a Christian monk, has music that is in Massenet's richest style, but her confidantes, and the various entertainments that pervade the opera, considerably heighten the oriental setting with devices similar to those employed in *Hérodiade*.

❋ SYMBOLISM OR IMPRESSIONISM?
∼ p. 297

Debussy considered these phrases 'useless terms of abuse' but they have been used a great deal to understand the different aspects of his work. On the one hand he set countless texts of the symbolist poets as songs, he chose a play from the greatest symbolist playwright for his only opera; and was fascinated by the symbolists' predecessors, the American writer Edgar Allan Poe and the poet Charles Baudelaire. On the other hand, he wrote pieces inspired by landscape: *La mer*, *Ibéria* and many 'water pieces' for piano. In his opera *Pelléas et Mélisande* both symbolism and Impressionism can be found. Symbolically, Debussy uses the Wagnerian *leitmotif* to represent both characters and deeper emotional states, to which definitive tags cannot be applied. Impressionistically he has to evoke the sea, the sun on the water, the forests and the stagnant water in the vaults under the castle, not to mention freshly watered roses. While he may have rejected connections with both movements, preferring to be himself, the ways in which he paralleled impressionism in *pointilliste* orchestration, and symbolism with questioning motives, are undeniable. Debussy was particularly in tune with the poets and painters of his time.

⊛ THE BIRTH OF THE
METROPOLITAN OPERA ∼ p. 364

In 1880 a meeting was held between a group of wealthy businessmen in New York. Their uniting cause was the limited number of box seats available at the Academy of Music, the city's primary venue for opera. The solution they posited was to build an entirely new opera house. A design was commissioned from J. Cleaveland Cady that included boxes on every level of the auditorium. Henry Abbey, an impresario from Ohio, was engaged as manager, and an impressive roster of artists drawn up. The power of the Italian repertoire at the time ensured that the orchestra and chorus were formed mostly from Italians – even American singers on the bill during the season changed their names to sound Italian.

On 22 October 1883 the Metropolitan Opera House was spectacularly opened with a performance of Gounod's *Faust* that took nearly $15,000 at the box office. This success was not to last, however, and the average takings per night that season levelled out at $3,500. There was no fear when it came to spending. The only recorded contract offers Polish soprano Marcella Sembrich $1,455 per night for a guaranteed 58 performances. Perhaps unsurprisingly, Abbey resigned at the end of the season. This building was demolished and a new uptown location developed at the Lincoln Center near Broadway and 63rd (where the action of Bernstein's *West Side Story* takes place). Opened in 1966, it can seat up to 4,000.

⌘ THE *SALOME* SCANDAL ~ p. 293

The premiere of *Salome* on 9 December 1905 was a scandal. Even before the work had been heard in public, there were serious problems. Rehearsals became increasingly difficult because of both the demands Strauss placed on the voice and the eroticism of the subject. At the first piano rehearsal, the entire cast handed back their scores, declaring it unsingable, with the exception of the Herod, who embarrassed everyone by claiming to know it from memory. The production's Salome, Marie Wittich, threatened to withdraw because she was 'a respectable married woman', and the orchestra said the piece was impossible to perform.

It was the shock effects of *Salome* that drew most attention to it. The sexual prurience of the subject, particularly the now-famous 'Dance of the Sevel Veils' and Salome's desire to kiss the severed head of Jochanaan, caused problems for many people. The work was immediately banned in Vienna and Berlin – where Strauss had attempted to calm frayed nerves by explaining that he was working on a biblical piece – and there was a two-year wait before permission was granted for a performance. *Salome* even caused ructions in Strauss's relationship with the Wagners. The royalties from the scandal, however, made Strauss a wealthy man and he was able to build the ultimate status symbol: his personal villa.

⌘ FAMOUS PERFORMANCES: *TOSCA* ~ p. 297

Stories of chaotic and bungled performances of *Tosca* abound, but there are two in particular that have become legendary. The first concerns a production in New York in 1960. The prima donna singing the title role had, through her various demands and irascibility, made herself unpopular with everyone – so much so, in fact, that the backstage crew decided to have their revenge on her. At the end of the opera, Tosca is instructed to leap from the battlements of the Castel Sant'Angelo, after her lover, Cavaradossi, has been executed. She would normally land safely on a specially constructed pad. In this instance, the crew apparently substituted the pad with a particularly springy trampoline. The tragedy of Tosca's dramatic leap was cut short as she reappeared above the parapets several times.

The other story reports that a set of under-rehearsed extras in a 1961 production in San Francisco was rushed in to be the firing squad. Instructed to come on stage, conduct the execution and exit with the principals, the squad was confused to discover both Tosca and Cavaradossi on stage and no clear indication of who should be shot. They finally settled on Tosca – she was, after all, the tragic eponymous heroine – only to see her lover collapse beside her. Further disarray followed when Tosca leapt off the parapet and the men were left on stage. True to their instructions, they exited with the principals, following one another as they too jumped from the castle.

THE MODERN ERA

Although the art of the classical singer has traditionally been perceived as the pursuit of technical perfection and tonal beauty, the twentieth century enabled a re-evaluation of what that art should be. Due in part to the technological advances and harrowing events of the times, much of the music was innovative, challenging, moving, powerful and, in many cases, an assault on the senses and sensibilities of the listener. Accordingly, twentieth- and twenty-first century opera has often provoked controversy, while opening the door to those who previously did not subscribe to its more bourgeois attributes.

The twentieth century's burgeoning spirit was not fully revealed until after the outbreak of the First World War in 1914. Many Europeans sought a new life in America, while others set about bringing a new order to the old regimes. A political vacuum in some countries would soon open the doors to Fascist opportunists, yet the US thrived, its economy boosted via the sale and distribution of products in Europe. America's own mushrooming population now included some of Europe's best and brightest talents from every walk of life, and this exodus continued throughout the 1930s. Music and modernism became inextricably linked, when various aspects of modernity – the avant-garde, Dadaism, surrealism, modernism and expressionism – began to explode across the socio-cultural landscape. The bourgeois aesthetic was replaced by a leaner, sparser, musical palette that was often driven by ethnically influenced rhythms and harmonies; music that defied explanation and flew in the face of traditional Western harmony.

As the upheaval of the world wars and various political movements died down, the individual came to prominence in art once more – or at least, an increased perception of the importance of the self. Certainly, grand statements about the 'big questions' are still a common presence on the operatic stage, such as social (in)justice and more recent global issues such as climate change, the increasing power of corporations and the fear of terrorism. As the new century settles, there is also an emerging trend towards a more intimate study of humanity. There is a clear fascination in many contemporary operas with psychological subtext and introspection; a number of chamber pieces explore the minutiae of everyday life.

KEY EVENTS

1917	February and October revolutions in Russia end in the Bolsheviks taking power
1918	End of the First World War
1921	First Salzburg Festival takes place
1929	Stock market crash on Wall Street
1933	Hitler becomes Chancellor of Germany
1936	The Spanish Civil War begins
1939	Britain and France declare war on Germany after its invasion of Poland
1941	Germany invades Russia; Japan's attack on Pearl Harbor leads to US entry into the war
1945	The Second World War ends
1953	Soviet leader Joseph Stalin dies
1956	Hungarian revolt is crushed by the USSR
1963	Martin Luther King leads the freedom March on Washington
1969	Man walks on the Moon
1980	Philips releases the first compact discs
1985	Gorbachev becomes president of the USSR
1989	End of communist rule in many Eastern European states – fall of Berlin Wall
1992	World Wide Web enters the public domain
2001	Terrorist attacks in the United States
2003	Second Gulf War begins
2009	Barack Obama is first black US president
2016	Britain votes to leave European Union
2017	Donald Trump inaugurated as US president

The Modern Era
INTRODUCTION

The opera house and, more specifically, opera audiences, were among the last to be receptive to the new musical language that developed during the twentieth century. Slow, as well as reluctant to vary their traditional musical tastes, perceptions and expectations, many viewed the opera house with nostalgia; as a symbol of the establishment, holding on to the last vestiges of a secure, civilized and supremely hierarchical culture. Early in the twentieth century, Richard Strauss's (1864–1949) *Salome* (1905), had pointed the way to the future, followed by *Elektra* in 1909, both of which employed new and bold musical language to push chromaticism to its breaking point and thrust tonality towards the edge of the abyss. For his part, Strauss subsequently resurrected his late-Romantic style and embraced musical conservatism, thus allowing other composers to ignite the torch of modernism. Whereas entertainment had always been light opera's strongest component, serious music drama could be divided into two categories: opera of ideas and opera of realism. Opera of ideas is derived from the Wagnerian model, while opera of realism springs from Verdi's style of dramatic realism, expressing inner feelings that adhere to the verismo (heightened realism) tradition.

THE BALLETS RUSSES

Ballet plunged headlong into the new sound, embracing theatricality and daring the Ballets Russes and their producer, Sergei Diaghilev (1872–1929), to commission **Igor Stravinsky**'s (1882–1971) compositions *The Firebird* (1910), *Petrushka* (1911) and *The Rite of Spring*

(1913). The riots provoked by *The Rite of Spring* are legendary, yet the opera world would have to wait another 12 years to experience that kind of boldness and theatricality in the form of **Alban Berg**'s (1885–1935) *Wozzeck* (composed 1917–1921). This opera, with its use of **atonality** and serialism and its story of an ordinary, troubled man, was nothing short of revolutionary. *Erwartung* ('Expectation', 1909), on the other hand, composed by Berg's serialist teacher, **Arnold Schoenberg** (1874–1951), was somewhat mired by a static monodrama format. The conflict during this period between theatrically conceived opera and the formalized structures of serialism would ensure the former's slow advancement in deference to the opera-cantata form.

AN ERA OF EXPERIMENTATION

Bold and original voices from outside western Europe were beginning to be heard: Russia's **Dmitri Shostakovich** (1906–75), **Leoš Janáček** (1854–1928), once viewed in Czechoslovakia as a 'rural, home-grown talent', but now poised for operatic immortality courtesy of his substantial *oeuvre*, and Hungarian composer **Béla Bartók** (1881–1945), whose sole opera, *Bluebeard's Castle* (1918), would also make an indelible mark. As others responded by breaking with Austro-German tradition, so new creative voices emerged, each bolder and more confident than their predecessors.

Western music, rather than crystalizing or formalizing, was expanding and in a state of total experimentation, and many individuals were emboldened by the ability to express themselves. However, some also paid the price by means of harsh and demeaning criticism of their work, as well as being banned from public performance. Shostakovich was one such victim, his creative lights having been dimmed after Stalin attended a performance in 1936 of *Lady Macbeth*

295

of Mtsensk (1932) and compelled him to observe the Communist Party's artistic guidelines, as laid down by its so-called cultural commission. **Sergei Prokofiev** (1891–1953) also suffered the same fate upon his return to the Soviet Union.

NAZI CULTURAL REPRESSION

Still, the ultimate repression of artistic expression was that meted out to Jews by the Nazi Party during the 1930s. All forms of Jewish music and artistic expression were outlawed, while any other artists who did not conform to party doctrine were also banned from public performance. The Party even commissioned a leading official, Hans Severus Ziegler, to curate an exhibition of 'Entartete Musik' (degenerate music). Opened in Dusseldorf in 1938, the exhibition displayed works by Jewish and other ethnic minority composers, musicians who were perceived as an ideological or political threat to the Third Reich, and those who embraced atonal or avant-garde writing styles. Some more astute, or fortunate, people departed Germany before it was too late (if indeed they had the money to escape or the financial and bureaucratic support from others to do so) but many, such as composer **Victor Ullmann** (1898–1944), could not foresee or otherwise escape the Final Solution and went unwittingly to their eventual extermination.

Musically, pre-war Berlin was a thrilling place to be, and produced some biting social satire in the form of what Germans called *Zeitoper* – among the earliest examples were Ernst Krenek's jazz-inspired *Jonny spielt auf* ('Johnny Strikes Up', 1926) and the groundbreaking **Bertolt Brecht** (1898–1956) and his collective of writers, and **Kurt Weill** (1900–50) collaboration, *Die Dreigroschenoper* ('The Threepenny Opera', 1928). Yet these great artistic and political talents were also suppressed, prompting them to leave for new frontiers.

NEW SOUNDS AND STAGE DESIGN

With new sounds came new designs for the stage, providing visual artists with a large canvas to express themselves by way of operatic set design. Brecht's revolutionary vision of the stage amounted to defining the theatre not as a place where realism is constructed, but rather as a place where illusions are produced, without any need to disguise the machinations of theatrical illusion. At the same time, others who followed the Expressionist trend tried to suggest the psychological inner world of thoughts and feelings, Surrealism and Dada impacting opera via Guillaume Apollinaire's *Les mamelles de Tirésias* ('The Breasts of Tirésias', 1947), composed by **Francis Poulenc** (1899–1963).

A VARIED REPERTOIRE

From grand venues to the intimate chamber settings of church halls, salons and small public theatres, operas varied radically, and so did the experience and perspective of each composer. Stravinsky's *The Rake's Progress* (1951) took its neo-classical style from Mozartian models; **Karlheinz Stockhausen** (1928–2007) ventured into completely uncharted territory, employing a grand scheme that had previously never been heard in opera; **György Ligeti** (1923–2006), dismissing formal structures, opted for a chaotic world of sound; and **Mauricio Kagel**'s (1931–2008) performance art created 'anti-opera' in *Sur Scène* (1962), which would evolve into his deconstruction of the operatic traditions. Indeed, the edifice of Bayreuth tradition would also be shattered by Wieland Wagner's modern interpretation of the Wagnerian repertoire. Since the Kroll Opera's emergence in the late 1920s, directors, designers and the avant-garde have reinterpreted the operatic canon with varying degrees of success. David Hockney, for one, has received considerable acclaim for utilizing his art to interpret for the stage. While North

America has been slower to incorporate these trends, modern adaptions are more often *de rigueur* in Europe.

THE LURE OF CHARISMATIC SINGERS

Despite the variety of ways in which opera is produced, the public is still enchanted by the power and charisma of the singers themselves. In his book *The Queen's Throat: Opera, Homosexuality and the Mystery of Desire* (1993), Wayne Koestenbaum describes the strange bond that audiences form with performers. Singers are those intangible elements, who, when involved in the creative process, can bring operas to life in ways that are unfathomable even to the composers. With offerings ranging from Bugs Bunny's *What's Opera, Doc?* (1957) to the Three Tenors (**Luciano Pavarotti**, **Placido Domingo** and **José Carreras**) singing in sports arenas in their concert garb in the 1990s, operatic music became popularized on a grand scale. Opera continues to enter the popular arena, notably at official and sporting events: in 2014, the much-loved soprano Renée Fleming was the first opera singer to perform the American national anthem at the Super Bowl.

✹ HOGARTH'S ENGRAVINGS
∾ p. 363

When Stravinsky attended a Hogarth exhibition at the Art Institute in Chicago, he was so captivated by the natural narrative of certain images that he wanted to use them as the basis for an English-language opera. At the recommendation of his friend Aldous Huxley, Stravinsky contacted the poet W. H. Auden, and the two of them subsequently set to work on *The Rake's Progress*. Hogarth's stock in trade was that of an artist; painting, drawing and making prints of his drawings. It was these prints that Stravinsky saw at the Art Institute, including an eight-image series featuring Tom Rakewell: *The young

heir taking possession; *Surrounded by artists and professors*; *The tavern scene*; *Arrested for debt*; *Marries an old maid*; *Scene in a gambling house*; *Prison scene*; and *Scene in Bedlam*. Rakewell's problem, according to Hogarth, was 'affectation' and the habit of misrepresenting himself. The artist had been inspired to create a series on *The Rake* after the success of his previous group of etchings and engravings, *The Harlot*.

✹ OPERA IN THE TEREZÍN CONCENTRATION CAMP ∾ p. 365

'The only thing worth emphasizing is that Theresienstadt has not hampered my musical activity, but actually encouraged it and supported it.' The final entry in Victor Ullmann's journal referred to 'Theresienstadt', the town of Terezín, 60 kilometres northeast of Prague, which was remote enough for the Nazis to pursue their barbarism in relative seclusion. Yet within the walls of the camp grew a small underground artists' colony. The Nazis did not condone the 'cultural life' that emerged in the ghetto, but they were also aware that it greatly reduced the chances of insurrection while serving as a useful propaganda tool that would mask their true intent.

Written by Ullmann and librettist Petr Kien, *Der Kaiser von Atlantis* ('The Emperor of Atlantis', 1943) is a biting political satire rather than an opera. Scored for seven singers and 13 instrumentalists, it is considered one of the most important works to emerge from the camp. Nevertheless, its subject matter also ensured that it was never performed at Terezín. (The premiere took place in 1975, conducted by Kerry Woodward, and it was later recorded for Decca's exceptional survey of Entartete Musik). Music and visual art abounded within the camp confines, and it is a testament to the doomed artists' creativity and strength of will that, in the face of extreme oppression, they produced work that spoke not just of pain but also of profound beauty.

The Modern Era
GENRES AND STYLES

Throughout the twentieth century, opera constantly re-evaluated and redefined itself. Two world wars created a crisis of national identities that was reflected in a series of artistic challenges within the world of music – tradition over pluralism, experimentation over formalization – as composers sought to free themselves from Austro-Germanic influences.

BOLDER ATTITUDES
Janáček is a case in point. Quitting his studies in Vienna, he returned to Brno and began to write in his own idiomatic way, utilizing a 'through-composed' style. Bartók similarly took the Hungarian language and, creating a declamatory style that followed the patterns of speech, applied it to Freudian tensions between man and woman. And then there was the work of French composers **Maurice Ravel** (1875–1937) and **Claude Debussy** (1862–1918), who moved away from the tonal and harmonic influences of **Richard Wagner** (1813–1883). Certainly, the nationalistic idiom prevalent before World War I was unsustainable after it: bolder attitudes were inevitable as composers sought to create musical dialects that could somehow express global post-war devastation and the new political and social orders that were emerging as a consequence.

NEW LANGUAGE AND DEVICES
Many devices, such as **recitative**, **aria** and **ensemble**, are a part of the neo-classical style that is prevalent in Stravinsky's *The Rake's Progress*. Yet, in spite of all its influences from **Wolfgang Amadeus Mozart** (1756–91), it still sounds like a modern opera. Such is

the result of pairing twentieth-century tonal and harmonic language with older organizational devices. Meanwhile, at the other end of the spectrum, performance art enters the realm of opera, courtesy of Kagel's approach to 'anti-opera' in his work *Staatstheater* (1971). The nine scenes, each self-contained, can be reorganized into any order the director wants.

THE SPLINTERING OF OPERA
With opera splintered into mainstream, alternative (experimental, chamber, contemporary) and **music theatre** (of the Broadway and West End variety), this raises the question of ongoing financial viability. Many regional opera houses are expanding their repertoire to include operetta and music theatre – some European houses have programmed *West Side Story* (1957) in their season, while even the German Staatstheater and Viennese Volksoper have hosted everything from operetta to Broadway musicals. As Théâtre de Châtelet, Paris, has demonstrated more recently, works from this genre (from Lerner and Loewe's *My Fair Lady* to major works by Stephen Sondheim) can be woven successfully into each season. As these venues are well aware, survival is dependent not just on a production's quality, but also on its perceived 'entertainment' value.

Accordingly, composers are often caught in a struggle to fulfil their artistic vision while attaining patronage for their work, usually in the form of commissions. Commissioned works often come with particular demands or constraints: operas can be a costly venture, often with high production values that do not just involve singers and an orchestra but lavish theatrical sets and effects, costumes, dancers and supernumaries. It is therefore little wonder that **Benjamin Britten** (1913–76) founded his English Opera Group (1947), whose mission was the performance of chamber opera.

CHAMBER OPERA

While there will always be a place for – and indeed an obsession with – *grand opera*, economic constraints in the early twenty-first century have in large part inspired what might be considered to be a golden era for chamber opera, with many opera houses using their studio theatres to commission lower-budget and more 'risky' new pieces. Because chamber pieces are usually performed in a more intimate setting than the grand opera house, this also enables singers and orchestras to engage in a subtly more detailed dialogue. Paradoxically, as the world becomes more 'connected' through technology, nothing can quite replicate the metaphysical connection that comes from live theatre. Audiences clamour for vivid, close-up theatrical experiences, and, through sheer proximity and perhaps also the often more close-up subject matter, chamber opera has the power to create a symbiotic relationship between audience and performers.

THE RESURGENCE OF REALISM

With the rise of smaller-scale works has come a renewed exploration of close relationships within more intimate scenarios, often with detailed reflections on the interior lives of the characters. Real-life, although heightened, stories are investigated in works such as Jake Heggie's *Dead Man Walking* (1995), which explores the relationship of a convicted murderer on death row, Joseph De Rocher, with his mother and Sister Helen Prejean, the nun who supports him in the days before his execution. Jonathan Dove's *Flight* (which premiered at Glyndebourne in 1998 and is now programmed regularly across Europe) was inspired by the tale of Mehran Karimi Nasseri, an Iranian refugee who, having been refused permission to enter France, lived in Charles de Gaulle airport for 17 years. In 2015, composer Tansy Davies collaborated with director Deborah Warner and librettist Nick Drake to address the events of 11 September 2001 in *Between Worlds*.

While these and similar stories are visceral and immediate, composers often temper this with surreal vocal elements: in particular, high coloratura soprano and countertenor voices are exploited to add an ethereal, other-worldly feel to tales of raw human experience.

THE RECORDED VOICE

The advent of recordings certainly made opera accessible to many more people than ever before, and Enrico Caruso (1873–1921) was single-handedly responsible for the proliferation of his art via this medium. By the end of his life, he had made over 250 recordings. When the film world finally developed talkies, opera once again stepped to the fore, both to entertain the uninitiated and also to record for posterity the performances of renowned artists; some at the height of their career, others clearly on the decline. While singers such as Leo Slezak (1873–1946), **Beniamino Gigli** (1890–1957) and **Ezio Pinza** (1892–1957) were featured on film and achieved fame thanks to their exposure in the popular arena, other opera luminaries were the subject of newsreels and popularized on the radio. Meanwhile, artists such as **Maria Callas** (1923–77), Herbert von Karajan and **Elisabeth Schwarzkopf** (1915–2006) also owe their fame in part to exposure through recordings – not of stage performances, but those conceived to encapsulate a presence and artistry.

Ultimately, recordings shifted from being historical documents to being an art form unto themselves. At the centre of this revolution was EMI record producer Walter Legge. Consequently, today's operaphile has an extensive catalogue of recorded works from which to select, whether purchased for historical, educational or entertainment purposes.

The Modern Era
PERSONALITIES

Adams, John
b. 1947, **AMERICAN**

One of the most influential musical figures of his generation, John Adams draws on numerous genres, including jazz, ragtime, swing, pop and rock. Indeed, although he has often been labelled a minimalist, Adams is more expressive than many such composers; his mature works blend the rhythmic energy associated with this style with the harmonic interest and colour of late Romanticism.

Adams eschews historical and mythological figures for modern-day characters. His first opera, *Nixon in China* (composed 1984–87) saw librettist Alice Goodman, stage director Peter Sellars and choreographer Mark Morris form a dynamic collaboration that resumed in 1991 with *The Death of Klinghoffer*, which addressed the 1985 Palestinian hijacking of an Italian cruise ship. His next full-length opera, *Doctor Atomic* (premiered in 2005), explored the life and work of nuclear scientist J. Robert Oppenheimer and borrowed the structure of 1950s sci-fi movies.

Commissioned jointly by San Francisco Opera, Dallas Opera, Dutch National Opera and Teatro la Fenice, Venice, *Girls of the Golden West* (composed 2016–17), is based upon contemporary accounts of the California Gold Rush era. Peter Sellars' libretto includes newspaper reports and the writing of Louise Amelia Knapp Smith Clappe and Mark Twain.

Nixon in China
by John Adams
Composed: 1984–87
Premiered: 1987, Houston
Libretto by Alice Goodman

ACT I
On 21 February 1972, representatives of the Chinese armed forces are waiting at an airfield outside Beijing in order to greet President Richard Nixon on his arrival. The presidential Boeing, The Spirit of '76, *taxies to a halt. Nixon disembarks with his wife, Pat, and greets Premier Chou En-lai. Nixon is excited. He compares his landing in Beijing, seen live by millions of Americans on prime-time television, with the 1969 landing of the astronauts on the moon. Henry Kissinger tells him he is to see Mao Tse-tung.*

One hour later Nixon meets Chairman Mao in his office. Official photographs are taken. Everything Mao says is repeated, parrot-style, by his three secretaries. Nixon cannot understand Mao's seemingly unfathomable political observations and gnomic jokes. At the evening banquet Chou offers a toast to future brotherhood. Nixon's reply is to the Chinese people and the hope of peace. The toasts become less formal.

ACT II
Next morning Mrs Nixon is given a glass elephant while visiting a factory. At a farm she reminisces about rearing a prize-winning boar. Her sightseeing continues to the Summer Palace and the Ming tombs. Their evening entertainment is The Red Detachment of Women, *a revolutionary ballet devised by Mao's wife, Chiang Ch'ing. The wicked overseer menacing the downtrodden peasant girl is played by Kissinger. Mrs Nixon is drawn into the action. The girl is rescued and joins the Red Women's Militia. Chiang Ch'ing asserts her place in Chinese history.*

ACT III
On the last night of the visit the five principal characters lie in separate beds. The Nixons remember their early marriage, including his hamburger stand. Mao and Chiang Ch'ing recall the film actress meeting the revolutionary, and their struggles for the Revolution. Chou En-lai, alone, ponders, 'How much of what we did was good?'

Adès, Thomas
b. 1971, ENGLISH

The operas of celebrated composer, conductor, pianist and curator Thomas Adès have rapidly entered the contemporary repertoire. His chamber opera, *Powder Her Face* (1995) – a tale of the scandalous behaviour Duchess of Argyll in the early 1960s – provides an excellent performance opportunity for a soprano with notable dramatic as well as vocal powers. *The Tempest* (2004), directed by Robert Lepage and conducted by Adès himself, was premiered at Covent Garden, swiftly followed by performances at the Metropolitan Opera.

Adès observed in an interview in 2012 that 'Operas that are worthily about something, some idea or ideal, and that try to make a point, especially a political point, are just absurd in an off-putting way ... Music should have no excuse, other than itself.'

Premiered in 2016 at the Salzburg Festival, *The Exterminating Angel*, in which Adès makes typically extreme demands upon the range and capabilities of every voice in the cast, received a rapturous response from critics and audiences alike.

Recommended Recording:
The Tempest, Orchestra of the Royal Opera House, Covent Garden; Thomas Adès, conductor; EMI 6952342; Soloists: Simon Keenlyside (Prospero), Kate Royal (Miranda), Toby Spence (Ferdinand), Ian Bostridge (Caliban), Cyndia Sieden (Ariel), Philip Langridge (Alonso), Donald Kaasch (Antonio), Jonathan Summers (Sebastian), David Condier (Trinculo), Stephen Richardson (Stefano), Graeme Danby (Gonzalo)

Auden, W. H.
1907–73, ENGLISH

Possessing an ironic wit and a supreme lyric gift, Wystan Hugh Auden, born in York, England, in 1907, was one of the great writers of the twentieth century. To

him, opera was 'the last refuge of the High Style', since it was the sole art that could survive the pessimism of modernity. In 1930, Auden completed his first volume of poetry. Later, he witnessed the rise of Nazism while living in the sexually liberated atmosphere of Berlin, and then was a civilian observer of the Spanish Civil War. Relocating to New York in 1939, Auden became a US citizen in 1946. It was during this period that he began to write opera libretti with his partner, Chester Kallman. Their most triumphant collaboration was with Stravinsky on *The Rake's Progress*, and the two men also wrote the libretto to *Delia*, which Stravinsky never set. Other Auden-Kallman collaborations included the libretti to *Elegy for Young Lovers*, *The Bassarids* and *Love's Labour's Lost* (1970). Auden died in Vienna in 1973.

Baker, Janet, DBE
b. 1933, ENGLISH

Known for her rich, expressive and intensely personal performances, Baker's voice is equally at home with Handel, Mozart, Donizetti, Berlioz and Walton. Britten wrote the role of Kate Julian for her in *Owen Wingrave*, while **William Walton** (1902–83) adjusted the part of Cressida in *Troilus and Cressida* to suit her voice. In 1966, she made her Covent Garden debut in Britten's *A Midsummer Night's Dream*, and performed her first major role at Glyndebourne in *Dido and*

Aeneas. Baker may be best known for her **Lieder**, which set her apart from her contemporaries. Championing the lesser-known works of Schubert, she recorded for the Hyperion label. Following her retirement from the operatic stage in 1982, and from the concert stage in 1989, she served as Chancellor of the University of York.

Barber, Samuel
1910–81, AMERICAN

Samuel Barber's talents were evident from a very young age. Musically conservative, his harmonic language was highly influenced by late nineteenth-century Romanticism and often criticized by modernists. Indeed, although his style defied label, and his dissonances and harmonies were not truly Romantic, his gifts as a supreme melodist served to pigeonhole him.

Barber established a lifelong personal and professional relationship with **Gian Carlo Menotti** (1911–2007), whose libretto for Barber's first full-length opera, *Vanessa* (1957), was based on Isak Dinesen's *Seven Gothic Tales*. Barber received the Pulitzer prize for *Vanessa*, yet *Antony and Cleopatra* (1966), commissioned by the Metropolitan Opera for its 1966 season opening, suffered from an overblown production that was nevertheless eclipsed by the venue itself. This disappointment slowed his momentum, and although he revised the work in 1974, it never achieved the success he so hoped for. Instead, he is best remembered for two non-operatic works: *Adagio for Strings* (composed 1936) and *Knoxville: Summer of 1915* (composed 1947–49, first performed 1950), for soprano and orchestra.

Bartók, Béla
1881–1945, HUNGARIAN

Widely recognized as one of the twentieth century's most important composers, Bartók was supremely original in terms of his musical language, creating a national style that merged folk melodies with the asymmetric patterns of Hungarian speech. His vocal lines, often punctuated by a heavy chordal style, are evident in *Duke Bluebeard's Castle*, whose libretto by Béla Balázs is based upon Maurice Maeterlinck's play *Ariane et Barbe-bleu*. Composed in 1911 and premiered in Budapest on 24 May 1918, this one-act opera with prologue was dedicated to Bartók's first wife, and probably gave her ample food for thought about a husband who evidently identified with the central character's feelings of loneliness and isolation. Bartók's psychodrama unfolds with Bluebeard's latest wife, Judith, accompanying him to his dark and ominous castle, where she unlocks seven doors that reveal the duke's pain and suffering. By the seventh door, having learned all of her husband's darkest secrets, Judith is doomed to take her place alongside the other wives. Bartók remarried in 1923 and later relocated to New York, where he died in 1945.

Duke Bluebeard's Castle
by Béla Bartók
Composed: 1911 (re. 1912; 1918)
Premiered: 1918, Budapest
Libretto by Béla Balázs, after a fairy-tale by Charles Perrault

Bluebeard and Judith appear in the doorway of his castle. She has left her family and declares she will never leave him. He closes the iron door. She offers to warm the stones and let in the light. There are no windows, only seven locked doors. She demands he opens them. The first opens with a cavernous sigh. It is his torture chamber: the walls are bleeding. He tells her to beware of the castle, and gives her the second key. It is his armoury, the weapons stained with blood. She may have three more keys, on condition that she asks no questions. The third and fourth doors reveal the treasury and his garden, the jewels smeared with blood and the flowers withering. The fifth opens onto the glory of his kingdom. All this is now hers. Judith cannot rest while two doors remain closed. She holds out her hand for the sixth key. The castle grows darker as a still white lake of tears is revealed. He kisses her. She asks if his previous love was more beautiful, was she different? Still he refuses to open the last door. Now she knows the tears are those of his murdered wives. She must open the seventh door. His three former wives appear, each wearing a crown, and he kneels before them. He found them at morning, noon and evening. He found Judith, the most beautiful of all, at night. While she begs him to stop, he dresses her in a starry cloak and a crown. She follows them back and the door closes behind them. Now the night will last for ever.

Bartoli, Cecilia

b. 1966, ITALIAN

Achieving fame at an early age with her vocal agility and warm tone, this **mezzo-soprano**'s studies began in Rome at the Conservatorio di Santa Cecilia. Bartoli is best known as a Baroque, Rossini and Mozart specialist, having collaborated with many of music's pre-eminent early music ensembles. She remains highly sought after for her compelling personality, dramatic flair and utter dedication to the score.

Benjamin, George

b. 1960, BRITISH

George Benjamin's teachers included Olivier Messaien, who compared his student with Mozart; although contrary to the febrile pace of much of Mozart's composing, Benjamin has always taken time over his work, often taking a number of years to complete works of a few minutes. His first full-scale opera, *Written on Skin*, became an instant classic after its premiere at Aix-en-Provence in 2012 and its transfer to the Royal Opera House, Covent Garden. Tickets in London

were impossible to come by (the ROH also used its occasional policy of lowering prices to make contemporary works more accessible to new audiences). Excitement about Benjamin's meticulous and dramatically sensitive work was palpable: it was seen by many as an operatic game-changer with its psychologically astute libretto by Martin Crimp, its dramatic tautness, and its fusion of musical styles. As well as praising the impeccable orchestration, the critic Alex Ross noted '*Written on Skin* feels like the work of a genius unleashed'.

His keenly-anticipated third opera, *Lessons in Love and Violence*, inspired by Elizabethan drama and exploring the conflict between love and politics, was commissioned by the Royal Opera House for its 2018 premiere in London.

Recommended Recording:

Written on Skin, Mahler Chamber Orchestra; George Benjamin, conductor; Nimbus Records NI 5885/6; Soloists: Barbara Hannigan (Agnes), Bejun Mehta (First Angel/Boy), Christopher Purves (Protector), Rebecca Jo Loeb (Second Angel/Marie), Allan Clayton (Third Angel/John)

Berg, Alban

1885–1935, AUSTRIAN

The composer of just two operas, Berg was a man who took atonality and stretched it to its expressionistic limits. While **Joseph Haydn** (1732–1809), Mozart and **Ludwig Van Beethoven** (1770–1827) are often referred to as the First Viennese School, the so-called Second Viennese School consists of Berg together with fellow student **Anton Webern** (1883–1945) and their teacher, Arnold Schoenberg.

SCHOENBERG'S STUDENT

Berg was born in Vienna into a wealthy family, but he did not have a formal musical education. He wrote his first composition in 1901, and three years later, after a short spell as a civil servant, he began studying under Schoenberg, whose style was advancing rapidly towards atonality. Berg's studies formed and crystallized Schoenberg's theories of harmony and serialism as laid out in *Harmonielehre* ('The Theory of Harmony', published 1911). And at a time when Vienna's cultural life was burgeoning, Berg also had numerous opportunities to take in all the important musical compositions and theatrical productions of the day. For instance, although the theatrical works of Frank Wedekind were regarded as shocking and were banned by the German authorities, in 1905 Berg saw a private performance of *Die Büchse der Pandora* ('Pandora's Box'), one of two Wedekind plays that he would later adapt for his setting of the incomplete *Lulu* (1929–35).

AUDIENCE RESPONDS RIOTOUSLY

The last of Berg's tonal vocal compositions, *Sieben Frühe Lieder* ('Seven Early Songs', composed 1905–08), was influenced stylistically by Romanticism and Impressionism. However, in 1913 two of his five *Altenberg Lieder* caused a riot when performed to an unruly audience, and the songs were not performed again until 1952.

SHOCKING SUBJECT MATTER

Unlike Schoenberg and Webern, Berg wrote in an instinctively theatrical style, and his first opera, *Wozzeck*, connects viscerally with the audience. The work was based on Georg Büchner's play *Woyzeck* (1836), which Berg saw in Vienna in 1914. Drawn to this work, he envisioned it as the basis for an opera and returned to see it numerous times. Although army service slowed its progress, the opera was completed in 1922 and performed in Berlin in December 1925. Friends and colleagues were surprised and shocked by

the subject matter, and even Schoenberg found the depiction of common people in degraded circumstances tragic and unappealing.

SECRETLY CODED COMPOSITIONS

Berg was fascinated by numerology, and serialism proved to be mathematical nirvana in terms of his compositional style. He often used the palindrome as a writing device, and when theorists delved into his work they unearthed personal messages that had been 'encoded' in his *Lyric Suite* (1925–26). Presumably, these secret messages were intended for Berg's mistress, Hanna Fuchs-Robettin, causing his wife to be so incensed that she subsequently tried to suppress information pertaining to such compositional devices.

Berg's final work, commissioned by Louis Krasner, was his famous violin concerto (1935). It was, in fact, commissioned while he was composing both Lulu and the concert aria *Der Wein* ('Wine', 1930), and he was not compelled to write it until the untimely death of Manon Gropius, the daughter of **Gustav Mahler**'s (1860–1911) widow Alma Mahler Gropius. Berg's final completed work, it was not performed until after his death on Christmas Eve, 1935, from blood poisoning caused by an insect bite.

Wozzeck

Composed between 1917 and 1922 and first performed in Berlin on 14 December 1925, this work features Berg's own libretto, based on the Georg Büchner play *Woyzeck*. Written a century earlier, the play recounts the true story of a soldier, barber and drifter who is executed for murder. Büchner may have read about Johann Christian Woyzeck as a case history in one of his father's medical journals. Suffering from paranoia and hallucinations, Woyzeck sought a pardon based on his mental condition, and the case's notoriety thus stemmed from his plea of diminished responsibility, or the 'insanity defence'.

Under the banner of 'wir arme leut' ('we poor folk'), Berg symbolically raises Wozzeck as a universal figure, creating a work that is one of the high points of German Expressionism. Berg creates three acts, each with five fast-paced scenes, each with its own musical form and linked by orchestral interludes, featuring wonderfully effective and meticulously notated use of *Sprechgesang* ('speech-singing'). Much of Berg's structural and thematic organization is not apparent unless studying the score, thus making the operations of these devices and techniques subliminal. However, the spoken score traverses numerous musical styles, from tonal to atonal, *Sprechgesang* to song, and from cabaret to dissonant counterpoint.

Wozzeck

by Alban Berg
Composed: 1917–22
Premiered: 1925, Berlin
Libretto by the composer, after Georg Büchner's play *Woyzeck*

ACT I

Wozzeck, an orderly, is shaving the captain, who tells him to slow down. What is he going to do with the rest of his life? Tired of Wozzeck's replies of 'Yes, sir', the captain calls him dim and worthy, but he has no morality. He also has a child 'not blessed by the Church'. Wozzeck replies that God will not spurn the mite because of that. Poor people cannot afford to have morals. The captain says that Wozzeck thinks too much.

Wozzeck and Andres are cutting sticks in the fields. Andres sings a hunting song, but Wozzeck senses the place is cursed. The sun sets with a final blaze of colour. Marie and her child are standing at her window watching a parade. Her neighbour Margret suggestively comments on the drum major's interest in Marie. She slams the window

SOUNDS FAMILIAR

MARIE'S LULLABY

In *Wozzeck*, Act I, Scene 3, Marie lusts after the drum major as she and her neighbour Margret watch the marching band pass by. Restless and self-absorbed, Marie's lullaby has the vocal grace that one might expect, yet her cold and detached words inform us that she is not a maternal figure.

shut and sings a lullaby, rocking the child asleep. Wozzeck briefly returns, still deep in gloomy thoughts, and pays little attention to their child. Marie declares that this cannot continue.

The doctor has been supplementing Wozzeck's army pay with a few coins from medical experiments, including living on a diet of just beans for three months. He is angry that Wozzeck has not been following orders. Wozzeck asks if there is anything to hang on to when everything is dark. The doctor boasts that his research will make him immortal provided Wozzeck follows instructions. The drum major is puffing himself out to impress Marie. She resists, but then succumbs, saying 'What does it matter?'

ACT II

Marie is admiring her new earrings from the drum major. Her child is frightened. She tells Wozzeck she found them, but he mutters that he's never found two together. He gives her money and she is full of remorse. The captain meets the doctor in the street and tells him to slow down. In reply the doctor sees the captain as an interesting medical specimen. They stop Wozzeck and taunt him, asking if he has found a hair from a drum major's beard in his breakfast bowl. He warns them not to make fun of him. The doctor declares him 'a real phenomenon'.

Wozzeck sees Marie in the street and accuses her of being unfaithful. She holds him off, saying it would be better if he were to kill her than beat her. Andres asks why Wozzeck is sitting alone in the tavern. The idiot tells Wozzeck that he smells blood. Marie dances with the drum major and Wozzeck sees a red mist before him. Wozzeck is trying to sleep in the barracks, but he keeps on seeing them dancing and a knife flashing. The drum major, drunk and boasting about Marie, nearly throttles him.

ACT III
Marie is looking for consolation in the Bible story of the adulterous woman. She begs God to show her mercy as he did to Mary Magdalene. Wozzeck brings Marie to a pool in the forest. She shivers when he kisses her. A blood-red moon rises as he cuts her throat. Wozzeck is drinking in the tavern but Margret sees blood on his hand as they dance and he rushes out. Wozzeck is looking for the knife and imagines Marie with a crimson necklace to match her earrings. He finds the knife and throws it into the pool, before wading out and drowning. The captain and the doctor hear sounds like someone drowning, but do nothing. Marie's child is playing with the other children when one of them tells him his mother is dead. Not understanding, he carries on playing before running after the others.

Lulu
First performed as an incomplete work on 2 June 1937 in Zurich, this opera boasts a Berg libretto that is based on two Frank Wedekind tragedies: *Erdgeist* ('Earth Spirit', 1895) and *Die Büchse der Pandora* ('Pandora's Box', 1904). Following the composer's death, controversy arose as to the fate of the incomplete third act. Berg's widow asked Schoenberg, Webern and **Alexander Zemlinsky** (1871–1942) to complete the opera but they all refused. From this point on, she withheld all of Berg's supporting materials. It was not until after her own death in 1976 that Berg's manuscripts were finally released, at which point the third act was completed by Friedrich Cerha. *Lulu*'s revival took place at the Paris Opéra in 1979, under Pierre Boulez.

Berg's opera studies the central character's victimization through a series of choices and unusual events that begin to spiral downward following her marriage to Dr Schön. He is jealous of Lulu's steady stream of lovers, who include the lesbian Countess Geschwitz and his own son, Alwa. When Schön responds to his son's involvement by demanding that his wife commit suicide, she kills him instead and is arrested. Her subsequent escape leads to the streets of London, with Alwa and the Countess Geschwitz in tow, but her life as a prostitute is brought to an abrupt and bloody end when she unfortunately solicits one Jack the Ripper.

Just as in *Wozzeck*, Berg ties this work together with a number of structural devices that operate on a subliminal level, while his masterful orchestration ranges from the dense and lush to the stark cabaret style popularized by Kurt Weill.

Lulu
by Alban Berg
Composed: 1929–35
Premiered 1937, Zürich (incomplete version); 1979, Paris (complete in three acts)
Libretto by the composer, after Frank Wedekind's plays *Erdgeist* and *Die Büchse der Pandora*

BACKGROUND
An animal tamer introduces the pride of his menagerie, Lulu the snake.

ACT I
Dr Schön has arranged a marriage for his mistress, Lulu. The painter attempts to seduce her while painting her portrait. Her husband interrupts them and dies from shock. Lulu has married the painter. Schigolch (perhaps

her father, perhaps her first lover) arrives. Schön tells Lulu he is getting married and must end their relationship. Schön reveals Lulu's past to the painter, who kills himself. Lulu is determined to marry Schön. Lulu is a dancer in a show written by Schön's son Alwa, who wants to compose an opera about her. An African prince offers to marry her. She refuses to perform when she sees Schön with his fiancée in the audience and orders him to break off his engagement.

ACT II

Lulu has married Schön. He disapproves of her latest admirer, the lesbian Countess Geschwitz. Schigolch introduces two more, an athlete and a schoolboy. They hide when Alwa enters and declares his love. Schön drags Alwa away but he returns and offers Lulu a loaded revolver. All the admirers try to escape when Lulu fires into the ceiling. He urges her to kill herself but she shoots him in the back. Lulu promises to be faithful to Alwa if he will help her. Lulu is sent to prison. Geschwitz infects her with cholera and changes places with her in hospital. The athlete wants Lulu for his new act and plans to blackmail Alwa. Lulu arrives, thin and weak. They are going to Paris.

ACT III

In Paris everyone has invested in railway shares and they are also winning at the casino. Lulu is blackmailed by the marquis and the athlete. Schigolch offers to dispose of the athlete for money. Fortunes change at the tables. They all lose and the banker, hearing that the shares have collapsed, demands payment in cash. Lulu changes clothes with a page and escapes with Alwa.

Lulu is a prostitute in London. Schigolch and Alwa hide when she appears with her first client. Geschwitz arrives with Lulu's portrait. Lulu's next client, the 'Negro', argues about money and kills Alwa. Lulu's last client is Jack the Ripper, who kills first Lulu and then Geschwitz, who dies with Lulu's name on her lips.

OPERAS

1917–22	Wozzeck
1929–35	Lulu (final act later completed by Friedrich Cerha)

TIMELINE

1885	Alban Berg born, Vienna, Austria
1904	Begins composition lessons with Schoenberg
1905	Sees performance of Wedekind's Die Büchse der Pandora
1907	Begins work on his Piano Sonata op. 1; performs some of his songs at a concert by Schoenberg pupils, Vienna
1909	Begins to explore atonality in his Four Songs op. 2
1910	Composes String Quartet op. 3, which combines atonality with large-scale formal structures
1913	Schoenberg conducts performance of his Altenberg Lieder in Vienna
1914	Attends performance of Büchner's play Woyzeck
1915	Three Orchestral Pieces op. 6 completed; enters Austrian Army for military service
1917	Commences work on Wozzeck
1923	Starts work on Chamber Concerto for Schoenberg's 50th birthday
1925	Premiere of Wozzeck in Berlin causes a furore
1929	Begins adaptation of two of Wedekind's plays for Lulu libretto
1934	Completes first stage of music for Lulu
1935	Dedicates his Violin Concerto to daughter of Mahler's widow; Berg dies, Vienna

Berganza, Teresa
b. 1935, SPANISH

Combining a rich, sensual voice with a refined onstage presence, Herbert von Karajan called Berganza 'the best mezzo-soprano in the world'. After studying at the Royal Conservatoire in Madrid, she made her operatic debut at the Aix-en-Provence Festival. This led to invitations from the world's leading opera houses. A Rossini specialist, Berganza's recitals have shown an extensive repertoire. In June 1994, she was elected a member of the Academia Real de Bellas Artes – the first time in the Royal Academy's 250-year existence that a singer was awarded Spain's highest artistic honour.

Bergonzi, Carlo
1924–2014, **ITALIAN**

Known as 'the tenor of all tenors', Bergonzi had a lyrical voice that was both refined and intense. Vocal lessons were interrupted when he was interred in a prisoner-of-war camp, but resumed upon his release and in 1947 he began to make a series of debuts as a baritone. Retraining his voice, he emerged four years later as a tenor in the title role of *Andrea Chénier*. Acclaimed as the foremost Verdi singer of his generation, Bergonzi sang with amazing technical fluency, although his high notes had a baritonal timbre. By the 1970s his voice showed signs of wear, but he continued to perform and then teach until the end of his life, much loved by his students.

Bernstein, Leonard
1918–90, **AMERICAN**

A hugely talented composer and conductor, Bernstein inspired the American music scene with his passion and flamboyance. Born in Massachusetts and essentially self-taught on the piano, he studied at Harvard and became an overnight sensation when stepping in for ailing New York Philharmonic conductor Bruno Walter in November 1943. Success as a composer followed, ranging from the movie score for *On the Waterfront* (1954), to the Broadway musicals *On the Town* (1944), *Wonderful Town* (1952) and West Side Story (1957). Bernstein also enjoyed plaudits for his initial foray into opera, the one-act *Trouble in Tahiti* (1951), which melded contemporary pop-music styles with conventional operatic vocal techniques while depicting the marital woes of a couple living in suburbia. However, his work in the field of opera rarely matched the success of that for the musical stage.

The comic operetta *Candide* (1956) never took off during its initial run, and it underwent numerous rewrites by Bernstein and no fewer than seven librettists over the course of more than 30 years. Its 1973, revival has become the standard performance version, although that by John Mauceri in 1988–89, a year before his death in New York, was actually Bernstein's own personal favourite. On the other hand, resurrecting the *Trouble in Tahiti* characters (and much of the music) for *A Quiet Place* (1983) was altogether less credible and compelling.

Birtwistle, Harrison
b. 1934, **ENGLISH**

Uniquely gifted amongst contemporary English composers, Birtwistle first made a splash on the opera scene with the acclaimed *Punch and Judy* (1968). Centring around the murderous activities of Punch, the work distinguished itself through a lack of straightforward narrative, repeating the story several times from numerous different perspectives. Musically evoking the traditions of the Baroque era by endowing each movement with its own mood, the work drew on the traditions of Greek drama by punctuating acts of extreme violence with lullabies, duets and dances.

A number of other works followed, before Birtwistle repeated the *Punch and Judy* formula in spectacular fashion with *The Mask of Orpheus*. Completed in 1984, this highlighted the composer's love of mythological characters and repetitive narratives, paving the way for *Yan Tan Tethera* (1986), a story that pits shepherds against the devil. *Gawain* (1991) focused on the knight of Arthurian legend, while *The Second Mrs Kong* (1994) was derided as pretentious by some critics, with its jazz references and characters such as King Kong, a beauty queen, Vermeer, Orpheus and Eurydice. However, *The Last Supper* (2000), once again focusing on the concept of ritual and the often-complex relationship between fact and fiction, signalled a welcome return to form.

Björling, Jussi
1911–60, SWEDISH

For sheer beauty of tone, Jussi Björling may have been the greatest lyric tenor of the twentieth century. He began singing professionally at the age of nine in the Björling Male Quartet, with his father and two brothers. He made his debut at the Royal Stockholm Opera in 1930 as Don Ottavio in *Don Giovanni*, and his international career took off immediately. In 1938, he made his Met debut as Rudolfo in *La bohème*. His reign at the Met lasted until 1959 when he walked out in a dispute over salary, but the rave reviews he received for his Carnegie Hall concert the next year solidified his legendary stature. Plagued by health problems, depression and alcoholism, he was ordered to rest, yet he was still singing when he succumbed to his final heart attack aged 49.

Brecht, Bertolt
1898–1956, GERMAN

A poet and playwright, Brecht was best known for his departure from the conventions of theatrical illusion to create 'epic theatre' as a tool for social commentary. At its least nuanced and most dogmatic, this amounted to a didactic forum for his communist cause. Eugen Bertolt Friedrich Brecht was born and raised in Bavaria, where he allied himself with the Dadaist movement. Living in Berlin from 1924 to 1933, he thrived among like-minded artists. His particular genius was in his poetic work and in his ability to draw together a group of exceptional dramatic talents to contribute to his artistic vision (a significant proportion of the content of his plays and libretti came not directly from his own pen, but from his collective of writers). It was in Berlin that he met composer Kurt Weill and their association produced *Die Dreigroschenoper*, based on **John Gay**'s (1685–1732) *The Beggar's Opera*; *Aufsteig und Fall der Stadt*

Mahagonny; and *Der Jasager*. By now a Communist, Brecht fled Berlin in 1933, and that same year his final collaboration with Weill, *Die sieben Todsünden* ('The Seven Deadly Sins', 1933), was produced in Paris. Following 15 years of exile in Europe and the United States, he returned to Germany in 1948.

Britten, Benjamin
1913–76, ENGLISH

Lord Edward Benjamin Britten was one of England's most important composers. Britten was a musical ambassador who, working with a close-knit group of collaborators, helped develop a thriving and vital British opera scene. Indeed, Peter Grimes (1945) heralded a new era for British music and for the post-war performing arts in general.

A MUSICAL START

Born in Lowestoft, appropriately on St Cecilia's Day (she is the patron saint of music), Britten started writing at the age of five. After being mentored by composer Frank Bridge, he attended the Royal College of Music in 1930 to study composition with John Ireland and piano with Arthur Benjamin. These men helped Britten to develop his compositional style, and so did long-time companion **Peter Pears** (1910–86), whom he first met in 1937.

PACIFISM AND PAINFUL THEMES

Pears was a BBC singer who also dabbled in composition, and together the self-declared pacifists left for the US in 1939, following in the footsteps of their friend W. H. Auden, with whom Britten collaborated on the American folk opera *Paul Bunyan* that same year. While in San Diego, Britten became enthralled with the poetry of George Crabbe, especially 'The Borough' and its brutish fisherman, whose apprentices die under mysterious circumstances. Isolation and pain would be recurrent themes in Britten's life and

THE MODERN ERA: PERSONALITIES

309

work, and since he and Pears identified with the central character of Peter Grimes, he was inspired to return to England and set the story to music.

CHAMBER OPERA

Following the success of *Peter Grimes*, Britten sought the more intimate realm of the 'chamber opera' and composed *The Rape of Lucretia*, which was produced at Glyndebourne in 1946. In addition to their dramatic and artistic merits, chamber operas were financially viable, and to that end Britten, Pears, Joan Cross and Eric Crozier founded the English Opera Group. *Albert Herring* (1947) was their first production, and they expanded on this success by creating the Aldeburgh Festival the following year, in the Sussex town where Britten and Pears would eventually live.

POPULARIZATION OF OPERA

Leading by example, Britten created interest in opera and the performing arts, and this in turn led to *The Little Sweep* (from *Let's Make an Opera*, 1949), *Noyes Fludde* ('Noah's Flood', 1958) and *The Children's Crusade* (1969). Meanwhile, commissioned by the Royal Opera, Britten's sequel to *Peter Grimes* was *Billy Budd* (1951). This was an instant success, yet not until the coronation of Queen Elizabeth II would Britten write his next opera, *Gloriana* (1953), before dramatically returning to psychological drama in the form of Henry James's ghost story *The Turn of the Screw* (1954).

It was because the church played an important role in his life that in 1958 Britten chose to adapt *Noyes Fludde* from the Chester cycle of miracle plays. Then, after he and Pears turned to Shakespeare, adapting and producing *A Midsummer Night's Dream* for the 1960 Aldeburgh Festival, Britten wrote a trio of religious parables for performance at a church in

Orford Ness, Sussex: *Curlew River* (1964), *The Burning Fiery Furnace* (1966) and *The Prodigal Son* (1968).

A TELEVISION PERFORMANCE

Owen Wingrave (1971), focusing on a young man's right to choose pacifism over war, echoed Britten's own decision to leave England in 1939. Conceived for television, it was seen by a large audience and exposed him to millions of viewers who, until then, had only heard his name. At the same time, Britten also wanted to compose a work that could employ the vocal talents of his companion Pears, and it was a Thomas Mann novella that inspired the ailing composer to fulfil his desire with *Death in Venice* (1973). Revisiting Britten's favoured themes of isolation, loss of innocence, and tension between society and the individual, this was a fitting end to an *oeuvre* of 15 operas, composed over a period spanning a third of a century.

Peter Grimes

Composed in 1944–45 and first performed on 7 June 1945, *Peter Grimes* reopened London's Sadler's Wells Theatre following the Second World War – at the request of managing director, **soprano** Joan Cross. This opera, and its success, provided the momentum that the post-war arts environment needed. From the moment Britten read 'The Borough' he began making plans to compose an opera, although unlike Crabbe's negative and villainous protagonist, Britten's title character is a partly misunderstood idealist and visionary. The brilliance of this realization is in the portrayal of 'The Borough' as a single entity, depicting the terror inflicted as people join in lock step with one another. Punctuating the prevarications of these small lives are the majestic sea interludes.

The hopelessness of Peter's plight is emphasized when we acquaint ourselves with Ellen Orford, whose civilizing presence is ultimately not enough to prevent his psyche from plunging into even deeper despair. Peter's aria 'The Great Bear and the Pleiades' affords us a rare glimpse into the soul of this unlikely hero.

Peter Grimes

by Benjamin Britten
Composed: 1944–45
Premiered: 1945, London
Libretto by Montagu Slater, after George Crabbe's poem 'The Borough'

BACKGROUND

An inquest is being held in the Moot Hall at Aldeburgh around 1830. Peter Grimes, a fisherman, describes how his apprentice died at sea in a storm. Swallow, the mayor and coroner, tells him that if he must have an apprentice he should get a woman to look after him. Ellen Orford, the schoolmistress, promises to help Grimes clear his name.

ACT I

Townspeople are gathered at the fish market. Only Balstrode, a retired merchant skipper, and Ned Keene, the apothecary, will help Grimes with his boat. Keene has bought a new apprentice for Grimes at the workhouse and Ellen agrees to fetch him with Hobson, the carter. The townspeople disapprove. Balstrode warns of an approaching storm. He suggests that Grimes should move away, to which Grimes replies that he belongs there. He intends to make enough money to become respectable, marry Ellen and open a shop.

Outside the Boar Inn, a storm rages. There has been a landslide on the cliff next to Grimes's hut. Grimes enters, drenched and wild-eyed. The customers react to him as though he is mad or drunk. Keene breaks in when Bob Boles, a preacher, squares up to Grimes. Ellen arrives with the boy. A bridge had collapsed and they had almost had to swim for it. Without waiting for the boy to get dry, Grimes drags him away.

SOUNDS FAMILIAR

PETER GRIMES' ARIA

Few moments in opera make the impression that Act II Scene 2 of *Peter Grimes* does. Seeing the protagonist on the beach following a storm, we learn that his second apprentice has died at sea and listen as Peter rambles on about the boy, Ellen Orford, money and the town gossips.

ACT II

A church service begins while Ellen sits knitting in the sun with John, the new apprentice. As Mrs Sedley, the local gossip, watches, Ellen finds a tear in John's coat and a bruise on his neck, observing 'Well... it's begun'. Grimes has spotted a shoal that no one else has seen. He comes to take John away, even though Ellen protests that he needs his day of rest She asks about the bruise. He strikes her and leaves with John. Keene, Boles and Auntie, the landlady of the Boar Inn, tell the townspeople that 'Grimes is at his exercise'. Balstrode tries to defend him, but the rest turn on Ellen. The men leave for Grimes's hut.

Grimes pushes John into his hut and orders him into his fishing clothes. This shoal is his chance to gain wealth and respect. Sometimes in his dreams, however, he sees his dead apprentice. The procession is approaching, led by Hobson's drum. Grimes accuses John of telling tales to Ellen and orders him to climb down to the beach through the cliff door. Distracted by the procession, he does not see John fall. He leaves the same way. The men find the hut empty. Balstrode senses that something is wrong and follows Grimes.

ACT III

Outside a dance at the Moot Hall, Auntie's 'nieces' are trying to escape from Swallow. Mrs Sedley tells Keene that Grimes and his apprentice have not been seen for two days.

She is certain it is 'murder most foul.' She listens as Balstrode tells Ellen that Grimes's boat has been tied up for an hour. Ellen has found John's jersey. Balstrode assures her they can still help Grimes. Mrs Sedley tells Swallow about the boat. Hobson gathers a search party.

Grimes enters, demented and shouting back at his pursuers, who are heard through the fog. Ellen and Balstrode find him and Balstrode tells him to sink the boat out of sight of land. He helps Grimes push the boat out. Dawn comes and the searchers have not found Grimes. Swallow hears that a boat is sinking far out at sea. Auntie says it is just a rumour.

Recommended Recording:

Peter Grimes, Orchestra of the Royal Opera House, Covent Garden; Benjamin Britten, conductor; Decca Originals 4757713; Soloists: Peter Pears (Peter Grimes), Claire Watson (Ellen Orford), James Pease (Balstrode), Jean Watson (Auntie), Geraint Evans (Ned Keene), Lauris Elms (Mrs Sedley), David Kelly (Hobson), Owen Brannigan (Swallow), Raymond Nilsson (Bob Boles), Marion Studholme, Iris Kells (Nieces)

Billy Budd

First performed at the Royal Opera House in London's Covent Garden on 1 December 1951, this adaptation of Herman Melville's short story saw E. M. Forster writing large portions of prose while Eric Crozier focused on the dramatic execution. Accordingly, *Billy Budd* was one of the most meticulously researched and well-written librettos of any Benjamin Britten opera.

Typically for a Britten protagonist, the seafaring title character is an outsider pitted unwittingly against Claggart, the master-at-arms, and it is the tensions and clashes between the two men that serve as the dramatic and musical focus. Contrapuntal in nature, the work is distinguished by motifs that are used throughout to develop characters and their psychological struggles. In addition to its compositional dissonances, the orchestration is thick and expansive, with Britten employing the largest orchestra that he ever used for one of his operas. Nevertheless, in stark contrast to this musical density and complexity is the character of Billy himself. Uncomplicated, he is an innocent caught up in – and ultimately destroyed by – the machinations and injustices of a microcosmic world at sea aboard the *Indomitable*.

Billy Budd

by Benjamin Britten
Composed: 1950–51
Premiered: 1951, London (original four-act version; revised 1961)
Libretto by E. M. Forster and Eric Crozier, after Herman Melville's story

BACKGROUND

Captain Vere reflects that all the good he has known has had some fault. He recalls the summer of 1797, shortly after the mutiny at the Nore, when he commanded HMS Indomitable.

ACT I

Sailors are scrubbing the deck. Squeak, a ship's corporal, is ordered to flog the novice for accidentally bumping into the bosun. Three men have been impressed from a passing merchantman, the Rights o' Man. Mr Flint, the sailing master, is unimpressed by the usual standard. The third man questioned by Claggart, the master-at-arms, is different. Billy Budd is an illiterate foundling, but a willing sailor who enjoys working in the foretop. His stammer, however, is evident under questioning. The officers mistake his farewell to the Rights o' Man for revolutionary talk. Mr Flint comments that there is always some defect. Claggart orders Squeak to make trouble for Billy. Billy is warned against Claggart, who

THE MODERN ERA: PERSONALITIES

calls him 'Beauty'. The sailors praise 'Starry Vere', the captain.

The officers, summoned to Vere's cabin, disapprove of anything French, especially revolutionary ideas. Vere says they need not worry about Billy's high spirits. Billy finds Squeak searching through his belongings in the berth-room. Trying to control his stammer, he fights Squeak, who pulls a knife. Claggart orders Squeak to be arrested and gagged. He praises Billy, saying 'handsomely done'. It is this 'handsomeness' that Claggart hates. He has Billy in his power and is doomed to destroy him. He bullies the novice into offering Billy money to lead a mutiny. Billy's stammer reappears when he realizes what is being suggested. He does not believe Dansker's warning to beware of 'Jemmy Legs' (Claggart).

ACT II

The mist lifts and a French warship is sighted. The Indomitable is prepared for action, but they remain out of range. Claggart tells Vere that someone is planning mutiny, offering gold to the novice. Vere does not believe that it is Billy and orders him to be summoned. The French ship has escaped.

Waiting in his cabin, Vere is determined that Claggart's evil will not overcome Billy's good. Billy hopes he is up for promotion, but accepts Vere's denial with good humour. Claggart formally accuses Billy of mutiny. Billy stammers, unable to answer. Uttering 'Devil', he kills Claggart with one blow. Vere blames himself. He summons a drumhead court. His description of the incident is brief and factual. Billy insists he is loyal, but when his 'tongue wouldn't work' he 'had to say it with a blow'. He calls on Vere to save him. The court decrees that he is to be hanged. Vere must accept the verdict. He is now the one to destroy 'beauty, handsomeness, goodness'.

Billy, in irons, waits for the dawn. Dansker brings him some grog and a biscuit. Some crewmen want to save Billy, but he tells Dansker to stop them. Vere needs their support. Billy accepts his fate and bids farewell to the world. The crew is gathered on deck. Mr Redburn, the first lieutenant, reads from the Articles of War. As he pronounces sentence Billy calls out, 'Starry Vere, God bless you!' The crew repeats his words, but begin to murmur as Billy is taken away to be hanged. The officers order them to disperse.

EPILOGUE

Old once more, Vere describes the burial at sea. He could have saved Billy, but was prevented by earthly laws. Instead it is Billy who has saved him, offering hope like a distant sail in a storm.

Recommended Recording:
Billy Budd, London Symphony Orchestra; Richard Hickox, conductor; Chandos CHAN9826; Soloists: Philip Langridge (Vere), Francis Egerton (Red Whiskers), Mark Padmore (Novice), Simon Keenlyside (Billy), Alan Opie (Mr Redburn), John Tomlinson (Claggart), Matthew Best (Mr Flint), Alan Ewing (Mr Ratcliffe), Clive Bayley (Dansker)

The Turn of the Screw

First performed in Venice on 14 September 1954 at Il Teatro La Fenice, this chilling ghost tale is based on Henry James's short story, with a libretto written by Myfanwy Piper. The action ignites as a new governess arrives at Bly House to take care of two children, Miles and Flora. Depending on the stage director's interpretation, the ghosts that haunt the house are either a figment of the children's imagination that the Governess is drawn into believing, or she herself creates a tempest that draws on actual events and people who once lived in the house. Either way, the role of The Governess is a dramatic and musical tour de force.

Although based on a row of 12 chromatically organized tones, this row, known as the 'Screw Theme', does not follow the rules devised by Schoenberg. Instead, it forms a series of variations based upon 16 scenes (divided equally between two acts), each with a different tonal centre. By reappearing in every scene, this theme tightens the tension, while Britten demonstrates his genius for orchestration when evoking an eerie, semi-real world that is punctuated with children's nursery rhymes.

The Turn of the Screw
by Benjamin Britten
Composed: 1954
Premiered: 1954, Venice
Libretto by Myfanwy Piper, after Henry James's tale

BACKGROUND
A governess has been engaged to look after two children. She may not contact their guardian, an absent uncle.

ACT I
The Governess is travelling to Bly House, worrying about her new post. Mrs Grose, the housekeeper, is waiting with Miles and Flora, who take the Governess to see the house and grounds. Miles has been expelled from school, but the Governess and Mrs Grose cannot believe that he is bad.

Out walking one evening, the Governess sees a man at a tower window. She describes the man to Mrs Grose, who says it must be Peter Quint, the former valet, who had an evil effect on the children and Miss Jessel, their former governess. Quint and Miss Jessel are both dead. The effect of the apparition on the children becomes more evident. She briefly sees Miss Jessel whilst walking with Flora beside the lake. Flora must have seen her, yet says nothing. She despairs that she cannot save them. Quint and Miss Jessel sing to the children, displaying the extent of their power over them.

ACT II
Quint and Miss Jessel appear, discussing their motives – a desire for power that will compensate for their previous lives.

Miss Jessel is rejected by Quint. He wants a follower, while she wants a soul to share her woe. The Governess feels the evil and, worse, imagines it. Flora and Miles have strange rituals that she doesn't understand. Mrs Grose urges her to write to their uncle, but Miles challenges her and she feels that she must flee the house.

The Governess confronts Miss Jessel, who waits for Flora in the schoolroom, threatening revenge. She cannot abandon the children, so writes to their uncle. She tells Miles about the letter and asks what happened here and at school. He acts almost possessed, screaming when he hears Quint calling. Quint urges Miles to steal the letter from her desk, which he does.

Miles is practising the piano. While Mrs Grose sleeps,, Flora slips away. The two women follow her, convinced she has gone to find Miss Jessel. They find her, but Mrs Grose cannot see the ghost. The Governess urges Flora to admit that Miss Jessel is there. Flora screams that she hates the Governess, who despairs that she has failed. Mrs Grose loses faith in the Governess, but later realises that Flora is deeply disturbed.

Mrs Grose has decided to take Flora away. She realises that the letter has gone and says that Miles must have taken it. The Governess stays to try and save Miles. Speaking as a friend, she asks what is on his mind. Quint urges the boy not to reveal his name. Hesitantly Miles admits he stole the letter. Quint comes to claim him. Miles at last cries out 'Peter Quint, you devil!' and the ghost is defeated, fading away. The Governess is triumphant until she realizes that Miles is dead.

A Midsummer Night's Dream
With only a limited time to create an opera for the opening performance at the Aldeburgh Festival on 11 June 1960, Britten and Pears selected Shakespeare's comic play, and by shortening and tightening it they were able to employ Shakespeare's own text rather than rewriting it. The

music, meanwhile, transforms the stage into the woods, and every nuance of the outdoors is beautifully captured in Britten's orchestral composition. The success of action and score stems from the highly organized formal scheme, as well as the brilliance of his writing for the natural and supernatural. Both Tytania's florid vocalizations and Oberon's counter-tenor give them an otherworldly quality, while the casting of an acrobat in the speaking role of Puck further enhances the variety of characters. However, the highlight is the move to the court of Theseus and we see the play-within-the-play as a highly structured operatic gem within the larger work.

A Midsummer Night's Dream

by Benjamin Britten
Composed: 1959–60
Premiered: 1960, Aldeburgh
Libretto by the composer and Peter Pears, after William Shakespeare's play

ACT I

Oberon and Tytania, King and Queen of the Fairies, are quarrelling. Oberon orders Puck, his sprite, to find a flower with juice that makes everyone fall in love with the first creature they see on waking. Hermia is to marry Demetrius, but she loves Lysander. They plan to elope and swear fidelity. Oberon encounters Demetrius, who is searching for the others and is himself pursued by Helena. Puck returns with the flower. Some of the juice is for Tytania, but Puck is told to drop some into the eyes of Demetrius, whom he will recognize by his 'Athenian garments'. Six working men arrive to rehearse Peter Quince's play about Pyramus and Thisbe. Bottom, a weaver, wants to play every part. They leave to learn their lines.

Puck discovers Hermia and Lysander sleeping and anoints his eyes. Demetrius escapes from Helena. She wakes Lysander, who immediately declares his passion for her.

Helena runs away, pursued by Lysander. Hermia finds she is alone and sets off to find Lysander. Tytania's fairies sing her to sleep. Oberon squeezes juice in her eyes.

ACT II

The play's rehearsal is not going easily. Puck puts an ass's head on Bottom and the others flee in terror. Tytania is woken by his braying song. She is rapturously in love and orders her fairies to do whatever he wishes. They fall asleep together. Oberon discovers that Puck has found the wrong Athenian. This time Demetrius is anointed, but he also wakes to see Helena. Soon both men are fighting over her while Helena and Hermia quarrel violently. Puck leads them a merry dance until they fall asleep. He ensures that Lysander will wake seeing Hermia.

ACT III

Next morning Oberon wakes Tytania, who is horrified to see that her dream of loving an ass was real. They are reconciled and prepare to bless Duke Theseus's wedding to Hippolyta. Puck removes the ass's head from Bottom. The lovers have also had strange dreams. The last to wake is Bottom. When he meets the others he tells them that their play has been chosen for performance at court. The lovers beg forgiveness from Theseus. It will now be a triple wedding. Quince and his troupe perform their play of tragical mirth. The three couples retire to bed. Oberon and Tytania bless them. Puck is left to wish the audience good night.

OPERAS

1941	Paul Bunyan
1945	Peter Grimes
1946	The Rape of Lucretia
1947	Albert Herring
1948	The Beggar's Opera (arr. after Gay)
1949	Let's Make an Opera (The Little Sweep)
1951	Billy Budd
1953	Gloriana
1954	The Turn of the Screw
1958	Noyes Fludde
1960	A Midsummer Night's Dream
1971	Owen Wingrave
1973	Death in Venice

THE MODERN ERA: PERSONALITIES

TIMELINE

1913	Benjamin Britten born, Lowestoft, England
c. 1925	Begins studying with Frank Bridge
1930	Enters Royal College of Music, London
1933	Completes *Sinfonietta*
1935	Begins work composing music for documentary films
1936	'Our Hunting Fathers' song-cycle is performed at the Norwich Festival
1937	Meets tenor Peter Pears
1939	Leaves England for the US with Pears
1940	Premiere of *Sinfonia da Reqiuem*, Carnegie Hall, conducted by Barbirolli
1942	Returns to England
1945	*Peter Grimes* performed, bringing international acclaim
1946	*Young Person's Guide to the Orchestra* completed
1947	Forms English Opera Group (EOG), a chamber-opera touring group; premiere of *Albert Herring*, EOG's first production
1948	Founds the Aldeburgh Festival, England
1951	Large-scale opera *Billy Budd* produced at Covent Garden
1958	*Turn of the Screw* shows enlarging musical style
1961	Writes *War Requiem* with central role for Pears
1973	*Death in Venice* premieres at Aldeburgh
1975	Completes masterpiece, Third String Quartet
1976	First composer to be awarded life peerage; Lord Britten of Aldeburgh dies, Aldeburgh, England

Caballé, Montserrat
b. 1933, SPANISH

This soprano's melting pianissimo has earned her a faithful following, but she is also one of the few operatic singers to have had a hit pop record – Freddie Mercury, of rock band Queen, wrote 'Exercises in Free Love' for her, which was featured on the award-winning album *Barcelona*. Caballé's training began at the Barcelona Liceo, where she won the gold medal in 1954. She joined the Basel Opera company two years later and sang an assortment of roles. Her detractors consider her to be overly focused on her tone, but her performances of *bel canto* rarities are exemplary. She has also brought *zarzuela* and Spanish songs to an international audience.

Callas, Maria
1923–77, AMERICAN-GREEK

Known as 'La Divina' (The Divine One), soprano Callas was regarded as the greatest singing actress of the twentieth century. She revitalized forgotten operas and her delivery combined technical precision with dramatic intensity. Born in New York City, Callas's family returned to Greece when she was 13. She made her debut in Athens at the age of 17, singing the role of Tosca. Her repertoire remained diverse until Italian conductor Tullio Serafin redirected her towards the *coloratura bel canto* works of Bellini and Donizetti. Callas's personal life and difficult temperament were often as dramatic as her stage roles. She married Giovanni Meneghini, which freed her from financial worry, but they separated in 1959. Her equally volatile relationship with tycoon Aristotle Onassis was also highly publicized.

Capek, Karel
1890–1938, CZECH

Czechoslovakia's most important playwright, novelist and essayist before the Second World War, Capek is probably best remembered for his satirical play *R.U.R.* ('Rossum's Universal Robots', 1920). Aside from introducing 'robot' into the English language (courtesy of his brother Josef), this caused an international sensation by depicting the replacement of man by machine in modern society. As Capek saw it: 'Man will never be enslaved by machinery if the man tending the machine is paid enough.'

When Janáček approached Capek for the rights to use his play *The Makropulos Affair* as the basis for his next opera, Capek was sceptical about how a man 35 years his senior would treat this modern work. Nevertheless, Capek was enthralled with the result, which retained the humanist and moral questions that were intrinsic to his writing. Refusing to eat or emigrate after the

Western Allies allowed Germany to invade Czechoslovakia, Capek died of double-pneumonia on Christmas Day, 1938.

Cappuccilli, Piero
1929–2005, ITALIAN

With a warm, expressive baritone voice ideal for Verdi, Cappuccilli had a superb technique that was still evident when he performed *Cavalleria rusticana* and Pagliacci in his last performance at Covent Garden, aged 60. Studying at the Teatro Giuseppe Verdi before graduating to the main stage, he made his professional debut in 1957 as Tonio in Pagliacci. In 1960, Walter Legge offered him a contract to sing Enrico opposite Maria Callas in *Lucia di Lammermoor*, and he made his Met debut the same year. His Enrico at La Scala secured his position as an international star, while working with Karajan and Abbado earned him critical recognition.

Christoff, Boris
1914–93, BULGARIAN

As the leading Boris Godunov of his generation, Christoff benefited from his Russian mother's insistence that he adopt her country's culture. A difficult personality meant that controversy followed him throughout his life. Having sung with a church choir and local opera company in Bulgaria, Christoff emigrated to Italy in 1942 to pursue an operatic career. By 1945 he was singing professionally, and the development of his international career was dominated by Verdi bass roles. Christoff had an antagonistic relationship with his brother-in-law, Tito Gobbi, and during a production of *Don Carlos* this reached its breaking point. Further disputes embittered his working relationship with Maria Callas – during a rehearsal of *Medea* in Rome, Christoff accused her husband, Meneghini, of reducing his role by two-thirds. Meneghini hired a claque to disrupt Christoff's scenes on opening night, while Christoff and Callas argued backstage. They never sang together again.

Cocteau, Jean
1889–1963, FRENCH

Cocteau was an exceptional and prodigious talent. Inspired by everything around him, he gained an international reputation as a playwright, novelist, poet, artist, opera librettist and filmmaker. After designing the set for Debussy's opera *Pelléas et Mélisande* (1926), Cocteau wrote his first libretto for a Stravinsky opera-oratorio. Based on the *Oedipus* trilogy of plays by Sophocles, *Oedipus Rex* was translated from French into Latin by Jean Daniélou, thus distancing the text from the audience and creating characters who appear both formal and imposing. For *Le Pauvre Matelot* ('The Poor Sailor', 1927), Cocteau teamed up with Darius Milhaud to create a three-act mini-tragedy about a woman who unwittingly murders her husband whom she has not seen in over 20 years. Posthumously, Cocteau's films and screenplays have contributed to a Philip Glass trilogy: *Orphée, La Belle et la Bête* and *Les enfants terribles*.

Crozier, Eric
1914–94, ENGLISH

Armed with his experience as a stage director and as a producer for BBC Television (1936–39), Crozier helped create a new national identity for British opera while lending his expertise to composer Benjamin Britten. After all, if opera were to become viable in theatrical terms, then the composer, librettist and stage director would have to be closely associated. Crozier's close association with Britten began when he directed the world premiere of *Peter Grimes* (1945). Crozier then directed the world premiere of *The Rape of Lucretia* at Glyndebourne, which in turn led to the creation of the English

Opera Group, a small company with limited resources. Crozier's own librettos, *Albert Herring* and *The Little Sweep*, were produced by the English Opera Group. A founder member of the Aldeburgh Festival in 1948, along with Britten and his long-time companion, tenor Peter Pears, Crozier also collaborated with E. M. Forster and Britten on the libretto for *Billy Budd*.

Dallapiccola, Luigi
1904–75, **ITALIAN**

At the forefront of Italian serialism, Dallapiccola was inspired to compose after attending a 1924 performance of Schoenberg's *Pierrot Lunaire* ('Moonstruck Pierrot', 1912); he made a complete analysis of Schoenberg's 12-tone system and used this when writing his first one-act opera, *Volo di notte* ('Night flight', 1940), based on Antoine de Saint-Exupéry's book *Vol de nuit*. Unfortunately, just as Dallapiccola's music was reaching a wider audience, he had to limit performances to neutral countries due to the threat faced by his Jewish wife in the face of Europe-wide anti-Semitism. This resulted in his post-Second World War political statement, *Il prigioniero* ('The Prisoner', 1949), which expressed a prisoner's point of view via Dallapiccola's own libretto and a score that employed three 12-tone rows symbolically connected to elements of the opera.

   Job (1950), written when Dallapiccola was travelling and lecturing in America, was yet another one-act opera; his final composition, *Ulisse* ('Ulysses', 1968), was his only full-length work. Performed at the Deutsche Oper, Berlin, this sombre and unwelcoming score did not gain the critical plaudits that the composer had hoped for. He then dedicated himself to writing about his work.

Devia, Mariella
b. 1948, **ITALY**

Mariella Devia's impeccable technique has sustained a beautiful vocal timbre of profound depth and still-youthful sheen, and her four-decade career continues apace. Particularly celebrated for *bel canto* soprano roles, she made her professional debut at Treviso in the title role of *Lucia di Lammermoor* in 1973, appeared at the Met throughout the 70s and 80s in various Verdi, Donizetti and Mozart roles, and made her La Scala debut as Giulietta in *I Capuletti e i Montecchi* in 1987. She performed *Norma* for the first time in 1913, the day after her sixty-fifth birthday, at Teatro Communale di Bologna.

DiDonato, Joyce
b. 1969, **AMERICAN**

A lyric *coloratura* mezzo-soprano, DiDonato is known especially for her interpretation of Handel, Mozart, and an increasing number of *bel canto* roles. An example of the resurgent trend towards 'personalities' in the opera world, DiDonato has embraced the internet and social networking, regularly recounting her performance experiences and career developments online, as well as inspiring younger singers with her video blogs on the art – and the many challenges – of being an opera singer.

Domingo, Plácido
b. 1941, **SPANISH**

Domingo holds a unique place in the world of opera as a singer, conductor and administrator. He is the most recorded tenor in history, which has allowed him to sing a wide variety of roles. Early in his career, his voice was light and lyrical, but over time it has acquired tremendous expression and power. His Don Carlos, Alvaro in *La forza del destino* and Manrico in *Il trovatore* are without peer, and he has more recently moved towards roles such as Verdi's Otello and Wagner's Siegmund. Having used great intelligence, stage presence and acting ability to sustain a distinguished career, Domingo began to run opera companies in Los Angeles and Washington while continuing to sing leading roles, more recently from the baritone repertoire.

Dukas, Paul
1865–1935, FRENCH

A contemporary of Debussy and Ravel who joined the French Wagnerian movement, Dukas is primarily known for his orchestral fantasy *L'apprenti sorcier* ('The Sorcerer's Apprentice', 1897), memorably featured in Disney's animated feature *Fantasia*. He was a perfectionist who spent years rewriting his partially written works. Two of Dukas' operas remained unfinished: the Wagner-inspired *Horn et Riemenhild* (1892) and *L'arbre de science* (1899), a lyric drama in four acts. His only complete opera was *Ariane et Barbe-bleue* ('Ariane and Bluebeard', 1908), based on Maurice Maeterlinck's play and featuring Maeterlinck's libretto, yet Dukas was only granted permission to set the text to music on the condition that Georgette Leblanc (Dukas' long-term companion) could sing the role of Ariane. He complied, and the work received its first performance at the Opéra-Comique in 1907. Borrowing from the chromaticism of Wagner and the use of the pentatonic scale – much employed by Debussy – *Ariane et Barbe-bleue* is a mixture of traditional *grand opéra* and the natural declamation of French *mélodie*. In later years, as a professor of music at the Paris Conservatoire, Dukas passed his knowledge on to composers such as **Isaac Albéniz** (1860–1909) and **Olivier Messiaen** (1908–92).

Enescu, George
1881–1955, ROMANIAN

Enescu was a true prodigy – a brilliant pianist, superb conductor, and a man whose memory for music rivalled that of Mozart. Born in Romania, Enescu studied in Vienna and Paris, where he sat alongside **Gabriel Fauré** (1845–1924), **Jules Massenet** (1842–1912) and other celebrated French composers. Working with some of the best musicians of his day, he led an active life on the concert platform. Yehudi Menuhin was among his students, as was fellow violin prodigy Arthur Grumiaux.

Enescu's opera, *Oedipe* ('Oedipus'), while still in manuscript form, was lost en route to Moscow in 1917. Four years later, he began reassembling the work, but it took 10 years to complete and another five to make it to the stage. Finally premiered at the Paris Opéra in 1936, *Oedipe* was a grandly conceived work, depicting the story of Oedipus from birth to the grave, and involving an orchestration that used three sets of timpani and a wind machine. Modern-day revivals have included the 2002 Edinburgh Festival, where the production's critical success renewed widespread interest in this neglected work.

Fischer-Dieskau, Dietrich
1925–2012, GERMAN

In great demand as an opera singer and recitalist, Fischer-Dieskau was the most recorded baritone of the twentieth century. His opera work is remembered for roles such as Berg's Wozzeck, Busoni's Faust and Reimann's Lear, for which he gave the first performance. He was not well suited to the Romantic Italian repertoire, but had a great affinity for the works of Mozart, Wagner and Strauss. Everything Fischer-Dieskau sang was profoundly connected to the text, and a driving intelligence can be heard behind his recordings. For this reason, his renditions of Schubert's *Lieder* were particularly popular. After retiring from singing in 1993, he continued to conduct, write, paint and teach to his own high standards until his death in 2012.

Flagstad, Kirsten
1895–1962, NORWEGIAN

Flagstad began her career singing at Stockholm Opera. She was considering retirement in 1932 when singing the role of Isolde in Oslo, but after her appearance at Bayreuth the following year, her success was immediate; she made her Met debut in 1935 at the age of 40. Following a series of triumphs, Flagstad returned to Norway, her husband's Nazi collaborations having made her unpopular in America. She then sang four seasons at Covent Garden from 1948 to 1951. Richard Strauss wrote his 'Four Last Songs' with her in mind and these were premiered in London, 1950. Flagstad's long awaited return to the Met did not take place until the 1950–51 season, when she appeared as Brünnhilde (*Der Ring des Nibelungen*), Isolde (*Tristan und Isolde*) and Leonore (*Fidelio*). Her final operatic performance was in *Dido and Aeneas* at London's Mermaid Theatre in 1953.

Fleming, Renée
b. 1959, AMERICAN
Fleming has taken a position in the American public consciousness similar to that of Beverley Sills in the twentieth century – a household name even to many people who are unfamiliar with opera as an art form. Much-loved for her radiant tone and expansive on-stage presence, the full lyric soprano's repertoire encompasses Richard Strauss, Mozart, *bel canto*, French opera, and also operetta, musical theatre and jazz. She is also a champion of contemporary music, with acclaimed premieres including the role of Blanche Dubois in André Previn's opera *A Streetcar Named Desire*. More recently, she has integrated artistic direction and curation into her eclectic career.

Floyd, Carlisle
b. 1926, AMERICAN
Born in South Carolina, writing and producing operas while on the faculty of Florida State University during the early 1950s – the locally popular *Slow Dusk* (1949) and *The Fugitives* (1951), which disappeared after its first performance –

Floyd created the work that became his calling card. Written in seven months and presented at the university in 1955, *Susannah* was, according to noted critic Winthrop Sargeant following its 1956 New York City Opera debut, 'probably the most moving and impressive opera to have been written in America – or anywhere else, as far as I am aware – since Gershwin's *Porgy and Bess*'.

Susannah was a timely piece during an era of McCarthy-inspired communist witch-hunts. In the apocryphal biblical Book of Susannah, upon which Floyd based his libretto, the central character's innocence is proven. Yet, empathizing with contemporary Americans who were not so lucky, Floyd ensured that Susannah is persecuted for a 'sin' that she did not commit.

The musical language of *Susannah*, while late Romantic in its harmonies and textures, is full of American folk references and Quaker hymns, reflecting the people and their times. Floyd subsequently enjoyed moderate success with his setting of Emily Brontë's *Wuthering Heights* (1958) and John Steinbeck's *Of Mice and Men* (1969), but other operas such as *The Passion of Jonathan Wade* (1962), *Markheim* (1966) and *Bilby's Doll* (1976) attracted little interest.

Gedda, Nicolai
1925–2017, SWEDISH
A lyric tenor whose live and recorded performances attest to his refinement and intelligence, Gedda was not only fluent in Russian but also well-versed in Italian, French, Latin and Hebrew. In 1954, he made his Paris Opéra debut and remained there to specialize in French repertoire. Although adept at singing in a variety of styles, he was best suited to French, Mozart and Russian music. Gedda remained actively singing into his seventies, attributing this feat to his teacher Paola Novikova.

Gershwin, George

1898–1937, **AMERICAN**

On the night of 12 February 1924, Gershwin became an instant sensation when performing his *Rhapsody in Blue* at New York's Aeolian Hall. Written in less than a month and advertised as 'An Experiment in Modern Music', Rhapsody melded Classical structures with jazz, ragtime and the blues, heralding a new era in American music.

While George and his lyricist brother Ira turned out a string of hit songs and successful stage musicals, George also wrote several highly acclaimed orchestral works. However, his initial operatic outing *Blue Monday* (1922), a 20-minute jazz opera, did not sit well with audiences and was dropped soon after opening. In 1926, Gershwin found the subject for his next opera. Gershwin regarded DuBose Heyward's novel *Porgy* as the perfect vehicle for a 'folk opera' incorporating jazz and blues phrases and rhythms. The result, co-written with Ira as well as DuBose and Dorothy Heyward, was *Porgy and Bess*, which premiered in Boston on 30 September 1935 after seven years of negotiations with Heyward. It opened on Broadway 10 days later, but despite using classically trained singers it was not well received. Only over time would it earn a place as one of the best-known of all American operas, emphasizing the tragic loss caused by Gershwin's untimely death from a brain tumour.

Porgy and Bess

by George Gershwin
Composed: 1934–35
Premiered: 1935, New York
Libretto by DuBose Heyward after his novel *Porgy*, with lyrics by Heyward and Ira Gershwin

ACT I

During a crap game in Catfish Row, Charleston, Clara sings a lullaby to her baby.

'SUMMERTIME'

George Gershwin's music and DuBose Heyward's lyrics have reached far beyond the scope of *Porgy and Bess*. As soon as the two men agreed to work on this project, Gershwin wrote the song that Clara sings as a lullaby in the show. Today, it is usually performed out of context and in myriad styles.

Porgy, a cripple, returns home in his goat cart. Crown, high on 'happy dust' provided by Sportin' Life, picks a fight with Robbins and kills him. Bess, Crown's woman, has nowhere to hide until Porgy opens his door. Serena, Robbins' widow, refuses Bess's money for a 'saucer burial' until told it is from Porgy. Peter the honeyman tells the detective that Crown did it and is taken away.

ACT II

Jake, Clara's husband, is preparing his nets. Porgy has nothing to complain about. Maria chases away Sportin' Life. Peter is to be released. Porgy and Bess pledge themselves to each other. Maria invites Bess to the picnic on Kittiwah Island. Sportin' Life has interesting ideas about Old Testament stories. Bess tells Crown, who has been hiding on the island, that she is now with Porgy. The fishermen set off. Bess is ill in bed after being lost on the island. When she wakes she declares her love for Porgy. The hurricane bell is heard. While everyone prays for the storm to cease, Crown returns, looking for Bess. Clara has seen Jake's boat upside down. She rushes out into the storm but only Crown goes to help, still threatening to 'get' Porgy.

ACT III

Jake and Clara have been drowned. Porgy is waiting when Crown returns and then kills him. The police take Porgy to identify Crown's body. Sportin' Life tempts Bess to come to New York. One week later Porgy comes home looking for Bess, and his neighbours eventually explain that she has gone with Sportin' Life. He sets off after her.

Gigli, Beniamino
1890–1957, ITALIAN

Caruso's successor at the Met, Gigli possessed a lighter but sweeter voice, and with the advent of recording he actually became more popular than his predecessor. Rodolfo in *La bohème* and Nemorino in *Don Pasquale* were perfect for his effortless tone. Gigli's association with the Met began in 1920 but, due to a salary dispute, ended in 1932. Including tours, he gave a total of around 500 performances, singing heavier repertoire in later years with mixed results. His Chénier and Canio in *Pagliacci* were vocal wonders, but some now consider his style – with its excessive sobs and *portamenti* – to be old-fashioned.

Ginastera, Alberto
1916–83, ARGENTINIAN

One of the most important South American composers of the twentieth century, Ginastera combined energetic Argentine rhythms with enchanting lyricism and an almost hallucinatory ambiance to forge his unique style. He lived in New York on a Guggenheim Fellowship from 1945–48 before returning to Argentina. Here, he experimented with advanced composition techniques, yet his three operas – *Don Rodrigo* (1964), *Bomarzo* (1967) and *Beatrix Cenci* (1971) – belong to his later neo-expressionistic period and are steeped in the school of serialism.

The most accessible of these, *Don Rodrigo*, is drawn from a Spanish legend about heroism and depicts this theme by way of a complete 12-tone row. Fragments of the row underscore the action as well as the feelings of the central characters. Contrived as the serial format may be, the opera has an immediate impact upon

the listener – in the final scene, 24 bells are placed throughout different parts of the theatre to proclaim the restoration of Christianity to Spain. *Bomarzo* and *Beatrix Cenci* were commissioned and performed in Washington, D.C., yet *Bomarzo* was banned in Buenos Aires due to its depictions of sex and violence.

Glass, Philip
b. 1937, AMERICAN

Philip Glass defies conventions of traditional music and performance practice. A minimalist who is constantly extending musical boundaries, Glass has written several slowly developing, repetitively patterned operas.

In the mid-1960s he became fascinated with Indian music when transcribing the work of sitarist Ravi Shankar, and he set off to explore the music of North Africa, India and the Himalayas. Returning to New York in 1967, he formed the Philip Glass Ensemble and teamed up with theatrical concept artist Robert Wilson. Their hallucinogenic four-hour opera *Einstein on the Beach* (1976) was a critical smash and brought **minimalism** to the mainstream. They then produced *Satyagraha* (1980), which used a traditional orchestra, and the more accessible *Akhnaten* (1984). They have also enjoyed many commissions, including *The CIVIL warS* for the 1984 Los Angeles Olympics; *The White Raven* for Portugal's Expo '98; and digital 3D opera *Monsters of Grace* (1998). Among Glass's other works are *The Voyage* (1992) and a trilogy based on Jean Cocteau films: *Orphée* ('Orpheus', 1993), *La Belle et la Bête* ('Beauty and the Beast', 1994) and *Les enfants terribles* (1996).

Einstein on the Beach
by Philip Glass
Composed: 1974–75
Premiere: 1976, Avignon
Libretto by Christopher Knowles, Lucinda Childs and Samuel M. Johnson

Einstein on the Beach is divided into four acts, separated by five **intermezzi**, which allow for set changes. The performance is continuous and the audience are at liberty to leave and return as they wish. There is no plot, but there are references to the life and work of Albert Einstein, who appears at various stages of his life, including as an elderly violinist and as a scientist writing mathematical formulae on a blackboard. The limited text, both spoken and sung, complements the visual images of Robert Wilson's original production. Some scenes are almost entirely composed of numbers and *solfège* syllables. There are four actors and a chorus of 13 voices.

ACT I
Train 1: a train appears and slowly travels into the distance, where it is transformed into a building.
Trial 1: incorporates the song 'Mr Bojangles' and the spoken text 'All Men are Equal' (Johnson).

ACT II
Dance 1 – Field with Spaceship.
Night Train.

ACT III
Trial 2/Prison: incorporates the spoken texts 'Prematurely Air–Conditioned Supermarket' (Childs) and 'I Feel the Earth Move' (Knowles).
Dance 2 – Field with Spaceship.

ACT IV
Building/Train
Bed: cadenza and aria for solo soprano.
Spaceship: as the chorus frantically chant numbers, the scene builds up to something that might be interpreted as a nuclear holocaust.

Gobbi, Tito
1913–84, **ITALIAN**
Gobbi's baritone voice, although accomplished, was overshadowed by his magnificent stage presence. After studying in Rome and making his debut in 1935, he enjoyed his first success as Wozzeck in the 1942 Italian premiere of Berg's opera. Gobbi's La Scala debut also took place that year, and he became popular in London for his interpretations of Verdi roles such as Rigoletto and Iago. His most memorable partnerships were with reigning diva Maria Callas; her Tosca and his Scarpia became part of opera lore.

Grümmer, Elisabeth
1911–86, **GERMAN**
Possessing a pure, ringing voice that could sing anything from Mozart to Wagner, this German soprano carved out a special place for herself in the operatic world. After starting out as an actress, she married violinist Detlev Grümmer, who became concert master at Aachen opera house, under Herbert von Karajan. The maestro heard her singing at a party and engaged her for a part at the opera house. Grümmer's success led to numerous engagements, including Bayreuth, the Salzburg Festival and Glyndebourne. She sang with all the legendary conductors of her day and became legendary within musical circles for her superlative performances of Donna Anna in *Don Giovanni* and Agathe in *Der Freischütz*.

Henze, Hans Werner
1926–2012, **GERMAN**
A prolific composer of many moods and changes, Henze was yet another 12-note serialist who nonetheless was influenced by neo-classicism, expressionism and jazz. His first full-length opera, *Boulevard Solitude* (1952), preceded his move to Italy the following year. There, having finally put distance between himself and the repressive Germany of his youth, Henze's music became more lush and sensual, and his output included operas such as *König Hirsch* (1956), *Elegy for Young Lovers* (1961) and *The Bassarids* (1966).

THE MODERN ERA: PERSONALITIES

323

The latter two, arguably his most important works, are notable for his collaborations with librettists W.H. Auden and Chester Kallman – *Elegy for Young Lovers* is a chamber opera with a 12-tone score, while one-act, full-length opera *The Bassarids*, an adaption of Euripides' *The Bacchae*, displays the composer's penchant for naturalistic emotion.

Increasingly dedicated to left-wing views, Henze dramatized class conflict in *We Come to the River* (1976), while *The English Cat* (1983) featured a cast dressed either as cats, rats or mice. His 2003 opera *L'Upupa oder Der Triumph der Sohnesliebe*, commissioned for the Salzburg Festival, afforded him the opportunity to write his very first libretto. He remained an outspoken critic of current affairs until his death.

Elegy for Young Lovers

by Hans Werner Henze
Composed: 1959–61
Premiered: 1961, Schwetzingen
Libretto by W. H. Auden and Chester Kallman

ACT I

Hilda Mack recalls how her husband set out to climb the Hammerhorn 40 years ago. Dr Reischmann and Carolina, physician and secretary to the poet Gregor Mittenhofer, agree that no one thanks 'the Servants of the Servant of the Muse'. Reischmann's son Toni meets Mittenhofer's mistress Elisabeth. Mittenhofer is fascinated by Hilda Mack's coloratura premonition of a young couple's death. Mauer, a guide, reports that a body, probably Hilda Mack's husband, has been found. Toni is entranced by the way Elisabeth gently leads Hilda Mack towards an understanding. He remembers his dead mother. Now the crystal is broken Hilda Mack may return to life. Toni wishes to return to life through Elisabeth's love.

ACT II

Elisabeth wants to choose when to tell Mittenhofer about her love for Toni. Reischmann and Carolina attempt to dissuade them. Elisabeth asks Toni to take her away. Over breakfast Mittenhofer tells Carolina he already knows about the lovers. He describes to Elisabeth how difficult it is to be a poet. He asks only that she should tell him before she leaves. While she hesitates, Toni tells Mittenhofer, who asks the lovers to find an Edelweiss flower that will enable him to finish his new poem. Left alone he rages against them all: 'Why don't they die?'

ACT III

Hilda says goodbye as the lovers leave for the Hammerhorn. Mittenhofer tells Carolina that his poem is an elegy. Mauer warns that a blizzard is coming, but Mittenhofer claims that no one is on the mountain. Toni and Elisabeth, caught in the blizzard, imagine the 40 years of married life they will be denied. They ask the God of Truth to forgive them and die together. Mittenhofer gives a public reading of his poem, but no words are heard.

The Bassarids

by Hans Werner Henze
Composed: 1965
Premiered: 1966, Salzburg
Libretto by W. H. Auden and Chester Kallman after Euripides' *The Bacchae*

FIRST MOVEMENT

Cadmus, King of Thebes, has abdicated in favour of his grandson, Pentheus, who intends to break with the traditional religious order and establish monotheism. An offstage voice announces that 'the God Dionysus has entered Boeotia'. If legend is to be believed, this is the son of Zeus by Cadmus's daughter Semele. Many Thebans follow the Voice to Mount Cytheron to become Bassarids. Beroe, Semele's old nurse, remains true to the old gods, but Pentheus' mother, Agave, welcomes the new cult. Pentheus extinguishes the flame on Semele's tomb. The voice calls Agave and her sister Autonoe to Mount Cytheron.

SECOND MOVEMENT

Pentheus fears the cult and orders the imprisonment of anyone celebrating the festival of the Bassarids. A group of devotees captured at Mount Cytheron includes Agave, Autonoe, Tiresias and a Dionysian priest, whom Beroe recognizes as Dionysus himself.

THIRD MOVEMENT

The prisoners escape following an earthquake. In an intermezzo, Pentheus is shown his hidden erotic fantasies: the Judgment of Calliope, with his mother and aunt as Aphrodite and Persephone. The stranger induces him to dress as a woman and go to Mount Cytheron to watch the Bassarids and Maenads. They hear the voice denouncing him as a spy and tear him apart.

FOURTH MOVEMENT

Agave brings Pentheus's head back to Thebes. Still in thrall to the cult, she believes it is a lion. Cadmus has not succumbed and is able to bring his daughter back to her senses. She identifies the priest as Dionysus. The god banishes the royal house of Thebes and burns the palace. He raises his mother Semele from the dead and has her transported to Olympus as the goddess Thyone. The new cult is established in Thebes.

Hindemith, Paul
1895–1963, GERMAN

A composer, solo performer, conductor, teacher and theorist, Hindemith's work boasted an eclectic array of musical styles, ranging from the expressionism of his first three one-act operas – now all but forgotten – to the polyphony of his later neo-Baroque output. The first signs of this transition could be heard in Cardillac (1926, revised in 1952), with its separate musical numbers, whereas

Mathis der Maler ('Mathis the Painter', 1938) embraces a wide range of musical expression, including medieval modality and traditional German folk melodies, underpinned by contrapuntal techniques. By this time, much of Hindemith's work was condemned as 'degenerate' by the Nazis and banned throughout Germany, so he relocated to Switzerland and then America, where he spent several years lecturing at Yale and Harvard before returning to Europe in 1953. Die Harmonie der Welt ('The Harmony of the World', 1957) marked the culmination of his neo-Baroque compositional style, similar to that of Mathis, but performed on a much grander scale with two orchestras. Hindemith's final opera, The Long Christmas Dinner (1961), featured an English libretto by Thornton Wilder. Unfortunately, however, neither this nor Die Harmonie have enjoyed repeated exposure.

Mathis der Maler
by Paul Hindemith
Composed: 1933–35
Premiered: 1938, Zürich
Libretto by the composer

SCENE I

Mathis is painting a fresco. Schwalb, a leader of the peasants' revolt, shelters in the monastery with his daughter Regina. He reproaches Mathis for ignoring his fellow men. Mathis helps them escape.

SCENE II

Catholics quarrel with Protestants. Riedinger, a wealthy Protestant, successfully protests to Cardinal Albrecht about an order to burn Lutheran books. Mathis and Ursula, Riedinger's daughter, declare their love. Pommersfelden, the dean of Mainz Cathedral, insists on enforcing laws against Protestants. Mathis is denounced for helping Schwalb. He is released but insists on leaving Albrecht's service.

SCENE III

Capito foils Protestant attempts to hide their books in Riedinger's house. He shows them a letter from Luther urging the cardinal to bring reconciliation by marrying a Protestant. Ursula is asked whether she would marry for the good of her faith. She pleads with Mathis to take her away, but he has decided to join the rebels.

SCENE IV

Mathis tries to stop peasants harming Countess Helfenstein and is himself attacked. Schwalb is killed. The countess begs the soldiers to spare Mathis. Regina weeps over her father's body.

SCENE V

Albrecht reproaches Ursula for considering the marriage plan. She replies that she agreed because he is an enlightened man who could reconcile the warring factions. He resolves to do so from within the Church, renouncing wealth and marriage.

SCENE VI

Mathis and Regina have fled the fighting. He sees visions relating to the Isenheim altarpiece with himself as St Anthony, and is tormented by devils. Appearing as St Paul, Albrecht urges him to use his painting skills to benefit mankind.

SCENE VII

Regina dies in Mathis's studio, tended by Ursula. The studio is almost empty. Mathis tells Albrecht that his work is done. He packs away his last possessions.

Horne, Marilyn
b. 1934, AMERICAN

One of the great mezzo-sopranos of the twentieth century, Horne studied with William Venard and dubbed the voice of Dorothy Dandridge in the 1954 film *Carmen Jones*. She was admired by Stravinsky, who invited her to perform in the 1956 Vienna Festival; she remained in Europe

for three seasons at the Gelsenkirchen Opera. She returned to America in 1960 to perform as Marie in Alban Berg's *Wozzeck*. Horne is remembered for her association with **Dame Joan Sutherland** (b. 1926) and Richard Bonynge in their performance of Rossini's *Semiramide* and other *bel canto* rarities. She also became a stylistic and technical expert on the music of Handel. She has spent the years since her performing career demonstrating her deep commitment to educating and mentoring young singers, notably with her Marilyn Horne Foundation, which has particular dedication to preserving the art of the song recital.

Hotter, Hans
1909–2003, GERMAN

Although he sang Mozart and Strauss, Hotter is best remembered for his definitive interpretations of Wagner. His powerful bass-baritone premiered as the Speaker in Mozart's *Die Zauberflöte*, and he returned to this and other small roles well into his eighties. Hotter made his debut in Munich singing Wotan in 1937, and this role, along with Hans Sachs in *Die Meistersinger*, led to a 12-year association with the Bayreuth Festival.

James, Henry
1843–1916, AMERICAN

The most influential American writer of the nineteenth century, James was known for a style that brimmed with psychological study and character analysis. Not too surprising, then, that his father was a writer of philosophy, while his brother was considered among the most important philosophers of his day.

After attending Harvard Law School for a brief spell, James chose literature as a career and subsequently wrote 112 stories, 20 novels, 12 plays and several works of literary criticism. His much acclaimed novella *The Turn of the Screw* (1898) came to the attention of Benjamin Britten during the early 1950s and was produced as an opera in 1954. Additionally, another short story, *Owen Wingrave* (1893), which James would later turn into a one-act play, was initially set to music by Britten and produced as a television opera. A dedicated anglophile, James became a British citizen in 1915, having made his home in Rye, Sussex, many years earlier. It was there that he died.

Janáček, Leoš
1854–1928, CZECH

Undoubtedly the greatest of all Czech opera composers, and perhaps one of the true geniuses of the opera world, Janáček utilized music and theatre to maximum effect. Born in Moravia, his national style was evident in all his scores, and he was particularly adept at listening and adapting. Having spent plenty of time in provincial obscurity, he was not a devotee of any musical 'camp'. Instead, he absorbed the folk tunes of the region where he was born, and incorporated their angular rhythms and textual hues within his own work.

CZECH VERNACULAR OPERAS

Janáček was the first composer to use the Czech language consistently in opera, with its characteristically dramatic weight and colour, recounting earthy stories about flesh-and-blood people. He was so interested in the sounds around him that he carried a notebook to record the nuance and inflections of everyday speech. As he stated, his goal was 'to compose a melodic curve which will, as if by magic, reveal immediately a human being in one definite phase of his existence'.

INSPIRATIONAL AFFAIRS

The ninth of 13 children, Janáček studied in Brno, Leipzig and Vienna, before returning to the Moravian capital and, in 1881, founding the Brno Organ School. This would later become the Czech State Conservatoire of Music. Fascinated by historical and political events, as well as stories about people within his immediate rural surroundings, Janáček devoted his life to teaching and composition. That same year of 1881, he married a 15-year-old piano student, Zdenka Schulzová, and together they had two children, Vladimír and Olga. However, both offspring died at a young age, and, as the already troubled relationship deteriorated further, Janáček had several affairs and eventually divorced Zdenka in 1917. Thereafter, his creativity appeared to be energized by – and harnessed to – his relationships and sexual attractions. The most important of these involved Kamila Stösslová, 36 years his junior. She was relentlessly pursued by Janáček , but the relationship was never consummated. Nevertheless, she remained his muse throughout the final 10 years of his compositional career, which accounted for the operas *Kátya Kabanová* (1921), *The Cunning Little Vixen* (1923) and *The Makropulos Affair* (1925). He died while still finishing *From the House of the Dead* (1928). Since Janáček's death, the scholarship of Sir Chares Mackerras and John Tyrrell has produced definitive editions from numerous versions of the composer's original scores.

FIRST SIGNIFICANT OPERA

The impetus for Janáček to write his first significant opera, *Jenůfa* (1903), came from an earlier, lesser work, his one-act *The Beginning of a Romance* (1891). *Jenůfa*'s bleak, depressing story of village life was based on Gabriela Preissová's drama, Her Foster Daughter, and the subject matter was widely regarded as too gruesome for an opera. However, after Janáček's family, friends and close associates managed to get it premiered in Prague, the opera was produced by other companies around the world, and two more operas followed: *Osud* ('Fate', 1907) and *The Excursions of Mr Brouček*

(1917). Neither captured public attention like *Jenůfa*, however.

Kátya Kabanová, based on Alexander Ostrovsky's play *The Thunderstorm*, signalled a return to more traditional subject matter, even though the composer could draw parallels between the title character and the object of his infatuation, Kamila Stösslová. He was clearly still charmed by her when composing *The Cunning Little Vixen*, a light-hearted Moravian folk tale that combined opera, ballet and mime, yet the feelings of endearment had evidently given way to impatience by the time of his penultimate operatic work, *The Makropulos Affair*. This tells the story of a woman, born in 1585, who needs a potion to prolong her life. Ultimately, she is torn between her immortality and the love of a man.

A SPARSER STYLE

With his final opera, *From the House of the Dead*, Janáček departed from his previous style. Much sparser in texture, it was originally thought to require major revisions to prepare it for its premiere following the composer's death. However, the doubts proved to be unfounded. This story of life inside a Siberian prison camp, featuring an all-male cast, indulged Janáček's desire to write about how, in the face of oppression, the inmates maintain their 'spark of life' and faith in God.

Jenůfa

First performed on 21 January 1904 in Brno, *Jenůfa* was later revised and in 1916 received its first performance in Prague under the direction of Karel Kovarovic. He only agreed to direct the opera after submitting to persuasive pressure from friends and colleagues, but he also insisted on making changes to the orchestration. Kovarovik's revised *Jenůfa* became the accepted version until the 1980s, when Sir Charles Mackerras recorded Janáček's opera in its original form.

The raw naturalism of the text and the declamatory sounds of the Czech language produced violent, sometimes shocking effects that contributed to a Czech literary movement called 'social realism'. In the play upon which this work was based, author Gabriela Preissovà did not sentimentalize the harsh and brutal realities of country life, and Janáček strived to create a more natural-feeling opera by 'through-composing' without including any stops or individual numbers.

Janáček's two-year-old son Vladimír died of meningitis four years before work commenced on this opera, and the composer completed the score and played it to his 20-year-old daughter Olga just four days before she too died.

Jenůfa
by Leoš Janáček
Composed: 1894–1903
Premiered: 1904, Brno
Libretto by the composer, after Gabriela Preissová's play

BACKGROUND
Grandmother Buryjovka owns a watermill. Her elder son's first wife had a son, Laca, by an earlier marriage. Her younger son, who had a daughter, Jenůfa, by his first wife, later married Petrona Slomková, the Kostelnicka (sacristan). Although he is the elder half-brother, Laca works as a hired hand for Steva, who will inherit the mill. Jenůfa is now pregnant by her cousin Steva.

ACT I
If Steva is not conscripted, Jenůfa can marry him without anyone discovering her secret. Laca accuses Grandmother Buryjovka of never showing him any love. The foreman sharpens Laca's knife. Laca is openly jealous of Steva. Jenůfa is overjoyed that Steva is coming home, but Laca rails at the injustice. Steva returns with the recruits and demands to know what gives Jenůfa the right to accuse him of being drunk: he owns the mill and all

the girls love him. He calls for dancing and grabs Jenůfa. Interrupting, the Kostelnicka declares that all the Buryja men are alike. Her own husband drank and beat her. Is that what Jenůfa wants? She may marry Steva only if he gives up drinking for a year. Jenůfa is horrified at the delay. She threatens to kill herself if he leaves her. Laca mocks Steva, but Jenůfa claims he is worth one hundred Lacas. He tries to kiss her. As she pushes him away his knife cuts her across the cheek. Barena has seen what happened and says it was an accident, but the foreman claims Laca did it on purpose.

ACT II

Jenůfa is hiding in the cottage of the Kostelnicka, who has told everyone she has gone to Vienna. Jenůfa's baby is now one week old. The Kostelnicka tells her to pray for the baby to die and gives her a sleeping-draught. While she sleeps, Steva offers to pay for the child's upkeep, but says he cannot marry her now she is disfigured. He is going to marry Karolka, the mayor's daughter. Laca thinks Jenůfa has come home and pleads to be allowed to marry her. In desperation the Kostelnicka tells him about the baby, claiming that it has died. When he has left she decides to save Jenůfa's honour. She drowns the baby and hides it under the ice. Jenůfa wakes and prays to the Virgin to protect her child. The Kostelnicka tells her that the baby died while Jenůfa was in a fever, and she has buried it. Since Steva no longer wants her, she should marry Laca. She accepts Laca's proposal, even though she can bring him no property, honour or love. The Kostelnicka hears the icy voice of death.

ACT III

It is spring, two months later. The mayor and his wife pay their respects before the wedding. The Kostelnicka is pale and exhausted. Jenůfa hopes she will soon recover, but she says that all she wants is for Jenůfa to be happy. Laca tells Jenůfa that he will spend his whole life making amends for what he did. When

Steva arrives with Karolka, the Kostelnicka is shocked to see him. Grandmother blesses the couple. The baby's body has been found under the melting ice. Distraught, Jenůfa identifies her baby's clothes. The women accuse her of infanticide, but the Kostelnicka confesses, saying she only did it for Jenůfa's sake. Karolka breaks her engagement to Steva. Jenůfa tells the others to forgive the Kostelnicka, who is taken away. Jenůfa offers to release Laca from his vow, but he declares that it does not matter what the world thinks so long as they are together.

Kátya Kabanová

Kátya belongs to the final decade of Janáček's work and was inspired by his muse, Kamila Stösslová. She was the magnificent obsession who received a steady stream of letters from the composer up until his death, some of them confirming that Kátya was written for her.

The opera was based on Ostrovsky's drama The Storm, which concerns a woman who emerges from her repressive environment by engaging in an adulterous affair. When her conscience is unable to bear the burden of her deceit, she confesses to her husband in front of his mother, Kabanicha. The harsh environment and the title character's humanism stand in stark contrast to one another. The music is 'through-composed' and unselfconsciously theatrical, the orchestration providing subtle motivic cells that develop slowly and flower magnificently. Music and drama blend seamlessly to forge a mature and profound opera.

Kátya Kabanová

by Leoš Janáček
Composed: 1919–21
Premiered: 1921, Brno
Libretto by the composer, after Alexander Nikolayevich Ostrovsky's play *The Storm*

ACT I

Kudrjáš is admiring the River Volga outside the Kabanov's house. Dikoj scolds his nephew Boris for laziness. Boris explains to Kudrjáš that he and his sister will only gain their inheritance if they obey Dikoj. He wants to leave, but he must remember his sister in Moscow. Kudrjáš says that Kabanicha is as bad – a hypocrite and tyrant. Boris confesses his love for Kátya, the wife of Kabanicha's son, Tichon. Kabanicha orders Tichon to go to Kazan. She accuses him of loving her less since he married Kátya. A wife should know her place. Tichon is too soft on her. His sister Varvara accuses him of drinking and not defending Kátya.

Kátya confesses to Varvara her dream of flying away. She used to see strange romantic visions and now she is being drawn to another man. She is horrified by Varvara's suggestion that she should see him when Tichon goes away. She pleads with Tichon not to go or to take her with him. She begs him to make her swear to be faithful to him alone. It is time for Tichon to leave. Kabanicha makes him repeat strict instructions that Kátya must observe. She orders Tichon to kneel and kiss her, but turns on Kátya when she tries to embrace him.

ACT II

Kabanicha tells Kátya that if she really loved Tichon she would display more grief. The garden is usually locked, but Varvara has found the key. Kátya wants to throw it in the river, but she hides it when she hears Kabanicha. She must see Boris. Dikoj drunkenly claims that only Kabanicha understands him. He describes how he once thrashed a peasant and then begged forgiveness. Kabanicha tells him to get better manners.

Kudrjáš is waiting for Varvara in the garden. Boris enters, explaining that he has been summoned. He has met Kátya only once, but he cannot help loving her. Varvara tells Boris that Kátya is coming and then disappears with Kudrjáš. At first Kátya cannot overcome her guilt and tells Boris to stay away. He declares that she is everything to him. She can resist no longer and falls into his arms. Varvara, returning with Kudrjáš, tells them to go for a stroll. Kabanicha will not disturb them. Besides, what is fun without some risk? Kudrjáš calls the others back.

ACT III

Two weeks later, Kudrjáš is sheltering from the rain. He points out that lightning is just electricity, but Dikoj claims it is God's fury. The rain stops. Varvara warns Boris that Tichon has returned and Kátya is out of her mind. Thunder is heard. Seeing that Boris is hiding behind Kudrjáš, Kátya asks whether he really cares so little for her suffering. She confesses everything to Kabanicha and Tichon, before running off into the storm.

Tichon is searching the riverbank at night. Varvara and Kudrjáš run away to Moscow. Kátya is looking for Boris so she can die happy, but she dreads the darkness. She calls to Boris and he answers. Dikoj is sending him away. He will be free, but Kátya knows she will have to face Kabanicha's bullying and drunken beatings from Tichon. As they part she asks him to give money to beggars to pray for her soul. She imagines the peace she will find in death and leaps into the river. Tichon accuses Kabanicha of killing her. She stops him going to the body, claiming Kátya was not worth it. She thanks the onlookers for their kindness.

The Cunning Little Vixen

First performed in Brno on 6 November 1924, this opera, based on a story by Rudolf Tešnohlídek, centres around a little vixen known as 'Sharp-ears'. Janáček's music is colourful, evocative, playful, full of Moravian folk references and often very moving, combining ballet, mime, vocalization without text, orchestral interludes, a chorus and sung dialogue to create a rich sampling of nature and its many layers of life.

Having bought a country home in Hukvaldy, where he was born and raised, Janáček enjoyed daily walks in the forest, and this work sees the natural cycle of the forest come full circle when, after giving birth to her own cubs, the little vixen dies at the hands of a poacher. Janáček doubled certain roles so that some of the animals play humans, and the final scene is a deeply felt tribute to the natural world. In line with the composer's request, the 'Forester's Farewell' was played at his funeral in 1928.

The Cunning Little Vixen

by Leoš Janáček
Compose: 1921–23
Premiered: Brno, 1924
Libretto by the composer after Rudolf Tešnohlídek's novel *Liška Bystrouška*

ACT I

The forester rests in the forest. A young vixen examines a frog, which jumps on the forester and wakes him. He seizes the vixen and takes her home. That autumn the vixen is in the forester's yard. The dog moans that he knows nothing about love, but the vixen has heard scandalous stories from the sparrows. She rejects the dog's advances. She fights back when two boys bait her. Tied up, she dreams she is a young girl. Provoked by the cock, she unsuccessfully urges the hens to rise against him. Fed up with their ignorance she kills them, bites through the rope and escapes.

ACT II

The vixen insults a badger so grossly, backed by a swarm of flies, that he abandons his comfortable home. As they play cards in the inn one winter night, the forester teases the schoolmaster about his love for Terynka, a gypsy. The parson glumly warns them against women. On his way home the schoolmaster drunkenly sees his Terynka in a sunflower, behind which the vixen is hiding. The parson recalls the girl who cheated on him when he was a student. The forester shoots at the vixen and misses. The vixen is smitten by a handsome fox, who is impressed by her exciting life and by her house-ownership. She wonders if she really is beautiful. He offers her a rabbit and courts her with increasing passion. The owl is shocked by their activities inside the den. When they come out she is crying. The fox arranges an immediate wedding.

ACT III

Harašta is going to marry Terynka. The forester warns him against poaching and sets a trap. The vixen and the fox are playing with their cubs. The trap does not fool them. The fox wants a larger family. Harašta returns and sees the vixen as a muff for Terynka. She pushes her luck too far and is shot. The forester has found her den empty.

The schoolmaster mopes about Terynka's marriage. The parson has moved away. Spring has returned, and the forester recalls his own springtime. He dreams that he sees the vixen as a cub. Promising to treat her better this time, he tries to catch her. A frog stammers that his grandfather told him about the forester.

The Makropulos Affair

Janáček referred to this opera's protagonist, Emilia Marty, as 'the icy one'. Perhaps he was thinking of Kamila Stösslová, the opera singer in Capek's comedy who so fascinated Janáček that he immediately requested the rights for a libretto. Capek was sceptical that the elderly composer could understand his play, yet the final result was superlative and Capek had to admit that it far surpassed his expectations.

The music opens with a prelude, with offstage fanfares that evoke the pageantry of a bygone era, before reverting to a much sparser musical texture. During the climactic ending, Janáček repeats and develops the opening's sweeping gesture. After Emilia renounces her immortality, the return to this sweeping gesture signals that she embraces the meaning of life in the face of death.

The Makropulos Affair
by Leoš Janáček
Composed: 1923–25
Premiered: 1926, Brno
Libretto by the composer, after Karel Capek's comedy

BACKGROUND
Baron 'Peppi' Prus died in 1827. His estate went to the Prus family, but Ferdinand MacGregor claimed it. The Prus and Gregor families have been in litigation ever since.

ACT I
The final legal judgment is expected. It is Kolenaty's legal office in Prague in 1922. Albert Gregor is anxious to hear the outcome. The famous opera singer Emilia Marty tells Kolenaty where in the old Prus house he will find a sealed will, leaving the estate to an illegitimate son, Ferdinand. Albert is bewitched and asks about Peppi's mistress Elian MacGregor. Taking advantage of his infatuation, she asks for a Greek document among the family papers. Kolenaty has found the will, letters from Elian MacGregor and something else. Marty promises to provide written evidence to prove Albert's case.

ACT II
Marty has sent a letter from Elian MacGregor confirming Ferdinand's parentage. In different ways, all the characters, including the present Baron Prus and his son Janek, are fascinated by her. She lets slip that she heard a soprano who died a century ago. Old Hauk-Sendorf says she resembles a gypsy for whom he gave up everything in 1870. Marty calls him 'Maxi'. He replies 'Eugenia'. She kisses him and he leaves sobbing. Prus has read the letters, which only refer to E. M. This could be Elian MacGregor, Elina Makropulos, named as Ferdinand's mother in the birth register, or Emilia Marty. She asks his price. Albert passionately declares his love. She tells him they need another will in the name of Makropulos. Prus agrees to fetch the document.

ACT III
After a night with Marty, Prus feels cheated by her coldness. He hears that Janek has killed himself for her. Hauk-Sendorf comes to take his Eugenia away. As Marty collects her luggage the others arrive. Kolenaty announces that the letter, dated 1836, has the same ink and handwriting as her own. In her luggage they find an E. M. seal, Hauk-Sendorf's crest and evidence of other names beginning with E. M. They demand to know her name. She is Elina Makropulos, born in Crete in 1585. She describes how her father, personal physician to Emperor Rudolf II, invented an elixir of life. The emperor insisted she should try it first. She has always kept the initials E. M. and is Albert's great-great-great-great-great-great-grandmother. She left the formula with Peppi and has come back for it. Her soul has died inside her. Now she seeks death itself. As the document burns in a candle she ages and dies.

Recommended Recording:
The Makropulos Case, London Philharmonic Orchestra; Andrew Davis, conductor; Warner Classics 2564636281; Soloists: Anja Silja (Emiliar Marty), Kim Begley (Albert Gregor), Victor Braun (Baron Prus), Andrew Shore (Dr Kolenatý), Anthony Roden (Vítek), Manuela Kriscak (Kristina), Christopher Ventris (Janek),

Robert Tear (Hauk- endorf), Susan Gorton (Chambermaid), Henry Waddington (Stage Hand), Menai Davies (Cleaner)

OPERAS

1888	Šárka
1891	The Beginning of a Romance
1903	Jenůfa
1905	Fate
1917	The Excursions of Mr Brouček
1921	Kátya Kabanová
1923	The Cunning Little Vixen
1925	The Makropulos Affair
1928	From the House of the Dead

TIMELINE

1854	Leoš Janáček born, Hukvaldy, Moravia
1872	Becomes master of Brno teaching college
1874	Enters Prague Organ School
1879	Enrols at Leipzig Conservatory
1881	Returns to Brno and founds Brno Organ School
1888	Completes first version of his opera Šárka
1894	Premiere of his one-act Beginning of a Romance
1894	Begins work on Jenůfa
1904	Jenůfa produced, Brno
1916	Triumphant Prague premiere of Jenůfa brings international recognition
1916	Meets Kamila Stösslová, who becomes his muse
1917	Revitalized Janáček composes The Excursions of Mr Broucek
1918	Completes Taras Bulba, orchestral rhapsody
1921	Kátya Kabanová is produced, Brno
1924	Receives doctorate from Masaryk University, Brno
1926	Composes buoyantly enthusiastic Sinfonietta
1927	Glagolitic Mass has its premiere in Brno
1928	Begins work on final opera, From the House of the Dead
1928	Janáček dies, Moravská Ostrava

Jeritza, Maria
1887–1982, CZECH-MORAVIAN

The most highly paid German-speaking soprano between the wars, Jeritza sang mainly at the Vienna State Opera between 1912 and 1935. She debuted numerous roles, including Ariadne in both versions of *Ariadne auf Naxos* and the empress in *Die Frau ohne Schatten* by Richard Strauss. She also sang Marietta in Korngold's *Die tote Stadt* and the title role in Janáček's *Jenůfa*, and performed at the Met between 1921 and 1932, where her Tosca was renowned. Whereas Jeritza's feminine allure proved irresistible to many of her conductors, composers and collaborators, her artistic temperament, perfectly suited to *verismo* roles, was usually channelled towards her on-stage performances.

Kagel, Mauricio
1931–2008, ARGENTINIAN

A self-taught composer, this 'prankster of the avant-garde' began writing at 18 and quickly became associated with music theatre and eclectic compositional techniques, encompassing both neo-classical and aleatoric styles. Humour, irony, double-meanings and a rejection of music's more pretentious conventions are omnipresent elements within Kagel's work.

Intent on the theatricalization of music, Kagel used his first opera, Staatstheater, to subvert the hierarchy of the opera house. A ballet is performed by non-dancers, each member of a 60-strong chorus sings a solo and the orchestra is not in the pit, but pre-recorded. What's more, there is no plot or libretto. Staatstheater's premiere at the Hamburg State Opera provoked uproar, which helped to establish Kagel's reputation as an *enfant terrible* of the operatic stage.

Kaufmann, Jonas
b. 1969, GERMAN

Kaufmann's mesmerising presence, fine acting and beautiful sound have secured his place in the operatic firmament. He sings a large number of spinto tenor roles, such as the title role in *Don Carlos*, Don Jose in *Carmen*, and Maurizio in *Adriana Lecouvreur*, alongside an increasing number of Wagnerian roles. His versatility in opera sits comfortably alongside his recital performances, for which he is equally fêted.

Korngold, Erich Wolfgang
1897–1957, AUSTRIAN

The son of music critic Julius Korngold, Erich was declared a genius aged nine by Gustav Mahler. Four years later, Korngold wrote a ballet pantomime, *Der Schneemann* ('The Snowman', 1910), orchestrated by his teacher Zemlinsky. The work drew the admiration of Puccini and Strauss, both of whom were already major influences on Korngold's compositional style.

Munich Staatsoper produced his first two one-act operas, *Der Ring des Polykrates* and *Violanta*, as a double bill in 1916. Conducted by Bruno Walter, these were stylistic forerunners of Korngold's great late-Romantic opera, *Die tote Stadt* (1920), featuring a wealth of melodic material as well as a libretto by him and his father. 1927 then saw the premiere of *Das Wunder der Heliane*, which he considered to be his finest work despite it being eclipsed by Krenek's opera *Jonny spielt auf*, produced the same year.

With anti-Semitism on the rise, Korngold left Vienna in 1934 to work in Hollywood, where his movie scores for *Robin Hood* and *Anthony Adverse* earned him a pair of Oscars yet tarnished his career upon returning to Austria in 1949. His opera *Die Kathrin* (1937), which the Nazis had cancelled before his departure to America, was a critical failure, and he returned permanently to Los Angeles. His work is currently enjoying a well-deserved resurgence in the repertoire, and a number of his arias (notably 'Tanzlied des Pierrot' and 'Marietta's Lied' from *Die tote Stadt*) appear frequently on concert programmes and recital discs.

Lehmann, Lotte
1888–1976, AMERICAN

One of modern opera's great singers, Lehmann's performances of Robert Schumann's songs were renowned. She created the roles of the composer in *Ariadne auf Naxos*, the Dyer's Wife in *Die Frau ohne Schatten* and Christine in *Intermezzo*, all by Strauss. Although her true artistic home was Vienna, she made an auspicious debut as Sieglinde in Wagner's *Die Walküre* at the Met in 1934. Unable to sing in Austria during the Second World War, she remained at the Met and recorded *Lieder* with musicians such as Bruno Walter. Lehmann's distinguished career spanned 93 lyric-dramatic soprano roles and all three of the leading parts in Strauss's *Der Rosenkavalier*. In later life, she inspired the creation of the Music Academy of the West, in Santa Barbara, California.

Ligeti, György
1923–2006, ROMANIAN

An Eastern European exile whose family was executed by the Nazis during the Second World War, Ligeti was a composer with a neo-Dadaist penchant for the absurd, and a musical style that varied wildly from one piece to another as each work became a world unto itself.

While in Germany, Ligeti acquainted himself with the avant-garde movement, immersed himself in electronic music and composed two short music theatre works – *Aventures* ('Adventures', 1962) and *Nouvelles Aventures* ('New Adventures', 1965) – before relocating to Vienna and becoming an Austrian citizen in 1967. Ligeti's sole opera, *Le Grand Macabre* ('The Grand Macabre', 1976), features a chaotic score as well as a libretto by himself and Michael Meschke that reflect the hedonistic excesses of the work's pre-apocalypse characters. Ligeti's use of musical illusion, borrowing themes or interludes from the works of other composers, can be compared to the lifting of material in the world of pop art.

Le Grand Macabre found a new and enthusiastic audience when it was revised by Ligeti and remounted for the 1997 Salzburg Festival by director Peter Sellars and conductor Esa-Pekka Salonen.

Le Grand Macabre
by György Ligeti
Composed: 1972–76
Premiered: 1978, Stockholm
Libretto by the composer and Michael Meschke after Michel de Ghelderode's play *La ballade du Grand Macabre*

ACT I

Piet the Pot, drunk as ever, watches Amando and Amanda making love. Nekrotzar, the Grand Macabre, rises from his tomb and prophesies doom for Breughelland at midnight. He rides off on Piet to spread the news, while the lovers take over his empty grave. Astradamors, the Royal Astronomer, has seen a strange red glow in the sky. Dressed in women's underwear, he is being abused by his dominatrix wife Mescalina. Piet arrives with Nekrotzar. Mescalina gets drunk and in a dream demands that Venus sends her a well-endowed lover. Nekrotzar obligingly rapes and kills her. Astradamors is happy to be master of his house again.

ACT II

The Black Minister and the White Minister are teaching Prince Go-Go the alphabet. They bully him and he has a disastrous riding lesson. He is always feeling hungry. The coloratura Chief of Secret Police enters, panic-stricken and unable to tell them intelligibly that a comet is about to fall on the city. Sirens sound the alarm. Nekrotzar terrifies the people by prophesying doom. They plead with him to spare them. Piet and Astradamors decide to make him drunk. By midnight he is paralytic. There is a loud explosion. The comet has presumably landed. Nektrotzar is as surprised as anyone, but he claims responsibility for averting disaster and collapses.

Piet and Astradamors believe that everyone is dead. Nekrotzar slowly realizes that he has failed. Mescalina reappears and accuses him. He shrivels away when faced with her, the ministers, Piet and Astradamors. Amando and Amanda surface from the grave, unaware how close they came to the end of the world. Since no one knows when he or she is to die, we are encouraged to live merrily until then.

Los Angeles, Victoria de
1923–2005, **SPANISH**

Possessing fine musicianship and a warm, sincere stage presence, soprano de Los Angeles gained recognition when she won first prize in the 1947 Geneva International Competition. She performed the following year in London, then at the Paris Opéra in 1949 and the Salzburg Festival in 1950. After her Met debut in 1951, she was regularly featured there for the next 10 years. Among her signature roles were Mimi in Puccini's *La bohème*, which she recorded with Jussi Björling, and Rosina in *Il barbiere di Siviglia* by Rossini.

Ludwig, Christa
b. 1924, **GERMAN**

An outstanding mezzo-soprano recitalist and concert singer, Ludwig was the daughter of two singers: tenor Anton Ludwig, and contralto Eugenie Besalla-Ludwig, who sang under Herbert von Karajan. Forced into early retirement, Eugenie became her daughter's voice coach. Making her debut at 18 as Prince Orlovsky in Frankfurt, Ludwig remained there until 1952, before joining the Vienna Staatsoper three years later.

From 1959 to 1990 she sang at the Met, where her roles included the Dyer's Wife (*Die Frau ohne Schatten*), Didon (*Les Troyens*), Ortrud (*Lohengrin*), Kundry (*Parsifal*), Marschallin (*Der Rosenkavalier*) and Fricka (*Das Rheingold*). She also sang Brangäne (*Tristan und Isolde*) and Kundry at Bayreuth. Her musicality made her a favourite of a number of conductors, and Ludwig formed her greatest collaborations with Karl Böhm, Herbert von Karajan and Leonard Bernstein.

Mann, Thomas
1875–1955, **GERMAN**

Mann was one of the most important German-speaking writers of the twentieth century, receiving the Nobel Prize for Literature in 1929. In 1933 he settled in Switzerland, his anti-fascist writings having repeatedly attracted opprobrium. In 1936 he was stripped of his German citizenship, effective retrospectively from July 1933. He eventually went to America, where in 1940 he settled in to a community of German intellectuals in California, before returning to Europe. Although Mann's name was added to the list of authors whose books were burned by the Nazis, he never lost his affinity for the German culture and language.

Britten chose Mann's *Der Tod in Venedig* ('Death in Venice', 1912) as the subject for his final opera. The novella's protagonist, Gustav von Aschenbach, develops an obsession for a beautiful young boy of 13. The story was a means for the author to explore his own intuition about subjective beauty and his 'celibate' homoeroticism.

Martinelli, Giovanni
1885–1969, **ITALIAN**

Born in a small Italian village, Martinelli scaled the heights of operatic fame, becoming Caruso's successor in *verismo* repertoire at the Met. After making his operatic debut in the title role of Verdi's *Ernani*, he achieved his breakthrough when engaged by Puccini to sing Dick Johnson in the 1911 European premiere of *La fanciulla del West*. In 1913, Martinelli joined the Met, where he eventually gave a total of 926 performances in 38 operas. His amazing stamina lent itself to taxing roles of high tessitura, such as Canio (*I pagliacci*), Radamès (*Aida*), Manrico (*Il trovatore*), Samson (*Samson et Dalila*) and Otello. Although his voice was failing by the 1930s, Martinelli continued to sing well into his seventies, making his final performance as the emperor in *Turandot* at the age of 81.

Martinu, Bohuslav
1890–1959, **CZECH**

One of the leading Czech composers of the twentieth century, Martinu produced 15 operas that display a penchant for vibrant innovation. After studying at the Prague Conservatory, Martinu moved to Paris in 1923 and was influenced by the sights and sounds of jazz, music hall and the avant-garde. As Western Europe regenerated itself following the First World War, Martinu created operas such as *The Soldier and the Dancer* (1927), the jazz-inspired *The Three Wishes* (1929) and *The Miracles of Mary* (1934) before turning his attention towards a new medium: radio. Of Martinu's two radio operas, the comic morality tale *Comedy on the Bridge* (1935) is the best known and most performed. However *Julietta* (1937), based on the composer's libretto, is his finest operatic achievement, as well as his personal favourite.

In 1940, while his career was flourishing following the premiere of his *Double Concerto*, Martinu was blacklisted by the Nazis and fled to America with his wife, a suitcase and his score of Julietta. After the war, he wrote a couple of operas for television, and then settled in France during the mid-1950s. His final operas *Ariane* (1958) and *The Greek Passion* (1956–59) were not produced until after his death.

Melchior, Lauritz
1890–1973, **DANISH**

Melchior was the most famous Wagnerian **Heldentenor** of the twentieth century, his large physique housing a larger than life voice that, in terms of stamina alone, was unstoppable; a deep baritonal tenor with ringing high notes. His musicianship was often questioned and he was famous for making the same mistakes year after year, yet for all his eccentricities he was the genuine article, rising effortlessly above the heaviest of orchestrations.

Melchior's Bayreuth legend was cut short due to Wagner's affiliation with the Nazis – following his conscience, he left, never to return. He sang at major opera houses around the world, but one season short of his 25th anniversary at the Met he was forced into retirement by a resentful Rudolf Bing.

Menotti, Gian Carlo
1911–2007, ITALIAN

One of the most important opera composers during the 1950s, Menotti had already written two operas by the time he entered the Milan Conservatory aged 13, and he would go on to write 23 more. He later moved to America and studied at the Curtis Institute, where he met his lifelong companion and inspiration, Samuel Barber.

Menotti's music is derived from the Puccini school of *verismo*, and his theatricality often verges on the melodramatic. His one-act *Amelia Goes to the Ball* (1937) was performed at the Metropolitan Opera, and other early successes included a Broadway pairing of *The Medium* (1946) and *The Telephone* (1947) that ran for 211 performances. His full-length, Pulitzer Prize-winning *The Consul* (1950) is a compelling drama of people seeking political asylum, while *Amahl and the Night Visitors* (1951), based on the story of the Three Kings and produced for television, became an instant classic.

By the time *The Saint of Bleecker Street* (1954) was first performed, Menotti's work was falling out of favour, and his artistic energies subsequently shifted from composing to working on the establishment of the Festival of Two Worlds in Spoleto, Italy in 1958, as well as its counterpart in Charleston, South Carolina. Nevertheless, in 1986 Menotti wrote *Goya* for the tenor Plácido Domingo, which was presented by the Washington Opera.

The Consul
by Gian Carlo Menotti
Composed: 1949
Premiered: 1950, Philadelphia
Libretto by the composer

ACT I

John Sorel has been shot by the secret police at a political meeting. His wife Magda and his mother hide him in their apartment. A secret police agent threatens Magda. John decides to escape abroad. Magda will need a visa to join him. If the window is broken they will know the glass cutter, Assan, has a message from him. Magda joins the others in the waiting room trying to see the consul, including Nika Magadoff, the magician. The secretary makes them fill in endless forms. Still no one can see him.

ACT II

Magda is exhausted after weeks at the consulate. Her son is very ill. While she sleeps the mother sings a lullaby. Magda has a nightmare about John and the secretary. The window smashes. The secret police agent hints at a visa as a bribe to betray John's fellow revolutionaries. She orders him to go. Assan tells her that John is hiding in the mountains, waiting until she has her visa. Not wanting to delay his escape, she says that she has it. Her son has died. The magician promotes his case with tricks and hypnosis. Magda quarrels with the secretary, asking whether the consul exists. She may see him when an important visitor has left. It is the secret police agent. Magda faints.

ACT III

Assan finds Magda at the consulate and tells her that John is returning. She writes a note to make him stay away and rushes out. John enters and is arrested by the police who have been following him. He asks the secretary to telephone Magda. Magda commits suicide. While the gas takes effect she hallucinates about her companions in the waiting room. As she dies the telephone rings.

Messiaen, Olivier

1908–92, **FRENCH**

One of France's greatest twentieth-century composers, Messiaen began writing at the age of seven, and studied at the Paris Conservatoire from the age of 11 under the tutelage of Paul Dukas, Maurice Emmanuel and Marcel Dupré. In 1931 he became the organist at L'Eglise de la Trinité, where he remained until his death. As a music professor at L'École Normale in Paris he founded La Jeune France, which promoted French music principles. Imprisoned by the Germans during the Second World War, he composed *Quatuor pour la fin du temps* ('Quartet for the End of Time', 1941), a work written under great personal stress and scored for the only available instruments – violin, clarinet, cello and piano. Upon his release he returned to the Conservatoire.

Although Messiaen's primary instrument was the organ, he was drawn to musical analysis and forged a very unique style. His only opera, *Saint François d'Assise* (1983), premiered at the Paris Opéra and reflected his faith in Roman Catholicism. Just under four hours in length, it was conceived on a grand scale with a vast orchestra and three Ondes Martenots.

Netrebko, Anna

b. 1971, **RUSSIAN**

Soprano Anna Netrebko made her operatic stage debut as Susanna in *Le Nozze di Figaro* at the Marinsky Theatre, conducted by Valery Gergiev. Netrebko's repertoire includes a number of *bel canto* and *verismo* operas, and she thrives in roles that require great vocal and dramatic commitment; her fearless and flamboyant Violetta (*La Traviata*) being a fine example.

Nilsson, Birgit

1918–2005, **SWEDISH**

Nilsson's impressive soprano voice boasted a focused yet powerful sound and an amplitude that could ride the grandest of Wagnerian climaxes with ease. Among Nilsson's most famous performances were her legendary 1950s and 1960s portrayals of Brünnhilde and Isolde. Both of these roles were recorded, with Karl Böhm conducting. She was equally powerful in roles such as Turandot and Minnie in *La Fanciulla del West*. She retired in 1982.

Norman, Jessye

b. 1945, **AMERICAN**

Boasting one of the most magnificent voices of her generation, Norman has received praise for her operatic, concert and recital performances. A scholarship student at Howard University at the age of 16, she then studied at the Peabody Institute and received her Masters Degree at the University of Michigan. Her 1969 operatic debut as Elisabeth in Wagner's *Tannhäuser* for Deutsche Oper Berlin catapulted her into the international arena, yet her repertoire has remained eclectic. Some of her memorable performances include the title roles of Aida and Alceste, Ariadne in *Ariadne auf Naxos,* Cassandra and Didon (*Les Troyens*), Judith in *Bluebeard's Castle* and Schoenberg's half-spoken, half-sung monodrama *Erwartung*.

Rene Pape

b. 1964, **GERMAN**

A bass who is renowned for his vivid performances and sumptuous tone, Pape first came to international attention in 1991 singing the role of Sarastro in a production of *Die Zauberflöte* conducted by Georg Solti. He has sung almost all of the great German bass roles and demonstrates great versatility in concert too, but he is particularly celebrated for his interpretation of Wagner, capturing the virility and vulnerability of Wotan, and winning Grammys for his recordings of *Die Meistersinger* and *Tannhäuser*.

Pavarotti, Luciano
1935–2007, **ITALIAN**

Pavarotti became a commodity that often belies his profound vocal gifts as one of the greatest-ever tenors. His career commenced as soon as he began to sing, for he possessed an extraordinary, effortless voice with ringing high notes. Early roles such as Rodolfo (*La bohème*) and Tonio (*La fille du régiment*) amounted to near vocal perfection. Enticed by heavier repertoire, Pavarotti would eventually lose the thrilling sparkle of his earlier years; it is his performances recorded during the 1970s that stand out. In his later years, his worldwide fame was promoted via stadium appearances and as a member of the 'Three Tenors', together with Plácido Domingo and José Carreras.

Pears, Peter
1910–86, **ENGLISH**

England's leading tenor from 1945 to 1960, Pears created many of Benjamin Britten's leading roles, including Peter Grimes, Albert Herring, The Male Chorus (*The Rape of Lucretia*) and Aschenbach (*Death in Venice*). An **oratorio** specialist, he performed the Evangelist in the Bach Passions with distinction, while in recitals, often accompanied by Britten, he was deeply affecting. His voice was not incredible, but he used it intelligently. He founded the Aldeburgh Festival with Britten.

Penderecki, Krzysztof
b. 1933, **POLISH**

Violin virtuoso Penderecki attended the Kraków Academy until 1959, when he entered a composers' competition several times and collected a first prize and two second prizes. Initially attracted to the avant-garde movement, Penderecki found international fame with *Threnody for the Victims of Hiroshima* (1960), written for 52 stringed instruments. This used tone clusters to convey the effects of a nuclear explosion, and it called upon the musicians to create interesting textures by playing on the wrong side of the bridge or bowing the tailpiece. Around the mid-1970s, however, Penderecki began imbuing his work with more traditional, melodic styles, and started to indulge in vocal writing, composing the first of his four operas: *The Devils of Loudun* (1969), *Paradise Lost* (1978), *Die schwarze Maske* ('The Black Mask', 1986) and *Ubu Rex* ('King Rex', 1991).

Typically, Penderecki's operas pose specific challenges to the singers, who must project over dense orchestrations and squawk, scream or spit while instruments are played with glissandi and vibrato. This makes for an interesting aural-visual experience, and one that has attracted a considerable following worldwide.

Pfitzner, Hans
1864–1949, **GERMAN**

Russian-born, yet once a popular German composer, Pfitzner has shrunk into the recesses of memory, not least because his esteemed position was promoted by a Third Reich that, like him, believed German culture was threatened by international Jewry. His works *Von deutscher Seele* ('Of the German Soul', 1921) and *Das dunkle Reich* ('The Dark Realm', 1929) were written as a means of expressing his interest in creating 'pure' German music.

Pfitzner's late-Romantic style was influenced, in large part, by Schumann and Wagner, the latter's presence being especially obvious in Pfitzner's first two operas: *Der arme Heinrich* ('Poor Heinrich', 1891–93) and *Die Rose vom Liebesgarten* ('The Rose from the Garden of Love', 1897–1900). Soon, along with Engelbert Humperdinck and Richard Strauss, he was regarded as one of Germany's leading opera composers, and this position was solidified when, as director of the Strasbourg Opera, Pfitzner wrote his masterpiece *Palestrina*. A large-scale work that, like Hindemith's *Mathis der Maler*, questions the artist's position within society, Palestrina clings to the past and its cultural traditions. It was hailed by German intellectuals throughout the next few decades, until 1945 when the country lay in ruins along with the remnants of Pfitzner's career.

Palestrina

by Hans Pfitzner
Composed: 1911–15
Premiered: 1917, Munich
Libretto by the composer

ACT I

The composer Palestrina used to serve the pope. He was dismissed when he married, but has written nothing since his wife died. His pupil Silla finds his music old-fashioned. Palestrina tells Cardinal Borromeo that Silla may be right. Perhaps the style of the old masters is obsolete. Borromeo assures him that, if he were to use his God-given talent again, his powers would return. Decisions must be made at the Council of Trent regarding ritual and the Mass.

Purists wish to abolish polyphony. Borromeo has persuaded the pope to permit Palestrina to compose a test-piece that would justify its use at Mass. Palestrina refuses. Left alone, nine apparitions of old masters remind Palestrina of his duty to God. He calls on God and hears an angel singing. He starts to compose, inspired by more angels and the spirit of his wife.

ACT II

The cardinals gather at Trent amid political manoeuvring. Borromeo has had Palestrina imprisoned, but doubts whether or not this will make him co-operate. The Italian delegates are opposed by other nations. Cardinal Morone proposes that they discuss church music. Borromeo's announcement about Palestrina's test-piece causes uproar, *with the Spanish the most vocal opponents. The delegates' servants riot outside. Soldiers shoot them down.*

ACT III

Silla has handed over the manuscript to have Palestrina released. He is waiting with his son Ighino to hear how the Mass has been received. It is a triumph. The pope arrives to ask him to return to papal service. Borromeo breaks down in tears. He never knew that God spoke through Palestrina. He tries to kiss Palestrina's feet and runs out. Ighino tells Palestrina that Silla has gone to Florence. He asks to join the celebrations in the street. Palestrina looks at his wife's portrait and asks God for peace.

Pinza, Ezio

1892–1957, **ITALIAN**
Pinza's bass voice was notable for its beauty of tone. Following the First World War, he sang at La Scala under Toscanini. His debut at the Met in 1926 began a run of 22 consecutive seasons as a leading bass. He sang all the bass roles, Don Giovanni and Figaro being among his most memorable portrayals and earning him the title of 'opera's sex symbol'. After leaving the Met aged 56, Pinza began a career in musicals, operettas and film. His most famous Broadway performance was in Rodgers and Hammerstein's *South Pacific*.

Plomer, William

1903–73, **SOUTH AFRICAN-BRITISH**
A man of letters who wrote poems, novels, short stories, essays and opera librettos, Plomer scandalized his native country when, at age 22, his novel *Turbott Wolfe* (1925) denounced South Africa's racist domestic policies. Born to English parents, and spurred by his love of literature and travel, he settled in England where, as a boy, he had received his formal education. While Plomer's travels inspired a number of books, his poetry expressed his geopolitical views, and after these talents

came to the attention of Benjamin Britten the two men collaborated on *Gloriana*, an opera celebrating the coronation of Queen Elizabeth II. Thereafter, they joined forces on a trio of parable-related works: *Curlew River* (1964) was modelled after a Japanese No play; *The Burning Fiery Furnace* (1966) was from the Old Testament; and *The Prodigal Son* (1968) was a parable from the New Testament.

Ponselle, Rosa
1897–1981, AMERICAN
Soprano Ponselle's auspicious debut took place in 1918 at the Met, as Leonore in *La Forza del Destino* with Enrico Caruso. That season, she sang 23 times, mainly in leading roles, and often with Caruso. Ponselle was soon the Met's leading Italian dramatic soprano, with a dark, ringing, sonorous sound not heard since Claudia Muzio. Her Norma in 1927 was a vocal triumph, yet in the wake of these magnificent performances there was criticism that her music had been transposed down. Commercially successful but critically maligned, she left the Met in 1937 and, after a failed Hollywood screen test for the role of Carmen, made her final concert appearances in 1939. She was just 42.

Poulenc, Francis
1899–1963, FRENCH
Born into social privilege, Poulenc was introduced to the Parisian art scene by his piano teacher and mentor, Ricardo Viñes, and struck out in a new direction when becoming part of a non-conformist group known as Les Six. Hardly members of the avant-garde, these young composers instead liked to combine popular music styles with repetitive, strongly accented rhythms, polytonality and a quality of informality and spontaneity.

A gifted vocal writer and lyrical melodist, Poulenc composed his first operatic work during the Second World

'ENVOLEZ-VOUS...'
Francis Poulenc and his Les Six colleagues were highly influenced by Parisian culture's popular music. Some of the melodies in his opera *Les mamelles de Tirésias* are strongly influenced by French music hall and cabaret, most notably Thérèse's 'Envolez-vous, oiseaux de ma faiblesse...' and the closing scene 'Il faux s'aimer...'.

War. *Les mamelles de Tirésias* was based on a surrealist comedy by Apollinaire, which Poulenc had seen in 1917. But even though it premiered at the Opéra-Comique with legendary soprano Denise Duval in the title role, it received a lukewarm reception.

A decade later, Poulenc composed his only full-length opera. Based on a true story about nuns who were beheaded during the French Revolution, *Dialogues des Carmélites* ('Dialogues of the Carmelites' or 'The Carmelites', 1956) further demonstrated his masterful writing for voice and orchestra. It was his final opera, the one-act tragedy *La voix humaine* ('The Human Voice', 1959) that was his most personal. His portrayal of a young woman's one-sided phone conversation with her disengaged ex-lover probably echoed the pain that Poulenc had experienced with his own complex relationships.

Dialogues des Carmélites
by Francis Poulenc
Composed: 1953–56
Premiered: 1957, Milan
Libretto by the composer after Georges Bernanos' play

ACT I
It is April 1789 and revolution is stirring. Blanche de la Force, timid and highly strung, announces her intention to become a nun.

The prioress of the Carmelite convent at Compiègne warns Blanche that this is not a refuge. She wishes to be known as Soeur Blanche de l'Agonie du Christ Blanche rebukes Soeur Constance for chattering when the prioress is dying. Constance suggests that they should offer their lives in exchange for the prioress's. She senses that she and Blanche will die young together. The prioress is dying. She entrusts Blanche to Mère Marie's care and bids farewell to Blanche. As she nears death she becomes delirious, seeing visions of the chapel's desecration. Blanche sees her die horribly.

ACT II

Blanche and Constance keep watch over the body. Blanche is terrified when left alone. Constance suggests that the prioress's death may mean that others die more easily. The new prioress, Madame Lidoine, warns that the sisters' future will be full of trials. They should not aspire to martyrdom. Blanche's brother has decided to leave France. He tries to persuade her to leave the convent, but she declares that she is in God's care. When he has gone she collapses. Mère Marie tells her to have courage. The chaplain has been banned from performing his duties. The new prioress contradicts Mère Marie's belief that they may preserve the Church by giving their lives. The civil powers take over the convent. Blanche is terrified by the sound of the mob.

ACT III

The chapel has been sacked. With the prioress in Paris, Mère Marie proposes a vow of martyrdom. There is only one vote against, which Constance claims. As Blanche weeps, Constance begs to take the vow alongside Blanche, but she flees. The community has been outlawed and Blanche returns home. Her father has been guillotined, but she is too frightened to go back with Mère Marie. The Carmelites have been imprisoned. The prioress takes the vow. Constance has dreamt that Blanche will return, but they are all condemned to death. The chaplain stops

Mère Marie rejoining the sisters by saying that perhaps she has another destiny. They are brought to the Place de la Révolution on 17 July 1794. The prioress leads them to the guillotine singing the 'Salve Regina'. Constance is the last, and Blanche steps out of the crowd to join her.

Recommended Recording:

Dialogues des Carmélites, Philharmonia Orchestra; Jérémie Rhorer, conductor; Soloists: Sophie Koch (Mère Marie de l'Incarnation), Patricia Petibon (Blanche de la Force), Véronique Gens (Madame Lidoine), Sandrine Piau (Soeur Constance de Saint Denis), Rosalind Plowright (Madame de Croissy), Topi Lehtipuu (Le Chevalier de la Force)

Price, Leontyne
b. 1927, AMERICAN

From the Mississippi to the concert stages of Europe, Price helped to pave the way for black American singers. Assisted by Paul Robeson and an affluent white family in her hometown, she gained entry to Juilliard, where she appeared in George Gershwin's *Porgy and Bess* and Virgil Thomson's *Four Saints in Three Acts*. When, in 1955, NBC produced Puccini's *Tosca* with Price in the title role, she became the first African-American to sing in a televised opera. She also righted the wrong committed when the Daughters of the Revolution stopped Marion Anderson from singing at Washington's Constitution Hall in 1939 – more than 40 years later, Price dedicated her performance there to Anderson. Her association with the role of Aida began in 1957 and ended in 1985, when she retired from the stage. A perfect instrument for Verdi roles, Price was one of the great singers of the twentieth century.

Prokofiev, Sergei
1891–1953, RUSSIAN

One of the most accessible and well known of twentieth-century Russian composers,

Prokofiev merged an experimental approach with melodic conventionality to create music that was distinct in its national style.

A fine pianist and impetuous personality who studied orchestration at the St Petersburg Academy with **Nikolay Rimsky-Korsakov** (1844–1909), Prokofiev wrote three childhood operas by the age of 16 and composed his first mature one, *Maddalena*, four years later. A short spell in London was followed by a piano tour of America, where the Chicago Opera commissioned him to write an opera based on Gozzi's play *The Love for Three Oranges* (1919). A rambunctious, comedic, surrealist fantasy, this received an enthusiastic response, yet many Americans considered the music of 'the Bolshevik' to be barbaric, and after several years of living in Paris he returned to his homeland for good in 1933. Unfortunately, this was a bad move.

Castigated as unpatriotic by the Soviet authorities after completing *War and Peace* (1944), an opera that he considered to be among his finest works, Prokofiev tried to court government approval with his final operatic project, *The Story of a Real Man* (1948). However, even this transparently partisan work was banned, and the composer died a broken man just five years later. In 1954 his opera *The Fiery Angel*, which he had written in 1922–23 and then worked on intermittently for the next 30 years, was premiered in Paris.

The Love for Three Oranges
by Sergei Prokofiev
Composed: 1919
Premiered: 1921, Chicago
Libretto by the composer, after Carlo Gozzi's *L'amore delle tre melarance*

BACKGROUND
Factions in the audience demand Tragedy, Romance, Comedy and Farce. The Cranks take control.

ACT I
The prince is ill. If he dies, the heir to the King of Clubs would be Clarice. This must be avoided. It has been prophesied that he will be cured by laughter. Clarice has promised to marry Leander, the prime minister, who plots against Truffaldino's attempts to amuse the prince. Leander is helped by the evil Fata Morgana and her sidekick Smeraldina.

ACT II
Truffaldino makes the prince attend the entertainments. Nothing offered raises a smile until Truffaldino collides with Fata Morgana. The sight of her waving her legs in the air makes the prince erupt with laughter. She curses him. He will be obsessed with a search for three oranges. He sets out with Truffaldino.

ACT III
Celio, the king's sorcerer, tells them that the oranges are in the kitchen of the enormous, ferocious cook Creonta, who has a weakness for ribbons. He gives Truffaldino a magic ribbon and warns that the oranges should only be cut open near water. Creonta captures Truffaldino and is entranced by the ribbon.

The prince rescues the oranges. On their way home they cross the desert. The oranges have grown enormously. Exhausted and thirsty, Truffaldino opens an orange. Inside there is a princess dying of thirst He opens the next. Both princesses die. The Prince opens the third. The Cranks intervene to save the princess, Ninetta. Fata Morgana turns her into a white rat and Smeraldina takes her place.

ACT IV
The Cranks abduct Fata Morgana. The rat is found on the princess's throne. Celio somehow changes it back into Ninetta. The traitors are condemned, but escape.

War and Peace

by Sergei Prokofiev

Composed: 1941–42; 1946–47; rev. up
to 1953
Final version (13 scenes) premiered:
1959, Moscow
Libretto by the composer and Mira
Mendelson after Tolstoy's novel

PART ONE

*1806: Andrey Bolkonsky is weary of life. He
overhears Natasha Rostova talking to her
cousin Sonya about the beauty of life. Her
words renew his belief in happiness.*

*1810, St Petersburg: Andrey meets
Natasha at her first ball. They fall in love.*

*February 1812, Moscow: Andrey and
Natasha are engaged, but he is abroad.
Natasha and her father are treated rudely
by Andrey's father and sister, who want to
prevent the marriage.*

*May: Pierre Bezukhov's wife, Hélène,
introduces Natasha to her brother Anatol.
She mistakes his practised seduction manner
for passion and is tempted to elope.*

*June: Despite misgivings, notably that
Anatol is already married, Dolokhov agrees to
help him. Natasha is waiting for Anatol, but
Sonya has betrayed the plan. Akhrosimova
lectures Natasha and persuades Pierre to tell
her about Anatol's marriage. She pleads with
Pierre to ask Andrey to forgive her. Moved by
her despair, he declares that he would marry
her if he were free. Natasha attempts suicide
with arsenic. Pierre confronts Anatol. He
forces him to hand over Natasha's letters
and leave Moscow. Denisov brings news that
Napoleon is about to invade.*

PART TWO

*August, Borodino: Soldiers are digging
defences. Denisov explains his partisan
tactics to Andrey. Peasants report French
atrocities. Pierre visits Andrey. The troops
parade before Field Marshal Kutuzov.
Andrey declines a post on Kutuzov's staff.
Napoleon, watching the battle, senses that
destiny is turning against him. The Russian*

*generals are gathered at a council of war.
Against their advice, Kutuzov decides to
withdraw and surrender Moscow, rather
than lose his army.*

*September–October: Moscow has
been sacked. Pierre intends to assassinate
Napoleon. Fires are started all over the city.
Pierre is arrested but is spared execution. He
is befriended by an old soldier, Karatayev.
Natasha has found Andrey among the
wounded near Moscow. He is delirious. She
asks him to forgive her. They declare their
mutual love but he dies.*

*November: The French are retreating,
defeated by 'General Winter'. They have
taken Russian prisoners with them, including
Pierre and Karatayev, who has been shot. The
others are rescued by Denisov's partisans.
Pierre is told that Hélène and Andrey are
dead, but life is returning to Moscow. The
Russian people, led by Kutuzov, celebrate
their victory.*

Ravel, Maurice

1875–1937, FRENCH

A meticulous craftsman whose constant
reworking and rewriting may have
accounted for his relatively small body
of work, Ravel composed music that
consciously moved away from the
influence of Richard Wagner. Along with
Claude Debussy, he invented a highly
personalized French style.

Ravel also imbued his music with his
love for Spanish culture (perhaps because
his mother was of Basque origin), and
this was very much evident in his first
opera, *L'heure espagnole* ('The Spanish
Hour', 1911). This one-act **opera buffa**
comprised an exceptionally brilliant
setting of text, with witty declamations
and double-entendres, while the
orchestration was replete with clever
sound effects such as clocks, machines
and a recurring cuckoo motif. In his
second opera, *L'enfant et les sortilèges*
('The Child and the Spells', 1925), Ravel
and his librettist, Colette, perfectly

capture the innocence and wide-eyed fantasy of youth, even though the story and its more fantastic elements make this work difficult to mount on-stage.

Tragically, in 1933 Ravel began suffering from a degenerative brain disease that affected his ability to write, play the piano and take musical dictation. After four years, he finally agreed to undergo surgery, but lapsed into a coma from which he never emerged.

L'heure espagnole

by Maurice Ravel
Composed: 1907–09
Premiered: 1911, Paris
Libretto by Franc-Nohain, after his own play

Ramiro, a muleteer, brings a watch for repair to Torquemada's workshop in Toledo. Concepcion reminds her husband that it is Thursday, when he has to wind all the municipal clocks. He asks Ramiro to wait until he gets back. Concepcion, however, is expecting her lover, the poet Gonzalve. She asks Ramiro to carry upstairs a large, heavy clock. She tells Gonzalve not to waste their time alone, but soon tires of his extravagant poetics. When Ramiro returns she says she has changed her mind. He should bring down the clock and take up another. She pushes Gonzalve into the second clock. Don Inigo, a banker and another admirer, enters. Ramiro returns with the first clock, picks up the second (with Gonzalve inside) and goes upstairs, followed by Concepcion. She cannot help admiring his muscles of iron, but is concerned that Gonzalve might get seasick. Inigo is feeling left out and squeezes into the first clock. Ramiro ponders on the complexity of clocks and women. Concepcion finds that the clock upstairs has stopped working and sends Ramiro to fetch it. She is not amused by Inigo's cuckoo imitations. The two clocks are swapped over. Gonzalve refuses to leave his clock. Ramiro is most taken with Concepcion's charms. It

takes only one word to make him go back for Inigo's clock. She delivers a tirade against her two hopeless lovers. She then invites Ramiro upstairs, without a clock. Inigo is stuck inside his. Gonzalve gets out, but hides inside again when Torquemada returns. Torquemada, noticing the remarkably close attention they are paying to the clocks, makes two immediate sales. Concepcion and Ramiro return. With one last effort Inigo is freed. It is the muleteer's turn for love.

L'enfant et les sortileges

by Maurice Ravel
Composed: 1920–25
Premiered: 1925, Monte Carlo
Libretto by Colette (Sidonie-Gabrielle Colette)

The child has been naughty. His mother does not think he deserves more than tea without sugar and dry bread. He must think about how sad he has made her. He shouts after her, 'I don't love anybody! I'm naughty!' He starts smashing and ill-treating everything in the room. Suddenly the armchair comes to life and dances off with a Louis-Quinze chair, happy to be free of that awful child. The grandfather clock is disorientated. The Wedgwood teapot and Chinese cup also dance away together, singing. The fire warms good children but burns naughty ones. The child is frightened. Shepherds and shepherdesses emerge from the wallpaper, separated now that the child has torn it. The princess has no idea what will happen to her, since the child has ripped out pages from her picture book. The only pages he can find summon up the exhausting 'arithmetic man'. He follows two noisily amorous cats into the garden, but even there everything has something bad to say about the child. The squirrel has not forgotten being imprisoned in a cage and prodded. The child says it was only to admire his eyes. He realizes that all the creatures are now ignoring him. He is alone and cries out, 'Maman!' Suddenly the creatures turn on him. Soon they are fighting among themselves and a squirrel is hurt. The child binds its injured paw with a ribbon and then collapses. The creatures are amazed that the dreadful child should have helped one of them. He is good and kind after all. They cannot help him themselves. Repeating the cry of 'Maman!', they carry him to the house. Recovered, he calls out to 'Maman!'

Recommended Recording:

L'enfant et les sortilèges, French Radio National Chorus and Orchestra; Ernest Bour, conductor; Testament SBT1044; Soloists: Nadine Sautereau (L'enfant), Denise Scharley (Maman), Solange Michel (La bergère Louis XV), Odette Turba-Rabier (Le feu), André Vessières (La fauteuil), Yvon le Marc'Hadour (L'horloge comtoise), Joseph Peyron (La théière), Martha Angelici (La princesse), Maurice Prigent (Le petit vieillard)

Rihm, Wolfgang
b. 1952, GERMAN

Initially a student of Stockhausen, Rihm, like several other German composers of the 1970s, moved away from the intellectual and structural forms of serialism, favouring a more expressive, flexible approach. Rihm was drawn to the work of Frenchman Antonin Artaud and his 'Theatre of Cruelty', which Artaud defines not as an artistic spectacle but as a communion of actors and spectators. Accordingly, Rihm has used orchestral texture, vocal shadings, range and dynamics to create an extremely accessible lyricism.

Of his six highly imaginative and ambitious stage works – the 40-minute *Faust und Yorick* (1976); *Jakob Lenz* (1978); *Die Hamletmaschine* ('The Hamlet Machine', 1986), in which a cross-dressing Hamlet and Ophelia clash with Lenin, Marx and Chairman Mao; *Oedipus* (1987); *Die Eroberung von Mexico* ('The Conquest of Mexico', 1992); and *Séraphin* (1994)

– both *Eroberung* and *Séraphin* stand as particular examples of Rihm attempting to illuminate the psychological, not through narrative or text, but through aural drama. Little known in Britain or America, he has had a significant impact on the European scene.

Sallinen, Aulis
b. 1935, FINNISH

Hailing from a country without a strong operatic legacy, Sallinen approaches the craft of composition with true dramatic flair, as well as a genuine understanding of how to create theatre-oriented music in a more traditional tonal language.

The first of his six operas, *Ratsumies* ('The Horseman', 1975), was such a huge national success that the Finnish National Opera then commissioned *Punainen viiva* ('The Red Line', 1978). The international buzz that followed in turn led to a joint commission from Finland's Savonlinna Festival, London's Royal Opera House and the BBC that resulted in *Kuningas lähtee Ranskaan* ('The King Goes Forth to France', 1983). A seriocomic parable on human violence, this ultimately divided the critics, yet by now Finland's opera scene was beginning to flourish as other young composers entered the scene.

Sallinen responded to a commission for the opening of a new opera house in Helsinki by writing *Kullervo* (1988), a collection of poems from the poetic song tradition that relate the powerful tale of a feud between two brothers. While the chamber-opera political satire *Palatsi* ('The Palace', 1995) was less critically successful, his setting of *King Lear* (2000), is regarded as the synthesis of his musical ideas and the themes that he holds dear.

Saariaho, Kaija
b. 1952, FINNISH

Having studied in Helsinki, Freiburg and Paris, composer Saariaho focused on writing chamber works in the early part of her career, often integrating live music with electronics. In recent years, her works have increased in stature, structure and orchestral forces. Saariaho has produced three operas with her librettist, Amin Maalouf: *L'amour de loin* (2000), *Adriana Mater* (2006, commissioned by the Opéra National de Paris), and *Émilie* (2010), based on the life story of Émilie du Châtelet, the French mathematician, physicist and writer during the Age of Enlightenment. In 2016, *L'amour de loin* was performed at the Metropolitan Opera, New York: the first time that the Met has staged an opera by a woman since their production of Ethel Smyth's *Der Wald* in 1903.

Schoenberg, Arnold
1874–1951, AUSTRIAN

One of the most important and controversial figures of twentieth-century composition, Schoenberg was a true visionary who paved the way for serialism – a system that, while abandoning traditional western harmony and melody, gave direction to the chaos of atonality. In so doing, he attracted plaudits and outright vitriol, for although serialism has resulted in some undeniable masterworks, more often than not it has further divided the intellectual composer from the listening public.

Schoenberg's monodrama, *Erwartung* ('Expectation', 1909), was one of his early atonal works and proved to be rather too forward-thinking for its time; the text and music were considered to be so disturbing by conductors and producers that the work was not premiered until 1924. Marie Pappenheim's libretto, focussing on the disturbed thoughts of a lovelorn woman (a vocal *tour de force* for soprano), drew on real-life events – just before Schoenberg began work on *Erwartung*, painter Richard Gerstl, who taught the composer and his wife Mathilde, had committed suicide after Mathilde ended their affair.

Schoenberg's other main opera, and his most expansive staged work that gave full expression to his serialist methods, was the biblical *Moses und Aron*. Partially composed between 1930 and 1932, Schoenberg had to abandon the work when his music was banned by the Nazis, and he never completed the third act. However, the work was finally performed in concert in 1954 and was then staged as an opera in 1957.

Moses und Aron
by Arnold Schoenberg
Composed: 1930–32
Premiered: 1957, Zurich
Libretto by the composer

ACT I

Moses prays in the desert. He is answered by voices from the Burning Bush telling him to become a prophet and the leader of the Israelites. He pleads that he does not have the eloquence to explain God's will in terms they can understand, but is told that this will be the task of his brother Aron. Moses meets Aron, to whom an understanding of God's purpose comes spontaneously, although Moses has to restrain his exuberance. When Aron describes how God can be swayed by offerings, Moses insists that sacrifices will not alter His purpose. They are intended to purify one's thinking, not change events.

Word spreads that the new god that Moses is bringing may be stronger than the Egyptian gods and will free them from captivity. A priest resists this idea and the people divide into two factions. Moses and Aron are seen approaching. The people offer to sacrifice to the new god if it will bring them hope. They are bewildered by Moses' command that they should fall down and worship something they cannot see. Aron throws down Moses' staff, which turns into a serpent, demonstrating how a rigid idea can become flexible. Two further miracles persuade the Israelites to pledge their allegiance to the new God and follow Moses.

INTERLUDE

Moses has been away for 40 days. The people wonder whether he has abandoned them.

ACT II

The elders warn Aron that the people are growing restless and demanding their old gods. To stop them killing the priests, he offers to make a golden image for them to worship. A golden calf is set up amid orgiastic rejoicing. Old men sacrifice themselves and four naked virgins are killed to appease the calf. A man who denounces the idolatry is murdered. Everyone succumbs to an orgy, until they are finally exhausted. Moses enters, carrying the tablets of the law. He destroys the calf.

Aron justifies his action by saying that he has heard nothing from Moses. The people cannot survive without his love. They need an image to follow, even the tablets. Moses smashes them. Aron claims to have kept hope alive. He leads the Israelites as they follow a pillar of fire towards the Promised Land. To Moses, however, this is just another image. Aron has falsified God's revelation to Moses.

Schorr, Friedrich
1888–1953, HUNGARIAN

Schorr's rolling Wagnerian bass was the model of grandeur and his poetic sensibility invaluable to his portrayal of Hans Sachs in *Die Meistersinger*. After studying in America, Schorr sang small roles in Chicago before returning to Europe. His real debut was in 1912, performing Wotan in *Die Walküre* and his tenure with the Berlin Staatsoper allowed him to sing the great Wagnerian roles. He sang extensively at Bayreuth, Covent Garden and the Met. Schorr's recording legacy confirms his stature as the greatest Wagnerian bass of the twentieth century.

Schreker, Franz
1878–1934, GERMAN

Schreker's work was once placed alongside that of Richard Strauss and Arnold Schoenberg, as all three were considered to be important avant-garde figures in the early years of the twentieth century. Influenced by the French musical style as characterized by Debussy, Schreker's music is notable for its harmony and sensual quality.

Schreker, who lived most of his life in Vienna, enjoyed his first real success with the ballet *Geburtstag der Infantin* ('The Birthday of the Infanta', 1908). Thereafter, Schreker became a leading proponent of the new music scene, conducting and introducing the works of his contemporaries. But although *Der ferne Klang* ('The Distant Sound', 1910) was a resounding success, pointing the way to Berg's masterwork, *Lulu*, it nevertheless amounted to Romanticism couched in modernism.

Immediately following the First World War, two of Schreker's most popular operas were *Die Gezeichneten* ('The Stigmatized', 1918) and *Der Schatzgräber* ('The Treasure-Seeker', 1920). However, his themes of isolation, ugliness, despair and sexual desire would soon become an easy target for the Nazis, who denounced the composer not only for his music, but also for the fact he was Jewish. The 1931 premiere of his opera *Christophorus* had to be cancelled, while *Der Schmied von Gent* ('The Blacksmith of Ghent', 1932) was heckled by anti-Semites. Schreker died of heart failure two days before his 56th birthday.

Schumann-Heink, Ernestine
1861–1936, AUSTRO-AMERICAN

Schumann-Heink's voice was renowned for its richness and wide range. Studies with Marietta von Leclair led to her concert debut in 1876 and her operatic debut in Dresden two years later, in *Il trovatore*. For many years she sang at Hamburg and Bayreuth, while also appearing at London's Covent Garden in Wagnerian roles. Schumann-Heink made her US debut in Chicago in 1898, and between 1899 and 1932 she sang regularly with the Metropolitan Opera Company. She created the role of Klytämnestra in Richard Strauss's *Elektra*, and boasted a repertory of 150 roles. Hailed as the world's greatest contralto, she sang Erda (*Siegfried*) at the Met in 1932 aged 70.

Schwarzkopf, Elisabeth, DBE
1915–2006, GERMAN

The great soprano Olga Maria Elisabeth Friederike Schwarzkopf was perhaps one of the greatest Mozart singers of the twentieth century. Trained as a mezzo before becoming a coloratura soprano and joining Berlin's Deutsche Oper in 1938, she was signed to an EMI recording contract by producer Walter Legge in 1946. Legge, who subsequently became her husband and manager, pointed out that she sang in too many different styles; she eventually focused on Mozart and Strauss roles. An artist of great musical intelligence, Schwarzkopf was sometimes prone to vocal and textual mannerisms. She was the first Anne Trulove in Stravinsky's *The Rake's Progress*.

Shostakovich, Dmitri
1906–75, RUSSIAN

Born in tsarist Russia, Shostakovich spent his entire career under the critical and often hectoring gaze of the Soviet regime, yet he still managed to produce some of his nation's most powerful and engaging twentieth-century music.

Studying composition at the Petrograd Conservatory from 1919 to 1925, he presented Symphony No. 1 as his graduation piece, a work that brought him international attention. His first complete opera was *The Nose*, completed in 1928. An excellent example of Russian post-revolutionary avant-garde theatre, it satirized the tsarist rule of Nicholas I. Following its 1930 premiere, the Soviet regime began to formulate its manifesto for 'Socialist Realism' and *The Nose* was duly abandoned after only 16 performances. It was rediscovered by the conductor Gennadi Rozhdestvensky and underwent a revival in 1974.

Arguably the greatest achievement of Shostakovich's career was *Lady Macbeth of the Mtsensk District* (composed in 1930–32 and premiered in 1934), after a novel by Leskov. A masterpiece that enjoyed great success overseas, its dissonant compositional style was blasted in the Soviet newspaper *Pravda* after Stalin attended a performance in January 1936. The work was revived in Moscow 1963, having being toned-down, as *Katerina Ismailova*. Outside Russia, the original version has now replaced the revised version.

Lady Macbeth of the Mtsensk District
by Dmitri Shostakovich
Composed: 1930–32
Premiered: 1934, Leningrad
Libretto by the composer and Alexander Preys, after the short story by Nikolay Leskov

ACT I

Katerina is married to Zinovy Ismailov. Despite his great wealth, she is bored. She has no children and Boris, her father-in-law, accuses her of being frigid. Zinovy has to go away on business. Boris makes Katerina publicly vow to be faithful to Zinovy. Katerina catches the men, led by Sergey, abusing Aksin'ya. Katerina pushes him away and is challenged to a wrestling match. Boris discovers them on the ground together.

Sergey knocks on Katerina's bedroom door and proposes another wrestling match. She protests, but eventually her resistance dissolves. After they have noisily made love, Katerina tells Sergey that he is now her true husband.

ACT II

A week later, Boris catches Sergey leaving Katerina and whips him. Boris demands some of his favourite mushrooms. She adds an extra ingredient, rat poison. He dies in agony, blaming Katerina. After making love, Katerina promises to marry Sergey. Zinovy returns and accuses Katerina of cuckolding him. Together they strangle him and hide his body in the cellar.

ACT III

A drunken peasant finds Zinovy's rotting corpse. Katerina is marrying Sergey. The policemen are annoyed at not being invited. The drunk tells them about the body. Katerina notices that the cellar lock is broken. The police arrive before she can flee. She confesses and Katerina and Sergey are arrested.

ACT IV

A convict column halts beside a river in Siberia. Sergey tells Katerina she has ruined his life. He flirts with Sonetka, who wants new stockings. He makes Katerina part with hers and gives them to Sonetka. As the convicts line up, Katerina pushes Sonetka into the river. Both of them are swept away.

Simoneau, Léopold
1916–2006, CANADIAN

One of the great Mozartian tenors of his age, Simoneau married French-Canadian soprano Pierrette Alarie. They went to Europe, where he sang at the Paris Opéra, Aix-en-Provence, Glyndebourne and London's Covent Garden. In 1952, Simoneau sang in a historic recording of *Oedipus Rex*, with Stravinsky conducting and librettist Jean Cocteau as narrator. He then gave recitals with pianist Glenn Gould, before making his Met debut as Don Ottavio in 1963. Following his retirement in 1970, Simoneau was appointed Quebec's Minister of Culture, which led to the opening of L'Opéra de Québec.

Smyth, Ethel
1858–1944, ENGLISH

Overcoming family resistance, Smyth studied composition at Leipzig Conservatory, where her early influences included Wagner and Berlioz and she met Grieg, Tchaikovsky and Dvořák. Her 1906 opera, *The Wreckers*, is now acknowledged to be an important contribution to British operatic repertoire. The performance of her short opera, *Der Wald*, at New York's Metropolitan Opera in 1903 accords her the disappointing honour of being one of only two women to have had their operas performed there (the second being Kaija Saariaho, whose *L'amour de loin* was staged there in 2016).

Stabile, Mariano
1888–1968, ITALIAN

Stabile was renowned for complete mastery of character, with almost unparalleled imagination and timing. Toscanini coached him for the role of Falstaff, which he sang nearly 1,200 times. During his 1926 debut season at Covent Garden, Stabile sang Falstaff, Iago and Don Giovanni. Eventually he switched to singing Gianni Schicchi and Scarpia, while his later years were distinguished by purely comedic and buffa roles. These included Dr Malatesta in *Don Pasquale* and Don Alfonso in *Così fan tutte*, both of which were remarkable for their exuberance and panache.

Stefano, Giuseppe di
1921–2008, ITALIAN

Possessing a beautiful voice that was recorded to great effect, di Stefano was renowned for performances of the bel canto repertoire. His speciality roles included Edgardo in *Lucia*, Nadir in *Les pecheurs de perles* and Fritz in *L'amico Fritz*. However, by the mid-1950s he began to sing heavier roles that robbed his voice of its warmth and tonal purity. Di Stefano was Maria Callas's leading tenor, and in 1973, long after their vocal prime, they began an international recital tour that was aborted the following year. Nevertheless, stamina was not an issue for di Stefano, who sang the role of the emperor in *Turandot* at Caracalla in Rome aged 71.

Stemme, Nina
b. 1963, SWEDISH
One of the most thrilling Wagnerians of the twenty-first century (and now rivalling even the legacy of twentieth-century legend Kirsten Flagstad), Stemme is adored by Wagner fans for the seeming ease with which she commands the score and the stage. Her repertoire also includes contemporary music and major Strauss and Puccini roles.

Stockhausen, Karlheinz
1928–2007, GERMAN
A master of electronic composition, Stockhausen forged a unique path by creating and reinventing musical forms while recasting the fundamentals of musical content. One of his works lasts 24 hours. Another mixes electronic sounds with the voice of a boy soprano. As composer-conductor Pierre Boulez said: 'He invented a new kind of relationship between music's components. He has changed our view of musical time and form.'

Stockhausen's desire to break with the past was more than justified. His father was reported missing in action during the Second World War, while his mother, hospitalized in 1932 for severe mental lapses, succumbed in 1941 to the Nazis' euthanasia programme. Raised in Cologne, he lived in a complex that housed his own theatre, rehearsal areas and music studio; an environment attuned to his ongoing operatic quest from 1977 to rival Wagner's *Ring* cycle. *Licht: Die Sieben Tage der Woche* ('Light: The Seven Days of the Week') was conceived as seven large sections, each corresponding to a day of the week. Each day is then divided into smaller sections, culminating in 'Sonntag aus Licht', the day on which all of the work's musical and dramatic elements come together.

Stravinsky, Igor 1882–1971, RUSSIAN
Stravinsky, who was born in Oranienbaum, Russia, and died in New York, is one of the most important composers of the twentieth century. A master of style, he could create sound palettes as extreme and varied as any written during his lifetime, even if these extremes stemmed from his refusal to associate himself with one particular style.

INFLUENCE OF RUSSIAN FOLKLORE
Three ballets written for impresario-producer Sergei Diaghilev and his Ballets Russes are among the most important in the repertoire. Inspired by French Impressionism, both *The Firebird* and *Petrushka* are replete with Russian folklore references, yet neither critics nor fans of the day were prepared for the stylistic leap that Stravinsky took with *The Rite of Spring*. Featuring a convulsive narrative, angular orchestral writing and primitive rhythms, this radical work provoked an instant riot at the Théâtre des Champs-Elysées.

As Stravinsky began to minimize instrumental resources within his compositions, so he created a new, leaner style. Then, with the operatic genre as his last frontier, he embarked on *The Nightingale* (1909), based on the Hans Christian Andersen fairytale. In this, Stravinsky melded his two evolving styles of composition – neo-Romantic (in Act I) and his aforementioned streamlined style – to create a work of highly oriental and exotic influences.

Still, of the many works that he produced for the stage, few can be classified as opera. *Renard*, a 15-minute burlesque (1915), and *Mavra* (1922) were programmed together in a 1922 performance, yet not too successfully.

Mavra had been composed as homage to the hallowed stylistic conventions of the old Russian school of Italian opera, and dedicated to **Mikhail Glinka** (1804–57), **Alexander Pushkin** (1799–1837) and **Pyotr Ilych Tchaikovsky** (1840–93).

WEIGHTIER WORK TO COME

Stravinsky's wish to produce a weightier work was then achieved with *Oedipus Rex* (1927). As translated into Latin, Cocteau's libretto underpins Stravinsky's neo-classical score – a narrator in contemporary concert attire recites the story scene by scene. However, as the opera-oratorio progresses, his role becomes more integrated within the musical texture. This ritualized and highly dramatic work is effective in both concert and fully staged renderings. Nevertheless, the apex of Stravinsky's operatic oeuvre and his neo-classical style is *The Rake's Progress*. Comprising three acts, this is his only full-length opera, and is among the most performed of all post-war operas.

The Rake's Progress

Based on a series of eight Hogarth paintings, this opera was first performed on 11 September 1951 at Il Teatro La Fenice in Venice. In *The Rake's Progress*, Stravinsky's neo-classical style maintains a clear delineation of musical numbers separated by recitatives (accompanied by harpsichord), and as such it has often been considered a stylistic companion to the works of Mozart and to Gay's *The Beggar's Opera*. While its form adheres to Classical ideals, certain basic elements such as melody are angular and disjointed, zig-zagging across the extremes of the singers' vocal resources.

The themes of *The Rake's Progress* are derived from literature and mythology – Nick Shadow is drawn from the Faustian character of Mephistopheles, and the young lovers are personified in a redemptive denouement as Venus and Adonis. Hogarth's satiric paintings have come full cycle, and our fallen 'hero' now resides in Bedlam. The cast returns to the stage under full house lights to present the story's epilogue-cum-moral, Mozart-like devices being used to disguise more serious post-war issues of morality.

The Rake's Progress

by Igor Stravinsky
Composed: 1947–51
Premiered: 1951, Venice
Libretto by W. H. Auden and Chester Kallman after William Hogarth's series of paintings

ACT I

Trulove is determined that his daughter Anne will never marry a lazy husband. Tom Rakewell scorns work and prefers to entrust himself to Fortune. At his words 'I wish I had money', Nick Shadow informs them that a previously unknown uncle has left Tom a fortune. Trulove urges him to go to London. Tom is reassured that he can settle Nick's wages in a year and a day. He promises to send for Anne and Trulove. Nick announces that 'the Progress of a Rake begins'.

The 'roaring boys' and whores are carousing at Mother Goose's brothel. Tom recites the definitions of Pleasure and Beautiful he has been taught, but hesitates at Love, which burns his lips. Nick turns back a cuckoo clock with a gesture. Tom's song of betrayed love interests the Whores, but Mother Goose claims him. Anne has not heard from Tom. Weeping will not do. Tom is weak and needs her help.

ACT II

Tom is sick of London and would-be mothers-in-law. He does not dare think of the only honest girl he knows. He longs for simple pleasures: 'I wish I were happy'. Nick suggests he should marry an attraction at St Giles Fair, Baba the Turk. Since he does not desire her and owes her nothing, such a marriage would guarantee Tom's happiness. Tom thinks it would also make him famous.

Anne hesitates outside Tom's London house. When he sees Anne and tells her to go home, indicating his new wife, the veiled Baba. Anne leaves. He tells Baba this was only a milkmaid he owed money to. To please the crowd Baba removes her veil, revealing a flowing black beard. Baba chatters through breakfast Tom glumly pushes her away. Suddenly jealous of Anne, she furiously throws everything in reach until Tom rams his wig on her head. She is immediately motionless. As Tom sleeps, Nick demonstrates a simple magic trick with bread and broken pottery. Tom has dreamt of inventing something to turn stones into bread. He wishes it were true. Nick's machine is the way to abolish hunger, but it will take other people's money. Already Baba is in the past.

ACT III

The financial scheme has collapsed. Everything is to be auctioned, including an unknown object. It is Baba, who comes back to life when Sellem, the auctioneer, lifts the wig. She tells Anne that Tom still loves her. She must go to him.

A year and a day have elapsed. Nick's wages are due. Beside an open grave he explains that Tom's soul will be forfeit on the last stroke of midnight. He may choose from knife, rope, poison or gun. Before the ninth stroke Nick stops time and suggests that if Tom can guess three cards correctly he will be free. Thinking of Anne, Tom calls the Queen of Hearts which is correct. Startled by a falling shovel, he calls 'the deuce!', also correct. Tom sees cloven hoof-prints. He calls on Love to rule once more. It is the Queen of Hearts. Nick sinks into the grave, taking Tom's sanity with him. He now believes he is Adonis.

Anne comes to Tom in Bedlam. He takes her for Venus and begs forgiveness. She rocks him to sleep with a lullaby. Trulove calls her away. They will not meet again on earth. Tom wakes, looks for Venus and dies. The inmates mourn for Adonis.

Recommended Recording:
The Rake's Progress, London Philharmonic Orchestra; Vladimir Jurowski, conductor; Opus Arte Glyndebourne OA1062D; Soloists: Miah Persson (Anne Trulove), Topi Lehtipuu (Tom Rakewell), Clive Bayley (Father Trulove), Matthew Rose (Nick Shadow), Susan Gorton (Mother Goose), Elena Manistina (Baba the Turk), Graham Clark (Sellem)

OPERAS

1909	The Nightingale
1922	Mavra
1927	Oedipus Rex
1951	The Rake's Progress

TIMELINE

1882	Igor Stravinsky born Oranienbaum, Russia
1902	Begins studying under Rimsky-Korsakov
1905	Starts work on his first symphony
1909	Chinese opera The Nightingale completed
1910	Composes The Firebird
1913	First performance of The Rite of Spring, Paris, causes a riot
1914	Stravinsky takes refuge in Switzerland after outbreak of First World War
1918	The Soldier's Tale marks Stravinsky's growing interest in non-Russian music
1922	Completes Mavra
1927	Oedipus Rex produced as oratorio, Paris
1039	Moves to USA
1051	Premiere of The Rake's Progress, Venice
1058	Serialist choral work Threni completed
1071	Stravinsky dies, New York

Supervia, Conchita
1895–1936, SPANISH

This Spanish contralto made her debut just before her 16th birthday at the Teatro Colón in Buenos Aires, Argentina. The following year she sang Octavian in the Rome premiere of Strauss's *Der Rosenkavalier*. She soon became associated with Rossini's heroines, Angelina, Rosina and Isabella, all of which she sang with irresistible charm and charisma. Her Carmen in Paris in 1930 was a triumph, but she could not translate the success to the Covent Garden stage. She died of complications following childbirth aged 40.

Sutherland, Joan, DBE
1926–2010, AUSTRALIAN

Dubbed 'La Stupenda' in Milan, this great coloratura soprano was capable of flawless trills and vocal pyrotechnics that were best suited to the *bel canto* repertoire, especially Bellini and Donizetti heroines. Sutherland's musical engagements began at a young age in Sydney and culminated in her winning Australia's foremost voice competition. Thereafter she studied at London's Royal College of Music and made her Covent Garden debut in October 1952. Coach-conductor and husband Richard Bonynge convinced her to focus on coloratura repertoire, and in 1959 her international career took off when she sang the title role in *Lucia di Lammermoor*, conducted by Tullio Serafin. Continuing to add *bel canto* roles to her repertoire, Sutherland was often criticized for her poor diction, yet she astounded the world with her expansive and stunning voice.

Szymanowski, Karol
1882–1937, POLISH

Szymanowski was the most important Polish composer of the twentieth century, even though his childhood home was in a territory annexed by the Russian Empire. While his early years were spent composing and playing piano, he later pursued his studies in Warsaw and Berlin, before returning to the family home that was subsequently destroyed by Bolshevik revolutionaries. A Polish patriot, Szymanowski became involved in the creation of a national style of music. Spending a great deal of time in the resort town of Zakopane in the Tatra Mountains, he adopted the region's syncopated rhythms, in addition to its tonal and melodic language.

Although his one-act opera *Hagith* (1913) derived its musical language from the German, French and Russian composers of the time, he scored one of the greatest successes of his career with *Krol Roger* ('King Roger', 1924), a full-length opera that centres around the clash between a church and a young shepherd's paganism. Greatly influenced by Ravel's *Daphnis et Chloe* (1912), Szymanowski ensured that, from the opening of *Krol Roger* to the many contemplative passages of its score, the music would be highly evocative, full of nuance and rich in orchestral colour.

After years of money struggles and failing health, Szymanowski died in a Swiss sanatorium, but he was afforded a huge state funeral in Krakow.

King Roger
by Karol Szymanowski
Composed: 1918–24
Premiere: 1926, Warsaw
Libretto by J. Iwaszkiewicz and the composer

ACT I

The archbishop and the abbess urge King Roger of Sicily to banish a shepherd who is proclaiming an unknown god. Queen Roxana and Edrisi, the King's Arab counsellor, advise Roger to speak with him. The crowd calls for him to be stoned. He rhapsodizes about his god as the Good Shepherd who protects his lost sheep. Roxana is entranced by his smile. Her pleadings and Edrisi's calls for justice persuade him to release the shepherd. He will, however, stand trial of a kind, since he is to visit Roger that night.

ACT II

Edrisi urges him not to be afraid, but Roger trembles at the fire in the shepherd's eyes. They hear Roxana pleading for mercy for the shepherd, who enters richly dressed. His answers, full of sensuous imagery, infuriate Roger. People gather round the shepherd. Roger declares that his powers must come from hell. The crowd begins to whirl and dance around. Roxana joins them. Roger orders the guards to seize him, but the chains shatter. The shepherd calls on the people to follow him and challenges Roger to judge him in his homeland. Roger resolves to follow as a pilgrim.

ACT III

Roger and Edrisi are beside an altar decked with a recent sacrifice. Roger calls and Roxana answers. It is the king's turn to stand trial. A vision of Roxana appears to tempt him to remain. They throw garlands into the altar's flame. The shepherd, now revealed as the god Dionysus, summons Roger to 'an endless journey, to the joyful dance'. Roger stands motionless, with his arms lifted high. The shepherd and his followers disappear with the dawn. Roger has not succumbed to the mysteries of the cult. He offers his heart to the sun.

Tebaldi, Renata
1922–2004, **ITALIAN**

Tebaldi studied at the Conservatory of Milan before auditioning for Arturo Toscanini in 1946. Impressed with her exceptional voice, Toscanini offered Tebaldi a concert engagement at La Scala, where she remained on the roster for the next five years. By the mid-1950s, both Tebaldi and Maria Callas were performing regularly at the Met and, despite their different repertoires, a famous feud developed. Loud slanging matches would occur between rival fans, but it all came to an end one night in 1969 when Callas went backstage to congratulate Tebaldi after a performance of *Adriana Lecouvreur*. There, in front of countless photographers, two of the twentieth century's most legendary voices embraced and resolved their differences.

Terfel, Bryn
b. 1965, **WELSH**

One of the most exciting bass-baritones currently performing, Terfel became a sensation after winning the Cardiff Singer of the World Lieder prize in 1989. In 1990 he made his operatic debut as Guglielmo in Così fan tutte at Welsh National Opera, before bursting onto the London scene as Figaro in *Le nozze di Figaro* with English National Opera in 1991. By 1993 he had signed a contract with Deutsche Grammophon and debuted with the Vienna State Opera. The Met was next in 1994, followed by La Scala in 1997, both as Figaro. Terfel has judiciously expanded his repertoire, introducing – and triumphing in – an increasing number of Wagner roles over the past decade.

Thomson, Virgil
1896–1989, **AMERICAN**

A composer of both originality and substance, Thomson produced what was arguably America's first major opera, *Four Saints in Three Acts* (composed 1927–28). Hailing from a Southern Baptist background where church music, marching bands and popular American tunes were a large part of his cultural heritage, Thomson attended Harvard and studied under Nadia Boulanger in France, where he met Satie, Cocteau and the members of Les Six.

He collaborated with writer Gertrude Stein on *Four Saints in Three Acts*, a rhythmically repetitive opera with no plot, which divorced words from their contextual associations and used them for aural and sequential effect. Following its premiere in Connecticut, *Four Saints* transferred to Broadway and ran for 60 highly acclaimed performances. Gertrude Stein said: 'I wanted to have four saints that did nothing and I wrote *Four Saints in Three Acts* and they did nothing and that was everything'.

More than a decade later, *The Mother of Us All* (1947), based on the life of feminist Susan B. Anthony, also achieved significant success. Stein died just months after completing the libretto, and for his third and final opera, Thomson collaborated with librettist Jack Larson. Commissioned in 1960 and intended for the Met, Lord Byron took seven years to complete and was finally premiered at the Juilliard Opera Center in 1972.

Four Saints in Three Acts
by Virgil Thomson
Composed: 1927–28
Premiered: 1934, Hartford, Connecticut
Libretto by Gertrude Stein with scenario by Maurice Grosser

BACKGROUND
The saints are introduced. Note that St Teresa of Avila is sung by two performers (soprano and contralto).

ACT I
Seven tableaux involving St Teresa II, described as a 'Pageant, or Sunday School Entertainment', are revealed behind a curtain on the steps of Avila Cathedral. She paints Easter eggs, talking with St Teresa I. St Settlement takes her photograph holding a dove. St Ignatius Loyola serenades her. He offers her flowers. They admire a model of the Heavenly Mansion. She is shown in ecstasy. She rocks an imaginary child in her arms.

ACT II
The formally dressed Compère and Commère comment on a garden party in the country near Barcelona. There is a Dance of Angels

and St Chavez organizes a game. The saints look at the heavenly mansion through a telescope, which St Ignatius refuses to give back to St Teresa I. St Chavez consoles her.

ACT III
St Ignatius is mending fishing nets in a monastery garden on the coast near Barcelona. Both St Teresas and St Settlement discuss the monastic life with St Ignatius. They see a vision of the Holy Ghost and St Ignatius reproves those who doubt the vision and predicts the Last Judgement. There is a storm and then the saints process out, chanting.

ACT IV
The Compère and Commère are arguing whether there should be a fourth act. The saints, now in heaven, recall their earthly lives. The Compère sings 'Last Act', and the saints reply, 'Which is a fact'.

Tippett, Michael
1905–98, **ENGLISH**

Tippett began his musical studies at the age of 18, wrote his first significant work aged 30, and was 41 when he embarked on his first opera, *The Midsummer Marriage* (composed 1946–52, premiered 1955). Despite his relatively late development in the operatic genre, he soon became a composer of international recognition.

Referencing Mozart's *Die Zauberflöte* (1791) with regard to how the protagonists must endure physical trials that test their spiritual love, so Tippett's couple in *The Midsummer Marriage* have to find the light of self and mutual understanding by way of knowledge and communication. Boasting a bucolic setting and lush, lyric and tonal beauty reminiscent of Elgar, *The Midsummer Marriage* was not an immediate success, yet it has become one of Tippett's most important operatic works.

In all, he composed five operas, each very different in terms of structure and theme. The ancient Greek legend of *King*

Priam (1962) examines the consequences of personal decisions, while *The Knot Garden* (1970) explores material economy by compressing 32 scenes into 90 minutes, melding traditional opera with jazz and blues. *The Ice Break* (1977), set in an airport lounge, draws on cultural and literary references in dealing with the topic of racial inequality, while his final opera, *New Year* (1989), is his most perplexing and contrived, uneasily merging classical themes with elements such as rap.

The Midsummer Marriage
by Michael Tippett
Composed: 1946–52
Premiered: 1955, London
Libretto by the composer

ACT I
Mark asks the Ancients of the sanctuary for a new dance for his wedding to Jenifer. They warn him of the danger in meddling with tradition. Jenifer has run away from her father, King Fisher. She claims to want truth, not love, and disappears up a broken staircase.

Mark plunges through gates into the hillside as King Fisher appears. His secretary, Bella, cannot persuade the Ancients to open them. She fetches her boyfriend, Jack, with his tools. Sosostris, within, warns King Fisher, but he instructs Jack to try again. Mark and Jenifer reappear, transformed by the experiences of heaven and earth. They quarrel and depart to experience the other's revelations.

ACT II
Bella proposes to Jack. They yearn for simple domestic bliss. Over three ritual dances a male dancer (Strephon) – as a hare, fish and bird – is hunted by a female dancer – in the form of a hound, otter and hawk. Bella screams as the hawk swoops on the injured, helpless bird. Jack comforts her. She shows him how the 'real' Bella is created with comb

and make-up. King Fisher has summoned them. Jack chases her off. The chorus is heard singing that 'she must leap and he must fall... on midsummer day'.

ACT III
King Fisher engages Sosostris, a clairvoyant, to reveal the truth, but is enraged by what she sees. He smashes her crystal ball and rips away the veils to reveal Mark and Jenifer. He aims a pistol at Mark. They turn to him and he falls dead. The dancers celebrate 'carnal love transfigured as divine consuming love'. Mark, Jenifer and the Ancients disappear in fire. Mark and Jenifer reappear as themselves for their wedding.

King Priam
by Michael Tippett
Composed: 1958–61
Premiered: 1962, Coventry
Libretto by the composer, after Homer's *Iliad*

ACT I
It is foretold that Paris will cause the death of his father, Priam, King of Troy. His mother, Hecuba, believes he should be killed. Priam orders this, but is troubled: he is both a father and a king. Priam and his elder son, Hector, encounter the young Paris while hunting. Priam accepts both his son and his fate. Hector, who resents Paris, has married Andromache. In Sparta Paris has fallen passionately in love with Helen. She must choose between Menelaus and him, but if he takes her there will be war. Ordered by Hermes to choose between Athene, Hera and Aphrodite (represented as Hecuba, Andromache and Helen), he gives the apple to Aphrodite. The others curse him.

ACT II
Hector accuses Paris of cowardice. Priam tells Hector to take advantage of Achilles' withdrawal following a disagreement with Agamemnon. Hector and Paris go to battle. Achilles is sulking in his tent with his friend

Patroclus. His singing moves Patroclus to tears. Patroclus offers to lead the counter-attack in Achilles' armour. Hermes, as a messenger, tells Priam that Hector has killed Patroclus and stripped his body. Hector enters in Achilles' armour. As the Trojans rejoice, Achilles' war cry is heard.

ACT III

Andromache and Hecuba turn on Helen, who defends her semi-divine status as the source of men's desire. Andromache senses that Hector is dead. Priam knows that Hector's death began the moment he spared Paris. Priam visits Achilles to plead for Hector's body in exchange for Patroclus. They foretell each other's death. Paris has killed Achilles. The Greeks are in the city. Priam will not speak to Hecuba or Andromache. He sends Paris to his death, but speaks gently to Helen. Greek soldiers burst in and Achilles' son kills him.

Turnage, Mark-Anthony
b. 1960, **ENGLISH**

One of the most important talents on the contemporary British opera scene, Turnage produces work that expertly captures the times and culture within which he lives. A jazz enthusiast who has served as Composer in Association with both the Birmingham Symphony Orchestra and English National Opera, he often attempts to combine numerous genres in his work.

Turnage's first opera, *Greek* (1988), features 21 orchestra members all doubling on percussion while singers are required to sound distinctly non-operatic in their sometimes-vulgar vocal declamations. Accorded a single staged performance with the London Sinfonietta, the production caused an immediate stir among critics who interpreted its modern spin on the tragedy of Oedipus as a thinly veiled denigration of Thatcherist ideals. Turnage insisted that the parallels were more broad-based than that, relating to

differing class cultures and the oppression that results, yet his reputation as a somewhat wayward operatic hotshot had seemingly been established. Other more recent works from this always-innovative composer include a 1997 opera adaption of the H. G. Wells short story *The Country of the Blind,* and an award-winning, critically acclaimed setting of Sean O'Casey's anti-war play *The Silver Tassie* (2000), with a libretto by Amanda Holden.

Ullmann, Viktor
1898–1944, **AUSTRIAN**

Among the most heart-breaking of musicians' stories is the brutally curtailed life and career of Viktor Ullmann. A Jewish victim of the Nazi genocide, he reached his creative zenith during two harrowing years inside Terezín (known as Theresienstadt by the Nazis). As he noted about himself and other musician prisoners before their death in the concentration camp, 'Our desire to create matched our will to live'.

Raised in a Moravian-Czech border town, Ullmann studied composition in Vienna under Schoenberg and developed a music style that, although not atonal, still exhibited the chromaticism of the Viennese school. Returning to Prague when Hitler seized power, Ullmann composed prize-winning works such as the opera *Der Sturz des Antichrist* ('The Fall of the Antichrist', 1935), whose Hitlerian central character ensured it was never performed during Ullmann's lifetime. Other projects met with a similar fate, before he was transported to the Terezín camp in September 1942.

As the Nazis encouraged artistic activity in order to fool visiting Red Cross delegates, within 24 months Ullmann composed an astounding 23 works, including the remarkable *Der Kaiser von Atlantis* ('The Emperor of Atlantis', 1943), an allegorical satire alluding to Hitler's downfall. It was not performed until the 1970s. Ullmann served as a concert organizer and music critic at Terezín until, on 16 October 1944, once he and the other musicians and composers had outlived their usefulness, they were transferred to Auschwitz and delivered to the gas chamber the following day.

Vickers, Jon
1926–2015, CANADIAN
A Heldentenor with a unique approach to the stage, Vickers had a compelling singing-acting style. Trained as a baritone, he brought a warmth to his tenor, but risked uncertainty at the top of his range. Vickers' Otello is arguably the greatest ever recorded. His Peter Grimes, while not approved by Britten, also stands as a benchmark interpretation.

Walton, William
1902–83, ENGLISH
Walton had a strong musical background and was the child of two musicians – his mother was a voice teacher and his father was a chorus-master. Walton as a young boy was a chorister at Christ Church, Oxford, later becoming an undergraduate there. His *Belshazzar's Feast* (1931) and *Symphony No. 1* (1935) assured him of his place in British music, and following the success of Benjamin Britten's *Peter Grimes*, the BBC wished to commission an opera by a British composer.

Walton was commissioned to write *Troilus and Cressida* for the reopening of the Royal Opera House at Covent Garden, and began work on it in 1947. It took him 6 years to complete, and its premiere was plagued by numerous setbacks. When the opera was finally performed in December 1954, it received a lukewarm reception. The verdict was that Walton had written some effective orchestral music but the work itself was old-fashioned. Walton revised and re-worked Christopher Hassall's libretto and re-scored portions of the opera, in addition to transposing the role of Cressida for mezzo-soprano Janet Baker.

His one-act comedy *The Bear* performed in June 1967 at the Aldeburgh Festival is a witty parody of the vocal excesses of the operatic style and the compositional mannerisms that are often used to underscore the action.

Warren, Leonard
1911–60, AMERICAN
Possessing a voice of exceptional ability, Warren was one of America's greatest opera stars. His voice eclipsed his contemporaries; he was the only dramatic baritone able to sing an open high C. Among his best performances were those in Verdi's *Il trovatore*, *Rigoletto*, *La traviata*, *Un ballo in maschera* and *Macbeth*. He collapsed onstage at the Met during a performance of 'Urna fatale' from *La forza del Destino*, and died of a cerebral haemorrhage.

Weill, Kurt
1900–50, GERMAN
A precocious compositional talent, Weill's early operatic works *Der Protagonist* ('The Protagonist', 1926) and *Der Zar lässt sich photographieren* ('The Tsar has his Photograph Taken', 1928) strengthened his resolve to invent a style of music theatre that used the finest playwrights and dancers.

In 1927, he collaborated with writer Bertolt Brecht on *Mahagonny Songspiel*, and this led to a string of massive successes that included *Die Dreigroschenoper* ('The Threepenny Opera', 1928), *Happy End* (1929), *Aufstieg und Fall der Stadt Mahagonny* ('Rise and Fall of the City of Mahagonny', 1929) and *Der Jasager* ('He Who Says Yes', 1930). *Die Dreigroschenoper*, a reworking of Gay's *The Beggar's Opera*, with its cast of thieves, pimps and prostitutes, perfectly captured the decadence of pre-Second World War Berlin and also brought Weill international fame.

He and Brecht quickly fell out, however, due to Weill's dominance, and the successful run of *Der Silbersee* ('The Silver Lake', 1933), for which Weill worked in partnership with expressionist playwright Georg Kaiser, was shut down by the Nazis. Weill and Brecht revived their partnership for the song-cycle *Der sieben Todsünden* ('The Seven Deadly Sins', 1933). But then Weill fled to America, where works such as *Love Life* (1948) and *Lost in the Stars* (1949) garnered critical acclaim but box-office failure. Weill enjoyed great critical and financial success with *One Touch of Venus* (1943) and *Lady in the Dark* (1941) and his American masterpiece, *Street Scene* (1946). His work enjoys regular revivals in European and American opera houses.

Aufstieg und Fall der Stadt Mahagonny ('Rise and Fall of the city of Mahagonny')
by Kurt Weill
Composed: 1927–29
Premiered: 1930, Leipzig
Libretto by Bertolt Brecht

ACT I

Leokadja Begbick, Trinity Moses and Fatty, all wanted by the police, found Mahagonny. They recruit men in search of whisky, gambling and women to join them in the 'city of gold'. Jenny's price, thirty bucks, is too much for Jack O'Brien but Jim Mahoney takes her for the night. Business is bad in Mahagonny and there is little to do. Begbick has to lower the price of whisky. Jim's friends stop him leaving. Begbick imposes many repressive rules. Jim rebels against the conformity and quiet life. As a hurricane approaches Mahagonny the others accept his philosophy: 'Do it!'

ACT II

The hurricane swings away. Life is now based on food, love, boxing and drinking.

Jack eats himself to death. The brothel is organized like a production line. Trinity Moses kills Alaska-Wolf Joe in the boxing ring. Jim is unable to pay for his round in the bar. He drunkenly imagines that he can sail away from there with Jenny and Bill. There is no escape. The only major crime in Mahagonny is not to pay your bills. Jim is arrested and his friends abandon him.

ACT III

With Begbick as the judge even a murder charge can be bought off with a bribe, but Jim has nothing to counter the charges of singing an illegal song, causing Joe's death, seducing Jenny and not paying for three bottles of whisky and a curtain rod. He is condemned to death. The people know they are already in hell. The city is in flames. Amid the turmoil four groups of demonstrators proclaim their beliefs, but nothing can help a dead man.

Die Dreigroschenoper
by Kurt Weill
Composed: 1928
Premiered: 1928, Berlin
Book by Bertolt Brecht, from a translation by Elisabeth Hauptmann after John Gay's *The Beggar's Opera*

PROLOGUE

The Ballad Singer sings the 'Ballad of Mack the Knife'.

ACT I

Peachum controls the begging business in London. His wife's description of their daughter Polly's lover, 'the Captain', fits the notorious gang leader Macheath (Mack the Knife).

Polly has married Macheath. The gang furnishes a stable for the celebrations. 'Tiger' Brown, the police chief and Macheath's old army friend, offers his congratulations. He leaves to prepare for the coming coronation. Their wedding night begins. Polly's marriage is enough to wreck Peachum's business. She knows too much.

ACT II

Peachum plans to inform against Macheath, who decides he should lie low. He tells Polly how to run the gang in his absence. His idea of lying low is to visit the whores at Turnbridge. Mrs Peachum bribes one of them, Jenny, to signal to the police while he is distracted. Brown visits Macheath in prison. He is sorry he could not prevent his arrest. The jealousy between Polly and Lucy, Macheath's secret wife and Brown's daughter, spills over into a violent quarrel. Mrs Peachum drags Polly away. Lucy helps Macheath escape. Peachum threatens to disrupt the coronation.

ACT III

Jenny comes to collect her money for betraying Macheath, who is now with Suky Tawdry. As Peachum is about to send his beggars out into the streets he is arrested by Brown, but is able to blackmail his way out of custody. The whores betray Macheath again. The crowds gather to enjoy his execution before the coronation. He begs their forgiveness. At the last moment Brown appears as a mounted messenger bearing a royal pardon, a peerage and an annual pension.

Weir, Judith
b. 1954, **ENGLISH**

Combining stylistic versatility with a strong compositional voice, Weir's interests in narrative, theatre and folklore are well suited to opera. She also writes her own libretti. With themes ranging from Chinese Yuan Dynasty drama, Icelandic sagas and German romanticism, and a fine understanding of the voice, her operas have earned a secure place in the repertoire. Weir's first full scale opera, *A Night at the Chinese Opera*, was premiered in 1987, with regular revivals since. Her more recent works are The *Vanishing Bridegroom*, *Blond Eckbert* and *Armida* (premiered as a television broadcast in 2005). She was appointed Master of the Queen's Music in 2014.

Recommended Recording:
Blond Eckbert, Orchestra of English National Opera; Sian Edwards, conductor; NMCD106; Soloists: Nicholas Folwell (Blond Eckbert), Anne-Marie Owens (Berthe), Christopher Ventris (Walter), Nerys Jones (A bird)

Wunderlich, Fritz
1930–66, **GERMAN**

Wunderlich was the ideal tenor. His powerful yet lyric timbre was effortless, and indicated that it would have grown considerably beyond his existing repertoire. Furthermore, he had remarkable breath support that he attributed to his French horn studies, and which he used to great effect in Mozartian arias. Wunderlich's appearances in Germany and Austria received rave reviews; he also undertook a highly successful US concert tour in 1964, and sang at Covent Garden and Edinburgh in 1965. However, just three weeks before he was scheduled to debut at the Met, he died after falling down a flight of steps at a friend's castle.

Zemlinsky, Alexander
1871–1942, **AUSTRIAN**

Dedicated to opera as a conductor and composer, Zemlinsky attracted critical acclaim, yet by the time of his death he was all but forgotten. He had his second opera, *Es War Einmal* ('Once Upon a Time', 1899), conducted and revised by Gustav Mahler for its first performance at the Vienna Court Opera in 1900. Zemlinsky assisted Mahler at the VCO and began planning the premiere of his next opera, *Der Traumgörge* ('Görge the Dreamer', 1906), but when Mahler resigned in 1907, Zemlinsky followed suit. The opera was not performed until nearly 40 years after his death.

Zemlinsky's next appointment, to the Neues Deutsches Theater in Prague, marked the beginning of a fertile 16-year stretch. It became one of Europe's most significant opera centres, and his own projects flourished. As well as his best-known work, the *Lyric Symphony* (1923), Zemlinsky wrote two beautiful one-act operas: *Ein florentinische Tragödie* ('A Florentine Tragedy', 1917) and *Der Zwerg* ('The Dwarf', 1922), with a libretto by Georg C. Klaren after Oscar Wilde's *The Birthday of the Infanta*. After Zemlinsky's last complete opera *Der Kreidekreis* ('The Chalk Circle', 1932) was suppressed by the Nazis, he moved to America and died in relative obscurity.

Zimmermann, Bernd Alois
1918–70, GERMAN

Attracted to the avant-garde, Zimmerman composed only one opera, yet it is one of the most powerful German-language works of recent years. The four-act *Die Soldaten* ('The Soldiers') premiered in Cologne in 1965. Zimmermann travelled outside Germany just once, when he was sent to France during the war. Here, he familiarized himself with the musical scores of Stravinsky, Honegger, Poulenc and Milhaud. On his return in 1942 he decided to study traditional composition with Jarnach, a former pupil of Busoni, but by 1950 he was using Schoenberg's 12-tone techniques.

Throughout the 1950s, he searched for a unique style. However, unlike Stockhausen and Boulez, who wanted to break with the past, he liked to explore aspects of Western culture. He blended acoustic and electronic sound, film, pre-recorded tape, dance and mime, in order to define his pluralism. Zimmermann's vision for *Die Soldaten* of 12 scenic onstage areas had to be modified for practical reasons, so he used a set consisting of five levels, sometimes staging three scenes simultaneously, involving different times and places. The originality of these techniques has frequently been emulated, but not yet surpassed.

Die Soldaten
by Bernd Alois Zimmermann
Composed: 1958–64
Premiered: 1965, Cologne
Libretto by the composer after Jakob Michael Reinhold Lenz's play

ACT I
Marie Wesener, the daughter of a Lille merchant, and Stolzius, a draper in Armentières, are in love, but his mother disapproves. Marie rejects the advances of Desportes, a nobleman. The officers at Armentières discuss seduction. Desportes sends Marie a love poem. Her father asks her to wait for a proposal. Meanwhile she should not forget Stolzius, whom she still loves.

ACT II
Officers tease Stolzius about Marie and Desportes. He writes a letter to Marie; she shows it to Desportes. He dictates a reply and seduces her. Stolzius vows revenge. Marie's grandmother foresees her downfall.

ACT III
Stolzius applies to become Major Mary's batman. Charlotte, Marie's sister, disapproves of Marie's interest in Mary. They notice the man's resemblance to Stolzius. The Countess does not consider Marie a suitable match for her son. Although she denies it, Mary has abandoned Marie. The Countess offers her a position and tells her to ignore gossip.

ACT IV
Mary confronts Marie, who flees. Desportes orders his huntsman to find her. Raped by the huntsman, she turns to prostitution. Stolzius buys poison. He overhears Desportes saying that Marie deserved her fate. He poisons Desportes' soup and swallows some himself. Wesener gives money to a beggar, remembering Marie. He does not recognize her. Marie's sobs are drowned by sounds of marching.

❈ SERIALISM ∿ p. 363

In order to expand on atonality while creating a formal structure and rules for its usage, Arnold Schoenberg invented a system of composition. Schoenberg's 12-tone technique, sometimes called dodecaphony, was founded as a replacement for the limiting traditions of formal Western harmony.

These 12 tones refer to the 12 chromatic pitches contained within an octave that are used to create a row or line of music, and it is essential that each of the tones is not repeated. This predetermined order or 'row' of tones may also incorporate any of a variety of other musical alterations, including transposition, inversion or retrograde (backwards).

Serialism would later be equated with composition that uses any ordered sets in combination with an application to any music element. Accordingly, 'total serialism' and 'integral serialism' are terms used to clarify and distinguish between the more rigorous form devised by Schoenberg. Two of the most distinguished composers who have followed this style and further developed it are Karlheinz Stockhausen and Pierre Boulez, while the first such operatic masterwork was Alban Berg's *Lulu*. Within the mathematical and formal structures he employed, Berg was able to create a world of intense expressivity. Today, serialism has enabled composers to experiment with sound much in the same way that explorations in the visual arts were regarded as 'abstract expressionism'.

❈ EXPRESSIONISM ∿ p. 363

Initially a facet of the visual arts, the Expressionist movement was best delineated by the painter Vincent van Gogh, when he consciously used different colours and forms to express his feelings about a particular subject. During the last two decades of the nineteenth century, the art world embraced expressionist works as created by the likes of Munch and Matisse, who utilized distortion as a means of higher expression. However, the movement would not become a key aspect of musical composition until the 1910s and early 1920s.

Büchner's play *Woyzeck* had already anticipated an eerie world of inner thoughts, fears and distortions, and the main feature of Berg's operatic adaption, *Wozzeck*, is that every character, every action, every locality is perceived from a single point of view. In Edvard Munch's painting *The Scream*, the central figure is shrieking and the surrounding environment echoes his pain. The painting's colours and shape, devoid of realism, reveal the anguish of a tortured soul; much the same is achieved musically in *Wozzeck*.

In Act III, Scene Four, after Wozzeck murders Marie, he searches for the murder weapon in a blood-red pool and quickly finds himself drowning in it. While he is still descending into the pool, the musical glissandi ascend rather than descend, providing us with Wozzeck's own perspective as his body sinks and his life fades away.

❈ MINIMALISM

Minimalism is a musical style of composition that began in the 1960s, seeking to convey musical ideas with few elements. It often involves musical patterns that repeat while their effect is manipulated through changes in duration, speed and volume. These alterations can create patterns that join together, overlap or phase. For its part, a pattern may consist of a rhythm, notes, chords, harmony, or samples that are looped and expanded through dynamics, layering and the adding or subtracting of additional elements. Often these elements consist of arpeggios and scales.

Originally an American movement, minimalism began as a reaction to the complex and dense structures and sounds used by European composers. With ideas derived from foreign sources such as African drumming and Javanese gamelan, the repetition of musical cells keeps revealing new details. While its application in the world of electronic music has endless possibilities, forms of minimalism exist within numerous genres, from classical to rock. The foremost opera composers of this style are Philip Glass (*Einstein on the Beach*) and John Adams (*Nixon in China*), although this compositional style has influenced the work of many more recent composers too.

⊛ KROLL OPERA ∿ p. 364

This unlikely opera house was the first avant-garde public arena and was funded by the Prussian Ministry of Culture. Built in 1844 by entrepreneur Josef Kroll, the theatre, with its large stage and fine acoustics, became the centrepiece for new music and production values that embraced modernity.

When Otto Klemperer was appointed musical director, he approached the project as a personal mission. Making all the important artistic decisions, he mounted both old and new works that eschewed a naturalistic production style. His first bold experiment, *Fidelio*, was a critical failure, but he followed with a Stravinsky triple bill – *Mavra*, *Oedipus Rex* and *Petrushka* – before operas by Hindemith, Schoenberg and Weill stirred public and critical evaluation of these new compositional voices.

The most radical production was of Wagner's *Der fliegende Holländer*. Since the composer's operas were highly descriptive in terms of how he dictated performance practice and staging, Klemperer and his design and directorial team decided to deconstruct Wagner's intentions and superimpose their own. This was a potentially dangerous concept, and one that necessitated 100 police officers

attending the premiere to prevent Nazis from smashing or torching the theatre.

Although the Kroll Opera continued until its grant ran out, its demise would have been imminent due to the Nazi Party's ban on the public performance of many new composers' works.

⊛ ENTARTETE MUSIK ∿ p. 365

In 1937, Arnold Schoenberg said, 'I have at last learned the lesson that has been forced upon me during this year, and I shall not ever forget it. It is that I am not a German, not a European, indeed perhaps scarcely a human being – at least the Europeans prefer the worst of their race to me – but I am a Jew.'

As the avant-garde exerted a greater cultural influence, so it brought new names to the public's attention. Nevertheless, many such artists, including Schoenberg and Weill, were Jews, and after the Nazis enacted race laws in 1933 to prevent Jewish voices from poisoning the expression of 'pure' German art, the Reichsmusikkammer (Reich's Music Chamber) decreed that all musicians must register. Consequently, hundreds of composers' works were suppressed.

The first outright attack on the artistic community took place in 1937 at Munich's exhibition of 'Entartete Kunst' ('Degenerate Art'), followed in 1938 by Düsseldorf's 'Entartete Musik'. Directed by one of propaganda minister Joseph Goebbels' puppets, Hans Ziegler, this latter exhibition targeted composers, performers, musicologists, theorists and teachers whose photos were hung alongside vicious printed critiques and moral attacks.

Black American musicians such as Louis Armstrong were singled out for particularly harsh criticism. Jazz was considered by the Nazis to be an evil form of music, and people were cautioned to keep away from it at all costs. However, Bartók asked the authorities to label his own compositions 'Entartete' as a show of support for German colleagues such as Hindemith, Berg, Weill, Krenek, Erich Korngold and Schreker.

✹ COMING HOME: ALDEBURGH AND LIFE ON CRABBE STREET

George Crabbe's poem 'The Borough' inspired Benjamin Britten's return to England from America. A self-proclaimed pacifist during the Second World War, Britten identified with the poem's protagonist, Grimes, and his views about military service, and he returned home with companion Peter Pears to set about working on the opera *Peter Grimes*. Britten strongly identified with the central character from 'The Borough', and he and his librettist, Montagu Slater, decided to set the opera in the period in which the poem had been written, the early 1800s.

A friend of Crabbe's son confirmed that 'The Borough' was based on the story of a real-life fisherman who lived in Aldeburgh during the mid-1800s. Britten himself resided in nearby Snape, but in 1947 he would move to a house in Aldeburgh, located on the aptly named Crabbe Street and overlooking the sea that is so vividly described in the original poem.

As the English Opera Group began to experience critical success, Britten and his co-founders, Pears and Crozier, felt they could provide it with a residency in Aldeburgh for public performances. With the aid of government funding, they subsequently created a viable festival; a proud achievement and a true labour of love. It was in Aldeburgh that Britten was to end his days.

✖ FROM OBSCURITY TO THE OPERATIC CANON ∽ p. 365

The twentieth century was replete with the names of composers hailing from every part of the western world, each boasting their own personal style. The conductor Sir Charles Mackerras was studying in Czechoslovakia in 1947 when he first heard Janáček's music being played in rehearsal. Mackerras was immediately drawn to the music, as well as to the challenge of making it accessible to western Europe, London in particular.

Janáček's career was not without success, but his four greatest works were written during the last 10 years of his life. The composer's most productive time was during the 1920s, after the prospect of a free Czechoslovak state had finally been realized in 1918, and his chosen themes and stories not only told intimate tales of humanity but also reflected world events.

Mackerras and various scholars worked tirelessly during the 1950s and early 1960s to revive Janáček's original orchestrations. To this end, most of the Prague performances underwent extensive re-orchestration, as during the preceding decades they had been doctored and smoothed out, removing much of their raw sonority.

It was these inconsistencies that motivated Mackerras to restore the scores in accordance with the composer's original intentions. The much-loved Mackerras conducted performances of Janáček's work all over the world for the rest of his life.

✖ PLATE-SMASHING AND SLAPSTICK: MAKING A MESS TO FIND MEANING ∽ p. 366

The almost uncategorizable Irish composer Gerald Barry, whose untrammelled imagination and irreverent wit is displayed in operas such as his 1990 'opera within an opera', *The Intelligence Park*, returned to the stage more recently with his take on Oscar Wilde's comedy of manners, *The Importance of Being Earnest*.

The Los Angeles concert premiere (conducted by Thomas Adès, a great champion of Barry's work) and the stage premiere in Nancy in 2013 revealed ideas that were strikingly counter to the refinement of Wildean wit: the aural slapstick of Algernon's appalling piano playing (although in reality making virtuosic demands on the pianist), Cecily Cardew and Gwendolen Fairfax expressing their loathing for each other with the rhythmic smashing of plates, and Lady Bracknell played by a bass, with no attempt to make his voice remotely feminine – this was a new flavour of comedy in modern opera. The piece entered the repertoire rapidly with productions at major venues across Europe and the US.

✖ ENTERTAINMENT ... OR WHAT?

John Adams, a purveyor of much-admired and accessible music has had his opera, *The Death of Klinghoffer* performed across the world. The troubling story, set on a cruise ship, addresses the murder of Leon Klinghoffer, a Jewish man, by Palestinian hijackers. While meeting controversy about its subject matter, it would seem that for previous productions the argument had prevailed that art should have the liberty to unsettle and perhaps provoke audiences with difficult, and sometimes upsetting, themes.

However, shortly before its 2014 production, the Met in New York announced that the performances would no longer go ahead. While some critics appreciated the work of Adams and his librettist, Alice Goodman, in considering the views of each 'side' in the story, others were distressed that Klinghoffer seemed to be an unsympathetic character, concluding that the piece was anti-Semitic and gave too much consideration to the Palestinian terrorists. Eventually, an awkward compromise was reached: the performances would stay, but the Met's international broadcast (a highly successful means of reaching new audiences) would be cancelled.

Funders of the Met had a strong voice in this debate, with some patrons threatening to withdraw their financial support if the production was not cancelled. This also brings to the foreground the sensitive matter of the power of patronage: should contributing financially to the arts give donors the authority to decide what the arts might be permitted to address?

♔ SUPERTITLES

Now an accepted part of going to any opera house, one of the more controversial additions to opera during the twentieth century was that of 'supertitles', the projection of a translation of the libretto to help audience members to understand the words that are being sung. Although supertitles are usually projected above the stage – antagonizing some lighting designers who are concerned about the light bleeding onto the stage and into the house – some venues feature them on small screens that are built into the backs of the theatre seats. The advantage of these built-in titles is that viewers have the option to turn them on or off, and in many houses they can also select a preferred language.

Since the size, acoustic or layout of certain opera houses already sets great challenges for singers' audibility (English National Opera's Coliseum is one example) even before one tackles the challenge of creating crystalline diction, it is often beneficial for supertitles to be used for English-language productions too. Marilyn Horne has even used them in her Lieder masterclasses.

While one concern is that supertitles can divert attention from the action or a singer's nuanced performance, audience members soon adjust to focusing on the stage while noting the translation simultaneously. There is little doubt that supertitles can help new audiences to enter the world of opera – particularly people who might otherwise be intimidated by the idea of hearing words sung in a language that is unfamiliar to them.

GLOSSARY

aria

- A self-contained solo song with a catchy melody and an instrumental accompaniment in a cantata, opera, oratorio or Passion.
- An independent solo song known as a concert aria.

ariette

- In early eighteenth-century France, a virtuoso operatic solo like its Italian counterpart, the aria.
- In the late-eighteenth century, a song from a comic opera.

arioso

- A passage of measured music in a recitative.
- An independent solo vocal movement that is shorter and less complex than an aria.

atonality

Music in which no one pitch assumes greater importance than another, so that it is impossible to feel a sense of tonality.

ballet de cour

An entertainment of the sixteenth- and seventeenth-century French court. It consisted of an overture followed by sets of dances, each introduced by a spoken prologue or recitative.

bass

- The lowest male voice.
- The lowest-sounding part of a composition for voices, instruments or both.

bel canto

'Beautiful singing': an Italian term originating in the nineteenth century and referring to an earlier 'golden age' of vocal

production coinciding with the flowering of the eighteenth-century operatic aria.

buffa, buffo

'Comical'. *Opera buffa* is the comic antithesis of eighteenth-century *opera seria*, while a *basso buffo* might well sing a comic patter song.

cabaret

A satirical singing and dancing entertainment staged in venues such as night clubs.

cantata

An instrumental and vocal genre, usually containing recitatives and arias. Lutheran cantatas were closely related to the prescribed biblical readings and sermon that preceded and followed them.

castrato

An emasculated male capable of singing operatic soprano or alto parts such as that of the eponymous hero in Handel's *Giulio Cesare*.

coloratura

- An elaborately ornamented soprano song like that sung by the Queen of the Night in Mozart's *Die Zauberflöte*.
- A virtuoso soprano capable of singing such music.

comédie-ballet

A French opera-cum-ballet of the late seventeenth and early eighteenth centuries, such as Lully's *Le bourgeois gentilhomme*.

commedia dell'arte

A comic entertainment including improvised songs. It originated in sixteenth-century Italy then spread throughout Europe. Some of the stock characters of the commedia dell'arte continued to appear in musical works through to the twentieth century.

contralto

The lowest female voice.

da capo aria

The *da capo* aria is a ternary structure (A-B-A) in which the repeat is rarely written out: instead the words *da capo* ('from the beginning') or the letters DC at the end of the second section are sufficient indication of the composer's intentions.

divertissement

- In seventeenth-century French opera, a group of pieces performed within or between the acts.
- In the late eighteenth century, an entertaining instrumental composition such as a divertimento, cassation or serenade.

ensemble

- A group of two or more performers.
- The degree of unanimity in group performance.
- An operatic movement involving several characters and sometimes a chorus.

entr'acte

Music performed between the acts of an opera or play.

entrée

- A group of dances in a *ballet de cour*.
- The entrance of an operatic character, or the music for such an entrance.
- The first movement of a suite.

Heldentenor

Translating from the German as 'heroic tenor', a heldentenor's range combines a brilliant top register with a strong lower voice, and is capable of singing long passages that require great vocal stamina. Some of the greatest heldentenors, such as Lauritz Melchior, originally trained as baritones, which gives their voices the crucial lower timbre. Heldentenors are generally associated with Wagnerian roles, notably Tristan and Siegfried.

incidental music

Music that adorns a dramatic production but which is not an essential part of it, for example Mendelssohn's music for *A Midsummer Night's Dream*.

intermedio

Vocal and instrumental music performed between the acts of a play. In sixteenth-century Florence, these could be elaborately staged dramas on allegorical

GLOSSARY

369

or mythical subjects involving more than 80 performers. In the next century, *intermedi* were performed between the acts of full-scale operas.

intermezzo

A comic version of the *intermedio* that was performed between the acts of eighteenth-century serious operas.

libretto

The text of an extended vocal work such as an opera or oratorio.

Lied

A German poem set to music by a composer; most popular during the late eighteenth and nineteenth centuries, usually for solo voice accompanied by piano.

madrigal

A medieval or late Renaissance song for several voices, often with a vernacular text of an amatory nature.

masque

A dramatic entertainment with vocal and instrumental music deriving from the Italian *intermedio* and reaching its apogee in seventeenth-century England.

Mass

- The Roman Catholic celebration of the Eucharist.
- A musical setting of texts that are common to most celebrations of the Mass (Kyrie, Gloria, Creed, Sanctus and Agnus Dei).

mezzo-soprano

A female voice, the range of which falls between the ranges of sopranos and altos.

minimalism

Late twentieth-century music that exploits the potential of very short and simple ideas, often employing a minimum of performers.

motet

- In the Middle Ages, a multi-voice vocal composition based on a pre-existent melody in long notes heard in one of the contrapuntal parts.
- In the Renaissance, an independent polyphonic vocal setting of a sacred Latin text. Most such motets were specific to a particular day in the church's year.

music theatre

A twentieth-century genre in which drama and music are combined in semi-staged performances that deliberately reject the traditions of conventional opera.

ode

An extended vocal composition written to celebrate the personification of an emotion or idea, or prowess of a person or a particular day.

opéra-ballet

An opera-cum-ballet that flourished in France in the late seventeenth and early eighteenth centuries.

opera buffa

Comic opera sung in Italian.

opéra comique

An opera based on a French text including music and dialogue; it developed from being light-hearted to incorporating more serious elements throughout the eighteenth century.

opera seria

Serious opera of the eighteenth century. It was a highly stylized art form, largely consisting of a series of recitatives and da capo arias presented in three acts. Later in the century, vocal ensembles, choruses and ballets figured more prominently.

oratorio

A religious drama first cultivated by the Congregation of the Oratory in sixteenth-century Italy. Like opera, it contains recitatives and arias, but most oratorios were not staged – relying to a greater extent on the dramatic use of choruses – and excluded ballet.

overture

An instrumental prelude to a dramatic work such as an opera or oratorio.

pastorale

A French operatic genre in one or more acts that evoked a golden age when heroes conducted their affairs in Elysian rural seclusion.

plainchant, plainsong

A corpus of unaccompanied melodies of great antiquity associated with the liturgical texts of the Catholic church.

recitative

A single vocal line designed to replicate the rhythms of spoken words and express their meaning through the use of appropriate melodic intervals. In Baroque opera and oratorio the resulting fragmented melody was usually supported by a continuo group, but in later periods orchestral accompaniments took over this role.

ritornello

- A passage of instrumental music heard in a Baroque vocal movement. In a da capo aria the instrumental *ritornello* heard at the start is often repeated at the end.
- A passage of music for the *ripieno* recurring in whole or in part in a Baroque concerto movement.

semi-opera

English dramas of the late seventeenth and early eighteenth centuries, in which the leading roles were spoken, but music was composed for lesser characters together with incidental instrumental music, for example Purcell's *Dioclesian*.

soprano

The highest female voice, or the uppermost part of an ensemble of voices or instruments.

tenor

A high male voice, or the third melodic line down in conventional four-part harmony.

tragédie lyrique

French seventeenth- and eighteenth-century tragic or epic opera.

treble

A high child's voice, or the uppermost part of a polyphonic composition.

verismo

A late Romantic style of opera in which violent and sordid events were realistically portrayed in contemporary settings.

BIBLIOGRAPHY

THE ROOTS OF OPERA

Binkley, T. and M. Frenk, *Spanish Romances of the Sixteenth Century*, Indiana University Press, 1995

Blackburn, B. J. et al (ed.), *A Correspondence of Renaissance Musicians*, Clarendon Press, 1991

Boone, G. M. (ed.), *Essays on Medieval Music*, Harvard University Press, 1995

Caldwell, J., *The Oxford History of English Music*, Clarendon Press, 1991

Fenlon, I. (ed.), *The Renaissance: From the 1470s to the End of the Sixteenth Century*, Prentice Hall, 1989

Fassler, M. and W. Frisch, *Music in the Medieval West*, Norton & Company, 2014

Freedman, R. and W. Frisch, *Music in the Renaissance*, Norton & Company, 2012

Knighton, T. and D. Fallows (eds.), *Companion to Medieval and Renaissance Music*, Dent, 1992

Mayer Brown, H. and L. K. Stein, *Music in the Renaissance*, Prentice Hall, 1998

Perkins, L. L., *Music in the Age of the Renaissance*, W. W. Norton, 1999

Reese, G. et al, *The New Grove High Renaissance Masters*, Macmillan, 1984

Wilkins, N., *Music in the Age of Chaucer*, D. S. Brewer, 1999

Wilson, D. F., *Music of the Middle Ages*, Schirmer, 1990

Woetmann Christoffersen, P., *French Music in the Early Sixteenth Century*, Museum Tusculanum Press, 1994

EARLY AND MIDDLE BAROQUE

Anderson, N., *Baroque Music from Monteverdi to Handel*, Thames & Hudson, 1994

Anthony, J. et al, *French Baroque Masters*, Macmillan, 1986

Arnold, D. and N. Fortune (eds.), *The New Monteverdi Companion*, Faber and Faber, 1985

Arnold, D., *Monteverdi (The Master Musicians)*, 3rd edition, Oxford University Press, 2001

Bokina, J., *Opera and Politics, from Monteverdi to Henze*, Yale University Press, 1997

Burdon, M., *Purcell Remembered*, Faber and Faber, 1995

Carter, T., *Jacopo Peri, His Life and Works*, Garland Publishing, 1989

Cessac, C., *Marc-Antoine Charpentier*, English translation, Amadeus Press, 1995

Demuth, N., *French Opera: Its Development to the Revolution*, Perseus Books, 1982

Gianturco, C., *Alessandro Stradella, His Life and Works*, Clarendon Press, 1994

Holman, P., *Henry Purcell* (Oxford Studies of Composers), Oxford University Press, 1994

Keates, J., *Purcell, A Biography*, Chatto and Windus, 1995

King, R., *Henry Purcell: A Greater Musical Genius England Never Had*, Thames & Hudson, 1994

Kurtzman, J., *The Monteverdi Vespers of 1610*, Clarendon Press, 1999

Mundy, S., *Purcell*, Omnibus, 1995

Price, C., Henry *Purcell and the London Stage*, Cambridge University Press, 1982

Price, C. (ed.), *The Early Baroque Era*, Prentice Hall, 1993

Rifkin, J. et al, *French Baroque Masters*, Macmillan, 1985

Sadie, J. A. (ed.), *Companion to Baroque Music*, Gale Group, 1990

Stevens, D., *The Letters of Claudio Monteverdi*, Clarendon Press, 1995

Tellart, R., *Claudio Monteverdi*, Fayard, 1997

Tomlinson, G., *Monteverdi and the End of the Renaissance*, University of California Press, 1985

Westrup, J. A., *Purcell*, Oxford University Press, 1995

Whenham, J., *The Cambridge Companion to Monteverdi*, Cambridge University Press, 2007

LATE BAROQUE

Adams, S. *Vivaldi: Red Priest of Venice*, Lion Hudson, 2010

Booth, J., *Vivaldi*, Omnibus Press, 1989

Brown, P., *Antonio Vivaldi*, Exley, 1992

Buelow, G. J. (ed.), *The Late Baroque Era*, Prentice Hall, 1993

Burrows, D., *Handel*, Oxford University Press, 1996

Burrows, D., *Handel* (The Master Musicians), Oxford University Press, 2001

Dean W. and J. M. Knapp, *Handel's Operas, 1704–1726*, Clarendon Press, 1995

Gossett, P. and C. Girdlestone, Jean-Philippe *Rameau: His Life and Work*, Dover Publications, 2014

Hogwood, C. and A. Hicks, *Handel*, Thames & Hudson, 2007

Keates, J., Handel, *The Man and His Music*, Hamish Hamilton, 1986

Landon, H. C. Robbins, *Vivaldi: Voice of the Baroque*, Thames & Hudson, 1993 Ledbetter, D., *Continuo Playing According to Handel*, Clarendon Press, 1990

Radice, M. A. (ed.), *Opera in Context: Essays on Historical Staging from the Late Renaissance to the Time of Puccini*, Amadeus Press, 1998

Talbot, M., *Vivaldi (The Master Musicians)*, Oxford University Press, 1993

Thompson, W., *Handel*, Omnibus Press, 1994

CLASSICAL

Boyd, M. (ed.), *Oxford Composer Companions: J. S. Bach*, Oxford University Press, 1999

Buller, J. L., *Classically Romantic*, Xlibris Corporation, 2001

Butt, J. (ed.), *The Cambridge Companion to Bach*, Cambridge University Press, 1997

Butterworth, N., *Haydn*, Omnibus Press, 1983

Cairns, D. *Mozart and His Operas*, Penguin, 2007

Catucci, S. et al, *Bach and Baroque Music*, Barron's, 1998

Charlton, D., *Grétry and the Growth of Opéra-Comique*, Cambridge University Press, 1986

David and Mendel (eds.), *The New Bach Reader*, Norton, 1998

Dreyfuss, L., *Bach and the Patterns of Invention*, Harvard University Press, 1996

Grey, C., *Johann Sebastian Bach*, Exley, 1994

Headington, C., *Johann Sebastian Bach*, Pavilion, 1997

Heartz, D., *Haydn, Mozart and the Viennese School, 1740–80*, Norton, 1995

Heartz, D. and T. Bauman, *Mozart's Operas (A Centennial Book)*, University of California Press, 1992

Hughes, R., *Haydn (The Master Musicians)*, Oxford University Press, 1950 (rev. 1989 and 1994)

Jenkins, J., *Mozart and the English Connection*, Cygnus Arts, 1998

Jones, D. W., *Oxford Composer Companions: Haydn*, Oxford University Press, 2009

Koerner, J., *Wolfgang Amadeus Mozart*, Friedman/Fairfax Publishing, 1997

Landon, H. C. Robbins, *1791: Mozart's Last Year*, Thames & Hudson, 1999

Pestellf, G., *The Age of Mozart and Beethoven*, Cambridge University Press, 1994

Rice, J. A., *Antonio Salieri and the Viennese Opera*, University of Chicago Press, 1998

Rosselli, J., *The Life of Mozart*, Cambridge University Press, 1998

Rushton, J., *The New Grove Guide to Mozart and His Operas*, OUP USA, 2007

Vernon, R., *Introducing Mozart (Introducing Composers)*, Chelsea House Publications, 2000

Zaslaw, N. (ed.), *The Classical Era*, Macmillan, 1989

EARLY ROMANTIC

Altman, G. S., Beethoven: *A Man of His Word*, Anubian Press, 1996

Ashbrook, W., *Donizetti and His Operas*, Cambridge University Press, 1982

Barzun, J., *Berlioz and the Romantic Century*, Columbia University Press, 1969

Cairns, D. (trans. and ed.), *The Memoirs of Hector Berlioz*, Cardinal, 1990

Cook, N., *Beethoven*, Cambridge University Press, 1993

Cooper, B., *Beethoven (The Master Musicians)*,

Oxford University Press, 2001

Cooper, B. (ed.), *The Beethoven Compendium*, Thames & Hudson, 1996

Gibbs, C. (ed.), *The Cambridge Companion to Schubert*, Cambridge University Press, 1997

Gossett, P. et al, *The New Grove Masters of Italian Opera*, W. W. Norton, 1997

Jones, D. W., *The Life of Beethoven*, Cambridge University Press, 1998

Kimbell, D., *Italian Opera*, Cambridge University Press, 1991

Landon, H. C. Robbins, *Beethoven: His Life, Work and World*, W. W. Norton, 1992

Matthews, D., *Beethoven*, Oxford University Press, 1997

McKay, E. Norman, *Franz Schubert: a Biography*, Oxford University Press, 1996

Newbould, B., *Schubert: The Music and the Man*, Victor Gollancz, 1997

Osborne, R., *Rossini*, Dent, 1993

Osborne, C., *The Bel Canto Operas: Of Rossini, Donizetti and Bellini*, Amadeus Press, 1994

Ringer, A. (ed.), *The Early Romantic Era*, Macmillan, 1990

Rosen, C., *The Romantic Generation*, HarperCollins, 1995

Servadio, G., *Rossini*, Carroll & Graf Publishers, 2003

Swafford, J., *Beethoven: Anguish and Triumph*, Faber & Faber, 2014

Thompson, W., *Composer's World: Beethoven*, Faber Paperbacks, 1990

Vernon, R., *Introducing Beethoven (Introducing Composers)*, Chelsea House Publications, 2000

Walton, B., *Rossini in Restoration Paris*, Cambridge University Press, 2011

Whittall, A., *Romantic Music: a Concise History from Schubert to Sibelius*, Thames & Hudson, 1987

HIGH ROMANTIC

Adorno, T. W., *In Search of Wagner*, trans. R. Livingstone, Verso, 2009

Berger, W., *Verdi with a Vengeance*, Vintage, 2001

Brown, D., *Tchaikovsky: The Man and His Music*, Faber & Faber, 2007

Budden, J., *The Operas of Verdi: From Oberto to Rigoletto*, Clarendon Press, 1992

Dalhauus, C., *Nineteenth-Century Music*, trans. J. B. Robinson, University of California Press, 1989

Emerson, C., *The Life of Musorgsky (Musical Lives)*, Cambridge University Press, 1999

Garden, E., *Tchaikovsky (The Master Musicians)*, Oxford University Press, 2001

Gregor-Dellin, M., *Richard Wagner: His Life, His Work, His Century*, Harcourt, 1983

Macdonald, H., *Bizet (Master Musicians)*, OUP USA, 2014

Millington, B., *The New Grove Guide to Wagner and His Operas*, Oxford University Press, 2006

Newman, E., *The Wagner Operas*, Princeton University Press, 1991

Nice, D., *Tchaikovsky*, Pavilion, 1997

Orlova, A. (ed.), *Tchaikovsky: A Self-Portrait*, Oxford University Press, 1990

Osborne, C., *The Complete Operas of Richard Wagner*, Da Capo Press, 1993

Plantigna, L., *Romantic Music: A History of Musical Style in Nineteenth-Century Europe*, W. W. Norton, 1984

Poznansky, A., *Tchaikovsky*, Methuen, 1993

Rosselli, J., *The Life of Verdi* (Musical Lives), Cambridge University Press, 2000

Samson, J., *The Cambridge History of Nineteenth-Century Music*, Cambridge University Press, 2014

Samson, J. (ed.), *The Late Romantic Era*, Macmillan, 1991

Spencer, S., *Wagner's Ring of the Nibelungen: A Companion*, Thames & Hudson, 2010

Vernon, R., *Introducing Verdi (Introducing Composers)*, Chelsea House Publications, 2000

Walsh, S., *Musorgsky and His Circle: A Russian Musical Adventure*, Faber & Faber, 2013

TURN OF THE CENTURY

Budden, J., Puccini: *His Life and Works*, OUP USA, 2006

Carner, M., *Giacomo Puccini: Tosca,*

Cambridge University Press, 1985

Gilliam, B. (ed.), *Richard Strauss and His World*, Princeton University Press, 1992

Groos, A. and R. Parker, *Giacomo Puccini: La Bohème*, Cambridge University Press, 1986

Jensen, E. F., *Debussy (Master Musicians Series)*, OUP USA, 2014

Kennedy, M., *Richard Strauss: Man, Musician, Enigma*, Cambridge University Press, 1999

Keolker, J., *Last Acts: The Operas of Puccini and his Italian Contemporaries*, Opera Companion Publications, 2000

Kramer, L., *Opera and Modern Culture: Wagner and Strauss*, University of California Press, 2007

Nichols, R. and R. Langham Smith, *Claude Debussy: Pelléas et Mélisande*, Cambridge University Press, 1989

Nichols, R., *The Life of Debussy*, Cambridge University Press, 1998

Osborne, C., *The Complete Operas of Giacomo Puccini*, Victor Gollancz, 1981

Puffett, D., *Richard Strauss: Salome*, Cambridge University Press, 1990

Thompson, W., *Claude Debussy*, Faber Paperbacks, 1993

Wilson, C., *Giacomo Puccini*, Phaidon Press, 1997

Youmans, C., *The Cambridge Companion to Richard Strauss*, Cambridge University Press, 2010

THE MODERN ERA

Beckerman, M., *Janáček and His World*, Princeton University Press, 2003

Cooke, M., *The Cambridge Guide to Twentieth-Century Opera*, Cambridge University Press, 2005

Hall, M., *Leaving Home: a Conducted Tour of Twentieth Century Music with Simon Rattle*, Faber & Faber, 1996

Cross, J., *The Cambridge Companion to Stravinsky*, Cambridge University Press, 2003

Kennedy, M., *Britten (The Master Musicians)*, Oxford University Press, 2001

Kildea, P., *Benjamin Britten: A Life in the Twentieth Century*, Penguin 2014

Martin, G., *Twentieth Century Opera: A Guide*, Limelight Editions, 1999

Sutcliffe, T., *Believing in Opera*, Faber and Faber, 1996

Taruskin, R., *Stravinsky and the Russian Tradition*, University of California Press, 1996

Zemanova, M., *Janáček: A Composer's Life*, Northeastern University Press, 2002

GENERAL REFERENCE

Abbate, C. and R. Parker, *A History of Opera: The Last Four Hundred Years*, Allen Lane, 2012

Boyden, M., *Icons of Opera*, Thunder Bay Press, 2001

Boyden, M., *The Rough Guide to Opera*, Rough Guides Limited, 2007

Dean, W., *Essays on Opera*, Oxford University Press, 1990

Forman, D., *A Night at the Opera: An Irreverent Guide to the Plots, the Singers, the Composers, the Recordings*, Modern Library, 1998

Holden, A. (ed), *The New Penguin Opera Guide*, Penguin Books, 2001

Macy, L., *The Grove Book of Opera Singers*, Penguin Books, 2008

Sadie, S. and L. Macy, *The Grove Book of Operas*, Oxford University Press, 2009

Sadie, S. (ed.), *The New Grove Dictionary of Opera (Vols 1–4)*, Grove's Dictionaries, 2004

Simon, H. W., *100 Great Operas and Their Stories*, Anchor, 2010

Snowman, D., *The Gilded Stage: A Social History of Opera*, Atlantic Books, 2010

Warrack, J. H. and E. West, *The Oxford Dictionary of Opera*, Oxford University Press, 1992

CONTRIBUTOR BIOGRAPHIES

Stanley Sadie
General Editor: Classical Introduction

Stanley Sadie was music critic for *The Times* for 17 years, editor of *The Musical Times* for 20 years and music consultant on the TV series *Man and Music*. From 1970 he worked as editor of *The New Grove Dictionary of Music and Musicians* (1980, new edition 2001), as well as its associated dictionaries on instruments, opera and American music. He was editor of the Billboard and Flame Tree *Encyclopedia of Classical Music* and wrote extensively on Handel and Mozart. He was president of the Royal Musical Association (1989–94) and the International Musicological Society (1992–97) and was appointed CBE in 1982. With his wife, Julie Ann Sadie, he completed a survey of European composer museums and memorials. He died in 2005.

Philip Langridge
Foreword

Philip Langridge studied violin and singing at the Royal Academy of Music, London. He is now one of the world's most distinguished singers, whose musical and dramatic qualities ensure that he is in constant demand throughout the world. His remarkable versatility and command of a wide variety of styles is reflected in his extensive discography and videos, ranging from the early classical period to the present day. He was appointed CBE in 1994. He appears regularly at the Royal Opera House, the Met in New York, Munich, Paris, Barcelona, Los Angeles and Amsterdam. In concert he has appeared with most of the well-known conductors of our time, and has given recitals with Maurizio Pollini, Andras Schiff, Steuart Bedford, John Constable, Peter Donohoe and more recently with David Owen Norris in a tour of Schubert's *Winterreise*, culminating in a performance at the Mozarteum in Salzburg to public and critical acclaim.

Jane Bellingham
The Roots of Opera

Jane Bellingham worked as commissioning editor for early opera at Grove. She is a writer and lecturer, and has contributed articles to leading musical journals and also to *Gramophone* and *The Times*. She is the Programme Book Editor for Aldeburgh Productions, home of the Aldeburgh Festival in Suffolk.

Sarah Gabriel
Consultant Editor

Sarah Gabriel is a singer and actor. She made her USA debut conducted by Lorin Maazel and her European debut as Eliza in *My Fair Lady* at Théâtre de Châtelet, Paris. Passionate about song, she has given recitals across Europe, the US and Asia, and in the UK at festivals and venues such as Glyndebourne, Cheltenham International Festival and Wigmore Hall.

Richard Langham Smith
Turn of the Century

Richard Langham Smith graduated from the University of York and studied with Wilfrid Mellers and Edward Lockspeiser. His critical translation of Debussy's complete articles appeared in 1977 and he has subsequently co-authored the Cambridge Opera Guide to Debussy's *Pelléas et Mélisande* as well as writing and broadcasting on French music in general. His completion of Debussy's unfinished opera *Rodrigue et Chimène* opened the new opera house in Lyons in 1993. He is Research Professor in Music at the Royal College of Music, London.

Dorothy-Jean Lloyd
The Modern Era

Dr Dorothy-Jean Lloyd began her musical studies as a mezzo-soprano at the University of British Columbia. Her studies continued at the Juilliard School, and culminated in a Doctor of Musical Arts Degree in opera direction and production from UCLA. After an apprenticeship at the Paris Opéra, she sang and toured throughout Canada and the US. As well as producing and directing many opera workshop productions, she developed an opera outreach programme for the Gluck Foundation at UCLA. She now teaches at universities in Chicago, while continuing to direct and produce.

Robin Newton
Turn of the Century
Robin Newton is active as a conductor, specializing in contemporary music. In 1997 he formed his own ensemble, e2k, with which he gives regular concerts in London. He has worked on several high-profile academic publications as writer and editor, chiefly for *The New Grove Dictionary of Music and Musicians* and the Northern Arts magazine Artscene.

Brenda Ralph Lewis
Early and Middle Baroque, Classical, Romantic
Brenda Ralph Lewis is a historian and musician. Having attended her first opera at the age of 14, it has been a life-long passion. She attended Trinity College of Music in London, where she studied music and theory. Since then she has written over 100 books and partworks, including *Discovering Opera* and *The Musicals*.

Julia Rolf
Synopses
Julia Rolf studied at University College, London and L'Università degli Studi, Pisa, and works in London as a music editor and writer. She has contributed to a number of Flame Tree music titles and is also involved in local musical activities as a singer and viola player.

David Rose
Synopses
David Rose is a book editor, and worked on *The Grove Dictionary of Art* and *The New Grove Dictionary of Music and Musicians* for

eight years. He is also a part-time character tenor, playing creeps, rotters and upper-class twits, performing in operas in London and the South-East. David is an avid collector of recordings and scores of opera, operetta and musicals.

Stewart Spencer
High Romantic
Stewart Spencer is an expert on Wagner, and is the editor of the Wagner Society's journal *Wagner*. He has translated many books on Bach, Liszt, Mozart and Wagner, and has also written extensively on Wagner and his contemporaries, including *Selected Letters of Richard Wagner* and *Wagner in Performance*.

David Vickers
Late Baroque
David Vickers is a musicologist specializing in the Baroque era – Handel in particular. As well as writing articles and reviews for publications including *The Guardian* and *Gramophone*, he is a research scholar at the Open University. In 2002 he formed the Kirklees Baroque choir, a chamber choir and period instrument orchestra that is one of the few ensembles dedicated to performing quality performances of Early Music across the north of England. He also gives lectures at international Handel Festivals.

Richard Wigmore
Classical
Richard Wigmore read modern languages at Cambridge and took a second degree in music theory and performance at the Guildhall School of Music. After a career as a professional singer he now works as a writer and broadcaster, specializing in the Viennese Classical period and in *Lieder*. He contributes regular features and reviews to *Gramophone*, *BBC Music Magazine* and *The Daily Telegraph*. His first book, *Schubert's Complete Song Texts*, was published in 1988, and he has recently worked on a new biography of Haydn for the *Master Musicians* series and one for the Faber pocket series.

INDEX OF WORKS

INDEX

GENERAL INDEX

Page references in **bold** indicate a
main entry.